W9-CEL-640

Sports Economics

SECOND EDITION

Rodney D. Fort

Professor, Department of Economics
Washington State University

PEARSON
Prentice
Hall

Upper Saddle River, NJ 07458

Library of Congress Cataloging-in-Publication Data

Fort, Rodney D.
  Sports economics/Rodney D. Fort.—2nd ed.
     p. cm.
  Includes bibliographical references and index.
  ISBN 0-13-170421-4
    1. Sports—Economic aspects—United States. 2. Professional sports—Economic
  aspects—United States. 3. College sports—Economic aspects—United States. I. Title.

GV716.F68 2005
338.4'77960973—dc22   2005055578

Acquisitions Editor: Jon Axelrod
MVP/Executive Editor: David Alexander
VP/Editorial Director: Jeff Shelstad
Manager, Product Development: Pamela Hersperger
Project Manager: Francesca Calogero
Editorial Assistant: Michael Dittamo
Media Project Manager: Peter Snell
AVP/Executive Marketing Manager: Sharon Koch
Senior Managing Editor (Production): Cynthia Regan
Production Editor: Denise Culhane
Permissions Supervisor: Charles Morris
Production Manager: Arnold Vila
Manufacturing Buyer: Michelle Klein
Cover Design: Bruce Kenselaar

Cover Illustration/Photo: Michael Melford/Image
  Bank/Getty Images, Inc.
Director, Image Resource Center: Melinda Reo
Manager, Rights and Permissions: Zina Arabia
Manager, Visual Research: Beth Brenzel
Manager, Cover Visual Research & Permissions:
  Karen Sanatar
Image Permission Coordinator: Rita Wenning
Manager, Multimedia Production: Christy Mahon
Composition: Integra Software Services
Full-Service Project Management: Elaine
  Lattanzi/BookMasters, Inc.
Printer/Binder: Hamilton Printing
Typeface: 10/12 Palatino

Credits and acknowledgments borrowed from other sources and reproduced, with permission, in this textbook appear on appropriate page within text. Photo Credits: Cover: Michael Melford/Getty Images Inc./Image Bank; Pages 8, 121: Getty Images Inc./Agence France Presse; Pages 9, 70, 155: Corbis/Bettmann; Page 18: Michael Conroy/AP/Wide World Photos; Page 40: AP/Wide World Photos; Page 65: Louie Psihoyos/Corbis/Bettmann; Page 76: Charles Bennet/AP/Wide World Photos; Page 105: Gerald Scully; Page 138: Clive Brunskill/Getty Images, Inc./Allsport Photography; Page 181: Ryan Remiorz/AP/Wide World Photos; Page 233: Chris Trotman/CORBIS; Page 240: Duomo/Duomo Photography Incorporated; Page 245: Jamie Squire/Getty Images Sport/Getty Images; Page 265: AP/Wide World Photos; Page 271: Elaine Thompson/AP/Wide World Photos; Page 322: Tim Boyle/AP/Wide World Photos; Page 358: Pete Cosgrove/AP/Wide World Photos; Page 395: James A. Finley/AP/Wide World Photos; Page 441: Hillery Smith Garrison/AP/Wide World Photos; Page 401: Eric Gay/AP/Wide World Photos.

Pearson Education LTD.
Pearson Education Singapore, Pte. Ltd
Pearson Education, Canada, Ltd
Pearson Education—Japan

Pearson Education Australia PTY, Limited
Pearson Education North Asia Ltd
Pearson Educación de Mexico, S.A. de C.V.
Pearson Education Malaysia, Pte. Ltd

10 9 8 7 6 5 4 3
ISBN 0-13-170421-4

BRIEF CONTENTS

CONTENTS

PREFACE

Sports Economics is the only text that provides enough content and rigor for a course taken primarily by economics majors.

INTENDED AUDIENCE

This book is intended primarily for upper-division undergraduate classes aimed at a general audience (usually composed of business and sports management majors) or for a specialized seminar for economics majors. It also provides the basics required for a graduate-level treatment of the subject, and the chapter references provide a good starting point for graduate students on any team sport topic. Students using this text should have an understanding of the principles of microeconomics.

These days, the business side of the playing field dominates the sports pages at times. Players, owners, local elected officials, and fans all seem at odds. This is a confusing state of affairs because Americans appear to have a nearly insatiable demand for sports and there appears to be more than enough money to go around. This book aims to clear up this messy topic by applying a dose of economic thinking to the business of sports. Sports truly are business, and off-field economic decisions determine on-field outcomes.

SPECIAL FEATURES

These features will facilitate student learning and understanding:

- *Learning Objectives* at the start of each chapter preview key content.
- *Pull quotes* and *"Did You Know?"* margin facts help pique and retain student interest.
- *Learning Highlights* present interesting and detailed examples and information relevant to the text material. These are intended to be informative and entertaining, often concerning sports business personalities and economic explanations of their actions.
- *Three levels of end-of-chapter questions:*
  - *Review Questions* are memory joggers that remind students of the important elements of the readings.

- *Thought questions* require students to work through the chapter content that requires higher-level thinking.
- *Advanced Questions* push students to actually apply sports economics rather than just think about it.

NEW TO THIS EDITION

All data are updated and put in common dollar denominations

- The extensive data from the first edition all are updated. And all dollar comparisons are done in 2004 dollars, adjusted by the consumer price index.

New and updated Learning Highlights

- New Learning Highlights add significantly to the discussions. And some previous highlights are updated to reflect evolving circumstances.

Original graphs for sports analysis

- In addition to the two-team diagram familiar to all, graphs have been added representing the break-even considerations for work stoppages (Chapter 9) and changes in revenues under new roster depreciation laws (Chapter 12).

Market outcomes are now covered in two chapters rather than one

- Following user input, this important topic is now discussed in more depth to give students more coverage, and therefore a better understanding.

The new Chapter 6 focuses exclusively on competitive balance in pro sports leagues

- The chapter ties together the uncertainty of outcome hypothesis from Chapter 2 and the actual outcomes in pro sports leagues. The material helps students apply economic reasoning to concrete sport examples.

FOR INSTRUCTORS

The following supplements are available to adopting instructors. For detailed descriptions, please visit www.prenhall.com/fort.

Instructor's Resource Centre (IRC) online: Log in at www.prenhall.com/irc.
PowerPoint slides: Visit the IRC for this text.
Electronic Solutions Manual: Visit the IRC for this text.

You can also link to Professor Fort's Web site from www.prenhall.com/fort for additional material and links related to the text.

Instructor's Resource Center

Register. Redeem. Log in. www.prenhall.com/irc is where instructors can access a variety of print, media, and presentation resources available with this text in downloadable, digital format. For most texts, resources are also available for course management platforms such as Blackboard, WebCT, and Course Compass.

It gets better. Once you register, you will not have additional forms to fill out or multiple usernames and passwords to remember to access new titles and/or editions. As a registered faculty member, you can log in directly to download resource files and receive immediate access to and instructions for installing Course Management content to your campus server.

Need help? Our dedicated Technical Support team is ready to assist instructors with questions about the media supplements that accompany this text. Visit 247.prenhall.com for answers to frequently asked questions and toll-free user support phone numbers.

ACKNOWLEDGMENTS

All shortcomings in this book are my fault, but many of the good things about the book came about with the help of others. Almost everything I know about practicing sports economics I learned from Roger Noll and James Quirk. As all sports economists should admit, Gerald Scully is the true pioneer. Whether it is demand, team and league behavior, the market for players, or the analysis of sports over time, Scully is nearly always first on the scene. The book benefited greatly from a number of reviewers. Their thorough comments helped shape this book and (hopefully) future editions. My heartfelt thanks to:

Katie Baird, *University of Washington, Tacoma*
Ross Booth, *Monash University*
Roger Blair, *University of Florida*
Stanley Engerman, *University of Rochester*
John Fizel, *Pennsylvania State University, Erie*
Jahn Hakes, *Clemson University*
Kevin Quinn, *St. Norbert College*
Tom Regan, *University of South Carolina*
Allen Sanderson, *University of Chicago*
John Siegfried, *Vanderbilt University*
Paul Staudohar, *California State University, Hayward*

Even though they don't know it, all of my sports economics students at Washington State University contributed fundamentally to this book. As I honed my lectures and approaches, the organization of the book came into being.

FEEDBACK

The author and product team would appreciate hearing from you! Let us know what you think about this textbook by writing to college_economics@prenhall.com. Please include "Feedback about Fort 2e" in the subject line.

If you have questions related to this product, please contact our customer service department online at www.247.prenhall.com.

Chapter 1

Warm-Up: The Business of Sports

Chapter Objectives

After reading this chapter, you should be able to:

- Explain why there is more to sports than the revenues they generate.
- Understand that because sports are actually businesses standard economic tools can enhance your understanding of sports off the field.
- Know why the business side of sports often befuddles fans.
- Understand the skepticism that players voice toward owners' claims of poverty.
- Explain why owners typically are exasperated at their treatment by players and fans.

> *If we do everything right this year and win again, we probably will be able to break even. And I'll tell you this much: I didn't buy this team to break even.*

—MINNESOTA TWINS OWNER CARL POHLAD
Sporting News, *August 24, 1992, p. 10*

In 1915, the New York Yankees were purchased for $7.8 million (in 2004 dollars). Eighty-three years later, in 1998, a bona fide offer of $733.8 million (also in 2004 dollars) was recorded for the team. Adjusting for inflation, that's a 5.6 percent return per year [$7.8(1 + r)^{83} = 733.8$ implies that r, the constant rate of return, is 5.6 percent]. The inflation-adjusted growth rate in the U.S. economy at large is typically about 3 percent annually. Thus, owning the Yankees was nearly twice as valuable as a diversified investment portfolio.

The Yankees' value serves to introduce the following warm-up on the business of sports. The world of sports is confusing. These days, the sports pages look more like the business pages, and judging from media reports, nobody seems happy about it. Players and owners fight over money; owners fight with each other over money; and the fans seem more hardened and cynical every day. To top it all off, a dizzying array of terminology drowns everybody—free agency, luxury taxes, lockouts, salary caps, arbitration, the National Labor Relations Board (NLRB), franchise free agency, local host blackmail, and public-private partnerships, to name just a few. Any sports fan needs more than the analysis offered in the newspaper to make sense of it all. In this chapter, I'll discuss these issues and a few basic ideas to set up the economic analysis of American sports that appears in the rest of the book.

PUTTING THE BUSINESS OF SPORTS IN PERSPECTIVE

Analysts differ in their opinions about the place of sports in society. Some argue that America's priorities are out of whack and that our preoccupation with sports is unhealthy. For example, in 1994, the U.S. House of Representatives held hearings on the labor-management tensions that had led to the Major League Baseball (MLB) strike that year. Brookings Institution economist Henry Aaron (believe it or not, there really is an economist with that storied sports name) almost scolded the House of Representatives subcommittee for spending its time on sports. He pointed out a number of facts about the relative **economic importance of sports**: MLB was about a $2 billion industry in terms of total revenue (at that time), and any given sports team typically represented only a fraction of 1 percent of the economic activity in its county. Professor Aaron went on to note that the envelope industry generated about $2.6 billion and the production of cardboard boxes generated $7.6 billion in annual revenues. Surely, he urged the committee, there had to be bigger things to worry about than baseball!

It cannot be denied that the importance of sports exceeds its total revenues. For example, there is no cardboard-box page in the daily paper or on the news each night. Further, the last time I checked, there was no cardboard-box equivalent of a cable network like ESPN devoted to reporting the minutiae of the industry. These news reports make it clear that the level of interest in sports goes beyond just their monetary contribution to team owners, employees, or local governments.

Did You Know?
Total revenues in MLB more than doubled from 1990 ($1.9 billion in 2004 dollars) to 2003 ($4.1 billion in 2004 dollars).

Did You Know?
The popular history text *Build Our Nation* covers the Depression in just a couple of paragraphs, whereas it devotes two pages to baseball player Cal Ripken, Jr.

Two of the many keys to understanding the way the sports world works are a little bit of economics and a modicum of common sense. Of course, having applied this approach to sports for over 20 years, I speak from experience. My aim is to show you how the business side of sports affects the game you see at the stadium or in the arena. So let's go ahead and start applying economics and common sense to the world of sports.

SPORTS REALLY ARE BIG BUSINESS

Sports are big business. Legends of owners who don't care about profits or players who play just for the love of the game are overblown. The romanticized Shoeless Joe Jackson character in the film *Field of Dreams* would have us believe he would have played for free. Well, sport was fun (and still is), but the money has never been bad either, even in the days of Shoeless Joe's Chicago Black Sox. Even before Harvard first rowed against Oxford, earning money from a contest has been the way in sports. As we'll see in the last chapter, this goes for so-called amateur sports as well.

Interestingly, many sports fans have a hard time understanding that sports really are big business. Some evidence and a little common sense help to drive the point home. Historically, teams that spend the most tend to win the most. So why don't team owners, some of the most successful and wealthy of all Americans, just buy a winning team or invest in winning players? We don't see wealthy owners toss their money around in this way very often. Even when we do, the strategy doesn't always work. Take Wayne Huizenga, who in 1997 invested big money in the Florida Marlins. By all accounts, he bought enough talent that year to win the World Series. In fact, the team did go on to win the World Series, but Huizenga sold off most of the important members of the team the following year. The reason? The city of Miami made it clear that part of the revenue Mr. Huizenga hoped to capture with his world champions, in the form of a new publicly financed stadium, was not going to be delivered. In the end, Huizenga's investment didn't pay off.

The stadium issue brings up more evidence that sports really are business. Why don't owners just build their own stadiums rather than pressuring state and local governments to foot the bill? Surely, these extremely wealthy people can afford their own stadiums. For example, Paul Allen, who owns both the National Basketball Association's (NBA) Portland Trailblazers and the National Football League's (NFL) Seattle Seahawks, built and owns the Trailblazers arena. However, he would only exercise his option to buy the Seahawks if public money was put toward a new football stadium in Seattle. Perhaps it had something to do with the fact that an arena can be built at a little less than half the cost of a stadium. That is clearly a bottom-line consideration important to a business decision.

For that matter, why do these eminently rich people even charge admission or sell broadcast and sponsorship rights? Why would they ever lock out players, as happened with the loss of nearly half of the NBA season in 1998? In fact, why would the owners negotiate player contracts at all? If sports are not businesses, wealthy owners could just give the players what they wanted, let fans into stadiums for free, and everybody would be happy. Players would be richer and fans wouldn't suffer any interruption in play. Speaking of players, if sports are not businesses, then why don't they just play for expenses?

The Power 100

The importance of the business aspect of sports can also be seen in the *Sporting News* "Power 100" list. Each year, the magazine lists whom it considers to be the 100 most powerful people in sports. Typically, fewer than 10 of these dominant sports personalities actually participate in their sport. The *Sporting News* list is dominated by sports officials (commissioners and league officers in pro sports, conference presidents and bowl officials for college sports, and presidents and organizers for the Olympics). Media moguls and other network officers are a close second. CEO/owners, agents, sponsors, and participants (players and coaches) round out the field. Fewer than half of these powerbrokers are directly responsible for the actual operation and playing of sports (officials, CEO/owners, and participants). In fact, in 2002, media mogul and New York Yankees owner George Steinbrenner was judged the most important person in sports. Incidentally, in 1995, Stanford University economist—and my former professor—Roger Noll made the list, ranked number 93. Although my old professor does have a pretty decent baseline jump shot, he didn't make the list because of his athletic prowess. Professor Noll's services are in demand by nearly every players' union in sports, as well as by the U.S. Congress for expert testimony. In fact, his analysis was instrumental in court considerations that eventually resulted in NFL free agency beginning in the 1994 season and during the MLB strike of 1994.

Did You Know?

Typically, fewer than 10 of the 100 most dominant sports personalities actually participate in their sport.

So sports are business, and big business at that. Sometimes owners make statements that appear to contradict this. Even a billionaire owner like Mark Cuban, owner of the NBA Dallas Mavericks, doesn't let his fans in for free, nor is he going to mismanage his personnel. He is going to treat his team as an investment. Part of the return may be in terms of his love of sports, but there is an undeniable business aspect to the investment as well. Cuban intends to make money on his team. In the next section, we'll look at the problems that the sports business poses for fans, owners, and players.

Did You Know?

"Say I'm worth $1.1 billion, and through a series of incredibly moronic moves, I lose $100 million. Oh, gee! What does that leave me?"—Mark Cuban, dot-com billionaire owner of the Dallas Mavericks (*Sports Illustrated*, November 6, 2000, p. 88)

BEFUDDLED FANS

Media accounts seem to indicate that the greed and hypocrisy of those involved in the sports business generate a great deal of **fan confusion** and skepticism. These common feelings about the sports business are worth mentioning. A review of the

Table 1.1 Fan Poll Results, 1984 and 1994

	OVERPAID	WORTH IT	NO OPINION
1984			
Players	81%	14%	5%
Owners	76%	14%	10%
1994			
Players	73%	18%	3%
Owners	52%	28%	3%

Source: *Business Week* for 1984 and *Time* for 1994.

causes of these views provides a nice point of departure for the economic explanations that we will discuss later in the book.

We've all heard sports fans lament that sports are not about the game anymore but all about money. Fans also believe that players and owners are overpaid—a belief that has been remarkably consistent over time. Table 1.1 shows the results of two polls conducted about 10 years apart on fans' opinions of player and owner earnings. As you can see from the table, the vast majority of fans agrees that owners and players are overpaid, and players more so than owners. But note that these feelings have eased a little over the years. It can't be known whether fan survey responses reflect concern that payment issues are spoiling the games or whether such responses just reveal **fan envy**.

Although overpayment may be in the eye of the beholder, there is no doubt that athletes make a lot of money. As you can see in Table 1.2, according to the *Forbes* Top 100 Celebrities list for 2003, top-earning athletes can make tens of millions of dollars annually. Even Yankees third baseman Alex Rodriguez, ranked 50th on the list by pay, made $26 million in 2003. Compare this with the average physician's income at the time, about $116,000. At that rate, the average doctor wouldn't earn A-Rod's $26 million for 229 years. A teacher with an average pay at

Table 1.2 Top-Paid Athletes in *Forbes* Top 100 Celebrities by Pay, 2003

NAME	RANK OUT OF 100	PAY ($MILLIONS 2002)
Tiger Woods	4	$78.0
Michael Schumacher	5	$75.0
Michael Jordan	23	$35.0
Shaquille O'Neal	37	$30.5
Oscar DeLaHoya	38	$30.0
Kevin Garnett	46	$28.0
Alex Rodriguez	50	$26.0
Grant Hill	51	$25.5
Andre Agassi	53	$24.0
Jacques Villeneuve	54	$23.0
15 other male athletes	—	—
Venus Williams	71	$14.0

Source: *Forbes*, 2003 (forbes.com/lists). Pay includes both salary and endorsement income.

Did You Know?
It would take the average teacher more than 591 years to earn the amount paid to Yankee star Alex Rodriguez for a single season.

that time of around $44,000 would take 591 years to match A-Rod's pay for just one year.

The wealth of owners also befuddles fans. *Forbes* (forbes.com/richlist2003) reported in 2003 that Paul Allen, owner of the Portland Trailblazers and Seattle Seahawks, had a net worth near $22 billion. Indeed, according to *Forbes*, there were more than a dozen billionaire owners, and many of them owned more than one pro sports team. Few of us can even imagine this type of buying power. On top of it all, these owners make choices that irritate fans. Fans perceive that owners let money get in the way of fielding winning teams. Then the owners have the gall (in the eyes of fans) to hold fans and local governments hostage in negotiations over public subsidies for stadiums and arenas. Some owners have even blamed their fans for lack of support when their subsidy demands are not met. Meanwhile, fans surmise that all of the money comes out of their pockets. The typical view is that greedy players hit up rich owners who bow to their demands and, in turn, raise prices for the fans. A little economic thinking shows that this commonly held path of causality is flat backwards: It just doesn't fit reality.

Imagine walking into your boss's office and demanding a pay increase that isn't tied to some sort of extra revenue that you have generated for the firm. Good luck! Unless the firm is earning more money and unless some of the increase can be directly tied to your performance, your demand won't be met. The same is true of sports stars. Team revenues continue to grow, providing the basis for such demands in the first place. Nonetheless, fans are befuddled and, at times, angry, and not all of them are taking it lying down. **Fan consumer movements** are detailed in Learning Highlight: Consumer Movements in Sports.

Player Skepticism and Owner Exasperation

As anyone who reads the sports pages knows, players are often portrayed as greedy in their pay negotiations and skeptical of owners' claims of poverty. Every year, players with multi-million-dollar contracts hold their teams and fans hostage during prolonged preseason holdouts. This lack of **player loyalty** is a common fan lament. But think about this from the players' perspective. There is plenty of justification for **player skepticism**. The value of teams continues to increase over time. In our first book, *Pay Dirt* (1992), James Quirk and I demonstrated that **franchise sale values** typically outperformed a portfolio of common stocks from the 1940s through the 1980s (for more information on this, see Learning Highlight: Buying the New York Yankees). In our second book, *Hardball* (1999), Quirk and I showed that, while the increase in sale prices slowed during the 1990s, teams still offered a pretty attractive investment. Team sale prices in the 1990s increased 11.3 percent in MLB, 12.7 percent in the NFL, 17.7 percent in the NBA, and 10.7 percent in the National Hockey League (NHL).

Did You Know?
Team sale values typically outperformed a portfolio of common stocks from the 1940s through the 1980s.

Table 1.3   Highest Expansion Franchise Rights Fees ($Millions 2004)

	MLB		NBA		NFL		NHL	
DECADE	FEE	YEAR	FEE	YEAR	FEE	YEAR	FEE	YEAR
1960s	$67.4	1968	$10.8	1968	$49.3	1965	$11.1	1967
1970s	$23.4	1976	$25.0	1974	$64.8	1974	$21.9	1975
1980s	—	—	$49.4	1989	—	—	—	—
1990s	$146.7	1998	$155.5	1994	$777.8	1999	$91.8	1997
2000s	—	—	$300.0	2004	—	—	$86.5	2000
Average yearly increase	2.6%		8.0%		21.4%		2.3%	

Source: Calculated from data in Quirk and Fort (1992, 1999) and recent popular reports.

Just recently, record payments for teams were set in every league—the NHL's New York Islanders, $196 million (2000, or $214 million in 2004 dollars); the NBA's Boston Celtics, $360 million (2002, or $374 million in 2004 dollars); MLB's Los Angeles Dodgers, $371 million (2004); and the NFL's New York Jets, $635 million (2000, or $692 million in 2004 dollars).

Further, as Table 1.3 shows, **expansion franchise prices** have grown astronomically. The amounts in Table 1.3 show what a new expansion team would have cost over the decades in the four major professional team sports. But let's be careful making comparisons over a 40-year history. In Table 1.3, expansion fees that involved league mergers in hockey and basketball in 1979 are excluded. On an annual basis, expansion franchise prices in the major leagues have increased from between 2.3 percent in the NHL to 21.4 percent in the NFL over the past 4 decades.

Did You Know?

The value of selling franchises in the major leagues has increased from between 2.3 percent in the NHL to 21.4 percent in the NBA over the past 4 decades.

From the players' perspectives, it is easy to see why owner claims of poverty are met with skepticism. These increases in sale values are public knowledge, and it is only natural for players to focus on their contribution to the rising values. After all, nobody pays to watch an owner own. So players are just like other workers when they try to collect their share of the value they help to create, and those values have been rising handsomely for quite a long while.

Owners receive the most mixed treatment from fans and the media. It is easy to paint a clear picture of **owner exasperation** with the business of sports. On the one hand, they pay an arm and a leg to get the team in the first place. Further, payments to players are increasing over time. It is small wonder owners claim that they aren't getting rich running these teams. From their perspective, being investment savvy, taking risks, and having administrative skill all contribute to success and increasing team values. So they, too, want their fair share. Many owners seem genuinely exasperated with the disapproval their actions garner from fans and players.

LEARNING HIGHLIGHT
Consumer Movements in Sports

In 1994, MLB fans lost the end of the regular season, both League Championship Series, and the World Series to a players' strike. NBA fans lost the first half of the 1998–1999 season to a lockout by the owners. Understandably, fans were upset. But not all fans are willing to take strikes and lockouts sitting down. A few have begun to organize via the Internet. Here are descriptions of a few of these groups:

Sports Fans of America Association. This organization aims to improve the quality of sports from a fan's perspective. In part, it tries to provide a collective voice for fans on issues such as college football playoff systems, official accountability, and affordable ticket prices (sportsfansofamerica.com).

We the Fans. They're mad as hell and they aren't going to take it anymore. Their aim is getting fans united, organized, and "into the game" of sports business. Their view is that fans are the most important part of sports and the sports business (wethefans.com).

The Baseball Fans Union. The union wants maximum fan participation to show the players and owners that they cannot take the fans for granted anymore. Membership is free. Their position is: no work stoppage, enhance competitive balance, committed fans can put effective pressure on players and owners in the long-term interest of the game (baseballfansunion.com).

Some fans do more than just cheer to support their favorite team.

LEARNING HIGHLIGHT
Buying the New York Yankees

The New York Yankees is one team that has been, for the most part, kind to its investors. The following table, adjusted to 2004 dollars from figures in *Sports Illustrated* (November 2, 1998, p. 40), shows the sale prices of the Yankees over 83 years. Remember that the real annual growth rate in the economy at large is about 3 percent per year.

The growth in sales value, even with the disastrous tenure of CBS, is truly amazing. A simple formula shows the annual rate of return: $P_0(1 + r)^t = P_t$, where P_0 is the original

sale price, r is a constant rate of return, t is the length of time to next sale, and P_t is the latest sale price. From this, it is clear that $r = [(P_t/P_0)^{1/t}] - 1$. Ruppert and Huston enjoyed about a 4.0 percent real annual return to sale in 1945, while the Triumvir enjoyed about a 5.3 percent real annual return to sale in 1964. Both of these early annual rates are substantially more than the usual 3 percent annual growth rate in the economy. CBS lost about 8.5 percent annually, but then look at George Steinbrenner's reign—the franchise increased

New York Yankees' Historical Sale Values

Year	Buyer	Amount ($Millions 2004)
1915	Ruppert and Huston	$7.80
1945	The Triumvir	$25.50
1964	CBS	$67.50
1973	Steinbrenner	$30.30
Spring 1998	Dolan (Cablevision) offer	$733.80
Fall 1998	Informed speculation	$1,016.10

at large. Overall, then, the 83-year average of about 5.6 percent is the real annual increase in the value of the New York Yankees. Nice work, if you can get it when the general growth rate of the economy is 3 percent.

In 1915, the New York Yankees were sold for $7.8 million (measured in 2004 dollars). In 1998, that figure had risen to about $1 billion (also measured in 2004 dollars).

in value conservatively at a whopping 13.6 percent per year based on an actual offer by one media provider. This is 4.5 times the typical 3 percent growth rate in the economy

The following is a selection of resources that up-to-date sports economists read:

Sporting News
Sports Illustrated
Street and Smith's Sports Business Journal
SportsBusinessNews.com (www.sportsbusinessnews.com. They'll even send a "daily dose" to your e-mail address.)

CHAPTER RECAP

Professional team sports generated revenues of about $13.9 billion in 2002–2003 (measured in 2004 dollars). This isn't much compared to other industries, but interest in sports goes way beyond revenues. Perhaps Americans are obsessed with sports to the detriment of other important areas of endeavor. The business of sports is the object of our analysis.

The bulk of the evidence shows that sports are big business. Even billionaire owners treat their endeavor as a business. The bottom line matters, revenues are of paramount importance, and costs are fought with grim determination. Millionaire players certainly behave the same as any labor supplier seeking to maximize the return on their efforts. At times sports may be about more than just money, but by and large, business aspects dominate off the field.

Fans believe it's all about money. They're jealous and amazed at player salaries and believe that both owners and players make too much from their sport. Finally, amid all this money making, the price of enjoying sports continues to increase. Part of this fan befuddlement has turned to anger and action in the form of fan advocacy groups.

Players and owners also are skeptical and exasperated. Despite the arguments of owners that they aren't getting rich at their sport, team values and expansion franchise prices rise at handsome rates, and players know that they contribute to these increases. Owners counter that high team prices are the albatross they bear through their entire term of ownership. They take all the business risks and provide no small amount of administrative skills, and they expect profits in return.

KEY TERMS AND CONCEPTS

- Economic importance of sports
- Sports are big business
- Fan confusion

- Fan envy
- Fan consumer movements
- Player loyalty
- Player skepticism

- Franchise sale values
- Expansion franchise prices
- Owner exasperation

REVIEW QUESTIONS

1. Why do some argue that America's preoccupation with sports is unhealthy? Think in terms of economics.
2. Why are sports important beyond the basic revenues that they generate? Why are they important to you?
3. What are some of the indicators of the importance of sports beyond the money?
4. List reasons why sports really are businesses.
5. Why do rich owners insist that the public share some of the burden of stadium remodeling or construction?
6. Do you believe that Mark Cuban, owner of the Dallas Mavericks, really doesn't care if he blows $100 million in management mistakes? What else is behind his statement?
7. List three reasons why fans are befuddled by the current sports landscape.
8. Why are players skeptical of owners' claims of poverty?
9. Why do owners have chips on their shoulders about team ownership?
10. With whom do you most identify—fans, players, or owners? Why?

THOUGHT PROBLEMS

1. Boston Bruins owner Jeremy Jacobs said (*Sporting News*, 1992), "In reality, professional sports in America simply could not have evolved to their current positions of extraordinary popularity without adopting contemporary business practices. Professional sports management has contributed greatly to the increased accessibility, enjoyment and vitality of American sports." How do you assess Jacobs's statements? What are the good things that "contemporary

business practices" have brought to pro and college sports? What are the bad things?

2. Why is it that fans perceive that the game is all about money? How would you respond if one of your friends started to spout off about how sports are all about the money? Be sure to include both pro and college sports in your answer.

3. In Table 1.1, what happened to the no opinion percentage between 1984 and 1994? Who bears the greater brunt of fan dissatisfaction with earnings over time, fans or owners? Why do you think this has happened?

4. How do you explain the rise of fan consumer movements on the Internet? Be sure to think both in terms of fan attitudes and the cost involved in organizing a group using the Internet. Check out some fan consumer movements and decide which one you would join. What influenced your selection?

5. If you were a professional athlete (pick your sport), would you behave any differently than today's players in your pursuit of pay? If so, why? How are you different from players, economically speaking?

ADVANCED PROBLEMS

1. How would you go about assessing the overall value of sports? For example, one component might be the difference between the size of circulation and price of newspapers in cities that have pro sports and those that don't. Can you think of other elements to get a handle on this value?

2. Can you think of actions by owners and players that indicate there is more to sports than just money? Are these actions outside the bounds of economic analysis?

3. How is player pay just like pay for, say, management information systems jobs?

4. Do owners have any incentive to misrepresent the economic welfare generated for them by team ownership? Think of the big picture in terms of all of the relationships that owners have with players, fans, and the state and local government officials with whom they must deal.

5. Why are the NHL expansion fees in Table 1.3 so much lower than those for the rest of the major pro sports leagues? The data in Table 1.3 for all leagues besides MLB share something in common. Identify the commonality and offer an explanation.

INTERNET RESOURCES

For a host of additional material and questions for thought, visit this book's Web site at www.prenhall.com/fort.

REFERENCES

Levin, Richard C., George J. Mitchell, Paul A. Volcker, and George F. Will. *The Report of the Independent Members of the Commissioner's Blue Ribbon Panel on Baseball Economics.* New York: Major League Baseball, July 2000.

Quirk, James, and Rodney Fort. *Pay Dirt: The Business of Professional Team Sports.* Princeton, NJ: Princeton University Press, 1992.

Quirk, James, and Rodney Fort. *Hardball: The Abuse of Power in Pro Team Sports.* Princeton, NJ: Princeton University Press, 1999.

SUGGESTIONS FOR FURTHER READING

Costas, Bob. *Fair Ball: A Fan's Case for Baseball.* New York: Broadway Books, 2000.

Helyar, John. *Lords of the Realm: The Real History of Baseball.* New York: Ballantine Books, 1994.

Klein, Gene. *First Down and a Billion: The Funny Business of Pro Football.* New York: St. Martin's Press, 1987.

Miller, Marvin. *A Whole Different Ball Game: The Inside Story of Baseball's New Deal.* New York: Simon and Schuster, 1991.

Noll, Roger G., and Andrew Zimbalist, eds. *Sports, Jobs, and Taxes: The Economic Impact of Sports Teams and Stadiums.* Washington, D.C.: Brookings Institution, 1997.

Chapter

2

Demand and Sports Revenue

Chapter Objectives

After reading this chapter, you should be able to:

- ■ *Explain the concept of demand for sports, why it varies for different types of sports, and why teams have market power.*

- ■ *Explain how demand functions yield estimates of sports fan welfare.*

- ■ *Discuss the relationship between demand, elasticity, total revenue, and marginal revenue in sports.*

- ■ *Explain why fans with more inelastic demand can be charged higher prices than those with more elastic demand.*

- ■ *Explain why revenue variation is the source of unbalanced competition on the field and tension between teams in a given league.*

> *I remember Arthur Wirtz (former owner of the Chicago Blackhawks, deceased, 1983) delivering his most famous line. Somebody said, "We need some paint for the seats," and Arthur said, "We don't need paint, we need asses."*

—STAN MIKITA, FORMER BLACKHAWK GREAT
Sports Illustrated, June 1, 1992, p. 68

*F*an decisions to attend games are one of the most important elements of the sports business, but fan decisions are a complex issue. Stephen Jay Gould, the eminent natural scientist, emphasizes this as follows:

> Old fans like me often argue that the hoopla and commercialism—with rock music between innings at the park, organized cheering and chanting, hyped selling of all conceivable paraphernalia—have greatly compromised the gentler game we loved (which can still be so beautiful in its execution between the between-innings hype). But who is buying the T-shirts, fawning (and pawing) over every utility infielder for autographs, acquiescing in each successive move to eliminate the free broadcasts we once enjoyed and substitute some new scheme of selective payment? Us, of course; nobody but us, or at least most of us. . . . How can we moan that baseball has fallen to mammon when we willingly rushed into each new purchase? (The *New York Review*, November 5, 1992, p. 44)

We analyze these interesting fan choices in this chapter. We will examine scarcity and rationing in sports, as well as the demand theory as it applies to sports. Because there are few close substitutes for sports team output, we will look closely at market power and its effect on sports and discuss willingness to pay and consumers' surpluses. Price elasticity, total revenue, and marginal revenue are also covered in this chapter. We will also see that price discrimination is the meat and potatoes of sports pricing decisions. Finally, we will close our discussion by analyzing revenue data.

SCARCITY IN SPORTS

Scarcity makes the economic world go round. Indeed, it is the foundation of the economic chain of events—the trinity, if you will—summarized in Figure 2.1. Scarcity leads to **rationing,** and rationing leads to competition. Although the press usually portrays owners in pursuit of fan dollars, it actually is a two-way street: Sports fans demand team output and are willing to pay for it.

But just what is it that is so scarce when we talk about sports? The answer, of course, is that all of the characteristics of the sports product—the beauty of athletic prowess, absolute and relative team quality, the commonality sports provide, and the thrill of victory—are scarce.

Athletic Prowess

We have all played the games and understand that we are observing far more than mere proficiency when we watch professional athletes in action. All of the other scarce elements aside, fans appreciate the beauty and seeming impossibility of athletic prowess.

Figure 2.1 The Economic Trinity
Scarcity is a fact of life. Because scarcity exists, rationing devices must be chosen. Once a rationing device is chosen, people will compete according to that choice in order to obtain the scarce good.

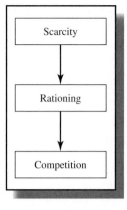

Frederick Exley put it this way describing a Sunday afternoon football game at the Polo Grounds in 1954:

> . . . when the play on the field seemed astonishingly perfect, we just fell quiet. That was the most memorable picture of all. Though we may not have had the background, or education, to weep at Prince Hamlet's death, we had all tried enough times to pass and kick a ball, we had on our separate rock-strewn sandlots taken enough lumps and bruises, to know that we were viewing something truly fine, something that only comes with years of toil, something very like art. (Exley, 1968)

Nearly every fan has felt what Exley has verbalized, and we are willing to pay in order to see it.

Quality of the Teams and Competition

The quality of teams, both absolute quality and relative quality, is a scarce commodity that generates the competition that fans enjoy. The **absolute level of quality** simply refers to the level of quality; for example, the difference between minor and major leagues. The **relative level of quality** describes the competitiveness of a team once the absolute level is determined; for example, the difference between a cellar dweller and a division champion.

Although fans enjoy the quality of competition at any level, they are willing to pay more for higher quality levels. Thus, the absolute level of quality matters. The level of competition that particular fans will eventually enjoy will depend on their willingness to pay for team quality. Those willing to pay more get to enjoy a higher level of quality than those willing to pay less. We will wait until Chapter 4 to analyze this in detail, but just think of the reason why one city only enjoys minor league competition whereas another enjoys a World Series champion. All of the elements behind that outcome concern the ability and willingness of fans to pay for different levels of competition in a given league.

Once the absolute level of quality is determined, relative competition becomes the object of fan attention. For the most part, an

"In order to maintain fan interest, a sports league has to ensure that teams do not get too strong or too weak relative to one another so that uncertainty of outcome is preserved."
— Quirk and Fort (1992, p. 243)

operational hypothesis in sports economics is that fans want their team to win in close games. And when it comes to the postseason, fans expect a reasonable chance that their team will appear, not every year, but often. This is sometimes called the **uncertainty of outcome** hypothesis. Even if the best that fans can support at a particular location is minor league sports, they still will care deeply about the competition at that level of play.

The uncertainty of outcome hypothesis is just that, a hypothesis. It is a prediction about preferences that cannot be examined directly. So those interested in the hypothesis must approach it indirectly by examining data related to fan choice. For example, in academic studies of the demand for attendance, investigators attempt to determine the impact of the usual demand variables on attendance, such as price, income, and winning, but also the impact the closeness of team records (even pregame betting odds) and how late in the season the ultimate playoff contenders are identified. The results of these studies are mixed. Some analysts find that these types of uncertainty of outcome variables matter, others don't.

Table 2.1 provides a bit of simple evidence concerning the uncertainty of outcome hypothesis and serves to emphasize that it is, after all, a hypothesis. Table 2.1 relates fans' willingness to pay (in terms of the average price of attendance), winning percent (wins divided by total games), and close games (plus or minus a touchdown). As you can see, there is some support for the uncertainty of outcome hypothesis. New England has the highest ticket price in the league, high winning percent, and a high percent of close games. To a somewhat lesser extent, so do Philadelphia and Green Bay. But, as with all things in the sports business, there is some variation. Kansas City is in the top-10 ticket price group, with a high winning percent but a relatively low percent of close games. St. Louis is in a similar situation, with the 12th highest ticket price, a relatively low winning percent, and a low percent of close games. Carolina, Seattle, and Tennessee are at the opposite end, relative to the uncertainty of outcome hypothesis. They have high winning percents and a high percent of close games but are in the bottom 10 in terms of ticket price.

This brings up an important operating principle for sports leagues that we will return to repeatedly in this book. If fans care about relative outcomes, there must be some balance in competition between teams. If the same teams always dominate the play-offs and the competitors in the championship are a foregone conclusion, then fan interest will wane. The Learning Highlight: Michael Jordan's Retirement, provides an introduction to why competitive balance is a big deal. In 1992, my coauthor and I put it this way:

> . . . For every fan who is a purist who simply enjoys watching athletes with outstanding ability perform regardless of the outcome, there are many more who go to watch their team win, and particularly to watch their team win a close game over a challenging opponent. In order to maintain fan interest, a sports league has to ensure that teams do not get too strong or too weak relative to one another so that uncertainty of outcome is preserved. (Quirk and Fort, 1992, p. 243)

Commonality

Another scarce sports characteristic is the commonality it provides. Yesterday's game and its coverage by the media provide a common bond among people. How often

Table 2.1

Willingness to Pay and Close Games, NFL 2003

Team	Price	Winning Percent	Close Ratio
New England	$75.33	0.875	0.625
Washington	$68.06	0.313	0.688
Chicago	$65.00	0.438	0.438
Philadelphia	$64.00	0.813	0.500
Jacksonville	$62.85	0.313	0.625
N.Y. Jets	$62.20	0.375	0.750
N.Y. Giants	$61.67	0.250	0.313
Minnesota	$59.00	0.563	0.250
Oakland	$58.89	0.250	0.563
Kansas City	$58.40	0.813	0.375
San Francisco	$58.00	0.438	0.438
Denver	$57.28	0.625	0.375
St. Louis	$54.92	0.750	0.438
Pittsburgh	$54.55	0.375	0.438
Green Bay	$54.40	0.688	0.500
Detroit	$53.91	0.313	0.313
Dallas	$53.06	0.625	0.375
Baltimore	$53.03	0.625	0.375
Houston	$50.67	0.313	0.625
Tampa Bay	$49.78	0.438	0.563
Indianapolis	$47.39	0.875	0.688
Cincinnati	$47.28	0.500	0.688
San Diego	$46.82	0.250	0.438
Miami	$46.46	0.625	0.438
Cleveland	$45.71	0.313	0.563
New Orleans	$43.87	0.500	0.563
Tennessee	$43.35	0.813	0.563
Seattle	$43.06	0.625	0.563
Buffalo	$42.55	0.375	0.250
Carolina	$42.27	0.875	0.875
Arizona	$35.99	0.250	0.375
Atlanta	$34.63	0.313	0.500

Notes: Includes playoff games. "Close" is defined as plus or minus 7 points. Price is the average ticket price from Team Marketing Report's Fan Cost Index (www.teammarketing.com).

have you heard, "Hey, how about those [favorite team here]?" The common bond of sports is also apparent in poetic epics such as Ernest Lawrence Thayer's "Casey at the Bat" (1888) and shared personal reflections such as Donald Hall's *Fathers Playing Catch with Sons* (1998). Finally, motion pictures ranging from the emotional (*Hoosiers* or *Field of Dreams*) to the tragic (*Brian's Song*) to the lighthearted (*Tin Cup*) bind us together. Once you've heard it, you'll never forget Terrence Mann (played by James

When Michael Jordan retired in 1998, reactions were mixed. On the one hand, the NBA lost arguably its greatest player ever, long before his talents were in decline. The beauty of the game suffered. Many argued that the absolute level of talent declined with the loss of just one player. In addition, one of the NBA's biggest draws was gone, leading to much hand wringing among observers of the financial welfare of the game. All of this was on the heels of the loss of half a season to a labor dispute that led to the first lost games in the league's history.

But fans in New York, Phoenix, San Antonio, and Utah had an entirely different take on MJ's retirement. With the demise of the Bulls, no longer led by Jordan, fans in these cities could look forward to an increased probability of successful postseason play for their own teams. Without Jordan, the absolute level of competition in the NBA may have decreased, but relatively speaking, more teams were in the hunt for the championship. The revenue impact across so many cities could potentially outweigh any other decline in fan interest due to the loss of Jordan to the league. If more fans are more interested in the enhanced chances for a wider variety of teams, the NBA could actually be better off without Jordan.

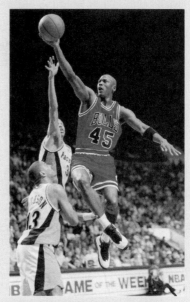

When Michael Jordan retired in 1998, many believed the absolute level of talent in the NBA declined.

Earl Jones) explaining the binding power of baseball to farmer Ray Kinsella (played by Kevin Costner) in *Field of Dreams*:

> The one constant through all the years, Ray, has been baseball. America has rolled by like an army of steamrollers. It's been erased like a blackboard, rebuilt and erased again. Baseball marked the time. This field, this game, is a part of our past, Ray. It reminds of all that once was good . . . that could be again. Ohhhh, people will come, Ray. People will most definitely come.

Winning

Let's not forget about winning. Depending on how you may have been coached, you probably remember those immortal words attributed to Vince Lombardi, NFL coaching legend and namesake of the Super Bowl Trophy: "Winning isn't everything. It's the only thing." Fans love the home team, but they love it even more when it is a winner.

The more bitter the rivalry, it seems, the sweeter the win. Thus, winning is very closely related to competition in the sense that victory over a bitter rival is the sweetest of all. Winning is such a pervasive motivation for fans that later in the book we will use it as a catchall for the characteristics of sports demanded by fans.

Rationing in Sports

From an economic perspective, the factors we just described are all scarce commodities; that is, there are not enough of them freely available to satisfy all desires. Thus, rationing must occur; some mechanism must be chosen to help discriminate between those who want sports. There are many rationing devices, but the most prominent is price. If fans are willing to pay ticket prices, they get to see the sports event. The more fans in a given location who are willing to pay for quality, the higher the quality of the team they will get to enjoy. Further, as long as fans pay a price through product purchases, advertisers will give media providers (networks, cable, and satellite stations) the financial incentive to put sports on television.

Those who are unhappy with price as a rationing device often seek to alter the terms of trade. In many lease agreements between professional teams and their city-hosts, clauses either restrict ticket prices or require that teams keep some seating sections affordable. In cases where the dollar price is kept artificially low due to agreements between the teams and the government, some fans are happier than they would be if ticket prices were higher. But the inescapable observation is that a price will be paid, either in dollars or as a combination of dollars and waiting. Many fans who are relatively slow to get in line lose out on attendance altogether.

Waiting in line is just one option; the black market is another. Black markets arise whenever the price mechanism is exchanged for another rationing method. Scalping reflects a fully functioning black market. Scalpers buy the cheap tickets and sell them to people who are willing to pay high prices in order to avoid waiting in lines. Such arbitrage from lower- to higher-price buyers usually is viewed as an important function of markets. However, scalping is often viewed so scornfully that it is illegal in many places.

Let's now turn to a more rigorous specification of scarcity and rationing, namely, demand theory. The basic idea of relating quantity to price generates the entire foundation of the revenue side of sports. If you seek answers to the many puzzles surrounding sports, you've got to follow the advice that "Deep Throat" gave to Bernstein and Woodward in *All the President's Men* (1974): "Follow the money." Following the money requires a thorough understanding of the demand for sports.

DEMAND THEORY IN SPORTS

Fans want to share in the excellence, competition, identification, and the vicarious "thrill of victory and agony of defeat" associated with sports teams. They are willing to pay in order to do so. The economic concept of **demand** quantifies willingness to

Table 2.2

Demand Schedules for Men's and Women's Basketball Season Tickets (Class size = 100)

SEASON TICKET PRICE ($)	# OF MEN'S HOOPS TICKETS	# OF WOMEN'S HOOPS TICKETS
0	100	100
10	85	70
20	70	40
30	50	20
40	20	5
50	12	0
60	8	0
70	2	0
80	0	0

pay and the scarcity implicit in that willingness. Demand is simply the relationship between prices and quantities demanded. But let's not forget that willingness to pay—and all of the elements that determine willingness to pay—is also captured in this deceptively simple concept. For the rest of this chapter, we will use attendance to measure the consumption of the scarce items in sports events. In later chapters, we'll expand to other measures, but for now will stick to just attendance.

Suppose we want to discover the relationship between price, or willingness to pay, and the number of season tickets to your school's men's and women's basketball teams that would be purchased by the people in your class at different prices. The data points that we would collect, relating prices and quantities of attendance demanded, are called a demand schedule. A typical pair of demand schedules for men's and women's basketball looks like the pair shown in Table 2.2. Graphing the data shown in Table 2.2 (remember, in economics the convention is to plot price against quantities demanded), one finds the demand functions for men's hoops and women's hoops shown in Figure 2.2.

Demand Determinants

The two-dimensional graph in Figure 2.2 can only show the relationship between two things. The demand for season tickets to men's basketball and women's basketball shows only how many tickets will be purchased at a variety of prices. Thus, if ticket price changes, **movement along the given demand function** shows changes in quantity demanded. Prices and quantities are inversely related; as the price of tickets increases, the quantity demanded decreases. However, what happens if something else changes?

Changes in other factors will cause a change in demand itself. What other factors determine the demand for attending the two types of basketball for this particular group of buyers? There are five main categories of **demand shifters:**

- Preferences, or sports fan tastes (especially for team quality)
- Fan income
- The price of other goods fans enjoy (especially entertainment substitutes)
- Fan expectations about the future
- Population in a team's city

Figure 2.2 Demand Functions for Men's and Women's Basketball Season Tickets (Class Size = 100)

A simple classroom experiment chooses a subset of the class and asks, "How many season tickets to men's or women's basketball would you buy at various prices?" Plotting price against their response gives two different demand functions for the two sports. For example, 70 students are willing to buy a men's ticket at a price of $20, but the price would have to fall to $10 before 70 students would buy a women's ticket.

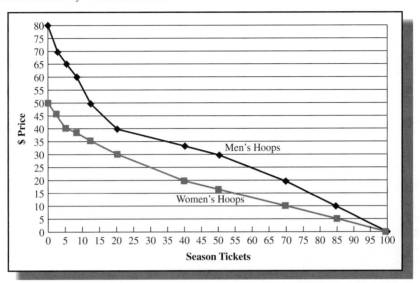

Fan Preferences Identifying the source of fan preferences for sports raises questions of both the "nature" and "nurture" variety. The natural joy of coordinated physical activity is apparent in the youngest of children. Are people competitive by nature, or is it a learned behavior? Certainly, experience contributes to our preferences for sports. It appears that fans love the games that they learned to play while growing up (baseball, basketball, soccer, football, and hockey) and continue to play as they age (tennis, golf, and bowling). Participation among high school students in various sports is shown in Table 2.3. Clearly, once grown, men and women are fans of the games they played when they were younger.

The relative number of people who have experience in different sports helps explain why it is only very recently that soccer has become an important spectator sport in the United States. Experience may also help explain why more sports fans seek the level of excellence and competition offered in men's sports rather than in the same sport played by women. Not that long ago, interest in women's basketball was so low that athletic departments did not even charge fans for admission! This would be one part of the explanation for the shape and location of the demand for women's hoops and men's hoops in Figure 2.2.

Did You Know?
Nearly a million more boys participate in the top-5 sports for boys than girls participate in the top-5 sports for girls.

It is essential to remember that preferences can change. Judging by the increasing fan interest in women's basketball at both the college and professional level, as experience with women's sports has increased, so has the attention of fans. Thus, one

Table 2.3 Sports Participation by High School Boys and Girls, 2001–2002

BOYS		GIRLS	
SPORT	PARTICIPATION	SPORT	PARTICIPATION
Football	1,023,712	Basketball	456,169
Basketball	540,597	Outdoor track & field	415,677
Outdoor track & field	494,092	Volleyball	395,124
Baseball	451,674	Fast-pitch softball	355,960
Soccer	339,101	Soccer	295,265
Wrestling	244,637	Cross country	160,178
Cross country	190,993	Tennis	160,114
Golf	163,299	Swimming	141,218
Tennis	139,483	Competitive spirit squads	94,635
Swimming	90,698	Field hockey	60,737
Total	3,678,286	Total	2,535,077

Source: National Federation of State High School Associations, 2001–2002 High School Participation Survey, Indianapolis, IN.

would expect that the demand for women's basketball has been increasing over time, shifting to the right and outward toward the demand for men's basketball. The recent staying power of women's professional basketball, the WNBA, stands as testimony to the importance of changing preferences.

Quality is one of the more important preference elements in the determination of demand. Although all of the other elements matter, they can be overcome by the intensity of preferences for quality. All fans enjoy higher quality relative to lower quality, but the intensity of that desire is reflected in willingness to pay. Fans in two different locales may be identical in all other regards, but if one set of fans puts a higher premium on winning than another, then they will have a greater willingness to pay for higher quality. This greater willingness to pay will be reflected in a greater demand than enjoyed at the other location.

It is a simple extension of this idea to see that preferences for quality can actually overcome other demand factors when comparing two locations. Even though the population may be larger in one city, fans in another city may have such intense preferences for quality, and willingness to pay for it, that their team is competitive even though it has a smaller population. For example, the NFL's Green Bay Packers come to mind. We'll see the details of how this happens later in the chapter.

Whether it's nature or nurture doesn't matter to economists, who simply take preferences as given. This bothers people who are more interested in the question of preference formation than in the question of how preferences affect choices. From the economic perspective, if preferences for a particular sport change over time, then the demand for that sport will shift. A change in preferences probably explains the increase in demand for NBA basketball over time relative to the demand for MLB baseball. Earlier in this chapter, we saw that NBA basketball and MLB are entertainment substitutes. This partially explains why fan interest in basketball increased at the same time as a decline in the interest in baseball. And, at least to hear MLB marketers tell it, this was especially true of young African-American sports fans.

Fan Income Income changes also cause sports demand functions to shift. An increase in income can cause demand to either increase for so-called normal goods or decrease for so-called inferior goods. If incomes rose and some sports fans shifted their purchases from college basketball to professional basketball available in the same area, then the pro version would be income normal and the college version would be income inferior for this group of consumers. It is extremely important to point out that any given sport can be a normal good for some fans and an inferior good for other fans. After all, income simply allows fans to pursue their preferences, and preferences certainly vary between sports for a given fan and among different sports for different fans. We will further discuss the influence of fan income later in this chapter.

Price of Other Goods Changes in the price of other entertainment alternatives also shift sports demand functions. All entertainment options can be considered as alternative consumption possibilities, from opera to Little League. Even professional sports in different leagues with different seasons can be substitutes. It all depends on how you view the planning process for sports fans. If they think over an extended period about how they will spend their money, then the NBA and MLB can be substitutes, even though they are played at different times during the year. Sports fans confront trade-offs as they plan their annual spending.

Whether demand decreases or increases with the price of another good depends on whether a sport and its entertainment alternative are substitutes or complements. If the price of season opera passes (a substitute) fell dramatically, some sports fans might well choose more opera and reduce sports attendance. On the other hand, if the price of a complement such as parking were to increase, fewer people would attend sports.

Fan Expectations Expectations about future prices also shift demand itself. If fans expect the price of a particular type of sports event to increase in the future, their demand for that event might increase today. Fans might consume more of it while it is cheaper. One example of the impact of expectations is the purchase of "lifetime" reservation rights. Some fans of pro teams will pay for a personal seat license, or PSL, that guarantees access to a particular location for a specified period of time. PSLs vary in price by seat location and the amenities offered for that particular type of seat. Fans would pay this price if they expected that the price of obtaining the same seat was at least as high as the PSL price. If they expected that the price would increase even more, then the license would be a bargain. Because fans can just wait and buy seats on an annual basis, we are led to conclude that they must be getting a price break on their seat, given their expectation that prices will increase over time.

Population The impact of population on demand is simple arithmetic. Suppose the class size in the example portrayed in Table 2.2 and Figure 2.2 was to double. With 200 students, there simply would be more people willing to pay at every price (as long as some of the added students were basketball fans!). Thus, as population increases, so does demand. Recall that an increase in demand is a shift to the right in the entire demand function.

Table 2.4 lists areas with major league teams and the number of teams, population, and per capita income for each area. The areas are listed in order of population. Because all of the factors that determine the shape and location of demand functions

Table 2.4 Teams, Per Capita Income, and Population of Major League Areas

City	Number of Teams	Population 2000	Per Capita Income $2004
New York—Northern New Jersey—Long Island	9	18,323,002	$28,466
Los Angeles—Riverside—Orange Country	5	12,365,627	$22,652
Chicago—Gary—Kenosha	5	9,098,316	$26,302
Washington—Baltimore	5	7,349,177	$30,147
Philadelphia—Wilmington—Atlantic City	4	5,687,147	$25,358
Detroit—Ann Arbor—Flint	4	5,211,593	$25,974
Dallas—Fort Worth	4	5,161,544	$25,269
Miami—Fort Lauderdale	4	5,007,564	$21,886
Houston—Galveston—Brazoria	3	4,715,407	$23,220
Boston—Worcester—Lawrence	4	4,391,344	$28,736
Atlanta	3	4,247,981	$26,785
San Francisco—Oakland—San Jose	3	4,123,740	$32,923
Phoenix—Mesa	4	3,251,876	$23,440
Seattle—Tacoma—Bremerton	3	3,043,878	$27,546
Minneapolis—St. Paul	3	2,968,806	$28,054
Cleveland—Akron	3	2,843,103	$23,881
San Diego	6	2,813,833	$24,531
St. Louis	1	2,698,687	$24,287
Denver—Boulder—Greeley	4	2,629,980	$27,832
Memphis, Nashville	1	2,516,993	$23,113
Pittsburgh	3	2,431,087	$22,400
Tampa—St. Petersburg—Clearwater	3	2,395,997	$23,309
Cincinnati—Hamilton	2	2,009,632	$24,553
Portland—Salem	1	1,927,881	$24,173
Kansas City	2	1,836,038	$24,959
Sacramento—Yolo	1	1,796,857	$23,863
Green Bay, Milwaukee	3	1,783,340	$23,961
San Antonio	2	1,711,703	$19,814
Orlando	1	1,644,561	$22,718
Columbus	1	1,612,694	$24,631
Indianapolis	2	1,525,104	$24,822
Salt Lake City—Ogden	1	1,411,514	$21,166
Charlotte—Gastonia—Rock Hill	2	1,330,448	$25,056
New Orleans	2	1,316,510	$20,152
Buffalo—Niagara Falls	2	1,170,111	$21,553
Hartford	1	1,148,618	$27,685
Jacksonville	1	1,122,750	$23,286
Min	1	1,122,750	$19,814
Max	9	18,323,002	$32,923
Ave	3	3,692,553	$24,824
Median	3	2,629,980	$24,531

Source: factfinder.census.gov.

Notes: Consolidated Metropolitan Statistical Area (CMSA) or Metropolitan Statistical Area (MSA) that included the main city name. Author matched population areas to income areas. Per capita income originally reported in 1999.

Did You Know?
On average, the top
10 population areas have
5.5 times the population,
1.1 times the income, and
three times as many pro
sports teams as the bottom
10 population areas.

are highly interactive, it isn't always just the greatest population or the highest income that leads to the highest demand. However, you should be able to trace some of the ideas we have just discussed. For example, the New York–New Jersey area has the greatest population, the largest number of teams, and the fourth highest per capita income of the 37 listed areas. Jacksonville, at the other end, has the smallest population, only one team (the NFL's Jaguars), and a below-average per capita income.

Although there is quite a bit of variation in Table 2.4, a look at the top 10 and bottom 10 cities proves insightful. The top 10 population areas average 7.7 million in population, 4.7 teams, and $26,833 in per capita income. The bottom 10 population areas (which include the smallest income area, San Antonio) average 1.4 million in population, 1.5 teams, and $24,012 in per capita income. Based on the averages, the top 10 population areas have 5.5 times the population, 1.1 times the income, and three times as many teams as the bottom 10 areas.

However, population is not static. Some areas grow in population while others decline. Because demand represents willingness to pay, owners are quite interested in the demand prospects in different locations as population changes. Given the limited number of teams, areas that are growing faster represent greener pastures for current sports team owners. Therefore, population also helps determine the migration of teams as owners seek areas with greater willingness to pay.

LESSONS FROM DEMAND

Let's pause and reflect on what you have learned thus far. The first important concept, to which we will often return, is that nearly all of the money in sports comes from fans. The single qualification to this statement concerns the money transferred through the political process. Typically, this money comes from nonsports fans and goes to fans, owners, players, and others who earn income from the presence of sports teams in a given location. We will spend a significant amount of time on this exception in Chapters 11 and 12. As for the rest of the money, even though it is collected from a variety of sources, such as ticket revenue, broadcast revenue, shares of stadium revenues, sponsorships, and the sale of licensed merchandise, the source of all these revenues is fans willing to pay for sports. In the next chapter, we'll talk extensively about advertising revenue, and even that comes from fans.

MARKET POWER

Perhaps the first thing you noticed about the demand functions in Figure 2.2 is that they are negatively sloped; that is, the functions slope downward. As price increases, fewer season tickets are demanded. That these demands slope downward implies that there are substitutes, although not perfect ones, for attendance at these college games. In the case of perfect substitutes, the market is perfectly competitive. Therefore, it follows that the demand curves in Figure 2.2 come from a less than perfectly competitive situation. To see this distinction based on economic competition, let's think about the substitutes for attendance.

Consumers view all manner of other entertainment as substitutes for sports. Opera, theater, movies, television shows, and concerts—all of these activities entertain us and are substitutes for sports. In fact, some sports are even substitutes for each other. For some fans, men's basketball and women's basketball may well be substitute goods. If there were perfect substitutes for sports attendance, one would not find the demand functions sloping downward, as in Figure 2.2. At some given price for season tickets, if prices were increased, fans would simply turn to the perfect substitutes for men's basketball or women's basketball. In this case, the athletic department would have no power over the price they could charge. This would be a perfectly competitive situation. But why aren't these other nonsports entertainment alternatives good substitutes for sports? In his book *Sports Marketing* (1999), Matthew Shank offers one explanation: Sports are the most spontaneous of all entertainment:

> A play has a script, and a concert has a program, but the action that entertains us in sport is spontaneous and uncontrolled by those who participate in the event. When we go to a comedic movie, we expect to laugh, and when we go to a horror movie we expect to be scared even before we pay our money. But the emotions we may feel when watching a sporting event are hard to determine. If it is a close contest and our team wins, we may feel excitement and joy. But if it is a boring event and our team loses, the entertainment benefit we receive is quite different. (p. 3)

Economists seldom delve into such explanations, but they are important in determining the shape of demand. Figure 2.3 shows the variety of shapes for demand functions based on the closeness and availability of substitutes. Suppose the demand function were like D_1. If a team raised its price by even a penny, it would

Figure 2.3 Varieties of Demand Functions

D_1 represents the case of demand with perfect substitutes; increasing the price just a little results in a complete collapse in attendance to zero. D_2 takes the polar opposite case of no substitutes at all; fans demand a particular level of tickets regardless of price. D_3 is the intermediate case of downward sloping demand; increasing price reduces attendance, but not completely.

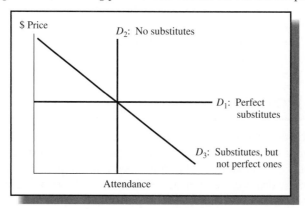

lose all of its fans. This is the perfectly competitive demand function. If there were absolutely no substitutes, the attendance demand function would be vertical, like D_2. Even if a team raised its price substantially, it would lose no fans. But for the teams depicted in Figure 2.3, the case is in between, more like D_3. There are substitutes for sports attendance but not perfect substitutes. It is this last type of demand that characterizes sports attendance.

In sports, this **market power** is derived from the fact that teams occupy **exclusive geographic territory.** At all levels of sports, even down to youth sports, there is a decision-making body that decides the number and location of teams in the organization. In baseball, for example, organizations such as Little League, Protect Our Nation's Youth (PONY) League, and Babe Ruth Baseball all grant specific locations to a certain number of teams. Because there are many competing youth sports organizations, which may sometimes include local park departments, there is little reason to suspect that any of these organizations are able to exercise much power over the price that they charge local sports organizations to belong.

Can the same thing be said as we move up the sports ladder? The Professional Baseball Agreement (PBA) governs the relationship between the minor leagues, organized as the National Association of Professional Baseball Leagues (NAPBL), and MLB. The PBA also governs the relationship between all of the various levels of minor league baseball, from short-season "rookie" leagues to AAA leagues, the level just below MLB. Although the PBA is complicated, the final result is very clear. Each league can assign exclusive geographical rights to a particular team. In the event of territory conflict between leagues, the PBA gives a clear prescription on how to settle the issue.

Outcomes under the PBA are well-defined, exclusive rights to a particular territory for a particular team. No other team may enter the territory and compete, economically speaking, with the exclusive franchise holder. In the case of minor league baseball, the lack of substitutes is engineered under the PBA to make sure that the franchise holder is the only game in town. Although there are some other entertainment substitutes for the local team, there are no other professional baseball substitutes. Here is an example with which I am familiar from some consulting work in the past.

In 1993, the AAA Salt Lake City Gulls folded and were replaced by the Salt Lake City Trappers. The Trappers were members of the Pioneer League, a short-season rookie league. They were phenomenally successful, hiring pretty good talent in a weak league, developing a large following, and even making the national news for the longest winning streak in professional baseball (a record that stands to this day).

The Portland Mavericks, playing at the AAA level just below Major League Baseball, weren't faring nearly as well. The Mavericks played in an oversized stadium in front of few fans. Under the rules of the PBA, all the owner of the Mavericks needed to do was inform the Trappers that the Mavericks would be taking over their territory. Under those same PBA rules, however, the Mavericks were required to compensate the Trappers, but the two teams could not reach an agreement as to the amount. In this case, the PBA rules dictate a formal arbitration hearing. Parties represent their cases and agree to live with whatever the arbitrator decides. Eventually, nearly $2 million in total compensation went to the Pioneer League, and the Mavericks moved to Salt Lake City. Under the arbitration settlement, the Pioneer League was allowed to place a team (the Raptors) in nearby Ogden, Utah, but the Trappers could no longer operate in Salt Lake City.

The highest-level professional leagues have complete control over the number and location of teams. The league decides when to expand, and rules for team movement require more than a simple majority vote among league members. Leagues (and the NCAA in the college case, as we'll see in Chapter 14) offer a number of explanations for their exclusionary practices. Essentially, the leagues' arguments all boil down to quality control—major leagues determine who gets to count themselves as major. Regardless of the justification, the result is that the number of close substitutes is reduced and individual teams are endowed with some market power. Through careful management by the league, the location and number of teams is controlled over time.

Consider the recent expansion of the NFL. The NFL's decision came down to two candidate host cities, Los Angeles and Houston. The league chose the latter, guaranteeing the Houston area to a single NFL team. In the meantime, fans in the Los Angeles area are without an NFL team. Surely, if the world were a bit more economically competitive, another league would have put a team in Los Angeles, the second largest market in the United States. As a result, the only real chance for economic competition facing teams in a given league comes from outside the sport. We'll see in-depth how this control effects league outcomes in Chapters 5 and 6, and just why it is that they continue to have this control in Chapter 12.

Given this careful management of team location to ensure market power, how can we explain multiple teams from the same league operating in the same location? There is a two-part explanation. First, there is the simple power of numbers. Some cities have more than enough people for the economic survival of more than one team. Thus, the greater Southern California metropolis clearly can support more than one team, as can the San Francisco Bay Area in Northern California, the New York/New Jersey area, and Chicago.

Second, just because artificial boundaries define a particular city or metropolitan area, that doesn't mean that these areas are just one big happy single entity. Chicago's North and South Sides, for example, are economically and ethnically distinct. So are the boroughs of New York City. San Francisco and Oakland couldn't be more distinct in terms of their economic situation. As the old joke among San Franciscans goes, there's a good reason why they collect the Bay Bridge toll as you leave Oakland. Nobody would pay to get in. And Oakland residents probably feel the same way about San Franciscans.

The upshot of all of this is that attendance demand for any particular sports team, at any level, slopes downward. This is the definition of market power. A firm has market power when it has few close substitutes for its product. A sports team does not have to be a monopoly in the strictest sense to have market power.

Preferences and Demand for Women's Sports

Let's return to Figure 2.2. It is clear that the demand for men's basketball tickets is greater than the demand for women's basketball tickets—at every price, a greater quantity of men's than women's tickets is demanded. What factors explain this difference in demand? The number of students is constant, and the rest of the factors influencing demand (income, the price of other goods, and expectations) do not change when turning from the demand for men's hoops to the demand for women's hoops. The answer lies with preferences. We will spend quite some time on sex and race issues in sports in Chapters 6 and 13. The important lesson here is that preferences are at the heart of this difference in demand.

Change in Demand versus Upward Sloping Demand

Note the difference between a change in the quantity demanded and a change in demand itself. It seems that the more expensive an event becomes, the greater the number of people who attend. Before jumping to the conclusion that demand slopes upward, remember that a given demand curve can change over time. The more likely outcome is that demand simply has increased over time and one has observed two different prices on two different demand functions.

The law of demand states that consumers buy fewer units when prices rise, but the typical observation is that both attendance and price increase over time. Indeed, the data show that this has been true over some time periods. In Table 2.5, covering the period 1999–2003, the adjusted correlation is the correlation between attendance and prices, adjusted for inflation in the prices. Note that all of the values are positive. These data appear to be consistent with the idea that higher prices go along with greater quantities.

However, our analysis of demand suggests a different answer. Be careful to distinguish between changes in the quantity demanded and changes in demand itself. To assume that the relationship between attendance and price over time represents a single demand function is to assume that no other demand shifters have changed over time. That seems pretty unreasonable. Instead, it's highly likely that income, the price of other goods, preferences, expectations, or population might have changed over the 14 years in the sample. Among these, it is most likely that an increase in income or an increase in population would lead to higher prices and attendance over time. The confusion is shown in Figure 2.4. At one time, an observed attendance-price pair might be (A_1, P_1) on demand function D_1. At another time, after any number of demand shifters may have changed, an observed attendance-price pair is (A_2, P_2) on demand function D_2. It would be careless to just connect the

Table 2.5

Correlations Between Attendance and Prices, 1999–2003

	ADJUSTED CORRELATION
LEAGUE	($2004)
MLB	0.28
NBA	0.16
NFL	0.13
NHL	0.04

Notes: Incomplete data through the entire period precluded inclusion of the NBA's Grizzlies and Jazz, the NFL's Oilers, and the NHL's Avalanche. The correlations are the average across the teams in each league. Ticket prices are from Team Marketing Report's FCI (www.teammarketing.com).

Figure 2.4 Upward Sloping Demand Versus Change in Demand

A change in demand from D_1 at one point in time to D_2 at a later point in time can be confused for a positive relationship between attendance and price. Rather than correctly identifying point (A_1, P_1) on demand D_1 and point (A_2, P_2) on D_2, one could mistakenly conclude that demand slopes upward by failing to account for factors that change demand itself.

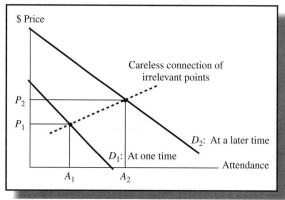

two points, as the dotted line in Figure 2.4 does, when the two different points might lie on different demand curves.

Demand and Large and Small Markets

Population is part of the explanation for what is known as the "large market–small market" conflict. We'll discuss this conflict later in the text, but it is worth introducing here. Historically, large-market teams win more often than small-market teams. Part of the reason has to do with the fact that teams with larger populations to draw from have the opportunity to earn higher revenues for any given level of quality. This means that teams in larger markets will buy better players because they can earn higher revenues from those players than teams in smaller markets could earn. Although it is revenue that ultimately drives this wedge between small- and large-market teams, population is one of the determinants of revenue differences.

Population is not the only factor that determines the demand for sports in a given location. A team owner might consider moving to another location, even if its population is smaller, as long as other factors such as income and preferences result in greater demand. This is especially true if this greater demand manifests itself through a city's offer to build a new stadium or arena to house the team.

WILLINGNESS TO PAY AND CONSUMERS' SURPLUSES

The market demand function for sports reveals consumers' willingness to pay. For example, in our derivation of the attendance demand functions for men's basketball and women's basketball in Figure 2.2, willingness to pay is higher for the men's version for every single level of season tickets.

Willingness to Pay

In Figure 2.2, the demand curve for women's hoops shows that the most any person is willing to pay for the fifth women's ticket is $40. The demand curve for men's hoops shows that somebody would be willing to pay $65 for the fifth men's ticket. Some people would be willing to pay even more than that for the first through fourth tickets for each type of basketball output. Moving farther down along the demand functions, some fan is willing to pay only $10 for the 70th women's season ticket, whereas the greatest willingness to pay for the 70th men's ticket would be $20.

These marginal changes in willingness to pay show us one measure of value of season tickets to fans. At the margin, the amount given by the two demand functions allows us to compare the dollar value that fans put on the two different versions of basketball. There is considerable variation in even this simple example. At the end of this chapter, we'll examine revenues within a sport and across the four major pro sports leagues. Considerable variation in willingness to pay, measured by actual revenues collected by teams, exists in all sports.

Consumers' Surpluses

A closely related idea concerns just how happy consumers are with their consumption. A dollar measure of this welfare is called **consumers' surpluses.** Consumers' surpluses are the sum of the difference between willingness to pay and the actual market price on all units of consumption. Figure 2.5 demonstrates consumers'

Figure 2.5 Consumer's Surpluses for Men's and Women's Basketball Tickets (Class Size = 100)

Consumers' surpluses are the area above a given price, but below the demand function, on the number of tickets sold. At a price of $20, 40 women's tickets are demanded. On each and every ticket, willingness to pay (along the demand function) lies above the price. The shaded area shows the Consumers' surpluses enjoyed by those purchasing the 40 tickets.

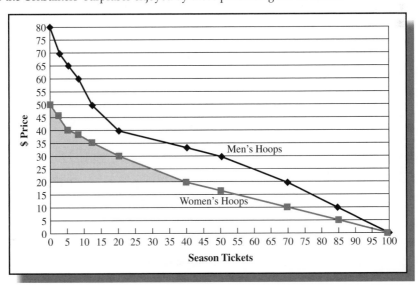

surpluses for the demand for women's season tickets. In the figure, the shaded area shows the consumers' surpluses for women's tickets purchased at $20. Clearly, because all 40 buyers are willing to pay more than $20 for each season ticket, the consumers' surpluses for women's tickets totals about $450 (just add up the differences between willingness to pay on the demand function and the actual price of $20). Remember, these values are dollar measures of welfare. In the most real sense of the word, they represent precisely how much buyers would be willing to give up to enjoy season tickets over and above the price, in dollar terms.

It also is possible to put a dollar measure on the change in welfare associated with a change in the price of tickets. This idea is demonstrated in Figure 2.6 for women's season tickets. At a price of $20, we've already seen that the consumers' surpluses are equal to the shaded area below the demand function and above the price of $20 (about $450). Now, suppose the price falls to $10 per ticket. Intuitively, buyers will be happier at a lower price. We can use consumers' surpluses to attach a dollar value to that increased welfare. The first part of the increased welfare concerns the savings that occur for those purchasing the original 40 tickets. Each ticket now costs $10 less. That's a dollar measure of increased welfare equal to $400, or the area in Figure 2.6 at the bottom left filled in with vertical stripes. The second part of the increased welfare occurs because the number of tickets demanded increases when the price falls to $10. In fact, 30 more tickets would be purchased at the lower price. The dotted area shows the consumers' surpluses on these tickets. A careful calculation of this area using the data in Table 2.2 yields an increase of $150. All told, the increased welfare enjoyed by

Figure 2.6 Price Change and Consumers' Surpluses for Women's Basketball Tickets (Class Size = 100)

Consumers' surpluses can be used to measure the value buyers put on changes in prices. At a price of $20, consumers' surpluses on the 40 tickets purchased are the shaded area above $20 and below the demand function out to 40 tickets. When price falls to $10, consumers' surpluses increase by the vertical-dash rectangle, plus the dotted triangle on the original 40 tickets, plus the shaded triangle because the number of tickets purchased increases by 30 to 70 total.

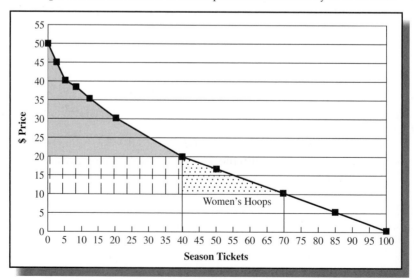

buyers of women's tickets when the price falls to $10 is equal to $550. Added to the $450 already enjoyed before the price fall, that's a total of $1,000.

Knowing the level of surpluses is interesting enough. But throughout this book we will use surpluses to analyze a number of important sports issues. For example, what could be more important to team owners than the fans' willingness to pay? Suppose owners decide to raise ticket prices. Consumers' surpluses give a measure of how this makes ticket buyers worse off. From the policy perspective, if a team is leaving a location, consumers' surpluses give one estimate of the losses to some fans. Another example of the usefulness of surpluses is in the analysis of the impact of market power on consumers, which is covered in Chapter 5. Also, owners of sports teams often demand subsidies from local communities. Elected officials might want to know if their constituents find a particular subsidy level to be worth it. Surpluses are one way to estimate willingness to pay for subsidies. We'll examine this issue in Chapter 10.

PRICE ELASTICITY, TOTAL REVENUE, AND MARGINAL REVENUE

The price elasticity of demand is one of the most important bits of information captured by the demand function. In this section, we develop the idea generally for use in subsequent sections to gain insight into particular sports economics issues, including attendance pricing by teams.

Price Elasticity

Let's stick with look at gate attendance, denoted A. From basic economics, the **price elasticity of demand** relates the percentage change in consumption to a percentage change in price. It is free of units of measurement. The elasticity of attendance for a sports event can be expressed as:

$$\varepsilon = -\frac{\%\Delta A}{\%\Delta P} = -\frac{\Delta A}{\Delta P}\frac{P}{A}$$

Because $\Delta A/\Delta P$ is always less than zero for a negatively sloped attendance demand function, the negative sign in the elasticity expression guarantees that we are only talking about the magnitude of elasticity. Notice that the elasticity of attendance demand contains the slope of the demand function, $\Delta A/\Delta P$, and depends upon where the elasticity is calculated, P/A.

The elasticity of demand is not constant over the entire range of attendance. At the attendance level associated with the linear midpoint of demand, $\varepsilon = 1$. The percentage change in attendance is just equal to the percentage change in price; demand is called unit elastic at this attendance level. At attendance levels below the unit elastic level, the percentage change in attendance exceeds the percentage change in price, $\varepsilon > 1$. Here, demand is called elastic. At attendance levels beyond the unit elastic level, the percentage change in attendance is less than the percentage change in price, $\varepsilon < 1$. In this range, demand is called inelastic. Keep these ideas about elasticity in mind when we discuss revenues.

Total Revenue

Total revenue is one of the two most important pieces of information that **owners** of a sports team must have. If we remember that demand slopes downward for sports teams with market power, then **total revenue** is defined as:

$$R(A) = P(A)A$$

Where R is total revenue, P is the price of attendance, and A is gate attendance. That price is a function of attendance incorporates the fact that sports team owners have market power. If the market were competitive, price would not depend on attendance. As you can see, total revenue, $R(A)$, is inextricably linked to demand, $P(A)$. If sports team owners know their demand function, then they know their total revenues for any level of attendance that might occur.

Even though demand is usually a curve, it is easy to work with the linear version. It supports everything we will do in this book. Such a demand function is defined as:

$$P(A) = a - bA$$

This demand function is in y-intercept form, with price on the y-axis. The parameter a is the y-intercept and parameter $-b$ is the slope of the linear attendance demand function. Figure 2.7 shows a generic attendance demand function, along with the elasticity regions described in the last section.

Let's examine total revenue for this linear demand function. As just noted, total revenue is defined as price multiplied by attendance. Multiplying the linear price function by attendance, we get the following:

$$R(A) = P(A)A = (a - bA)A = aA - bA^2$$

Figure 2.7 Demand and Elasticity

A linear demand function is defined as $P = a - bA$, where P = price, a is the y-intercept, $-b$ is the slope, and A is attendance. Elasticity is $\varepsilon = -\dfrac{\%\Delta A}{\%\Delta A} = -\dfrac{\Delta A}{\Delta P} \dfrac{P}{A}$. Above the linear midpoint,

demand is elastic ($\varepsilon > 1$). At the midpoint, demand is unit elastic ($\varepsilon = 1$). Below the midpoint, demand is inelastic ($\varepsilon > 1$).

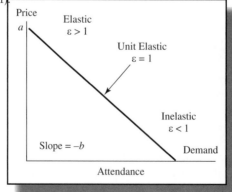

This quadratic function is a parabola, concave to the x-axis, starting out at zero with a unique, positive maximum point. Thus, total revenues increase at first as price falls, but eventually, past some level of attendance ($A > a/b$), total revenues fall back to zero.

Marginal Revenue

Important economic intuition comes from the slope of the total revenue function, defined as $\Delta R/\Delta A$. You probably recognize this as the definition of **marginal revenue,** or $MR(A)$ for short. If we go ahead and calculate this from the revenue function, we find:

$$MR(A) = a - 2bA$$

Notice that the only difference between marginal revenue and the demand function is that marginal revenue is twice as steep. Figure 2.8 shows the relationship between demand, marginal revenue, and total revenue. In addition, based on our findings in the previous section, regions of the elasticity of demand also are identified in Figure 2.8.

Another important thing to notice is that the following three things all occur at attendance level A_0 in Figure 2.8:

- $R(A_0)$ is at its maximum level
- $MR(A_0) = 0$
- $\varepsilon = 1$ (i.e., demand is unit elastic)

Given Figure 2.8, it is easy to tie some economic insight to the mathematics. In the elastic range of attendance demand ($\varepsilon > 1$), $MR(A)$ is positive but falling. Even though price falls, attendance increases enough in percentage terms to increase

Figure 2.8 Demand, Marginal Revenue, and Total Revenue
A linear demand function is defined as $P = a - bA$, where P = price, a is the y-intercept, $-b$ is the slope, and A is attendance. Marginal revenue has the same y-intercept but twice the slope $-2b$. Total revenues are $R(A) = P(A)A$. Total revenues rise to a maximum through the elastic region of demand ($\varepsilon > 1$), reach their maximum at the unit elastic point ($\varepsilon = 1$) associated with attendance A_0, and fall through the inelastic region of demand ($\varepsilon < 1$).

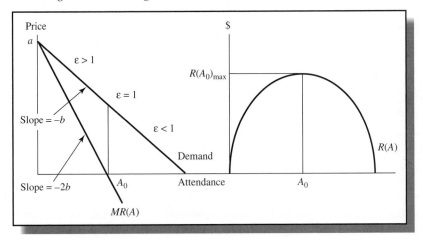

revenue. But because marginal revenue is falling $MR(A)$ is positive but getting smaller in this region of demand, total revenue will continue to increase but at a decreasing rate. Once attendance reaches the unit elastic point ($\varepsilon = 1$) at A_0, marginal revenue is zero. No addition to total revenue is made, and we must be at the maximum point of total revenue. Once into the inelastic region of demand, added attendance no longer is large enough to overcome the decrease in price, in percentage terms. Marginal revenue is negative, and total revenue must start to fall away from its maximum. As price falls even more, marginal revenue becomes increasingly negative. Total revenue must fall at an increasing rate to zero.

Marginal Revenue, Price, and Elasticity

There is one last concept to develop that will be useful later in the chapter. Generally speaking, price is just a function of attendance, say, $P = P(A)$. Total revenue is just $R(A) = P(A)A$. Marginal revenue is the change in total revenue when output increases by a unit. Using the basic chain rule for a derivative,

$$MR(A) = \frac{\Delta P}{\Delta A} A + P$$

If we pull a P out of the right-hand side, then we get:

$$MR(A) = P\left(\frac{\Delta P}{\Delta A}\left(\frac{A}{P}\right) + 1\right)$$

The first term inside the parentheses is the reciprocal of the negative of the elasticity of demand. Remember? The elasticity of demand is:

$$\varepsilon = -\frac{\%\Delta A}{\%\Delta P} = -\frac{\Delta A}{\Delta P}\frac{P}{A}$$

In summary, we can write:

$$MR(A) = P\left(1 - \frac{1}{\varepsilon}\right)$$

This is just another outcome that demonstrates how prices, revenues, and the elasticity of demand are inextricably linked. Remember this result for later use when we discuss price discrimination.

LESSONS FROM TOTAL AND MARGINAL REVENUE

Let's review some important insights from what you have learned so far. The relationship between elasticity and total revenues offers important insights for team owners. Owners may only know a few price and quantity pairs for a very limited portion of their demand function, but elasticity always can be calculated. The result of that calculation reveals two important things: where the owner's pricing decision lies on the demand function and the impact of changing price.

Figure 2.9 Production in the Inelastic Region of Demand

A linear demand function is defined as $P = a - bA$, where P = price, a is the y-intercept, $-b$ is the slope, and A is attendance. Marginal revenue has the same y-intercept but twice the slope, $-2b$. Total revenues are $R(A) = P(A)A$. Total revenues rise to a maximum through the elastic region of demand ($\varepsilon > 1$), reach their maximum at the unit elastic point ($\varepsilon = 1$) associated with attendance A_0, and fall through the inelastic region of demand ($\varepsilon < 1$). If all that matters is attendance revenue, production in the inelastic region of demand, at A_1, has lower total revenue than production at the unit elastic point, A_0. Reducing ticket sales increases total revenues.

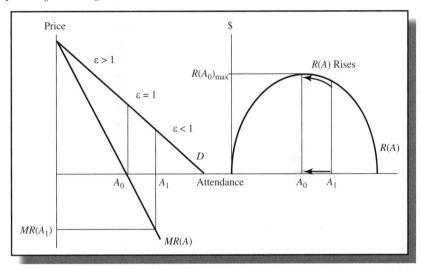

For example, suppose you own a sports team and wonder what the effect on your revenues would be if you raised your ticket price. Your research staff investigates ticket pricing for the team. There isn't much to go on because prices really haven't changed much over time. But the small amount of information they do have allows them to calculate the elasticity of demand. It ends up at about 1.6. What will happen to revenues if you raise the ticket price? Refer to Figure 2.9 and you will remember that revenues will decrease if you increase your price in the elastic portion of demand. You don't have much to go on, but at least calculating elasticity gives you a clue as to what will happen if you increase the ticket price.

Pricing in the Inelastic Region of Demand

Here's another insight from the relationship between elasticity and revenue. I'll pose it as a puzzle. The economics literature that analyzes the demand for attendance consistently finds **inelastic ticket pricing.** But in the inelastic portion of the demand function, marginal revenue is negative. Reducing output will increase total revenue. In Figure 2.9, attendance level A_1 is in the inelastic portion of demand. Notice that its associated marginal revenue, $MR\,(A_1)$, is less than zero. As output is reduced toward attendance level A_0, total revenue increases. Even though we haven't developed the cost side of sports, it is intuitive that costs fall as attendance is reduced (if for no other reason than fewer service personnel are needed to serve fewer fans). So if revenues are rising and costs are falling, profits must be increasing. The puzzle is just why owners would price attendance in such a fashion if by increasing price they can increase profits. But pricing in the inelastic portion of demand is just what demand analysts have discovered.

Of course, one explanation for this could be that owners don't care about profits. If this were true, then pricing where $MR(A) < 0$ can happen based on owner preferences alone. But if owners care about profit, like all good business people do, then such a pricing choice can only make sense if there is some other, nongate revenue gained as an offset. There certainly are other types of revenue tied to attendance. If an owner lowers ticket prices to increase attendance, then attendance revenue falls in the inelastic range of demand. However, parking, concessions, and licensed merchandise sales may more than make up for the reduction in gate revenue. The owner will continue to reduce ticket prices as long as the added revenue from parking, concessions, and merchandise sales makes up the difference. With these other revenue sources, ticket pricing in the inelastic portion of attendance demand is consistent with profit pursuits. One simply must count all of the sources of revenue.

Changes in Demand and Changes in Total Revenue

There is one more essential observation to be had here. What happens when the demand function shifts? Let's suppose that income or population increases or the price of parking falls or prices for sports are expected to increase in the future. The demand function would shift to the right, say, from D_0 to D_1 in Figure 2.10, so that greater attendance would be demanded at every ticket price. What does this do to total revenue? Clearly, total revenue must increase, as illustrated in Figure 2.10. As the revenue function expands from R_0 to R_1, both the range along the x-axis and the new maximum of total revenue increase. Why is $A_1 > A_0$? Remember, the maximum of total revenue occurs at the unit elastic level of output, and that point on the demand curve has increased from A_0 to A_1.

Figure 2.10 Total Revenue and an Increase in Demand
An increase in demand from D_0 to D_1 increases total revenues from $R_0(A)$ to $R_1(A)$. It is important to note that the maximum of the new total revenue, $R_1(A_1)$, occurs at a higher level of attendance, $A_1 > A_0$.

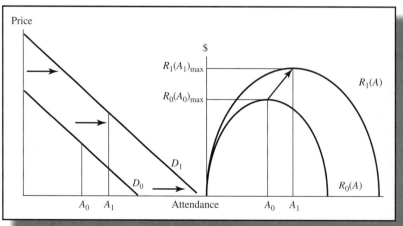

Putting all of these pieces together, you can probably fill in the last insight. A common lament is that a sports team would be much better off if it could only increase attendance. As developed here, increasing attendance can mean one of two things, either increasing the quantity of attendance demanded or increasing demand for attendance itself. Let's look at each of these.

Does it make sense to increase attendance along a given demand curve? Let's refer back to Figure 2.9 and assume that stadium capacity is at fixed size, A_1. Now, given capacity A_1, does it make sense to fill the stadium? Suppose that ticket revenue increases at a greater rate than other revenues are lost. In that case, the answer would be no. If a team inherits such a capacity, it will never admit more than the revenue maximizing level of attendance, A_0. In fact, as long as costs increase with output, the team will operate to the left of the maximum revenue point. Teams like this will simply have excess capacity as long as profits drive their decisions.

Can Team Owners Shift Their Demand Function? Another way to increase attendance would be to try to shift the demand function to the right, rather than lowering price along a given demand. If demand shifts right, both the range and the maximum of total revenue shift to the right. If the increase is large enough, stadium capacity may be below the revenue maximizing level of attendance. Even though profits, not revenues, drive decisions, there is at least a chance that filling the stadium can make sense. One surefire way to increase demand is to increase the quality of the team—lay out enough money to bring a winner to the fans. But as we'll see in subsequent chapters, this can be risky if demand doesn't increase enough. Other ways of increasing demand are well known. Nearly all were created by one of sports' most interesting entrepreneurs, Bill Veeck (see Learning Highlight: Bill and Mike Veeck).

Stadium Reconfiguration

Another approach to excess stadium capacity is simply to reconfigure the stadium—make it smaller. This idea doubtless is behind the downsizing of stadiums in MLB as the cookie-cutter facilities of the early 1970s have been replaced. The Ballpark at Arlington for the Texas Rangers, Jacobs Field for the Cleveland Indians, and Safeco Park for the Seattle Mariners all followed the important example set by Camden Yards for the Baltimore Orioles. All seat in the 40,000 to 50,000 range, down dramatically from the monsters they replace. In addition to getting out from under other types of costs, these capacities are more in keeping with the market characteristics of these areas.

Sellouts and Other Oddities

There are other interesting puzzles, such as the phenomenon of sellouts. First, from our discussion thus far, it's unlikely that sellouts ever should happen because stadium capacity is a short-run outcome. For sellouts to occur, profit maximization would have to coincide with a very particular level of admissions. There is the additional question of why it would make sense to price tickets so that waiting in line is the norm, either for any given game or for years in the case of some season tickets. Filling the stadium is one thing, but filling it at a lower price than you could otherwise get begs some extensions of the analysis. We'll get to that analysis in subsequent chapters.

LEARNING HIGHLIGHT
Bill and Mike Veeck

As owner of the Cleveland Indians, the St. Louis Browns, and the Chicago White Sox at various times from 1946 to 1980, Bill Veeck (rhymes with *wreck*) was a marketing genius who loved the game of baseball. Veeck introduced to baseball such attractions as ladies night, straight-A night (kids just had to bring their report cards), and scoreboard fireworks. On grandstand management night, fans "helped" the manager make important calls like pitching changes by holding up cardboard signs supplied under their seats. Perhaps his most memorable gambit was signing the adult, 3' 7", 65 lb., Eddie Gaedel to a major league contract and sending him to the plate as a pinch hitter in a game between his St. Louis Browns and the Detroit Tigers in 1951. Gaedel drew a walk and was pulled from the game. His still stands as the shortest career in MLB, according to his listing in *The Baseball Encyclopedia.*

Following in his father's footsteps, Mike Veeck built the St. Paul Saints into one of the most profitable independent minor league teams in history, and right in the backyard of the MLB Minnesota Twins! He once hired five mimes at $300 each to act out instant replays (reported by Tim Kurkjian on ESPN.com, February 4, 1999, "Baseball's Back, from A to Z"). "The crowd hated them, but we sold 42 hot dogs per paid customer, and they threw everything they had at the mimes," Veeck

recalls. "They left in the fifth inning . . . crying." Veeck also served as marketing man for MLB's Tampa Bay Devil Rays for a spell. There, Veeck touted his team's newest promotion, lawyer appreciation day (*Sports Illustrated*, February 22, 1999, p. 34): "We're going to charge them double, bill them by the third of an inning, and generally berate them." His father would have been so proud.

Bill Veeck, the self-described baseball hustler, added a great deal of business creativity to the sport of baseball.

Sources: Veeck (1962) and *Sports Illustrated* (February 22, 1999, p. 34).

ELASTICITY AND PRICE DISCRIMINATION

Elasticity is the primary determinant of attendance pricing decisions by team owners. The most notable characteristic of attendance prices is their variation between fans. This type of variation is a characteristic of **price discrimination.** In its most basic form, price discrimination means charging different people different amounts for the same consumption. However, we must exercise caution in determining whether price variation really is price discrimination in any particular case. For example, a difference in price to different people may reflect that it costs different amounts to serve different customers. Or different fans may not actually be buying the same quality experience even though they enjoy the event at the same time. Thus, if quality or costs of service vary by consumer, charging them different prices need not be price discrimination.

In sports, the variation in price at an event based on seat location is not price discrimination because different seats have different qualities (view, closeness to the action, access to other amenities). It is also the case that, on average, walk-up customers are more expensive to serve than fans who buy their tickets in advance. In order to save seats for walk-up buyers, owners must estimate the right number of tickets to reserve for walk-up fans. If they guess wrong, seats may sit empty. Thus, walk-up fans must be charged the implicit cost of saving them a seat as opposed to selling it in advance, including the risk of seats sitting empty.

However, the cost of providing sports does not vary by the time of day, day of the week, or ages of fans. Neither does a person who attends a baseball game between the same two teams, sitting in a particular seat, in a particular section, on a particular day consume a different quality good when the same consumption happens on another day. Variation in price according to these factors is price discrimination.

True Price Discrimination

Let's look in detail at a case of true price discrimination, namely, lower attendance prices for elderly fans. We'll see that the elasticity tool proves valuable once again. What is different about elderly fans that would lead an owner to charge them differently to sit side by side with younger fans at the same game? Recall that the determinants of elasticity are pretty much the same ones that determine willingness to pay along a demand function—income, closeness and availability of substitutes, expectations, and adjustment time. Because the elderly have lower disposable income, they are much more responsive to price than younger fans.

Using some of our previous results, we can see that owners will charge more elastic demanders, such as the elderly, lower prices. In an earlier section, we showed that $MR(A) = P(1 - 1/\varepsilon)$. Suppose for simplicity that an owner confronts two types of demanders, the elderly, denoted E, and the rest of the younger fans, denoted Y. It is clear that the owner will make as much money as possible by selling seats so that $MR_E(A_E) = MR_Y(A_Y)$, that is, when the marginal revenue from elderly and younger fans is equal. (Suppose instead that $MR_E(A_E) > MR_Y(A_Y)$. In that case, the owner rearranges seat sales away from younger fans toward elderly fans for a net increase in revenues.)

Let's substitute in for the MR earned from our two types of buyers and set the two MR relations equal to each other. In order to make as much money as possible, the owner will find that

$$MR_E(A_E) = P_E\left(1 - \frac{1}{\varepsilon_E}\right) = MR_Y(A_Y) = P_Y\left(1 - \frac{1}{\varepsilon_Y}\right)$$

Clearly, if $\varepsilon_E = \varepsilon_Y$, then $P_E = P_Y$. Unless there is some difference in the elasticity of demand between the two types of buyers, the owner will charge them the same price. But suppose that $\varepsilon_E > \varepsilon_Y$, so that $P_E < P_Y$. Elderly fans have more elastic demand than younger fans, and owners charge the elderly the lower price.

Remember, this differential price outcome is based on willingness to pay for an identical product, not seat quality or differential cost of service. Does price discrimination describe any actual outcomes in sports? Elderly (and very young) fans pay less than the rest of the fans. They have lower disposable income and so have more elastic demand; an increase in ticket price will drive more of them away than the rest of the demanders. Price discrimination can also be used to sell weekday tickets. The value of foregone alternatives is higher during the week than on the weekend. Prices are lower for weekday buyers in the form of special deals off the regular ticket price. This is especially true for daytime games on weekdays.

Lowering Prices Another type of price discrimination is ticket deals that appear to lower the average price of a ticket. Roll-your-own multiple ticket packages during the season are of this variety. In order to get the seemingly lower unit price, a fan must buy a specified number of tickets. However, because demand slopes downward, subsequent tickets are worth less than the first ones bought, and there really is no deal for the fan. The appearance is a lower average ticket price, but fans don't get to see what price would be charged in the absence of the owner's knowledge about willingness to pay. As always, be careful. Advance season tickets are not a form of price discrimination because they have a reservation of a given seat included in the price. This is a distinct quality difference.

Personal Seat Licenses While we're on the topic of reserved season tickets, let's examine a recent seat pricing phenomenon in pro sports, the personal seat license (PSL) (in Chapter 13 on college sports, we'll see that this actually is quite an old idea). Let's suppose that an owner has already taken advantage of price discrimination and is charging accordingly. For some given fan, the result might be as shown in Figure 2.11. At price P^*, from our previous development, the consumers' surpluses for this fan are the triangle XP^*Z. Suppose the owner discovers which fans, in general, enjoy this type of surplus. Relative to just selling tickets for P^*, the owner might charge P^* for the tickets and then charge an annual fixed fee equal to XP^*Z. If you think this sounds just like a PSL on season tickets, it is. The owner has been able to extract just a bit more revenue from each fan.

The additional fixed charge, as close as possible to XP^*Z for fans like the one depicted in Figure 2.11 in addition to the ticket price, P^*, will exhaust the fan's willingness to pay. This two-part pricing mechanism is just an extension of price discrimination to collect even more of the consumers' surpluses across all fans. Different fans pay different ticket prices and different PSLs based on willingness to pay. Some of the difference might be due to seat quality or the value of reserving a particular seat, but the remainder is price discrimination.

Figure 2.11 PSL for a Typical Fan

PSLs are a form of two-part price discrimination. In addition to charging a ticket buyer the ticket price. *P**, an additional charge equal to consumers' surpluses (the shaded triangle *XP*Z*) also is sought. It is the additional charge that discriminates between higher willingness to pay and lower willingness to pay among different buyers.

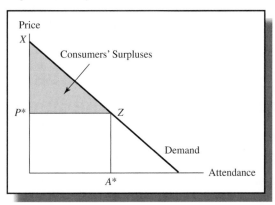

REVENUE DATA

The pro team sports revenue data that are generally available appear in *Forbes* (earlier versions of the data were published in the now defunct *Financial World*). (Because we'll treat college sports separately, in Chapter 13, we won't go into it here. Suffice it to say that precisely the same type of relationships characterize college revenues.) Revenues come from ticket sales at the gate, TV (from national contracts for all sports and from local contracts for a few sports), shares of league property sales (licensed merchandise and memorabilia), sponsorships, and from the nature of the team's stadium arrangement. Some teams own their own stadium so that concession and parking revenues and revenues from any other use of the stadium belong to the owner.

However, even if a team doesn't own its own stadium, the same types of revenues can flow to a team, depending on how profitable an arrangement the team has made with its host city. We'll get into the gruesome details of leases in Chapters 10 and 11.

The data in *Forbes* come from a survey of team owners, who often are bargaining with their hosts for subsidies. Thus, it is in the owners' best interests to understate revenues and overstate costs in order to convince their hosts of the need for such assistance. This means that we should view the survey responses with some skepticism.

We could try to guess a team's revenue by using other available data. Gate revenues can be "guesstimated" pretty easily from attendance and posted ticket prices. TV revenues are also commonly known and published in a variety of places. Shares of league merchandise revenues are less well publicized, and the only way to know the details of stadium revenues is to dig into actual stadium lease documents. However, leases are difficult to obtain

Table 2.6 2003 *Forbes* Data (All figures in $ millions)

LEAGUE	SMALLEST REVENUE	TEAM	LEAGUE AVERAGE	LARGEST REVENUE	TEAM
MLB	$81	Montreal	$129	$238	NY Yankees
NBA	$70	Seattle, Golden State, Milwaukee	$94	$149	LA Lakers
NFL	$126	Arizona	$155	$227	Washington
NHL	$48	Edmonton	$70	$113	NY Rangers

Source: www.forbes.com.

and, perhaps, even more difficult to understand. So the survey data are the best numbers that we have.

Table 2.6 and Figure 2.12 show a summary of the revenue data available from *Forbes* for 2003. Clearly, there are haves and have-nots. In each league, that is, there is significant **within-league revenue variation.** Those at the low end of the scale can have as little as 63 percent of the mean, such as in MLB, whereas those at the top end typically have revenues of well over 1.5 times the mean. The greatest dispersion between the haves and have-nots also occurs in MLB.

Figure 2.12 2003 Forbes Revenue Data
Each line in the chart shows the smallest, average, and largest team revenues for each of the four major pro leagues. Revenue variation among teams is shown along a given line. Revenue variation between leagues is apparent from a comparison among the lines. The low-end NFL team earns much more than the low-end NHL team. The NFL and MLB averages are the highest, and MLB clearly has the largest revenue team at the high end.

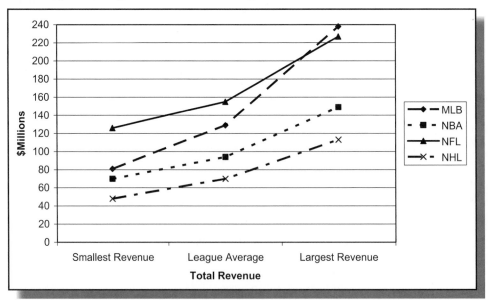

Figure 2.12 also shows that there is substantial **between-league revenue variation.** Some sports are simply worth more to their fans than others. For example, at the averages, NFL fans spend over twice as much on their sport as hockey fans spend on theirs (including the value of TV advertising). At the top end, MLB fans spend just over twice as much as hockey fans. With an understanding of the basics of demand, this is no mystery. Fan preferences, population, and income situations drive these types of demand differences.

This revenue disparity is the source of a lot of tension in sports. Although the world of sports is an uncertain one, revenues translate into strong on-field performance when owners use revenue to purchase talent. Owners in large revenue market locations can earn higher revenues from a given level of talent than can owners in smaller revenue markets. As long as revenues are unbalanced, it is quite likely that there will be unbalanced talent choices between teams and unbalanced outcomes on the field. If these types of imbalances become too great, some teams will be unable to survive.

Which teams should survive and which should not? That, ultimately, becomes a challenge for owners in two ways. First, their individual incomes depend upon whether they are one of the teams that can compete. Second, the very existence of the league depends upon the relative competitiveness between teams in the eyes of fans.

CHAPTER RECAP

The beauty, competition (both absolute and relative), commonality, and vicarious enjoyment of winning are scarce characteristics of sports. Fans pay the most for the highest level of absolute competition, but once that is decided, relative competition is extremely important. Scarcity requires some means of rationing. In sports, both price and waiting time are common rationing devices.

The demand function is a representation of fan willingness to pay for different quantities of sports. The demand for any given team's sports output slopes downward, meaning that there are only imperfect substitutes for that team's output. As price increases, fans demand less of the sports output. Changes in fan preferences, income, prices of other goods, expectations about the future, and population all will shift the demand for sports. Examples that appear to contradict the law of demand in sports can be explained by changes in demand over time.

Market power dominates sports demand functions. The source of the market power lies mostly in the fact that individual teams are granted exclusive franchise areas.

Demand functions contain an astonishing amount of information. The economist's tool of consumers' surpluses produces one type of dollar estimate of the value of sports consumption. The demand function also demonstrates responsiveness, or elasticity, of fan demand to changes in price.

An important piece of information that comes from a knowledge of demand is total revenue. Price decreases through the elastic portion of demand will increase total revenue. At the unit elastic point on the demand function, total revenues are at a maximum. Even lower prices increase quantity, but total revenues fall through the inelastic portion of demand. Marginal revenues are defined as the change in total revenue as output increases. Marginal revenues are positive but falling through the elastic portion of demand. They are zero at the unit elastic point on the demand function (i.e., the maximum of total revenue). Finally, marginal revenues are negative through the inelastic portion of demand.

Even though owners may not know their entire attendance demand function, they will know the impact on revenue of changing their ticket price by a small amount if they know the elasticity of demand. Sports teams would only price in the inelastic portion of attendance demand if other revenues offset reduced gate revenues. Finally, price discrimination involves charging different fans different prices for the same attendance. When real price discrimination occurs, those fans with the highest elasticity of demand receive the lower price.

The data on sports team revenues reveal substantial variation between teams in the same pro sports league. The data on revenues also reveal that there is substantial variation in revenues between different sports.

KEY TERMS AND CONCEPTS

- Scarcity
- Rationing
- Absolute level of quality
- Relative level of quality
- Uncertainty of outcome
- Demand
- Movement along demand

- Demand shifters
- Market power
- Exclusive territory
- Consumers' surpluses
- Price elasticity of demand
- Total revenue
- Marginal revenue

- Inelastic ticket pricing
- Price discrimination
- Within-league revenue variation
- Between-league revenue variation

REVIEW QUESTIONS

1. What are the scarce elements of sports demanded by fans?
2. What are the typical rationing devices used in sports markets? If price is eliminated as a rationing device, is competition for tickets eliminated? Why or why not?
3. Explain the uncertainty of outcome hypothesis. According to this hypothesis, what will happen to a league that becomes too competitively unbalanced on the field?
4. Explain the effect that each of the following would have on the demand for NFL football games in Chicago:
   a. All else constant, some Bears fans find the violence in football less to their liking.
   b. All else constant, incomes of Chicago residents increase.
   c. All else constant, the price of a season ticket to the Chicago Opera falls to equal the price of a Bears season ticket.
   d. All else constant, Bears fans expect season ticket prices to increase next year.
   e. All else constant, due to hard times, the Chicago population is expected to decline.
5. Why does the demand for attendance at sports events slope downward?

6. Define consumers' surpluses for those attending sports events. Discuss the two components of changes in consumers' surpluses when the price of attendance falls.
7. Define the price elasticity of attendance demand. What does it measure?
8. Define total revenue. In a graph, show and explain the relationship between a downward sloping demand curve and a team's total revenues. Identify the elastic, unit elastic, and inelastic regions of attendance on the total revenue function you drew.
9. On a graph of total revenue, show what happens to total revenue if demand increases.
10. On a graph of total revenue, show a team that has stadium capacity below the maximum of total revenue. Should this team operate to capacity? Why? If demand falls drastically, so that capacity is now above the maximum of total revenue, should this team still operate to capacity? Use the graph to demonstrate your answer.
11. Define marginal revenue. Beginning at a price where quantity demanded equals zero and lowering the price to zero, describe how marginal revenues change along the demand function.
12. Where is marginal revenue equal to zero? Are total revenues positive or negative in the inelastic portion of demand?
13. Will sports teams ever price in the inelastic portion of demand? Explain.
14. What is price discrimination in sports attendance? Why do senior citizens pay a lower ticket price than other fans for a given game and seat?
15. Why do members of a sports league keep a close eye on within-league revenue variation? Relate this to your answer in Review Question 3.

THOUGHT PROBLEMS

1. Think about your favorite sports team using the scarcity, rationing, and competition outline (Figure 2.1). What are the scarce commodities supplied by the team? Is attendance rationed by price only? If the price of attending a game were reduced to $1 for all seats, would any of your team's fans be unhappy? Explain.
2. Consider the following statement, paraphrasing one lament by fans: "Fans can never catch up with the vicious cycle of sports event pricing. As fan income rises, they can finally afford the high price of sports events. But this increase in demand for sports just raises prices again, and fans are right back where they started. It's a vicious circle that drives the everyday fan out of the arena." What is the error in this statement? Explain.
3. Discuss why competitive balance is an important characteristic of team sports leagues. What role does the uncertainty of outcome hypothesis play? In your discussion, cover what would happen if three teams came to dominate a league. In closing your discussion, address whether the end of the NBA Bulls dynasty of the 1990s was a good or bad thing for the NBA.
4. Explain why it must be preferences that explain the difference between the demand functions in Figure 2.2.
5. If you look at the movement of teams from one city to another, you will find that some teams move to cities with smaller populations. For example, the owner of

the NFL's Los Angeles Rams moved her team to St. Louis for the 1997 season (examine Table 2.4 for population and income characteristics of areas). Is this a bad business decision? Explain.

6. A student intern discovers the following about the demand by local businesses for attendance at a pro sports team's games:

$$P_B = 140 - 4A_B$$

where P_B is the ticket price paid by businesses, measured in dollars, and A_B is their attendance, measured in thousands of fans. Draw this demand function. Does this team have market power over business buyers? Why or why not?

7. In the most recent PBA between the majors and the minors, MLB imposes minimum stadium quality specifications for all affiliated minor league teams. What does this restriction accomplish from the perspective of market power?

8. The consumers' surpluses for the women's basketball demand functions in Figure 2.5 when the price was $20 was calculated earlier in the chapter. At the same price of $20, calculate the consumers' surpluses for the men's basketball attendance demand function in the same figure. Is the amount larger or smaller than for women's games at this price? Why?

9. Calculate the price elasticity of attendance demand for women's hoops for a price decrease of $30 to $20 in Figure 2.2. Will revenues for the team rise or fall for this price change? Explain.

10. Teams earn revenue from a variety of sources: ticket sales, parking fees, concession sales, sales of licensed products, and broadcast rights sales. Explain how all of these revenues actually come from fans.

11. Explain the role of the inflation rate in comparisons of team revenues over time.

12. Return to the business attendance demand function in Thought Problem 6. Find the total revenue function. What is the shape of the total revenue function? What is the highest possible total revenue that the team can hope to collect? At what level of attendance? At what price?

   a. Find the marginal revenue function. At what level of attendance is marginal revenue equal to zero? At what price?

   b. What is the elasticity of demand at the revenue maximizing attendance level?

   c. If capacity at the team's stadium is 25,000 seats, should the team owner fill the stands with business buyers? Why or why not?

13. PSLs reserve the rights to a particular seat for a lump sum payment in addition to the price of tickets. Is it price discrimination to charge for this extra reservation value through a PSL charge? Why? Is it price discrimination if two different people in approximately the same seating area pay different PSL charges? Why?

14. In addition to the business demand function in Thought Problem 6, our clever student also discovers that the demand by families for attendance at the same games and the same seat types is as follows:

$$P_F = 80 - (2/3)A_F$$

where P_F is the price of a ticket for individual family members, measured in dollars, and A_F is the attendance by individual family members, measured in thousands. Show why individual family members will be charged a lower price than business buyers for the same games and seat types. What is the ratio of business buyer to family member prices if the team owner cares about the bottom line? Is this price discrimination?

15. Using the data from Figure 2.12 and Table 2.6:
    a. What is the range of total revenues in the NFL? What is the ratio of highest to lowest total revenue?
    b. Identify the team with the smallest total revenues in the NFL. This team is not very successful, but the MLB team for this city is very successful. How can this be?
    c. Given your answer in part a, do you expect play on the field to be balanced in the NFL? Why or why not?
    d. Based on revenue dispersion, which of the leagues covered in Figure 2.12 and Table 2.6 do you think would be the most competitively balanced? Why?

ADVANCED PROBLEMS

1. In his book *Getting It Right* (1997), economist Robert Barro argues that the only thing that matters to fans is the relative level of competition. Given this, many behaviors in sports, such as the escalation in training routines and the growing use of performance-enhancing drugs, are socially wasteful because they are costly but do not alter relative competition. At the heart of the issue is that fans would pay the same with or without these behaviors because the outcome on the field is unaltered. With these behaviors, resources are spent without any value being added from the fan perspective.
   a. Barro's view is at odds with the arguments about absolute and relative quality in this chapter. What is the strongest argument in sports favoring that both absolute and relative quality matter?
   b. Using Barro's logic, is the existence of both major league and minor league levels of sports socially wasteful? After all, there are really close minor league games, so why invest in attaining major league status? Do you reach the same conclusion using the argument given in this text? Why or why not?
   c. Barro uses his logic to argue that strict drug testing and punishment of offenders would be beneficial from society's perspective, not because it punishes bad behavior, but because it reduces wasteful use of resources. Would Barro's logic also support strict limits on the amount of time that school kids can spend on sports? How would the time limit be determined and by whom? Would parents of gifted student athletes agree with this idea? Why or why not?

2. How might you measure the uncertainty of outcome between your team and its next scheduled opponent? (Hint: Uncertainty probably increases with expected closeness of the outcome.) How would you measure it for teams in a league after a given season? How about over the longer run?

3. Is the price of attendance just the dollar value of the ticket and PSL (if any)? How would you measure the full price of attendance? (Hint: Be careful. Why are

prices lower during the week than on the weekends? Is the price of a Los Angeles Lakers game higher for someone living in San Diego than it is for someone living in adjacent Orange County?)

4. The NFL's Houston Oilers left Texas to become the Tennessee Oilers for the 1997 season. They changed their name to the Tennessee Titans and moved into their new Adelphia Stadium for the 1999 season. Interestingly, their lowest-priced individual tickets were priced at $12 while their lowest-priced season ticket cost $250. Given that there are only 8 home games, why didn't fans just buy individual tickets rather than season tickets? Is this price discrimination or not? Explain.

5. In addition to the lowest-priced arrangements in the last question, the Tennessee Titans' highest-priced individual tickets in 1999 were $52 while the highest-priced season ticket was $2,500. Relative to the lowest-priced arrangements, is the highest-priced arrangement price discrimination? Why? Suppose that the $2,500 included a $1,000 personal seat license. Is this price discrimination compared to charging no personal seat license? Explain.

6. If fans in one location are willing to pay more for higher quality than fans in another location, why will it never make sense for the point spread between their teams to be zero?

7. Thinking about Figure 2.1 and your basic economics training concerning price ceilings, evaluate the impact of a lease requirement that the price of some seats be kept at "a family-affordable" level. In particular, think about:
   a. The quality of family-affordable seats.
   b. The amenities that will be offered at family-affordable seats.
   Who will capture the difference between the family-affordable price and the price at which these seats would otherwise have sold?

8. Recall the business attendance demand function in Thought Problem 6. Answer the following questions.
   a. Calculate consumers' surpluses at $P_B = \$80$ and $P_B = \$60$.
   b. What is the dollar value of the increased happiness enjoyed by business fans at the lower price of $60?
   c. Even though fans would be happier, why would you not expect the price to fall from $80 to $60?

9. Why would it be inadvisable for sports teams to sell all of their seats as season tickets even if they could? That is, why don't as many teams as possible aim for season-ticket only sellouts for the season?

10. The full revenue data are at the Web site for this text (www.prenhall.com/fort). Describe the relative contributions of gate, TV, and venue in pro sports. Which one has been growing relative to the others over time? Why?

INTERNET RESOURCES

For a host of additional material and questions for thought, visit this book's Web site at www.prenhall.com/fort.

REFERENCES

Barro, Robert. *Getting It Right: Markets and Choices in a Free Society.* Cambridge, MA: MIT Press, 1997.

Bernstein, Carl, and Bob Woodward. *All the President's Men.* New York: Simon and Schuster, 1974.

Exley, Frederick. *A Fan's Notes: A Fictional Memoir.* New York: Harper & Row, 1968.

Hall, Donald. *Fathers Playing Catch with Sons.* New York: North Point Press, 1998.

Quirk, James, and Rodney Fort. *Pay Dirt: The Business of Professional Team Sports.* Princeton, NJ: Princeton University Press, 1992.

Shank, Matthew D. *Sports Marketing: A Strategic Perspective.* Upper Saddle River, NJ: Prentice Hall, 1999.

Thayer, Ernest Lawrence. "Casey at the Bat." *San Francisco Examiner,* June 3, 1888.

Veeck, Bill. *Veeck as in Wreck.* New York: Simon and Schuster, 1962.

Chapter 3

The Market for Sports Broadcast Rights

Chapter Objectives

After reading this chapter, you should be able to:

- Describe the functioning of advertising and the market for rights to sports programming.

- Understand that the market power lies with leagues; broadcast, cable, and satellite media providers merely channel money competitively from advertisers to leagues.

- Explain how buying advertising and sports rights may become very complicated.

- Explain why advertising revenues can be large enough to cover a team's entire payroll but also are highly variable across different leagues and across teams in a given league.

- Understand that the commercialization of sports increases compensation to athletes, raising their incentive to excel, but that it can have an adverse effect on fan perceptions.

- Recognize that outright team ownership by media providers may increase the distance between revenue haves and have nots, leading to increasing competitive balance problems.

It would not be good public relations for baseball to have the Series sponsored by the producer of an alcoholic beverage.

—MLB COMMISSIONER HAPPY CHANDLER
Refusing beer ads on the first televised World Series (Helyar, 1994, p. 393)

*I*n its original bid to break into network TV, FOX spent so much obtaining NFL rights that its sports division took a $350 million loss on its 1994 contract. However, the network as a whole showed an increase in profits (after the $350 million loss solely by its sports division) from $511 million for the last 6 months of 1993 to $610 million for the last 6 months of 1994. Despite losing hundreds of millions of dollars on the NFL, FOX profits rose 16 percent (in 2004 dollars).

As you saw in Chapter 2, teams generate revenue from a number of sources. In this chapter, we will focus on advertising because it offers interesting economic lessons and because media revenues are growing in importance for all sports leagues. We will take a look at the basics of the sports broadcast rights market and sports leagues' rights. Our discussion will also cover media providers and advertising, as well as media ownership. We will examine firms and how they make their advertising choices, with a focus on the "beer wars" and sponsorship. Finally, we will look at the impact of all this money on sports.

SETTING THE STAGE: THE MEDIA IN SPORTS

Media are the second most important source of revenue in all major sports. The willingness of advertisers to pay for sports programming has altered the revenue side of pro and college sports forever. Especially since the advent of cable and satellite TV in the early 1980s, teams are richer by tens of millions of dollars than they otherwise could have been. Firms use advertising to sell their products. Media providers have ad slots on so-called free TV, cable, and dish feeds. Sports leagues (and, as we'll see in Chapter 13, college conferences) have rights to the programming that reaches particular audiences of interest to some of the advertisers.

The increase in the number of cable and satellite TV providers, reflecting underlying fan demand for sports viewing, has driven sports rights values up and also has made media markets extremely competitive. No single media provider has the power to extract more than a normal return to its endeavors. Advertisers also are many and compete for ad slots. The massive sums that change hands include monopoly profits that can be charged by leagues. After all, they are in the market power position in the first place.

As with all inputs, ads are purchased until the extra benefit equals the extra cost. However, figuring out the marginal benefits is complex. Some would say that media providers are cursed to lose money if they win broadcast rights. We will see in this chapter that such an analysis fails to include the entire array of benefits that go to media providers when they win sports broadcast rights. Similar puzzles exist for firms that purchase ad slots from media providers.

Sports leagues structure the bidding process to extract the highest possible amount from media providers. The results can be staggering for sports leagues, but they are a mixed blessing. The variation in media revenue across teams in a league contributes to the current competitive balance woes of some pro leagues. Ultimately, revenue imbalances can lead to competitive imbalance in the eyes of fans.

The most recent media-driven phenomenon in sports concerns sponsorship of events and arenas and the outright ownership of teams by media providers. Although many lament this commercialization of sports, it is valuable. The payoff to athletes engendered by this money generates much more intense competition on the field, producing athletes like none seen before. However, in addition to any possible overcommercialization, a shift to outright ownership by media providers brings other concerns. Not the least of these concerns is that as the market for team owner-ship moves away from individual ownership some teams are left behind in the short run. This could further exacerbate revenue disparity and the competitive balance problems that follow.

ADS AND PREFERENCE FORMATION

To understand the power of advertising in sports, it is worth pausing for a moment to ponder just how ads work. When firms use ads, they think about how the ads impact new consumers and consumers already purchasing their product. Of course, the objective is to reach consumers and increase sales. Evidence is mixed on whether ads generate new consumers who have never tried a product before. That is, do ads lead to **start-up consumption**? For example, noted sports management expert John Crompton (1993) observes that alcohol ad bans don't appear to have any impact on consumption, because countries with ad bans show little difference in alcohol behav-ior than those without bans. Generally speaking, Crompton points out that the impact of ads on alcohol consumption is weak, at best. It appears that price, availability, and family/lifestyle are more likely to affect consumption.

Did You Know?
Alcohol ad bans don't appear to have any impact on consumption. Countries with ad bans show little difference in consumer behavior toward alcohol than those without bans.
—Crompton (1993)

Conversely, if individuals never have been exposed to a particular type of consumption, advertisements might make them aware, heighten their awareness, or shape their preferences. This certainly is the belief behind regulations aimed at stopping partic-ular types of ads that may influence children. The ban on cigarette television advertising in 1971, the "Kid Vid" crusade of the 1970s and 1980s, and the more recent movement against advertising icons (such as Joe Camel) all are aimed at advertisements pur-ported to lead young people (new consumers) to unhealthy consumption. If adver-tisements generate new consumers, then they clearly are valuable to the producers of these products.

Ads and Brand Choice

Advertisements play another important role. Once people have decided which goods to consume, advertisements clearly present the array of possible choices for a particular good. So, ads may help consumers make **brand choices.** How many brands of cigarettes, beer, or cars are there? Consumers appear to identify very heavily with being a particular kind of consumer; we might consider ourselves Pepsi drinkers as opposed to Coke drinkers. Thus, ads also generate brand loyalty. We will return to this second important function of advertising later in the chapter when we address advertising choices by firms.

Aiming Advertisements at the Right Target

Ads must be aimed at the group of consumers most likely to care about them. This group is referred to as a **target demographic group.** For sports programming, the typical viewer is a male between the ages of 18 and 34 (women typically are less than one-third of a sports audience). Advertisers interested in reaching this male target demographic purchase sports program ad slots. Ads that are actually seen by large numbers of the intended demographic group are said to have good **advertising reach.** As you can see in Table 3.1, beer and automobile ads dominate football and baseball broadcasts because males aged 18–34

Table 3.1   Top 20 Sports Advertising Companies, 2003

RANK	COMPANY	TOTAL SPORTS ADS ($MILLIONS)	TOTAL ALL ADS ($MILLIONS)	%SPORTS ADS
1	Anheuser-Busch Cos.	$218.2	$284.9	77%
2	Ford Motor Co.	$136.2	$437.9	31%
3	Chevrolet Motor Division	$135.9	$295.0	46%
4	Miller Brewing Co.	$125.4	$140.5	89%
5	Microsoft Corp.	$93.0	$280.6	33%
6	Coors Brewing Co.	$85.2	$115.4	74%
7	Southwest Airlines Co.	$84.5	$88.1	96%
8	IBM	$83.7	$171.9	49%
9	Visa International	$79.0	$260.8	30%
10	Pepsi-Cola Co.	$77.1	$255.7	30%
11	Verizon Communications, Inc.	$71.4	$356.3	20%
12	Procter & Gamble Co.	$70.3	$1,407.9	5%
13	Toyota Motor Sales USA, Inc.	$68.2	$261.4	26%
14	Nike, Inc.	$66.3	$123.5	54%
15	Nissan North America, Inc.	$66.3	$311.5	21%
16	MasterCard International, Inc.	$65.7	$221.5	30%
17	Coca-Cola USA	$64.5	$166.9	39%
18	Doctor's Associates, Inc. (Subway)	$63.2	$163.8	39%
19	Universal Pictures	$59.0	$221.1	27%
20	Dodge Car-Truck Division	$58.5	$136.9	43%
	Total	**$1,771.6**	**$5,701.6**	**31%**

Source: Adapted and excerpted from *Sports Business Journal*, March 22, 2004, p. 9.

Table 3.2 Sports Programming, Revenues in Excess of $100 Million, 2003

RANK	PROGRAM TYPE	2003 AD REVENUE ($MILLIONS)	2002 AD REVENUE ($MILLIONS)	% CHANGE
1	Professional football*	$2,000.5	$1,881.1	6%
2	Professional basketball*	$579.4	$769.4	−25%
3	Golf	$578.8	$525.7	10%
4	College basketball*	$521.7	$498.0	5%
5	Auto racing	$472.6	$441.8	7%
6	College football*	$449.5	$423.9	6%
7	Sportscast	$444.9	$355.8	25%
8	Professional baseball*	$438.5	$409.5	7%
9	General sports show	$361.6	$302.4	20%
10	Tennis	$156.1	$150.8	4%
11	Hockey	$127.1	$99.8	27%

*Includes pre- and/or postgame programming.
Source: Adapted and excerpted from *Sports Business Journal*, May 3, 2004, p. 21.

Did You Know?
Of the top 20 sports advertisers, car manufacturers spend the most and outspend the second-highest spenders, beer companies, by about $36 million. However, Anheuser-Busch, a beer company, spends the most of any single advertiser.

tend to drink beer and buy cars—and watch sports. More expensive consumption items, such as luxury vehicles, dominate golf advertising because golfing males are typically more affluent. Table 3.2 demonstrates the different types of sports viewers that advertisers try to reach when they allocate their advertising dollars.

Of course, it's not just who watches, but how many watch, as well. Table 3.3 shows the results of a poll of fans' favorite spectator sports. NFL football tops the poll, but there is some variation in the popularity of other sports among male and female fans. Also, the NBA has declined in popularity while others have grown. Table 3.4, showing Super Bowl **ratings** and ad rates, makes it clear that these

Table 3.3
Sports Programming Poll Results, 1998

FAVORITE SPORT TO WATCH	% RESPONSE MALES	% RESPONSE FEMALES
Pro Football	24.4	22.1
Pro Baseball	12.4	13.6
Pro Basketball	12.3	12.6
None	8.6	
Figure Skating		6.5
College Football	6.4	4.3
College Basketball	5.6	
Auto Racing	4.2	
Pro Hockey	3.5	

Source: (Males) *NFL Report*, Spring 1998, p. 2; (Females) NFL.com.

Table 3.4 Super Bowl Ratings and Advertising Rates

Year	Super Bowl	Network	$/30-Second Slot ($2004 Millions)	Rating	Game Matchup
2003	XXXVII	ABC	$2.14 million	40.7	Tampa Bay 48, Oakland 21
2002	XXXVI	FOX	$1.94 million	40.4	New England 20, St. Louis 17
2001	XXXV	CBS	$2.34 million	40.4	Baltimore 34, New York Giants 7
2000	XXXIV	ABC	$2.40 million	43.3	St. Louis 23, Tennessee 16
1999	XXXIII	FOX	$1.82 million	40.2	Denver 34, Atlanta 19
1998	XXXII	NBC	$1.50 million	44.5	Denver 31, Green Bay 24
1997	XXXI	FOX	$1.41 million	43.3	Green Bay 35, New England 21
1996	XXX	NBC	$1.45 million	46.0	Dallas 27, Pittsburgh 17
1995	XXIX	ABC	$1.23 million	41.3	San Francisco 49, San Diego 26
1994	XXVIII	NBC	$1.15 million	45.5	Dallas 30, Buffalo 13
1993	XXVII	NBC	$1.11 million	45.1	Dallas 52, Buffalo 17
1992	XXVI	CBS	$1.14 million	40.3	Washington 37, Buffalo 24
1991	XXV	ABC	$1.11 million	41.9	New York Giants 20, Buffalo 19
1990	XXIV	CBS	$1.01 million	39.0	San Francisco 55, Denver 10
1989	XXIII	NBC	$1.03 million	43.5	San Francisco 20, Cincinnati 16
1988	XXII	ABC	$994,500	41.9	Washington 42, Denver 10
1987	XXI	CBS	$997,560	45.8	New York Giants 39, Denver 20
1986	XX	NBC	$948,090	48.3	Chicago 46, New England 10
1985	XIX	ABC	$921,060	46.4	San Francisco 38, Miami 16
1984	XVIII	CBS	$880,566	46.4	Los Angeles Raiders 38, Washington 9
1983	XVII	NBC	$664,020	48.6	Washington 27, Miami 17
1982	XVI	CBS	$636,480	49.1	San Francisco 26, Cincinnati 21
1981	XV	NBC	$572,220	44.4	Oakland 27, Philadelphia 10
1980	XIV	CBS	$573,750	46.3	Pittsburgh 31, Los Angeles Rams 19
1979	XIII	NBC	$481,185	47.1	Pittsburgh 35, Dallas 31
1978	XII	CBS	$506,940	47.2	Dallas 27, Denver 10
1977	XI	NBC	$466,650	44.4	Oakland 32, Minnesota 14
1976	X	CBS	$414,375	42.3	Pittsburgh 21, Dallas 17
1975	IX	NBC	$421,056	42.4	Pittsburgh 16, Minnesota 6
1974	VIII	CBS	$409,275	41.6	Miami 24, Minnesota 7
1973	VII	NBC	$425,340	42.7	Miami 14, Washington 7
1972	VI	CBS	$451,860	44.2	Dallas 24, Miami 3
1971	V	NBC	$466,140	39.9	Baltimore 16, Dallas 13
1970	IV	CBS	$486,540	39.4	Kansas City 23, Minnesota 7
1969	III	NBC	$218,484	36.0	New York Jets 16, Baltimore 7
1968	II	CBS	$230,622	36.8	Green Bay 33, Oakland 14
1967	I*	CBS	$240,159	23.0	Green Bay 35, Kansas City 10
1967	I*	NBC	$240,159	17.8	Green Bay 35, Kansas City 10

* The first game was broadcast by both networks, which had separate AFL and NFL broadcast rights to the Super Bowl.

Source: Street & Smith's *Sports Business Journal*, January 26, 2004, p. 26.

poll results are backed up by actual data taken from Street & Smith's *Sports Business Journal*. A rating point equals about 954,000 viewing homes. This means that about 46.8 million homes tuned in to Super Bowl XVI in 1982 (the highest-rated Super Bowl ever). According to the NFL Report (Spring, 2004), far more people watched the 2004 Super Bowl (about 144.4 million viewers) but its rating was far down the line in Super Bowl history at 41.4.

The data show that sports programs are very popular with the target demographic that advertisers wish to reach. The ad rates in Table 3.4 indicate how much networks think advertisers are willing to pay for this type of reach. As you can see, measured in 2004 dollars, a 30-second Super Bowl slot has hit as high as $2.4 million (Super Bowl XXXIV, 2000), and those 30 seconds have been worth more than a million dollars for the last 15 years (again, measured in 2004 dollars).

Table 3.5 demonstrates exactly which companies were willing to pay these rates for such exposure during Super Bowl XXXVII in 2003. Not surprisingly, beer and car companies are on the list. But the full range of companies runs from motion pictures and entertainment to major charities to drugs.

Table 3.5 Super Bowl XXXVII Advertisers and Amounts, 2003

COMPANY	TOTAL SECONDS	30-SECOND SLOTS	APPROXIMATE EXPENDITURE ($MILLIONS)
Anheuser-Busch Cos.	360	12.0	$25.20
PepsiCo	180	6.0	$12.60
General Motors Corp.	120	4.0	$8.40
Sony Pictures Entertainment	90	3.0	$6.30
AT&T Wireless Services, Inc.	60	2.0	$4.20
DaimlerChrysler AG	60	2.0	$4.20
Levi Strauss & Co.	60	2.0	$4.20
NFL	60	2.0	$4.20
Reebok	60	2.0	$4.20
Sony Corp.	60	2.0	$4.20
Universal Studios	60	2.0	$4.20
Visa International	60	2.0	$4.20
Walt Disney Co.	60	2.0	$4.20
Warner Bros.	60	2.0	$4.20
W. B. Mason	60	2.0	$4.20
White House Office of National Drug Control Policy	60	2.0	$4.20
ESPN, Inc.	50	1.7	$3.50
FedEx Corp.	45	1.5	$3.15
American Honda Motor Co.	30	1.0	$2.10
Computer Associates International Inc.	30	1.0	$2.10
Coors Brewing Co.	30	1.0	$2.10

(Continued)

(Continued)

COMPANY	TOTAL SECONDS	30-SECOND SLOTS	APPROXIMATE EXPENDITURE ($MILLIONS)
Fair, Isaac & Co.	30	1.0	$2.10
Ford Motor Co.	30	1.0	$2.10
Gallery Furniture	30	1.0	$2.10
H&R Block Inc.	30	1.0	$2.10
MasterCard International, Inc.	30	1.0	$2.10
Philip Morris Cos.	30	1.0	$2.10
Quizno's	30	1.0	$2.10
Salton, Inc.	30	1.0	$2.10
Sara Lee Corp.	30	1.0	$2.10
Doctor's Associates, Inc.	30	1.0	$2.10
TMP Worldwide, Inc.	30	1.0	$2.10
Toyota Motor Corp.	30	1.0	$2.10
20th Century Fox	30	1.0	$2.10
United Distillers & Vintners	30	1.0	$2.10
United Way	30	1.0	$2.10
Yahoo!, Inc.	30	1.0	$2.10
AOL Time Warner, Inc.	15	0.5	$1.05
Pfizer, Inc.	15	0.5	$1.05
The *New York Times*	15	0.5	$1.05
Total	**2180**	**72.7**	**$152.60**

Notes: Condensed from original report; all values calculated by the author; reported 30-second amount is $2.1 million.
Source: Original data from *Sports Business Journal*'s *By The Numbers*, 2004, p. 34.

BASICS OF THE SPORTS BROADCAST RIGHTS MARKET

Let's begin our analysis of the market for sports broadcasting rights by identifying the participants and their roles, which are displayed in Figure 3.1. At the top of Figure 3.1 sit professional sports leagues. As you can see on the left side of the figure, these leagues provide programming that they sell for a **rights fee. Media providers** pay the rights fee for programming in the form of games to be broadcast. These media providers, which include the major networks (ABC, NBC, CBS, and FOX), cable (ESPN, FOX SportsNet), and satellite and Internet companies, then sell **advertising slots** associated with this type of programming to the advertisers most interested in those slots. Advertisers interested in reaching the male target demographic purchase sports program ad slots, paying the media providers **slot fees.** These fees represent dollars that media providers can then pay to the professional sports leagues for the rights to broadcast their games. Then, the cycle continues from league to media provider to advertiser and back.

Note that there is no box for fans in Figure 3.1. So how does the figure square with our view that all the money comes from fans? From the relationship shown in Figure 3.1 we can make the following observation: The only reason that advertisers

Figure 3.1 The Sports Broadcasting Rights Market

The sports broadcasting rights market performs two important functions. It sends programming from teams and leagues to media providers that, in turn, sell ad slots to advertisers. It also moves money from advertisers that pay slot fees to media providers to teams and leagues in the form of rights fees.

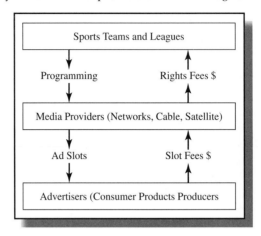

buy ad slots is to increase and/or preserve the sales of their products to consumers. In the case of advertising on sports programs, the consumers also happen to be sports fans. Therefore, it is fan willingness to pay that is the point of interest, albeit indirectly in this case, through their purchase of advertised products.

Where Does the Money Go?

We'll use Figure 3.1 to analyze sports advertising from the perspective of each participant in the figure later in the chapter, but let's jump straight to the $64,000 question: "Who gets the money?" The answer lies in identifying the economically competitive sectors of the advertising market. Because audiences can be enormous, many people mistakenly assume that this means that individual media providers have market power. It is easy to confuse the power of the media to influence people with market power. However, my consulting experience with media providers, briefly working with lawyers for ABC, indicates a high level of **media provider competition.** Remember, market power is driven by a lack of close, readily available substitutes. Back in the days when ABC, CBS, and NBC were the only major networks, there weren't very many close substitutes for advertisers wishing to purchase ad slots. However, times have changed. Since the early 1980s, national and regional cable and satellite networks have proliferated. In addition, radio, the corner newsstand, and even the newspaper rack at the local library are all substitutes for each other (not necessarily perfect substitutes, but substitutes nonetheless). Can you believe that there were once only two dominant sports publications, *Sporting News* and *Sports Illustrated*? And these were usually obtained at specialty news stores or by subscription. Now you can find entire shelves of magazines devoted to the topic in the supermarket.

Did You Know?

At one time, there were only two dominant sports publications. Today, there is a sports publication for just about every sport.

TV media providers maintain their audiences by airing programs that audiences want to watch, and they do so in a very competitive environment. This means that, ultimately, the competitive media market only has one power, namely, the power to give viewers what they want as measured by ratings. If a media provider loses in the ratings, advertisers move to higher-rated slots from other providers. The media provider that loses advertisers suffers lower profits. Consumers have the ultimate power of switching channels or turning off the set.

SPORTS LEAGUES AND THEIR BROADCAST RIGHTS

Teams and leagues sit at the top of Figure 3.1. Individual teams have exclusive home game broadcast rights, which they eventually sell to television, radio, or Internet media providers. Teams sell their sports broadcast rights in one of two ways (things are bit different in college, as we'll see in Chapter 13). First, teams sell some home games through their league. This type of sale occurs through what is called a **national broadcasting contract.** Usually, the national contract includes only television rights, but recently, leagues started to market some of their video and audio rights at the national level through firms on the Internet. The proportion of games sold through national contracts varies by league. MLB teams sell only a few games nationally; NBA and NHL teams sell a larger share; and NFL teams sell all of their games through the league's national contract.

Did You Know?
The MLB markets some of its audio rights at the national level through the Internet firm RealNetworks.

Second, broadcast rights to games that are not covered under the national contract are left to the individual teams to sell as they see fit. Typically, teams sell to television and radio providers, but the Internet is a rising force. Contracts covering these games are called **local broadcasting contracts.** MLB teams sell nearly all of their games through local market contracts. NFL teams, in contrast, have no local market sales except by radio. However, given the level of broadcast technology that exists, both leagues actually end up broadcasting a very similar product. In MLB, where local contracts dominate, all locations get their local team nearly nightly, along with a general interest game a couple of times each week. In the NFL, where there is literally no such thing as a local television broadcast, fans get approximately the same thing. They can be reasonably sure that they will see their home team every week, along with a couple of games of broader interest. We'll return to this outcome and discuss why teams sell some of their games through leagues when we cover the behavior of leagues in Chapter 5.

MEDIA PROVIDERS AND ADVERTISING

As you can see in Figure 3.1, media providers pay rights fees for programming. These media providers are involved in what can be characterized as an auction for broadcast rights. The most interesting thing about sports rights auctions is how much providers eventually end up paying for the rights. Many observers think that the rights go for more than they are worth based on their contribution strictly in terms of ad slot revenue. These same observers condemn such purchases as folly. Are such purchases really silly? If not, how have observers missed the point? We'll discuss these questions in this section.

From an economic perspective, media providers would consider the extra costs and benefits of rights fee purchases. As long as a sports broadcast right generates at least as much revenue as it costs, then it is worth buying. Otherwise, it's not worth the price of the broadcast right. Table 3.6 reveals that these revenues are sizable. For example, three out of four of the general major networks (only NBC is left out), along with the exclusively sports ESPN, generate revenues in excess of $1 billion from their sports programming. On the other hand, beside ESPN, only FOX collects more than 25 percent of its revenues from sports programming. So sports programming is

Table 3.6 Network Advertising Revenues, 2003

NETWORK	SPORTS REVENUE ($MILLIONS)	NONSPORTS REVENUE ($MILLIONS)	TOTAL AD REVENUE ($MILLIONS)	SPORTS REVENUE % OF TOTAL
CBS	$1,435.6	$4,392.0	$5,827.6	24.6%
ABC	$1,330.2	$3,797.2	$5,127.4	25.9%
FOX	$1,176.2	$1,824.8	$3,001.0	39.2%
ESPN	$1,163.5	$0.0	$1,163.5	100.0%
NBC	$472.3	$5,103.7	$5,576.0	8.5%
TNT	$221.6	$508.5	$730.1	30.3%
ESPN2	$219.2	$0.0	$219.2	100.0%
The Golf Channel	$88.4	$0.0	$88.4	100.0%
Speed Channel	$62.9	$0.0	$62.9	100.0%
USA	$44.3	$522.7	$567.0	7.8%
FX	$43.5	$230.7	$274.2	15.9%
TBS	$34.4	$718.5	$752.9	4.6%
Outdoor Life Network	$34.1	$16.3	$50.4	67.7%
ESPN Classic	$19.8	$0.0	$19.8	100.0%
Galavision	$19.6	$60.9	$80.5	24.3%
Spike TV	$14.1	$275.8	$289.9	4.9%
MTV	$7.5	$828.0	$835.5	0.9%
CNBC	$6.7	$416.2	$422.9	1.6%
BET	$4.7	$257.0	$261.7	1.8%
Discovery Channel	$4.2	$408.6	$412.8	1.0%
Pax	$1.2	$161.0	$162.2	0.7%
TLC	$1.1	$347.9	$349.0	0.3%

Source: Adapted and excerpted from *Sports Business Journal*, May 3, 2004, p. 23.

important, but the rest of the programming purchased by media providers provides the vast majority of network revenues.

Often, however, the sports division of a media provider actually loses money! Sports rights fees can be greater than the sports division revenues generated by selling ads on sports programming. Despite these losses, the rights are still worth having. The reason is that the value of broadcast rights to media providers is only partly in the advertising slot revenue that the programming generates. Thus, the **marginal revenue product of broadcast rights** extends beyond just the value of ad slots sold to advertisers.

Let's examine these other values. First, marginal revenue will be earned both by selling ad slots to advertisers and by advertising the provider's own shows during the broadcast. In addition, placing the sports program close to other programs may provide some "sequencing value"; people who tune in to the broadcast may leave their sets tuned to the same channel and watch a subsequent show and vice versa. In addition, the media provider's local affiliates receive ad revenues from local ads that appear during the sports program. The returns to the major media providers are earned here through franchise contracts with affiliates. The marginal revenue gained from all of these sources must be included in the calculation of the value of a sports broadcast right.

In a recent NFL broadcast rights go-round, NBC lost out to CBS. Dick Ebersol of NBC claimed that they bailed out of the bidding because, at the final level of bidding, the eventual winner would suffer annual "catastrophic losses" of $150 to $200 million. Sean McManus, president of eventual bid winner, CBS Sports, argued, "We are not going to lose money on this deal . . . because of the value it brings to our stations, the savings in promotional time, the extra value to our affiliates" (Quirk and Fort, 1999, p. 40). All of these factors generate revenue that appears on the overall CBS balance sheet but may not show up on the CBS Sports balance sheet. This is an essential point that bears repeating: Media providers place their bids based on the contribution that programming makes to their overall revenue structure, not just to the sports division from ad revenue.

Another example, which we mentioned at the start of the chapter, is FOX. In its original bid to break into network TV, FOX spent so much obtaining NFL rights that it took a $350 million loss on its 1994 contract. But don't shed any tears for Rupert Murdoch. The network as a whole showed an increase in profits (after the $350 million loss solely by its sports division) from $511 million for the last 6 months of 1993 to $610 million for the last 6 months of 1994 (Quirk and Fort, 1999, p. 41). Despite losing hundreds of millions of dollars on the NFL, FOX profits rose 16 percent (in 2004 dollars). Surely, some of that increase was from NFL spillover and affiliate values.

The Winner's Curse

Generally, apparent losses on sports rights actually turn into positive contributions to the overall revenues of the media provider once spillover values are included in the calculation. However, in some auction settings rights prices might be forced to a level that exceeds their overall contribution to media provider revenues. Typically, auctions among well-informed buyers move broadcast rights to the highest bidder, with the media provider passing the vast majority of the value through to the league. A typical auction has many bidders who are both experienced and well informed about the product up for auction. The bids are essentially the same and close to the true underlying value of the rights.

However, in some sports broadcast rights auctions, these usual circumstances don't hold. Suppose that there is not much information on which to build any subjective evaluation of the probable value of the ads and other contributions to media provider revenues. This could happen for a number of reasons. Media providers may be facing very different situations than in the past, or there may be providers that are new to the process. In such cases, providers still must develop some sort of estimate of the broadcast rights value, but it is very likely that the bids won't be bunched around the true expected value. Such a setting is ripe for what is called a **winner's curse.** In such a setting, a competitive bidding system would elicit the most optimistic—and therefore wrong—highest bid. The winner in such a situation would be cursed by having won because the true expected value is most likely much less than the winning bid. A recent possible example of the winner's curse in action is covered in the Learning Highlight: The Curse of Monday Night Football?

LEARNING HIGHLIGHT
The Curse of Monday Night Football?

At its inception in 1970, only (then) president of ABC Sports Roone Arledge saw what Monday Night Football would become. Indeed, Arledge built part of his legend on the show. But the rights belong, of course, to the NFL, and the league put them up to bid for the 1998 season. ABC eventually won the MNF rights for 8 years for $4.4 billion in the face of a hard charge by NBC. Because NBC should have pretty good knowledge of the value of MNF rights, did ABC necessarily win? Or was ABC a cursed winner?

One analysis would have it that ABC was cursed because of its winning bid. NBC had very experienced sports people in the bidding process and had carried NFL games for many years. Surely, those people must have known the value of these rights as well as ABC? Because NBC dropped out, ABC must have ended up paying too much for the rights. Reinforcing this view were public statements by NBC at the time that it expected ABC to lose more than $100 million per year with the winning bid. This is the usual notion of a winner's curse and reminiscent of Dick Ebersol's quote concerning the horrible prospects facing the winner in the battle over NFL rights between NBC and CBS.

The argument against a winner's curse for ABC rests solely on an evaluation of the setting because only ABC can know if they took a loss or not. First, that NBC dropped out doesn't mean that it had a better guess than ABC. Think about it like this. If NBC had won the bid, they would have been the cursed winner by the same argument. Further, the setting here just doesn't fit the requirements for a winner's curse. How likely is it that either bidder would have only a weak estimate of the true expected value of the rights? In fact, ABC had the rights to sports programming in the past and MNF broadcasts in particular. So the bidders are neither uninformed nor neophytes, and the setting for a winner's curse is questionable given that NBC and ABC were informed bidders.

An alternative assessment is that, based on its expenditures, ABC expected to make about $500 million each year for the 16 MNF games that it would televise. That's just a bit over $31 million per game. This seems a pretty tall order if one looks only at the revenues generated by MNF broadcasts. However, some of the MNF ad slots will be filled with ads for ABC shows. Further, one program leads into another, and the sequence of programming can affect viewing levels. For example, CBS had rights to NFC games before the most recent contract. CBS moved their Sunday Game of the Week to a lead-in position just before *60 Minutes*, and ratings for the latter jumped. When FOX won the rights to the NFC games away from CBS in the recent contract, the ratings for *60 Minutes* fell right back down again. Presumably, ABC knew that MNF could have the same effect on its Monday night programming.

By this explanation, ABC must have expected that the actual MNF ad revenues, plus the value of advertising its own programs, plus the sequencing value of MNF, would exceed the $31 million per game price tag. However, the winner's curse cannot be dismissed without a close look at the specific setting and the outcome.

ABC's Steve Bornstein managed to hold on to Monday Night Football in the face of NBC's hard charge in 1998 but was he the victim of the winner's curse?

Source: Inspired in part by "Thrown for a Loss," *Time*, January 16, 1998, p. 52.

MEDIA PROVIDER OWNERSHIP OF SPORTS TEAMS

The phenomenon of **media provider ownership of teams** provides one of the most interesting unsolved puzzles in the business of sports. The phenomenon itself is clear. Except in the NFL, corporations can own teams outright (we'll talk about why it makes sense to restrict corporate ownership in the next chapter), and some corporate owners are media giants themselves. In MLB, FOX Sports own part of the Colorado Rockies, and AOL-Time Warner owns the Atlanta Braves. In the NBA, Bell Globemedia owns the Toronto Raptors; Comcast owns the Philadelphia 76ers; and FOX and Cablevision have shares of the New York Knicks. In the NHL, Bell Globemedia also owns the Toronto Maple Leafs, and Cablevision owns the New York Rangers. Until recently, Rupert Murdoch's News Corp. owned the Los Angeles Dodgers, and Disney, which owns ABC and ESPN, owned the NHL Anaheim Mighty Ducks and the MLB Anaheim Angels.

Why buy the entire team instead of just its broadcast rights? What is gained? The decision to buy a sports team is just one of the many choices a media provider must make concerning the structure of its firm. All media providers obtain programming in one of two ways—either they purchase it from another programming producer (firms like Carsey-Warner, Stephen J. Cannell Productions, Bright-Kauffman) or they can produce it in-house (nearly all network news shows are in-house productions). A similar organizational choice confronts media providers when it comes to sports programming. Media providers can purchase the broadcast rights for a given team or purchase the team itself. In a sense, the latter choice can be thought of as bringing the production of actual sports programming in-house. Whether to buy a team rather than just its broadcast rights is quite close to the question of what to produce in-house versus what to outsource to other production companies.

CBS and the Yankees: A Historical Example Against Media Provider Ownership

The puzzle is best presented with the single historical example of an economically tragic media provider ownership—CBS and the New York Yankees (the Yankee sale prices are in Quirk and Fort [1992], but the calculation of losses is original here). In 1964, then-owners Dan Topping and Del Webb sold 80 percent of the New York Yankees to CBS for about $11 million. By 1967, CBS had bought them out completely for about another $3 million, for a total of about $14 million. CBS did so poorly with the team that the current majority owner, George Steinbrenner, was able to put together a syndicate in 1973 and buy the team for $10 million. This was exactly the price of an expansion franchise in 1968. Two existing teams, the Seattle Pilots and Washington Senators (arguably the worst teams ever in the history of MLB) each sold for about $10 million in 1970. The Yankees under CBS weren't much better than an expansion franchise. The Yankees led their division in 1963, with a 0.611 winning percent. However, they never led their division during the entire tenure of CBS (the best they did was second in 1970).

Did You Know?

Historically, the sale price of the New York Yankees has risen about 5.6 percent annually in real terms, but during its tenure of ownership (in 2004 dollars), from 1964 to 1973, CBS lost $69.9 million, or about 62 percent of its investment.

In nominal terms, the $4 million loss represents about 29 percent of CBS's original purchase price of $14 million. However, let's not forget about inflation and the opportunity cost of the funds. Putting it all into 2004 dollars, the 1964 amount is $66.5 million, the 1967 amount is $16.8 million, and the total is $83.3 million. The sale price in 1973 becomes $42.2 million. In addition, the original $66.5 million spent in 1964 would have accrued interest over CBS's 9 years of ownership. According to the usual formula, and using a 3 percent real interest rate, $65 million invested at the beginning of the ownership period would have been worth ($66.5 million) $\times (1.03)^9 =$ $86.8 million. The additional $16.8 million invested at the end of 1967 would have been worth ($16.8 million) $\times (1.03)^6 =$ $18.6 million. Over the entire ownership period, the opportunity cost of funds was $86.8 million + 18.6 million = $105.4 million. After selling the team to Steinbrenner's group for $42.2 million, the actual loss compared to the opportunity cost of the funds was a whopping $63.2 million, or 60 percent of the opportunity cost of the investment. For a little perspective, on average, owners who bought teams in the 1960s essentially broke even at the next sale episode in real terms (Fort, 2006), even when the Yankees are included in the calculation, but CBS managed to suffer a 60 percent loss.

Presumably, there is no reason to believe that CBS would be any better or worse at hiring front office talent, a field manager, coaches, and players than anybody else, especially for 10 years running. Just why the network failed so miserably as an owner of one of the most storied franchises in MLB history is something of a mystery. This is especially interesting because Steinbrenner turned the team around on the field and in the marketplace. In Chapter 1 we saw that an actual offer of $733.8 million (in 2004 dollars) was made for the team in 1998.

Possible Advantages to Media Provider Ownership

Buying a team secures local broadcast rights for the owner. These rights are less expensive than the only alternative to a network, namely, the national contract. Because many areas have no local team, a network-level media provider can attempt to fill that gap with a team that may have nationwide appeal. All that those fans would get, otherwise, would be the scattered few games on national TV, plus cable superstation offerings.

This is just what Ted Turner did when he bought the Atlanta Braves in 1976 (through his Turner Broadcasting). The Braves provided programming for Turner's fledgling regional cable company that eventually grew into TBS. TBS reached millions of viewers nationwide who didn't have any other "every day" baseball alternative. In addition, the Braves were cheap, making them especially appealing to Turner, whose staples were syndicated reruns.

Did You Know?
Through his company, News Corp., Rupert Murdoch paid $350 million for the Los Angeles Dodgers.

News Corp./FOX and Disney/ABC/ESPN were a completely different situation. In their media provider role, both News Corp. and Disney were already well established when they entered into team ownership. Their programming was of the more expensive, original variety rather than the syndicated reruns aired by TBS. Further, Turner and other superstations that followed already were beaming their teams nationwide. So News Corp./FOX and Disney/ABC/ESPN couldn't fill the same niche with their baseball offerings. In addition, News Corp./FOX and Disney/ABC/ESPN did not purchase bargain-basement sports teams. Murdoch paid $311 million for the Los Angeles Dodgers in 1998 (or $357 million in 2004 dollars).

This leads to the puzzle mentioned at the beginning of this section. News Corp./FOX or Disney/ABC/ESPN could pursue exactly the same policy just by buying a team's broadcast rights rather than by buying the entire team outright. If these media providers just bought the rights to the games left over after the national contract, they could accomplish the same end without paying hundreds of millions of dollars for the team itself. So why buy a team?

The obvious economic answer would be that Murdoch and Disney are of the opinion that it's more profitable to own the team than it is to purchase residual broadcast rights. However, none of the reasons for increased profitability that come to mind are very convincing. We've already gone through the CBS/Yankee episode, so we know that corporate ownership doesn't guarantee profits. Some of the possible reasons for corporate ownership include:

- Avoidance of the high price of broadcast rights
- Production efficiency gains through control of the process
- Tax advantages
- Alteration of the competitive environment confronting the media provider
- Enjoyment gained from owning a team and making money

Avoiding the High Price of Broadcast Rights Contrary to the opinion of some very good reporters (who turn out to be poor economists), ownership has nothing to do with whether a media provider can avoid the high price of broadcast rights. If the media provider buys the broadcast rights on the open market, then it pays the market price. If, on the other hand, the media provider owns the team, it must implicitly account for this forgone price if it chooses to broadcast the programming itself. This is no different from the logic of opportunity cost underlying every decision that has to do with using something of value rather than selling it.

Gaining Production Efficiency Does some gain in production efficiency reduce the cost of putting games over the air if a network owns the team? If so, then the network would get to keep the balance of value over the reduced cost. But how can owning the team lead to lower broadcast costs? One way would be if owning the team reduces contracting costs (e.g., legal costs between the media provider and the team as well as the costs of making sure that all elements are in place in order to produce a broadcast). However, this does not decrease the stages of production or reduce the number of people who must be hired. As we saw in the Yankees case, there is no reason to suspect that media providers have some sort of specialized talent that would lower costs. Further, it would seem that the same sorts of economies are available under long-term contracts.

Securing Possible Tax Advantages The tax benefits of owning a team are an interesting possibility. In this situation, there would have to be a connection between the media provider's tax payments and the tax liability of the owned team. Suppose that the media provider itself (the parent company) makes high profits subject to the corporate income tax. If the team it owns shows a loss, then transferring some of the taxable profit to the team would reduce the tax obligation of the overall operation.

This is a possibility, but there are other things to consider. First, for this tax avoidance scheme to be of value to the parent company, as opposed to the team itself, the savings would have to come back to it somehow. However, the revenue would have been shown on the team's books, and that would go into the team's net value. Indirectly, because the media provider owns the team and its net value would rise, the media provider now has a more valuable team in its overall portfolio. But because the revenue of the media provider fell, how can the overall value rise? Second, if there was a tax advantage to one type of firm-team relationship over another, then all team owners could simply incorporate, like Disney, and gain the same advantage. We simply don't see this happening. Finally, the idea of transferring value would argue that media providers buy teams that are likely to show losses (or, at most, very low revenues). This hardly seems to characterize the Yankees, Braves, Dodgers, Angels, or Mighty Ducks.

Changing the Competitive Environment   Sometimes owning the team may change the competitive environment of the media provider. Cornering the market on local rights can be of very high value. However, a few mitigating factors apply to this approach. First, it simply is very hard to do. Competition among media providers is fierce. Second, such a move invites regulatory scrutiny. An international example of how media provider ownership can draw the scrutiny of antitrust oversight is featured in the Learning Highlight: Murdoch's Bid for Manchester United. The Federal Trade Commission (FTC) and the Federal Communications Commission (FCC) closely watch the behavior of media providers in the United States. Finally, if team owners see what the media provider is up to, they will simply raise the price of the team to try to capture the expected future value of the reduced competition. The value of such an action just gets bid into the price of the team and the current owner collects it, rather than the media provider. Obtaining an environment of decreased competition is simply a difficult thing to pull off.

Having Fun and Making Money?   There is one other explanation that works for the actual people behind the media provider firms. Perhaps they just wanted their firms to own baseball teams for the same reason that other owners buy their teams—team ownership has significant fun and profit aspects. The associated broadcast rights just follow along at the same cost as buying them, but the other aspects of ownership might have driven their choice.

But don't forget that a corporation cares only about profits. Fun doesn't enter into the picture. And the people running these corporations could pay a high price for fun—if profits fall, they could lose control of their firms. Just why is it that owning the teams is more profitable than buying rights to their local broadcasts? Given that media provider ownership is taking on international dimensions, figuring out the answer takes on added significance.

The Possible Problems with Media Provider Ownership

Whatever the reasoning by media providers, their ownership of sports teams may signal the beginning of a dilemma. If teams are worth more to media providers than they are to individual owners (and this is a big *if* because it is difficult to find any advantages to owning versus buying broadcast rights), then media providers will start bidding up the price of sports teams. If this really is the beginning of a trend, media provider ownership could lead to two problems.

First, if it is true that teams are most valuable as a division of media providers, then revenues will be higher for those teams owned by media providers. In the short run, at least, the impact of media provider ownership may be to further exacerbate revenue differences among teams. Unless all teams end up as divisions of media providers, the revenue gap between teams would widen. Wide enough gaps would lead to less competitive balance, risking lost fan interest, except for the fans of teams owned by media providers.

None of the usual explanations for media provider team ownership seems to fit the case of Rupert Murdoch's buying the Los Angeles Dodgers through his company News Corp. But additional insight into media provider ownership of teams lies in another of Murdoch's moves. Recently, his international ambitions led to his tendering an offer for Manchester United in the English Premiere League (European football), for $1 billion through his international cable system, BSkyB. In this particular instance, the answer to why buy the team rather than just the rights is supplied by the British Monopolies and Merger Commission (MMC).

The MMC concluded that ownership of the best team in the Premiere League might have reduced competition for the broadcasting rights to all English Premier League matches. After all, it is precisely the Manchester United home games that everybody wishes to see. The upshot might have been fewer choices for the Premier League in the broadcasting of soccer games. The MMC also concluded that the move would improve BSkyB's ability to secure rights to Premier League matches, would reduce competition in the market for sports premium television channels, and would lead to reduced competition in the wider pay-TV market.

These competition concerns were the main reasons for the MMC's conclusion that the proposed merger was not in the public interest. The British secretary of state for trade and industry, Stephen Byers, nixed the sale, citing the MMC conclusions. Such an acquisition might have altered the competitive situation for broadcast rights, as BSkyB is the dominant player in that market in England, with a contract for 670 million pounds with the Premiere League already. Eventually, through BSkyB, Murdoch did gain control of 10 percent of Manchester United, which he sold in October 2003, for around $113 million. We can only contemplate how much more valuable the team would have become if competition had been reduced dramatically, as the MMC feared.

Rupert Murdoch tendered an offer of around $1 billion for the Manchester United English football team.

Sources: James Walker, "Give Us Back Our Man United," *SportsJones*, www.sportsjones.com, April 23, 1999; sportsbusinessnews.com, October 9, 2003.

The second problem concerns changes forecast by some observers. If the move toward media provider ownership is the front end of a trend, then current owners of teams will have to live with an interesting, mixed result. The price of franchises will increase and current owners will be wealthier, but they may well no longer be in the sports business. This is because they would have to sell their teams to collect. Although resources move to a more highly valued use, not all will be happy with the outcome. What will happen to the mix of over-the-air and cable or satellite sports?

Surely, those willing to pay the most will get the sports. But won't some current fans be displaced? Finally, local fans may find it difficult to identify with absentee media provider owners who care only about ratings.

However, let's remember that a few instances (currently two in MLB, three in the NBA, and two in the NHL) do not, in and of themselves, signal a trend. Indeed, Disney sold the Angels to billboard magnate Arturo Moreno, and Frank McCourt recently completed the purchase of the Dodgers from News Corp. Bob Daly, chairman, general manager, and 5% owner of the Dodgers put it bluntly, "The Dodgers are not a core asset for News Corp. They are not making money, and you don't have to control the team to control the sports rights" (sportsbusinessnews.com, accessed January 23, 2003). Only the passage of time will sort out these issues.

FIRMS AND THEIR ADVERTISING CHOICE

Let's move on to the last (or first, depending on your perspective) rung on the ladder in Figure 3.1, firms that buy ad slots from media providers. At the most basic level of economic analysis, advertisements are just another input in any firm's production process. How do firms determine the amount of advertising to buy and how much they will pay for it?

Because advertisements are "just another input," the usual logic of input hiring holds. If the revenue earned from the additional sales generated by ads exceeds the extra cost of the ads (production costs plus the purchase of ad slots), then the advertisements are worth it. The contribution to revenue made by an additional unit of input is called its marginal revenue product (MRP). In the case of advertising, the logic is precisely as stated, but figuring out the marginal benefits is complex. Here is an example that shows why.

Did You Know?
Kellogg's, Nuprin, and 7-Up did not advertise in the Super Bowl in 1991 but did in 1992. Only Kellogg's enjoyed any increase in sales; the other two firms actually had much smaller sales despite their very expensive Super Bowl ads.

Firms often have a devil of a time figuring out the value of ads. Advertising results of the 1991 and 1992 Super Bowls are shown in Table 3.7. Clearly, the results are highly variable. Gillette and Advil advertised during both games and saw significant sales increases in 1992. Budweiser and Pepsi did the same but enjoyed a much smaller increase in 1992 compared to 1991. The interesting outcome concerns the remaining firms. Kellogg's, Nuprin, and 7-Up did not advertise in 1991 but did in 1992. One would expect an increase in sales given the high price of Super Bowl ads. However, only Kellogg's enjoyed any increase. The other two firms actually had much smaller sales despite their very expensive Super Bowl ads.

How can a firm spend millions on Super Bowl advertising and not show an increase in sales? How did a firm decide whether a 30-second ad during the 1992 Super Bowl was worth $850,000 (about $1.1 million adjusted to 2004 dollars)? Maybe the winner's curse is in operation. There would have to be a very broad distribution of estimates of Super Bowl ad values among inexperienced bidders for ad slots. If the bidding for sports programming ad slots is very competitive, the most optimistic, highest—and therefore wrong—bid would be the winner. The winner

Table 3.7 Super
Bowl Advertising
Results for 1991
and 1992

FIRM/PRODUCT	SALES 6 WEEKS AFTER SUPER BOWL 1/91 ($MILLIONS)	SALES 6 WEEKS AFTER SUPER BOWL 1/92 ($MILLIONS)	% CHANGE 1991 TO 1992
Gillette Sensor	$15	$17.8	18.7
Advil	$30.7	$35.4	15.3
Kellogg's Corn Flakes	$27.7*	$29.5	6.5
Budweiser	$136.9	$145	5.9
Pepsi	$296.6	$306.4	3.3
Nuprin	$7.6*	$7.3	−4.8
7-Up	$59.3*	$55.2	−6.8

*Did not advertise on televised Super Bowl.
Source: Wall Street Journal, January 26, 1993, pp. B1, B6.

would then be cursed by having won because the true expected value must be less. In this Super Bowl ad context, some firms guessed high and took the ads. Others, like Coke, took no ads. The outcome revealed that the true expected value was lower than those who "bid"—or paid—the most. The sales just weren't there.

This is an appealing piece of logic but, as with our analysis of media providers, does it make sense? After all, who knows more about the value of advertising than firms like Kellogg's and 7-Up? One might as well throw in Pepsi, because its increase in revenue was only about 3 percent. Surely these firms are neither naïve nor inexperienced. On the face of it, a winner's curse explanation goes wanting.

EXTENDING THE DEFINITION OF THE MRP OF ADS FROM THE ADVERTISER'S PERSPECTIVE

An alternative explanation expands the idea of the MRP of ads in an important way. Implicitly, in assessing the value of Super Bowl ads, we have assumed that the MRP of ads is just in terms of additional sales per dollar spent. This misses an essential point about advertising that we learned in the first section of this chapter. Sales can come from both new consumers and established consumers that choose to switch brands. What if most of a firm's advertising budget actually impacts the latter? In this situation, the net result of advertising by one firm depends on the advertising choice of other, competitive firms. Thus, the net result of advertising, given advertising by rivals, is the point of analysis. Let's see where this leads.

If one firm advertises its brand, some consumers will choose it. But if another firm advertises its competing brand, some consumers will choose it instead. If advertisements were at equal levels for the two firms, and each firm had equal access to the same quality of ads, equal numbers of consumers would choose each brand. Thus, the

Did You Know?
The net result of one firm's ads depends on how much advertising is done by its rivals.

net result of one firm's ads depends on how much advertising is done by its rivals. In this case, MRP can be portrayed as follows:

$$MRP_1\ (A_1, A_2, X_1) = MP_1\ (A_1, A_2) \times MR_1\ (X_1)$$

A_1 and A_2 stand for the amount of advertising by the two firms. The other element in MRP is X_1, the level of sales of the actual product being advertised. This is the general form of MRP because marginal revenue depends on the level of sales of the good generated by advertising. In this specification of advertising MRP for Firm 1, the firm's additional sales revenue depends on its own advertising and advertising by the other firm. For any given level of advertising for Firm 1, greater advertising by Firm 2 would reduce sales. We could state the same type of MRP for Firm 2 that would depend on the advertising choices of Firm 1.

Game Theory This insight leads us to cast the choice of advertising in strategic terms. This is the realm of **game theory.** In the portrayal of the game used here, two firms must choose simultaneously whether to increase their advertising. Simultaneous choices are easily portrayed in a game matrix, like the one shown in Figure 3.2. In this model of **strategic advertising,** our assumptions are (1) simultaneous choice by the two firms, and (2) the firms are trying to decide whether to increase their advertising spending by $5 million. Each of the cells in the matrix shows the net payoffs after paying the cost of advertising that will result from each firm's choices. If neither firm advertises (bottom-right corner), then nothing happens, and each enjoys its current level of, say, $15 million in net revenue.

The rest of the payoffs make use of our insight about the interdependence of advertising. If Firm 1 were to increase its advertising and Firm 2 didn't follow suit, then Firm 1 would increase its sales at Firm 2's expense. In such a case, let's put Firm 2's hypothetical losses at $7 million. This would mean that the net position of Firm 2 in this case would be $15 million (its starting point) minus $7 million for a net

Figure 3.2 The Advertising Game
Each firm starts at a revenue level of $15 million. Advertising costs $5 million. If one firm advertises and the other doesn't the advertising firm gains $7 million. In the off-diagonal cells, the result is $15 million minus $7 million lost sales for the firm that doesn't advertise and $15 million plus $7 million minus the $5 million ad cost for the firm that does. If both advertise, no net change in sales occurs, but both firms fall to $10 million each for advertising (upper-left diagonal cell). If neither advertises, no change occurs (lower-right diagonal cell).

		Firm 2	
		Increase	Don't Increase
Firm 1	Increase	Firm 1: $10 mil. Firm 2: $10 mil.	Firm 1: $17 mil. Firm 2: $8 mil.
	Don't Increase	Firm 1: $8 mil. Firm 2: $17 mil.	Firm 1: $15 mil. Firm 2: $15 mil.

of $8 million. But Firm 2's loss is Firm 1's gain. So Firm 1's position is calculated as follows: $15 million (its starting point) plus $7 million gained at Firm 2's expense minus the cost of its increased ads, $5 million. On net, Firm 1's result is $17 million. This outcome is depicted in the upper-right cell of the diagram in Figure 3.2. Because we assume that the situations are exactly symmetric for the two firms, just the opposite outcome would happen if Firm 2 increased its advertising and Firm 1 didn't. This is shown in the lower-left cell of Figure 3.2.

That leaves the upper-left cell. If Firm 1 increased its advertising at the same time that Firm 2 increased its advertising, the following would occur. Starting from its initial $15 million position, Firm 1 would pay the $5 million ad price. It would gain the $7 million return from customers previously buying from Firm 2. One would think that the outcome would be, again, $17 million. But remember that ads are interdependent. Firm 2 would have also paid its $5 million ad cost and earned the $7 million return from customers previously buying from Firm 1. The gains of $7 million for each firm are canceled out by the identical amount lost to their rival.

So for Firm 1, starting from $15 million, $7 million would be gained from previous customers of Firm 2, but an equal amount would be lost to Firm 2. There would be no net change in sales revenue. However, Firm 1 would have paid the $5 million in ad costs, so its net position would be $10 million. The same goes for Firm 2. This is depicted in the upper-left cell of Figure 3.2.

The Best Strategy in the Advertising Game

What are the strategies in this case, and is there an equilibrium result? From the matrix, Firm 1 knows that if Firm 2 were to increase its advertising, then Firm 1 would earn $10 million if it increased advertising and $8 million if it didn't. Firm 1 would, therefore, increase its ad spending. Conversely, if Firm 2 stood pat, Firm 1 would earn $17 million if it increased its advertising and $15 million if it didn't. Again, Firm 1 would increase its ad spending. Thus, Firm 1 has a dominant strategy. Regardless of what Firm 2 decides to do, Firm 1 will increase its advertising.

Turning to the question of equilibrium, we need only note that the payoffs are exactly symmetric for Firm 2. Thus, increasing advertising also is the dominant strategy for Firm 2. Because increasing ads is the dominant strategy for both players, each firm increases its advertising and the equilibrium result puts the players in the top left-hand corner of the matrix in Figure 3.2. Both increase their advertising and earn $10 million. For the purposes of discussion later in this section, note that both firms would rather be in the lower-right cell than in the upper-left cell. However, their individual actions keep them in the inferior $10 million position.

The game theory depiction of advertising choice reveals that the extra benefits of advertising can be difficult to figure out. Although, technically, the equilibrium follows from a consideration of extra revenue, the complicating factor is that the result for one firm depends on the choices of the other. Thus, one consideration can be that failing to advertise (or to increase advertising) means lost revenue as customers move to a rival. Simply put, increasing advertising yielded no increase in sales in our example in Figure 3.2. However, failing to advertise would have been even worse for each firm.

Did You Know?
Increasing advertising may not yield an increase in sales, but failing to advertise may lead to decreased sales.

Going back to our Super Bowl advertising puzzle, one could come away with the impression that the ads are useless, but this misses the important point that failing to advertise would lead to an even lower payoff. Perhaps this was the consideration by Pepsi and 7-Up, highly competitive soft-drink firms. Thus, an explanation of the outcome in our Super Bowl ad example doesn't require a winner's curse. All it requires is a careful consideration of the marginal value of ads, including the value of preserving sales in the face of rivals.

The Advertising Dilemma

The game theory portrayal of advertising offers another insight. If they could, the two firms would rather not advertise, and each would enjoy a $5 million net revenue increase and no change in market share.

Both firms would rather be in the lower-right cell of the payoff matrix than in the upper-left cell. If they could, both would stop and escape this **advertising dilemma.** However, each expects the other to simply continue the escalation, and neither can risk being left behind. In such a case, the two firms are trapped in an advertising dilemma that will be difficult to escape through their own actions.

Escaping the Dilemma Without Outside Intervention Escaping the advertising dilemma without outside intervention may be difficult, but it can occur. One of our assumptions is that the game is played one time. One way out of this

Did You Know?
Tacit advertising cooperation may explain why Coke and Pepsi typically do not advertise in major events at the same time.

dilemma involves learning over time. Each firm knows the game matrix in Figure 3.2. Thus, each can look forward to such a game and know the eventual, noncooperative outcome. There is some evidence that firms in this type of situation can tacitly reach an understanding that avoids escalation. A typical type of **tacit cooperation** would be to advertise alternately and split the market. Perhaps this tacit type of result also helps explain why Coke and Pepsi typically do not advertise in major events at the same time. Note that this is a tacit type of agreement; firms do not get together and collude, they simply realize independently that splitting the market is in their mutual interest.

Escaping the Advertising Dilemma Through Outside Intervention There is another, more direct way out of this advertising escalation trap. The firms could hope for or obtain some sort of external constraint on advertising. For example, if the firms are beer companies, the government might be convinced to impose an **ad ban** on beer ads on TV. Government has already outlawed cigarette advertising on TV, as detailed in the Learning Highlight: Is Beer Next? Lessons from the Cigarette TV Ad Ban. The result of an ad ban would be favorable to existing firms for at least two reasons:

1. They do not have to spend as much to maintain sales. They would continue to advertise, but in lower impact and, hence, lower cost media (print, radio, and billboards).

LEARNING HIGHLIGHT
Is Beer Next? Lessons from the Cigarette TV Ad Ban

The cigarette industry was under attack from antismoking forces such as the American Lung Association and the March of Dimes. It also was stuck in the advertising game described in Figure 3.2. Then an amazing thing happened. The FTC stepped in to impose the surgeon general's warning that "Smoking Cigarettes May Be Hazardous to Your Health." Shortly thereafter, the FCC enforced the fairness doctrine in the case of cigarette ads. This doctrine stated that if local stations allowed any advocacy advertising, they must also allow equal access to opposing viewpoints. Equal access extended to helping the opposing group produce its response. Local stations were suddenly in the antismoking commercial business, and public service announcements took a novel step forward.

Thus, in addition to its own advertising escalation dilemma, the cigarette industry now suffered lost sales due to antismoking ads produced at nearly no cost to advocacy groups by local stations. What happened next is that the FCC stepped in to ban cigarette ads on television. Among antismoking forces, there was much rejoicing. But analysts have since pointed out that a number of good things happened to cigarette companies as a result of the TV ad ban. Cigarette company profits soared; there was no decline in consumption; and there hasn't been a challenge to the existing structure of the industry since. One wonders if the antismoking advocates ever saw what hit them.

Antismoking ads may have taught the beer industry some important lessons.

Sources: Gideon Doron, *The Smoking Paradox* (New York: University Press of America, 1984), and A. Lee Fritschler, *The Politics of Smoking* (Upper Saddle River, NJ: Prentice Hall, 1995).

2. Because TV ads are necessary to introduce competing brands, the elimination of TV ads would raise a barrier to entry for new firms. For example, when cigarette ads were banned from TV, profits of existing firms rose and entry into the market essentially ended for many years.

THE BEER WARS

John Helyar, in his book *Lords of the Realm: The Real History of Baseball* (1994), details the strategic interplay between advertisers and a pro sports league, with media providers right in the middle. The example concerns the **"beer wars"** of the late 1970s and their impact on the value of MLB broadcast rights. MLB's first commissioner, Kenesaw Mountain Landis, once said, "Not in my lifetime or yours will you ever hear a beer advertisement during a World Series broadcast." Later, Commissioner Happy

Chandler refused beer ads on the first televised World Series, saying, "It would not be good public relations for baseball to have the Series sponsored by the producer of an alcoholic beverage." Helyar emphasizes how things changed:

By the 1980s, beer was the mother's milk of baseball. Anheuser-Busch, which in 1976 sponsored the telecasts of twelve teams, in 1986 sponsored those of all twenty-six. Its war with Miller [the introduction of Miller-Lite in 1975 cut Anheuser-Busch's market share from 23.7 percent to 19.4 percent] was also a huge factor in driving up the value of baseball's broadcast rights. TV could pay big for baseball rights, knowing Anheuser-Busch and Miller would pay big to advertise. Baseball was summer; summer was beer; and beer was huge money. (Helyar, 1994, p. 393)

Beer advertising was huge money indeed. In 1983, the new contract for MLB's national broadcasting rights (to last over the period 1984–1989) went for $1.125 billion ($2.1 billion in 2004 dollars), approximately four times the previous contract. As you might guess, MLB played both ends against the middle and encouraged the escalation between Anheuser-Busch and Miller. First, NBC was offered the entire contract for $1 billion. They refused. Said Ken Schanzer, "number two" at NBC Sports at the time, on their beer wars strategy, "Either we succeeded in getting the whole package, or we so crippled our competitor, we made his life hard" (Helyar, 1994, p. 395). Eventually, the $1.125 billion was paid in two pieces, $575 million from ABC and $550 million from NBC.

"The money is so big, given the current ratings, that the (proposed) increase is amazing. But there are always two decisions in something like this. One is purely economical. The other is strategic: What does the other guy lose if we take something away from them?"
—A senior vice president at Turner Sports (*USA Today* Online, www.usatoday.com, August 6, 1998)

By 1992, the beer wars ended. Their end signaled the end of the dramatic rise in MLB broadcasting rights values. Indeed, the MLB contract has never come close to the dramatic level reached during the beer wars. But the logic that fueled that escalation appears to be gaining steam in another sport. About Disney's recent win in the competition over NHL broadcast rights, a senior vice president at Turner Sports said, "The money is so big, given the current ratings, that the (proposed) increase is amazing. But there are always two decisions in something like this. One is purely economical. The other is strategic: What does the other guy lose if we take something away from them?" (*USA Today* Online, www.usatoday.com, August 6, 1998.)

There couldn't be a clearer statement of the strategic underpinnings of advertising escalation. The "purely economical" part is just the ad slot revenue. The strategic part is winning the rights away from rivals and the spillover values to the overall revenues of a network.

The advertising war between Bud and Miller bid up the value of ad slots above their usual value. Media providers are perfectly happy to take more for the slots they have to offer. However, competition at the media provider level actually just sent a substantial portion of the overblown ad slot revenue to MLB through an extremely lucrative rights fee contract. The beer wars simply made MLB teams much richer than they already would have been.

SPONSORSHIP

One other interesting item deserves treatment while we're on the subject of advertisers, namely, sponsorship. Sponsorship is just another form of advertising by firms, where firms buy the right to have their name affiliated with a particular event or facility. Many fans find this form of commercialization especially irritating. Perhaps this is because we long for the nostalgic; people would much rather conjure up images of "The Stick" (Candlestick Park) and its San Francisco Giants history than the newer, growing legacy at SBC Park.

Despite the common perception that sponsorship is just the latest in commercialization, it actually has been around for a long time. The longest-standing examples are sponsors of individual sports (sponsorship and college sports are covered in Chapter 13). In men's golf, just take a look at the PGA Tour Schedule (www.pga.com). The list includes important car companies (e.g., Buick has four: the Buick Invitational, the Buick Classic, the Buick Open, and the Buick Challenge), energy companies (e.g., the Shell Houston Open), communications companies (e.g., the AT&T Pebble Beach National Pro-Am), and a host of others. The list of major sponsors is just as impressive for women's golf (LPGA Tour Schedule: www.lpga.com), and Nationwide Insurance sponsors an entire tour of men's PGA hopefuls (previously, the Buy.com Tour).

Turning to pro team sports, sponsorship of a sort actually has existed for quite some time. The tie is in name recognition with a particular product. Busch Stadium, named after the previous owners of the MLB St. Louis Cardinals, has obvious name recognition with Anheuser-Busch beers. The same type of name recognition worked for Wrigley Field, named after the original owners of the MLB Cubs. The relationship to their line of chewing gum is inescapable.

Sometimes name recognition fails. Labatt Breweries owned the MLB Blue Jays from 1991 to 2000. One of the owner's major regrets is that the nickname Jays caught on instead of the Blues, which would have obvious ties to the brewery's top-selling Labatt's Blue Label.

More recently, sponsorship has grown into an explicit, big business. In addition to sponsoring events or individual teams, many very large firms now purchase the right to have their name attached to stadiums and arenas to enhance their advertising. Table 3.8 shows recent stadium and arena sponsorship arrangements. It's possible for such rights to go for as much as $10 million per year (adjusted to 2004 dollars).

Did You Know?
Of sponsorship fees at or exceeding $3 million per year, the split between arenas and stadiums is nearly equal (six arenas and five stadiums).

Although lease arrangements vary, sponsorship rights fees commonly go to the primary tenant of the facility. For baseball stadiums and arenas, this is always the single tenant team owner. For arenas that may have double or triple occupancy, the owner with the highest revenue often receives the value of sponsorship rights. Even in the $2 million range, as with Safeco Field in Seattle, this type of revenue is more than enough to obtain an especially able coach, field manager, or front office general manager.

Table 3.8 Recent Naming Rights

NAME	CITY	YEARS	$MILLION PER YEAR (2004)	EXPIRES	# EVENTS
Phillips Arena	Atlanta, GA	20	$10	2019	82
FedEx Field	Washington, DC	27	$8.5	2025	9
American Airline Center	Dallas, TX	30	$6.9	2030	95
Staples Center	Los Angeles, CA	20	$6.3	2019	136
PSINet Stadium	Baltimore, MD	20	$6	2018	8
Gaylord Entertainment Center	Nashville, TN	20	$4.5	2018	48
Lowe's Motor Speedway	Concord, NC	10	$3.8	2009	16
Pepsi Center	Denver, CO	20	$3.7	2019	82
Enron Field	Houston, TX	30	$3.5	2030	83
Raymond James Stadium	Tampa, FL	18	$3.5	2016	32
Xcel Energy Center	St. Paul, MN	25	$3.3	2024	N/A
Edison International Field	Anaheim, CA	20	$2.8	2018	81
National Car Rental Center	Sunrise, FL	10	$2.8	2008	50
Continental Airlines Arena	East Rutherford, NJ	12	$2.8	2008	101
Bank One Ballpark	Phoenix, AZ	30	$2.5	2028	83
MCI Center	Washington, DC	20	$2.5	2017	116
Fleet Center	Boston, MA	15	$2.4	2010	82
Comerica Park	Detroit, MI	30	$2.3	2030	81
American Airlines Arena	Miami, FL	20	$2.3	2019	34
Ericsson Stadium	Charlotte, NC	10	$2.3	2006	8
Pro Player Stadium	Miami, FL	10	$2.3	2006	87
Pacific Bell Park	San Francisco, CA	24	$2.2	2024	81
Miller Park	Milwaukee, WI	20	$2.2	2020	78
Conseco Fieldhouse	Indianapolis, IN	20	$2.2	2019	53
Safeco Field	Seattle, WA	20	$2	2019	42
PNC Park	Pittsburgh, PA	20	$2.2	2021	80
Adelphia Coliseum	Nashville, TN	15	$2.2	2013	9
TransWorld Dome	St. Louis, MO	20	$2.2	2015	10

Notes: Events are for 1999–2000. Values are in $2004 calculated based on the beginning year of the contract.
Source: Excerpted from *Sports Business Journal*, July 3, 2000, pp. 24–25.

BIG RIGHTS MONEY AND ITS IMPACTS

In this closing section, we will look at the data on broadcast right fees and the impact of big money on sports. We will examine two important questions:

1. How much money is involved in broadcasting sports?
2. How does the level of this type of revenue shape both our perceptions and the actual outcomes in sports markets?

Table 3.9 All Media Revenues, 1990 through 2001 ($2004 Millions)

LEAGUE	1990	1991	1992	1993	1994	1995	1996	1997	1998	1999	2000	2001	GROWTH RATE
MLB	965	991	955	1006	407	635	840				1033	1368	3%
NBA	272	515	525	523	635	700	733						18%
NFL	1118	1242	1345	1503	1363	1567	1609	1630	2337	2395			9%
NHL	150	153	94	165	175	177	195						4%

Sources: forbes.com for MLB 2000; Selig Report for MLB 2001; *LA Times* for NFL 1995–1999. The rest are from Fort and Quirk (1999). All calculations by the author.

Here's how my coauthor and I characterized the contribution that media providers have made to the sports business:

> It's a no-brainer: the networks, the superstations, the cable sports stations, and local TV stations have inundated pro team sports with a veritable monsoon of dollars, which has affected everything and everyone involved in pro team sports. Over the past 20 years, from 1980 on, the most important single factor responsible for the wild explosion in franchise prices and in player and coaching salaries is the huge increase in pro sports' television income. (Quirk and Fort, 1999, p. 29)

Did You Know?

NBA media revenues increased 18 percent in real terms from 1990 to 1995, roughly six times the average U.S. economy growth rate.

Table 3.9 shows all media revenues in professional sports (national and local, if any) from 1990 to 1996, plus additional years for MLB and the NFL. For the NBA and the NFL, the increase in these values over time is phenomenal. On an annual average basis, adjusted to 2004 dollars, NBA media revenues grew 18 percent per year in real terms. Remember that, on average, this is a staggering six times the average rate of annual real growth in the U.S. economy. Interestingly, MLB and the NHL about equaled the economy-wide average growth rate.

The NHL and MLB data offer an interesting comparison concerning the impacts of fan disillusionment over work stoppages. A strike occurred in MLB impacting both the 1994 and 1995 seasons (more in Chapter 9). Media revenues fell dramatically during both of those seasons and really hadn't rebounded by 1996 (although, ultimately, media revenues are healthy recently). The lockout in the 1991–92 NHL season had much less impact on hockey fans. Media revenues rebounded immediately and grew at a 4.3 percent real rate in the following four years. Perhaps it was the fact of a strike by players in MLB versus a lockout by owners in the NHL, but whatever the reason hockey viewers were more forgiving than baseball viewers.

Table 3.10, which provides recent contract amounts, shows that things have kept right on going into the present for the NBA, NHL, and NFL, and that MLB has rebounded quite nicely. With regard to national contracts, the NFL is the heavy hitter at a $2.2 billion annual average, followed by the NBA at $657 million annually and MLB at about $550 million. The NHL, at the end of a $120 million

Table 3.10 Most Recent Contract Details, National Contracts Only

LEAGUE	DURATION	BUYER	PROPERTY PURCHASED	AMOUNT ($)
NFL	1998–2005	ABC	Monday Night; 3 Super Bowls	4.4 billion
		ESPN	Sunday and Thursday Nights	4.8 billion
		FOX	NFC Sunday; 3 Super Bowls	4.4 billion
		CBS	AFC Sunday; 2 Super Bowls	4 billion
				Total: $17.6 billion
NBA	2002–2008	ABC/ESPN		2.4 billion
		AOL/TimeWarner		2.2 billion
				Total: $4.6 billion
NHL	2004–2006	ESPN/ABC	200 matches named later	Total: Unknown
		NBC	No fee, revenue sharing	
MLB	2001–2006	FOX	Postseason and All-Star Game	2.5 billion
		ESPN	Regular Season	800 million
				Total: $3.3 billion

Source: sportsbusinessnews.com, April 20, 2002.

Did You Know?
Congressional Hearings in the 1960s show that the New York Yankees' radio contract in 1950 was worth $416,000 (about $3.2 million 2004 dollars) and the New York Giants contract in 1952 was worth $158,000 (about $1.1 million 2004 dollars).

per year contract in 2004, has only a $67 million annual promise from ABC/ESPN and has embarked on a revenue sharing arrangement with NBC. By way of detailed comparison, the previous MLB contract (1996–2000) with FOX, ESPN, and NBC generated about $1.69 billion over 5 years, or just over $2 billion in 2004 dollars (Quirk and Fort, 1999, p. 43).

The national contract data also make it clear that each pro sports league spreads the wealth among media providers. There always are multiple winners in the bidding game, but not all win, which makes it clear that the bidding must remain competitive for these monopoly broadcast rights.

Media Revenues and Player Cost Comparisons

An even more important aspect of media contracts can be seen when we include all media revenues, shown in Tables 3.11 and 3.12 for MLB and the NFL. Similar data for the NBA and NHL, unfortunately, end at 1996. (This really is a behind the scenes look at the totals listed in Table 3.9.) The sum of media revenues would include individual team negotiations with regional and local media providers, as well as the national contracts. The tables also show total

Table 3.11 All Media Revenues and Player Costs, MLB, 2001 ($2004)

TEAM	LOCAL MEDIA	NATIONAL MEDIA	MEDIA TOTAL	PLAYER COSTS	MEDIA TOTAL/ PLAYER COSTS
N.Y. Yankees	$60,155	$25,865	$86,020	$125,012	0.7
N.Y. Mets	$49,026	$25,865	$74,891	$105,093	0.7
Seattle	$40,132	$25,865	$65,997	$88,983	0.7
Boston	$35,354	$25,865	$61,219	$125,579	0.5
Chicago White Sox	$31,898	$25,865	$57,763	$70,724	0.8
Los Angeles	$28,983	$25,865	$54,848	$123,042	0.4
Texas	$26,801	$25,865	$52,666	$98,361	0.5
Chicago Cubs	$24,973	$25,865	$50,838	$82,776	0.6
Cleveland	$22,341	$25,865	$48,206	$108,640	0.4
Baltimore	$22,254	$25,865	$48,119	$84,570	0.6
Atlanta	$21,187	$25,865	$47,052	$105,651	0.4
Detroit	$20,217	$25,865	$46,082	$60,615	0.8
Philadelphia	$20,076	$25,865	$45,941	$52,347	0.9
Colorado	$19,292	$25,865	$45,157	$74,182	0.6
San Francisco	$18,229	$25,865	$44,094	$76,516	0.6
Florida	$16,274	$25,865	$42,139	$44,609	0.9
Toronto	$15,328	$25,865	$41,193	$88,829	0.5
Houston	$14,545	$25,865	$40,410	$75,872	0.5
San Diego	$13,182	$25,865	$39,047	$48,854	0.8
St. Louis	$12,619	$25,865	$38,484	$84,957	0.5
Anaheim	$11,583	$25,865	$37,448	$55,373	0.7
Oakland	$10,025	$25,865	$35,890	$46,450	0.8
Tampa Bay	$16,442	$19,353	$35,795	$60,420	0.6
Pittsburgh	$9,643	$25,865	$35,508	$56,421	0.6
Arizona	$15,024	$19,588	$34,612	$105,400	0.3
Cincinnati	$8,333	$25,865	$34,198	$48,135	0.7
Minnesota	$7,709	$25,865	$33,574	$32,324	1.0
Kansas City	$6,895	$25,865	$32,760	$45,266	0.7
Milwaukee	$6,273	$25,865	$32,138	$54,234	0.6
Montreal	$568	$25,865	$26,433	$39,937	0.7
Total	$605,361	$763,161	$1,368,524	$2,269,172	

Notes: Player costs include payment to benefit plan. National media in all likelihood also includes some MLB properties income.
Source: Selig Report, 2001.

player costs and the ratio of media revenue to player costs in order to provide a comparative benchmark of the value of media revenues and spending on talent. A ratio equal to or greater than one means that media revenues are enough to cover player costs. All other revenues (gate, concessions, and venue) would simply go to pay the rest of the team costs, including remaining player costs and owner profits.

Table 3.12 All Media Revenues and Player Costs, NFL, 1999 ($2004)

TEAM	LOCAL TV/ RADIO	COMMON REVENUE	TOTAL MEDIA	PLAYER COSTS	TOTAL MEDIA/ PLAYER COSTS
New England Patriots	$9,648	$73,127	$82,775	$79,754	1.0
Washington Redskins	$9,575	$72,558	$82,133	$81,992	1.0
Dallas Cowboys	$7,388	$73,911	$81,299	$74,183	1.1
San Francisco 49ers	$6,490	$73,799	$80,289	$79,563	1.0
Cleveland Browns	$7,597	$72,527	$80,124	$50,878	1.6
Denver Broncos	$4,958	$74,453	$79,411	$73,633	1.1
Carolina Panthers	$6,364	$72,586	$78,950	$82,478	1.0
Chicago Bears	$6,410	$72,455	$78,865	$74,095	1.1
New York Giants	$5,738	$73,117	$78,855	$71,431	1.1
Baltimore Ravens	$5,425	$72,471	$77,896	$78,637	1.0
Seattle Seahawks	$4,456	$73,127	$77,583	$66,991	1.2
Philadelphia Eagles	$5,143	$72,415	$77,558	$72,680	1.1
New York Jets	$4,336	$73,214	$77,550	$72,121	1.1
Detroit Lions	$4,906	$72,619	$77,525	$69,975	1.1
Tampa Bay Buccaneers	$4,683	$72,567	$77,250	$70,308	1.1
Tennessee Titans	$3,863	$73,071	$76,934	$74,621	1.0
Miami Dolphins	$4,188	$72,742	$76,930	$80,126	1.0
St. Louis Rams	$4,174	$72,399	$76,573	$69,070	1.1
Pittsburgh Steelers	$3,725	$72,623	$76,348	$70,766	1.1
Green Bay Packers	$2,520	$73,743	$76,263	$84,951	0.9
Jacksonville Jaguars	$2,822	$73,274	$76,096	$67,155	1.1
San Diego Chargers	$2,802	$72,959	$75,761	$73,796	1.0
Atlanta Falcons	$2,452	$73,183	$75,635	$74,570	1.0
Minnesota Vikings	$2,208	$73,293	$75,501	$77,199	1.0
Kansas City Chiefs	$2,182	$73,127	$75,309	$86,043	0.9
Oakland Raiders	$1,548	$73,158	$74,706	$72,116	1.0
New Orleans Saints	$2,023	$72,527	$74,550	$72,540	1.0
Indianapolis Colts	$2,056	$72,399	$74,455	$74,364	1.0
Buffalo Bills	$1,599	$72,598	$74,197	$69,925	1.1
Cincinnati Bengals	$1,669	$72,399	$74,068	$68,472	1.1
Arizona Cardinals	$236	$72,583	$72,819	$70,487	1.0
Total	$133,184	$2,261,024	$2,394,208	$2,284,921	

Note: Common revenues are national TV/radio, international TV, NFL properties.
Source: LA Times.

As you can see from Tables 3.11 and 3.12, just about as many teams at the lower end of the media revenue distribution are able to cover their player costs as at the top end. This can only be true if those teams at the low end of the revenue distribution spend less on players than those at the top end. Clearly, salary level is a choice, an issue that will be addressed in the next chapter.

If you calculate the average player costs for the top five media revenue teams in MLB (the Yankees, Mets, Mariners, Red Sox, and White Sox in Table 3.11), you will get about $103.2 million. The middle six MLB teams average about $68.8 million, and the bottom five teams average about $43.8 million. It is pretty clear that media revenue is a major determinant of the ability of teams to spend money on talent in MLB.

As one would expect in a league where nearly all revenues are shared, the NFL teams in Table 3.12 break the mold (top five, $73.4 million; middle five, $72.5 million; and bottom five, $70.8 million). Also note that the percent of player costs covered is nearly equal and exceeds 1.0 for all NFL teams except the Green Bay Packers and Kansas City Chiefs. So broadcast rights money is big. Further, certain sports are more important to advertisers and, consequently, to media providers and sports leagues. The NFL typically leads the way, followed by MLB and the NBA. The NHL always is a distant last. Why would a sport like the NFL, with so many fewer broadcast slots, make so much more money than the other sports in total? Of course, the answer is that the NFL provides better reach to the important target demographic of advertisers. Media providers collect this value and pass it through to the NFL.

Variation in Media Revenue for Teams and Leagues

In any given sport, the same type of variation witnessed earlier for total revenue also holds for media revenue. There is substantial **media revenue disparity** around the mean in any sport. In every sport except the NFL (with its nearly complete revenue sharing), the vast majority of teams are below the average in media revenue. Ultimately, this imbalance contributes to one of the major problems for sports. Recall the implications of the uncertainty of outcome hypothesis: more balanced competition is more interesting to fans than less balanced competition. But when fans are willing to pay more money to watch high quality teams, if owners give the fans higher quality, then the owners will have the money to spend on talent. As with the conclusion for revenue in general, variation in media revenues contributes to less balanced competition.

If these differences continue to grow over time, as they have in recent years, then leagues run a real danger of losing one of the things that fans demand, namely, an acceptable level of competitive balance on the field. The common lament is that we all may end up watching nothing but larger-revenue teams in the championship games of every sport. This is a very real possibility if no other teams can compete economically. Leagues are quite aware of this danger and have invented a variety of mechanisms to take care of it. We'll discuss this in more detail in Chapter 6. For now, you only need to understand the source of the potential problem.

Other Problems with Big Media Money

Competitive balance problems are just one issue concerning the commercialization of sports, but there are other big money problems in sports. Some argue that "It's not about the game anymore," it's all about TV. However, sports have always been big business. The only difference from the past is in terms of magnitude. For example, TV does intrude on the actual play on the field, directly. There weren't any TV time-outs through most of the history of sports broadcasts, and the length of games clearly diminishes fan satisfaction.

Another downside of commercialization concerns the behavior of players. Players are freer to behave as they please because their value is so high. When problem players misbehaved in "the good old days," getting rid of them wasn't nearly so expensive as it is today. Leagues tend to put up with problem players who happen to be stars much more than in the past. The revenues they generate make it so.

Another important talent issue is that the absolute level of competition would be lower if it weren't for the commercialization of sports. According to Michael Roarty, Executive Vice President for Corporate Marketing and Communications for Anheuser-Busch:

> While the basic spirit of sports has remained true, other aspects of the game have changed—and matured—for the better. For instance, with the involvement and advertising support of American business, sports have expanded and improved. Today, there are more games for the enthusiast to participate in, more events to view on television, more competitions for national sports media to cover. (*Sporting News*, May 11, 1992, p. 9)

Clearly, without this involvement and the subsequent elevation in player value to teams, we would not see the very high absolute level of quality that we currently enjoy. This is evident in the investment that athletes now make in their own careers, especially after they make it to the pros. Pro athletes used to consider their sport to be a part-time endeavor, and all had other jobs in the off-season. Given the immense returns driven in part by commercialization, training and preparation are full-time occupations. Roarty goes on (remember, this is in 1992, and the $100 million ESPN package, $133.4 million in 2004 dollars, was a tremendous event):

Did You Know?
Pro athletes used to consider their sport to be a part-time endeavor and all had other jobs in the off-season.

> In 1979, Anheuser-Busch became the charter advertiser for a fledgling organization called ESPN, with a $1.4 million contract. Last year, our company and ESPN signed the largest sponsorship commitment in cable advertising history, a five-year, $100 million package.

Measured in 2004 dollars, that's an increase from $3.6 million to $133.4 million. Along with players, fans clearly are beneficiaries of this type of corporate commitment to sports.

The pursuit of money by athletes has its downside. First, in order to win the big prize, nearly obsessive levels of training and practice are required of athletes from their earliest age. However, only a very few will ever actually win the prize, so much of this effort may be wasteful. Especially, because young people are assessing the possible outcomes, the losses are in terms of the fundamentals of education that lead to job skills. This lost lifetime earnings stream is extremely costly to society if young people are overly optimistic about their chances. We'll revisit this in Chapter 7.

Another problem occurs when the intensity of competition over a potentially lucrative prize leads to risky health choices by athletes. Performance-enhancing drugs and playing hurt can lead to long-term disability. It is always easy to say that it is the athlete's choice in these matters. However, many of the athletes making these choices have not reached the age of legal consent.

There is an economic logic to these choices. Performance-enhancing drugs, if universally adopted, would raise the absolute level of performance. Fans value higher levels of absolute performance over lower levels. However, if all athletes were using the drugs, relative outcomes wouldn't change. The final question becomes, "How much is society willing to give up to obtain higher absolute quality levels?" An offset is the decreased value that fans might place on the behavior that leads to performance enhancement in the first place. If enough fans feel this is bad behavior, then any gains fans enjoy by increased absolute performance are offset.

In any event, some fans may lament the huge amounts paid to athletes and even begrudge them that pay. Society may come down in its final analysis against the lamentable loss of human potential that goes into the making of a very few star athletes. We are forced to note our recurrent theme: The money comes from fans in the first place. Apparently, while it might be viewed as a mixed blessing, the vast majority of fans enjoy the fruits of commercialization in the form of higher quality competition than they would enjoy otherwise.

CHAPTER RECAP

The willingness of advertisers to pay for sports programming fundamentally shapes the revenue side of the sports business. Firms use advertising to sell their products. Some advertisers wish to reach particular target demographic groups most likely to watch sports. Media providers purchase broadcast rights and supply advertisers with ad space for that demographic. Sports leagues provide the programming to the media providers. All of the money that changes hands during sports advertising comes from fans, who purchase the goods and services that are advertised.

Media markets are extremely competitive. No single media provider can extract more than the normal return to its endeavors. The massive sums that change hands reflect the market power of teams and leagues.

Sports teams possess the broadcast rights to their home games. Some games are sold through their leagues in the form of a national contract, others are sold by the team through local contracts. The proportion of games sold in each type of contract varies by league.

Media providers pay rights fees to leagues and teams for programming. Through an auction system, media providers compete for these rights. Some observers criticize this process because rights fees typically end up being greater than the value of ad slots. However, programming provides other types of values to the media provider. Media providers advertise their own programming, as well as the products of paying advertisers, and sequence other programs around the sports broadcast. Finally, local affiliates also enjoy the same types of values in their own local advertising markets. The overall value of sports programming should be compared to rights fees if one wants to judge their net economic contribution to media providers.

In some cases the net value of sports broadcasting rights is negative, even from the overall perspective of media provider revenues. If bidders are inexperienced and do not have enough information to guess broadcast rights values, then a winner's curse may arise. A broad range of estimates of the expected value of the rights and competitive bidding will elicit the highest bid and the wrong value. The winner is cursed to have paid too much relative to the true underlying value of the rights. One must evaluate each case in order to see if the special circumstances that would yield a cursed winner hold before assuming this explanation.

Much has been made of media provider ownership of teams. Why does it make sense for a media provider to actually own a team rather than just buy its broadcast rights? It is a difficult case to make on profit grounds. CBS's ownership of the Yankees shows that profits are not guaranteed to a media provider owner. Subsequent sale of the Dodgers and Angels by media producers serves to reinforce this claim. The media provider pays the same cost for broadcast rights, and it is difficult to see any cost reduction in the actual production process. Any tax advantages would usually be offset. In addition, it would be both difficult and expensive to try to reduce competition with rival media providers by buying up teams. A much simpler explanation is that teams are just a good, solid financial investment when all of the values of team ownership are considered.

Advertising MRP determines how much advertising a firm will purchase. At first look, some ads don't appear to be worth it because they do not increase sales. In such cases, rival firms see the value of advertising as saving the current level of sales as opposed to increasing sales. If a firm doesn't advertise, it may lose sales to its rivals. Bidding is structured by leagues and conferences to elicit the most that such advertising wars can generate for the ultimate holders of market power, the leagues themselves. Sometimes, firms can tacitly recognize ways to avoid such a disastrous situation, but at other times, only outside intervention can save them.

Sponsorship is another form of advertising. In team sports, the newest manifestation of sponsorship is in the naming rights to venues. These rights can be upward of $10 million annually. These amounts certainly make a difference in terms of the financial health of team owners.

Media revenues are often large enough to cover team payrolls. In the NFL, it is common for team owners to cover all of their team payroll solely with TV revenues. On the downside, substantial variation in media revenue contributes to the current lack of competitive balance in many leagues. The commercialization of sports causes many a great deal of anguish.

KEY TERMS AND CONCEPTS

- Start-up consumption
- Brand choice
- Target demographic group
- Advertising reach
- Ratings
- Rights fee
- Media providers
- Advertising slots
- Slot fees

- Media provider competition
- National broadcasting contract
- Local broadcasting contract
- Marginal revenue product of broadcast rights
- Winner's curse
- Media provider ownership of teams

- Game theory
- Strategic advertising
- Advertising dilemma
- Tacit cooperation
- Ad ban
- Beer wars
- Sponsorship
- Media revenue disparity

REVIEW QUESTIONS

1. Explain the role of advertisements in both (a) start-up consumption and (b) brand choice after start-up consumption. What other factors matter in each case?
2. What determines advertising reach?
3. What are ratings? How are they measured? Why do they matter to advertisers?
4. Which of the participants in Figure 3.1 ends up receiving most of the money from advertising (over and above their costs)? Why?
5. Explain the difference between a national broadcasting contract and a local broadcasting contract.
6. Describe the different approaches to selling broadcasting rights used by the NFL and MLB.
7. Define the marginal revenue product of broadcast rights to media providers. Why does this marginal revenue product exceed the value of ad slots that media providers sell to advertisers?
8. What factors must exist in an auction to generate a winner's curse? Do these factors characterize sports broadcast rights auctions? How?
9. What are the possible advantages to media providers of owning a team rather than just buying that team's broadcast rights? What problems might be caused if this type of ownership takes over in sports?
10. Define the marginal revenue product of ad slots to advertisers. Why does this marginal revenue product exceed just the additional sales generated by running an advertisement in an ad slot?
11. In the advertising game matrix in Figure 3.2, describe each payoff pair in each cell, starting clockwise from the top-left cell. Why does one player do better than the other in the off-diagonal cells?
12. Explain Firm 1's best strategy in the advertising game in Figure 3.2. Is it different from Firm 2's best strategy? Why?
13. In what way is the equilibrium of the game in Figure 3.2 a dilemma?
14. Which team in MLB has the highest, middle, and lowest media revenue in Table 3.11? What types of competitive balance issues arise from this difference in media revenue?
15. Beside competitive balance, what other problems arise with big media money?

THOUGHT PROBLEMS

1. Try the following small experiment on your own. Of your friends and classmates, how many think that advertisements can induce start-up consumption? How many would fall into the brand-influence camp?

2. Males ages 18–34 drink beer and buy cars. But they also buy ice cream and nonathletic shoes. Why aren't these types of companies among the top 20 sports advertisers?

3. Here are some companies that have measured the importance of their brand name and rate it highly (*Sports Business Journal*, November 6, 2000, p. 31): Intel, GE, Disney, Cisco Systems, Citibank, Kodak, Heinz, Xerox, The Gap, and Kellogg's. Even though they seem just like the firms in Table 3.1, only Disney even advertises on the Super Bowl (Table 3.5). Why?

4. In Table 3.4, what was the largest percentage increase in Super Bowl advertising rates between years? What explains this large increase?

5. Why would a media provider advertise its own other shows during one of its sports broadcasts rather than sell the ad slots to paying advertisers? Why allow local affiliates to advertise on national broadcasts?

6. What characteristics of the ABC/NBC competition for Monday Night Football would lead to a winner's curse? (Refer to the Learning Highlight: The Curse of Monday Night Football?) Do you think the result was a winner's curse outcome? Why?

7. If you were a media provider, would you buy a team or just buy its broadcasting rights? Why? Are all your reasons economic?

8. Use the idea of the marginal revenue product of advertising slots to explain why advertisers put so much more into professional football than into other sports (see Table 3.2). Does this explanation also explain the amount advertisers put into the sport with the lowest amount? Explain.

9. How much more valuable in percentage terms is sports advertising to Anheuser-Busch than it is to Ford Motor Company (use the data in Table 3.1)?

10. Why isn't a Super Bowl ad slot even more expensive than the amount listed in Table 3.4? (Be careful to think about both sides of the market! For example, Table 3.5 shows Toyota Motor Corp. spending on a recent Super Bowl, but what share of Toyota's total ad spending is the Super Bowl for this advertiser [check Table 3.1]? What would happen if the price of an alternative to Super Bowl advertising fell?)

11. Does the outcome in Figure 3.2 depend upon the price of advertising? Suppose the price of ads rises to $8 million. What is the new outcome? Instead of an ad price increase, suppose an ad costs $5 million and that the ad brings $6 million in new start-up consumption for either firm that advertises. What is the new outcome? Given these results, do you always expect to find the kind of sports advertising dilemma described in the text?

12. Who gained most from the beer wars? Why?

13. What roles do attendance and TV play in the value of a sponsorship agreement? Are the data in Table 3.8 consistent with your answer?

14. Why can nearly all NFL team owners cover all of their player costs with media revenues while nearly none of the owners in MLB can do so?

15. Does the ability to cover at least half of the total player cost also correlate to the ranking of revenues by league? Why or why not?

ADVANCED PROBLEMS

1. Is there really any difference between the NFL and MLB broadcast rights approach? After all, in either case, fans are pretty much guaranteed to see nearly all of their home team's games. Also in either case, fans will get other games of broad, national interest as well. What is the difference in their approach?

2. Using the data in Table 3.1, devise an index of the relative importance of sports advertising for Anheuser-Busch versus Proctor and Gamble. What determines this relative importance of sports advertising between different advertisers?

3. What determines the ranking of favorite sports to watch in Table 3.3? Why isn't soccer in the top five? If you took this same poll 10 years from now, what might be different? Why?

4. A number of very prominent firms are not even listed in Table 3.5 (e.g., other beer and soft drink firms), but both Universal Studios and Sony Pictures are there. Why? (Hint: Think strategically.)

5. How would one discover whether there really was a winner's curse result in the ABC/NBC bidding over Monday Night Football? (See the Learning Highlight: The Curse of Monday Night Football?)

6. What was the key to Ted Turner's success using the Atlanta Braves as a programming anchor for TBS? Why couldn't Rupert Murdoch replicate this success by using Fox to purchase the Dodgers?

7. Refer to the Learning Highlight: Murdoch's Bid for Manchester United. What lesson does the European example rejecting Rupert Murdoch's bid to buy Manchester United hold for his purchase of the Dodgers through FOX? (Think carefully about the relationship between his regional FOX networks and local MLB broadcast contracts.)

8. Discuss the major impacts of TV on sports in terms of club revenues and profits, wages, and competitive balance. In your answer, distinguish between outcomes in the NFL and MLB.

9. Calculate the following ratios from Tables 3.11 and 3.12: the highest to lowest media revenues and the highest to average media revenues. Show how these simple ratios help to enlighten a discussion of the relationship between competitive balance and media revenues across leagues. What data would you need in order to use these ratios to discuss the relationship between competitive balance and media revenues within a given league?

10. Economist Robert Barro, in his book *Getting It Right* (1997), has argued that it is efficient to regulate/ban the use of performance-enhancing drugs because they have no effect on relative performance by players. If all used drugs, the result would be that all players would be stronger and there would be no difference in outcome on the field. Critique this view.

INTERNET RESOURCES

For a host of additional material and questions for thought, visit this book's Web site at www.prenhall.com/fort.

REFERENCES

Barro, Robert. *Getting It Right: Markets and Choices in a Free Society*. Cambridge, MA: MIT Press, 1997.

Crompton, John L. "Sponsorship of Sports by Tobacco and Alcohol Companies: A Review of the Issues," *Journal of Sport and Social Issues* 17 (1993): 148–167.

Doron, Gideon. *The Smoking Paradox*. New York: University Press of America, 1984.

Fort, Rodney. "The Value of Major League Baseball Ownership," *International Journal of Sport Finance* 1 (2006): forthcoming.

Fritschler, A. Lee. *The Politics of Smoking*. Upper Saddle River, NJ: Prentice Hall, 1995.

Helyar, John. *Lords of the Realm: The Real History of Baseball*. New York: Villard Books, 1994.

Quirk, James, and Rodney Fort. *Pay Dirt: The Business of Professional Team Sports*. Princeton, NJ: Princeton University Press, 1992.

Quirk, James, and Rodney Fort. *Hardball: The Abuse of Power in Pro Sports*. Princeton, NJ: Princeton University Press, 1999.

Walker, James. "Give Us Back Our Man United," *SportsJones Magazine*, www.sportsjones.com, accessed April 23, 1999.

Chapter 4

Team Cost, Profit, and Winning

Chapter Objectives

After reading this chapter, you should be able to:

■ *Explain the difference between the short- and long-run decisions that confront sports team owners.*

■ *Understand that, subject to the usual real-world allowances for uncertainty, the short- and long-run choices made by sports team owners are consistent with profit maximization.*

■ *Explain how profit maximization creates tension between those who want champions (fans, players, and on-field managers) and owners, who also want to win but have to pay attention to the revenues and costs associated with doing so.*

■ *Express how variation in profits across teams in a given league contributes to competitive balance problems within a league.*

■ *Identify how acceptable sports accounting techniques can make a profitable sports team appear unprofitable, and why sports team owners may prefer it that way.*

> *Owners are never the most popular sports figures in a city. When a team loses consistently, the owner is the person the fans blame; when the team wins, the owner is the person the fans want to get out of the way so that the announcer can interview the coach and star players. There is a reason that no owner has ever been pictured on a football card.*

—GENE KLEIN, FORMER OWNER OF THE SAN DIEGO CHARGERS
(Klein and Fisher, 1987, p. 12)

*W*ayne Huizenga, owner of the MLB Florida Marlins, a team in a major media market, claimed losses in 1997 of $34 million after just winning the World Series. When Broward and Miami-Dade Counties refused to build him a new, retractable-roof ballpark, Huizenga made it clear that if the revenues he expected in order to field a champion weren't forthcoming he wouldn't try to field a champion. He sold off the players responsible for the series victory, ostensibly to reduce losses. The Marlins' payroll fell from $53 million in 1997 to $13 million the next year. The team fell from winning the World Series to last place and, with a winning percent of 0.333, was the worst team in baseball in 1998. Considering the introductory quote by Gene Klein, is it any wonder that the fans often despise owners for their business choices?

In this chapter, we'll explore the reasons behind team owners' business choices. Our guiding assumption will be that team owners maximize profits. In exploring these choices, we'll develop the cost side of producing sports outputs. Bringing in the revenue side developed in the last chapter, our profit maximization assumption will allow us to identify some of the important business choices of owners. In particular, we'll analyze the quality of the teams that they put on the field. One of our most important discoveries will be that there is a clear conflict between winning, costs, and profits. We will see that in some cities, where revenues are insufficient to cover the costs of fielding a winning team, there will always be unhappy fans, players, and coaches. We also will look at some real-world accounting data on sports teams and see how certain acceptable accounting practices can make a team worth millions of dollars look like it is losing money.

PROFIT MAXIMIZING OWNERS?

Ultimately, we are going to need to know what motivates owners to understand the level of winning that they choose to put in front of their fans. Some view owners as gentle sportspeople. The Yawkee family, whose trust once owned the Boston Red Sox, and the Haas family, previous owners of the Oakland Athletics, are perfect examples. This view would have it that the fun of being involved with the sport, the coaches, and the players is the main payoff. Or perhaps owners want to be famous— many owners are better known as owners than they are as real estate or industry magnates. A variation on the gentle sportsperson view is that owners simply wish to maximize the number of wins their team achieves.

One needn't go far to find owners complaining about the lack of money involved, painting themselves as benevolent sportspeople. Here's Gene Klein, the irascible former owner of the NFL's San Diego Chargers, on the subject:

> For almost 20 years I owned and ran a National Football League team, the San Diego Chargers. When I bought the Chargers I believed I could apply to professional sports the same principles of good business

management that had enabled me to succeed in the corporate world. I'm not ashamed to admit that. There was also a time when I believed in Santa Claus, the Easter Bunny, and the Tooth Fairy . . . I thought that a pro-football team was just about the best toy anyone could ever have. I learned. Oh, how I learned. Some toys just keep on giving—a pro-football team keeps on taking. Possibly the two happiest days of my life were the day I bought a controlling interest in the Chargers and the day I sold a controlling interest in the Chargers. (Klein and Fisher, 1987, p. 12)

Clearly, Klein describes a love-hate relationship and makes it plain that the money wasn't that great. That might have been true in his case, but it doesn't matter that profits weren't large. What matters for our purposes is that profits are pursued.

The Profit Maximization Hypothesis and Its Implications

It should be clear from the first three chapters that the most common economic view holds that owners pursue profits in the usual way, total revenues minus total costs. Under the **profit maximization hypothesis,** owners make decisions about their venues, players, and media contracts in order to maximize the difference between total revenues and total costs. Even if actual observed levels of profits are not always great, owners pursue them, and their choices are made in order to make profits as large as possible. Their choices involve the quality of the team to be fielded, the quality of the fan experience in the venue, and pricing.

Owners would love to field winning teams if there is money in it. Otherwise, owners are quite content to keep costs low, field second-rate teams, and make as much profit as possible. The "as possible" part has to do with the willingness of fans to pay for some level of quality. Later, we will turn to some data to determine how much money is involved.

Sports business analysts have gained important insights using the idea that owners are motivated by profit. This is true no matter how wealthy an owner might be. Profit maximization is a common and powerful abstract in economics, even if it only approximates behavior or only covers the behavior of some. Its usefulness is in the insights it generates.

Profit maximization can seem too strict an imposition on real-world decision makers. However, there is nothing in an economic view of team owners that precludes them from making mistakes. It may well be that an owner intends to win the pennant some year, makes the deals to put the level of talent on the field that is required, and is simply wrong about the talent that was hired. For example, as teams near the playoffs, they trade for particular players that are expected to put their receiving teams over the top and into postseason play. However, some of these players may be nursing injuries unknown to their receiving teams. As a result, owner expectations go unmet and the trades and the final result disappoint fans. There is also room for plain old bad luck. Over time, mistakes and bad luck should even out so that talent choices meet expectations. If not, another owner would buy the team and do better.

The Short Run versus the Long Run

Every market has two sides. We discussed the demand side in Chapters 2 and 3. The other side, the supply side, requires producer knowledge of the costs of production. We will start by examining the basics of production. Then we will see how knowledge of player physical contributions to team success, along with the price of players, results in the costs of winning that owners face.

Teams produce what fans want. As we saw in Chapter 2, fans want, among other things, grace and beauty, a sense of commonality, and relative and absolute competition. All of these items are also highly correlated with winning. Winning teams tend to have more grace and beauty, and winning tends to be a stronger common bond than losing (although fans of lovable losers also share commonality, albeit of the miserable type). We can all probably agree that competitiveness is the essence of a winning team and that winning stands as a reasonable proxy for team output. Because of this, we will use the terms *winning percent* and *team quality* interchangeably.

Winning percent is the number of games won by a team divided by the total number of games played. However, this winning percent misses the championship incentive inherent in the structure of all team sports. Some think that fans only care about winning the championship. However, winning matters—a team cannot make it to the championship without a high winning percent.

Owners actually can be in two different situations when they think about the level of winning they will put in front of fans, what economists refer to as the short run and the long run. In the **short run**, elements of the team production function are fixed. This includes anything covered by contractual obligation in force during production. For sports teams, the primary fixed inputs are talent, on and off the field, and the facility in which the team plays.

One difficulty with this economic distinction concerns the relationship between the short run and actual physical time. In terms of actual physical time, the short run for team quality choices tends to correspond to a given season, from preseason on through the regular season, playoffs, and championships. In contrast, the short run for the stadium or arena corresponds to the economic life span of the facility. This means that the short run for a stadium might be 30 years or more. To clarify, if any of the resources used to produce winning are fixed, the owner is in a short-run situation. So, in the short run, the owner makes decisions about the number of season tickets to sell and the price to charge (because demand slopes downward) or the number of games to put on local television, given that the quality of the team is fixed; that is, it has been more or less determined prior to league play.

However, teams often alter their level of on- and off-field talent during the season. Negotiating player trades, changing managers or front office personnel, and even moving into a new stadium will alter the quality of a team. When an owner changes the quality of their team, the team is in a new situation of different fixed inputs. Note that the short run is not associated with any specific period of time, but is a period where team quality is held constant.

In the **long run**, everything about the team's production process is variable—a new stadium may be built, the lineup may be completely altered, or the head coaches and management may be replaced. Perhaps the easiest way to think about the long run is in terms of an owner's planning process. Despite the short-run situation confronting owners, they can always step back and think about how they would alter their team and stadium. This long-run planning process captures the essence of exactly what the long run means economically. Whenever all elements of the process are variable, then the long run is under consideration.

SHORT-RUN PRODUCTION AND COSTS

The essence of the short run is that some decisions about putting winning in front of fans have already been made. In this section, we discuss in detail the elements of the winning production process that are fixed and the elements that remain variable in the short run. When combined with knowledge about the price of these inputs, short-run costs can be determined.

Fixed Inputs in Sports Production

In the sports team production process, **short-run fixed inputs** include the player roster, the stadium, other contracted personnel such as the front office general managers and on-field managers and coaches, insurance coverage, and loans to cover investments. A team also has certain obligations to its league that are fixed, such as participation payments.

All of these elements have costs attached to them. Because the factors are fixed, the costs associated with them are called **short-run fixed costs.** They must be paid whether or not the team ever plays a game.

Variable Inputs in the Short Run

Other elements in the team production process are **short-run variable inputs.** These include team operations expenses. In the movie *Major League*, the owner decided to punish the team to get them to lose by busing them and, when she couldn't bus them, flying them on a rickety airplane charter. She also cut off the hot water to the locker room. However, she didn't cut off team spending on her own enjoyment and comfort. These are extremes, but you get the idea. These are all examples of short-run variable team operating expenses.

Teams often control stadium operations, at least during their tenancy and often for all nonsports events as well. These stadium expenses also are variable. A team can pour resources into quality stadium experiences for fans regardless of the quality of play it has chosen to put on the field. For example, entertaining mascots and between-innings music and video presentations enhance the stadium experience. Recently, some teams have begun to sponsor live musical entertainment after the game, even including portable dance floors. Because any of these inputs can be cancelled at any time, they are variable.

Scouting and player development expenses also are variable. They have a great deal to do with the future quality of the team, but are not fixed for any given quality choice. For example, in the extreme, a team could stop all scouting and player development. Finally, advertising and marketing are variable inputs. The teams can market like crazy or not.

Just as with short-run fixed inputs, short-run variable inputs have costs attached. Because the factors are variable, the costs associated with them are called **short-run variable costs**. The level of these costs will vary, depending on the level of short-run outputs offered to fans. For example, the greater the level of attendance, the more labor that must be hired to manage ticket sales, turnstiles, clean up, and parking and to sell concessions.

Short-Run Total Costs

Short-run total costs are the sum of short-run fixed costs and short-run variable costs: Short-Run Total Costs = Total Fixed Costs + Total Variable Costs, or:

$$SRTC = TFC + TVC$$

Did You Know?
The expense data set for the Seattle Mariners is one of only a few very detailed accounts available to the general public, and nearly half of that data set is tainted by revenue sharing changes and a strike impacting the 1994 and 1995 seasons.

Table 4.1 shows total operating expenses for the Seattle Mariners from 1993 to 1998. These data may seem old, but believe it or not this is one of only a couple of data sets generally available that provide the detail we need to investigate short-run costs. Because a strike shortened both the 1994 and 1995 seasons and revenue-sharing practices in MLB changed after the 1995 season, we'll restrict ourselves to the period 1996 to 1998 in order to make observations about the levels of modern short-run costs. The time period is also short enough that we'll ignore inflation. Can you determine which spending categories are included in *TFC* and which are included in TVC? Table 4.2 shows which operating costs fall under the fixed, variable, and mixed headings.

As you can calculate from Table 4.2, *TFC* averaged about $58.6 million a year for the Mariners from 1996 to 1998. General and administrative expenses averaged $7.2 million a year. These general and administrative expenses pose a problem in identifying fixed and variable costs. Although it is difficult to know which portions of general and administrative expenses are fixed or variable, it seems reasonable that the majority are fixed (legal expenses, etc.) and don't change much over time. That puts *TFC* in the neighborhood of $65.8 million annually, whereas *TVC* averaged $20.8 million a year. Therefore, *SRTC* averaged around $86.6 million a year from 1996 to 1998.

Did You Know?
Fixed costs dominate the sports production process. For example, for the Seattle Mariners, fixed costs were 76 percent of total costs from 1996 to 1998, primarily because player compensation was 52 percent of the total.

Tables 4.1 and 4.2 show that player compensation dwarfed all other cost elements, fixed or variable, at about $45.2 million on average per year. Player compensation thus represented about 52 percent of *SRTC* for the Mariners over the years 1996 to 1998, whereas *TFC* averaged about 76 percent of the *SRTC*, and *TVC* made up the remaining 24 percent. Although outside analysts are

Table 4.1 Operating Expenses for the Seattle Mariners, 1993 to 1998 ($Thousands)

	1993	1994	1995	1996	1997	1998
Baseball Operations						
Player compensation	$32,612	$20,918	$29,732	$39,313	$43,815	$52,392
Team operations	$5,200	$3,825	$5,219	$4,530	$5,353	$6,281
Scouting/player development	$6,458	$5,205	$6,030	$6,375	$7,017	$7,606
Other Operating Expenses						
Kingdome operations	$1,898	$1,388	$1,864	$2,777	$3,383	$3,888
Marketing, publicity, ticket operations	$3,186	$2,663	$2,819	$4,239	$4,859	$5,990
General and administrative	$5,501	$4,798	$5,385	$6,765	$7,395	$7,430
Net interest and other expenses	$411	$178	$1,324	$1,274	$1,197	$1,230
King County settlement[a]		−$4,204				
ML revenue sharing agreement[b]				$613	$3,364	$3,417
Total Operating Expenses	$55,266	$34,771	$52,373	$65,886	$76,383	$88,234
Other Expenses						
Signing bonuses	$4,540	$2,049	$5,019	$5,164	$5,025	$3,572
Depreciation and amortization[c]					$9,237	$6,176
Total Expenses	$59,806	$36,820	$57,392	$71,050	$90,645	$97,982

[a]One-time settlement in a political agreement between the team and King County.
[b]The so-called luxury tax that shares revenues among MLB owners.
[c]Only reported for 1997 and 1998.

Source: Personal correspondence from Angelo Bruscas, *Seattle Post-Intelligencer*, 1999.

not privy to many sports teams' expense ledgers, the little data that are known, combined with reports from consultants, indicate that this relationship holds for nearly all sports teams, with TFC dominating the expense side of the ledger.

General Graphical Analysis of Short-Run Costs

Table 4.2 shows just one example of short-run cost outcomes for a team, the Seattle Mariners. Note that it only presents 3 years' data. If we use the typical economic reasoning about short-run costs, along with the representative data in Table 4.2, we can make a rough approximation of how short-run costs might look, in general. From Table 4.2, for the Mariners, on average, *TVC* = $20.8 million, *TFC* = $65.8 million, and *SRTC* = $86.6 million. In addition, let's have attendance proxy for short-run output. Average yearly attendance for the Mariners from 1996 to 1998 was 2.9 million.

Let's think about how *TFC*, *TVC*, and *SRTC* vary with attendance. In general, depicting *TFC* is easy. These costs are fixed, as represented by the horizontal line in Figure 4.1. Using the Mariners' data as our guide, fixed costs are about $65.8 million. However, this number is particular to our data. The Mariners were a pretty good

Table 4.2 Fixed and Variable Costs for the Seattle Mariners, 1996 to 1998 ($Thousands)

	1996	1997	1998
Short-Run Fixed Costs			
Player compensation	$39,313	$43,815	$52,392
Signing bonuses	$5,164	$5,025	$3,572
ML revenue sharing agreement[a]	$613	$3,364	$3,417
Net interest and other expenses	$1,274	$1,197	$1,230
Depreciation and amortization[b]		$9,237	$6,176
Total Short-Run Fixed			
* Costs*	$46,364	$62,638	$66,787
Short-Run Variable Costs			
Marketing, publicity, ticket operations	$4,239	$4,859	$5,990
Scouting/player development	$6,375	$7,017	$7,606
Team operations	$4,530	$5,353	$6,281
Kingdome operations	$2,777	$3,383	$3,888
Total Short-Run Variable			
* Costs*	$17,921	$20,612	$23,765
Mixed Category			
General and administrative	$6,765	$7,395	$7,430
Total Short-Run Costs	$71,050	$90,645	$97,982

[a]The so-called luxury tax that shares revenues among MLB owners.
[b]Pooled sharing began in 1996.

Source: Adapted from Table 4.1.

Figure 4.1
Hypothetical Short-Run Cost Functions Based on the Mariners' example in the text, at attendance of about 2.9 million; total variable costs (*TVC*) equal $20.8 million; total fixed costs (*TFC*) equal $65.8 million; and their sum, short-run total costs (*SRTC*), equals $86.6 million. The shapes are hypothetical, based on the idea of diminishing returns to variable inputs.

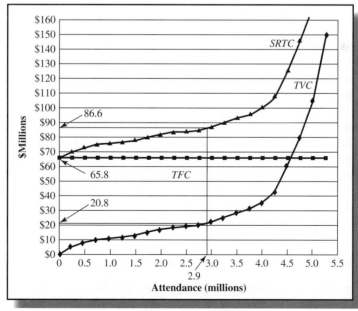

team through the late 1990s, finishing second in the American League West in 1996, first in 1997, and third in 1998. Better teams will have a higher *TFC* because they will choose to put together a more expensive set of players during a given season.

What about *TVC*? **Diminishing returns to variable inputs** characterize all production functions. Diminishing returns means that, given the level of fixed inputs, increasing the use of variable inputs eventually will result in decreased marginal product. For example, given that the dimensions of the stadium are fixed in the short run, adding more and more labor to the fan experience will mean that an additional vendor eventually will not enhance the stadium experience as much as the last one hired. If so, then *TVC* might rise at a decreasing rate over some low range of output, but once diminishing returns set in, *TVC* must begin to increase at an increasing rate.

TVC are shown in Figure 4.1 for a reasonable hypothetical range of these types of costs relative to attendance. In Figure 4.1, diminishing returns set in when attendance is about 3.5 million. Because we don't have much data, this is simply a rough guess. In actuality, diminishing returns could set in at higher or lower levels of attendance. Finally, in Figure 4.1, *SRTC* is the vertical sum of total fixed and total variable costs.

We used our data on the Mariners to anchor the location of these costs functions in Figure 4.1. At an average attendance of 2.9 million, *TVC* = $20.8 million, *TFC* = $65.8 million, and *SRTC* = $86.6 million.

LONG-RUN PRODUCTION AND COSTS

In the long run, all inputs are variable, including the team's level of talent. What must the team consider when it investigates altering its quality? There are two ways to look at this long-run concept. First, we could compare a series of short-run outcomes for a given team. In fact, we could use the Mariners' data in Table 4.2 in just this way. Using winning percent as a proxy for quality, we would just look at teams that got better over time and see how much more they spent in terms of fixed costs as they improved. This series of short-run outcomes would be the result of long-run planning at the beginning of every season. This long-run choice pretty much boils down to purchasing more talent.

The problem with this approach is that we would only see a restricted set of relationships between costs and winning percent. Why restrict our look at costs to just one team? Each season, we get to observe all of the teams and the variation in costs across teams of differing quality. There is an abundance of data to investigate the relationship between owners' spending and team quality. Of course, one season will have its exceptions; some teams will be better than their payroll/talent choice would indicate, and some teams will be worse. To see how these factors even out over time, we'll have to look at the same types of choices over a longer time period.

Team Quality Analysis in a Given Season

The 2003 MLB season is as good as any for our purposes. As Table 4.3 shows, there were really bad teams, such as the Tigers (a team that won just over a quarter of its

Table 4.3 MLB Standings in 2003

AMERICAN LEAGUE	FINAL WINNING PERCENT	NATIONAL LEAGUE	FINAL WINNING PERCENT
East			
1. Yankees	0.623	1. Braves	0.623
2. Red Sox	0.586	2. Marlins	0.562
3. Blue Jays	0.531	3. Phillies	0.531
4. Orioles	0.438	4. Expos	0.512
5. Devil Rays	0.389	5. Mets	0.410
Central			
1. Twins	0.556	1. Cubs	0.543
2. White Sox	0.531	2. Astros	0.537
3. Royals	0.512	3. Cardinals	0.525
4. Indians	0.420	4. Pirates	0.463
5. Tigers	0.265	5. Reds	0.426
		6. Brewers	0.420
West			
1. Athletics	0.593	1. Giants	0.621
2. Mariners	0.574	2. Dodgers	0.525
3. Angels	0.475	3. Diamondbacks	0.519
4. Rangers	0.438	4. Rockies	0.457
		5. Padres	0.395

games), and teams like the Yankees, Braves, and Giants (who won just over 60 percent of their games).

As the averages in Table 4.4 show, teams at the bottom of their divisions won about 38 percent of their games in 2003, that is, an average winning percent of 0.377. To move up to the fourth-place position in their division, the losing teams would, on average, need to increase their winning percent by about 0.078 points, to 0.455. An additional 0.061 points moves the team from fourth place to third place in its division, whereas adding 0.037 points moves the team from third place to second place. Adding 0.041 points facilitates the jump to first place at a winning percent of about 0.593, on average, across the divisions in 2003.

Table 4.4
Winning Percents
in MLB in 2003

	AVERAGE PERCENT	CHANGE IN POSITION	INCREASE NEEDED TO MOVE UP PLACES
1st-place team	0.593	2nd to 1st	0.040
2nd-place team	0.553	3rd to 2nd	0.037
3rd-place team	0.516	4th to 3rd	0.061
4th-place team	0.455	5th to 4th	0.078
Bottom-ranked teams	0.377		

Table 4.5

Winning Percents in
MLB from 1999 to
2003

	Average Percent	Change in Position	Increase Needed to Move Up Places
1st-place team	0.597	2nd to 1st	0.046
2nd-place team	0.551	3rd to 2nd	0.050
3rd-place team	0.501	4th to 3rd	0.054
4th-place team	0.447	5th to 4th	0.039
Bottom-ranked teams	0.408		

Did You Know?

From 1999 to 2003, it was more difficult to move from fourth to third place (which required a 54 point increase in winning percent), and from third to second (which required a 49 point increase in winning percent), than it was to move out of the basement (which required a 40 point increase in winning percent) or from second to first (which required a 46 point increase in winning percent).

Here is an essential point: The teams at the top of the winning percent heap are better than other teams because they hire better players. Sometimes, a historically dominant team ends up with interrupted success for a short period. Sometimes, a team that never had success has a brief, shining moment. Winning is uncertain, even for teams loaded with talent. However, on average, over time, higher quality teams win more games.

Team Quality Analysis Over Time

Although analyzing statistics from one season provides interesting information, it doesn't demonstrate how hiring talent averages out over time. So let's look at the 1999 to 2003 seasons. Table 4.5 shows the same information regarding average team winning percents by place in the final standings. It also shows the average increases teams need to advance through the standings for those five seasons. You can see that the pattern in Table 4.5 is similar to the one shown in Table 4.4. It would seem that a low-quality team has an average winning percent of about 0.408. Successively, such a team must add about 0.039 points in order to move up the ladder one rung, 0.054 points to move into third place, 0.050 points to move up to second place, and 0.046 points to make it to first place.

Let's use this historical view of winning to characterize how teams typically think about increasing their output of winning, that is, their **long-run quality choice.** Essentially, this involves adding increasingly better players who move teams up in the standings. Even teams that end up choosing a low winning percent can at least consider how they might have a higher winning percent. For our purposes, we'll characterize these increasingly better players as stars. The idea of stars is clear—they are a cut above the average player. We will now examine the positive relationship between stars and winning percent.

At the bottom rung on the winning percent ladder, a team either has no stars (but may produce a few in the future) or only older, faded stars at the end of their careers. The data in Table 4.6 are my best guess about how adding more stars to a team will increase that team's winning percent. Looking at the data in the table, it seems reasonable that a team would have to add a star to get close to a winning percent of 0.429. Just as reasonably, to move from a weak 0.420 winning percent to contention,

Table 4.6 A
Hypothetical
Production Schedule
of Winning Percent
for MLB

STARS	TOTAL WINNING PERCENT
0	0.420
1	0.429
2	0.448
3	0.466
4	0.490
5	0.528
6	0.598
7	0.646
8	0.680
9	0.695
10	0.700

a 0.528 winning percent, a team probably would need to add five star players. Let's be very clear: Table 4.6 is just an intuitive snapshot of the relationship between adding stars and winning; it is not the result of any more extensive analysis than you have just read.

The data in Table 4.6 portray a long-run relationship between adding talent and increasing winning percent. Adding stars increases the output of winning that fans pay to see. The **long-run winning percent production function** in Figure 4.2 is a graphical presentation of this relationship. Apparently, there is some limit to management abilities when more than four stars are on a given team. After five stars are added to any team, winning percent increases at a decreasing rate. There must be some sort of **limit to management ability in the long run** once a large enough number of stars is on one team. This is the same type of argument that is made of all production functions in the long run. Once a process reaches a particular scale, it becomes unwieldy.

Looking Inside the Production of Winning

In our discussion thus far, culminating in Figure 4.2, we glossed over an underlying production process: In a nutshell, player talent and managerial or coaching skill is mixed to produce winning on the field. It takes a keen awareness of ability and how to combine it in order to produce winning. Is the bundle of talent in a given roster a power team (e.g., hitting or pitching in baseball, running in football)? Is the talent better suited to finesse (e.g., hitting and speed in baseball, deceptive passing offense in football)? An entire process underlies the observed winning percent produced by some level of talent.

Economists have extensively analyzed this production activity. On the one hand is the analysis of individual player contributions in a team environment. On the other is the impact of managerial skill on the field. We'll look at individual player contributions in Chapter 7. The impact of managerial skill is covered in the Learning Highlight: Gerald Scully, Pioneering Sports Economist. Research on **managerial efficiency** in sports (Scully, 1989; Kahn, 1993; and Singell, 1993) finds that baseball managers contribute substantially to the process of winning, that these managers

Figure 4.2 Hypothetical Winning Percent Production Function for MLB in the 1990s

Star players are added to a standard lineup in order to increase winning percent in the long run. The relationship between the number of stars and winning percent, deduced from real-world data on stars and winning over time, is the winning percent production function. For example, adding the first star increases winning percent by .009 (from Table 4.6). The shape of the curve cannot be dictated by diminishing returns because winning percent is a long-run choice and all inputs are variable. Limits to managing more and more stars must be the explanation for diminishing returns.

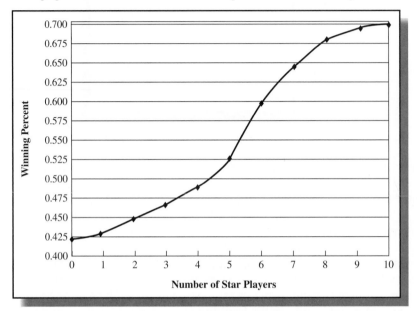

improve with tenure on a given team, and that players appear to respond more to better managers. Similar research is currently underway in other pro sports.

In the real world, stars are not added to a lineup in the nice orderly fashion portrayed in Figure 4.2. Some are added early on, others are added only if teams need them at particular times, for example, in the playoffs. Still others are added subject to market availability. In an attempt to gain understanding of a complex issue, economic analysis reduces the problem to a much simpler setting. At least we have captured just how it is that adding more stars will alter winning percent, even if we've abstracted a bit on when they are added. One way to keep this clear is to remember that we are thinking of production in the long run as a planning process. Player and coaching talent is used to produce winning on the field, on the ice, and on the court. Adding more stars raises winning percent.

The Long-Run Costs of Talent and Winning

A production function like the one shown in Figure 4.2 allows us to derive the cost of winning to an owner. Because talent is one of the most important long-run choices for owners, the cost of talent will represent the largest element in the team's long-run total cost function. Cost functions relate costs to output. Earlier, we chose winning percent as the long-run team output. Thus, **long-run total cost** is the relationship between winning percent and the cost of obtaining it.

LEARNING HIGHLIGHT
Gerald Scully: Pioneering Sports Economist

Pioneering sports economist Gerald Scully was at the forefront of the study of sports economics, contributing to the very first book on sports economics, Roger Noll's (1974) *Government and the Sports Business*. Scully analyzed the pro sports business for most of his career, and his numerous articles and two important books are obligatory reading for all sports economists. Although his most famous work was an analysis of player pay, his work also covered nearly every aspect of the baseball business.

Especially important was his work on managerial efficiency, which he began with Phil Porter (Porter and Scully, 1982), but carried on alone after that. Managerial efficiency is the analysis of how far actual winning outcomes are from the maximum winning possible given the level of talent a given manager has to work with. The lower the manager's actual winning relative to the highest possible winning, the less efficient the manager is.

In his original work with Porter (1982), Scully estimated the maximum winning possible for various rosters. He then compared actual managers to this estimated maximum. The most efficient managers, such as the legendary managers Earl Weaver, Sparky Anderson, and Walter Alston, were within a few percentage points of the maximum. The less efficient managers were up to 20 percent off the mark. Interestingly, and not surprisingly, managerial efficiency correlated quite highly with longevity. This leads to the notion that

learning with a given team happens over time, illustrating that systematic improvements in managerial efficiency occur the longer a manager is with a team.

Later, in *The Business of Major League Baseball* (1989), Scully extended the idea of managerial efficiency to expansion teams. He contends that expansion teams start out very inefficient but improve substantially over their first 10 years. By the 10th year, Scully claims, expansion teams are about as efficient as any average team.

Putting the idea of managerial efficiency in a general social science context, Scully (1994) later showed that MLB tenure is directly and significantly related to managerial efficiency. This casts doubt on the organization sociology view that managerial efficiency has more to do with the firm and market environment than with individual talent—at least in sports!

Pioneering sports economist Gerald Scully.

Before we move on, a few comments about the costs of winning are in order. In economics, costs relate to output. However, many people mistakenly refer to costs in terms of the price of inputs. For example, you can often find newspaper stories on the "costs" per at bat, a player's salary divided by that player's number of plate appearances. Similarly, columnists sometimes list "costs" per game pitched or the "cost" per minute played by basketball or hockey players. These are just interesting ways to portray the price of the talent input. Teams do not produce at bats, pitching appearances, or minutes played any more than a fast food restaurant owner produces clean tables. Player tasks are performed not as individual products but as part of an effort to win games.

It is important not to confuse input prices with output costs. For example, the easiest way to make the "cost" per at bat smaller would simply be to have inexpensive players appear at the plate most often. However, such a strategy would prove very expensive in terms of long-run output, namely, winning. When one puts weak players at the plate, the team loses more often.

While input prices are not the costs of winning, they do matter in terms of determining those costs. It's easy to find the costs of winning once we introduce the price of star players. Continuing with our baseball example, at the top end, Alex Rodriguez of the New York Yankees earned about $22 million in 2003, whereas lesser stars earn less. The data for 2003 suggest that the going price of baseball stars is between $9 million and $19 million per year. The data on 2003 team payrolls suggest that an owner spends about $9 million in total on a lineup that doesn't have any stars. Finally, let's measure winning percent in whole units, that is, multiply by 1,000 (e.g., a winning percent of 0.700 in whole units would be 700). Table 4.7 combines the long-run relationship between stars and winning with our assumptions about the price of obtaining stars. The cost with no stars is $9 million; the first few stars come at a price of $9 million each; and so on, up to the very last superstar at $19 million. The result in Table 4.7 is the team's long-run total cost schedule. (Remember: All costs are variable in the long run, and the talent level of a team, or its quality, is a long-run consideration.)

Long-run total costs are simply the sum of the player costs (salaries) as more stars are added and winning percent increases. It is the cost of winning percent that the team owner seeks to find. For example, in order to play at a winning percent of 528, the team would have to add five stars to a "no-star" lineup. The total cost of playing 528 ball becomes $9 million (the cost of a team with no stars) + $9 million (the cost of one star) + $9 million (the cost of the second star) + $9 million (the cost of the third star) + $10 million (the cost of the fourth star) + $11 million (the cost of the fifth star) = $57 million.

Technically speaking, the salary column in Table 4.7 is not the long-run marginal cost of talent, or winning percent. If we measured talent in terms of winning percent, then the marginal cost of each unit of talent from the first star would be $9 million divided by the

Table 4.7

Hypothetical Total Cost of Winning for MLB

Number of Stars	Team's Total Winning Percent	Player Annual Salary ($Millions)	Total Cost of Team ($Millions)
0	420	$9	$9
1	429	$9	$18
2	448	$9	$27
3	466	$9	$36
4	490	$10	$46
5	528	$11	$57
6	598	$12	$69
7	646	$13	$82
8	680	$14	$96
9	695	$15	$111
10	700	$19	$130

increase in winning percent—that is, 429 minus 420—for 9 more winning percent points. Marginal cost in this range would be about $1 million per winning percent point added. Because we're talking more in terms of the actual way that talent is added to a team, player-by-player, then one simply adds up the salaries that produce any given level of winning in order to obtain the total talent cost of that level of winning percent.

The example in Table 4.7 is an abstraction of the way talent actually is hired. Owners don't simply line players up in a row, from worst to best at higher prices, and make their choices. Instead, talent is groomed in either the minor leagues or college or traded back and forth between teams. Plans to reach a particular level of winning can take time. The portrayal in Table 4.7 is an abstraction representing the thought process that owners go through when considering the level of talent they would want to hire. The real world, as always, is much messier.

The total cost data in Table 4.7 are portrayed graphically in Figure 4.3. The 2003 total salary bill for the most probable 25-man rosters of MLB teams varied between $19.6 million and $149.7 million. Our talent cost function pretty much mirrors actual outcomes in MLB.

Figure 4.3 Hypothetical Long-Run Cost of Winning for MLB
Star players are added to a standard lineup in order to increase winning percent in the long run. If the price of stars is known, then the long-run cost of winning percent is also known. For example, buying enough star talent to play 0.429 costs $18 million, and so on (from Table 4.7). The shape of the curve where the total cost of winning percent rises at a decreasing rate at first, but eventually rises at an increasing rate. follows from the same limit to managing more stars that characterized the winning percent production function in Figure 4.2.

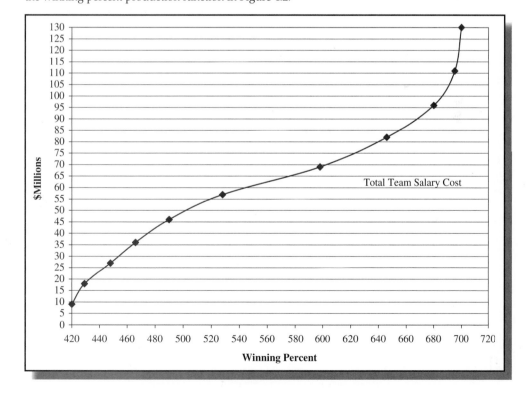

Cost Comparisons Between Lower- and Higher-Quality Teams

To get a clear picture of the level of quality ultimately chosen by an owner, it is instructive to look at the short-run situations associated with each level of long-run total cost. Each point on the long-run total cost function is associated with a particular short-run production setting. This means that an owner will face a particular set of short-run cost functions, as shown in Figure 4.1, for any given level of winning that is chosen. Thus, one can think about the short-run as a particular choice of team quality. For a team to alter its quality, it is choosing to face higher fixed costs in its next short-run setting.

We will use this simplification to talk about two kinds of teams. A lower-quality team has similar variable costs but much lower fixed costs (primarily on-field player and management talent) than does a higher-quality team. Of course, there are a few other long-run cost function elements beside player costs. These elements include other types of off-field talent that help determine the long-run winning chances for a team. According to the annual *Forbes* magazine report for 2003, MLB team total costs were between $89 million and $264 million, with an average of $131 million. Therefore, we need to shift our long-run costs of winning percent up as shown in Figure 4.4.

The Tension Between Winning and Costs

At this point, students typically ask me, "We've developed all of this structure, but what have we learned?" The answer is an important insight. As teams choose higher

Figure 4.4 Hypothetical Long-Run Total Costs for MLB
In addition to the long-run total costs associated with players at different winning percents an owner might choose, other long-run considerations, such as stadium quality, also have a cost. The sum of all of these considerations is the overall long-run total cost function.

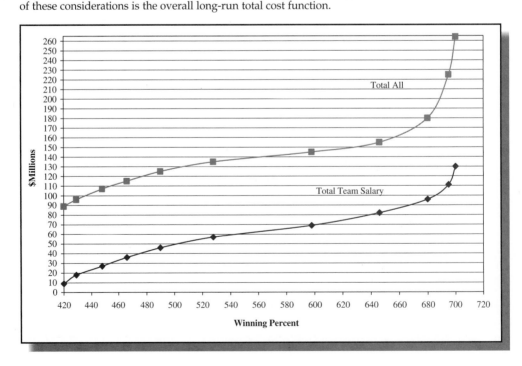

winning percents, in the long run total costs rise. A look at Figure 4.4 shows they rise only gradually through a range of the winning percent at first, but eventually, they rise at an increasing rate. Remember that the argument for the long run is that costs eventually rise at an increasing rate due to diseconomies that seem reasonably attributed to management, either in the front office or on the field.

This means that there is a **tension between winning and costs.** The more an owner wants to win, the more it's going to cost. Perhaps because owners tend to be wealthy, fans, players, and on-field managers often miss this crucial limitation on winning. Hiring talent to put a team in position to win can raise costs by $50 million or more relative to a team with an average winning percent of 0.500.

For example, suppose that a team owner determines that talent sufficient for 640 winning percent points must be hired in order to win the pennant (not unusual in the American League Eastern Division, for example). As shown in Table 4.7, the owner would have to hire seven stars at a total cost of about $82 million. On average, that's about $128,125 per point. It may well be true that a wealthy owner would have that kind of money, but whether that level of talent is worth it to a profit maximizing owner depends on the team's revenue structure. If fans are willing to pay enough to cover the costs of hiring this level of talent, then it is worth it. But if the fans are not willing to pay, the owner will lose money. If the owner cares about the bottom line, don't expect the team to win at that level. This can really grate on fans and on-field managers. Lou Piniella, manager of the Tampa Bay Devil Rays, voiced a common hope of fans and on-field managers, "It's a Catch-22 situation. If you don't win, people just (don't come). But if you put a good team on the field and compete with any team that comes in here and win your share of ballgames, people will come out. It won't happen overnight, but you'll see a steady progression" (*St. Petersburg Times*, June 29, 2003, from their Web page, www.sptimes.com, accessed June 29, 2003). If Piniella is right, everything he says will follow. But if he is wrong, then following his prescription could lose the owner of the Devil Rays millions of dollars.

If the owner doesn't care about the bottom line and gets large amounts of satisfaction out of winning, then the talent may be hired even if the fans are unwilling to pay for it. Given that fans, players, and managers often butt heads with owners over their choices about winning, the evidence seems pretty clear that the bottom line does matter to nearly all owners.

PROFIT ANALYSIS

Generically, profits are defined as the difference between total revenue and total cost. We discussed the cost side earlier in this chapter. We found that team quality, using the winning percent proxy, is the owner's long-run decision variable. We can imagine (or, if we're lucky enough to have the data, calculate) the owner's long-run cost function. An example appears in Figure 4.4.

Once the level of quality is chosen, the team will be in a short-run situation, with a specific set of short-run cost functions that depict *TFC* (primarily player compensation) and *TVC* (primarily team operations and player development). Output in the short run concerns the selling of seats at the stadium (and parking that goes along with it), other parts of the attendance experience (concessions and other types of shopping,

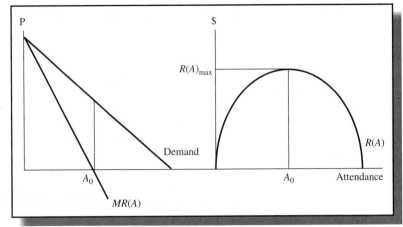

Figure 4.5
Owner Total Revenue for a Given Winning Percent
The relationship between demand, marginal revenue, and total revenue in the short run from Chapter 2, Figure 2.8.

restaurants), and games on television. In what follows, we'll use gate attendance as our unit of measurement, recognizing that these other outputs also are important.

Downward sloping demand functions dictate marginal revenue and total revenue functions, as is shown in Figure 4.5. One of the determinants of the shape and location of demand functions is fan preferences, especially for quality. When the owner chooses a higher level of team quality, fan demand increases and so do total revenues. However, quality is determined by the choice of winning percent—depending on its winning percent, the team will sell different amounts of attendance at different prices. Therefore, the particular set of demand, marginal revenue, and total revenue functions shown in Figure 4.5 would hold for a particular choice of winning percent.

Team owners who maximize **long-run profits** seek to determine the highest level of profit that can be obtained at any winning percent they might choose. Thus, while each demand function gives the team's short-run revenue potential, a look across all of these opportunities will allow the team owner to find the team's long-run profit possibilities. All the owner has to do is pick the winning percent with the highest profit. The result is maximum profit in the long-run. It is easiest to derive the long-run profit function by comparing profits at two particular quality levels.

Short-Run Profits When a Team Chooses Lower Quality

Let's find the profit maximizing level of output for a particular winning percent, or the team owners' **short-run profits** at that winning percent, for a team considering a lower-quality choice. This decision is shown as W_L in the left-hand side of Figure 4.6 (W stands for winning percent; subscript L denotes lower quality). Note that the $SRTC$ function is for a lower-quality team, as is the total revenue function. For example, a lower-quality level might be $W_L = 0.270$. The owners know the least that can be spent on on-field and off-field talent according to the long-run total cost function. If the owners were to choose a winning percent of 0.270 and the long-run cost function were as in Figure 4.4, then long-run total costs would be less than $90 million.

Figure 4.6 Total Revenue, Short-Run Total Cost, and Profit for Lower- and Higher-Quality Team Choices for a Given Owner

In the left-side panel, the difference between revenues and costs for a lower-quality team (subscript L) gives the owner's short-run profits, $\Pi(A)_L$, where Π is profit and A is attendance. Losses occur below A_L^0 and profits reach a maximum at A_L^*. Losses also are incurred if attendance goes beyond A_L^1. In the right-side panel, a higher-quality team will generate higher revenue than a lower-quality team and higher costs because higher fixed costs are incurred in order to hire more talent. The owner's short-run profits in this case also are the difference between revenues and costs, $\Pi(A)_H$. Similarly, losses are incurred at too low an attendance level, A_H^0, profits are a maximum at A_H^*, and losses again occur at too high an attendance level, A_H^1.

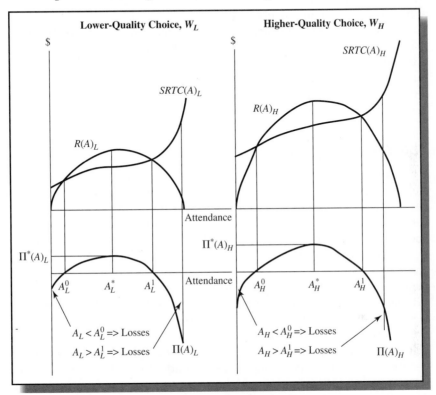

If the owners made that choice and spent less than $90 million, they would put themselves in the short-run situation of a 0.270 ball club. In that situation, the owners will confront a particular set of short-run costs. A representative $SRTC$ function for this lower-quality choice appears in the left-hand side of Figure 4.6.

On the demand side, quality is one of the primary preference determinants of the shape and location of the demand function for sports teams. If the team owners made the lower-quality choice, they would confront a given demand and its associated total revenue function. A hypothetical total revenue function for a lower-quality choice also appears in the left-hand side of Figure 4.6. The $SRTC$ and total revenue functions are shown in the abstract, without any scale on the axes of the graphs. We would be able to put actual numbers on the axes only if we had data on revenue and cost over the possible levels of attendance in the short run.

The short-run profit function simply plots short-run profits as the difference tween short-run revenues and total costs at all different levels of attendance, A,

$$\Pi(A) = R(A)_L - SRTC(A)_L$$

where the L subscript signifies profits, revenues, and costs at the lower-quality choice. The profit function is shown in the lower portion of the left-hand side of Figure 4.6.

The shape of the short-run profit function should make sense to you. For example, at attendance below A_L^0 the team loses money because $SRTC(A) > R(A)$; the same is true to the right of attendance level A_L^1. Between these attendance levels, profits rise at first, reach a maximum, and then fall.

For a given level of quality, it is clear that choosing very high attendance leads this team to lose the most money. The costs incurred with ever-increasing attendance for a given team quality eventually dwarf the revenues. A profit maximizing owner chooses the highest possible profit, given this lower level of quality, which occurs at attendance level A_L^*. Remember this combination for future reference: For a lower-quality winning percent, W_L, the profit maximizing attendance and profit combination is (A_L^*, Π_L^*).

Short-Run Profits When a Team Chooses Higher Quality

If we examine another possible quality choice for the owner, we'll see almost immediately how long-run profits come into play in determining just how good a team will be. Let's suppose that the same team owner calculates profits if a higher quality is chosen, denoted W_H in the right side of Figure 4.6 (with the H subscript standing for higher quality). For example, the right side might represent a team that chooses $W_H = 0.375$.

Higher quality will alter both the costs and revenues from attendance. On the one hand, TFC for a higher-quality team are much larger because better on-field players and management talent must be purchased. The result is that $SRTC$ is shifted to a higher level for a higher-quality choice. On the other hand, the demand for this higher-quality team shifts to the right relative to a lower-quality choice. Thus, the revenue function for a higher-quality choice also is higher. In the right-hand side of Figure 4.6, a new profit function is derived for this possible higher-quality choice.

Again, a profit maximizing owner would choose that level of attendance for a team of higher quality with the highest short-run profits. This is at attendance level A_H^* in the right side of Figure 4.6. Remember this combination for future reference as well: For a higher-quality winning percent, $W_H > W_L$, the profit maximizing attendance and profit combination is (A_H^*, Π_H^*).

Notes of Caution

Two notes of caution are in order at this point. In the hypothetical results of Figure 4.6, attendance is higher when the owner chooses a higher-quality level, that is, $A_H^* > A_L^*$. This seems to be an intuitive outcome. However, it needn't be so. For example, if revenues rose less than portrayed in the right side of Figure 4.6, it is possible for attendance to be lower even though quality rises.

The same caution should be applied to the profit outcome. In Figure 4.6, profits are depicted as larger if the owner chooses the higher-quality level, that is, $\Pi_H^* > \Pi_L^*$. Again, this seems intuitive. However, profits could be higher for a lower-quality choice. If revenues rise less than depicted in the right side of Figure 4.6, profits could be lower even though quality rises. Given the paucity of actual data on revenues and costs, we are left with observed owner behavior and a bit of analysis that you will see later in this chapter to settle this issue.

The Downside: Talent Dumping

The tension between winning and profits helps explain **talent dumping** and why owners will continue to make trades or sales of player talent that are destined to irritate the fans who want a champion regardless of the owner's bottom line.

The history of talent dumping goes way back, indicating that the pursuit of profits has always dominated the thinking of MLB owners. The "Curse of the Bambino" plagued the Boston Red Sox from the time owner Harry Frazee sold Babe Ruth to New York in 1920 in order to finance a Broadway play (he also sold a bunch of other players and, in 1923, the team itself) until the Red Sox's World Series win in 2004. Boston didn't win a World Series over the intervening 84 years. Connie Mack sold off his champion Philadelphia Athletics, one at a time and in groups, because he wouldn't meet the rising salaries caused by the rival Federal League in 1915. Another sell-off of the three-straight-pennant-winning Philadelphia A's by Mack occurred in 1931 due to declining revenues during the Depression. Charlie O. Finley peddled most of the dynasty Oakland A's in the mid-1970s—they won big but couldn't draw fans. Recently, San Diego, Houston, and Florida all have dumped talent. The reason in every case (except for Babe Ruth) is clear. The cost of winning wasn't worth the revenue generated.

PROFITS AND QUALITY CHOICE IN THE LONG RUN

The calculations in the preceding section cover only two of many different levels of winning percent between zero and one that team owners might choose. The same type of analysis would hold for each potential team quality level. Each will have its total revenue, short-run cost, and profit functions, and each will yield a particular level of attendance that maximizes profits in the short run.

A comparison across all short-run profit opportunities will determine the best winning percent of all from the profit perspective. In the long run, that's the one a profit maximizing owner will choose. This choice can be directly at odds with maximizing winning percent. This helps explain how teams like MLB's Milwaukee Brewers, the NFL's New Orleans Saints, or the NBA's Denver Nuggets have survived quite nicely from the profit maximization perspective by being lovable losers for so very long.

The Long-Run Profit Function

Figure 4.7 shows the two results for the lower- and higher-quality choices in Figure 4.6. Winning percent is on the x-axis and profits on the y-axis showing the long-run trade-off confronting this owner. In each case, there also will be an associated short-run profit maximizing output level. Let's suppose that we went through the same exercise,

Figure 4.7 The Owner's Long-Run Profit Opportunities

In the long run, the owner compares all possible profits that can be earned from all quality choices in the short run. This is the definition of the long-run profit function, $\Pi(W)$, where Π is profit and W is winning percent, or team quality. As depicted here, profits are higher at higher winning percents, like 0.375 compared to 0.270. That is, $\Pi^*(W_H) > \Pi^*(W_L)$. Profits eventually reach a maximum at W^*, that is, $\Pi(W^*)$, and decline thereafter. In adopting this shape, we assume that, eventually, rising costs of quality overtake rising revenues earned from higher-quality teams.

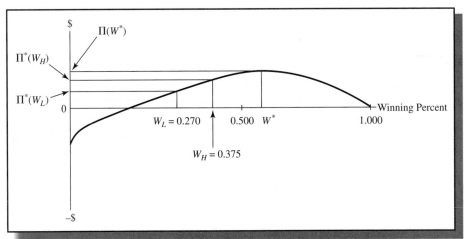

finding the profit maximizing result for all possible levels of quality (winning percent). We would find the rest of the combinations of winning percent and profit shown in Figure 4.7. This is the long-run profit function confronting the team owner. Notice that the relationships from the last section are intact in Figure 4.7: $W_H > W_L$ and $\Pi^*(W_H) > \Pi^*(W_L)$, but remember this was by deliberate choice and that you should heed the notes of caution in the last section.

The long-run profit function in Figure 4.7 has a very particular concave shape. For the long-run profit function to be concave, fan willingness to pay for winning percent would have to increase at a slower rate than costs. If this were the case, then revenues would continue to rise, but eventually costs would rise faster. If this relationship between increasing revenues and costs holds, then profits will rise at first with winning percent, and then eventually fall at higher winning percent levels. In the figure, profits fall long before the team gets anywhere close to winning all of its games. This is the source of the fundamental tension between winning and profits.

The Long-Run Profit Maximizing Level of Team Quality

An owner who maximizes profits will choose that level of winning percent associated with the highest profits in the long run. In Figure 4.7, the peak in profits occurs at a winning percent denoted W^*, and the best that the owner can do in the long run is a profit level of $\Pi(W^*)$. For this particular owner, the long-run outcome is a team that consistently strives for a winning percent greater than 0.500. There are three important observations from this outcome—profits can constrain winning, profits influence competitive balance, and small market teams are not necessarily economic losers.

Profits Can Constrain Winning   In the long run, if costs eventually rise faster than revenues, then profit maximization constrains owners in their pursuit of winning. This means that the owner will not hire talent in order to win an outrageously large share of games unless that is what fans will pay the most, on net, to see. Some owners may be willing to violate profit maximization, but they may pay dearly. Losses will mount and other potential owners will start to make overtures to buy the team. This is the fundamental tension between owners, fans, players, and managers. Owners who care about profits are constrained in their pursuit of winning.

Competitive Balance   For our second insight, we return to the competitive balance issue. The fact that profits constrain the pursuit of winning can harm competitive balance on the field. When one team is located where fans will pay far more for quality than the fans of another team are willing to pay, then the higher-profit team will win more, on average, over time. Not all team owners will choose to be lovable losers and some, with relatively larger demand and large potential revenues, will choose to win the most. As with revenue variation and competitive balance, **profit variation can harm balance.**

   This concept is shown in Figure 4.8. Here, the long-run profit opportunities for two different owners are shown. They are referred to as small market (S) and big market (B) owners. The big market owner has greater profits through most of the range of winning percent than does the small market owner. Accordingly, the big market owner chooses the larger long-run winning percent, $W_B^* > W_S^*$. As long as this relationship between small and big market teams goes unchanged, the big market team will dominate, competitively speaking. Eventually, small market fans may revise their willingness to pay downward over time. This observation relies on the idea that big market teams actually do have higher profits.

Figure 4.8   Long-Run Profit Opportunity Comparison of Big and Small Market Owners

Big market owners and small market owners have different profit opportunities. As depicted here, the maximum long-run profit for the big market owner is greater than for the small market owner, $\Pi^*(W_B^*)_B > \Pi^*(W_S^*)_S$. This also depicts the big market owner winning at a much greater level than the small market owner, that is, $W_B^* > 0.500 > W_S^*$.

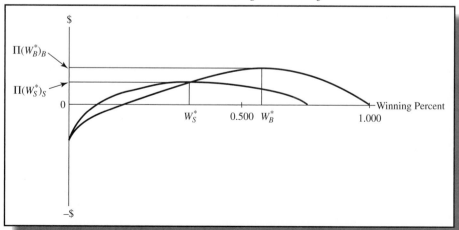

However, remember the notes of caution from the last section before jumping to any conclusions.

Small Market Does Not Necessarily Mean Economic Losses The competitive imbalance problem does not necessarily mean that small market teams are not profitable. It's just that they may not be as profitable as their big market counterparts. Don Fehr, Major League Baseball Player Association director, has been quoted as saying, "This whole thing is not really an issue of big market, small market. It's larger revenue teams, with smaller revenue teams complaining about not making as much as their bigger partners" (*Sporting News*, August 24, 1992, p. 10). Note that the outcome in Figure 4.8 echoes these sentiments. The small market owner still earns positive economic profits, just not as much as the big market owner.

"This whole thing is not really an issue of big market, small market. It's larger revenue teams, with smaller revenue teams complaining about not making as much as their bigger partners."
—MLBPA Director Don Fehr

A big market owner can correctly calculate demand and revenue, know costs, choose the level of talent to maximize profits, and then have the whole thing fall apart. Team chemistry, unexpected injuries to key players, off years in key player lifetime performance, and just plain bad luck can all wreck a perfectly rational economic plan. The same goes for some small market teams. The owner can correctly calculate small revenues, know their costs, choose the level of talent to maximize profits, and then have the team do much better than had been planned. On-field outcomes are uncertain in the sports world. The analysis of profit maximizing owners gives insight only in terms of averages. There will be exceptions every year, which is what makes sports fun. However, we would expect the exceptions to even out over time. On average, big market teams will have profit maximization occur at a higher level of winning percent than small market teams.

Alterations in Long-Run Profits

Why would a given team try to improve its quality? From the economic perspective, the answer lies in the owner's perceptions of how profits might change in the future. Profit maximizing owners will beef up on talent if they believe that doing so will raise revenues at a greater rate than the costs of making it happen. An owner might expect that something about demand has changed or is about to change. If that change will increase revenues at a greater rate than would previously have been the case relative to costs of winning, then a higher winning percent will generate greater profits than before.

Similar logic holds for the opposite scenario. If demand is expected to decrease, then a lower winning percent will maximize profits. If you are catching on to the power of the insights gained from profit maximization, then the Learning Highlight: When Can a New Owner Change a Team's Fortunes? should make perfect sense to you.

Based on the Learning Highlight, we can see that only if the last owner made horrible mistakes or has the same vision as the new ownership but no money should we expect the new owner to alter the level of team quality. Otherwise, the next owner will run the team at pretty much the same level of quality as chosen by the former owner. That would be the profit maximizing level of team quality.

Based on profit maximization, should we expect a new owner to behave any differently from previous owners? Let's look at a real-world example.

The title of a 1995 article in *Baseball Weekly*, when the Disney corporation took over the helm of the Anaheim Angels, was "Sale to Disney Spawns Anaheim Optimism." Given the massive resources at Disney's command, the article predicted that the Angels' payroll would rise and the team's chances for consistent postseason play would improve. In addition, because marketing is Disney's cup of tea, it seemed reasonable that the team's budget for enhancing the fan experience during the game would increase. In short, "Mickey Ball" would be better and more fun than the brand of baseball provided by the previous owners, the "Old Cowboy," Gene Autry, and his heirs.

Let's look just at attendance impacts. In the first 3 years of Mickey Mouse's tenure with the Angels (1996–1998), attendance averaged 2.0 million annually. In the 3 years prior, it averaged 1.8 million—about a 15 percent average increase. In those same 3 years prior to Disney's purchase, the team averaged 0.462, in the 3 years after, 0.493, for a 7 percent performance improvement. There was no change in playoff appearances with Disney's ownership. The Angels were not in the playoffs in any of the 6 years.

However, Disney spent, on average, about 28 percent more on players (in real terms) than Autry did in the 3 years prior. Now, just in terms of attendance, was it worth an additional $5.5 million in real terms to generate another 200,000 fans each year? Because these figures translate into $27.50 in spending (without including any of the variable costs) for each of these additional fans at the gate, the answer is yes, if fans spend more than that when they visit. The Fan Cost Index, published annually by *Team Marketing Reports*, is a spending index of admissions, concessions, parking, and memorabilia. For 1998, the index averaged $28.33 per person for the Angels. Therefore, Disney cleared $0.83 per fan. If variable costs were less than that on a per fan basis (or about $166,000 per game), then the bump in quality paid off. But also remember that other revenues were produced as well.

Eventually, the team improved, winning the World Series in 2002. But Disney had been trying to sell it for a few years prior to that and did sell the team to Arturo Moreno in 2003. Mr. Moreno immediately invested in a higher quality team, landing free agent Vladimir Guerrero. Moreno clearly believes that he sees something in the market for Angels' success that Disney missed.

REAL-WORLD CASE STUDY: THE SAN ANTONIO SPURS

Many team owners and league commissioners claim large losses for some of the teams in their leagues. Are these claims believable? For example, in Chapter 1, you saw that franchise prices and expansion fees for new entrants into sports leagues have grown— sometimes astronomically. How can this be if teams lose money? In this section, we'll examine the economic data of the San Antonio Spurs to attempt to untangle the confusion. We'll also try to square our theory of profit maximization with the real world of taxation.

The San Antonio Spurs Annual Operations

Tables 4.8 and 4.9 show the annual operating revenues and expenses of the San Antonio Spurs for the 1993–1994 and 1994–1995 seasons, respectively. The information on the Spurs was supplied to me by a reporter at the *San Antonio Gazette* when the owner of the Spurs was pursuing public funding support for a new arena. Again, while these data are old, they comprise a large part of what precious little information exists in detail about team revenues and expenses.

As discussed in Chapter 2, revenues come from the gate, broadcast rights, the Spurs' stadium arrangement, and royalties on NBA properties. The Spurs made the playoffs in both seasons, and they also operate their stadium for both basketball and non-NBA events through a wholly owned subsidiary, SAOne, Inc. Spurs' revenues totaled $50.8 million in 1993–1994 and $53.3 million in 1994–1995. Note that the play-offs are lucrative, grossing $9.4 million for the 1993–1994 season and $4.9 million the next. Finally, arena operations earned another $4.0 million and $2.2 million in each of the years on all other non-NBA events. Because the playoffs are attributable to the team and the team owner wholly owns the stadium management firm, it is reasonable to add up all the revenues across the board. The result is right around $64.2 million for 1993–1994 and $60.3 million in 1994–1995.

Operating expenses also follow the categories you would expect. Far and away the largest expense is player compensation. Teams also promote themselves, pay

Table 4.8   San Antonio Spurs' Annual Operations Statement for the Year Ending June 30, 1994

	REGULAR SEASON	PLAYOFFS	SAONE, INC.
Revenues			
Gate revenue	$19,125,159	$6,637,135	$2,178,570
Broadcast revenue	$22,271,712	$1,918,529	$1,288,629
Stadium revenue	$4,515,221	$495,688	$182,778
NBA royalties and other income	$4,855,346	$381,890	$303,105
Total Revenue	$50,767,438	$9,433,242	$3,953,082
Costs/Expenses			
Team salaries	$23,753,729	$45,000	
Broadcasting, advertising, and promotion	$6,510,759	$257,490	$430,600
Other salaries	$5,565,703	$731,129	$178,532
Interest expense	$3,655,426	0	0
NBA and indirect expenses	$3,566,484	$2,925,364	$536,439
Sales and other taxes	$2,305,618	$504,985	$36,186
Shared revenue			$2,038,596
Other general and administrative	$5,255,528	$607,432	$334,152
Total Expenses	$50,613,247	$5,071,400	$3,554,505
Net Operating Revenue Before Depreciation	$154,191	$4,361,842	$398,577

Source: Personal correspondence from Charlotte Anne Lucas, *San Antonio Gazette*, 1997.

Table 4.9 San Antonio Spurs' Annual Operations Statement for the Year Ending June 30, 1995

	REGULAR SEASON	PLAYOFFS	SAONE, INC
Revenues			
Gate revenue	$20,055,648	$3,020,335	$797,559
Broadcast revenue	$24,126,334	$1,275,017	$1,127,701
Stadium revenue	$4,497,040	$296,999	$111,810
NBA royalties and other income	$4,577,065	$283,905	$172,485
Total Revenue	$53,256,087	$4,876,256	$2,209,555
Costs/Expenses			
Team salaries	$26,917,914		
Broadcasting, advertising, and promotion	$7,311,916	$349,459	$468,378
Other salaries	$5,574,112	$233,452	$260
Interest expense	$3,180,312		
NBA and indirect expenses	$3,569,964	$1,366,242	$182,041
Sales and other taxes	$2,233,891	$187,883	$28,617
Shared revenue			$892,901
Other general and administrative	$7,047,850	$389,299	$101,335
Total Expenses	$55,835,959	$2,526,335	$1,673,532
Net Operating Revenue Before Depreciation	–$2,579,872	$2,349,921	$536,023

Source: Personal correspondence from Charlotte Anne Lucas, *San Antonio Gazette*, 1997.

salaried employees, cover interest expenses and their obligation to the league as NBA members, pay their taxes and, as always, the famous "other" category gobbles up a hefty amount. In addition, SAOne, Inc., pays its obligation to the city of San Antonio, which built the Alamodome, in terms of shared revenues. Adding up across the board, expenses for the 1993–1994 season totaled around $59.3 million and around $60.0 million for 1994–1995.

Net operating revenues available to cover longer-term expenses and profits (if any) for the owners were about $4.9 million for the 1993–1994 season. However, the team made only $306,000 for the 1994–1995 season. On average, over these 2 successful years for the Spurs, including arena operations, the owners' net was about $2.6 million per season. How can there be such a dramatic difference in just one season, especially when the team was about equally successful with nearly the same roster in each of these seasons?

Economics versus Accounting

The answer lies in taking an economic view of team accounts rather than the accounting view. The accounting information goes to the IRS and must satisfy IRS rules. However, the question we're addressing is the value of owning this team. There are a host of reasons why the data reported in Tables 4.8 and 4.9 don't tell the whole story of the value of owning the Spurs.

Related Business Opportunity   First, there are other values to team ownership that will only appear on another annual operations statement. When you are the owner of the local team, doors to business opportunities are opened that otherwise might not be. Much as what happens on the golf course, business deals are made and business connections are reinforced in the owner's box during and after basketball games. There also is the political clout that comes with team ownership. All of these are values that would occur only because of team ownership. However, they do not appear on the team annual operations statement; they are only found on other annual operations statements to which we are not privy.

> "Being able to share the ownership experience with clients is extremely rare and a huge competitive advantage in business."
> —Raul Fernandez, part owner of the Washington Capitols

Raul Fernandez, 10 percent owner of the Washington Capitals and part owner of the Washington Wizards, put it this way, "It's not just taking people to the luxury box, it's taking them to the locker room. . . . Being able to share the ownership experience with clients is extremely rare and a huge competitive advantage in business" (*Washington Post*, October 14, 2003, from their Web page, washingtonpost.com).

Costs That May Not Be Costs   An examination of the cost side also turns up some interesting values to team ownership. It ends up that not all costs are costs. Other salaries for some teams include salaries to owners or dependents. For example, during the court hearings on free agency in the NFL in 1994, it came out that Norm Braman, owner of the Philadelphia Eagles, paid himself a salary of $7 million in 1990 (Reingold, 1993). Similarly, the Griffith family populated all of the main management positions for the Minnesota Twins for many years. Without doubt, services were provided in each case. But to the extent that Braman's $7 million was above the going rate or the Griffiths were paid above the going rate, these expense entries may be excess direct payments to owners (and their family members).

There are other ways profits can be taken. Those same NFL free agency trials revealed that Hugh Culverhouse, then owner of the Tampa Bay Buccaneers, borrowed $22.7 million from the team in 1990 for investment and debt reduction (Reingold, 1993). Some expenses can be direct revenues to other activities of the owners themselves. For example, suppose a member of an owner group also is a principal in a law firm. That owner might "sell" the team the firm's legal services so that the cost of legal services (in the "other general and administrative expenses" category) becomes a revenue entry on the law firm's annual operations statements.

Revenue Shifting and Tax Advantages from Cross-Ownership   Another way that the value picture can be clouded concerns **revenue shifting and cross-ownership.** Suppose a media provider is a majority stockholder of a team (not the case for the Spurs). The total taxes of the two entities may be lower if the media provider, by virtue of its majority ownership of the team, pays the team nothing for local broadcast rights. This means that operating revenue is higher for the media provider than it would be if it paid for the rights. However, if the media provider's revenues are already such that it shows losses, and the additional revenues do not push net revenues to a positive amount, then the media provider pays no taxes. In this scenario, the team's revenues fall by the amount of the unpaid rights fee. This reduces the tax liability of the team. On net, the total tax liability of the two entities is lower.

LEARNING HIGHLIGHT
Wayne Huizenga's Fish Story

The introductory story to this chapter lists the woes of former Florida Marlins owner, Wayne Huizenga. Noted sports economist Andrew Zimbalist (1998) couldn't resist shooting fish in a barrel. Recall that Huizenga claimed to have lost $30 million winning the World Series in 1997. But looking at the data with an economist's eye rather than an accountant's, Zimbalist notes that most of the losses actually are nothing but an artifact of Huizenga's ownership of both the stadium that the Marlins play in and the team's local broadcast outlet.

On the stadium, Huizenga does not report luxury box or club seat revenue as team revenue, presumably putting these revenues under stadium operations instead. Zimbalist estimates this value at around $16.5 million. Other revenues generated by the Marlins (naming rights, parking, signage, major league merchandise) but put under the stadium account Zimbalist estimates at around another $13.9 million. Zimbalist also notes that concession revenue appears to be understated by about $7.6 million. In addition, Huizenga charges $5 million to cover stadium expenses. However, because the stadium is shared with the NFL Dolphins, it seems reasonable that no more than half of this amount rightfully should be paid by the Marlins. Thus, on the stadium, it is reasonable that about $38 million actually was generated by the Marlins and that costs should be $2.5 million less. On the stadium alone, the $30 million in the red turns into $15.5 million in the black.

But that's before Huizenga's cross-ownership of the Marlins' media outlet is considered. Zimbalist reports that the media outlet paid $2.1 million under market estimates for the Marlin's local broadcast rights. Estimates cited by Zimbalist show that the value of the media provider rose from $85 million to $125 million. The underpayment was worth $40 million to the media provider, but Zimbalist sticks with the $2.1 million. With a few other small discrepancies, Zimbalist suggests that instead of a $30 million loss, an operating profit of $13.8 million was more likely. Zimbalist argues that the Marlins were more profitable as losers in 1998 than they were as World Series champions in 1997, even though they were quite profitable that year as well. Huizenga hid all of this through cross-ownership of the stadium and the media provider.

Wayne Huizenga claims to have lost $30 million on his Florida Marlins, but a certain economist doesn't agree.

Source: Andrew Zimbalist, "Just Another Fish Story," *New York Times*, October 18, 1998. Online version (www.nyt.com).

Moreover, the taxes that are avoided are just as easy to spend as an increase in revenue. Note that this cannot occur if the media provider wholly owns the team. In this case, the firm at large is the taxpaying unit and there is no value to the shifting approach. The Learning Highlight: Wayne Huizenga's Fish Story details other aspects of cross-ownership that allow a team to look like a financial loser when, in reality, it generates tens of millions of dollars.

Pass-Through Firm Organization and Personal Income Tax Savings

There is a bottom line. If book profit is positive, the owners get that amount, net of taxes. For example, if the story ended in Tables 4.8 and 4.9 for the Spurs' owners, they would have the $4.9 million and $306,000 from these 2 years' worth of ownership.

And, believe it or not, even if the bottom line is negative, the value of owning the team can still be millions of dollars. Let's look at that case next.

Suppose that net operating revenues are negative. In this case, the owners pay no taxes on team operations. However, they must eat the losses, right? Well, not completely, as long as their team is organized as a **pass-through firm** for tax purposes. Subchapter S corporations and partnerships are pass-through forms of business organization that allow both income and losses to carry over to individual 1040 forms where personal income is reported to the IRS. So if net operating revenues are negative for the sports team, the losses appear on the owners' individual 1040 forms, and these losses reduce the owners' tax liability. Reduced taxes spend just like income.

For example, suppose the owners of the Spurs were in the 33-percent tax bracket. Their tax on the $4.9 million in net revenue for 1993–1994 would be about $1.6 million. Thus, their net would be $3.3 million. However, a loss of about $9.9 million would be just as valuable. Sheltering $9.9 million in other earnings on their 1040 forms is worth—you got it—0.33 × $9.9 million, or about $3.3 million, a savings that spends just the same as income earned. Owners would be indifferent between earning $3.3 million or losing $9.9 million on the team and saving $3.3 million in taxes on their personal 1040 forms.

Roster Depreciation and Personal Income Tax Savings

Actual accounting practices in sports in fact do this idea one better. What if there were an acceptable accounting practice that reduced the team's income for tax purposes but not in actuality. Then, the net income wouldn't really be lost, but taxes on personal 1040 forms could be reduced anyway. There is just such a practice, and we will explore how it works.

Amortization is the divvying up of the cost of a longer-term project over a number of years. It covers intangibles rather than the tangible depreciation of machinery. For example, a firm might want to invest in a new piece of capital but not have the money it needs. In this case, the firm saves up the money over a number of periods, faithfully charging itself for its future purchase. The opportunity cost of the money set aside for these purposes is tax deductible.

Depreciation refers to the loss of productive capacity that happens to capital assets, such as machines, buildings, and equipment, as they age. In a sense, over a known period of time, capital assets will wear out completely or be completely depreciated. This loss in productive capacity is tax deductible. Teams can own physical capital that depreciates, such as cars, computers, and buildings. In that way, they are just like other firms.

The acceptable tax practice that allows owners to reduce team income for tax purposes, but not in actuality, concerns another kind of depreciation. Bill Veeck, the famous baseball owner and entrepreneur, successfully convinced the IRS that the player roster is a piece of capital that wears out over time. As such, this so-called **roster depreciation** should be tax deductible. At the time of our Spurs example, when an owner bought a team the IRS allowed half of the purchase price to be a physical capital asset, depreciable for up to 5 years after the initial purchase (the rules have become more liberal, see Chapter 12). Thus, in 1993, the current owners bought the Spurs for $75 million. This means that they could deduct half the purchase price, or $37.5 million, for 5 years, as lost productivity of the players they bought. For reasons known only to the Spurs' owners, a 3.5-year depreciation schedule was chosen, or about $10.7 million annually—and this amount is deducted before taxes are calculated.

Here is why roster depreciation doesn't really reduce income but reduces taxes paid by owners: Over nearly their entire career, players actually increase in productivity. That simply is how people are different from machines. We learn and gain experience—essential components to enhanced production. Eventually, physically, players begin to decline. However, there is a perfectly good substitute waiting in the shape of other players available at about the same price. So if there is any "depreciation," it doesn't cost the owners a thing. Team income is reduced for tax purposes but not in actuality. There really isn't any loss. If roster depreciation is large enough to cause a loss (for tax purposes) and the team is organized as a pass-through, then the loss amount goes to the owner's 1040 forms, producing a tax savings. So there really isn't any diminution in net revenue, but taxes are reduced on the team. If accounting losses are large enough, there also is a tax savings for the owner. Pretty slick.

Roster depreciation also provides a second puzzle. Let's play along with this facetious logic and assume, for the moment, that players do depreciate. Then they must either be depreciated or count as a current business expense but not both. But the IRS allows precisely this sort of double counting to occur. Player compensation is carried in the expense column, and the roster depreciation allowance also is subtracted from net operating revenues.

Despite the fact that players don't actually depreciate and, even if they did, depreciating and expensing represents double counting, the IRS continues to allow this practice today. Truth really is stranger than fiction, especially the truth of sports accounting. But it gets even better, as we learn looking just a bit further into the Spurs example.

Sports Accounting Practices and the Spurs' Accounts

The data for 1993–1994 in Table 4.8 cover the first year that the owners group took possession of the team. It would be the first year that they could take a $10.7 million roster depreciation deduction. If one looks at the Mariners' data in Table 4.1, knowing published accounts of the team's payroll, the Mariners simply add roster depreciation into their player compensation expense category.

Table 4.10

San Antonio Spurs'
Depreciation and
Tax Savings
1993–1994 and
1994–1995
($Millions)[a]

Category	1993–1994 w/o RD	1993–1994 w/RD	1994–1995 w/o RD	1994–1995 w/RD
NOR[b]	$4.9	$4.9	$0.3	$0.3
DEP[c]	$3.5	($3.5 + $10.7)	$3.5	($3.5 + $10.7)
NAD[d]	$1.4	−$9.3	−$3.2	−$13.9
Taxes	$0.5	$0	$0	$0
NADT[e]	$0.9	−$9.3	−$3.2	−$13.9
Tax Savings	$0	$3.2	$1.1	$4.9

[a]Data in table assume the following: team purchased in 1993 for $75 million; 3.5-year roster depreciation schedule ($10.7 million/year); 1993–1994 and 1994–1995 depreciation equals $3.5 million; tax rate 35 percent; and team organized as a pass-through.
[b]NOR is net operating revenue.
[c]DEP is depreciation.
[d]NAD is net after depreciation.
[e]NADT is net after depreciation and taxes.

We can deduce that the Spurs' owners did not use the same method, because that would leave only about $13 million for actual payments to players in 1993–1994 ($23.7 million in team salaries minus $10.7 million in roster depreciation) and about $16.2 million in 1994–1995. In addition, we know actual current salary payments were larger than that in each of the years. Therefore, we must calculate what roster depreciation would do to the tabled Spurs' reports. The calculation of the value of the roster depreciation is in Table 4.10.

Suppose there were no roster depreciation (RD, for short, in Table 4.10). For the 1993–1994 season, net operating revenue (NOR) before depreciation and amortization for the regular season, playoffs, and non-NBA arena activities was about $4.9 million. Actual depreciation (DEP) was reported at $3.5 million for the 1993–1994 season. This means that the owners would start to report net after depreciation (NAD) $1.4 million to the IRS. Assuming the team is organized as a partnership pass-through, the $1.4 million would be divided among the owners, reported as income individually, and taxes would be paid. At this income level, a 35 percent tax would make the net after depreciation and taxes a total of $910,000 for the owners.

But things are dramatically different for 1993–1994 with the roster depreciation in place. The $1.4 million minus roster depreciation of $10.7 million reduces NAD to a loss of $9.3 million. This isn't an actual loss but rather a loss only in the eyes of the IRS. Even though there is no real loss of productive capacity, and even though the owners already get to expense player compensation, they still will report a loss of $9.3 million to the IRS.

This has two effects. First, the owners' tax liability on the team itself is reduced to zero because it no longer shows any positive net revenue. That returns the net value of owning the team, after real depreciation, back to $1.4 million. Second, and this is an accounting practice that is completely legal, NADT for the year falls to a loss of $9.3 million. Because we assume that the team owners carry profits or losses through to their personal 1040 forms, the tax savings are 35 percent of $9.3 million, or about $3.2 million across all owners. Roster depreciation turns $910,000 into $4.6 million ($1.4 million plus $3.2 million).

The next year is even better despite the fact that net operating revenue, before depreciation, is lower. Assuming that real depreciation and amortization is another $3.5 million, one gets the following chain of value if there were no roster depreciation: Roughly $300,000 in net operating revenue minus $3.5 million in depreciation results in an operating loss of about $3.2 million. There would be no tax obligation for the team owner on the team itself, and the tax savings from the pass-through loss on the 1040 forms would be about $1.1 million.

What happens in the presence of the roster depreciation should be clear. Adding another $10.7 million in depreciation increases the total pass-through loss to $13.9 million. That raises the tax savings from $1.1 million to about $4.9 million. Only in the world of sports accounting can a team be more valuable when it shows a book loss of $3.2 million on operations (as was the case with the Spurs in 1994–1995) than when it shows a book profit of $1.4 million (as was the case with the Spurs in 1993–1994)!

When we try our hand at the real world, some elements are missing from our exploration of roster depreciation. Other reductions in net operating revenue also occur, but there is no way of knowing their level to make even a wild guess. In addition, there is no accounting for amortization (how can we know about the investment plans of the Spurs?). Other reductions include deferred bonuses and other types of deferred player compensation. All of these reduce net operating revenue for the team, but also increase the amount of the pass-through to owners' 1040 forms.

If one were to summarize the value of owning the Spurs over the 1993–1994 and 1994–1995 seasons, the list would include the following items:

- All of the values in other business activities in each year
- Any direct payments to owners or their businesses that are shown in the expense section of the annual operations statement each year
- A profit of $1.4 million for 1993–1994 because taxes were driven to zero
- A loss on the Spurs of $3.2 million for 1994–1995
- Tax shelters worth $3.2 million and $4.9 million in 1993–1993 and 1994–1995, respectively

We can't know the value of other business activities or payments to owners and/or their businesses. In addition, remember that we don't know about any other long-term obligations that would reduce net operating revenue and raise tax savings. But, at least in terms of roster depreciation, a ballpark figure is $1.4 million plus the two tax shelter values worth $7.8 million minus the $3.2 million loss in 1994–1995 for a spendable total of $6.3 million. The roster depreciation allowance makes the team a loser on the books in both years; however, there was only an actual loss in the second season. The roster depreciation allowance only lasts up to 5 years, but in the first 2 years, it was worth about $8.6 million to the owners of the Spurs ($490,000 in saved taxes on $1.4 million in net revenues in 1993–1994 plus $8.1 million in taxes saved on other 1040 income across both seasons).

Why Do Owners Plead Poor?

Most of this discussion concerns the difference between allowed accounting practices and economic value. The essential question about team ownership, from the economic perspective, is whether the bottom-line result is enough to keep owners and their resources engaged in team sports. Acceptable accounting practices in sports, plus contributions to other income, actually make the team more valuable than a simple calculation of net operating revenue would indicate.

We can only assume that owners know that their actual position is much better than their team accounts indicate (otherwise, there are some very rich accountants out there!). Economists have been pointing out this fact for quite a few years. Team values have risen quite handsomely, and this doesn't happen typically to assets that lose money over time. Just as typically, very wealthy people do not line up to gain access to an asset at a price of hundreds of millions if they anticipate large losses.

Why do owners persist with their claims of losses? First, some teams really may be suffering losses, especially small market teams that no longer have a roster depreciation allowance. But there is another explanation. Owners may be posturing. Pleading poor and showing the public their book losses may be helpful to owners as they deal with players at the bargaining table. If players can't figure out revenues or team profits, then they may be at a bargaining disadvantage. However, whereas players can hire analysts to figure out the actual financial position of owners, the general public cannot. Thus, claiming losses may help bolster owners' positions as they bargain for new stadiums with their current host cities; remember these data on the Spurs came from just such a setting. If their claims of losing tons of money are convincing, then chances for a stadium subsidy or favorable lease contract may increase. We'll return to these issues in Chapters 10 and 11.

CHAPTER RECAP

Most wealthy team owners have become wealthy by watching the bottom line in all of their business endeavors. In this chapter, we have assumed that profit maximization is the guiding principle for team owners' decisions concerning their sports teams.

In the long run, all inputs in the sports production process are variable. The most important variable in the long run is the player roster. Regardless of the state of all other variables, once the player roster is chosen, so is team quality.

Winning percent is the usual measure of quality. Once team quality is fixed, the team is in the short-run, economically speaking. As a result, the short run is characterized by a fixed amount of on- and off-field personnel. Once this is determined, teams consider short-run outputs such as attendance, concessions, parking, logo properties, and the stadium experience for fans.

In the short run, fixed costs are pretty much identical to roster costs, plus the costs of contractual front-office talent and any contractual obligations associated with the stadium. Fixed costs do not change with the level of output in the short run. Variable inputs include team and stadium operations, player development, and advertising and promotion. The costs associated with variable inputs determine variable costs. Variable costs increase at a decreasing rate over some initial range of output but must increase at an increasing rate due to diminishing returns to variable inputs.

For every quality choice, there will be a particular short-run cost structure as well as a particular revenue structure because quality is a primary determinant of fan demand that, in turn, determines revenues. Profits are the difference between revenues and costs. For each short-run situation there will be a maximum amount of profit that the owner could choose. Long-run profit maximization requires the owner to compare all of these possibilities and select the level of quality with the highest profits. As long as costs of increased quality eventually rise faster than revenues, then there will be one, and only one, highest profit quality level.

Sometimes great teams will falter and weak teams will surprise. However, over the long haul, teams with greater talent win the most. Owners wishing to maximize profit will only choose higher quality if it pays off. The highest level of talent is not necessarily concentrated where profits are highest. This only happens if large-revenue markets are also large-profit markets. However, as long as there is a wide range of payoffs among teams, competitive imbalance will be a problem. In addition, there is also tension between some owners whose profit maximizing level of winning is low and their fans, players, and on-field managers. How often have we heard the lament of long-suffering fans of lovable losers? But as long as profits dictate talent choices and some locations support only low levels of quality, there will always be unhappy fans, players, and coaches.

In the real world of sports, the revenue side of annual operations statements may not show all of the team's value. There can be related business opportunities for sports owners; some expenses may not be costs at all; and when there is cross-ownership of media providers and/or stadiums, sports team owners can put revenues generated by teams on different annual operations statements. Finally, the ability to both expense and depreciate the team roster, a perfectly legal sports accounting practice, can make a team that is worth millions of dollars to its owner both in terms of net operating revenue and personal tax reductions look like it is losing money. Owners might find it advantageous to show a loss when they confront players' unions and when asking a city for upward of a few hundred million dollars in stadium subsidies. *For example the RDA.*

So data over time will smooth out the statistics.

KEY TERMS AND CONCEPTS

- Profit maximization hypothesis
- Short run
- Long run
- Short-run fixed inputs
- Short-run fixed costs
- Short-run variable inputs
- Short-run variable costs
- Short-run total costs
- Diminishing returns to variable inputs

- Long-run quality choice
- Long-run winning percent production function
- Limit to management ability in the long run
- Managerial efficiency
- Long-run total cost
- Tension between winning and costs

- Long-run profits
- Short-run profits
- Talent dumping
- Tension between winning and profits
- Profit variation can harm balance
- Revenue shifting and cross-ownership
- Pass-through firm
- Roster depreciation

REVIEW QUESTIONS

1. What is the profit maximization hypothesis? If teams earn very low profits or lose money, does this mean the owner does not maximize profit? Can owners who make systematic mistakes survive in a league of profit maximizing owners? How?

2. Why is winning a useful way of describing sports team output? What are the limitations of this abstraction?

3. Define the short run in economic terms. What do owners sell in the short run? What is fixed in the short run? How long does the short run last?

4. Define the long run in economic terms. What is long-run output? What are the primary long-run decision variables for sports team owners? If an owner alters the roster during the season, when is the team back in the short run again?

5. What are the short-run fixed inputs for a sports team? The short-run variable inputs? What distinguishes the team's short-run fixed costs from the team's short-run variable costs?

6. Define short-run total costs. What type of expenditure represents the largest element in short-run total costs? Graphically, what is the vertical distance between short-run total costs and short-run total variable costs equal to?

7. Why are the functions for short-run total costs and short-run variable costs shaped as in Figure 4.1? What would change to shift short-run total fixed costs up? What would change to shift short-run variable costs up?

8. What is the main determinant of where teams end up in the standings; that is, what determines whether they win more or not? For our purposes, what is the definition of a star player? Explain how star players contribute to a roster that has no stars.

9. Describe the long-run winning percent production function. What role does managerial efficiency play?

10. Define long-run total cost. What determines its shape in Figure 4.3?

11. Define long-run profit. Define short-run profit. Why are profits negative, then positive, and then negative again as attendance increases?

12. Why is there conflict from the owner's perspective between winning and costs? What is talent dumping? Why does it occur?

13. How do profits constrain winning? How can profit variation harm competitive balance?

14. List the five elements that, from the economic perspective, contribute to the value of owning a team but do not appear on the team's annual net operating revenue report. You should be able to give an example for three of the elements.

15. What is a pass-through firm organizational structure? Why is such a structure valuable to sports team owners? What is roster depreciation? Why is it valuable to a team owner?

THOUGHT PROBLEMS

1. In the section on short-run costs, general and administrative costs for the Seattle Mariners were eventually characterized as fixed costs. How would you determine where they truly belong?

2. In Figure 4.1, at an attendance of 2.9 million, what is the dollar value of the vertical distance between the short-run total cost function and the short-run variable cost function? What does this dollar value represent? What is the vertical distance equal to if attendance is 3.5 million? Why?

3. In the long run, everything is variable. How can it be, then, that there is some "limit to management ability" that gives the long-run winning percent production function its shape? Doesn't this limit mean that management ability is fixed? Explain.

4. Use a graph to explain what happens to short-run costs as a team owner increases quality. What type of expenditure is made by owners to make this shift occur?

5. Use a graph to explain what happens to revenues in the short run when a team increases quality.

6. A team owner tries to decide quality level. By spending another $12 million, the owner expects that the team will finish one place higher. Does this mean that the owner can raise the team's place in the standings by one place for each $12 million spent? Why or why not?

7. Graph a short-run situation where a big market team has lower profits at its profit maximizing level of attendance than a small market team has at its profit maximizing level of attendance. In your graph, be sure to identify the profit maximizing attendance and profit in each case.

8. Using a carefully labeled graph of long-run profit opportunities, answer the following:
   a. What determines the shape of the profit function that you drew in your graph?
   b. Is this a long- or short-run graph? Explain.
   c. With reference to different points on your graph in part (a), explain why no profit maximizing team will ever want to win all of its games.
   d. Draw the profit function for a team owner who would rationally choose to win fewer than half the team's games in the long run.

9. Graph a small market team's long-run profit function when it is possible to earn profits in the long run. Suppose that economic hard times befall the fans; incomes fall dramatically. The result is that the owner can't figure out any way to break even. In your graph, show this new profit outcome. What would you do if you were this owner?

10. When a player says that an owner doesn't want to win, what is really being said?

11. Fans always crave a better team. Often they grow weary of ownership that won't give them one. If the team changes owners, when will fan expectations of improvement be met? Relate your answer to the Disney example in the Learning Highlight: When Can a New Owner Change a Team's Fortunes?

12. What is the crucial characteristic of cross-ownership that determines whether revenue shifting can occur? What is the gain to cross-ownership to be had from revenue shifting?

13. Suppose a team is organized as a pass-through firm. Further, suppose that there are no physical depreciation or roster depreciation or other long-term obligations. Both the tax rate on the team and the tax rate on the owner's personal income are 33 percent. Explain why the owner would be indifferent between making $7.98 million on the team before taxes and losing $16.2 million on the team after taxes.

14. Give the arguments in support of roster depreciation. Give the arguments against it. How do you come down on the issue? Why?

15. How would you determine whether a given pro sports team owner tries to maximize profits? Why would the team's annual net operating revenue statement not be very helpful in your analysis?

ADVANCED PROBLEMS

1. Examine the data in Table 4.4. Why did it take an increasing amount of points at the margin to move up through the standings (once out of the basement)? Now, examine Table 4.5. The same pattern appears to hold over a longer time period. Why is that?

2. Even though we gloss over the underlying production function for winning in this chapter, it's still fun to think about. True or false, and explain your answer thoroughly: The best football coach is the one who always chooses the play that will gain the most yardage.

3. Why use the data across a few seasons in Table 4.5 rather than the single season data in Table 4.4 to ascertain movements through the standings? What is gained by examining the data over time?

4. Suppose you hear the following: "Arenas are multipurpose buildings. If NBA and NHL owners could just afford to own their own stadiums rather than rent them, two things would happen. First, they'd be able to get out from under high arena rental costs, reducing their costs per game. Second, they'd gain control over the revenues earned on other nonsports events. This would improve their net revenue picture and they'd be able to buy better basketball or hockey talent." There are three things wrong with this statement. Identify and correct each one.

5. "Our costs rise each year as they would in any household or business. Like any NFL team we have operating costs and player costs. We also are in a unique situation because, unlike a lot of teams, we have a privately funded stadium and there are costs associated with that"—Phil Youtsey, Director of Ticket Sales, Carolina Panthers, on increasing ticket prices by 2.5 percent for the 2002 season (sportsbusinessnews.com, accessed March 25, 2001). Are there really cost differences between owning a stadium and renting a stadium? What are they?

6. Use the following schedule of stars, winning, and salary to answer the questions.

STARS	TOTAL WINNING PERCENT	SALARY ($MILLIONS)
0	420	$7
1	429	$5
2	448	$5
3	466	$5
4	490	$6
5	528	$6
6	598	$7
7	646	$8
8	680	$8
9	695	$9
10	700	$10

   a. Graph the total cost of winning percent (from player compensation only). Be sure to label the points in your graph.

   b. Is this the long-run or short-run total cost structure for this team? Why?

   c. What costs are missing from the complete picture of the costs of winning?

   d. How would inclusion of the costs you list in part (c) alter your graph in part (a)? Show the revised graph.

7. A team owner learns from a research firm that the demand for winning looks like this: $P = (36 - 2A)W$, where P is ticket price, A is attendance, and W is the quality of the team measured by winning percent. To focus on the long run, the team owner sets marginal cost equal to zero, but the owner knows that fixed costs determine quality in the following way: $TFC = 65W^2$, where W is winning percent. With this information, answer the following:

   a. What are the owner's profits if a low-quality team is chosen, say $W = 0.350$.

   b. What are the owner's profits if a high-quality team is chosen, say $W = 0.650$?

   c. Comparing your answers, above, should the owner choose the high-quality or low-quality alternative?

   d. Graph the relationship between quality (remember, $0.000 \le W \le 1.000$) and profits. What is the precise winning percent that earns the owner the greatest possible profit?

8. What dissatisfied you about the analysis in the Learning Highlight: When Can a New Owner Change a Team's Fortunes? What additional data or analysis would make the example more satisfying?

9. Here's a simplified team accounting problem (round your answer to whole numbers). Suppose an owner buys a football team for $200 million. The team is organized as a pass-through firm. The corporate and individual tax rates are equal at 33 percent. Physical depreciation is $4 million. The team has no other long-term obligation. In the first year of ownership, operating revenues minus expenses equal $16 million. Show that the team loses $8 million after taxes and all depreciation. Show that the actual value of the team to the owner, just from these calculations, is a positive $15 million. Finally, show that the value of roster depreciation to the owner was $7 million. (Hint: There are two positive components to this last part.)

10. What was Wayne Huizenga's goal in rearranging revenues, as Zimbalist (1998) claims he did in the Learning Highlight: Wayne Huizenga's Fish Story? How did all of the shenanigans cited by Zimbalist contribute to that goal? In particular, how did the revenue shifting due to Huizenga's cross-ownership of the Marlins' local cable outlet support his goal? Did revenue shifting have any other advantages? Under what circumstances?

INTERNET RESOURCES

For a host of additional material and questions for thought, visit this book's Web site at www.prenhall.com/fort.

REFERENCES

Kahn, Lawrence M. "Managerial Quality, Team Success, and Individual Player Performance in Major League Baseball," *Industrial and Labor Relations Review* 46 (1993): 531–547.

Klein, Gene, and David Fisher. *First Down and a Billion: The Funny Business of Pro Football.* New York: St. Martins Press, 1987.

Noll, Roger. *Government and the Sports Business.* Washington, D.C.: Brookings Institution, 1974.

Porter, Philip K., and Gerald W. Scully. "Measuring Managerial Efficiency: The Case of Baseball," *Southern Economic Journal* 48 (1982): 642–650.

Reingold, Jennifer. "When Less Is More," *Financial World*, May 25, 1993, 38.

Scully, Gerald W. *The Business of Major League Baseball.* Chicago, IL: University of Chicago Press, 1989.

Scully, Gerald W. "Managerial Efficiency and Survivability in Professional Team Sports," *Managerial and Decision Economics* 15 (1994): 403–411.

Singell, Larry D., Jr. "Managers, Specific Human Capital, and Firm Productivity in Major League Baseball," *Atlantic Economic Journal* 21 (1993): 47–59.

Zimbalist, Andrew. "Just Another Fish Story," *New York Times*, Sunday, October 18, 1998. Online version (www.nyt.com, accessed October 18, 1998).

5

Sports Market Outcomes, Part I: Leagues, Team Location, Expansion, and Negotiations

Chapter Objectives

After reading this chapter, you should be able to:

- ■ *Understand that leagues facilitate play on the field and maintain the business structure of sports.*

- ■ *Explain how the business structure of sports leagues establishes and maintains territorial exclusivity for member teams.*

- ■ *Understand the financial and strategic components of expansion and team relocation choices by the league.*

- ■ *Understand the role that rival leagues have played in the formation of today's modern leagues.*

- ■ *Discuss how owners act in joint ventures through their leagues, including TV contract negotiations, labor negotiations, and dealings with their host cities.*

Free market economics is the process of driving enterprises out of business. Sports league economics is the process of keeping enterprises in business on an equal basis. There is nothing like a sports league. Nothing.

—NFL COMMISSIONER PAUL TAGLIABUE
(*Sports Illustrated*, September 10, 1990)

*C*ommissioner Paul Tagliabue could not have been more correct about there being nothing like a sports league. For example, when MLB's Brooklyn Dodgers and New York Giants left for California in 1957, they left a big hole in the fans' hearts. In 1959, after failing to convince either an existing MLB team to move or MLB to expand, William Shea decided to form the new Continental League with Branch Rickey, perhaps the most famous baseball businessman in history, as president. However, Shea and Rickey couldn't get the existing American League and National League teams to agree to Continental League team locations under MLB rules for a new league to join the existing American League and National League, and the Continental League folded in 1960. Not 2 months later, the National League announced two expansion teams for Houston and, you guessed it, New York. The American League agreed to expand to Los Angeles and to the just vacated Washington, D.C., market. All of the MLB owners had joined forces and determined that there was no room for Continental League teams in cities that they then immediately occupied after the Continental League folded. Had firms in any other industry behaved this way, they arguably would have run afoul of antitrust laws.

In this chapter, we investigate the behavior of team owners as members of leagues. We will see that owners seek to enhance their individual welfare through coordinated league action and that leagues set the stage for play on the field as well as the business structure of member teams. We will also look at how leagues establish and protect the team territories of owners and negotiate for member owners in a more profitable way than owners would be able to individually.

WHY LEAGUES? MAKING PLAY AND PROFITS

Leagues enable owners to pursue economic goals and objectives that they cannot pursue as successfully acting alone, such as setting a season schedule, organizing championships, and implementing rule changes. Coordinated league activity makes league play happen, but it also provides owners with many profit opportunities off the field. We cover the idea behind such coordinated cooperation in this section, but the actual elements deserve subsequent sections of their own.

Single-Entity Cooperation: Making League Play Happen

Some cooperative actions among teams must happen for league play to occur at all. This type of activity is called **single-entity cooperation**. Single-entity cooperation defines the actions that owners must take to make league play happen in the first place—setting schedules, the rules of play, and the structure of championships. However, even at this seemingly innocuous level of creating league play, economic issues arise.

Setting the Schedule Setting the schedule is the most basic form of single-entity cooperation. If team owners cannot cooperate with each other to set a schedule, then league play, by definition, cannot occur. Even this type of single-entity cooperation has economic impacts. George Halas, one of the NFL's founding fathers and original owner of the Chicago Bears, described the original scheduling of the NFL to Congress:

> "We had to have official scheduling. . . . By making the season more interesting to the fans, this action benefited each member club and helped to stabilize each club." —George Halas, NFL owner-icon

Naturally, each team wanted to play a team which would draw the most fans. . . . It reached the point where the Giants, Green Bay and the Bears (the most successful teams) became the most sought after teams to play. . . . We had to have official scheduling. . . . By making the season more interesting to the fans, this action benefited each member club and helped to stabilize each club. (*NFL Report*, 1999, p. 2)

Thus, leagues need to act in their single-entity capacity to include all teams in the schedule. If only larger teams played each other, smaller-market teams would fail economically. In trying to generate widespread fan interest and league growth, Halas understood that stronger teams must play weaker teams as well as other strong teams in order to cultivate broad fan interest, especially in championship play at the end of the season.

Another important element in setting the schedule is establishing season length. There is nothing magic about the length of seasons except that it helps determine profits from the regular season and the playoffs. Season lengths certainly have changed over time. The season length in the American League increased from 154 games to 162 games in 1961, a 5 percent increase (the National League followed suit the next year). The most recent change in the NFL season was from 14 to 16 games after 1976, a 14 percent increase.

Setting the Rules If teams play under different rules, they aren't playing the same game. In addition, there must be officials and appeals for the sake of fairness. Once again, however, even this basic single-entity determination has economic elements. Rule changes alter the balance between offense and defense in producing winning margins. In turn, this changes the pattern of winning between teams, which is what fans pay to see.

Gerald Scully (1989) details the economic implications of changes in playing rules. For example, narrowing the strike zone would be expected to favor hitting relative to pitching. In Table 5.1, the "predicted" column shows what Scully predicted would happen to batting average and earned run average due to narrowing the strike zone in 1969. Batting averages should rise because a good pitch is easier to detect in a smaller zone. Pitchers should fare worse, with a higher earned run average. As Table 5.1 shows, both of these results did occur in 1969.

The designated hitter rule was another important change in the American League, relative to the National League. In the American League, teams are allowed to designate a hitter to take the pitcher's place in the lineup. This means that there is one more skilled batter in American League lineups than National League lineups.

Table 5.1 Predictions About Rule Changes and Performance

CHANGE	YEAR	PREDICTED	BATTING AVERAGE	ACTUAL EARNED RUN AVERAGE	RUNS PER GAME
Walk reduced to eight balls	1880	−	−	−	−
Mound moved back to 50′	1881	+	+	+	+
Walk reduced to seven balls	1882	−	−	+	+
Walk reduced to six balls	1884	−	−	−	−
Walk increased to seven balls	1886	+	+	+	+
Strikeout changed to four strikes	1887	+	+	+	+
Strikeout reduced to three strikes	1888	−	−	−	−
Walk reduced to four balls	1889	−	+	+	+
Mound moved back to 60′6″	1893	+	+	+	+
Lively ball introduced	1920	+	+	+	+
Strike zone narrowed	1950	+	+	+	+
Strike zone widened	1963	−	−	−	−
Strike zone narrowed	1969	+	+	+	+
Designated hitter in the American League	1973	+	+	+	+

Source: Gerald Scully, *The Business of Major League Baseball* (Chicago, IL: University of Chicago Press, 1989).

Scully (1989) points out that measures of hitting, especially slugging average, increased significantly in the American League over the National League after the designated hitter rule was implemented.

What do all of these rule changes have to do with economics? In narrowing the strike zone or adopting the designated hitter, the offense was favored because that's what owners thought fans would want and pay to see. If fans get bored with the length of games, shorten them. If fans want more action, institute more offense if it is affordable relative to the value created.

Cooperation and Championships The ultimate indicator of fan demand for winning is the crowning of a league champion. Therefore, determining a champion is very economically valuable. However, the way championships are structured also produces economic incentives for team owners. Relative to a league that just crowns the team with the highest winning percent as its champion, adding playoffs does two things: (1) It extends the season and fan interest for a few teams, and (2) it reduces the returns to buying talent.

Did You Know?
Adding playoff rounds reduces the chances that the team with the highest winning percent will eventually be the league champ, but those chances still remain greater than 50/50 (Fort and Quirk, 1995).

James Quirk and I (Fort and Quirk, 1995) found that playoffs reduce the chances that the team with the highest winning percent will become the eventual league champion, even though those chances remain higher than 50/50. This means that the expected value of talent falls, too, causing owners to choose lower talent levels. One implication of this is that owners have a greatly reduced incentive to hoard talent to ensure the highest winning percent relative to the rest of the teams in the league.

Finally, the number of playoff games also is a choice variable for leagues. For example, prior to 1968, there were no playoffs in MLB. Indeed, there were no divisions in either the American League or National League, so the winners of each league just met in the World Series. The American League and National League championship series started after divisions were created in 1968. With the 1992 expansion, MLB added another round of playoffs after three divisions were created in each league. Once again, these rounds generate additional revenues for a few owners and impact the talent choices of all owners in the league. Similar increases in the number of championship rounds have been adopted by the other major professional leagues over time as well.

Joint Venture Cooperation: The Economics of League Behavior

Walter Neale (1964) was the first to recognize the important relationship between single-entity action and economic outcomes, naming it the peculiar economics of team sports. But this peculiar economics only begins with the single-entity actions of owners in leagues. Once owners act together in pro leagues to set the stage for competition on the field, they may also act together to raise profits for member owners.

All cooperative actions that do not make play happen are called **joint ventures**. In this section, we will set up the idea of joint ventures, the main categories of which are covered later in the chapter. In a joint venture, all owners in the league surrender part of their autonomy to allow the league to act on their behalf. However, joint ventures can also be pursued individually by owners rather than through the league. Given that, economic intuition suggests that joint ventures are cooperative acts aimed at increasing profits relative to acting individually. Single-entity action helps create efficient schedules, rules, and championships. However, since the time of Adam Smith, we've known that joint venture cooperation can facilitate market power and its inefficiency. Market power doesn't have to be the result of joint venture actions; it just ends up that way. Owners really do control their leagues. If leagues do not make owners better off than if they were acting alone, the owners will simply leave the league. This doesn't happen often because leagues are good at doing what owners require, but it does happen. In the 1940s, the National Basketball League (NBL) faced a rival, the Basketball Association of America (BAA) (Quirk and Fort, 1992). The BAA, composed primarily of arena owners, had a lock on the largest and most valuable venues. Defection to the BAA by NBL teams because their own league could not secure these profitable venues led to the demise of the NBL. After the 1947–1948 season, the four strongest NBL franchises went over to the BAA. After the next season, six more NBL teams defected. The NBL died because it hadn't satisfied one of the most basic requirements for its member owners, namely, a chance to play in the most lucrative venues. The Learning Highlight: Challenging European Football's Power Structure presents an international case where a sports organization is failing to give its members what they want most and the likely repercussions.

Did You Know?
Over the 1947–1948 and 1948–1949 seasons, the National Basketball League died because almost all of its teams jumped to the Basketball Association of America in order to get better playing venues.

The Union of European Football Associations (UEFA) organizes the European football (soccer) championship at the level just below World Cup competition. Essentially, the champions from each European country meet to decide the champion of Europe. The prize to the participants is the chance at becoming the European champion, and a rather substantial payday from the TV revenues for the tournament. An important feature of these payments is that they are larger for the finalists than they are for teams that do not make it past the early rounds. Herein lies a problem for UEFA. Smaller countries, such as Scotland, Belgium, and Luxembourg, usually make early exits from UEFA cup competition. However, the teams in these smaller countries are media dynamite in their own markets.

This has recently led to a movement by national European sports organizations, at the behest of their most winning teams, for a "small country" European championship. Of course, such defection would reduce the value of the UEFA tournament. UEFA responded that any teams that participate in such a championship will be banned from UEFA cup play and, quite possibly, World Cup consideration.

One would think that this ultimatum would end the quest for a small-country championship. However, the smaller countries responded that they would push forward anyway. One of two things must be true:

1. This group of small-country malcontents may just be pushing UEFA's hand to see if the threat actually will be carried out.

2. It may actually be worth enough to the small-country teams, in terms of added TV revenue, to break off and start their own championship round.

Either way, UEFA is not meeting the needs of these small-country teams; therefore, these teams are seeking a structure that will.

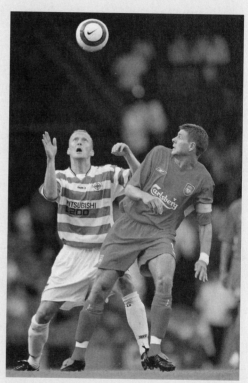

Teams from small countries are pressing for their own UEFA cup to capture a larger return from postseason play.

Source: *Sports Business Journal*, December 25, 2000, p. 33.

In the following sections, joint venture activity is divided into three main categories: territory definition and protection; expansion and team relocation; and league-level negotiations with TV, players, and host cities. Joint action is not required for any of these activities. Acting together on these issues must simply be more valuable to owners than acting individually would be.

TERRITORY DEFINITION AND PROTECTION

The first joint venture activity with implications for other teams, other leagues, and fans is the definition and protection of individual owner territory. Leagues have been allowed to grant **exclusive territories** to their members. This means that the league is allowed to define a territory and ensure that no other members locate within that territory. The result is that exclusive territories are the primary determinant of the revenue structure that any owner will enjoy. Protection of that revenue structure is a fundamental reason to join a league in the first place. Let's examine how leagues perform this essential task and its impacts.

Exclusive Territories and Market Power

How many times have you heard it said that in the hearts of fans there is no substitute for the home team? Packers fans are not Vikings fans, and Yankees fans couldn't care less about the rest of MLB except insofar as they are the competition. Leagues rely on this fan identification when setting exclusive territories for member teams.

Franchise Agreements Leagues manage exclusive territories through **franchise agreements** with their member owners. A franchise agreement is a contract between the league and an owner that clearly specifies what it means to own a pro sports team. The owner names the franchise, enters the season schedule and playoff schedule, agrees to abide by the league operating rules, and eventually shares in league-wide broadcasting revenues and expansion fees. The franchise agreement also specifies the responsibilities of the league to enforce operating rules and to protect the franchise territory from other league members.

The courts endow leagues (even though each league really is just a collection of owners who benefit from joint ventures) with the rights to their franchises, logos, and properties. Leagues, in turn, license logo rights and other properties to various sellers, and they sell franchises to owners. This ability to define territories has survived over time subject to judicial review under the antitrust laws (see Chapters 8 and 12 for more on antitrust). The rules in every pro sports league strictly govern the ability of any member of the league to encroach on existing territories. Teams cannot simply move to a new territory without careful review and approval by their league according to its bylaws.

Economic Impacts of Exclusive Territories

Nothing about franchise arrangements necessarily restricts competition. For example, when McDonald's grants a franchise, there is plenty of other competition from other fast service providers (Burger King, etc.). Indeed, the competitively determined customer base acceptable to potential franchise buyers often is such that quite a few McDonald's restaurants are located in the same city.

This situation is not often found in pro sports leagues. First, leagues themselves only put more than one team in a very few of the largest markets in the country. And we've already discussed how multiple teams in the same *area* are not necessarily in the same *market*! Second, once a league is in place, competition from competing leagues is either squelched or reduced in such a way that no meaningful economic competition to the dominant league's teams ever will be forthcoming. Finally, and crucially, remember that all of the individual McDonald's owners do not comprise the decision-making body for that corporation as owners do in their respective leagues.

Economically speaking, careful management of exclusive geographic territories by leagues provides owners with market power. Once exclusive territories are created and protected, there literally is no substitute team, in that sport, in that area for fans. There are other entertainment substitutes, but not another team in the same sport. From an economic perspective, this managed absence of substitutes allows individual teams to maximize profits as monopolies in their sport in their territory (although they still compete with entertainment providers in general). You know from your general economics training that firms with market power reduce output and raise prices relative to a more economically competitive outcome. You also know that this type of firm earns positive economic profits.

Quantity Restrictions Leagues impose two types of **quantity restrictions.** One that we have already discussed is season length. The second and more important output restriction in sports follows directly from the maintenance of exclusive territories. Owners acting through their leagues limit the number of teams in their league by choice rather than through the forces of competition. There are two important indicators that the number of teams is smaller than a more economically competitive sports world would give to fans. First, rival leagues do form occasionally. This indicates that the previous league size was too small in the eyes of the fans of the rival league.

Second, every time a league announces that it plans to expand, a long line of candidate-owners forms in the hope of becoming the newest addition to a league. Wealthy people typically do not line up to get assets that generate low returns. This suggests that the expansion team will be economically viable or, in turn, that the number of teams prior to expansion was smaller than the set of possible markets could support. Because the line is long, economic intuition suggests that savvy business people would snap up more than just the expansion team(s) being offered. Either way, the number of teams, even after expansion, is smaller than competition would provide.

Did You Know?
After the initial round of identifying candidates for MLB expansion teams in 1992, the pool was narrowed to owner groups in 15 cities.

High Prices The remaining effects of the market power generated by exclusive territories can be seen in sports pricing and profits. In Chapter 2, we saw how sports teams facing downward sloping demand functions employ a variety of price discrimination mechanisms to increase fan expenditures. The cost of providing on-field competition does not vary by seat location, time of day, day of the week, or the age of fans, but fans' willingness to pay does vary along each of these dimensions. Profits are higher when owners can price discriminate. In Chapter 4, we also saw how profits can be positive in the long run for sports teams. Territorial exclusivity, controlled by leagues, maintains the market power of teams in a given location, leading to all of these pricing outcomes.

EXPANSION AND RELOCATION

Leagues expand and member owners relocate their teams for two reasons. First, there can be money in it. **League expansion**, increasing the number of teams in the league, pays because the franchise right is valuable to potential owners. **Team relocation** to a more profitable location also is good for the owners who move their teams. Other teams in the league may earn any spillover value in the national TV contract. In addition, expansion and relocation also protect existing owners from outside competition. As some cities grow and prosper and others fade economically, the most valuable locations for pro sports franchises change. New York Giants owner Horace Stoneham knew this only too well when he moved his team to San Francisco with this parting shot, "Tell the kids I haven't seen their fathers at the ballpark lately" (*Sporting News*, October 5, 1992).

Leaving some viable locations without teams enhances the bargaining power of existing owners with their current host cities, but if an existing league is slow to move, a rival league may move into these new economic centers. Expansion and relocation can preclude this possibility. Let's examine these components of a league's expansion and relocation decisions.

Expansion and Relocation: The Direct Financial Component

Suppose an existing league is considering a candidate for expansion or relocation. We would expect the league to approve the expansion or move if, on net, the current team owners in the league will be better off because of the expansion. Selling the franchise right to an owner can generate hundreds of millions of dollars for current owners. The important dollar elements include the expected **ownership value** of the expansion team, gate impacts for member teams, and the impacts of expansion on league television rights values. Although this is just as true for a team move, it is easiest to see with an expansion, so let's stick with that example.

Net Present Value of the Expansion Team Members of the current league, really just the current team owners, decide the expansion fee to charge. Actually, they are trying to estimate the net value of ownership that we just covered in Chapter 4. Thus, the current owners must estimate revenue sources in the expansion city (gate, television, venue) and costs (operations, player costs, and the owner's opportunity cost). In addition, there will be values to any related business operations, "costs" that are actually profit-taking, cross-ownership tax advantages, pass-through tax advantages, and shares of any future league expansions. These can be summarized as the expected net present value of expansion team ownership, NPV_e:

$$NPV_e = \sum_{t=0}^{T} \frac{V_t - C_t}{(1 + r)^t}$$

where e denotes the expansion team; V is the overall value of ownership; C is cost; t indexes time into the future from the base year "zero" to the end of the planning horizon, T; and r is the interest rate.

The *t* subscripts on the right-hand side of the *NPV* expression make it clear that value, costs (including the owner's opportunity cost), and the interest rate all vary over time. To the extent that the league can make such an estimate, the expansion fee will include the chance to capture NPV_e. But there are other financial impacts from expansion that owners must consider that are not captured by NPV_e.

Other Expected League Impacts Expected local revenue impacts (gate, concessions, parking, and in some cases, local television) for member owners represent another element in the expansion fee consideration. Typically, expansion teams are not very successful at first, as shown in Table 5.2. On average, in MLB, it takes an expansion team more than 7 years to win more than half its games. It takes between 5 and 6 years in the other three pro leagues. There are a few bright spots, such as the recent and successful Arizona Diamondbacks in MLB and the Jacksonville Jaguars in the NFL, but on average, expansion teams barely win 40 percent of their games over their first 5 years. Because fans love a winner, all else constant, this means revenues that depend on the quality of opponents will be lower when teams play expansion clubs. Expansion clubs simply tend not to be very good, and fans will be less inclined to pay as much to watch them. Of course, if this lag period to becoming an average team is shorter or longer in other leagues than MLB, the impacts would be adjusted accordingly.

In addition, there may be **expected national TV impacts**, especially important in the NFL where there is only a national contract. Here we must be careful to distinguish between expansion and relocation impacts. Expansion impacts would be expected to be positive because adding a team expands the total market for the

Table 5.2 MLB Expansion Team Records for the First 5 Years

Team	Year Expanded	First Year	Average First 5 Years	Number of Years to Reach 0.5
Senators	1961	0.379	0.383	9
Angels	1961	0.435	0.474	2
Mets	1962	0.25	0.322	8
Colt45s/Astros	1962	0.400	0.412	8
Padres	1969	0.321	0.368	10
Expos	1969	0.321	0.436	11
Royals	1969	0.426	0.478	3
Pilots/Brewers	1969	0.395	0.420	10
Mariners	1977	0.395	0.385	15
Blue Jays	1977	0.335	0.358	7
Rockies	1993	0.414	0.485	3
Marlins	1993	0.395	0.474	5
Diamondbacks	1998	0.401	0.543	2
Devil Rays	1998	0.389	0.374	Not as of 2004
Averages		0.375	0.422	7.2

league's games. But some expansion candidates will contribute more to the value of the national television contract than others, depending on those elements important to sports advertisers. As discussed in Chapter 3, advertisers care about the size of target demographic groups and how often these groups are expected to watch the sport in the expansion location. However, this is a consideration at the margin. Fans in every city watch sports. Granting a franchise to a potential owner in a particular city will increase interest in that city, but it is unlikely that everybody in that location is just going to stop watching if they do not get an expansion team. Thus, the current owners in the league compare the additional value to the national TV package between competing franchise locations. This was particularly important in the most recent NFL expansion, detailed in a subsequent section of this chapter.

Relocation, in comparison, may or may not enhance the value of the national contract. It all depends on the value of the audience in the original and new locations. This can make relocation a vexing problem for leagues. Owners would only consider relocating their team if it were in their personal best economic interest. But impacts on the national contract could be harmful to the league as a whole. It becomes a difficult league decision process in this case.

Because these local and national TV impacts are an identifiable estimated dollar amount, they can be included in the expansion fee consideration process as the change in the net present value to existing owners, ΔNPV_n:

$$\Delta NPV_n = \sum_{i=1}^{n} \sum_{t=0}^{T} \frac{V_{it} - C_{it}}{(1 + r)^t}$$

where Δ denotes change and there are $i = 1, \ldots, n$ total current owners. The rest of the variables and notation are as in the calculation of the net present value of the expansion team.

The Expansion Fee   It is now easy to see how the expansion fee would be determined, in general. Suppose that the impact of expansion on national TV is positive and outweighs the impact of expansion on local revenues. In this case, $\Delta NPV_n > 0$, and expansion has a net positive effect on the group of current owners. The **expansion fee** (F) would have to be:

$$NPV_e \le F \le NPV_e - \Delta NPV_n$$

The actual outcome would depend on the level of competition over expansion franchises. Suppose there were only one potential buyer. With a strong bargaining position, this single buyer might be able to bargain the price down to $F = NPV_e - \Delta NPV_n$ because that buyer would know the positive value of expansion and try to extract it from the league. More realistically, and more consistent with actual outcomes, there are many buyers and heavy competition for the expansion franchise. In this case, $F = NPV_e$. The league would be able to keep the positive value of expansion and extract the value of ownership from the competitive buyers.

Another very interesting case does exist. Suppose that, instead of producing a net positive value for current owners in the league, expansion actually imposes net costs, that is, $\Delta NPV_n < 0$. In this case, it is clear that under the more likely setting where there is brisk competition for the franchise that $F \geq NPV_e - \Delta NPV_n$. The current group of owners would extract the value of ownership and cover the net negative impact of expansion through national TV and local revenues. But this raises the very interesting question, what type of potential buyer would pay more than the owners' best guess at the value of the franchise to the buyer? There are a couple of possibilities. First, the owner may not seek to maximize profits. If there are consumption benefits, then this type of owner would pay more than the net present value as we've set it up here. Second, the potential buyer may think the estimate made by the current group of owners is less than the true underlying value over time. If so, this buyer would pay more than $F = NPV_e$ for the expansion franchise.

The upshot of all this, given that competition among potential buyers usually is heated, is that the most likely expansion franchise price is $F = NPV_e$. The current group of owners would be expected to keep the net positive value spilling over to them and extract the value of ownership from potential buyers. Note also that the expansion fee will vary across all of the locations under consideration during any expansion episode. Large-revenue markets would have higher expected profits and less negative impact on local revenues than small-revenue markets. Using B for a potential big-revenue-market location and S for a potential small-revenue-market location, we would expect $F_B > F_S$.

A Few Practical Considerations

There are additional practical considerations about the expansion fee. First, because fees tend to run from tens to hundreds of millions of dollars, they typically are paid to the league on an installment plan. Second, one would suspect that the length of time over which negative local revenue impacts occur would not be as long as the horizon used by member teams to estimate expected profits. After all, even expansion teams eventually got close to the league average winning percent after about 7 years.

A second practical consideration concerns **owner viability**. Suppose that two potential owners represent the same financial value of expansion for the league, but one is riskier in terms of making expansion fee payments. This might lead the league to reject one seemingly similar potential owner in favor of another on owner-viability grounds alone. Even in this era of franchise free agency, the leagues prefer stability. Demand for team sports requires time to mature. Mature demand, with loyal fans, usually is the type that generates the most revenue in the long run.

Two other values to expansion do not vary across potential expansion owners. First, under league bylaws governing expansion, the new team(s) must draft a specific number of players from existing teams. This is called an **expansion draft**. Of course, the rules also allow existing owners to protect nearly all players of any real value. Thus, the players eligible for the expansion draft typically are high-priced players at or nearing the end of their careers and in the final years of long-term contracts. As always, there may be a few bargains in an uncertain world, but by and large, we would expect players in the expansion draft to be overpriced.

The evidence on this is pretty clear. In the 1992 MLB expansion, neither the Colorado Rockies nor the Florida Marlins drafted a single eligible player with contracts over $2 million. They chose much cheaper, younger prospects and filled the rest of their lineups with free agents and trades. Apparently, the expansion teams found all of the older expansion-draft-eligible players to be overpriced and did not take a single one of them at the going rate.

Finally, sharing of national TV contract revenues can be postponed for new expansion team owners. In their 1992 expansion franchise agreements, Colorado and Florida agreed to receive no share of MLB's national TV contract until 1994. Alas for them, just as they were about to receive their first share of the national TV contract, the MLB strike occurred. Large portions of the national TV contract were not collected, a bitter pill for the Rockies and Marlins, who had waited 2 years for their shares.

Profit Extraction and Owner Behavior   The logic behind the determination of expansion fees raises an interesting issue. The expansion fee, F, includes the expected net ownership value of the expansion team. In the 1990s, these fees averaged close to $200 million in the NFL, $100 million in MLB, $82 million in the NBA, and $36 million in the NHL. They have grown at extraordinary rates in the last few decades (as high as 70% annually in the NBA). To the extent that league estimates are close to the true value of ownership, existing owners extract the largest possible payment with just enough left to cover the expansion owner's opportunity costs. This means that one of the expansion owner's costs is the **imputed expansion fee**; owners must include covering the expansion fee in their fixed costs. Only unexpected changes alter the outcome. For example, if stadium needs were unknown at the time the expansion was granted and the new owner discovers that the local host city will pay a generous stadium subsidy, then the new owner may earn profits that the existing owners did not expect at the time of expansion.

This extraction of value by the existing league owners forces the expansion franchise owner to exploit market power just to break even economically. If the new owner does not fully exploit market power but the league included profits from that type of behavior in the expansion fee, then the owner will lose money. Collected profits over time will not cover the imputed expansion fee. To the extent that the new owner is able to exploit market power better than league owners anticipated at the time of expansion, profits over and above the expansion fee can be had. We expect owners to maximize profits, and the expansion fee is a cost that must be covered by the full exploitation of their market power position.

Expansion and Relocation: Strategic Issues

The foregoing discussion considered only the financial value of expansion to member owners. The introduction to this section mentioned that there also are two strategic issues associated with expansion and relocation. Expansion and relocation can be carefully managed to enhance the bargaining power of existing owners with their host cities. Expansion and relocation also can be used to preclude competition from existing or potential rival leagues. The money issues just discussed, plus consideration of these strategic values, give the complete account of the values that go into the expansion decision.

Expansion, Relocation, and Owner Bargaining Power Leaving economically viable team locations empty is valuable to current members of the league in bargaining with their host cities. If the host city, county, or state fails to meet an owner's subsidy demands, the owner can simply threaten to move to the open viable location. If elected officials do not want to lose the team, the owner's upper hand can be worth millions of dollars. The strategy here concerns the preservation of **believable threat locations**. A believable threat location is an alternative location for the team that politicians in the current host city would believe is truly a viable location.

To see just how important this threat value is, consider the case of Tampa Bay/St. Petersburg during the 1990s. Despite spending nearly $200 million on the Suncoast Dome stadium (the forerunner of today's Tropicana Field) to prove that they were worthy, owner-hopefuls in Tampa Bay/St. Petersburg did not get an MLB expansion team in 1993. Owners in Denver and Miami received the teams for that expansion round. The MLB owner-hopefuls in Tampa Bay/St. Petersburg let it be known that they would be willing to host an expansion team or buy an existing team.

Immediately following this failed attempt, in rapid succession, the Chicago White Sox, San Francisco Giants, and Seattle Mariners used Tampa Bay/St. Petersburg as a believable threat location against their host cities. The White Sox threatened to move to Tampa Bay/St. Petersburg, with its "ready, willing, and able" empty Suncoast Dome unless they received a new publicly funded ballpark. The hopefuls in Florida printed up Tampa Bay White Sox tickets and mocked up a few hats, joyful at the thought of a team. But with extraordinary participation by then Illinois governor James R. Thompson, at midnight of the last day of the session the legislature capitulated, and the financing groundwork was laid for the new Comiskey Park in Chicago (now named U.S. Cellular Field).

The Giants, after losing a few referendum votes for new stadiums in San Francisco and the surrounding area, also invoked the Tampa Bay/St. Petersburg ploy. Tampa Bay Giants hats were mocked up and season tickets were printed. After a cooling-off period, commanded by then National League president Bill White, the team was sold and kept in San Francisco. The new owner immediately began to press for a new ballpark and, eventually, significant infrastructure support for the privately funded PacBell Park (now SBC Park) was granted by the city.

Last, but not least, the owner of the Mariners threatened to sell the team to the Tampa Bay/St. Petersburg hopefuls in order to raise enough money to pay the interest on loans to keep his local radio network financially afloat. Once again, there was much rejoicing in Florida. At the last minute, a new ownership group kept the Mariners in town and immediately began pressing for a new stadium. Shortly thereafter, the state legislature produced a funding package for Safeco Field.

Did You Know?
After failing to get an expansion team that would have begun play in 1992, Tampa Bay/St. Petersburg was passed over by the White Sox, Giants, and Mariners as a potential new home before an owner group eventually landed an expansion team that began play in 1998.

Clearly, as an open, believable threat location, Tampa Bay was valuable to the owners of the White Sox, Giants, and Mariners. Hundreds of millions of public dollars were allocated to keeping these teams in their cities. Heavy bargaining leverage was assured for three member owners when MLB expanded to Miami and Denver rather than Tampa Bay. Eventually, the value of that leverage must have declined because an owner group in Tampa Bay did get

LEARNING HIGHLIGHT
Keeping the Oilers in Edmonton

Once the team of the "Great One," Wayne Gretzky, and a five-time Stanley Cup champion, the NHL Oilers needed a neat hat trick to remain in Edmonton in 1997. The example also ties together lessons from Chapter 4 on sports accounting and the value of team relocation or, more technically in this case, the battle against relocation.

Then owner Peter Pocklington claimed that the Oilers had lost $60.75 million since 1990 (all values in this learning highlight are converted to US$ at the then prevailing rates). This was despite the fact that he had used the threat of moving to a believable alternative location in 1993 to get federal, provincial, and local governments to remodel Northlands Coliseum (currently Skyreach Centre) and Pocklington's minor league baseball field. That public contribution was about $20.25 million. In addition, Pocklington reportedly was $162 million short on taxes owed to the province of Alberta. He put the Oilers up for sale asking $85 million.

But the federal, provincial, and local governments that helped rebuild Skyreach Centre had exhibited a modicum of foresight. A clause in the remodeling agreement (good until 2004) stated that if a local group could muster $70 million then the team was theirs. The timing of the $70 million went like this. First, a $5 million nonrefundable payment had to be made within 30 days of any offer made for the team. An acceptable payment plan for the remaining $65 million had to be reached in two months after the $5 million payment. This clause would play a crucial role as events unfolded.

Enter Cal Nichols, president of the Edmonton Investor Group (EIG). Nichols made his fame with a string of gas stations in western Canada and had been instrumental in helping to keep the Oilers in Edmonton in the past. He began to rally the troops, and EIG started learning some interesting sports accounting lessons covered in Chapter 4. Remember, one lesson from Chapter 4 was that not all is as it seems on sports annual operations reports. Werner Baum, an eventual investor in EIG and former accountant for the Oilers, went on the record saying, "Those numbers [Pocklington's claimed losses], I knew, weren't anywhere near what the actual situation was." Baum claimed that Pocklington was including accounts not related to the hockey team in order to paint a bleak picture for those who wanted the team to stay in Edmonton. Apparently Pocklington hoped that frightening away smaller local buyers with scary stories of mounting massive losses would allow a bigger offer than $70 million from an outside buyer who would probably move the team to the U.S.

EIG also discovered that the Canadian tax authorities permitted a roster depreciation allowance that was even more generous than the one for U.S. team owners discussed in Chapter 4. In Canada, 60 percent of the purchase price could be declared player roster depreciation over a reasonable period, a sizable tax shelter for a pass-through firm. Cal Nichols noted, "If we did nothing more than break even over the first four years, at least we would be in a position where we could get almost 100 percent of the investment as a tax write-off against other income and still have the paper, the shares of the Oilers."

In the meantime, that bigger outside offer was made by NBA Houston Rockets owner Les Alexander. He placed his $82.5 million bid in

(Continued)

early 1998. EIG knew it was coming, but unless they could come up with the $70 million, it looked like a pretty good bet that the Houston Oilers would resurface but in the NHL as another occupant of Houston's arena. Through the force of Baum's arguments that losses were not as they seemed, and the lure of lucrative tax advantages, EIG made the $5 million deposit in the nick of time. They used the remaining two months to try to get part of the remaining $65 million from local government officials.

EIG tried to pressure the city council for $14.2 million and part ownership but failed. They did manage to obtain a rent subsidy of $2.4 million annually through 2004. The mayor of Alberta suggested that this was a no-brainer given the huge economic spin-off to the city area generated by the team. (Stay tuned for more on the economic value of sports teams to cities in Chapter 10.)

Now, of course, everyone wonders if EIG will keep the team in Edmonton after the restrictions on outside team sales end in 2004. After all, expansion NHL franchises recently went for about $80 million, and there was a genuine offer of $82.5 million for the Oilers (similar to the $80 million paid for the San Jose Sharks in 2002). When the tax breaks that fueled most of the private support run out, coincident with the 2004 release date, will EIG just cash in on the additional $12.5 million? Without the careful restriction on the number of teams, viable alternative threat locations wouldn't even exist in the first place, and there wouldn't be any profit to be had.

Source: Inspired by *CAmagazine*, October 1999, pp. 24–32.

a team in the 1998 MLB expansion. The Learning Highlight: Keeping the Oilers in Edmonton is quite instructive on the value of believable threat locations in another league, the NHL.

Expansion, Relocation, and Precluding Competition from Rivals

Maintaining believable threat locations is valuable to existing owners. However, there is a downside to this practice. By leaving viable locations empty, the league puts out the welcome mat to the possibility of competition from **rival leagues**. As we will see, rival leagues have actually formed around just one or two teams in large-revenue markets also occupied by another league's team. The rival league gains initial access in one or two large-revenue markets and puts the rest of its teams in smaller markets uncovered by the dominant league. The result is competitive economic pressure on the dominant league. With competition, some fans shift to the rival league. Demand and revenues decline for teams in the dominant league. In addition, the rival league can begin bidding up the price of players so that costs rise for the dominant league. When prices fall and costs rise, profits must also fall.

Expanding the league to include the viable location or moving an existing team to that location should reduce the attractiveness of formation of a rival league. **Strategic expansion and relocation** can preclude rival competition. The same would be true of putting another team in a market large enough to support two

Table 5.3 Pro Sports League Coverage of the Top 30 Cities by Population

LEAGUE	# TEAMS	# COVERED	% COVERED
MLB	30	26	87
NBA	29	22	76
NFL	32	24	75
NHL	30	21	70
All Leagues	121	30	100

Did You Know?

MLB has been better at keeping its teams in the top 30 large markets than any other league despite the fact that MLB has been better at keeping its teams in the top 30 large markets than any other league. Overall, there is at least one major sports team in all top 30 large markets left to become the Texas Rangers in 1971. Overall, there is at least one major sports team in all top 30 large markets.

Did You Know?

The Pacific Coast League was in the process of obtaining official major league status when the Dodgers and Giants moved to California in 1957. Immediately after that, of four previous PCL teams in California, only the San Diego Padres remained as a PCL team. Nearly all of the teams in the revised PCL became wholly owned by MLB teams.

teams. If the rival league cannot gain access to some large-revenue-market areas, it is unlikely to form. Table 5.3 shows how well pro sports leagues have done at keeping a presence in the top 30 population centers. MLB always has been best at covering the top 30 (Fort and Quirk, 1995), whereas some cities are just not basketball or hockey towns, as the NBA and NHL have the worst coverage of top 30 population centers. As you can see in Table 5.3, the NFL also has plenty of room to expand.

Let's look at an example of strategic relocation. Up until the 1950s, the majors had simply ignored moving west of the Mississippi River. However, population grew steadily in the West, especially in California. The Pacific Coast League (PCL) thrived with teams in Los Angeles, San Francisco, Vancouver (BC), San Diego, Hollywood, Seattle, Portland, and Sacramento. During U.S. House of Representatives antitrust hearings in the early 1950s, members of the Celler Committee scolded MLB for its reluctance to move west and told MLB to design a procedure that would show how a rival league could obtain officially sanctioned MLB status. MLB responded with a procedure and a set of requirements, based on attendance, that nearly none of its own teams could meet (the same rules that the Continental League tried to use in the example at the beginning of the chapter).

The PCL was so prosperous that its principals actually tried to gain official recognition as a third major league under these guidelines. However, the clearly unreasonable requirements stalled the PCL's campaign for major league status. In the meantime, MLB's Brooklyn Dodgers and New York Giants moved west in 1957, occupying what were clearly the anchor cities for the PCL, Los Angeles and San Francisco. With this ready-made historical MLB rivalry now in their area, baseball fans shifted loyalty away from their old PCL teams and toward the MLB's new Los Angeles Dodgers and San Francisco Giants.

Shortly after the Dodgers and Giants appeared, the PCL was almost entirely out of California, with only the Padres remaining in San Diego. The other California teams moved to Phoenix, Salt Lake City, and Spokane. After losing their anchor cities, the PCL was relegated to AAA minor league status. Indeed, most of the remaining teams in the AAA version of the PCL were either purchased by MLB teams or entered into close contractual relations with MLB teams.

Clearly, the relocation of the Dodgers and Giants ended all chances, however unreasonable, for the PCL to obtain major league stature. If there's one thing we know, it is that in every pro sport, even though rivals sometimes appear, the **single dominant league** outcome always prevails. MLB, the NBA, NFL, NHL, and even the WNBA have all confronted rival leagues, and one dominant league always is the result.

The 2000 NFL Expansion The 2000 NFL expansion into Houston serves to illustrate nearly all of the elements in the decision by league owners to expand. The decision boiled down to two locations that had recently lost their NFL teams, Los Angeles (which had lost the Rams to St. Louis and the Raiders to Oakland) and Houston (which had lost the Oilers to Nashville, later renamed the Tennessee Titans).

The Houston owners group raised the $700 million expansion fee. In addition, it was a top 10 population center and a large TV market. The owner group was financially solid, and Houston taxpayers had committed to a new stadium. Added to the expansion fee, the stadium commitment raised the dollar value of the amount offered by the Houston owner group to nearly $1 billion. In addition, Houston had a team before and the fans were hungry for another. *Sports Illustrated* reported that $48 million in PSL revenues were collected by the expansion Houston club in just 21 days (January 16, 2000, p. 23). Los Angeles, also with a viable owner group but with many unresolved stadium issues, relied on its strength as an economic and TV powerhouse but lost its bid for a team. The Houston Texans began play in September 2002.

Did You Know?
In the first 21 days of PSL sales, the expansion Houston Texans earned $48 million.

This is a marvelous example of how a league evaluates the value of TV markets at the margin, as described earlier in this chapter. According to the *Los Angeles Times* (June 6, 2003), the NFL enjoyed a 9.5 rating on broadcast television in Los Angeles in 2002, a season when there were no NFL teams in the area. This rating was 58 percent better than that enjoyed by the NBA Lakers, 188 percent better than the MLB Dodgers, and a whopping 764 percent better than the NBA Kings. Overall, the Los Angeles rating was better than New York's 9.3 with two NFL teams. At the margin, it is entirely possible that ratings in Houston were better with a team there than ratings could possibly have increased in Los Angeles.

In addition to all of the other comparisons, strategically there was quite a bit of value to NFL owners in keeping the Los Angeles market open. It is a completely believable threat location for other teams in the league to use against their hosts. Of course, the NFL owners also run the risk associated with leaving Los Angeles open. Such a location probably could hold two teams, easily. Rival leagues have certainly started with less, a topic to which we now turn.

History of Rival Leagues The history of rival leagues is too long to include in this book. (The interested reader can find a pretty complete account in Quirk and

Table 5.4 Pro Sports League Rivalries

DOMINANT LEAGUE (YEAR ESTABLISHED)	RIVALS	DURATION	DISPOSITION
National League (1896)	American Association	1883–1891	Assimilated
	Union Association	1884	Assimilated
	Players League	1890	Assimilated
	American League	1901–1902	Merger
MLB (1903)	Federal League	1914–1915	Buyout by MLB
	Negro Leagues	1923–1950	Folded
	PCL	mid-1950s	Assimilated (AAA ownership)
NFL (1922)	American Football League I	1926	One-team merger
	American Football League II	1936–1937	Partial merger
	American Football League III	1940–1941	Folded
	All-American Football Conference	1946–1949	Partial merger
	American Football League IV	1960–1969	Partial merger
	World Football League	1974–1975	Folded
	U.S. Football League	1983–1985	Folded
NBA (1949)	ABL	1960–1961	Folded
	ABA	1967–1976	Partial merger
NHL (1917)	World Hockey Association	1972–1979	Partial merger

Source: Author additions to information in Quirk and Fort (1992).

Did You Know?
Both baseball and football have faced seven rival leagues each. Basketball has faced only two and hockey only one.

Fort [1992 and 1999].) Although the current structure of leagues in professional sports has been fairly stable for nearly 20 years, rival leagues have formed and have been successful. Table 5.4 lists rivals for the four major U.S. team sports.

How these rival leagues formed is quite clear. First, the artificial restriction on the number of teams by leagues often leaves room for a rival league to put a team in the largest revenue markets. How do you convince the sole occupant of a market with vast revenues to act in the interests of the league and accept another close neighbor? Expansion into an existing team's franchise area requires unanimous consent, typically. If that team cannot be compensated or the behavior of existing teams is to not pay compensation to the current single-occupant owner even if they could, then a protective expansion can be vetoed. If the league fails to get that second team in place, then the door is open to a rival league in a large market.

A classic example occurred in 1960. To that time, the NFL left the pro-football hungry fans in Dallas without a team. The upstart AFL (version IV) made it clear that one of their original teams would be in Dallas. True to its word, the AFL began play in 1960, and one of its original teams was the Dallas Texans. Interestingly enough, the NFL also granted an expansion franchise that began play as the Cowboys in that same year. The battle for Texas was on. Eventually, the NFL brand proved too strong and the AFL Texans moved on to become the Kansas City Chiefs. But clearly the AFL gained substantially from having one of its original teams in such a strong market.

The second part of the answer has to do with pushing a good thing too far. An open viable market provides valuable bargaining leverage to member owners. However, if you leave a plum hanging on the tree for too long, a rival league is quite likely to pick it. Any type of miscalculation on the part of the league about how long it can leave a viable location open can lead to the formation of a rival league.

The case of the PCL and MLB is just one example of how relocation protects against rival leagues. Leagues have always moved their teams around quite a bit, except for the last 30 years in MLB. Table 5.5 shows team moves by league. No league beats the NBA in team moves, either by the number of examples or the number of times a given team has moved. Two NBA teams have been in four different cities, and there are four three-city teams. Although teams typically move less in the NHL, we do have the very interesting example of the Dallas Stars. If you count the merging of the original Minnesota North Stars with the Cleveland Barons, that team has moved five times. All of this movement should be to higher-valued locations, helping to preclude the formation of rival leagues.

One observation about the history of rival leagues that must be emphasized is that they simply do not survive. The single dominant league outcome has always prevailed. As shown in Table 5.4, partial mergers and assimilations characterize nearly every rival league episode. Mergers and assimilations typically occurred by offering the owners of the most successful teams in the rival league very inexpensive franchises in the dominant league. Those owners then just moved their entire team, lock, stock, and barrel, into the dominant league. Sometimes assimilations happened by melding some teams in the rival league with dominant league teams. Let's examine this single dominant league outcome in more detail.

The Single Dominant League and Game Theory

The earlier section on the history of rival leagues makes it clear that dominant leagues have confronted competition. But why haven't any of these rival leagues been able to make a go of it over the long haul? The first part of the explanation involves a simple game theory explanation that suggests rival leagues that might be operating on a shoestring may not be able to survive the competitive struggle for existence (Fort and Quirk, 1997). The rest of the explanation concerns lack of enforcement of laws designed to foster economic competition. Let's begin with the game theory portion of the explanation.

Table 5.5 Team Movement in Pro Sports

TEAM	MOVES
MLB	
Angels	Los Angeles—Anaheim
Athletics	Philadelphia—Kansas City—Oakland
Braves	Boston—Milwaukee—Atlanta
Brewers	Seattle—Milwaukee
Dodgers	Brooklyn—Los Angeles
Expos	Montreal—Washington, D.C.
Giants	New York—San Francisco
Orioles	Milwaukee—St. Louis—Baltimore
Rangers	Washington, D.C.—Arlington
Twins	Washington, D.C.—Minnesota
Yankees	Baltimore—New York
NFL	
Cardinals	Chicago—St. Louis—Phoenix
Colts	Baltimore—Indianapolis
Oilers	Houston—Tennessee
Raiders	Oakland—Los Angeles—Oakland
Rams	Cleveland—Los Angeles—St. Louis
Ravens	Cleveland—Baltimore
Redskins	Boston—Washington, D.C.
NBA	
76ers	Syracuse—Philadelphia
Bullets	Chicago—Baltimore—Washington, D.C.
Clippers	Buffalo—San Diego—Los Angeles
Grizzlies	Vancouver—Memphis
Hawks	Tri Cities—Milwaukee—St. Louis—Atlanta
Hornets	Charlotte—New Orleans
Jazz	New Orleans—Salt Lake City
Kings	Rochester—Cincinnati—Kansas City—Sacramento
Lakers	Minneapolis—Los Angeles
Pistons	Fort Wayne—Detroit
Spurs	Dallas—San Antonio
Warriors	Philadelphia—San Francisco—Golden State
NHL	
Avalanche	Quebec—Denver
Coyotes	Winnipeg—Phoenix
Devils	Kansas City—Colorado—New Jersey
Flames	Atlanta—Calgary
Stars[a]	Oakland—California—Cleveland—Minnesota—Dallas
Whalers	New England—Hartford

[a]Cleveland Barons merged with the Minnesota North Stars in 1978.
Source: Quirk and Fort (1992), and online team histories.

Figure 5.1 Rival League Talent Dilemma

The dominant strategy in this game is for both leagues to spend high and obtain major-league status. For example, if League 1 spends high, so should League 2. If League 1 spends low, League 2 should still spend high. The same strategy holds for League 1 because the payoffs are symmetric. However, if the costs of maintaining major-league status are too high over time, only one dominant league will survive.

		League 2	
		Spend High	Spend Low
League 1	Spend High	1 & 2 Major	1 Major 2 Minor
	Spend Low	2 Major 1 Minor	1 & 2 Minor

Suppose two rival leagues, each with two strategy choices, spend high on talent and become a "major" league in the eyes of fans or spend low on talent and remain a minor league. This idea focuses on the idea from Chapter 2 that fans care about the absolute level of play in their identification of what it means to be a major league. The matrix of outcomes is in Figure 5.1.

Let's examine choices by League 1 in Figure 5.1. If League 2 spends high, then the best that League 1 can do in response is to also spend high (if League 1 spends low, League 2 will be perceived as a major league in the eyes of the fans). If League 2 spends low, then the best that League 1 can do is, again, to spend high (and become the only major league in the eyes of fans). Because the rewards are symmetric, we would expect League 2 to always choose to spend high as well. Given this dominant strategy for each league, the result is that both spend high and are seen as equal in the eyes of fans, and we have rival leagues.

The question from the perspective of the single dominant league outcome is whether this equilibrium can survive. Because both leagues are spending high but the rival probably doesn't have teams located in as many large-revenue markets, the rival league could fail. Competition may not be self-sustaining if the returns are too low for the rival league. Owners in a league can use revenue sharing, the draft, luxury taxes, or salary caps to transfer money among themselves and enhance survival. Alternatively, they can use scheduling penalties and playoffs that reduce the certainty of payoffs to talent stocking against the most powerful teams. However, implementing these mechanisms between leagues is more difficult and possibly illegal. So rivals may fail.

This idea also leads to some speculation about whether the dominant league can intentionally kill a rival by bidding up the price of talent. If the dominant league, with a huge war chest from past and future expected profits, starts to bid up the price of talent against a rival, then the rival may not survive. If the rival league is not as profitable or it was poorly funded at the outset, bidding up talent prices could be the end. Although there is no definitive proof of intentional strategy, this sounds an

A reasonable argument can be made that African-American baseball leagues (AABLs) were killed by the integration of MLB. Not to downplay the significant historical role of the integration of MLB, but the shenanigans killed a pretty successful entertainment enterprise, namely, AABLs. Joel Maxcy and I (Fort and Maxcy, 2001) show a number of interesting things about the relationship between MLB and AABLs. AABLs were profitable and viable. Owners did well, and star players in the AABLs were paid on a par with their white MLB counterparts. There is some evidence that AABLs were a thorn in the side of major league owners from the attendance perspective.

Integration, after Jackie Robinson joined the Brooklyn Dodgers in 1947, occurred in a brutal fashion from the perspective of AABL owners. MLB teams raided the AABLs relentlessly for talent, typically paying nothing, but at most paying pennies on the dollar. Unlike most rival leagues, AABLs were precluded from responding by just bidding up the price of talent because MLB stars did not want to play in AABLs (although there were a few MLB stars that did tour with AABLs in the off-season). Branch Rickey, president and general manager of the Brooklyn Dodgers, who signed Jackie Robinson, simply called AABLs a "racket" to justify paying no compensation for players in that league. Finally, the minor leagues were locked up by MLB, typically through ownership of minor league teams by MLB teams, so the few remaining AABL owners really had nowhere to turn for organized league play.

The result? Unlike other rival leagues, AABLs received no cheap offers to join MLB, and a profitable league endeavor simply died on the vine within 3 years of integration, by about 1950. Literally hundreds of professional baseball players were precluded from earning a living at their sport, and countless hundreds of thousands of fans lost their only access to professional baseball. Almost. MLB did expand into the previous AABL strongholds of Kansas City and Baltimore within a few years of the demise of the AABLs. However, even across color lines, the relentless single dominant league outcome prevailed.

MLB integrated with Jackie Robinson in 1947, but the aftermath was the end of a proud legacy of African-American baseball leagues.

Source: Fort and Maxcy (2001).

awful lot like what might have happened to African-American baseball leagues after integrating with MLB, as covered in the Learning Highlight: African-American Baseball Leagues as an MLB Rival.

James Quirk and I (1999) sum up the single dominant league outcome in this way:

> The profit potential of additional franchises in the megalopolis cities has been one factor driving the entry of rival leagues in the past, and might in the future as well. Still, all in all, it appears that leagues have managed to expand sufficiently to deter entry while still preserving enough vacant sites to make move threats believable, which is bad news, of course, for fans and taxpayers. (p. 136)

Enforcement of the Antitrust Laws

One last observation is that owners, acting through leagues, do not have to be allowed to behave this way. Antitrust laws are over 100 years old and are designed to handle precisely these problems. Indeed, it has often been the case, from the famous Standard Oil of Ohio case on down to the recent Microsoft case, that dominant firm outcomes have drawn the scrutiny of regulators and the courts. However, the courts and Congress have not acted to stop the single dominant league outcome in pro sports. We'll talk about this in Chapter 12.

Economic Impacts of League Expansion and Relocation Choices

The upshot of this careful management of location by and for the benefit of member owners is to keep the price of franchises quite high. As fan demand for the league's product increases over time, revenue growth is channeled to existing teams. This raises franchise prices in a way that would not happen if new teams were formed to satisfy increasing fan demand. If new teams were formed, some new owners would earn part of that increase in revenues. So, from the league's perspective, only occasionally is expansion the better way to increase the value of the league enterprise, and one would have to say that leagues have cultivated this value expertly. Refer back to Table 1.3 and refresh your memory on just how much the very judicious use of expansion has led to dramatic growth in the value of expansion franchises over time.

In addition, leagues exercise caution in this choice because it can be very difficult to undo expansion even if the economic situation warrants it. MLB made a big noise in 2001 about trying to reduce the number of teams in the league by two but never followed through. Some argue that the NHL has allowed expansion to get out of hand and may face the prospect of league contraction in the near future. Yet another reason for caution is whenever there is an expansion decision in professional sports, government scrutiny is brought to bear on the league decision process. Nothing is surer to generate House and Senate hearings on the market power position of pro sports leagues than expansion. Representatives all want the expansion franchise to go to the group in their political jurisdiction. It should come as no surprise that sports leagues would rather not have their exercise of market power under the Congressional microscope.

NEGOTIATIONS

The impacts of joint venture behavior also occur as leagues negotiate with media providers, players, and their host cities. The most striking observation about these **joint venture negotiations** is the exercise of market power. Because individual owners could handle these negotiations, economic intuition leads us to suspect that leagues produce better results for owners than they could get on their own. Let's examine the three joint venture negotiation settings: broadcasting, players, and host cities.

Joint Venture: Broadcast Rights

League negotiations with media providers are a joint venture that could be done individually by team owners. Indeed, in all leagues except the NFL, which only offers national rights, individual teams negotiate their own local TV agreements. Owners act together through their leagues to confront media providers (network, cable, and dish TV) with a league monopoly on national broadcast rights. If media providers want to broadcast a major league sport, they have no alternative but to deal with the league as a whole. This leads to value extraction by the major leagues through national TV contracts. The profits flow primarily from advertisers to the teams in sports leagues through media providers.

Joint Venture: Players

Nothing requires team owners to deal as leagues with players. In the automobile industry, for instance, GM, Ford, and Chrysler do not confront organized labor through joint venture activity. So, once again, we are led to conclude economically that the joint venture provides a better outcome for owners than acting individually toward players' labor unions.

Labor relations are such an important topic that they deserve their own chapter, Chapter 9. However, in a nutshell, the object of negotiations with players is for owners to try to keep as much of the revenues as they can while lowering costs as much as possible. Player payments are the largest cost to owners, and one aim of negotiations is to reduce this cost as much as possible. Players also produce value at the gate and on TV, and owners would like to keep as much of that revenue as they possibly can. Historically, by sticking together in negotiations as a joint venture, pro owners have been very successful at keeping the vast majority of the economic value produced by players. This was especially true prior to free agency, as we will see in Chapter 8.

Joint Venture: Host Cities

Finally, leagues produce an especially controversial joint venture outcome in the dealings of owner members with host cities. We'll devote Chapters 10 and 11 to the relationship between teams and their hosts, but they are so much in the news that you probably already have some understanding of stadium issues. There were hints about it earlier in this chapter in the Learning Highlight: Keeping the Oilers in Edmonton.

Teams put demands on their host cities for improved lease terms, stadium renovation, and even publicly funded new stadiums and arenas. As state and local governments are understandably reluctant to subsidize sports enterprises generating hundreds of millions of dollars in revenue, the teams threaten to leave for one of the viable locations their league may have kept open. Because owners, acting as leagues, have controlled the location of teams so well, the city is at a bargaining disadvantage. Hosts are unable to appeal to some other team to replace their current team. Invariably, then, it is an all-or-nothing proposition, and cities usually (but not always) give in. It should come as no surprise that teams make out like bandits.

We have covered all of the ways that leagues deal with the external environment confronting their member team owners. In the next chapter, we move on to probably the most important issue that owners must deal with among themselves, namely, competitive balance.

CHAPTER RECAP

Leagues facilitate play on the field and the business structure of sports. Coordinated behavior through leagues provides teams with opportunities they could not exploit acting alone. Teams act together but not in an anticompetitive fashion as a single entity when leagues determine play on the field. This single-entity behavior has economic consequences through scheduling and rule changes.

Nearly all of the major economic impacts on owners occur through league joint ventures. Because owners could perform most of these same functions individually, economic intuition suggests that joint ventures generate greater profits. Owners maintain exclusive territories through league cooperation. This is the fundamental source of team market power.

Expansion and relocation are important joint ventures used by leagues to maintain market power for existing teams. Leagues decide on team location based on a few important factors. The financial value of expansion is important, but so is the trade-off between leaving a location open for its believable relocation threat value against existing host cities and the chance that rival leagues will occupy viable locations. An especially troublesome issue is expansion and relocation when a location will economically support more than one team. If the single team in such an area is protected, the league is less profitable than it could be, and a rival league is offered a location where it can establish a beachhead.

All major sports leagues face rivals, but the single dominant league outcome always prevails. For fans, the result is always the same. They get less of a sport, in fewer locations, at a higher price as a result of the careful management of team locations by leagues. How is it that the single dominant league outcome remains so pervasive over time? Simple game theory shows that rival leagues can fail if, in the face of stiff competition over player talent, the resources available to the rival are insufficient. In addition, the dominant league might just be able to bid up the price of talent enough that rivals must bow out.

There are other joint ventures as well. Leagues typically negotiate TV deals, bargain with players individually and with unions, and set the bargaining position of teams relative to their host cities. In all of these situations, the league provides a superior outcome for teams than they could obtain acting alone.

KEY TERMS AND CONCEPTS

- Single-entity cooperation
- Joint ventures
- Exclusive territories
- Franchise agreements
- Quantity restrictions
- League expansion
- Team relocation
- Ownership value

- Expected local revenue impacts
- Expected national TV impacts
- Expansion fee
- Financial value of expansion
- Owner viability

- Expansion draft
- Imputed expansion fee
- Believable threat locations
- Rival leagues
- Strategic expansion/ relocation
- Single dominant league
- Joint venture negotiations

REVIEW QUESTIONS

1. What is single-entity cooperation? How is it essential to league play?
2. How can single-entity cooperation have economic impacts on member owners through scheduling? Through the setting of rules? Through setting up championships?
3. What is joint venture cooperation? What distinguishes it from single-entity cooperation?
4. Is cooperation required for owners to do the things they do as joint ventures? Give an example.
5. Explain territory definition and protection. What do member-owners get through the definition and protection of territory by their league?
6. What is a franchise agreement? Why is it necessary?
7. Describe the impact of exclusive territories on team quantity and price.
8. Define the net present value of an expansion team to a potential buyer. Define other expected league impacts due to expansion. Explain what is meant by national TV impacts at the margin due to expansion.
9. What determines the expansion fee?
10. What is an imputed expansion fee? Is it a fixed or variable cost?
11. How do expansion and relocation help owners in their negotiations with host cities? Discuss the role of believable threat locations in your answer.
12. What is a rival league? How do expansion and relocation help owners to preclude rivals?
13. List the economic impacts of strategic expansion and relocation choices by leagues.
14. List the three types of joint venture negotiations done by owners acting through leagues.
15. Is cooperation required for such negotiation to occur? If so, why? If not, then why do owners negotiate through joint venture activities?

THOUGHT PROBLEMS

1. In Table 5.1, explain the pattern of predicted impacts for widening the strike zone in 1963. After that change, which would you expect to enjoy an increase in value, relatively speaking, hitters or pitchers? Explain.

2. What does a new owner gain when purchasing a franchise from another (remember the lessons of Chapter 4 in terms of the values of ownership)? What is the most that anybody would pay in order to have a pro sports franchise?

3. What essential service did the NBL fail to provide its teams that led them to jump to the BAA? Why didn't the NBL just respond to these owner needs? What does this say about the ability of rival leagues to form?

4. Why does market power result from territory definition and protection by owners acting as leagues? Provide a nonsport example where such protection does not generate market power. What is the crucial difference between your example and a pro sports league?

5. A league is considering expansion into two different markets, A and B. Suppose all else is constant in these two markets except for each of the following differences, considered one at a time. For each difference, what happens to the expansion fee in Market A relative to Market B?
   a. Market A is a larger revenue market than Market B.
   b. Population growth is greater in Market A than in Market B.
   c. Currently, city politicians and voters are hostile to any consideration of subsidies for a sports team in Market A, but not so in Market B.
   d. Interest rates are higher in Market A than in Market B.

6. What factors determine the difference between the expected financial value of expansion and the franchise fee? Is it possible that an expansion decision could rest on one of these factors rather than on the expansion fee itself?

7. What must be true about other league impacts due to expansion for the expansion fee, F, to be $NPV_e \leq F \leq NPV_e - \Delta NPV_n$? Explain fully, including a definition of all terms in this expression. What determines the eventual actual value of F in this situation? Again, explain fully.

8. What must be true about other league impacts due to expansion for the franchise fee, F, to be $F \geq NPV_e + \Delta NPV_n$? Explain fully, including a definition of all terms in this expression. What could possibly lead a potential team owner to pay such a franchise fee in excess of the league owners' estimate of the net present value of owning the expansion team?

9. List all of the differences in the current league owners' estimate of the net present value of owning an expansion team versus selling an existing franchise and relocating it to another city. Also list the differences in the other league impacts that would occur due to relocation as opposed to expansion.

10. Ultimately, what is the most likely value of the expansion fee, F, in actual practice? Why?

11. Owners are often criticized as rapacious monopolists. Defend their behavior in terms of the expansion or franchise fee that they paid for their teams.

12. Suppose you are a league consultant. What guiding principles would you use to help plan the league's future expansion and relocation decisions? Why is a presence in the top 30 cities so important?

13. The Los Angeles market is an important market for any league. Explain how a complete comparison of the Los Angeles and Houston markets led the NFL to grant an expansion franchise to Houston rather than Los Angeles. Be sure to include in your explanation the information in the text on television ratings in Los Angeles compared to other cities in 2002.

14. Why is the NFL so much worse than MLB at covering the top 30 population centers? Does this mean they run a greater risk of a rival league? Why or why not? In your answer, be sure to present how a rival league can even get started in the first place (remember, there are two components).

15. Suppose that joint venture negotiations were not allowed on the part of owners. Explain the expected outcome on the value of TV contracts for the league members.

ADVANCED PROBLEMS

1. There are official rule changes made by agreement among owners (some require the consent of players as well). But there also are changes in the way that rules are enforced. Using Scully's (1989) ideas concerning the reasons for rule changes, why would owners alter the enforcement of particular rules. Pick an example in a single pro sport and apply that logic.

2. As detailed in the Learning Highlight: Challenging European Football's Power Structure, why would UEFA fail to give small-country teams their own championship round? Think along the lines of giving members what they want.

3. It seems these days that everybody wants a pro sports team. But, almost universally, expansion teams are weak competitors and stay that way for quite some time. For example, Quirk and Fort (1992, pp. 251–252) offer the following evidence on the number of years that it takes expansion teams to reach 0.500 over the period 1900 to 1989:

LEAGUE	SHORTEST TIME TO 0.500	AVERAGE TIME TO 0.500	LONGEST TIME TO 0.500
MLB	2 years (Angels)	8.2 years	15 years (Mariners)
NFL	3 years (Bengals, Seahawks)	5.5 years	13 years (Saints)
NBA	2 years (Bucks)	5.6 years	10 years (New Orleans Jazz)
NHL	2 years (Blues)	6.3 years	14 years (Devils)

Given the bleak prospects for an expansion team on average in any league, how would you explain the high demand for new teams on the part of the residents of some cities?

Given the data, what do you think expansion does to the overall quality of league play from the fans' perspective? How does this enter into the determination of the expansion fee by a league?

What factors would explain the difference between the shortest time to 0.500 and the longest time to 0.500 in each league? (Hint: Think about the lessons from Chapter 2.)

4. When free agency was introduced in the NFL after the 1992 season, some argued that expansion teams would have an easier time competing than in the past because new owners could just buy great talent and enter the league with a running start. Using the data in Table 5.2, would you have made the same prediction? (Hint: Remember that free agency started in 1976 in MLB. Compare expansion team success before and after that year.) Derive the same information shown in Table 5.2 for NFL expansion and see if your prediction would have been correct. Explain this outcome in terms of the optimal choice of talent for expansion teams.

5. What possible economic justification was there for MLB's expansion Colorado Rockies and Florida Marlins to agree to forgo a share of the national TV contract for their first two years of existence? Explain in terms of both the current league owners' estimate of the net present value of the expansion teams to the new owners and in terms of the other expected league impacts due to expansion.

6. We saw in Chapter 2 that sports team owners use price discrimination to raise their profits above the level that could be made by charging fans a single price. This is especially true of so-called quality game pricing where some teams now charge more when a popular opponent comes to town or late in the season when playoffs are being decided. Critics have described these price discrimination mechanisms as "gravy" on top of the usual profits that could be made. The critics suggest that owners could do quite nicely without them and garner goodwill from fans. Use the logic of imputed expansion fees to show that profits from price discrimination are not just extra, over and above the profit that could be made without price discrimination.

7. Refer to Learning Highlight: Keeping the Oilers in Edmonton.
   a. Why did the Canadian government officials mentioned in the highlight impose the rule that local owners had a chance to buy the team at what would surely be an artificially low amount relative to prices that typically come out of the market for NHL franchises? What was Peter Pocklington's response when he put the team up for sale in 1997?
   b. How did the accounting lessons from Chapter 2 figure into EIG's success at generating the required $70 million payment?
   c. What was the source of a potential windfall gain for EIG if it does sell the Oilers after 2004? Would you sell the Oilers if you were EIG? Why or why not?

8. What led the NFL and the AFL (version IV) to both put teams in Dallas, Texas, in 1960? Be careful to distinguish the motivation of the NFL from that of the AFL. Ultimately, the AFL Texans left to become the Kansas City Chiefs. Does that necessarily mean that the NFL won in the battle for territorial rights against the AFL in this case? Why or why not?

9. Al Davis, now owner of the Oakland Raiders, was commissioner of the AFL (version IV) at the time of the merger between the NFL and the AFL in 1969. He urged the AFL owners not to merge, arguing that in a very short time the AFL would become the dominant professional football league. Using a version of Figure 5.1, what was Davis thinking in terms of the rival league talent dilemma?

10. Recount the death of the PCL. How is it related to the end of AABLs in the Learning Highlight: African-American Baseball Leagues as an MLB Rival? And how is the death of both leagues related to game theory and the single dominant league given in the text? Explain using Figure 5.1.

INTERNET RESOURCES

For a host of additional material and questions for thought, visit this book's Web site at www.prenhall.com/fort.

REFERENCES

Fort, Rodney. "Revenue Disparity and Competitive Balance in Major League Baseball." Statement for the U.S. Senate Subcommittee on Antitrust, November 17, 2000.

Fort, Rodney, and Joel Maxcy. "The Demise of African-American Baseball Leagues: A Rival League Explanation," *Journal of Sports Economics* 2 (2001): 35–49.

Fort, Rodney, and James Quirk. "Cross-Subsidization, Incentives, and Outcomes in Professional Team Sports Leagues," *Journal of Economic Literature* 23 (1995): 1265–1299.

Fort, Rodney, and James Quirk. "Introducing a Competitive Economic Environment into Professional Sports," in *Advances in the Economics of Sports*, vol. 2, ed. Wallace Hendricks. Greenwich, CT: JAI Press, 1997.

Neale, Walter C. "The Peculiar Economics of Professional Sports," *Quarterly Journal of Economics* 78 (1964): 1–14.

Quirk, James, and Rodney D. Fort. *Pay Dirt: The Business of Pro Team Sports*. Princeton, NJ: Princeton University Press, 1992.

Quirk, James, and Rodney D. Fort. *Hardball: The Abuse of Power in Pro Team Sports*. Princeton, NJ: Princeton University Press, 1999.

Scully, Gerald. *The Business of Major League Baseball*. Chicago, IL: University of Chicago Press, 1989.

Sports Market Outcomes, Part II: Leagues and Competitive Balance

Chapter Objectives

After reading this chapter, you should be able to:

- ■ *Use the two-team diagram of a pro sports league to determine equilibrium winning percents and payrolls.*

- ■ *Understand that the cause of winning imbalance and payroll imbalance is the underlying imbalance in revenue potential across the league.*

- ■ *Repeat the lessons of the historical data on competitive imbalance in pro sports leagues.*

- ■ *Understand whether the various mechanisms touted to enhance competitive balance—such as revenue sharing, the draft, luxury taxes, and salary caps—actually will accomplish that task.*

- ■ *See why it is imperative that leagues be able to discipline member teams to follow league policies, especially those affecting competitive imbalance.*

*It's too late merely to view with alarm the mess into which base-
ball has managed to get itself. The time has come to sound the
alarm before the national pastime, as it still calls itself, collapses
under the weight of its own archaic rules, mismanagement, lack
of leadership, greed, and plain stupidity. If this sounds like
a harsh indictment of what was once America's "only game in
town"—well, I mean it to be just that. Only a rude awakening,
followed by drastic action, can save the sport from oblivion. . . .
The symptoms of near disaster are plain enough: The Yankees
make an almost annual farce of the American League pennant
race—a most unhealthy condition. . . . Interest in big-league
baseball is on the downgrade. So is attendance generally, in spite
of glowing Yankee, Brave, and Dodger figures. An even greater
portion of the Nation's amusement dollar is being diverted from
baseball to other spectator sports and to participation sports
such as golf, bowling, boating, and hunting and fishing.*

—BILL VEECK

*As told to Murray Robinson, "I Know Who's Killing Baseball," article 1 in a series for the
Hearst newspapers. Found in Hearings Before the Subcommittee on Antitrust and Monopoly,
Committee on the Judiciary, U.S. Senate, 85th Cong., 2nd Sess., July 1958, p. 717.*

Perhaps you were surprised to see that this statement was made in
1958. It sounds almost exactly like the lament you could find in the
press or popular accounts of the problems in pro sports, such as
Bob Costas's impassioned assessment of MLB in his book *Fair Ball*.
In this chapter, we address the primary internal issue confronting owners in a pro sports league, namely, competitive imbalance. We will see
how, at times, individual owner actions can be detrimental to overall
league welfare, spurring pro leagues to develop mechanisms ostensibly
designed to enhance competitive balance. But, as with most things, we
will also see that things are not always as they are touted to be. Some
of these mechanisms actually do not affect competitive balance at all.
Instead, they reallocate sports revenues from some owners to others
and from players to owners.

COMPETITIVE IMBALANCE

So far, it looks like the world is a sports league's oyster. Exclusive territories are carefully maintained to the dramatic economic benefit of the current group of owners. One
of the downsides to territorial exclusivity is the possibility of rival leagues. Owners

acting together as a league must be careful to avert rival leagues. However, the maintenance of exclusive territories also has another potential downside, called **competitive imbalance**. A league suffers from competitive imbalance if, year after year, there are very strong and very weak teams and the mix of strong and weak teams doesn't change. The danger is that competitive imbalance, if bad enough, can reduce fan interest in the league product and, eventually, individual team profits. This potential danger follows from the uncertainty of outcome hypothesis from Chapter 2. Under that hypothesis, fans prefer closer games to blowouts and a changing mix of teams in postseason play. If the hypothesis holds for fans, competitive imbalance would drive fans of losing teams that nearly never appear in postseason play away from watching home games. Those teams would become economically unviable, owners would get out of the game, and the league would not be able to find replacement owners. The spillover losses to the remaining owners would come in the form of lost shared revenue and a reduction in the total fan base that would watch postseason play. In short, the entire league would suffer economically. The *Blue Ribbon Panel Report* (Levin, Mitchell, Volcker, and Will, 2000) argues the case for MLB:

"The presence in the game of clubs, perhaps a majority, that are chronically uncompetitive, alongside clubs that routinely dominate the postseason, undermines the public interest and confidence in the sport."
—*Blue Ribbon Panel Report* (Levin, Mitchell, Volcker, and Will, 2000)

> While most fans do not demand or expect that their team will reach postseason play each year, some have ample reason to believe that the club they root for will remain chronically uncompetitive. Because revenue Quartile III and IV clubs have not been winners and have barely been participants in the postseason for the past 5 years, many fans have come to believe that it is unlikely these clubs will reverse that fate in the next few years. The presence in the game of clubs, perhaps a majority, that are chronically uncompetitive, alongside clubs that routinely dominate the postseason, undermines the public interest and confidence in the sport. (p. 42)

But whether competitive imbalance is a problem begs an examination of competitive imbalance in the first place. For the rest of the chapter, let's examine three things. What causes competitive imbalance in the first place? What do the data on competitive imbalance tell us (has balance worsened over time in pro sports)? Finally, how have pro sports leagues tried to handle competitive imbalance and what other techniques could be used to enhance league balance?

The Theory Behind Competitive Imbalance

Revenue disparity drives competitive imbalance in all leagues. Revenue disparity is guaranteed once owners are granted exclusive geographic franchises because different franchise areas have different drawing power. This generates different revenues and different abilities to buy the talent required to win. Subject to the usual caveats concerning uncertainty, higher revenues yield better teams on average. Exclusive territories do provide market power positions for owners, but they lead to competitive imbalance.

Graphical Analysis of League Winning Percents It is easy to show the winning percent outcome in a league with a simplified graphical analysis of a two-team league.

Figure 6.1 Smaller- and Larger-Revenue Market Teams in a Two-Team League

The small-market team has lower marginal revenue for all levels of winning percent than the large-market team. $MR_L(W) > MR_S(W)$ for all W. An example is shown at $W = 0.250$.

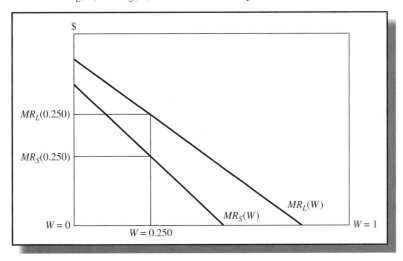

Figure 6.1 shows the marginal revenue functions of two owners. Following our simplification from Chapter 4 that owners produce winning for fans, the x-axis measures winning percent from 0 to 1. If we measure talent in units that it takes to produce one more unit of winning percent, then the x-axis also measures the amount of talent hired by each owner. We'll assume that talent is measured in these units.

Both a larger-revenue market owner and a smaller-revenue market owner are shown in Figure 6.1. Remember, the only way it makes sense to talk about larger-market and smaller-market owners is in terms of the revenues that they can generate in their respective locations. $MR_L(W)$ is the marginal revenue from winning percent for the larger-revenue market owner and $MR_S(W)$ is the marginal revenue from winning percent for the smaller-revenue market owner. The idea of smaller- and larger-revenue markets is purposely exaggerated in Figure 6.1 to make the point clearly. Every level of winning is more valuable to the larger-revenue market owner than it is to the smaller-market owner; that is, $MR_L(W) > MR_S(W)$ for all levels of winning percent, W. For example, at $W = 0.250$ (the teams were to win one-fourth of their games) $MR_L(0.250) > MR_S(0.250)$, and the same would be true for every other level of winning percent.

Figure 6.2 is a useful device in this simplified, two-team world. It shows exactly the same information that was contained in Figure 6.1, but it makes it easy to present the equilibrium winning percents for the two owners. Winning for the larger-market team is measured from zero to one on the x-axis from left to right. Winning for the smaller-market team is measured from zero to one on the x-axis from right to left. The two marginal revenue functions, $MR_L(W)$ and $MR_S(W)$, show precisely the same relationship between winning percent and marginal revenue as before; they are just relocated with respect to their new graphical origins. The origin for the smaller-revenue market team is in the lower-right corner, and the origin for the larger-revenue market team is in the lower-left corner.

Figure 6.2 Two-Team League Revised

This depiction of the two-team league is a useful adaptation of Figure 6.1. The large-market team is portrayed from left to right, and the small market team is portrayed from right to left. The sum of winning percents in a two-team league equals one, $W_L^1 = 1 - W_S^1$. At that winning percent outcome, $MR_L^1 > MR_S^1$; therefore, the market cannot be at equilibrium because the large-market team wishes to buy more talent and the small-market team will sell it.

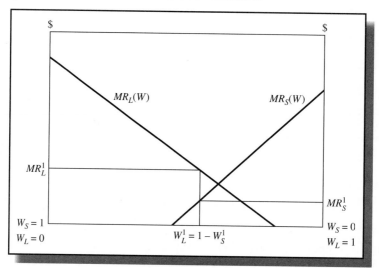

We will assume that each of the owners in our two-team league must compete for talent. We will also need to remember a useful fact: The sum of the winning percents in any league must equal half the number of teams. The average winning percent in any league is 0.500. The formula for the average is $\frac{1}{n}\sum_{i=1}^{n} W_i = 0.500$, where n is the number of teams and W_i is the winning percent of team i. Multiplying both sides by the number of teams, n, gives $\sum_{i=1}^{n} W_i = 0.500n$; that is, the sum of the winning percents is equal to half the number of teams. Thus, in this two-team world, the sum of winning percents must be equal to one. This means that $W_L + W_S = 1$ everywhere along the x-axis, or that $W_L = 1 - W_S$. With these preliminaries out of the way, we're ready to examine winning percent outcomes.

Equilibrium Winning Percents   Suppose that talent has been chosen so that the winning percent for the larger-market team is W_L^1. Because the sum of winning percents must equal one, we know that $W_L^1 = 1 - W_S^1$, as shown in Figure 6.2. However, this cannot be an equilibrium winning percent outcome. At this outcome, we know that $MR_L^1 > MR_S^1$. This means that the larger-market owner would make more money than the smaller-market owner on the last unit of talent hired by the smaller-market owner. The most that the smaller-market owner will pay is MR_S^1, but the larger-market owner can afford to pay up to $MR_L^1 > MR_S^1$. Thus, the larger-market owner can make an offer to the player supplying that last unit of talent that is greater than the amount the smaller-market owner will pay. That unit of talent would move to the larger-market team, and the outcome would be an increase in the winning percent of the larger-market team. This would be true as long as the teams were to the left of the intersection of the marginal revenue functions.

The same logic, but in the opposite direction, would hold if talent is chosen so that $MR_S(W) > MR_L(W)$. In that case, the smaller-market owner would bid talent away from the larger-market owner. This may seem odd at first since every unit of talent is worth more to the large-market owner. But remember we're comparing between the two *at the margin*. Once the larger-revenue owner has a high level of talent, the very next unit under consideration could be worth more to the smaller-revenue owner. This would be true for all talent combinations to the right of the intersection of the marginal revenue functions.

There is only one place where the two owners no longer try to bid talent away from each other. That allocation will be the **winning percent equilibrium**. In equilibrium, it must be the case that $MR_L(W) = MR_S(W)$, that is, at the intersection of the two marginal revenue functions. This is shown in Figure 6.3 at $MR_L^*(W) = MR_S^*(W)$ so that $W_L^* = 1 - W_S^*$.

Important Features of the Competitive Equilibrium There are three important features in the equilibrium winning percent outcome shown in Figure 6.3:

1. Marginal revenues are equal across teams, that is $MR_L^*(W) = MR_S^*(W)$.
2. Revenue imbalance causes competitive imbalance.
3. Revenue imbalance causes payroll imbalance.

The first feature describes equilibrium and provides an important observation. Both owners confront the same price of talent, and that price equals marginal revenue for both teams. While the total amount of talent hired by the larger-revenue owner is greater, the marginal value to both owners of another unit of talent is equal. The important

Figure 6.3
Market Equilibrium
Because the sum of winning percents in a two-team league equals one, $W_L^* = 1 - W_S^*$. The result is an equilibrium outcome. At $MR_L^* = MR_S^*$, neither team wishes to alter its talent choice. The market equilibrium price of talent is $P = MR_L^* = MR_S^*$.

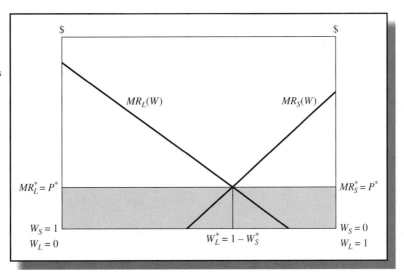

observation is that there is a limit on talent purchases by the larger-revenue market owner. The larger-revenue market owner will not buy all the great talent because, eventually, the marginal unit of talent is more valuable to the smaller-revenue owner.

The second feature of the competitive talent equilibrium is that the larger-revenue market team has a higher winning percent than the smaller-revenue market team. This also is easy to see in Figure 6.3 because equilibrium is to the right of 0.500 for the larger-revenue market team. This only makes sense; every single unit of talent hired produced winning that was more valuable to the larger-market owner. The larger-revenue owner therefore hires more talent and wins more.

Don't lose sight of this important distinction. A common statement about imbalance is that larger-market owners buy all of the great talent because they have such high revenues. This actually clouds the true line of causality. Profit-maximizing owners evaluate the revenue potential of their market. If that market will pay the most for a high quality team, the owner buys the talent to make it so. Only then can the owner collect the high level of revenues from fans at the gate and from TV rights fees. As long as there are markets that generate different amounts of revenue for different quality teams, there will be owners who choose talent so as to generate competitive imbalance.

The final important feature of the equilibrium winning percent outcome can be seen as follows, using Figure 6.3. P denotes the price of one unit of talent. Because we measure talent in terms of units that generate one more unit of winning percent, in equilibrium $MR_L(W) = MR_S(W) = P^*$. To buy that last unit of talent, each owner paid P^*. Given this result, it is easy to see how much each owner pays, in total, for the winning percent that they choose. The bill for the larger-market owner is the left-hand shaded rectangle, calculated as $P^*W_L^*$; that is, the price of each unit of winning multiplied by the number of units of winning. This amount also represents the payment to talent because we have measured talent in units that produce each unit of winning percent. Therefore, the shaded rectangle also represents the total payment to talent hired by the larger-revenue market owner. Similarly, the right-hand shaded rectangle is the smaller-market owner's talent bill, calculated as $P^*W_S^*$. The conclusion is that the larger-revenue market owner spends more on talent than does the smaller-revenue market owner. So, along with competitive imbalance, there will be **payroll imbalance** as long as there are large- and smaller-revenue market areas. Again, don't lose sight of this line of causality. The existence of market areas that generate different amounts of revenue for different quality teams drives both competitive imbalance and payroll imbalance.

Note that this equilibrium outcome suggests that the larger the revenue imbalance, the larger the competitive imbalance. Suppose that $MR_L(W)$ shifts to the right. Perhaps incomes in the larger-revenue market increase or population rises. You should be able to convince yourself that the following will occur. First, the price of a unit of talent will increase. Second, talent spending by the larger-revenue market owner will increase; they buy more talent at the new higher price. Third, because the price of talent is rising in the inelastic portion of the smaller-revenue owner's marginal revenue function, spending by the smaller-revenue market owner also rises. Finally, the winning percent of the larger-revenue market team increases.

The Data on Competitive Imbalance The theory informs us that there will be competitive imbalance and payroll imbalance as long as owners have unequal earning power and that competitive imbalance worsens the more imbalanced revenues become.

Before we turn to the remedies that have been suggested for this competitive imbalance, let's look at the data of actual competitive balance outcomes in pro sports leagues. We touched on revenue imbalance in Chapters 2 and 3. Here, we extend the idea by looking at imbalances in revenues, payrolls, winning percents, and championships. But first we must specify just how we're going to measure competitive imbalance.

Competitive Imbalance Measurements We will use three measures of competitive imbalance in pro sports leagues. A brief overview of these measurements is given here (your instructor may point you to more in-depth treatments as needed). We will use the **Gini coefficient** to measure revenue and payroll inequality. You may have seen the Gini coefficient used to describe income inequality in your basic economics course. The Gini coefficient lies between zero and one; the larger the Gini coefficient, the greater the inequality in revenues or payrolls between owners in a league. For example, if the Gini coefficient were equal to one, a single owner would have literally all of the revenue in a league. In practice, this won't happen, but such an outcome is the theoretical limit on revenue inequality.

The Gini coefficient proves problematic in measuring the inequality in winning (see Utt and Fort, 2002, for a complete discussion). If there are more than two teams in a league, it is theoretically impossible for one owner to have all of the wins due to the zero-sum nature of league play. For example, in a three-team league where each team plays the other only once, there are three total games. But the most that a single team can win is two games. So for winning percent we turn to another measure.

The standard deviation of winning percent is a statistical measure of the spread of winning percent around its league-average value of 0.500. The smaller the standard deviation, the lower the spread and the closer should be the winning outcomes. If we check the behavior of the standard deviation of winning percent over time, any increase represents growing competitive imbalance whereas any decrease means the league has become more balanced over time. There is one added complication.

The standard deviation is sensitive to season length. For example, think of a two-team league playing a ten game schedule. One team wins nine games and the other team only wins one. The standard deviation of winning percent is 0.566. Now suppose the two teams play a twelve game schedule. The same team wins only one game and the other eleven. Now the standard deviation is 0.589 even though it is reasonable to say the imbalance is the same. The following invention controls for this characteristic of the standard deviation and provides a tidy comparison of winning percents over time.

The invention is the standard deviation of winning percent in a perfectly balanced league. Suppose that the probability any team in the league beats another literally is 0.5 (the proverbial "on any given day any team can beat any other" actually is true here). It ends up (an easy presentation is in Fort and Quirk, 1995) that the standard deviation of winning percent in this version of a perfectly balanced league is $\frac{0.5}{\sqrt{m}}$, where m is the length of the season measured in games. If we divide the actual standard deviation by the standard deviation for a perfectly balanced league, we have controlled for any changes in season length by the denominator $\sqrt{m}$. This **standard deviation ratio** of actual to perfectly balanced standard deviations is greater than or equal to one. The closer the measure is to one, the more balanced the league is. We will use this ratio to compare winning percents over time in pro sports leagues.

Our final measure of competitive imbalance concerns the postseason. Suppose a division in a league has fifteen teams. If playoff appearances were equally likely, we'd expect to see each team win the division once every fifteen years. Naturally, then, a measure of postseason balance is the average number of years between championships for each of the teams in the league. This measure has the added advantage of controlling for the fact that some teams that were in the league longer had a greater number of chances to get to the postseason. We could calculate the Gini coefficient (Quirk and Fort, 1992), but this one is easier. And off we go.

Revenue Imbalance. Table 6.1 shows Gini coefficients for **revenue imbalance** in the four pro sports leagues. Because league choices on team location help determine revenues, the data are shown at the league level. The revenue data used to calculate

Table 6.1 Gini Coefficients for Revenue Imbalance in Pro Sports Leagues

YEAR	MLB	AL	NL	NBA	NFL	NHL	SPORTS ECONOMY AVERAGE
1930s average	0.242	0.241	0.224				
1940s average	0.182	0.182	0.170				
1950s average	0.210	0.217	0.180	0.214	0.151	0.155	0.190
1980s average	0.184	0.184	0.176				
1990	0.158	0.173	0.137	0.139	0.047	0.119	
1991	0.154	0.157	0.141	0.151	0.051	0.162	
1992	0.149	0.158	0.119	0.158	0.037	0.184	
1993	0.140	0.147	0.128	0.135	0.054	0.197	
1994	0.161	0.176	0.140	0.137	0.061	0.198	
1995	0.186	0.195	0.168	0.157	0.077	0.181	
1996	0.193	0.220	0.153	0.172	0.059	0.156	
1997	0.201	0.222	0.170		0.067		
1998				0.189	0.072		
1999	0.209	0.221	0.191	0.141	0.081	0.150	
1990s average	0.172	0.185	0.150	0.153	0.061	0.168	0.146
Pre-stoppage average	0.150	0.159	0.131	0.150		0.172	
Post-stoppage average	0.201	0.221	0.171	0.165		0.153	
2000	0.176	0.176	0.172		0.075		
2001	0.153	0.166	0.136	0.119	0.070	0.160	
2002	0.158	0.165	0.148	0.125	0.072	0.146	
2003	0.126	0.145	0.102		0.070		
2000s average	0.153	0.163	0.140	0.122	0.072	0.153	0.133

Notes: Pre-stoppage and post-stoppage are calculated according to the following work stoppages: MLB 1994–1995; NBA 1998; NHL 1994.

Sources: All author's calculations, according to the formula in the text, from revenue data in the Congressional Hearings discussed and referenced in Chapter 12; *Financial World* (typically the June and July volumes, 1989–1997); *Forbes* (www.forbes.com, annually since 1998); and Scully (1989).

these coefficients came from Congressional hearings in the 1950s, from Professor Gerald Scully for the some of the 1980s in MLB, and more recently from reports in *Financial World* and *Forbes* magazines. We need to be clear about this from the outset: Different analysts have different feelings about the veracity of the data behind this analysis. For example, each year, team owners dispute the *Forbes* reports. Also note that there weren't enough data to yield averages for some decades. However, these data are all we have, so let's see what they suggest about revenue inequality. First, we'll examine each league individually.

MLB typically battles the NHL as the league with the worst revenue imbalance. However, revenue balance has steadily improved in MLB from the 1950s to the present. A look at the past fifteen years shows revenue imbalance on a roller coaster ride, rising after the strike of 1994–1995 and falling again into the 2000s. In summary, as measured by the Gini coefficient, revenues have become more balanced by about 27 percent in MLB since the 1950s.

In the NBA, revenue balance has also improved steadily since the 1950s. While it suffered the worst revenue imbalance of all leagues in the 1950s, only the NFL now exhibits more revenue balance than basketball. Indeed, NBA revenues have become more balanced by about 43 percent since the 1950s, and its most dramatic gains occurred after the lockout of 1998.

The NFL always is the most balanced league in terms of revenues. This is no surprise given that the team owners in the league share nearly all of its revenues. While the league enjoyed a 52 percent improvement in revenue balance since the 1950s, imbalance has been climbing through the 2000s.

Finally, we come to hockey. The NHL has shown literally no improvement in revenue balance over the period in Table 6.1. Revenue imbalance increased in the 1990s but has shown some recent improvement; however, the NHL is now tied with MLB as the league with the most revenue imbalance among all pro sports leagues.

Overall, suppose we think of the four major leagues as a "sports economy" of sorts. On average across the decades where there are data for all four sports, revenue balance has improved without fail since the 1950s. Indeed, as measured by the Gini coefficient, there has been a 28 percent improvement in revenue balance in this sports economy. There are two general reasons why this may have occurred. On the one hand, leagues have enacted policies designed to enhance revenue balance. But this has always been the case in the NFL, and that league still shows steady improvement. Other underlying factors have to do with the source of revenues in the first place, namely, fan willingness to pay. As population centers grow larger and perhaps richer, one would expect the willingness to pay by fans to also begin to equate between team locations. But only future research will answer this question.

Payroll Imbalance.   Gini coefficients for payroll imbalance, again at the league-wide level where these amounts are determined by competition in the market for talent, are shown in Table 6.2. These data also are from Congressional hearings, popular media accounts, and open to the same type of disagreement noted earlier for revenues. But they are what we have, and here is what the data appear to tell us about payroll imbalance.

Table 6.2 Gini Coefficients for Payroll Imbalance in Pro Sports Leagues

YEAR	MLB OD	MLB EOS	AL EOS	NL EOS	NBA	NFL	NHL	SPORTS ECONOMY AVERAGE
1950s average		0.133	0.144	0.112	0.116	0.062	0.103	0.133
1980s average	0.153	0.144	0.158	0.119	0.116	0.078		0.119
1990	0.123	0.131	0.155	0.096	0.068	0.083	0.133	
1991	0.141	0.162	0.172	0.145	0.086	0.070	0.128	
1992	0.165	0.164	0.167	0.155	0.084	0.078	0.130	
1993	0.167	0.181	0.149	0.200	0.084	0.108	0.157	
1994	0.147	0.150	0.115	0.174	0.118	0.048	0.147	
1995	0.151	0.186	0.161	0.199	0.102	0.068	0.135	
1996	0.176	0.208	0.243	0.158	0.136	0.072		
1997	0.189	0.197	0.212	0.171	0.132	0.082		
1998	0.210	0.238	0.231	0.235	0.112	0.067	0.137	
1999	0.250	0.258	0.279	0.233	0.122	0.068	0.139	
1990s average	0.172	0.188	0.188	0.177	0.104	0.074	0.138	0.149
Pre-stoppage average	0.149	0.160	0.161	0.149	0.101		0.139	
Post-stoppage average	0.206	0.225	0.241	0.199			0.138	
2000	0.221	0.239	0.237	0.233	0.131	0.037	0.195	
2001	0.213	0.225	0.211	0.185	0.088	0.095	0.208	
2002	0.202	0.204	0.228	0.177	0.116	0.104	0.220	
2003	0.212				0.134	0.059	0.197	
2004	0.243					0.080		
2000s average	0.218	0.223	0.225	0.198	0.117	0.075	0.205	0.174

Notes: Pre-stoppage and post-stoppage are calculated according to the following work stoppages: MLB 1994–1995; NBA 1998; NHL 1994.

EOS = end of season.
OD = opening day.

Sources: All author's calculations, according to the formula in the text, from payroll data as follows.

MLB: Congressional hearings discussed in Chapter 12; *USAToday; New York Times; San Francisco Chronicle; Baseball Weekly;* the Associated Press; Forbes.com; and the *Los Angeles Times.* Latest possible publication date criterion. USAToday.com.

NBA: Fort and Quirk (1995); Patricia Bender's "Various Basketball Stuff" (www.dfw.net/~patricia/), and USAToday.com.

NFL: NFLPA 2000 and USAToday.com.

NHL: *Financial World, Hockey News,* USAToday.com.

MLB has always had the most payroll imbalance of all leagues, except for the NFL in the 1950s. Payroll imbalance has worsened about 67 percent in baseball since the 1950s. Only the NHL shows more growth in payroll imbalance than baseball. Interestingly, while not shown in Table 6.2 (no table can show everything!), the imbalance has been worse in the AL than in the NL in every tabled decade.

Only the NFL shows more payroll balance than the NBA. The level of payroll balance in basketball has remained pretty much unchanged since the 1950s, despite a bit of an improvement early in the 1990s. This should come as no surprise because we just saw how the NBA also has shown no change in revenue imbalance over the same time period.

Football has been the most balanced league in terms of payrolls except for the 1950s when it was the most unbalanced in all of pro sports. In the period from the 1950s to the 1980s, the data clearly show that the league found a different path, and payroll balance among owners in the league improved 60 percent. Note that this is well before the NFL salary cap of 1994. Interestingly, since the 1980s payroll balance in the NFL has remained static.

Finally, we turn to hockey. Since the 1950s, payroll imbalance in the NHL worsened nearly 100 percent, and there were record-setting increases in every decade. Clearly in the last five years the NHL has come to rival even MLB in its level of payroll imbalance.

Taking our sports economy viewpoint, payroll imbalance has worsened in pro sports overall, despite an improvement between the 1950s and the 1980s. As measured by Gini coefficients, payroll imbalance has worsened by 34 percent across the four major pro sports leagues. The only improvement was in the NFL, and that all occurred up to the 1980s. We are left with the conclusion that there must be a significant and growing gap in the value of talent between smaller- and larger-revenue markets in nearly all pro sports leagues.

Winning Percent Imbalance   Recall that our measure of winning percent imbalance is the ratio of the actual standard deviation to the standard deviation of a perfectly balanced version of the league. Here, for MLB, we must be careful to calculate this measure only over the games where it is created. Because there are no games between the AL and NL until very recently, and few of them even now, we will calculate our ratio measure separately for the AL and NL. For the other three pro sports leagues, play occurs between nearly all teams in each league, so the measure is calculated league wide. Remember that there need be no apology for the source of these data—anybody can find game outcomes on a daily basis.

In MLB for both the AL and NL winning percent imbalance has fallen significantly (13% in the AL and 42% in the NL). But look carefully at Table 6.3 and you'll notice that winning percent imbalance is creeping upward in both the AL and NL. Indeed, in the AL, this measure of imbalance has climbed back to near historic levels in the 2000s. Although the AL has almost always been more imbalanced than the NL, it is 18 percent more so over the last five years shown in Table 6.3.

Since it began play in 1947, winning percent imbalance in the NBA has remained virtually unchanged to the present day. The NBA has been the most unbalanced league in terms of winning percent in every decade except the 1950s, when the Yankees reigned supreme in MLB's AL. In the years of the current decade, however, there has been a slight improvement in the NBA over the previous two decades, the 1980s and 1990s.

Winning percent imbalance in the NFL is completely consistent with our earlier observations about revenue and payroll imbalance for the league. Except for the earliest two decades in Table 6.3, the NFL has had the most balanced winning

Table 6.3 Standard Deviation Ratio of Winning Percent Imbalance in Pro Sports Leagues

YEAR	MLB–AL	MLB–NL	NBA	NFL	NHL	SPORTS ECONOMY AVERAGE
1901–1909 average	2.55	3.28				
1910–1919 average	2.71	2.36			1.34	
1920–1929 average	2.40	2.31		1.96	1.79	
1930–1939 average	2.79	2.37		1.70	1.63	
1940–1949 average	2.29	2.50	2.58	1.85	1.91	2.16
1950–1959 average	2.52	2.06	2.18	1.52	2.04	2.06
1960–1969 average	2.01	2.18	2.90	1.68	2.00	2.15
1970–1979 average	1.96	1.84	2.39	1.62	2.64	2.09
1980–1989 average	1.75	1.69	2.72	1.52	2.02	1.94
1990	1.45	1.45	3.15	1.62	1.69	
1991	1.54	1.56	2.86	1.74	1.87	
1992	1.61	1.68	2.89	1.65	1.72	
1993	1.39	2.37	2.87	1.28	2.66	
1994	1.72	1.82	3.21	1.40	1.87	
1995	2.12	1.54	2.92	1.22	1.54	
1996	1.77	1.42	3.10	1.47	2.09	
1997	1.58	1.49	3.46	1.46	1.41	
1998	2.06	2.24	3.43	1.71	1.74	
1999	1.93	2.01	2.88	1.49	1.75	
1990–1999 average	1.72	1.76	3.08	1.51	1.83	1.98
Pre-stoppage average	1.50	1.76	3.06		1.96	
Post-stoppage average	1.83	1.79			1.75	
2000	1.37	1.76	2.92	1.58	1.88	
2001	2.41	1.65	2.85	1.63	1.95	
2002	2.69	2.06	2.50	1.32	1.66	
2003	2.48	1.78	2.27	1.54	1.69	
2004	2.11	2.20	2.65		1.73	
2000s average	2.21	1.89	2.64	1.52	1.78	2.03

Notes: Pre-stoppage and post-stoppage are calculated according to the following work stoppages: MLB 1994–1995; NBA 1998; NHL 1994.

Sources: All author's calculations, according to the formula in the text (ties count as half a winning percent point), from final standings at baseballreference.com, basketballreference.com, pro-footballreference.com, and (hockey) USAToday.com.

percents among teams of all pro sports leagues. On top of that, winning percent imbalance has declined 23 percent since its inception in 1922. Notice that no substantial gains were associated with the institution of the salary cap in 1994. The gains in balance occurred after extensive revenue sharing was already in force. This suggests that the revenue base of NFL markets has been gradually equalizing over time.

Our last look at the NHL shows it to be quite unbalanced as measured by winning percents up to the 1970s. Indeed, measured overall, the league looks to have worsened in terms of winning percent imbalance by a full 33 percent since it began play in 1918. But such a conclusion misses the improvements that have occurred since the 1970s, when winning percent imbalance was at its historically worst levels ever. Since the 1970s, winning percent balance has improved 33 percent in the NHL. Indeed, through the 2000s, play in the NHL is only marginally less balanced than in the NFL.

We close out our investigation with a quick look at winning percent imbalance across the sports economy. Since the 1940s, when all four leagues first existed simultaneously, winning percent imbalance has declined a modest 7 percent, and it has been a continual up-and-down process. The forces determining the distribution of team quality have changed a bit in favor of a more equal distribution but not much and not by much in any given decade since the 1940s.

Did You Know?
Championship outcomes are dominated by a small number of teams in all leagues. The NFL is the most balanced of all pro sports leagues in terms of championships. The NBA and the NHL have the least championship balance.

Championship Imbalance.   Our investigation of imbalance thus far has concerned outcomes during a given season—revenues are tallied at the end of the season, payrolls are set prior to the start of a season, and winning percents are calculated after the last regular season game is played. But **championship imbalance**, or postseason imbalance, also matters to fans. It's not just whether play during the season was competitively balanced; it also matters which teams make it into the playoffs.

Remember we have chosen a simple way to analyze the data on championships—the amount of time between titles. Table 6.4 shows years per title for AL and NL champions in MLB, and conference champions for the other three pro sports leagues. The entries are restricted to relatively more successful teams with less than ten years between championships. The data strongly indicate that titles are unequally distributed and, typically, go in favor of larger-revenue market teams. Teams in New York and Los Angeles have the lowest years per title in all leagues except hockey, and the larger-revenue market Canadian cities of Ottawa and Montreal dominate that league. It's always a judgment call as to which teams fall into the larger-revenue and smaller-revenue markets, but here goes.

Did You Know?
On average, MLB teams in New York (Yankees and Giants) typically have won league championships every 3 or 4 years over the history of the league.

Only remotely resembling smaller-revenue markets are Florida and Oakland in MLB; Syracuse and Rochester in the NBA; Miami, Tennessee, Buffalo, and Carolina in the NFL; Edmonton, Hamilton, and Carolina in the NHL. Which teams have larger-revenues can change over time, as with the Atlanta Braves and Seattle Mariners in MLB. But larger-revenue market teams simply always have dominated the playoffs in pro sports leagues.

Back to the Theory   Our simple two-team theory suggests that revenues should be highly positively related to both payrolls and winning percent. Further, if revenue imbalance increases, so should payroll imbalance and competitive imbalance. We can appeal to simple general statistics to get a basic understanding of the power of these relationships in actual practice.

A simple correlation statistic shows how two variables are related. Correlation coefficients are between zero and one, and the closer the coefficient is to one the stronger the relationship between the two variables under consideration.

Table 6.4 Years per League or Conference Title in Pro Sports Leagues

MLB (11 TEAMS)	TITLES	YEARS	YEARS/ TITLE	NBA (14 TEAMS)	TITLES	YEARS	YEARS/ TITLE
New York Yankees	39	102	2.6	Los Angeles Lakers	22	44	2.0
New York Giants	15	57	3.8	Minneapolis Lakers	6	12	2.0
Los Angeles Dodgers	9	47	5.2	Boston Celtics	19	58	3.1
Florida Marlins	2	12	6.0	St. Louis Hawks	4	13	3.3
Brooklyn Robins/ Dodgers	9	57	6.3	Chicago Stags	1	4	4.0
Milwaukee Braves	2	13	6.5	Syracuse Nationals	3	14	4.7
St. Louis Cardinals	16	104	6.5	Washington Capitols	1	5	5.0
Arizona Diamondbacks	1	7	7.0	Philadelphia Warriors	3	16	5.3
Oakland Athletics	6	44	7.3	Chicago Bulls	6	38	6.3
Atlanta Braves	5	39	7.8	Philadelphia 76ers	6	41	6.8
Baltimore Orioles	6	51	8.5	New York Knicks	8	58	7.3
Boston Pilgrims/ Red Sox	11	104	9.5	Washington Wizards	5	41	8.2
				Rochester Royals	1	9	9.0
				Detroit Pistons	6	56	9.3

NFL (20 TEAMS)	TITLES	YEARS	YEARS/ TITLE	NHL (17 TEAMS)	TITLES	YEARS	YEARS/ TITLE
New York Giants	17	71	4.2	Ottawa Senators I	8	18	2.3
Dallas Cowboys	10	44	4.4	Montreal Canadiens	27	88	3.3
St. Louis Rams	2	9	4.5	Detroit Red Wings	22	79	3.6
Cleveland Browns	11	54	4.9	Toronto Maple Leafs	22	88	4.0
Boston Redskins	1	5	5.0	Edmonton Oilers	6	26	4.3
Denver Broncos	6	34	5.7	Boston Bruins	17	81	4.8
Green Bay Packers	12	71	5.9	Colorado Avalanche	2	10	5.0
Oakland Raiders I	2	12	6.0	Montreal Maroons	3	15	5.0
Baltimore Colts	5	31	6.2	Philadelphia Flyers	7	38	5.4
Chicago Bears	11	71	6.5	New Jersey Devils	4	23	5.8
Miami Dolphins	5	34	6.8	Dallas Stars	2	12	6.0
Tennessee Titans	1	7	7.0	Hamilton Tigers	1	6	6.0
Washington Redskins	10	71	7.1	New York Islanders	5	33	6.6
Buffalo Bills	4	34	8.5	Calgary Flames	3	23	7.7
New England Patriots	4	34	8.5	Chicago Blackhawks	10	79	7.9
Minnesota Vikings	5	43	8.6	New York Rangers	10	79	7.9
Carolina Panthers	1	9	9.0	Carolina Hurricanes	1	8	8.0
Cleveland Rams	1	9	9.0				
Oakland Raiders II	1	9	9.0				
Los Angeles Rams	5	49	9.8				

Notes: Actually, it's the Brooklyn Robins/Dodgers, Baltimore/Capital/Washington Bullets-Washington Wizards, Ft. Wayne/Detroit Pistons, Ottawa/Eagles Senators I, Detroit Cougars/Falcons/Red Wings, and Toronto Arenas/St. Patricks/Maple Leafs. NFL calculated relative to 2003. MLB, NBA, and NHL calculated relative to 2004. Finally, only teams winning less than every ten years are shown.

Sources: All author's calculations, according to the formula in the text (ties count as half a winning percent point), from final standings at baseballreference.com, basketballreference.com, pro-footballreference.com, and (hockey) USAToday.com.

Table 6.5

Correlation
Coefficients and
Competitive Balance
in MLB

AVERAGES	REVENUE AND PAYROLL	REVENUE AND WINNING	PAYROLL AND WINNING
Pre-1950s	0.657	0.693	0.530
1950s	0.633	0.667	0.713
1990s	0.688	0.346	0.453
Pre-1994	0.578	0.151	0.287
Post-1995	0.848	0.608	0.644
2000s	0.887	0.474	0.463

Notes: Payrolls are "end-of-season" only because that is most useful for this purpose; ends 2002. No revenue data for 1998.

Sources: All calculations by the author from the data in Tables 6.1, 6.2, and 6.3.

A negative correlation shows that variables move apart, whereas a positive correlation shows that they move together. We'll examine just MLB here and leave an examination of the rest of the leagues to a project your instructor can assign.

In MLB, shown in Table 6.5, the correlation between revenues and payrolls always has been quite strong, although a bit less so in the prestrike years in the 1990s. This strong, positive result supports the theory. Owners evaluate the revenue potential in their market and hire talent accordingly. Turning to the impact on winning percent, we see the correlation between revenues and winning follows nearly the same pattern. Higher revenue teams actually then do pretty much perform up to expectations. Finally, it also is true that competitive imbalance increases as revenue imbalance increases. From the data in Tables 6.1 and 6.3, the correlation coefficients for the 1990s were 0.568 and −0.103 in the AL and NL, respectively. The former is reasonably strong and adheres to the theory. In the NL, however, the result is essentially zero. But a look inside the decade reveals something quite interesting. In the NL, while the overall correlation is essentially zero, it was 0.936 in the years after the strike (1996–1999).

Even with such a simple statistic, it appears the simple two-team league theory has strong explanatory power. This is nothing new, however. Scully (1989) states the conclusion of his analysis of the relationship between team expenditures, revenues, and winning for the early 1980s: "[W]hat can be concluded is that both club revenues and costs are positively related to team quality and that they tend to increase at about the same rate" (p. 126). The lesson is clear. Despite arguments in the popular press and by owners that the problems plaguing sports leagues are due to payroll imbalance, it is actually the unequal revenue potential in different geographic locations that drives both payroll imbalance and competitive imbalance. As we saw in the last chapter, this unequal revenue potential is in part due to the careful maintenance of territorial exclusivity by owners acting as leagues.

REMEDIES FOR COMPETITIVE IMBALANCE

Feelings are strongly mixed among analysts about whether the preceding evidence shows that there is a competitive balance "problem" in any pro sports league because research on just how imbalanced leagues ought to be is in its infancy. The issue is further complicated from what we learned in Chapter 2. Even if balance had improved over the decades, fans could be simply more dissatisfied than ever with the current level of imbalance they see.

In addition, you know from reading the last chapter that competitive imbalance is too large from the perspective of general sports fans (not just the ones who have a team now). This follows from the fact that owners, acting together through leagues, artificially restrict the number of teams fans get to enjoy. Regardless of the current measurement of competitive imbalance, there always is the market power problem to consider. In any event, let's have a look at the more familiar mechanisms pro sports leagues have implemented to ostensibly reduce competitive imbalance—gate and national TV revenue sharing, more general local revenue sharing, the draft, luxury taxes, and salary caps. A rather unusual alternative, not tried since the National League contracted from 12 to 8 teams at the end of the 1899 season, is described in The Learning Highlight: Shrinking MLB.

Gate and National TV Revenue Sharing

Gate revenue sharing is touted as a solution to competitive imbalance. With gate revenue sharing, the home team and the visiting team split a specific set of attendance revenues according to an agreed-upon formula. Currently, NFL owners share gate revenue at a 40 percent rate, and MLB owners share gate revenues through an aggregate sharing of all local revenues. Gate sharing may help teams with regard to team talent choices but at the expense of players. Moreover, gate sharing won't alter competitive imbalance. An analysis of our two-team league reveals this.

Graphical Analysis of Gate Revenue Sharing   Suppose that teams only keep a portion, $0 \leq \alpha \leq 1$, of their home gate. If $\alpha = 0$, the home team keeps none of its own gate revenue. If $\alpha = 1$, the home team shares nothing. Until quite recently, revenue sharing arrangements in MLB set $\alpha = 0.8$, approximately, whereas $\alpha = 0.6$ in the NFL. In the NHL and NBA, $\alpha = 1.0$ because there is no revenue sharing in those leagues (although this is expected to be altered in the newest NHL collective bargaining agreement). The actual practices of MLB and the NFL are treated shortly.

Figure 6.4 demonstrates the impact of revenue sharing. Each MR curve is shifted down by $1 - \alpha$ because each of the teams now can only keep αMR of their revenues. In addition, the new equilibrium is determined where $\alpha MR_L^* = \alpha MR_S^*$. However, precisely the same winning percent outcomes occur as without gate sharing. You can see this in Figure 6.4 because the parallel and equal shifts in the MR functions yield the same winning percent combination. Or, you can just cancel the α on each side of the equal marginal revenue equilibrium condition.

LEARNING HIGHLIGHT
Shrinking MLB

Only once has a league reduced the number of its member teams. That was in the National League in 1900, a few years before the formation of the modern MLB. More typically, a merger between rival leagues results in a larger single league than existed prior to the rivalry. Some of the rival league teams disappear after the merger, but a few join the dominant league.

Not long ago, talk of shrinking MLB arose. Jerry McMorris, owner of the Colorado Rockies, raised the question during an owners' meeting in 1999, "What would happen if instead of relocating and expanding, we considered consolidating teams?" (*Sports Illustrated*, August 20, 1999, p. 65). The particular targets at that time were teams in financial trouble, Montreal, Minnesota, Kansas City, and Oakland. The threat to shrink MLB earned some credence when the league recently killed the sale of some of these teams to what appeared to be reasonable owner groups.

Why shrink MLB? Shrinking the number of teams spreads shared revenues over fewer teams, raising the amount per team. Presumably, with increased shared revenues, those teams would become stronger. In addition, quality of play would improve with talent concentrated in fewer teams. Not surprisingly, the idea has not been brought up that closing down these existing franchises would open up new threat locations for the remaining MLB owners.

However, there are quite a few arguments against shrinking the league. Suppose that the idea of shrinkage had occurred 10 years ago. Likely candidates at that time would have included Cleveland, Atlanta, and Seattle, which are all now playoff-contending teams. It also is not at all clear that MLB can contract under the antitrust laws. Even if it can, other obstacles lie in the way. Eliminating teams would open a few more places for potential rival leagues to add to their list of possible cities. In addition, the players would be unlikely to sit idly by while upward of 180 jobs were eliminated. Finally, senators and members of Congress representing the fans who lose their teams could easily tie MLB up in hearings for years.

Eliminating MLB teams will do two things. First, it will open viable threat locations for the remaining owners to use against their host cities. Second, it directs revenue increases in the future to the smaller number of remaining owners. Some fans and observers like the idea because it will "raise quality." Tell that to the fans in Oakland and Kansas City who may end up without any major league baseball to enjoy of any quality level at all.

If MLB contraction occurs, the Expos will be history, and it could be many years before Canadian fans see the likes of Vladimir Guererro again.

Source: Sports Illustrated, August 20, 1999, p. 65.

Figure 6.4 Gate Revenue Sharing in a Two-Team League

Under gate revenue sharing, if the home team keeps a share equal to α, then both MR_S and MR_L shift down to αMR_S and αMR_L. The new equilibrium occurs at the same winning percents, $W_L^* = 1 - W_S^*$, but the price of talent falls from P to P'. The amount of revenue shared by the larger-revenue market owner is the area of the parallelogram *abcd*. The amount of revenue shared by the smaller-revenue market owner is the area *fbcg*. The difference between the two is the net gain to the smaller-revenue market owner, which is easy to see since *abcd > fbcg*.

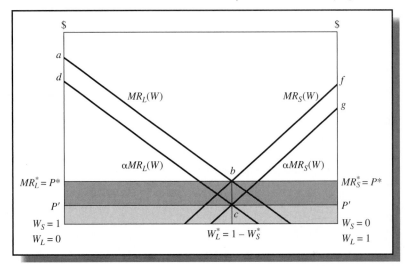

The amount of revenue shared by the larger-revenue market owner is the area of the parallelogram *abcd*. That area represents the difference in revenue with and without sharing. Similarly, the amount of revenue shared by the smaller-revenue market owner is area *fbcg*. The difference between the two is the net gain to the smaller-revenue market owner, which is easy to see because *abcd > fbcg*.

Thus, even though wealth is transferred to the smaller-revenue owner (because the shared base of total revenue is larger from the larger-revenue market owner), the talent choice is the same for both owners. Gate revenue sharing has no impact at all on competitive balance. The same is true of sharing the national TV contract, because owner shares of that contract do not depend on how well their team performs. All teams get an equal share of the national TV contract in all leagues. It is interesting to note that our view of pro sports team owners as profit maximizers is truly important for this observation about gate revenue sharing. In a league of winning-percent-maximizing teams, gate revenue sharing can improve competitive balance, as shown by Kesenne (1996; 1999; 2000).

Gate Sharing Impacts on Player Pay It is easy to see from Figure 6.4 that the revenue sharing payments by each team actually come from players, the providers of talent. In the presence of revenue sharing, payment per unit of talent falls from P^* to P'. Thus, the larger-market owner pays their talent less by the amount of the rectangle $(P^* - P')W_L^*$. However, that area is equal to the area of its sharing, *abcd*. Similarly, the small-market owner pays their talent less by the amount of the rectangle

$(P^* - P')W_S^*$, and that area is just equal to its sharing area, *fbcg*. After all, the owners collect the same amount of revenues on the same amount of talent. Payment to talent falls, and that is the amount shared by each team.

Pay falls because, at the margin, talent is less valuable. Each team now keeps a smaller proportion, $\alpha < 1$, of every dollar that talent helps create. Thus, the value of talent falls, as does the willingness of teams to pay for it. However, this is because revenue sharing makes teams bear a part of the burden of their talent choice on other teams. This is a good thing for league owners. Therefore, gate sharing reduces the urge to overinvest (from the league's perspective) in talent for some teams. However, it does not alter competitive balance, and the payment comes from reduced payments to players.

Recent Gate Revenue Sharing Changes: The NFL The NFL changed its revenue sharing plan for the 2001 season, but because owners already share nearly all local TV revenues, the league only altered its gate-sharing plan. Now, instead of sharing gate revenue on a visitor-by-visitor basis, 40 percent of all gate revenue goes into a pot that is shared equally by all teams. This is called straight-pool sharing. The most recent data on gate revenue in the NFL, from the 2004 *Forbes* report on team values, indicate that higher-gate teams usually make about $50.6 million, lower-gate teams about $29.6 million, and the median-gate teams around $37.6 million. Let's suppose one of each of these teams is in the league and focus on the change this will have on owners.

The calculations are shown in Table 6.6. Before the change, the owner of the high-gate team sent 40 percent of its revenues, or $20.2 million, to the other owners and received half of the 40 percent that each of the other owners contributed, or $13.4 million. On net, the high-gate owner made a net contribution of $6.8 million. By the same steps, the owner of the median team sent $15.0 million to the other two and received $16.0 million for a net income of $1 million. The owner of the low-gate team also is a beneficiary. That owner sends $11.8 million into the pot and gets back

Table 6.6   NFL Gate Revenue Sharing Through the Years

OLD 60/40 GATE SHARING

TEAM	GATE REVENUE ($MILLIONS)	AMOUNT PAID ($MILLIONS)	AMOUNT RECEIVED ($MILLIONS)	NET ($MILLIONS)
High revenue	$50.6	$20.2	$13.4	−$6.8
Median revenue	$37.6	$15.0	$16.0	$1.0
Low revenue	$29.6	$11.8	$17.6	$5.8
Sums	$117.8	$47.1	$47.1	$0.0

2001–PRESENT, STRAIGHT-POOL SHARING

TEAM	LOCAL REVENUE ($MILLIONS)	AMOUNT PAID ($MILLIONS)	AMOUNT RECEIVED ($MILLIONS)	NET ($MILLIONS)
High revenue	$50.6	$20.2	$15.7	−$4.5
Median revenue	$37.6	$15.0	$15.7	$0.7
Low revenue	$29.6	$11.8	$15.7	$3.9
Sums	$117.8	$47.1	$47.1	$0.0

Source: 2003 gate revenue data from in the 2004 *Forbes* Report on Team Values at Forbes.com.

$17.6 million for a net income of $5.8 million. This seems logical because the order of the net outcome varies inversely with gate; the owner of the lowest-gate team gets paid and the owner of the median-gate team receives less and the owner of the high-gate team actually pays, on net.

One problem with sharing so much revenue is that some owners might decide to scrimp on players because they are going to receive the same share of league revenues. There is an incentive to field a weaker team than the market will support and let the other owners field good teams, generating large revenues. The result is that the weaker team's share of revenue remains pretty much the same, but the team will have an even larger net financial result because costs have been lowered. Even 12 years ago, this was well recognized. Sports writer Paul Attner put it this way: "The NFLPA [Players Association] has maintained since the days of former executive director Ed Garvey that all of the league's revenue sharing has stripped owners of the incentive to spend what it takes to build winners. Nonsense, reply the owners, who claim they were just practicing fiscal responsibility in their efforts to keep salaries under control" (*Sporting News*, March 8, 1993, p. 20).

This problem of free riding on other owners is one of the reasons there is no corporate ownership in the NFL. Because owners are individually responsible for their team's bottom line, rather than just passing off the costs to operating revenues for a corporate owner, the incentive for other owners to monitor that behavior is greater. Fleisher, Shughart, and Tollison (1989) investigated this idea and found that teams in the hands of fewer owners had a greater degree of revenue sharing. Let's see if the new NFL sharing strategy helps.

Impacts of the New NFL Arrangement   Because the gate revenue sharing percentages have not changed under the new straight-pool sharing arrangement, all three team owners contribute the same amounts as before. As shown in Table 6.6, the total in the pool is $47.1 million. The new plan has each team owner receiving an equal share, or about $15.7 million. Under this scheme, the high-gate team owner remains a net contributor at $4.5 million. The owner of the median-gate team now earns a lower net payment of $700,000 on net. The owner of the low-gate team remains a beneficiary, receiving a net of $3.9 million.

Notice what has changed. First, the net payment to the owner of the low-gate team has fallen by 33 percent and the net payments to the owner of the median-revenue team fell by 30 percent. Of course, this means that the high-revenue team owner's net contribution fell by about 34 percent. The result should reduce the incentive for the low-gate owner to scrimp on talent. However, it is interesting that the reduction in payment is a bit higher for the high-gate owner than for the low-gate owner. Further, from Table 6.3, we see that there was no detectable impact on competitive balance in the league. Our ratio measure of the standard deviation is practically identical in the 1980s, 1990s, and on in to the 2000s.

Did You Know?
The alteration in the NFL's gate sharing that occurred for the 2001 season will reduce both the size of the net payment made by strong teams and the size of the net income to weak teams.

Local Revenue Sharing

Can **local revenue sharing**—adding concession revenue, parking revenue, and local TV revenue to gate revenue—drive a more balanced outcome on the field? We already know that the gate revenue portion will not have any marginal impact on competitive balance. The answer for the other elements of local revenue is complicated. The sharing must involve revenues that actually are based on how well the team performs. Otherwise, sharing revenue will not impact winning. Let's focus on local TV revenue.

The value of local TV contracts partly depends on population. From our discussion in Chapter 2, we know that advertisers seek to "hit" particular target demographics. In larger areas, the number of advertising hits would be expected to be greater; thus any team's contract would be worth more in a larger market. However, if population was the only factor that mattered, sharing would have no impact on competitive balance because no team owner can expect to cause the population of the team's fan area to increase based on winning.

However, population is not the only thing that matters. What really matters is the number of people watching out of a given possible population. That number does depend on the team's fortunes and available substitutes. If two teams were relatively equal in terms of target-group size at their respective locations, the more successful team would draw more target-group viewers and sell a higher-priced local TV contract because more hits would be produced per advertisement. A really good team in a small-gate-revenue market might have a larger local TV contract than a poor team in a large-gate-revenue market.

If the marginal revenue derived from local TV in one location is larger than in another, then sharing local TV revenues can increase competitive balance. In this case, forcing revenue sharing would indeed change the marginal value of talent for relatively more successful teams. One of the reasons the team with the higher local TV contract was investing in talent was to generate that higher-valued local contract in the first place. Sharing will decrease that value, and the team will choose less talent. That is, the league will be more balanced with local TV revenue sharing.

Variation in Local Revenue Sharing: The NFL versus MLB A comparison of the NFL, which shares all TV money, with MLB, which only began sharing some of its local revenues in 1996, and the NBA, which shares no local revenues at all, provides a little insight on this issue. We have to be careful to recognize that the NFL shares local TV revenue in a way that never allows us to see what the value of local TV contracts would have been in the absence of sharing because there is only a national contract in the NFL, equally shared. If sharing local TV equally drives more competitive balance, then we would expect the NFL to be more balanced than MLB and the NBA.

Our look at competitive balance across leagues back in Table 6.3 shows that the NFL is more balanced than MLB, and much more balanced than the NBA. In addition, we saw in Table 6.4 that championships are more balanced in the NFL. This is pretty strong evidence that local TV sharing does foster competitive balance, suggesting that the conditions under which that will happen are met in pro sports leagues.

Recent Changes in Local Revenue Sharing: MLB

MLB abandoned its old 80/20 gate sharing plan during the negotiations that ended the strike of 1994–1995. Since 1996, MLB owners contribute a percentage of all local revenues (gate, concessions, parking, and local TV) into a common pool shared by all teams. As we'll address shortly, the percentages and sharing rules have changed since 1996. From 1996 to 2001, about 17 percent of all local revenues, net of stadium charges, were shared under a split-pool arrangement. Seventy-five percent of the pool was shared equally among all owners. The remaining 25 percent was shared equally only among owners with below league average total revenues. From 2002 on, 34 percent of all local revenues, net of stadium charges, were shared under the same straight-pool arrangement used in the NFL—all owners simply get an equal share of the pool. In either case, the idea was to put more money in the pockets of weaker owners in order to give them a better chance to compete for talent. In addition to extending sharing to include all forms of local revenue, the commissioner's office also retained $30–$40 million to distribute to lower-revenue owners that made significant strides in improving the quality of their team. Let's see how it shakes out.

Again, let's adopt a comparison as if there were one high-revenue owner, one median-revenue owner, and one low-revenue owner. The calculations are in Table 6.7 based on the 2004 *Forbes* magazine report on team values. To determine the outcome under the old (approximately) 80/20 split, the data in Table 6.7 indicate that gate

Table 6.7 MLB Gate and Local Revenue Sharing Through the Years

OLD 80/20 GATE SHARING

TEAM	GATE REVENUE ($MILLIONS)	AMOUNT PAID ($MILLIONS)	AMOUNT RECEIVED ($MILLIONS)	NET ($MILLIONS)
High revenue	$82.6	$16.5	$6.0	−$10.6
Median revenue	$39.6	$7.9	$10.3	$2.3
Low revenue	$20.0	$4.0	$12.2	$8.2
Sums	$142.2	$28.4	$28.4	$0.0

1996–2001, SPLIT-POOL SHARING

TEAM	LOCAL REVENUE ($MILLIONS)	AMOUNT PAID ($MILLIONS)	AMOUNT RECEIVED ($MILLIONS)	NET ($MILLIONS)
High revenue	$81.0	$13.8	$8.7	−$5.0
Median revenue	$67.4	$11.5	$8.7	−$2.7
Low revenue	$57.0	$9.7	$17.5	$7.8
Sums	$205.4	$34.9	$34.9	$0.0

2002–PRESENT, STRAIGHT-POOL SHARING

TEAM	LOCAL REVENUE ($MILLIONS)	AMOUNT PAID ($MILLIONS)	AMOUNT RECEIVED ($MILLIONS)	NET ($MILLIONS)
High revenue	$81.0	$27.5	$23.3	−$4.3
Median revenue	$67.4	$22.9	$23.3	$0.4
Low revenue	$57.0	$19.4	$23.3	$3.9
Sums	$205.4	$69.8	$69.8	$0.0

Sources: 2003 gate revenue data in the 2004 *Forbes* Report on Team Values at Forbes.com. Adjusted "Other Data" category in the same report for the value of the 2003 national TV contract to get local revenue.

revenues are around $121 million for the highest-revenue owners, $47 million for the median-revenue owners, and $14 million for the lowest-revenue owners. With these data in hand, the calculations for the old 80/20 gate sharing approach follow the same steps as in the NFL case in Table 6.6. The highest-revenue owner would have contributed 20 percent of gate revenues, or $16.5 million, to the other owners and received half of the 20 percent that each of the other owners contributed, or $10.6 million. That makes the net contribution $10.6 million. The owner of the median-revenue team would have sent $7.9 million to the other two and received $10.3 million for a net income of $2.3 million. The owner of the lowest-revenue team would have paid $4.0 million and got back $12.2 million for a net income of $8.2 million. Once again, this seems logical. The owner of the weakest-revenue team is paid the most and the owner of the highest-revenue team foots the bill.

Under the local revenue sharing arrangement in place for the 1996–2002 seasons, each team contributed 17 percent of all local revenues net of expenses for ballpark financing. The split-pool sharing arrangement described above generated the results in the center panel of Table 6.7. The *Forbes* report suggests that the largest-market teams had local revenues of about $81.0 million whereas the median- and smallest-revenue teams had local revenues of $67.4 million and $57.0 million, respectively. The total in the pool would have been $34.9 million (17% of summed local revenues across all teams), about 23 percent more than was shared under the old 80/20 plan. The new plan has each team owner receiving a share of about $8.7 million, that is, (0.75 × 34.9)/3. In addition, in our three-team illustration, the lowest-revenue owner would also receive the entire remaining 25 percent, an additional $8.7 million. Under this scheme, the largest-revenue owner's contribution falls by more than half the previous amount and the median-revenue owner is now a net contributor rather than a net beneficiary of revenues sharing. Finally, the lowest-revenue owner's net receipt falls by 5.5 percent.

The change in the distribution of revenues is clear. However, the impacts of the change in revenue sharing on competitive balance are difficult to determine. The reason is twofold. First, a portion of the increase is coming out of gate revenues, and that sharing cannot alter competitive balance. Moreover, even for the portion that does come out of local TV revenues, the choice of how much to win will only be changed for some teams as covered in our earlier discussion of whether sharing local TV revenues accomplishes anything. Finally, revenues have increased over time in MLB. If they increase too much, they may swamp the shared portion and alter owners' decisions about winning.

Nonetheless, here is how competitive balance behaved during the split-pool arrangement. The data in Table 6.3 suggest that competitive balance was improving in the AL in the 1990s prior to the strike in 1994–1995. For example, the 1980s standard deviation ratio, on average, was about 1.75 and fell to 1.50 for 1990–1993. The opposite was true in the NL, but only slightly (1.69 for the 1980s and 1.76 for the 1990s prior to the strike). Through the duration of the split-pool approach, competitive balance worsened in the AL (the ratio increased from 1.50 to 1.85) and remained the same in the NL. Remember, what we can't know, given all of the other changes that happened over these years, is what would have happened to these measurements if MLB had retained its old 80/20 gate sharing only arrangement.

Let's move on to the straight-pool local revenue sharing arrangement in place in MLB since 2002. Sharing was increased to 34 percent of all local revenues, net of ballpark expenses, and all owners receive an equal share. Cutting straight to the chase, the last column in the last panel of Table 6.7 makes it clear that even though the total amount going into the pool increases 100 percent, the net contribution of the highest-revenue owner falls, the median-revenue owner becomes (slightly) a net beneficiary as under the old 80/20 arrangement, and the net receipt for the lowest-revenue owner falls again by a whopping 50 percent. The indications are that competitive balance has worsened. The standard deviation ratios, on average over 2002–2004 have risen to 2.43 and 2.01 in the AL and NL, respectively. The last time these statistics were greater than 2.0 for both leagues was the decade of the 1960s. While our three-team illustration is useful, the actual revenue transfer under the straight-pool approach, compared to the previous split-pool approach, is known for all teams. Table 6.8 contains the results. A few things jump out in the comparison. First, the size of the transfer, the number of net contributors, and the average size of the contributions they make did not change at all when the straight-pool approach was implemented for the 2002 season. The total transfer rose by about one-half of one percent, and the average transfer paid actually fell by about 5 percent. This means that the payment became more concentrated among the payers than it had been under the split-pool arrangement. But the average transfer receipt increased by just over 8 percent, so the receipts also were more densely concentrated than before. Finally, it appears that our three-team illustration truly was insightful. After the straight-pool approach had been in effect for just a year, the total transfer rose dramatically, there were many more owners enjoying a net payment than paying one, and the average transfer changed little. While these changes are consistent with the illustration in Table 6.7, they also suggest that revenues have risen dramatically again for MLB.

The Draft

Can we add the **reverse-order-of-finish draft** to local TV revenue sharing as a mechanism that might increase competitive balance? Under such a draft, the worst teams from the preceding season get first choice of the new talent coming into the league. This is highly touted as a remedy to competitive imbalance. After all, poor teams draft the better players and should be able to close the gap with richer teams, right?

Nearly all sports economists would say no. We are going to save a full-blown treatment of the draft for Chapter 8, but the idea is that talent always moves to its highest valued use in the league. Therefore, weak teams draft strong talent, but stronger teams in larger-revenue markets then pay to move that talent toward them. In this way, the talent ends up in the same place as it did without a draft. The only differences are that

- The draft reduces the amount that players are paid up front to join a given team because they must play for the owner that drafted them (again, details are in Chapter 8).
- Weaker teams get paid by larger-revenue market teams for the talent they bring into the league through the draft.

The data tend to support the view that reverse-order-of-finish drafts do not alter competitive balance. Table 6.9 shows a before-and-after look at the NFL and MLB

Table 6.8 MLB Revenue Sharing Comparisons, Split-Pool and Straight-Pool

TEAM	2001 ($MILLIONS)	2002 ($MILLIONS)	2003 ($MILLIONS)
N.Y. Yankees	−$26.5	−$26.6	−$52.7
Seattle	−$18.8	−$19.9	−$31.0
Boston	−$16.4	−$17.9	−$38.7
N.Y. Mets	−$15.7	−$17.4	−$21.5
Cleveland	−$13.3	−$10.6	−$4.8
Atlanta	−$10.6	−$9.8	−$11.3
Los Angeles	−$9.1	−$9.3	−$9.5
Texas	−$8.7	−$8.2	−$7.2
St. Louis	−$8.2	−$8.4	−$9.2
Baltimore	−$6.8	−$5.3	$0.3
Chicago Cubs	−$6.6	−$8.3	−$16.7
San Francisco	−$6.3	−$9.6	−$13.0
Colorado	−$6.0	−$5.1	$2.5
Houston	−$5.2	−$4.3	$1.2
Arizona	−$4.4	−$3.3	$1.5
Chicago White Sox	−$4.2	−$3.8	−$4.8
Milwaukee	$1.7	$8.5	$16.6
Pittsburgh	$1.8	$6.4	$13.3
Detroit	$5.1	$11.6	$16.7
San Diego	$8.7	$6.3	$13.3
Anaheim	$9.6	−$1.3	$1.9
Toronto	$9.8	$13.7	$18.7
Oakland	$10.5	$9.2	$11.8
Philadelphia	$11.8	$9.8	$9.0
Tampa Bay	$12.4	$14.7	$20.5
Cincinnati	$13.4	$9.8	$6.5
Kansas City	$16.0	$16.6	$19.0
Florida	$18.6	$20.9	$21.0
Minnesota	$19.1	$13.0	$17.2
Montreal	$28.5	$28.5	$29.5
League transfer	$167.0	$169.1	$220.4
Net contributors	16	17	12
Average net contribution	$10.4	$9.9	$18.4
Average net receipt	$11.9	$13.0	$12.2

Notes: League transfer is the sum for the net gainers. Average contribution equals league transfer divided by number of net contributors.

Sources: 2001 from Commissioner Selig's 2001 *MLB Report*. 2002 and 2003 from sportsbusinessnews.com, Daily Dose, May 19, 2004. sportsbusinessnews.com lists MLB Commissioner's office as point of origin.

drafts. For the NFL, our standard deviation ratio measure of competitive balance increases 7.2 percent from the before period (Period 2, in Table 6.9) to the after period (Period 3, in Table 6.9). One might be inclined to think this means balance worsened with the draft. But this really isn't much of a change, especially if we look at an

	PERIOD 1	% CHANGE	PERIOD 2	% CHANGE	PERIOD 3	AVE. % CHANGE
L	2.38	−2.1%	2.33	−18.9%	1.89	−10.5%
.L	2.43	−9.5%	2.20	−14.5%	1.88	−12.0%
NFL	2.03	−18.2%	1.66	7.2%	1.78	−5.5%

Notes: MLB periods are 12 years long; draft in place beginning Period 3, 1964. NFL periods are 6 years long; draft in place beginning Period 3, 1936.

Source: See Table 6.3.

additional period prior to the draft (Period 1 in Table 6.9). With this additional period, you can see that the average change yields an improvement of 5.5 percent in competitive balance. Once again, this isn't much of a change and provides evidence that the draft has no effect on competitive balance.

Turning to baseball, Table 6.9 shows that our measure of competitive balance decreases 18.9 percent from the before period (Period 2, in Table 6.9) to the after period (Period 3, in Table 6.9) in the AL. The NL statistic also decreases by 14.5 percent. These changes seem large enough to suggest that there were significant improvements in competitive balance due to the draft in baseball. Once again, however, let's look at one additional period prior to the draft. There is a downward trend in our statistic measuring competitive balance that had nothing to do with the draft. In the NL, the decline before and after the draft is only 2.5 percent greater than the trend, essentially no change. But in the AL, the decline before and after the draft is still 8.4 percent greater than the trend.

Reasonably, the AL result is worth pondering because it appears to refute the idea that the draft has no impact on competitive balance. One explanation is that there may have been something else changing at the same time (always a possibility when you look at very simple statistical comparisons like averages). Another is suggested by the CBS ownership of the Yankees incident detailed in Chapter 3. This period coincides with the imposition of the draft and was an uncharacteristically weak time for the Yankees. That alone may have been enough to make it appear that the draft was effective at redistributing talent in the AL.

So, although these draft cross-subsidies share the wealth created by players with lower-revenue teams, they do not generally lead to any change in competitive balance (although a more detailed analysis of the AL after the draft would prove interesting). Players end up distributed through the league roughly as they would without the draft.

The Luxury Tax

The so-called **payroll luxury tax**, (MLB calls it the competitive balance tax) can improve competitive balance. In its current form in MLB (the only league where such a tax is in use), the luxury tax is a progressive charge on the amount of talent hired. Essentially, the league and the union establish spending thresholds (starting at $117 million in 2003, growing to $136.5 million by 2006), and teams are free to spend as they choose on talent. However, if they spend more than the thresholds, they pay a progressively larger tax rate on spending past each threshold (eventually up to 22.5 percent for first-time violators, 30 percent for second-time violators, and 40 percent for third-time violators). By taxing talent differentially based on how much is purchased, competitive balance definitely will be altered.

Graphical Analysis of the Luxury Tax   The essential elements of the luxury tax outcome are in Figure 6.5. In a two-team league, an effective luxury tax would simply tax the larger-revenue owner's talent choice. This abstraction really does no harm because the effective talent spending level in the real-world version typically is chosen to affect only the few largest spenders. Let the tax on the larger-revenue owner be equal to t_1. This has the effect of making each unit of winning percent worth $(1 - t_1)$ $MR_L(W_L)$ to the larger-revenue market owner. The dotted-line segment in Figure 6.5 shows this impact for $t_1 = 0.5$, a 50 percent tax on spending.

The imposition of the luxury tax reduces the larger-revenue market owner's profit-maximizing winning percent to $W_L^t < W_L^*$ (equilibrium still must occur at the intersection of the larger- and smaller-revenue owner marginal revenues). Because the tax reduces the net value of talent at the margin and only for one of the teams, it also alters the amount of talent chosen by both teams; the smaller-market owner has an increased winning percent. The price of talent falls, the smaller-market owner purchases more talent, and the sum of the two winning percents must equal one. Note, too, that payments to talent are now smaller shaded rectangles because the price of talent has fallen in equilibrium to P'. When the net value of hiring talent falls, less of it is used and payment falls. Thus, larger-revenue market owners and players share the burden of the tax.

Figure 6.5   The Impact of Luxury Taxes in a Two-Team League

A tax of $t_1 = 0.5$ (50% on talent chosen beyond the threshold W_1) is imposed on the larger-revenue market owner. The new equilibrium choice by the larger-revenue owner is W_L^t. Because the sum of winning percents is one, the talent choice by the smaller-revenue market owner must increase. In addition, the price of talent falls to P'.

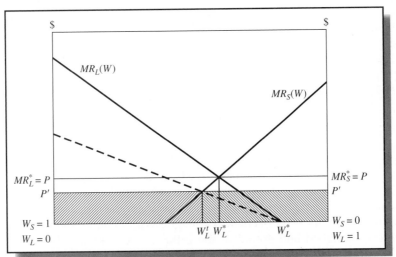

Total tax revenues collected from the larger-revenue owner will be equal to $t_1(P'W_L^*)$, that is, the tax rate applied to that owner's total expenditure on talent. In the real-world case of the MLB luxury tax, the 2001 labor agreement between the owners and the players dictates that tax revenues go to player benefits, the industry growth fund (a public relations drive to "grow" the fan base), or player development in countries lacking organized high school baseball.

It is extremely important to note the following. The luxury tax will reduce competitive imbalance, but what are the chances that it can reduce imbalance by very much? Refer back to Figure 6.5. For a tax of 50 percent, the reduction in competitive imbalance was quite small. If you get out your ruler, the gain in winning percent for the smaller-revenue team was about 0.045. The limiting factor is, as always, how much more talent the smaller-market owner will buy when the price of talent falls. Indeed, the 22.5 percent rate applied to first offenders seems unlikely to have much impact at all. Even at very prohibitive tax rates, like the 40 percent rate for third offenders, the gains in competitive balance may not be all that large.

Salary Caps

Salary caps in North American pro sports leagues are poorly named. Actually, they are the result of revenue sharing between owners and players and should more properly be named "revenue sharing payroll caps." In fact, this type of cap on payrolls does not include any cap on individual player salaries (although those do exist for some players in some leagues). First, during collective bargaining (Chapter 9), owners and players agree upon the portion of league-wide revenues that they will share. In the NFL, this amount is called defined gross revenues (*DGR*). In the NBA, the revenues shared between owners and players are called business-related income (*BRI*). The NHL is just in the process of working out these details after their prolonged lockout of the entire 2004–05 season. Then they agree upon the split between owners and players. In the 2001 extension agreed upon between NFL owners and players, the share for players is destined to increase from 63 percent to 64.5 percent by 2006. The minimum is 56 percent, and owners must pay players any amount below that. Let's label the players' share s. In a league of n teams, the following formula determines the cap on owner spending on talent, C (we use DGR, here, but BRI would do just as well):

$$C = \frac{1}{n} \times s \times DGR$$

Thus, the "salary cap" is actually a cap on payroll spending that is equal across all teams. The hope is that, by equalizing talent spending, team quality also will equalize across teams and enhance competitive balance.

Did You Know?
Salary caps in the NFL and NBA actually are revenue sharing agreements between owners and players. The cap is calculated based on a percentage share of each league's defined gross revenues that goes to players.

The salary cap was saved for last because it provides an introduction to the other problems confronting leagues. The cap, like local TV revenue sharing and the luxury tax, can enhance a league's competitive balance outcome. In fact, if properly designed and enforced, these three can eliminate the impacts of revenue imbalances completely.

Figure 6.6 The Impact of a Salary Cap in a Two-Team League

A cap on the price per unit spent on talent, C, along with the imposition of equal spending, has the following impact. First, the price of talent falls and payments to talent are reduced by the shaded rectangle, $P^* - C$. At equal spending, $W_L^C = W_S^C = 0.500$, and spending by each team is equal at $0.500 \times C$. However, because $MR_L > MR_S$ on all units between 0.500 and W_S', both teams have an incentive to violate the cap.

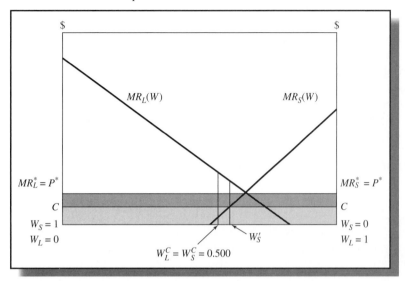

Graphical Analysis of Salary Caps   Figure 6.6 shows the intended impact of the salary cap's equal spending limitation. For our diagrammatic exposition, the cap is shown on a per unit talent basis as the line CC below the competitive price P^*. Equal spending, guaranteed by the presence of a minimum close to the cap, means an equal outcome, thus, $W_L^C = W_S^C = 0.500$. If this outcome lasts, the sizes of the shaded rectangles that measure team spending are the same.

There are two intended impacts of the cap. First, the cap lowers total spending on talent by the amount $P^* - C$ per unit of talent purchased by each team. The total reduction is the darker-shaded rectangle. Second, spending should be equalized across all teams. Thus, teams should all close in on a winning percent of 0.500, and complete competitive balance should reign.

There is some careful wording in the preceding paragraphs—*intended* impact, *if* this outcome lasts, spending *should* be equalized. These qualifiers were chosen because salary caps are subject to cheating. Given the cap C in Figure 6.6, both owners would rather not be at a winning percent of 0.500. The smaller-revenue market owner would rather choose an amount of talent W_S', where $C = MR_S$ and a winning percent lower than 0.500. This is because $C > MR_S$ for all units beyond W_S'. Thus, to accomplish its competitive balance goals, the payroll cap must also be a payroll floor. Both the NBA and NFL cap agreements have very specific language dictating a minimum amount of spending very close to the cap amount. Of course, this minimum requirement only matters if the cap is chosen so that $C > MR_S$.

In addition, the larger-revenue market owner would be happy to buy the talent that the smaller-revenue market owner wishes to relinquish because $MR_L > C$ on each unit between 0.500 and W_S'. When owners on both sides of the cap wish to cheat, one would expect them to try. In addition, fairness clauses in cap agreements allow some cap violations. It is typical to allow some cap overruns when owners attempt to retain their most treasured free agent players, for example. In cap language, caps that have more of these exceptions are referred to as "soft" caps and caps that have fewer exceptions are called "hard" caps.

Thus, the salary cap presents the league with a monitoring and enforcement problem. All of this creates a need for "cap police." The 0.500 equal winning percent outcome cannot be maintained without league monitoring and enforcement. In both the NBA and NFL this job has been given to the commissioner's office. The commissioner is allowed to punish cap violations with monetary fines, voided contracts, lost draft picks, and suspension of team officers involved in the violation.

Analysis of Cap Effectiveness   Given the enforcement problem posed by caps, as well as the fairness clauses that make it legal for some owners to spend more than the cap, it is natural enough to check to see if spending actually is anywhere near the cap. Table 6.10 shows caps and payrolls for the NBA and NFL. Two things are clear. First, even the average NBA and NFL payroll has been larger than the cap almost every year of its existence (Staudohar [1999] was the first to notice this). Of course, because this is an average, there also are teams far below and far above the cap.

James Quirk and I (Fort and Quirk, 1995) originally showed about ten years ago that it is only by happy coincidence that any NBA owner actually spends anywhere near the cap in any given year. Larger-revenue market owners typically violate it by as much as 25 percent. Table 6.11 shows that nothing much has changed since our initial analysis. Fully 86 percent of NBA teams are recently over the cap with not a single larger-revenue team at or below the cap and the largest-revenue New York Knicks lead the way. In the NFL, a much lower 69 percent of teams are recently over the cap. As one would expect given the breadth of revenue sharing, even the larger-revenue New York Jets are below the cap.

Did You Know?

In the NFL, the average team payroll has exceeded the league's salary cap every year of the cap's existence but one, beginning in 1993. In the NBA, the average team payroll has exceed the league's salary cap in all but 2 years since the 1985–1986 season.

The NFL and NBA caps are not met, even on average. This means that caps cannot be generating equal playing balance, but they may be making improvements. It is hard to tell in the NFL, because it is the most balanced of all the leagues. The NBA, on the other hand, is not balanced. It is not clear why caps are ineffective. As mentioned earlier, it is partly due to the fairness clauses that allow some teams to spend over the cap. However, cheating on salary caps cannot be ruled out as part of the explanation for both the NBA and the NFL. The league offices, charged with enforcing the caps, may not have been watchful for violations. Or league offices may simply have found it impossible to actually impose caps because the largest-revenue owners want to violate the cap away.

Interestingly, the point of the 1998 NBA owners' lockout of the players was to gain a hard cap, which they did through collective bargaining that year. The little data that we have indicate that it still isn't working. Both the 1998 and 1999 seasons have mean salaries well in excess of the cap, and the data in Table 6.11

Table 6.10

Salary Caps in the
NBA and NFL

Salary cap

	NFL		NBA	
YEAR	CAP ($MILLIONS)	AVG. TEAM PAYROLL ($MILLIONS)	CAP ($MILLIONS)	AVG. TEAM PAYROLL ($MILLIONS)
1984			$3.6	
1985			$4.2	$4.6
1986			$4.9	$5.7
1987			$6.2	$6.0
1988			$7.2	$6.8
1989			$9.8	$11.3
1990			$11.9	$13.7
1991			$12.5	$15.8
1992			$14.0	$18.5
1993			$15.2	$22.2
1994	$34.6	$36.6	$16.0	$25.0
1995	$37.1	$42.6	$23.0	$28.5
1996	$40.8	$45.7	$24.4	$32.7
1997	$41.5	$43.6	$26.9	$38.1
1998	$52.4	$61.4	$30.0	$45.1
1999	$58.4	$66.1	$34.0	$51.6
2000	$62.2	$68.1	$35.5	$53.3
2001	$67.4	$70.8	$42.5	$57.3
2002	$71.1	$66.0	$40.3	$57.2
2003	$75.0	$77.0	$43.8	$56.0
2004	$78.0		$43.9	
2005	—			
2006	—			
2007	—			

Sources: Cap values from USAToday.com, insidehoops.com, and Patricia Bender's "Various Basketball Stuff" (www.dfw.net/~patricia/). For payrolls, see Table 6.2.

Did You Know?

The point of the 1998 lockout of players in the NBA was for the owners to obtain a hard salary cap. However, the ratio of the average to the cap in the 1998–1999 and 1999–2000 seasons was higher than it had been since 1994.

indicate that larger-revenue teams remain the primary violators. It appears the league has not come to grips with the problem it sought to solve with the lockout.

In summary, old-fashioned gate revenue sharing and the reverse-order-of-finish draft won't reduce competitive imbalance. Local revenue sharing, the luxury tax, and salary caps all have the potential to reduce imbalance. All of the mechanisms discussed so far have one thing in common. Whether or not theory suggests that they will reduce competitive imbalance, they all will reduce payment to players. Small wonder then that each of these mechanisms has been a bone of contention in labor negotiations between owners and players, as we'll see in Chapter 9.

There are two other ways to reduce competitive imbalance in pro sports leagues. The historically unique contraction approach of 1899 in the Learning Highlight:

Table 6.11 Caps and Actual 2003 Payrolls in the NBA and NFL

NBA (2003–04 Season)	Cap = $43.8 Million	NFL (2003 Season)	Cap = $75.0 Million
Team	Payroll	Team	Payroll
New York	$84,523,891	New Orleans	$95,103,350
Portland	$84,304,778	Tampa Bay	$88,084,700
Dallas	$79,099,293	Minnesota	$85,719,851
Minnesota	$72,385,947	Cincinnati	$85,457,225
Sacramento	$69,567,889	Atlanta	$84,861,253
Los Angeles Lakers	$65,510,147	Washington	$84,826,189
Phoenix	$65,176,684	Seattle	$84,227,732
Atlanta	$63,536,207	Chicago	$82,803,517
Toronto	$60,307,176	New England	$82,128,250
Boston	$59,112,919	Dallas	$81,042,307
Memphis	$58,233,851	Arizona	$81,034,928
Philadelphia	$57,763,301	St. Louis	$80,224,050
Indiana	$57,548,489	Jacksonville	$78,735,117
Detroit	$52,942,639	New York Giants	$78,125,309
Houston	$52,354,437	Detroit	$77,662,097
Chicago	$52,150,699	Houston	$77,591,518
Golden State	$51,804,638	Philadelphia	$77,436,900
Seattle	$50,624,368	Kansas City	$77,394,073
New Jersey	$48,579,883	Green Bay	$77,230,121
New Orleans	$48,125,452	Baltimore	$76,154,450
Orlando	$47,696,731	Tennessee	$75,575,947
San Antonio	$46,879,322	Carolina	$75,004,350
Cleveland	$46,513,187	Indianapolis	$74,998,224
Washington	$45,681,942	Oakland	$74,904,848
Miami	$45,529,862	Buffalo	$73,299,382
Milwaukee	$42,452,361	San Diego	$73,230,536
Los Angeles	$37,547,054	New York Jets	$69,209,828
Denver	$36,004,731	Miami	$67,439,147
Utah	$28,320,329	Denver	$64,826,919
		Pittsburgh	$63,571,735
		San Francisco	$60,519,309
		Cleveland	$53,849,750
Average	$55,526,835	Average	$76,946,029
% of teams over cap	86%	% of teams over cap	69%

Sources: Caps, see Table 6.10. Payrolls are from USAToday.com player salary databases.

Shrinking MLB is one. Not a single pro sports league has ever used the other, harnessing the power of economic competition to reduce competitive imbalance. Why this method never will be used is discussed in the Learning Highlight: Competitive Imbalance and the Power of Economic Competition.

LEARNING HIGHLIGHT
Competitive Imbalance and the Power of Economic Competition

Theory suggests that the root cause of any competitive imbalance problems is that some owners are led to choose greater talent levels than others in order to collect the vastly larger revenues offered in their markets.

Local revenue sharing, luxury taxes, and salary caps all aim to reduce the marginal value of talent to owners, holding constant the fact that leagues have maintained exclusive territories of vastly differing revenue potential. But territorial exclusivity is the domain of the league, and there is a perfectly direct mechanism to address the problem at its root cause. Just put more teams in the largest-revenue "megamarkets."

This approach and its historical origins are discussed in great detail in my book with James Quirk, *Hardball: The Abuse of Power in Pro Team Sports* (Quirk and Fort, 1999). Suppose that only one team occupies the market with the greatest revenue potential. The owner creates the league's highest quality team to collect that revenue and competitive imbalance ensues. If the league allowed another franchise in the same location, competition should reduce the current owner's advantage. Fans now have more substitutes and the demand for the current team's product shifts left. So does the marginal revenue function for the current owner. As a result, that owner chooses a lower level of talent and competitive imbalance is eased.

Clearly, owners understand the forces of this type of competition. After all, it is the very essence of their joint venture activity to keep those forces at bay. The careful management of team location both protects the territory exclusivity of the larger-revenue market owners and impedes any possible rival leagues from putting franchises in the most valuable territories.

This also makes it easy to see why leagues have never harnessed economic competition to reduce competitive imbalance on the field. Some owners will face reduced economic circumstances as the value of their exclusive (but smaller) territories falls. Indeed, whenever a league moves a team to even remote proximity of an existing owner, long discussions ensue concerning compensation to the owner who perceives a loss of territory.

The idea of harnessing economic competition to reduce competitive imbalance isn't just held by academicians in their ivory towers, sharpening their heads to a fine point. At this writing, MLB had just decided to relocate the Montreal Expos to Washington, D.C. This is the first time a team has moved since 1971, when the last incarnation of the Washington Senators (the irony drips, doesn't it?) left for Texas. The move was aided by the fact that MLB had purchased the franchise from its previous owner just a couple of seasons earlier.

During the MLB owners' deliberations on what to do with their Expos, John Shea of the *San Francisco Chronicle* (August 24, 2003; or www.sfgate.com) plainly put it that moving the Expos to New York (!) would have important virtues:

> It has been 46 years since three [MLB] teams played in New York, and it might be another 46 years before it happens again. But by moving the Expos to the biggest city this side of Tokyo, baseball would help achieve two of its goals. It would give the Expos a home. It would give the Yankees a headache . . . MLB would not propose a three-team New York market . . . Even though a Gotham trifecta would be good for baseball, the Yankees and Mets aren't interested in helping the game as much as themselves . . . The 29 other teams own the Expos, and they'd draw top dollar by

(Continued)

selling to New York ownership. They'd also guarantee high attendance, which wouldn't be a lock in Washington, D.C., Northern Virginia or Portland.... Move the Expos to New York, and the Yankees, along with the Mets, would be forced into a regional form of revenue-sharing, and that would go a long way toward balancing the economic playing field.

Comparing the movement of teams to the largest-revenue markets with the contraction alternative (covered in the Learning Highlight: Shrinking MLB), Jim Caple at ESPN.com (November 7, 2001) put it as follows:

Contraction won't solve anything, it will just cost hundred of jobs in two communities and turn off fans by the hundreds of thousands. If baseball was really serious about addressing economic disparities, it would put the Expos in New York, where there are more than enough fans and corporate sponsors to support a third team. That also would reduce George Steinbrenner's [that is, the Yankees] competitive advantage over every other team. ... But

the owners won't do that. They would rather kill off baseball in two communities than work toward a meaningful solution.

In order for owners acting as a league to use economic competition to reduce competitive imbalance, the owners themselves would have to vote in favor of it. But it probably will never happen. In pro sports leagues, supermajorities are required for important league actions. In a league of 30 teams, if a 75 percent majority is required, then it would only take 8 owners to kill a move toward economic competition if such a movement ever arose in the first place. And moving a team into the actual territory of an existing owner requires unanimous consent. Along with compensation demands by harmed owners, supermajorities have operated for nearly 50 years to keep a third team out of New York. If the forces of economic competition were at work, there would already be a third team in that megalopolis market.

CHAPTER RECAP

Exclusive territories generate different revenue streams that lead to payroll imbalance and competitive imbalance. Theory predicts this outcome, as we discovered by analyzing the two-team league case. However, whether or not this is a problem is an empirical issue. Revenue imbalance, payroll imbalance, and competitive imbalance have always been part of league play, and it isn't clear that any of these types of imbalance is any worse than ever, historically speaking.

The data on competitive balance within the season, analyzed with Gini coefficients and the standard deviation ratio, reveal that generally revenue imbalance has improved steadily in pro sports leagues since the 1950s. Payroll imbalance has worsened. Finally, winning percent imbalance has declined modestly while taking a roller coaster ride through the decades. Championship imbalance has always plagued pro sports leagues; although the teams that one would identify as larger-revenue teams have changed over time, they nonetheless dominate the playoffs.

The data on revenues, payrolls, and winning percent also are correlated in just the way suggested by theory. Examining MLB, the correlation between revenues and payrolls is typically strong and positive. The same can be said for the correlation between revenues and winning percent. This suggests that arguments by the press and owners that payroll imbalance drives whatever problems leagues face are in error. It actually is, as theory predicts, the difference in revenue potential across teams that explains competitive imbalance.

However, even if competitive imbalance had improved over the decades, fans could dislike whatever level of competitive imbalance they saw. If they responded at the gate and in their viewing choices, leagues could face a reduced financial future. While the debate on the feelings of fans toward competitive balance continues, leagues have taken actions in the name of reducing competitive imbalance.

Joint venture remedies for competitive imbalance include gate and national TV revenue sharing, local revenue sharing, player drafts, luxury taxes, and salary caps. Theory suggests that gate and national TV revenue sharing and player drafts will have no impact whatsoever on competitive balance. However, they will redistribute money from players to the owners of weaker teams. Recent changes in gate sharing in the NFL show about the same amount of money collected in total. But there is a dramatic reduction in the net payment by the largest-revenue owners to the other owners in the league. This should reduce the incentive for lowest-revenue teams to skimp on talent, raising the quality of their teams.

Local revenue sharing can improve competitive balance if the marginal revenue derived from local revenue in one location is larger than in another. A comparison of the NFL, where all local TV is shared, and MLB, where none was shared until 1995, indicates that, all in all, local TV revenue sharing does improve competitive balance. In addition, changes in the way local revenue sharing mechanisms actually are designed in MLB show that league moving toward a larger pool for sharing but reduced transfers to lowest-revenue owners. The standard deviation ratios for the 2002–2004 seasons indicate that the most recent change in revenue sharing rules, to the straight-pool system, may be leading to a worsening of competitive imbalance.

Graphical analysis shows that luxury taxes, set high enough, also will lead richer teams to choose less talent. But this type of tax is unlikely to be applied to very many teams. At the current tax rates, large gains against competitive imbalance seem unlikely.

Salary caps, theoretically, can eliminate competitive imbalance entirely. However, the evidence is overwhelming that even average-team payrolls exceed the cap in both the NBA and the NFL. Even though caps can reduce competitive imbalance, they simply have not done so in their current forms. Either caps simply are designed with too many concessions in the name of fairness, or there is significant cheating on the caps in both leagues.

One method of reducing competitive imbalance would be to harness the forces of competition to that end. Leagues could locate more teams in the largest-revenue markets, reducing the value of those territories to owners currently occupying them and shifting marginal revenues to the left. The result is more balanced competition on the field. However, given that the largest-revenue owners would be opposed and that leagues are organized with supermajority decision rules, there is little reason for optimism about the implementation of this method.

KEY TERMS AND CONCEPTS

- Competitive imbalance
- Winning percent equilibrium
- Payroll imbalance
- Gini coefficient

- Revenue imbalance
- Championship imbalance
- Gate revenue sharing
- Local revenue sharing
- Standard deviation ratio

- Reverse-order-of-finish draft
- Payroll luxury tax
- Salary caps

REVIEW QUESTIONS

1. What is competitive imbalance? What danger can competitive imbalance pose to a pro sports league? Be sure to use the uncertainty of outcome hypothesis in your answer.
2. Why does theory predict that marginal revenues will be equal across all teams in a winning percent equilibrium? (Hint: Suppose they weren't? What would happen?)
3. What is the root cause of both payroll imbalance and competitive imbalance?
4. What is a Gini coefficient? How is a Gini coefficient used to identify revenue imbalance or payroll imbalance?
5. What is the standard deviation of winning percents? What advantage is there to using the standard deviation of winning percent, divided by the hypothetical standard deviation from a balanced league, rather than just the standard deviation of winning percent alone?
6. What measure is used to identify competitive imbalance in championships? Briefly summarize the evidence on championship imbalance in pro sports leagues.
7. Briefly summarize the evidence on the following aspects of pro sports leagues:
   a. Revenue imbalance
   b. Payroll imbalance
   c. Within-season competitive imbalance
   d. Championship imbalance
8. What does the theory presented in this chapter suggest about the correlation between revenues and payrolls? Revenues and winning percents? What do the data show for MLB?
9. Define each of the following and state what the theory predicts about whether each mechanism can reduce competitive imbalance. Explain fully:
   a. Gate and national TV revenue sharing
   b. Local revenue sharing
   c. Reverse-order-of-finish player draft
10. What is the difference between split-pool revenue sharing and straight-pool revenue sharing? Be sure to define each in your answer.

11. Define each of the following and state what the theory predicts about whether each mechanism can reduce competitive imbalance. Explain fully:
    a. Luxury tax
    b. Salary cap
12. Summarize what the theory predicts will happen to player pay under gate revenue sharing, local revenue sharing, the draft, a luxury tax, and a salary cap.
13. Briefly summarize the evidence on salary cap effectiveness.
14. Give two reasons for your answer in the preceding question. Can we tell which of the reasons you just gave explains more of the evidence than the other? Why?
15. How can economic competition be harnessed to reduce competitive imbalance? (See the Learning Highlight: Competitive Imbalance and the Power of Economic Competition.)

THOUGHT PROBLEMS

1. How do today's pro sports leagues resemble MLB as described by Bill Veeck back in 1958? What do you think is the primary cause of the similarities?
2. How does economics allow us to judge whether competitive imbalance is "too large" in some sports league? What are the limits of the economic way of thinking on this issue?
3. Is the two-team league winning percent equilibrium model a short-run or long-run model? Explain.
4. Graphically demonstrate that the marginal revenue from hiring talent is equal across larger- and smaller-revenue markets in equilibrium. In the same graph, show how revenue imbalance leads to competitive imbalance and payroll imbalance.
5. Starting from Figure 6.3, suppose that general employment opportunities in the smaller-revenue market increase dramatically so that population begins to increase. Show the following:
    a. The price of a unit of talent will increase.
    b. The smaller-revenue market owner buys more talent.
    c. Spending on talent by the smaller-revenue market owner will increase.
    d. Spending on talent by the larger-revenue market owner falls. (Hint: Is demand elastic or inelastic for the larger-revenue market owner?)
    e. Competitive imbalance is less than it was prior to the population increase.
6. What is the real-world importance of the three characteristics of the winning percent equilibrium demonstrated in Figure 6.3?
7. The Gini coefficient was used in the text to examine both revenue imbalance and payroll imbalance. Why wasn't the Gini coefficient used to examine winning percent imbalance as well? (You may wish to consult the paper by Utt and Fort [2003].)
8. Show why each of the remedies for competitive imbalance listed in the text will or will not improve balance. Where possible, use Figure 6.3 to make your point. On local revenue sharing, be sure to include how a comparison of

MLB and the NFL can aid in the judgment of that mechanism's chances to support balance.

9. Describe all of the steps involved in calculating a salary cap. Why is the term *salary cap* misleading in terms of what the mechanism actually does? What name does your author prefer?

10. The Learning Highlight: Shrinking MLB refers to a contraction in baseball that actually occurred after the 1899 season. The NL contracted from 12 to 8 teams. What teams were dropped? How did the teams that were contracted come to join the NL in the first place? What happened to competitive balance after they were dropped?

11. Does contraction necessarily mean that competitive balance will improve? Use the definition of the mean and standard deviation of winning percent as a guide. (You might also think about your answer to question 10 as well.)

12. The table below shows the years per title data for all of the NBA teams not displayed in Table 6.4:

NBA	TITLES	YEARS	YEARS/TITLE
Houston Rockets	3	33	11.0
Portland Trail Blazers	3	34	11.3
Seattle SuperSonics	3	37	12.3
Utah Jazz	2	25	12.5
San Francisco/Golden State Warriors	3	42	14.0
New York/New Jersey Nets	2	28	14.0
San Antonio Spurs	2	28	14.0
Orlando Magic	1	15	15.0
Milwaukee Bucks	2	36	18.0
Phoenix Suns	2	36	18.0
Indiana Pacers	1	28	28.0

What additional insight does this table give on championship imbalance? For example, how many teams really have been out of contention, relative to the total number of teams in the league in each year? (Hint: Remember to include all teams in this table and Table 6.4.)

13. Why is the minimum payroll in the cap system important from the perspective of improving competitive balance? What are the two reasons that a cap may not be very effective? How can these be overcome?

14. What arguments can you muster against moving the Expos to New York? (Hint: You may need to revisit the Learning Highlight: Competitive Imbalance and the Power of Economic Competition.)

15. Let's investigate the implications in the Learning Highlight: Competitive Imbalance and the Power of Economic Competition a bit more rigorously. Starting from Figure 6.3, how does entry into the larger-revenue market alter the marginal revenue functions? What happens to the price of talent and, subsequently, to the quality choice by the smaller-revenue market owner? What is the predicted impact on competitive imbalance?

ADVANCED PROBLEMS

1. What is the "right" level of competitive imbalance? Your answer to Thought Problem 2 suggests that competitive imbalance is too large relative to the level that would exist under freer entry and exit into pro sports leagues. But there also can be too much of a good thing. Using your basic economic training about comparing marginal benefits and marginal costs, portray the efficient level of competitive balance. Can you describe a situation where a perfectly balanced league is efficient?

2. Compare pro sports team quality to, say, the quality of opera (your author's favorite nonsports entertainment). We don't get upset when larger-revenue markets have higher quality opera alternatives (indeed, most would agree that it would be a waste if the New York Metropolitan Opera had its home base in a small town). So why do we get so involved with the variation in team quality across the cities in a league?

3. Imagine a league is comprised of a larger- (L) and smaller-revenue (S) team. W_L and W_S are their respective winning percents, and their marginal revenue functions are (values in millions of dollars):

$$MR_L = 90 - 90W_L$$
$$MR_S = 60 - 60W_S$$

    a. What is the equilibrium price of winning percent? Show it graphically as well.

    b. What will be the values of W_L and W_S in equilibrium? Show them graphically as well.

    c. What will be the equilibrium total talent bill for each? Identify them graphically as well.

4. The data show that revenues are typically significantly positively correlated with both payrolls and winning percents in MLB. Is the same true in, say, the NBA? (Warning: While the question is short, the time involved in finding the answer won't be!)

5. Examine the NFL's newest gate sharing arrangement. What were the impacts on larger- and smaller-revenue market owners? Which do you think favored the change? Explain fully.

6. Examine MLB's newest local revenue sharing arrangement. What were the impacts on larger- and smaller-revenue market owners? Which do you think favored the change? Why?

7. According to Table 6.1, revenue imbalance jumped 38 percent in MLB's AL, 39 percent in MLB's NL, 72 percent in the NFL, and 26 percent in the NHL. What can explain this? What was different about the NBA where revenue imbalance remained practically unchanged? What happened to winning percent imbalance in each league over the decade? Does this pose a problem for the application of theory to the data?

8. Return to our two-team league described in Advanced Problem 3. With the same marginal revenue functions:

    a. What if a luxury tax is imposed of $45,000 on each point (.001) over .500. What is the new price of winning percent?

    b. What are the new W_L and W_S in equilibrium?

    c. What are the new equilibrium talent bills for each team?

9. Baseball's Blue Ribbon Panel reached the following conclusions (reiterated in the MLB Updated Supplement, December 2001, p. 3). Using the summary conclusions from the text, based on the data in Table 6.1 through Table 6.4, comment on these findings:

   a. Large and growing revenue disparities exist and are causing problems of chronic competitive imbalance.

   b. These problems have become substantially worse during the five complete seasons since the strike-shortened season of 1994 and seem likely to remain severe unless Major League Baseball undertakes remedial actions proportional to the problem.

   c. The limited revenue sharing and payroll tax that were approved as part of MLB's 1996 collective bargaining agreement with the Major League Baseball Players Association (MLBPA) have produced neither the intended moderating of payroll disparities nor improved competitive balance.

10. A recent *Sports Business Journal* editorial (July 12, 2004, p. 30) listed five major unresolved problems for MLB. The fourth is fascinating:

    > Ensure that revenue sharing isn't profit-taking. Owners on the receiving end of revenue sharing ought to be putting the money back into their teams, not into their pockets. Spend it on payroll, on scouting or on marketing, but spend it on making the organization more competitive. That benefits both the individual team and the business of baseball overall.

    Suppose that revenue sharing is chosen in such a way that the desired level of competitive balance is achieved. Using Figure 6.3, show what happens if owners actually follow the editorial suggestion. What else do you expect owners will do with the shared revenues?

INTERNET RESOURCES

For a host of additional material and questions for thought, visit this book's Web site at www.prenhall.com/fort.

REFERENCES

Fleisher, Arthur A. III, William F. Shughart II, and Robert D. Tollison. "Ownership Structure in Professional Sports," in *Research in Law and Economics*, vol. 12, ed. Richard O. Zerbe. Greenwich, CT: JAI Press, 1989.

Fort, Rodney. "Revenue Disparity and Competitive Balance in Major League Baseball." Statement for the U.S. Senate Subcommittee on Antitrust, November 17, 2000.

Fort, Rodney, and Joel Maxcy. "The Demise of African-American Baseball Leagues: A Rival League Explanation," *Journal of Sports Economics* 2 (2001): 35–49.

Fort, Rodney, and James Quirk. "Cross-Subsidization, Incentives, and Outcomes in Professional Team Sports Leagues," *Journal of Economic Literature* 23 (1995): 1265–1299.

Fort, Rodney, and James Quirk. "Introducing a Competitive Economic Environment into

Professional Sports," in *Advances in the Economics of Sports,* vol. 2, ed. Wallace Hendricks. Greenwich, CT: JAI Press, 1997.

Kesenne, Stefan. "League Management in Professional Team Sports with Win Maximizing Clubs," *European Journal for Sport Management* 2 (1996): 14–22.

Kesenne, Stefan. "Player Market Regulation and Competitive Balance in a Win Maximizing Scenario," in *Competition Policy in Professional Sport: Europe after the Bosman Case,* eds. Stephan Kesenne and Claude Jeanrenaude. Antwerp: Standaard Uitgeverij, 1999.

Kesenne, Stefan. "Revenue Sharing and Competitive Balance in Professional Team Sports," *Journal of Sports Economics* 1 (2000): 56–65.

Levin, Richard C., George J. Mitchell, Paul A. Volcker, and George F. Will. *The Report of the Independent Members of the Commissioner's Blue Ribbon Panel on Baseball Economics.* New York: Major League Baseball, 2000.

Neale, Walter C. "The Peculiar Economics of Professional Sports," *Quarterly Journal of Economics* 78 (1964): 1–14.

Quirk, James, and Rodney D. Fort. *Pay Dirt: The Business of Pro Team Sports.* Princeton, NJ: Princeton University Press, 1992.

Quirk, James, and Rodney D. Fort. *Hardball: The Abuse of Power in Pro Team Sports.* Princeton, NJ: Princeton University Press, 1999.

Scully, Gerald. *The Business of Major League Baseball.* Chicago, IL: University of Chicago Press, 1989.

Staudohar, Paul D. "Salary Caps in Professional Team Sports," in *Competition Policy in Professional Sport: Europe after the Bosman Case,* eds. Stephan Kesenne and Claude Jeanrenaude. Antwerp: Standaard Uitgeverij, 1999.

Utt, Joshua, and Rodney Fort. "Pitfalls to Measuring Competitive Balance with Gini Coefficients," *Journal of Sports Economics* 3 (November 2002): 367–373.

Chapter

7

The Value of Sports Talent

Chapter Objectives

After reading this chapter, you should be able to:

■ *See that marginal revenue product theory provides a general and insightful explanation of pay and hiring in sports.*

■ *Explain why the winner's curse explanation of pay in sports does not fit any real-world sports situation.*

■ *Explain why the bidding war explanation of player pay only holds as a few teams approach the playoffs.*

■ *See that the winner-take-all logic might explain individual sport outcomes but that it does not explain player pay in team sports.*

■ *Recognize the variety of impacts that discrimination can have in sports labor markets and appreciate the limits of economics in the analysis of gender and racial discrimination in sports pay and hiring.*

> *I don't think anyone's worth this type of money, obviously.*
> *But that's the market that we're in today.*

—MLB PLAYER ALEX RODRIGUEZ UPON SIGNING AT OVER $20 MILLION PER YEAR
CNN.com, *Alex Rodriguez Profile*

The first NFL draftee, selected by the Chicago Bears, was Heisman-winner Jay Berwanger of the University of Chicago (then a member of the Big Ten Conference). However, Berwanger did not sign with the Bears because the pay they offered could not beat his starting salary with a prestigious degree! Things have changed since then. In 2003, the number-one draft pick, quarterback Carson Palmer, signed for an average of $3.1 million for 7 years and a $10 million signing bonus. But under the most optimistic circumstances covered in the contract, he could make as much as $49 million over 6 years plus the original $10 million bonus.

Many look at the market for athletic talent and shake their heads—they see both outlandish levels of pay for players and hiring discrimination in coaching and in the front office. In this chapter, we will explain the workings of the market for sports talent. The tried and true marginal revenue product (MRP) explanation gains us the most yards in terms of explaining talent market outcomes. We will also use the MRP explanation to clarify a few misconceptions, for example, the idea that salary increases lead to increased ticket prices. In addition, we will analyze three alternatives to the MRP explanation of player pay: the winner's curse, bidding wars, and winner-take-all logic. Although these are appealing explanations, we will see that they actually explain very little. Finally, we gain some insights about race and gender discrimination using the MRP explanation. But these results are limited to the market outcomes for which the MRP explanation was designed.

THE VALUE OF ATHLETES

Let's start the chapter by documenting just how large player earnings are. Earnings for a number of athletes, and salaries for some of them, are reported in Table 7.1. For most of us, these are unimaginable figures. The highest salary in Table 7.1 is $28 million for basketball player Kevin Garnett. Earning an average of $100,000 per year—a respectable wage—a person would have to work 280 years to match that single-year figure. And that isn't even the highest contract offered to a pro team sports player. Michael Jordan was offered $33.14 million (about $38.4 million in 2004 dollars) by Chicago Bulls owner Jerry Reinsdorf to play the single 1998 season—and Jordan turned that down in favor of retirement (*Sports Illustrated*, April 27, 1998). The amount Jordan was offered in 1998 would be enough to put over 200 students through 4-year degree programs at prestigious universities. The size of pro player earnings is not just an American phenomenon. According to www.worldtransfers.info (March 2, 2005), Real Madrid paid $45.6 million just to acquire the rights to Zinedine Zidane from Juventus of Italy in 2001. The source claims this is the world record transfer fee.

Did You Know?
Even though Michael Jordan chose not to play, the owner of the Chicago Bulls offered Jordan over $38 million (in 2004 dollars) to play with the Bulls in 1998. That's enough to put 200 students through 4-year degree programs at prestigious universities.

Table 7.1 50 Highest-Earning Athletes and Pay 2003–2004

RANK	NAME	SPORT	EARNINGS ($MILLIONS)	SALARY ($MILLIONS)
1	Tiger Woods	Golf	$80.3	
2	Michael Schumacher	Auto racing	$80.0	
3	Peyton Manning	Football	$42.0	$11.3
4	Michael Jordan	Basketball	$35.0	
5	Shaquille O'Neal	Basketball	$31.9	$26.5
6	Kevin Garnett	Basketball	$29.7	$28.0
7	Andre Agassi	Tennis	$28.2	
8	David Beckham	Soccer	$28.0	
9	Alex Rodriguez	Baseball	$26.2	$22.0
10	Kobe Bryant	Basketball	$26.1	$13.5
11	Grant Hill	Basketball	$25.9	$13.3
12	Derek Jeter	Baseball	$23.2	$15.6
13	Barry Bonds	Baseball	$22.7	$15.0
14	Manny Ramirez	Baseball	$22.1	$17.2
15	Oscar DeLaHoya	Boxing	$22.0	
16	Lebron James	Basketball	$21.1	$4.2
17	Vince Carter	Basketball	$20.2	$11.3
18	Dale Earnhardt, Jr.	Auto racing	$20.1	
19	Arnold Palmer	Golf	$20.0	
20	Phil Mickelson	Golf	$19.8	
21	Allen Iverson	Basketball	$19.7	$13.5
22	Champ Bailey	Football	$19.6	$2.1
23	Jeff Gordon	Auto racing	$19.3	
24	Lance Armstrong	Cycling	$19.2	
25	Tracy McGrady	Basketball	$19.0	$13.3
26	Ronaldo	Soccer	$18.5	
27	Carlos Delgado	Baseball	$18.0	$18.7
28	Ichiro Suzuki	Baseball	$17.8	$4.7
29	Randy Johnson	Baseball	$17.5	$15.0
30	Mike Piazza	Baseball	$17.3	$15.6
31	Jevon Kearse	Football	$17.2	$4.1
32	Sammy Sosa	Baseball	$17.0	$16.9
33	Pedro Martinez	Baseball	$16.8	$15.5
34	Jason Giambi	Baseball	$16.6	$11.4
35	Lavar Arrington	Football	$16.5	$4.7
36	Brian Urlacher	Football	$16.4	$15.1
37	Carson Palmer	Football	$16.3	$11.1
38	Greg Norman	Golf	$16.2	
39	Ernie Els	Golf	$16.1	
40	Ralf Schumacher	Auto racing	$16.0	
41	Jason Kidd	Basketball	$15.9	$13.2
42	Zinedine Zidane	Soccer	$15.8	

(Continued)

(*Continued*)

RANK	NAME	SPORT	EARNINGS ($MILLIONS)	SALARY ($MILLIONS)
43	Yao Ming	Basketball	$15.7	$4.1
44	Grant Wistrom	Football	$15.6	$1.6
45	Shawn Green	Baseball	$15.5	$15.7
46	Charles Rogers	Football	$15.4	$10.1
47	Rasheed Wallace	Basketball	$15.3	$17.0
48	Kevin Brown	Baseball	$15.2	$15.7
49	Anfernee Hardaway	Basketball	$15.1	$13.5
50	Andre Miller	Basketball	$15.0	$6.4

Notes: Totals include salaries, bonuses, prize money, endorsements and appearance fees.
Source: Collated by the author from data at www.forbes.com and USAToday.com.

Did You Know?
At the top end of the salary distribution, the highest-paid NBA superstar, Shaquille O'Neal, makes 31 percent more than the highest paid MLB star (Manny Ramirez), 2.4 times more than the highest paid NFL star (Antoine Winfield), and 2.7 times more than the highest paid NHL stars (Jaromir Jagr and Peter Forsberg).

Did You Know?
All major professional sports leagues witnessed at least a doubling in salaries in the 1990s, and salaries quadrupled in the NHL over that decade!

Did You Know?
In 2004, 21 MLB players earned more than $13.5 million, and $13.5 million was the average payroll for entire teams in MLB in 1989, just fifteen years earlier.

Salaries

Table 7.2 shows descriptive salary statistics for all four major pro sports leagues by decade but with recent years shown in detail. From the data in Table 7.2, you can see that there always have been top-end skewed salaries. First, as shown in Table 7.2, the median is always dramatically less than the average salary. Second, the top salaries have been more than ten times the median since the 1980s. For example, in 2004, the top-heavy ranking is as follows: Manny Ramirez at $22.5 million in MLB, just over 21 times the median; Antoine Winfield at $12.4 million in the NFL, nearly 18 times the median; Shaquille O'Neal at $29.5 million in the NBA, nearly 12 times the median; Jaromir Jagr and Peter Forsberg at $11 million in the NHL, just over 9 times the median.

The data in Table 7.2 also show extraordinary salary growth over time. The average has grown steadily in real terms over the decades. The rate of growth through the 1990s shown in Table 7.2 is nothing short of astonishing because the average rate of growth in the U.S. economy is typically around 3 percent. Even more astonishing is the fact that salaries have more than doubled in all four major leagues (and quadrupled in the NHL!). Few industries have ever witnessed a doubling of salaries in any single decade.

The data in Tables 7.1 and 7.2 also raise a number of interesting questions. How can athletes be worth this much? What happened to cause the jumps in salaries in various sports in different years? We will also look at why players of different sports are paid less than others later in this chapter. Clearly, from Table 7.2, NBA superstars are paid the most, followed by hockey and baseball players. NFL superstars are paid the least. We will try to answer these questions in this chapter. However, let's first look at what else we can deduce about sports compensation.

Table 7.1 Average and Median Salaries in Pro Sports Leagues ($2004)

	MLB		NBA		NFL		NHL	
Year	Average	Median	Average	Median	Average	Median	Average	Median
1970s	$205,307		$386,514		$141,400		$228,801	
1980s	$631,889	$453,170	$680,428		$321,942		$260,783	
1990s	$1,503,383	$538,662	$2,319,320		$843,451		$941,602	
2000s	$2,446,179	$1,144,254	$4,356,385	$2,525,417	$1,199,984	$573,797	$1,797,983	$1,164,315
1990	$901,433	$544,974	$1,302,005		$525,142		$417,343	
1991	$1,331,605	$615,607	$1,527,078		$588,619		$530,060	
1992	$1,572,962	$569,331	$1,751,989		$660,365		$537,440	
1993	$1,577,727	$523,208	$2,224,471		$867,544		$710,562	
1994	$1,632,298	$617,942	$2,424,103		$799,954		$714,472	
1995	$1,430,209	$367,224	$2,481,365		$903,217		$938,760	
1996	$1,505,664	$383,782	$2,651,217		$970,105		$1,084,766	
1997	$1,689,422	$488,421	$2,637,695		$868,237		$1,264,857	
1998	$1,448,853	$497,060	$2,857,147		$1,093,880		$1,553,192	
1999	$1,943,657	$779,069	$3,336,131		$1,157,454		$1,664,565	
2000	$2,186,837	$1,058,169	$3,264,875		$1,044,186	$547,560	$1,669,739	$1,011,450
2001	$2,422,911	$1,179,764	$4,815,000	$2,411,855	$1,177,535	$602,528	$1,757,571	$1,168,242
2002	$2,502,397	$1,243,492	$4,773,300	$2,627,323	$1,190,700	$531,953	$1,879,719	$1,258,994
2003	$2,632,140	$1,182,778	$5,064,510	$2,537,074	$1,287,500	$613,146	$1,884,900	$1,218,576
2004	$2,486,609	$1,057,069	$3,864,241		$1,300,000			

Note: For the NBA and NHL, year is the beginning year of the season (e.g., 2000 is for the 2000–2001 season).
Sources: See the data note in the references.

Endorsements

On top of player salaries, many players earn substantial endorsement income. That is the reason for the difference between salaries and earnings in Table 7.2. For example, in September 2000, golf pro Tiger Woods signed endorsement contracts for $100 million over 10 years (*Sports Illustrated*, September 25, 2000, p. 27). The real sports endorsement giant is former heavyweight champion of the world, George Foreman. He signed a deal with Salton grills for $137.5 million over 5 years. Other top endorsement earners are Grant Hill with Fila (September 1997: $80 million over 7 years), Allen Iverson with Reebok (June 1996: $50 million over 10 years), and Davis Love III with Titleist (September 2000: $50 million over 10 years). Most recently, according to ESPN.com, NBA man-child LeBron James signed with Nike (May 2003: $100 million over 7 years). A *Sports Business Journal* (October 9, 2000) survey shows that endorsement earnings typically double the income of male superstars. For female superstars, the impact is staggering. WNBA players such as Sheryl Swoopes and Lisa Leslie added 10 times their sports earnings through endorsements. Skater Michelle Kwan quintupled her income, and

Did You Know?
Former heavyweight champion George Foreman signed a 5-year, $137.5-million endorsement contract with Salton grills. On average, that's $27.5 million a year.

tennis players Serena Williams and Martina Hingis added four times their sports earnings with endorsements.

Comparisons with Other Entertainers

Even though these figures seem astronomical, when you look at Table 7.3, which lists the *Forbes* top 50 celebrity earnings of 2004, with only a couple of exceptions sports superstars do not reach the lofty compensation heights enjoyed by other entertainment superstars. Even though ten athletes make the list, only Tiger Woods makes the top 10. Indeed, the sports stars that even make the list typically are "bigger than their sport" (e.g., Tiger Woods, Michael Jordan, and Shaquille O'Neal). Even Tiger Woods earned only about 38 percent of what Mel Gibson earned in 2004. For a final bit of perspective, in 2004 the entire New York Yankees team, the highest-paid team in all of sports, earned $184.2 million, about 88 percent of Oprah Winfrey's earnings for that year. Even though sports superstars are paid handsomely, they are not even in the same league with other entertainment superstars, generally speaking.

Did You Know?
In 2004, the entire New York Yankees team made about 12 percent less than entertainment icon Oprah Winfrey.

Enough said about the impressive earnings of sports stars. What is the answer to the first question: How can athletes be worth so much? There are a few competing explanations for how sports stars get paid. Let's look at the marginal revenue product explanation of input payment. After all, sports talent is just an input to the sports production process.

Table 7.3
Celebrity Pay 2004

NAME	EARNINGS RANK	EARNINGS ($MILLIONS)
Mel Gibson	1	$210
Oprah Winfrey	1	$210
J. K. Rowling	3	$147
Michael Schumacher	4	$80
*Tiger Woods	4	$80
Steven Spielberg	6	$75
Jim Carrey	7	$66
Bruce Springsteen	8	$64
Nora Roberts	9	$60
David Copperfield	10	$57
Rolling Stones	11	$51
Tom Cruise	12	$45
Fleetwood Mac	12	$45
Ray Romano	14	$44
The Eagles	15	$43
*Peyton Manning	16	$42
Jerry Bruckheimer	17	$40
David Letterman	17	$40

(Continued)

(Continued)

NAME	EARNINGS RANK	EARNINGS ($MILLIONS)
Kelsey Grammer	19	$39
Robert De Niro	20	$35
Peter Jackson	20	$35
*Michael Jordan	20	$35
Metallica	20	$35
James Patterson	20	$35
Simon and Garfunkel	25	$33
Cameron Diaz	26	$32
*Shaquille O'Neal	26	$32
Howard Stern	28	$31
Dan Brown	29	$30
Sandra Bullock	29	$30
*Kevin Garnett	29	$30
Paul Harvey	29	$30
Rush Limbaugh	29	$30
Joel Silver	29	$30
*Andre Agassi	35	$28
*David Beckham	35	$28
Johnny Depp	35	$28
Celine Dion	35	$28
Michael Flatley	35	$28
Dave Matthews Band	35	$28
The Olsen Twins	35	$28
Cher	35	$28
Steve Martin	35	$28
Tom Hanks	44	$27
Angelina Jolie	44	$27
Siegfried & Roy	44	$27
*Kobe Bryant	47	$26
*Grant Hill	47	$26
*Alex Rodriguez	47	$26
Jennifer Aniston	50	$26

*Denotes sports stars.
Source: www.forbes.com.

THE MARGINAL REVENUE PRODUCT EXPLANATION

In almost all spheres of economic endeavor, payments to inputs, such as sports talent, are determined by the inputs' **marginal revenue product**, or MRP for short. Remember from Chapter 4 that talent is hired to produce winning percent in the long run. Given that, *MRP* for sports talent is defined as:

$$MRP(W) = MP(W) \times MR(W)$$

W is the level of team winning percent. $MP(W)$ is marginal product, or the player's contribution to winning percent. For example, from Table 4.6, a team currently with five stars and a winning percent of 0.528 could raise its winning percent by 0.070 by adding another star. $MR(W)$ is the marginal revenue generated by the player's contribution to winning. Again, revenue at the margin will depend on the level of winning percent that is being added to the level W. In sports, where market power leads to downward sloping demand functions, MR decreases with output. Therefore, the MR function slopes down for the individual team at any level of W that might be chosen in the long run. But what does MRP represent? Essentially, MRP is the input's contribution to the revenues earned by the team owner. In Chapter 4, you calculated the cost of winning in Table 4.7. MRP is the other side of the comparison. This is the essential decision made by all producers: Discover the cost of winning and compare it to those players' MRP in order to determine whether they are worth hiring.

One of the contributions of sports economics is the actual calculation of MRP. Once again, we return to one of the true pioneers in sports economics, Gerald Scully (1974; 1989). In Chapter 4, we discussed his contribution to the analysis of coaches and managers. Scully also devised a way to calculate the value of a baseball player's MRP. Basically, playing statistics translate into wins, and wins are sold to fans. Scully found that particular players added value in obvious ways and actually estimated the value of slugging, hitting, and pitching, holding everything else about the composition of the team and the performance of teammates constant. This makes the calculation truly an MRP calculation.

Did You Know?

Economist Gerald Scully (1989) has estimated that a strong (but not superstar) MLB slugger, just for his power contribution, adds about $3.9 million (in 2004 dollars) to team revenues each year. A strong (but not superstar) pitcher can add around $7.1 million.

In *The Business of Major League Baseball* (1989), Scully shows that a one-point increase in winning percent raised 1984 revenues by $31,696. In 2004 dollars, that is about $57,626. Because a win is 6.2 winning percent points, a win is worth $357,281 in today's dollars. A solid slugger would add 63 points, or about 11 wins. The marginal revenue from just those games is worth $3.9 million in today's dollars. A strong pitcher can add 20 net wins, or $7.1 million in extra revenue to an owner holding everything else about the team constant. These are precisely the elements that determine the MRP of players.

In a **competitive talent market**, we expect that players get paid pretty close to their MRP. In all pro sports leagues, rules agreed upon by owners and players through collective bargaining (covered in Chapter 9) allow players to sell their services to the highest bidder after a fixed number of years. In MLB, for example, it is 6 years. After that period, players are **free agents**, and they can sell their services to the highest bidder. The NHL has the most cumbersome formula for free agency, where free agency is determined both by experience and by age. Of course, players become free agents only if they are not bound by a long-term contract to their current team. In this free-agency setting, we would expect players to play where they will be the happiest. Most often, this is the place where they will be paid the most.

In order to get players to move from their current team, an owner will have to offer more than they make with that team. If competition over the player is brisk, then the eventual payment will be between the highest- and second-highest offer of the two top-bidding owners. Of course, competition works on both sides of the market. If good substitutes exist for any given player's services, one would expect this competition to dampen the size of the payment that would entice the player to change teams. Even though this amount will not be quite the entire MRP at the highest-valued location, it will be between that value and the second-highest value across the entire league.

If you have caught on to the MRP idea, then you can answer one of the questions posed in the last section. Why do NBA players make more than, say, NFL players? If you answer because NBA players play about 90 games (including the preseason) whereas NFL players play about 18 games (including the preseason), you need to think again. The MLB season is twice as long as the NBA season, but MLB players earn less than NBA players, as shown in Table 7.2.

According to the MRP theory of player pay, it must be either because an NBA player has higher marginal product on a basketball team than an NFL player has on a football team or because NBA fans are willing to pay more for added winning so that marginal revenue is higher or both. Both explanations do seem reasonable. With a smaller number of players on NBA teams than on NFL teams, it is possible that the contribution to team winning is larger for each individual NBA player than for each individual NFL player. The marginal revenue collected by NBA owners also may be larger if the demand by NBA fans is greater. The MRP deck seems stacked in favor of a given NBA player earning more than a given NFL player.

Case Study: The Barry Bonds Show, 2001

In 2001, Barry Bonds of the San Francisco Giants was paid $10.3 million. He was the 22nd highest-paid player in the league, in the top 3 percent. That year, Bonds hit 73 home runs, eclipsing the single-season home run record of 70 held by Mark McGwire. Bonds' record chase didn't seem to draw the same press enthusiasm as the earlier run by McGwire in 1998, but fans around the league were interested, especially in San Francisco—and to the tune of quite a few million dollars for the owner of the Giants.

It's pretty easy to see that Bonds' record chase was worth about the same amount to the Giants' owner as winning the division. In 1999, the Giants finished second in the National League West Division and drew 2,078,365 at the gate. In 2000, the team won their division, and attendance increased to 3,315,330. In 2001, Bonds' record-breaking season, the Giants again finished second but still drew 3,311,958. When the Giants won their division, they enjoyed an attendance increment of 1,236,965. Suppose that the Giants would still have drawn 2,078,365 finishing second in 2001 without Bonds' record. If so, then Bonds' record-breaking performance added 1,233,603 fans. In their "Fan Cost Index" resource, Team Marketing Report (www.teammarketing.com) lists the Giants' average ticket price in 2001 at $19.24. The fan cost index itself is given as $163.89 for two adults and two kids. The additional attendance was worth conservatively $23.7 million, just multiplying the average ticket price by the attendance increment. But the value could have been upward of $50.5 million, dividing the increment by 4 and multiplying by the Fan Cost Index.

Did You Know?
During Barry Bonds' pursuit of the single-season home run record in 2001, San Francisco attendance increased by around 1.2 million fans. This generated a revenue increase for the Giants' owners of between $23.7 million and $50.5 million. Bonds was paid $10.3 million that year.

Here's the kicker: Because seasons like this do not come along even once in a life-time, it is unlikely that the owners of the Giants had built the record chase into Bonds' contract to cover 2001. This means that Bonds' contribution to these unexpected revenues was over and above what the owners of the Giants thought he probably would be worth, on average, for the 2001 season, and we haven't included any revenues beyond those at the stadium. This bonus to the owners makes it clear that Bonds was worth his $10.3 million (and then some) in 2001.

The value of the Barry Bonds Show also spilled over to the rest of the league. Prior to a visit by Bonds and the Giants toward the end of the season, the San Diego Padres hosted the Arizona Diamondbacks (August 31 through September 2) and then the St. Louis Cardinals (September 3 through September 5) in a seven-game home stand (there was one double-header). The total paid attendance for both series was 154,013, or about 22,002 fans per game. Just after those seven games, in a three-game series against the Giants, 156,183 fans attended the San Diego–San Francisco games. That is 52,061 on average, per game, or an additional 30,059 per game over the immediately preceding series. Again, the Team Marketing Report average ticket price for San Diego was $13.74, and the Padres' fan cost index was $127.46. So the conservative estimate of the Barry Bonds Show's value to the owner of the Padres was $413,013 per game ($1.24 million total), and the top end could have been as much as $957,830 per game ($2.87 million total). Even with any other variation that might have occurred, such as the weather or a particularly interesting visiting team, it is clear that the increase in revenue can be attributed mainly to the history-making performance of Barry Bonds.

The Experience–Earnings Relationship

MRP develops over time. In economics, this is called the **experience–earnings relationship.** MRP on all jobs starts low, increases rather quickly, tops off, and then may decline as skill diminishes or health declines with age. This applies to sports as well.

Table 7.4 shows data on experience, performance, and earnings for a particular MLB pitcher, Randy Johnson. The table shows that Johnson's lifetime record is 246 wins and 128 losses, a 0.658 winning percent. His per-game earned run average (ERA, or on average the number of runs he would usually give up in nine innings) shows a typical pattern—erratic at the beginning and improving over time. Of particular interest to us, however, is the way that pay and experience are related.

Figure 7.1 charts Johnson's pay as compared to his experience; this is called an **experience–earnings profile.** It is clear that the relationship between pay and experience is as we would expect with any job. But there is a special sports twist. Through his first 3 full MLB years (1989–1991), Johnson's salary was very low. In the third year, something special happens for baseball players. They become eligible for **arbitration** (covered in detail in Chapter 9). If a player and team owner cannot reach an agreement in the third year, then the decision may go to an independent arbitrator, who must choose either the amount the player is asking or the amount offered by the owner. The effect, even for players who do not go to arbitration, is a dramatic increase in salary. Johnson's salary increased nearly four-fold in the fourth year, from $486,500 to nearly $1.9 million (both in 2004 dollars). Apparently, his improvement after that was sufficiently impressive that the Mariners' owners increased his salary steadily. Johnson's road to fabulous riches had a bump in 1998. He couldn't reach an

Table 7.4 Randy Johnson's Pay and Performance

YEAR	TEAM	WINS	LOSSES	PCT	ERA	PAY ($MILLIONS 2004)
1988	Mon	3	0	1.000	0.242	
1989	Mon/Sea	7	13	0.350	0.482	$106,400
1990	Sea	14	11	0.560	0.365	$268,250
1991	Sea	13	10	0.565	0.398	$486,500
1992	Sea	12	14	0.462	0.377	$1,879,875
1993	Sea	19	8	0.704	0.324	$3,438,750
1994	Sea	13	6	0.684	0.319	$4,159,250
1995	Sea	18	2	0.900	0.248	$5,797,000
1996	Sea	5	0	1.000	0.367	$7,230,000
1997	Sea	20	4	0.833	0.228	$7,463,500
1998	Sea/Hou	19	11	0.633	0.328	$6,960,000
1999	Ariz	17	9	0.654	0.248	$10,565,500
2000	Ariz	19	7	0.731	0.264	$14,685,000
2001	Ariz	21	6	0.778	0.249	$14,284,500
2002	Ariz	24	5	0.828	0.232	$14,017,500
2003	Ariz	6	8	0.429	0.426	$15,450,000
2004	Ariz	16	14	0.533	0.260	$16,000,000
Lifetime		246	128	0.658		

Source: Salaries are from the *USAToday* baseball salary database.

Figure 7.1
Randy Johnson's Experience–Earnings Profile
Charting salary against experience for Randy Johnson (the data are in Table 7.4) generates his experience–earnings profile. It is common for such profiles to increase slowly at first, then rise quite rapidly, tailing off toward the end of a worker's earning years.

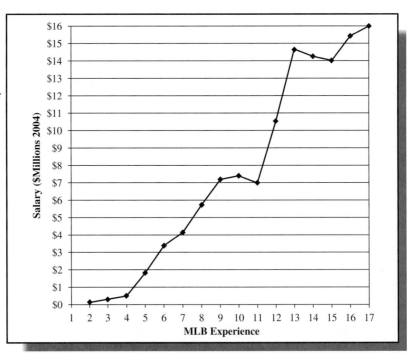

agreement with the Mariners' owners and took a short stay with the Houston Astros. But immediately he was grabbed by the Arizona Diamondbacks at 1.5 times his previous salary. Ultimately, he became the highest-paid pitcher in MLB.

People are often surprised that the pattern of earnings (although not the level) over time for pitchers is similar to that of any other job. This pattern of earnings and experience, except for the level of pay, looks just like the experience–earnings profile of any other employee hired on the basis of MRP, from starting at minimum wage on through middle-earnings years and ultimately to peak years. The similarity of this profile with those working in other jobs adds another piece of evidence in favor of the MRP explanation of pay in pro sports.

The MRP of Coaches and Managers

The MRP explanation works for other pro sport talent as well. Red Auerbach, coach of the NBA Boston Celtics during the Bill Russell dynasty years, earned $10,000 for the 1950–1951 season, whereas recent Celtics coach Rick Pitino was paid $7 million for the 1997–1998 season (*Sports Illustrated*, May 19, 1997, p. 57). That's a 700-fold increase in 47 years (almost exactly 15% per year), well above the average rate of inflation. How can this tremendous increase be explained?

In Chapter 4, the work of Porter and Scully (1982) and Scully (1989) on managerial efficiency was described. Essentially, managers become more efficient the closer they get to the theoretical best they can get out of their players in terms of winning. One would expect, by the MRP theory of pay, that better managers would make more. This work shows that there is some evidence that managers who make the most of their talent do get paid more.

However, this dramatic increase in pay for Pitino over Auerbach was not due to the relative success of the two coaches. Auerbach was clearly the more successful of the two, with Auerbach having the NBA record for championships. Part of the difference is that Pitino's job description included executive responsibilities that Auerbach did not have as a coach. The rest of the difference, according to MRP theory, simply follows from the dramatic increase in fan willingness to pay for NBA basketball. Nowhere is there a better example that the value of an input has risen because the marginal revenue aspect of MRP has skyrocketed. We saw in Chapter 2 that the NBA is now a $2 to $3 billion industry. Even though today's coaches may not be any better than their counterparts in the past, what they are doing has simply become much more valuable over time.

EQUILIBRIUM IN THE TALENT MARKET: GRAPHICAL ANALYSIS

Our conclusion thus far is that MRP theory provides a general explanation of pay in pro sports. It may be hard to believe that the MRP of coaches and players can be so high, but it is. As long as competition for coaches and players is brisk, they will be paid close to the value of what they produce (in Chapter 8, we will see what happens when the players' labor market competition is limited). Owners are forced to pay up to nearly the highest MRP of players across all teams in the league in the presence of strong competition over talent.

We can determine equilibrium winning percents and talent prices in a league with a graphical analysis of a competitive talent market. We will use the same graphical tool that we used in Chapter 6, namely, the two-team league with an exaggerated large-revenue market and a small-revenue market. We begin from an equilibrium in that league and remember two important points. First, we are measuring talent in units, so that hiring one more unit of talent increases winning percent by 0.001. As in Chapter 6, when we measure talent in units that produce one more unit of winning percent, the x-axis measures both winning percent for the teams and the amount of talent it takes to generate that winning percent. Using this measuring convention, the marginal revenue functions are also MRP functions. This means that we can find both the winning percent for teams and their talent choice at the same time. Second, the sum of the winning percents in our two-team league must be equal to one. We begin with Figure 7.2, market equilibrium.

From Chapter 6, we know that equilibrium can only occur at $MR_L^*(W) = MR_S^*(W)$ so that $W_L^* = 1 - W_S^*$ in Figure 7.2. Because of our convention of measuring talent in units that generate one more winning percent point, the price of winning and talent are both equal to P^*. Therefore, in equilibrium, $MR_L^*(W) = MR_S^*(W) = P^*$. P^* becomes the price of one unit of talent. We also have our three important features of a competitive **talent market equilibrium:**

- Marginal revenues are equal across teams, that is, $MR_L^* = MR_S^*$.
- Revenue imbalance means that there will be payroll imbalance.
- Revenue imbalance means that there will be competitive imbalance.

Figure 7.2 Market Equilibrium
In a two-team league, equilibrium in the talent market occurs where marginal revenues are equal and determine the price of talent, $MR_L^* = MR_S^* = P^*$. It is easy to see that the imbalance of revenues between the two teams ($MR_L > MR_S$ for all levels of winning percent) generates competitive imbalance since the large-market team has a higher winning percent in equilibrium, that is $W_L^* > W_S^*$. Further imbalance in revenues also generates payroll imbalance. Spending on talent by the large-market owner is larger than spending on talent by the small-market owner, that is, $P^*W_L^* > P^*W_S^*$.

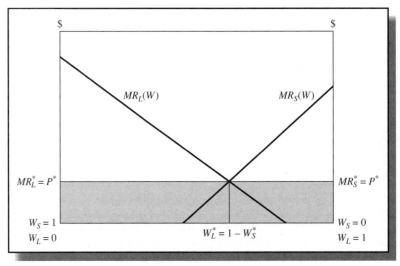

Given this result, it is easy to see how much each owner pays in total for the winning percent that they choose. The bill for the larger-market owner is the left-hand shaded rectangle in Figure 7.2, calculated as $P*W_L^*$; that is, the price of each unit of winning multiplied by the number of units of winning. This amount also represents the payment to talent because we have measured talent in units that produce each unit of winning percent. Thus, the left-hand shaded rectangle in Figure 7.2 also represents the total payment to talent hired by the larger-revenue market owner. Similarly, the right-hand shaded rectangle in Figure 7.2 is the smaller-market owner's talent bill, calculated as $P*W_S^*$. The clear conclusion is that the larger-revenue market owner spends more for talent than does the smaller-revenue market owner. Therefore, along with competitive imbalance, there will also be **payroll imbalance** as long as marginal revenues are not equal.

The second important feature of the competitive talent equilibrium is that the larger-revenue market team has a higher winning percent than the smaller-revenue market team, that is, in equilibrium, $W_L^* > W_S^*$ in Figure 7.2. Of course, this makes sense. Every single unit of talent hired produced winning that was more valuable to the larger-market owner. Therefore, that owner hires more talent and wins more. It is this important feature that leads us to the conclusion that **competitive imbalance** is a fact of life as long as there is **revenue imbalance**.

REAL-WORLD MRP INSIGHTS

MRP theory provides insights into a number of important and (otherwise) confusing sports outcomes. The very first insight is that our description of the competitive equilibrium at the end of the last section actually does portray outcomes in real sports leagues. Table 7.5 shows the payroll imbalance that MRP theory predicts will follow from revenue imbalance for the 2004 MLB season. The average payroll is about $69 million. Note that the Yankees' payroll is 6.7 times larger than the Brewers' and 2.7 times the average. As you might suspect, this type of imbalance also goes hand in hand with outcomes on the field. If you check the top payroll teams in Table 7.5, it will come as no surprise that they are, for the most part, successful teams from large-revenue markets.

A second real-world observation is that, in every sport, reporters usually take a shot at owners by pointing out the "busts and bargains" of the year. Busts are highly paid players performing below their usual level, whereas bargains are less-expensive players having unexpectedly good years. Reporters are especially unkind to owners burdened with busts when other teams in the leagues have a few bargains. Is the talent market subject to consistent owner mistakes, as reporters would have us believe? Or are reporters just selective in their presentation of bargains and busts, playing to the analytical weaknesses of fans in general?

Actually, these reporters are just pointing out that, in an uncertain world, some players will perform at levels above their current payment and some will perform at levels below their current payment. On average over time, one would not expect these outcomes to be predictable. Owners who repeatedly hire busts in the talent market will either absorb large losses or lose their team to a more astute owner. If some owners really do make systematic mistakes, another owner, with the same information, would make predictions closer to the actual performance of players.

Table 7.5

Payroll Imbalance in
MLB, 2004

TEAM	OPENING DAY PAYROLL
New York Yankees	$184,193,950
Boston	$127,298,500
Anaheim	$100,534,667
New York Mets	$96,660,970
Philadelphia	$93,219,167
Los Angeles	$92,902,001
Chicago Cubs	$90,560,000
Atlanta	$90,182,500
St. Louis	$83,228,333
San Francisco	$82,019,166
Seattle	$81,515,834
Houston	$75,397,000
Arizona	$69,780,750
Colorado	$65,445,167
Chicago White Sox	$65,212,500
Oakland	$59,425,667
San Diego	$55,384,833
Texas	$55,050,417
Minnesota	$53,585,000
Baltimore	$51,623,333
Toronto	$50,017,000
Kansas City	$47,609,000
Detroit	$46,832,000
Cincinnati	$46,615,250
Florida	$42,143,042
Montreal	$41,197,500
Cleveland	$34,319,300
Pittsburgh	$32,227,929
Tampa Bay	$29,556,667
Milwaukee	$27,528,500
Average	$69,042,198
Median	$62,319,084

Source: USAToday.com baseball salary database.

In this light, players are paid their **expected MRP** and, in an uncertain world, on average owners have **unbiased expectations** about eventual performance. Thus, if you watch a given team over time, you would expect that team's bargains and busts to offset each other. Across an entire league, this would almost certainly be the case. If you still have trouble relating to this, try the following. At the beginning of the season (not the end), make your predictions on bargains and busts. Check your predictions at the end of the season. If you do better than owners over a season or two, then there were systematic errors. If not, then the results are just due to the fact that performance is an uncertain, but unbiased, outcome.

The Relationship Between Ticket Prices and Salaries

MRP theory also helps unravel the faulty logic behind the idea that higher player salaries drive up ticket prices. How often have you heard this one? Greedy players demand higher salaries, so owners, eager to retain their talent, raise ticket prices. This type of argument clearly casts players as the villains behind the increase in costs to fans.

However, MRP theory dictates that players can only earn more if (1) they become more productive (that is, marginal product increases) or (2) fans increase their willingness to pay for the result. An increase in fan willingness to pay would lead to an increase in the marginal revenue (MR) portion of MRP, even though the marginal product (MP) part of MRP stays about the same (just as we saw with coaches in the last section).

If this is the effect, then players are more valuable than they used to be in the eyes of fans. This means that owners will raise prices because fans are willing to pay more. Then, player pay will rise as long as there is competition for their services between teams. If one team does not increase pay and the revenue is there among a few teams, then others will bid that talent away causing salaries to increase. Therefore, the reason players make more is that a change in some demand parameter (income, population, preferences) has increased fans' willingness to pay.

The data on payrolls and ticket prices bear out this theoretical prediction. Figures 7.3 through 7.6 show how ticket prices and payrolls (both adjusted for inflation) behaved for the pro sports teams in the Boston area since 1990. Of course, the first

Figure 7.3 Ticket Prices and Payrolls, Boston Red Sox ($2004)
Adjusted for inflation, the average salary paid by the owner of the Boston Red Sox shows two significant episodes of decline. But ticket prices increased over nearly the entire period in the figure. The idea that rising salaries can cause rising ticket prices is not supported.

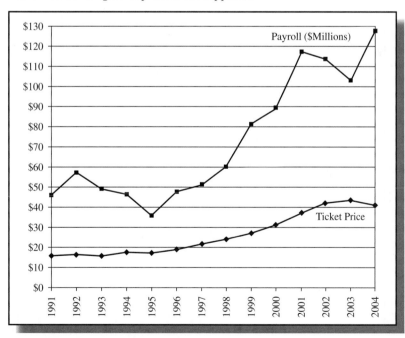

Sources: Ticket prices from Teammarketing.com; payroll data from USAToday.com Baseball Salary Database.

thing to note is that ticket prices in real terms did not increase uniformly over the time period studied for these four teams. Salaries increased steadily in real terms only for the NHL's Bruins, although a general increase over time for all teams is more apparent than it is for ticket prices. In the figures, it is clear that salaries move in the opposite direction of ticket prices as often as they move in the same direction as ticket prices. In fact, for the NFL's Patriots, salaries and ticket prices move in the opposite direction two-thirds of the time. If salaries cause ticket prices to change, then they should almost always be moving in the same direction. As the data show, this is not the case, so salaries do not drive ticket prices up.

However, it is interesting to note the correlation between real salaries and real ticket prices in Boston, ranging from 0.952 for the Red Sox to 0.645 for the Celtics, 0.494 for the Patriots, and −0.080 for the Bruins (essentially, zero). Thus, it ends up that salaries and ticket prices are highly correlated for the Sox and the Celtics, but not so for the Patriots and the Bruins. This makes a very nice case for thinking about the difference between causation and correlation. MRP theory dictates that players foresee larger contributions to revenues and ask for corresponding increases in salary. Judging from the correlations, the increase in MRP in baseball and basketball is observed partly at the gate. But other increases in MRP, especially in football and

Figure 7.4 Ticket Prices and Payrolls, Boston Celtics ($2004)
Adjusted for inflation, the average salary paid by the owner of the Boston Celtics had some significant ups and downs early on. But ticket prices increased steadily over that time. The idea that rising salaries can cause rising ticket prices is not supported.

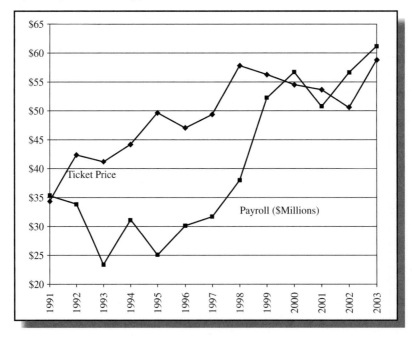

Sources: Ticket prices from Teammarketing.com; payroll data from USAToday.com Basketball Salary Database.

Figure 7.5 Ticket Prices and Payrolls, New England Patriots ($2004)
Adjusted for inflation, the average salary paid by the owner of the New England Patriots showed a number of periods of decline. But during those, there always was at least one significant increase in ticket prices. The idea that rising salaries can cause rising ticket prices is not supported.

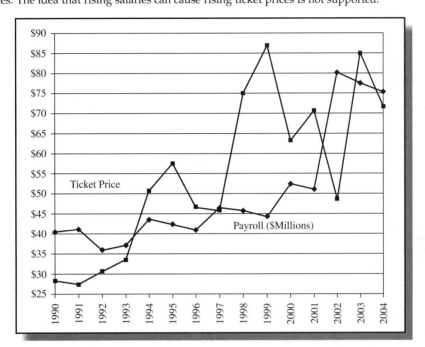

Sources: Ticket prices from Teammarketing.com; payroll data from USAToday.com Football Salary Database.

hockey, must be coming from a different impact on revenue, for example, impacts on the value of broadcast rights.

This was especially true of one particular episode for MLB teams in general. The explosion of player salaries in the 1980s was due to the proliferation of media providers, especially local and regional cable. The MR part of MRP, and as a result salaries, rose as media providers entered the scene with increased payment of broadcast rights fees. Therefore, the answer to our earlier question, "Why did MLB salaries rise steadily and in a huge cumulative amount during the 1980s?" is media provider payments. I'll say it again: Salaries do not drive ticket prices, but revenues are one of the determinants of how much players get paid.

Social Values: Ballplayers versus Teachers

MRP theory also helps us to understand some larger social issues related to sports. Many people abhor the obsession with sports in the United States. They deplore spending precious resources that could otherwise go to more "worthy" endeavors. How is it (they ask) that sports stars can be so highly valued when other people working at these more worthy endeavors are so poorly paid? Demand is certainly one side of the explanation for sports outcomes. However, we cannot forget the supply side, for in this particular case the supply side explains the outcome.

Figure 7.6 Ticket Prices and Payrolls, Boston Bruins ($2004)

Adjusted for inflation, the average salary paid by the owner of the Boston Bruins almost continually increased over time. But ticket prices did not. The idea that rising salaries can cause rising ticket prices is not supported.

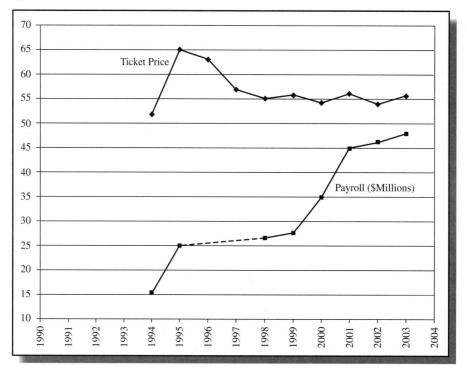

Sources: Ticket prices from Teammarketing.com; payroll data from USAToday.com Basketball Salary Database.

Figure 7.7 shows hypothetical demands for teaching and athletic services. Each of these demand functions is an MRP function. The figure is set up so that the MRP of teachers lies everywhere above the MRP of athletic services. In this hypothetical example, the MRP functions are located consistent with a society that values every single unit of teaching services more than it values the services of sports stars (willingness to pay is higher). This is the same thing as saying that society generally agrees that teachers are "worth more" than ballplayers. This really does appear to be how society places this value. For example, earlier in this chapter we saw how Barry Bonds was paid $10.3 million in 2001. But the value per fan is really quite low. Even if we only count the 3,311,968 fans at the gate, that's only around $3.11 per fan. If we add television viewers, the value per fan falls dramatically. But for teachers, the value per student is much higher even though their salaries are much lower. The U.S. Department of Labor gives the average salary of teachers in 2001–2002 as $44,327. With around 30 students per class, that means an elementary school teacher is worth at least $1,478 per student, or 475 times as much as Barry Bonds on a per customer basis.

Alas for teachers, there is plenty of quality teaching supplied at low pay relative to pro athletes. This is portrayed in Figure 7.7 by a flatter supply function of teaching

Figure 7.7 Hypothetical Demands for Teaching and Athlete Services

Even though society is willing to pay more for teachers than for sports stars, as revealed by the higher demand for the former, supply also matters. Equilibrium in the market for teachers occurs with S_T units of teaching services hired at a wage equal to W_T. In the market for stars, the result is S_T units of star services hired at W_S. Because many more teachers than stars are available at each possible wage, earnings by teachers are lower, that is, $W_T < W_S$.

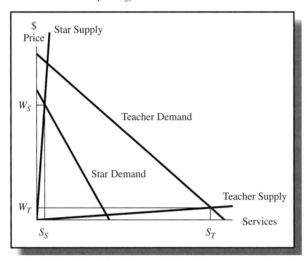

services relative to the steeper supply of pro sports star services. The intersection of teaching supply and demand results in a wage, W_T, for teachers. That wage is much less than the wage result at the intersection supply and demand for sports stars, W_S. Thus, the MRP of teachers can swamp that of sports stars generally, but sports stars can still end up being paid more. It is especially important to understand the underlying source of the outcome if public resources are going to be aimed at changing the outcome. Here, efforts should go toward increasing the MRP of teachers or decreasing their supply if one wishes to raise their compensation.

International Competition for Talent

Lately, owners of NHL teams in Canada argue that they cannot compete for talent because the Canadian dollar is weak against the U.S. dollar. Canadian NHL teams pay the same salary as U.S. teams but in weaker Canadian dollars. However, the weak Canadian dollar cannot be the explanation for the inability of Canadian owners to compete for talent; why don't Canadian owners just simply make up the difference with higher salaries in Canadian dollars or just write player contracts in U.S. dollars? The weakness of the Canadian currency is only a symptom of the actual problem from the Canadian owners' perspective.

The reason the Canadian dollar is weak is a macroeconomics lesson, but the upshot is that real income in Canada is lower than in the United States. Thus, relative to U.S. fans, the demand for hockey by Canadian fans is lower because willingness to pay is based on the lower Canadian real income. The lesson from Chapter 2 is that lower Canadian demand reduces the entire revenue function for Canadian teams. The lesson in this chapter is that Canadian players are paid according to their MRP.

With relatively lower revenues for Canadian owners (due to lower relative Canadian incomes), the value of talent also declines (the MR element in MRP is lower for Canadian owners). In essence, some Canadian teams are playing in smaller-revenue markets relative to some U.S. teams.

As long as relative real income is lower in Canada, owners of teams in Canada will lose talent (at the margin) to U.S. teams whose fans have higher real income. Owners of NHL teams can only pay less, even if they do pay U.S. dollars, because their fans' incomes are lower. Losing talent to U.S. teams is just the large-revenue market versus small-revenue market problem, in an international context.

Differences in MRP also explain the international migration of talent across formal leagues in different countries. For example, outfielder Hideki Matsui earned a Nippon Professional Baseball League record $4.7 million in 2002 (*Sports Illustrated*, January 7, 2002, p. 28). But he left the Yomiuri Giants for MLB's New York Yankees for $6 million in 2003 and then $7 million in 2004. Of course, the reason players are worth so much more in the United States is explained completely by MRP. Just examining the situation at the gate, Yomiuri Giants 2002 attendance of 3,783,500 was similar to 2002 Yankee attendance of 3,465,807. But ticket prices were dramatically higher in New York. The average ticket price in Yankee Stadium was $24.26 while a general admission ticket in the Tokyo Dome was $10.48. So there is quite a large difference in revenues generated by players in the United States even before we get to media revenues. Given the greater player MRP in the United States, the migration of top sports talent to the United States is of growing concern to pro sports leagues abroad, not just in baseball but also in basketball and hockey.

Overvalued Rookies?

Here is one last way that MRP theory can provide information on a typical confusion about sports markets. How can rookies be worth their huge bonuses and starting salaries? Rookies are untested at the professional level, and they often are paid more than established veterans. Let's look at an example, LeBron James.

As a rookie in the 2003–2004 season, LeBron James was paid a salary of $4 million. His contract also specified an additional $14.8 million through his fourth season. So just what did the Cleveland Cavaliers get in return? Home attendance jumped 59 percent from 471,374 to 749,790. Ticket revenue increased 80 percent from $15 million to $27 million. And the Cavaliers went from eighth place to fifth place, more than doubling their winning percent and missing the playoffs by one game. While it's a bit clouded by the unknown signing bonus, it is pretty clear that James was worth every cent the Cavaliers paid.

Did You Know?
During LeBron James's rookie season, regular season attendance revenue increased by $12 million, and the Cavaliers missed the play-offs by one game. James was paid "only" $4 million.

Let's consider what MRP theory suggests concerning the value of rookies, generally speaking. We look at the NFL because the most extensive data are available on those players. Signing bonuses and salary packages for top NFL rookie draft picks are shown in Table 7.6. Let's narrow our look to just the cream of the crop, those players offered a 7-year contract. On average, their package includes a $4.9 million signing bonus and a $1.9 million salary annually for 7 years. At 6 percent,

Table 7.6 Compensation Packages for Top NFL Draft Picks, 2003

Pick	Team	Position	First	Last	Signing Bonus	Salary	Duration
1	Cincinnati	QB	Carson	Palmer	$10,010,000	$21,710,500	7 years
2	Detroit	WR	Charles	Rogers	$9,100,000	$20,438,600	7 years
3	Houston	WR	Andre	Johnson	$9,000,000	$20,135,500	7 years
4	New York Jets	DT	Dewayne	Robertson	$3,000,000	$24,579,250	7 years
5	Dallas	CB	Terence	Newman	$6,510,000	$20,104,000	7 years
6	New Orleans	DT	Jonathan	Sullivan	$7,400,000	$16,599,330	7 years
9	Minnesota	DT	Kevin	Williams	$4,000,000	$12,798,000	7 years
10	Baltimore	LB	Terrell	Suggs	$2,000,000	$9,040,000	5 years
11	Seattle	CB	Marcus	Trufant	$3,500,000	$10,160,000	7 years
12	St. Louis	DT	Jimmy	Kennedy	$1,000,000	$8,750,000	5 years
13	New England	DT	Ty	Warren	$3,000,000	$10,800,000	6 years
14	Chicago	DE	Michael	Haynes	$1,000,000	$10,225,000	6 years
15	Philadelphia	DE	Jerome	McDougle	$3,000,000	$9,492,500	6 years
16	Pittsburgh	SS	Troy	Polamalu	$445,000	$8,310,000	5 years
17	Arizona	WR	Bryant	Johnson	$1,850,000	$6,420,500	5 years
18	Arizona	DE	Calvin	Pace	$3,000,000	$8,007,500	5 years
19	Baltimore	QB	Kyle	Boller	$2,200,000	$7,041,000	5 years
20	Denver	OT	George	Foster	$3,000,000	$8,313,750	6 years
21	Cleveland	C	Jeff	Faine	$2,350,000	$9,143,730	7 years
22	Chicago	QB	Rex	Grossman	$2,050,000	$6,895,000	5 years
24	Indianapolis	TE	Dallas	Clark	$3,800,000	$7,607,000	7 years
25	N.Y. Giants	DT	William	Joseph	$3,725,000	$8,890,000	7 years
26	San Francisco	OT	Kwamie	Harris	$3,600,000	$9,787,200	7 years
27	Kansas City	RB	Larry	Johnson	$3,310,000	$8,847,000	7 years
28	Tennessee	CB	Andre	Woolfolk	$2,500,000	$6,450,350	7 years
29	Green Bay	LB	Nick	Barnett	$3,210,000	$7,750,000	7 years
30	San Diego	CB	Sammy	Davis	$3,300,000	$7,710,000	7 years
31	Oakland	CB	Nnamdi	Asomugha	$3,200,000	$6,795,000	6 years
32	Oakland	DE	Tyler	Brayton	$3,150,000	$6,720,000	6 years
33	Cincinnati	OG	Eric	Steinbach	$1,760,000	$3,190,000	4 years
34	Detroit	LB	Boss	Bailey	$2,200,000	$4,600,000	5 years
35	Chicago	CB	Charles	Tillman	$2,055,000	$4,321,400	5 years
36	New England	CB	Eugene	Wilson	$2,000,000	$4,137,500	5 years
37	New Orleans	OT	Jon	Stinchcomb	$1,845,000	$3,215,000	4 years
38	Dallas	C	Al	Johnson	$1,820,000	$3,190,000	4 years
39	Jacksonville	FS	Rashean	Mathis	$1,800,000	$3,170,000	4 years
40	Minnesota	LB	EJ	Hendersen	$1,750,000	$3,120,000	4 years

Notes: Bonuses include option, roster, workout, and reporting. Salary total is the outcome if none of the option clauses voiding the contract are exercised. Data on Byron Leftwich, 7th; Jordan Gross, 8th; and Willis McGehee, 23rd, were not made public.
Source: ESPN.com.

the discounted present-value of the $1.9 million in salary paid for 7 years is around $10.6 million. That makes the present value of the package, including the bonus paid up front, about $15.5 million. Is this amount outlandish?

Let's think of it from the MRP perspective using just attendance revenues. Average attendance in 2003 for the owners drafting these players was 538,202. If they drew the same on average over 7 years, total attendance would be 3,767,414. In discounted present-value terms, each fan in attendance only has to spend $3.61 to cover this average top draft pick ($13.6 million divided by total attendance over 7 years). As a current point of reference, the Team Marketing Report data give an average ticket price for the owners of the drafting teams of $51.80. Again, even if that ticket price stayed constant over the 7 year contract, that's enough to pay for over 14 players just like our top draft pick over 7 years. And we haven't even gotten to TV revenue yet. Of course, the owners must also pay for the rest of their players, but it appears that there is ample gate and TV revenue to take care of them all.

The level of rookie compensation depicted in Table 7.6 stretches the imagination of sports writers and others who do not think that anyone untried can be worth so much. However, these players enter the league and, often as not, perform at a level equal to their pay, especially the highest-paid rookies. Basic MRP theory suggests that this should be so, and it is. Some falter, but most meet expectations.

Here's a note of caution: Contracts in sports, both rookie and veteran alike, are full of *ifs*, and contract clauses must be read with care. When you hear of a sports star getting paid over $100 million, read the small print. For example, from the reports in Table 7.6, we wouldn't be surprised if news reports put the value of Carson Palmer's contract at $31.7 million (although it would be economically correct to discount the $21.7 million salary portion to present-value). But it ends up that a news reporter could put the value of the contract at $49 million! Here's how. If minimum playing time levels specified in Palmer's contract are met, two things happen. First, the last year of the contract, 2009, is voided. Second, the base salaries in all years from 2004 through 2008 are increased so that the total salary amount becomes $39 million. And there you have the $49 million possibility. But the contract also specifies that only the original signing bonus and salaries from 2005 through 2007 are guaranteed. In the event of injury after that, Palmer gets nothing. Whew. Take what you read about stratospheric rookie contracts with a grain of salt.

THE VALUE OF ATHLETES: SPECIAL CASES

The large salaries in sports seem so outlandish that one might be tempted to abandon the MRP explanation. How can the same theory that explains pay and hiring from minimum wage to middle management work for sports stars? There are a few competing explanations for how sports stars get paid: the winner's curse, bidding wars, and winner-take-all outcomes. Let's explore these special situation explanations one at a time.

The Winner's Curse

Chapter 3, discussed the idea of a **winner's curse** in broadcast rights bidding. Some have used this same logic to argue that a winner's curse exists in the market for players, too. It is easiest to see how a winner's curse explanation works in the talent market by thinking of the free agent market as an auction. Owners are the bidders and free agent players the prize. Suppose that most owners are informed and experienced bidders in the free agent auction, but that a few are not. In such a case, most owners would only bid the true expected MRP of a player. However, the other inexperienced, uninformed bidders would bid well below or well above the true expected MRP. Under a vigorous competitive free agent auction, the highest of these inexperienced/uninformed guesses will be the winning bid. But as we discussed in Chapter 3, it will be wrong in terms of informed guesses about the player's MRP. In this situation, the winner is cursed by the size of the winning bid, and player salaries would be well above their actual MRP.

Early on during free agency in MLB, Cassing and Douglas (1980) found some support for the winner's curse. Lehn (1984) also found that owners sometimes lack all of the information they need when they make bids and may, for example, get stuck with an injured player at a high price. However, it does not seem reasonable that this special situation could apply to sports stars over an extended period of time.

It is true that the eventual performance of players is subject to uncertainty (deviations from career averages due to slumps or injury or the beginning of the eventual long-term decline in ability that happens to every player). But it also is true that no single productive input is monitored and checked more closely or more often than sports stars. Their performance often is tracked on a minute-by-minute basis. Player injury histories are well known and publicized. Medical specialists are always available to check on a player's status. This is just as true for incoming rookies. From the time they show any potential as youngsters and on through college, scouts follow players with the eye of a detective. Pro sports combines, where all teams get together, put the incoming talent crop through workouts, and observe their performance, reveal any weakness or deviation from perfect status.

When the free agent market first opened, nearly everybody was inexperienced in the process. It is hard to believe that there would be any systematic overbidding for players based on either inexperience or misinformation as time went by. It is reasonable to expect that inexperience in the free agent market on the part of owners was short-lived.

Bidding Wars

A **bidding war** is a special case of the MRP explanation where a very special circumstance is in operation. Essentially, a bidding war ensues when coming in second place is very costly. For example, suppose the season is closing in on the playoffs and that two teams need just one player to clinch a playoff spot and its rewards. At such a time, there may be very few substitutes that satisfy the playoff needs of these two teams. Coming in second in bidding for a single player who can swing the playoff hopes for either team would be expensive. The situation is compounded the more valuable that playoff appearance becomes.

In a bidding war situation, we have to be careful to include all elements of the player's MRP—nothing has changed about the player's ability, but the value during the playoffs raises the MR part of MRP, and coming in second is very expensive. However, although this situation may occur for some teams as each playoff is reached, it only happens at a particular time during the season, and most teams do not buy their talent under such pressures.

The Winner-Take-All Explanation

The **winner-take-all explanation** of Frank and Cook (1995) is our final special circumstance version of how players get paid. The winner-take-all explanation is easy to see for individual sports, such as golf or tennis. Suppose that fans want to see only the best compete against each other. Because television allows fans to simultaneously enjoy matches between the best players, only those best players would ever be on TV. As a result, some players who are only marginally worse than the best competitors will get nearly nothing and the best players will get nearly all of the prize money. In such a situation, fans will only see the best compete against each other for all the marbles. This is important: It must be the case that winners actually do take all.

We can take a quick empirical look at the winner-take-all idea in golf. Figure 7.8 shows the Lorenz curves for recent tournament outcomes in men's and women's pro golf. In both the men's and women's tournaments, the figure shows that the top 10 percent of players (between 7 and 9 golfers, typically) earn well over 50 percent of the total event purse. The Gini coefficients index this inequality as 0.656 and 0.620 in men's and women's golf, respectively. For comparative purposes, Gini coefficients in team sports can be as high as 0.500 (Chapter 6) and, in the economy at large, are typically around 0.300. It certainly looks like winners take nearly all in men's and women's pro golf.

Did You Know?
In both men's and women's golf tournaments, 10 percent of the players earn well over 50 percent of the total purse.

However, there are other explanations for this tournament prize structure. Suppose that pay were not structured with a huge payoff for the top ten in any given golf tournament. One could envision the top players deciding it was easier to just take turns winning the tournaments in a given year. Everybody shows up to play, but nine of the top 10 miss a putt here, shank a drive there, and the winner for the week takes home the check. Golf seems like an especially likely sport for this to happen because it is so difficult to be consistent over time and, as a result, fans would have a difficult time detecting this behavior.

This flies in the face of what both tournament directors and pro golf organizations are trying to do, namely, maximize profits from attendance and TV broadcast contracts for the year's tournaments. If it becomes known that players have colluded to share tournament purses, fan confidence in the integrity of play would disappear and, with it, the value of fan interest at the gate and on TV. Just imagine if a "hot hand" like Tiger Woods had agreed to such a purse-sharing scheme. The streak of majors in 2000–2001 would never have happened, and the value of selling

Figure 7.8 Men's and Women's Golf Lorenz Curves

The farther the actual Lorenz curve bows away from the 45-degree line, the more unequally shared is the purse. The Gini coefficient is the ratio of the area between the 45-degree line and the Lorenz curve to the area under the 45-degree line. The closer the Gini coefficient is to one, the more unequal the outcome. Gini coefficients of 0.620 and 0.656 are very high, indicating unequal outcomes in both women's and men's golf purses.

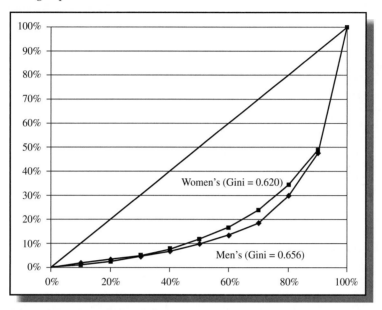

Notes: Men's tournament is the Players' Championship, 2004. Women's tournament is the 2004 U.S. Open.
Source: Author's calculations from data at www.golfweb.com.

tournaments would be much lower. So how can directors and associations overcome this type of behavior?

Ehrenberg and Bognanno (1990a; 1990b) show that the concentrated structure of pay at the top protects against these problems. When pay is highly concentrated for the top 10 finishers, moving up one spot on the leader board for players close to the top means a high expected return. By making the value of outdoing the other top golfers so large, the incentive to collude is reduced. These researchers found that players do perform better in their last round if they are close to the leader after three rounds; why waste huge effort moving from 53rd to 52nd? However, the increased effort to move from sixth to fifth pays off immensely. In addition, they found that higher prize money concentrated at the top leads to better scores. Thus, there may be a winner-take-all aspect to tournaments in individual sports, but concentrated prize money also maintains integrity of competition. Without that, tournaments would not be worth very much to fans.

The winner-take-all explanation at least sounds like it can characterize individual sports, but does it make any sense for team sports? First, do fans want to see only the best? If they did, then very poor teams might cease to exist. However, in all leagues, lovable losers have always existed. At the very least, if fans only wanted to see the very best, many home games for most baseball teams would never be broadcast. This casts doubt on the winner-take-all scenario for team sports. The real deciding fact on whether the winner-take-all explanation can be applied to team sports relates to the outcome: Do winners indeed take all?

Let's look at the player most likely in recent times to be such a winner, Michael Jordan. He was worth about $33 million to the Chicago Bulls had he played his final year, 1998. The *Forbes* magazine survey data show that total revenues in the NBA were about $3 billion at that time. Historically, NBA players receive around 60 percent of league total revenues, say, $1.8 billion through the salary cap process.

Jordan's $33 million is only about 1.8 percent of the total amount enjoyed by players. This hardly sounds like a winner taking all—especially compared to a single player taking the majority of a purse in individual sports. However, the pursuit of the large pay-offs to pro athletes does have some characteristics in common with the primary troublesome result of winner-take-all markets. Many who will never get the high payoff still invest extraordinary amounts of time and resources trying anyway. Sadly, this means that much of it is wasted, as shown in the Learning Highlight: Investing in an Athletic Career.

LEARNING HIGHLIGHT
Investing in an Athletic Career

Frank and Cook (1995) in *The Winner Take All Society* point out the tragic consequences of wasting youth in pursuit of athletic achievement in order to be one of the winners. One must exercise extreme caution in evaluating young people's choice to invest their time and energy into athletic careers. First, only the individuals investing in the sport know how much fun is involved, the subjective probability of making it, and their own opportunity cost. Second, it does not take a winner-take-all explanation to foster overinvestment. Overinvestment may occur just because young people make mistakes evaluating the benefits, chances of advancement, and costs of pursuing a pro career.

It seems reasonable to think that at least some of the young people investing in athletic careers are making a mistake. Richard Lapchick, University of Central Florida sociologist and director of its Institute for Diversity and Ethics, reports informal sampling that reveals nearly half of all high-school senior football players think they are going to get a college scholarship. Noted sports economist Roger Noll (1998) points out that a 15-year-old who is a good prospect to be a football player stands a 3 percent chance of a college scholarship and a 0.25 percent chance of a pro career. It would appear that many high-school seniors overestimate their chances.

However, those with a good chance of making it can be behaving quite rationally in pursuing a pro career. Noll (1998) estimates that the present value of the college shot is $200,000 in additional lifetime earnings and that the discounted present value of the pro shot is $2 million in additional lifetime earnings. The expected value calculation gives .033 × 200,000 + .0025 × 2,000,000, or about $11,000. Noll also estimates that to have a chance, the hopeful player would need to devote 2,000 hours of effort through high school. That's about $5.50/hour ($11,000/2,000 hours) as an expected return for 3 years of hard physical work. If the alternative has a lower expected value, it is rational for the hopeful to invest during high school for the chance at a top-level college scholarship that would result in a good chance at a pro career. However, note that $5.50 an hour identifies only those with approximately a minimum-wage potential through high school. For others who can make more than $5.50 an hour, the effort is not worth it unless the joy of playing makes up the difference, and joy can be had without devoting the effort required for a potential pro career.

Further, from a societal standpoint, having hundreds of thousands of teenagers dedicate their lives to a career in athletics is a waste of resources that could be better put to developing academic and job-related skills. Suppose the financial payoff to the best pro athletes would stay the same if tens of thousands, rather than hundreds of thousands, took their shot at the big payoff (with fewer trying, there is a chance that the level of

absolute competition would fall and, with it, the value of a pro career). The waste in resources is measured by the added income that the rest would have gained, net of their investment in earning it, learning another marketable skill. There would have to be an awful lot of nonmonetary joy for the rest in order to make up for the difference.

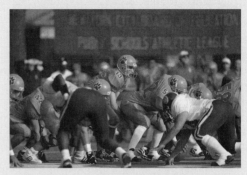

Nearly half of all high-school senior football players may think that they are going to get a college scholarship, but in reality around 3 percent actually do.

Sources: Frank and Cook (1995) and Noll (1998).

DISCRIMINATION IN PAY AND HIRING: INTRODUCTION

Before we move on, we need to examine one more important market outcome. To this point, competitive markets for talent have resulted in players earning close to the MRP with the team that values their talent the most. However, in some situations lacking this competitive vigor, it is possible for individuals with identical productive potential in sports to end up with very different economic outcomes because of their gender, race, or ethnicity. These outcomes are commonly referred to as **discrimination in pay and hiring**.

The Limits of Economic Analysis of Discrimination

Economics, by the nature of its focus on market outcomes and incentives, can address only a subset of the issues of interest in the study of discrimination. The tools of economics will be useful mainly in detecting discrimination in pay and hiring in sports. Economic tools will also be useful in analyzing how individuals respond to the discrimination that might occur. However, discrimination can permeate all social interactions, not just economic ones. The attitudes passed along among friends and business contacts influence referrals and other "network" outcomes that, in turn, influence economic outcomes. Thus, the tools of economic analysis come up a bit short, analytically speaking, in the direct examination of network outcomes.

A historical episode helps make this limitation clear. In 1961, the first version of MLB's Washington Senators moved to Minneapolis–St. Paul and became the Minnesota Twins. Attendance in Washington, D.C., had been abysmal—for the 5 years prior to their first season in Minnesota, the Washington Senators had the lowest attendance in all of baseball. Then-owner Calvin Griffith made the following remark at the time of the move in 1961 about the economics of gate attendance in the two locations:

> I'll tell you why we came to Minnesota. It was when I found out you only had 15,000 blacks here. Black people do not go to ball games, but they'll fill up a wrassling ring and put up such a chant it'll scare you to death. . . . We came here because you've got good, hard-working white people here. (Nelson, 1984, p. 95)

Many took these to be racist remarks. However, Griffith claimed he was being misinterpreted. He said he was not a racist, he was just explaining the demographics and buying habits of some fans in the market for baseball in Washington, D.C., compared to the market in the Twin Cities. The depth of intense emotion that such issues raise immediately pushes any economic insight into the background. Griffith had offered an explanation of his statement as a purely economic one. But one of his black stars, Hall of Famer Rod Carew, responded with outrage:

> I won't be a nigger on his plantation anymore. I will not ever sign another contract with this organization. I do not care how much money or how many options Calvin Griffith offers me. . . . The days of Kunte Kinte [of Roots fame] are over. . . . He respects nobody and expects nobody to respect him. (Nelson, 1984, p. 95)

Discrimination is an extremely emotional issue and economics is the antithesis of that way of thinking. That makes the application of economics to discrimination important but limited. Any statement about discrimination in general, based on a very small subset of the outcomes from discrimination such as pay and hiring, will certainly be invalid. For example, even if economic analysis suggests that there is no discrimination in pay or hiring, that does not mean that discrimination is no longer a problem in American society.

MRP Theory and Discrimination

From the economic perspective, discrimination is primarily an issue of compensation and hiring. Therefore, the foundation of analysis is still MRP theory. Because $MRP = MP \times MR$, anything causing variation in either MP or MR will cause variation in observed payment. Let's first examine MP. There are three factors that may explain variation in pay among individuals: innate ability, training, and experience.

Innate Ability   Innate ability matters in the world of sports, just as in other areas. Some individuals just are lucky at birth; they have a greater ability or aptitude or their body is of the proper proportion for a sport. All else constant, those with greater ability contribute more of what fans pay to see and are, therefore, expected to earn more. A seven-foot, well-coordinated basketball player should be expected to go at a premium relative to a tall, uncoordinated player. At the highest levels of sports, a 250-pound offensive lineman is not very valuable at all relative to equally able 300-pound players. Note that there is no ground for discrimination based strictly on innate ability. The idea itself is color-blind.

Training and Experience   Innate ability is not enough to succeed in pro sports. If those with the most innate ability did not train, then the rest of the players would close the gap through training and even overtake those with innate ability. Further, ability typically increases with experience. Thus, these two factors, training and experience, also contribute to earnings. Interestingly, variation in willingness to train or gained experience will contribute to variation in income. Presumably, those with innate ability also can train and gain experience, making them just that much more valuable. If those with less innate ability are able to close the gap, or if those of like ability forge ahead, then there must have been some hindrance to training and experience for those with greater ability. Perhaps it is a person's willingness to work hard. Perhaps it is a rational economic calculation about the returns to hard work.

Training and experience require investment of scarce time, energy, and monetary resources. The willingness to make these investments can vary between people for many reasons. Some may not choose athletic training because their opportunities in other endeavors are too great. As we saw in the Learning Highlight: Investing in an Athletic Career, the expected monetary value of a shot at a lucrative rookie bonus and contract may not meet the returns to other endeavors. In such a case, one would expect some people simply not to make the investment in sports, even if they could have enjoyed a modicum of success there.

Therefore, training choices can be due to willingness to work or calculation of the payoff to working hard. However, there may be a discrimination-based explanation for variation in training and experience. If minority and women players have less access to training, they may then fall behind in the race for athletic success. Without training, their chances of competing are limited. Therefore, they never catch up in the experience department. Without the training, they never had the chance to compete. This can affect their future opportunities.

If discrimination is pervasive, the resources needed to compete successfully on the field as players or off the field as coaches and front office executives may be denied to minorities and females. On average, because their training opportunities and experience have been reduced, one would expect those who were the object of discrimination to have less to offer at the hiring table. Here is the crux of the issue: Sports team owners and personnel directors, bigoted or not (more on this shortly), do not know whether any particular player has been disadvantaged in this way. The cumulative impact of past discrimination is an unobservable characteristic.

Statistical Discrimination

In such a hiring situation, owners and personnel directors may adopt a rule of thumb based on past performance of the group as a whole—but that past performance builds on the cumulative effects of past discrimination! People of color and women may lag behind, generally, because discrimination limited their access to training. Although not all people of color or women necessarily lag behind, the rule of thumb based on a group's past performance lumps all members of the group together. Thus, some players who are not below average get thrown in with the rest. Their talent does not get the attention it deserves. This is called **statistical discrimination**.

The result of statistical discrimination is clear. Rules of thumb adopted in the face of uncertainty about a player's ability are based on that player's membership in a demographic group. This leads to a perception of lower *MP* for members of particular groups. Fewer members of those groups will be hired, and they will be paid less. Until this "perception barrier" is broken, the biased outcomes will continue.

Robert Peterson (1970) repeatedly points out that nearly all MLB players and owners felt that Negro League players did not really have what it took to play in the white major leagues. As it has now been conclusively demonstrated that black players are every bit as able as white players, this is a perfect example of statistical discrimination. As the color barrier fell, rules of thumb about race were abandoned. However, you can also see that an alternative explanation is that these people in MLB may simply have been bigots. The difficulty in discerning between economic explanations of differential pay and hiring and plain old bigotry will be a recurrent observation in this section.

Perception barriers may also be falling in women's sports as well. Recent policies aimed at gender equity in the United States are the result of changing cultural expectations and attitudes. Full participation for women is not just a goal, it is the law (see Chapter 13 on Title IX). Markets for female talent have begun to take off, with the number of new women's pro sports teams growing. Previously, returns were low for team sports, so few women made the investment. But the underlying barrier—attitudes toward women in sports—appears to be crumbling, and both the value of talent in women's sports and training by women is increasing.

Fan Discrimination

So goes the *MP* element in the explanation of discrimination. For the *MR* component of MRP, the impacts will all be based on fan demand and its determinants. **Fan discrimination** occurs when fan preferences result in lower pay and reduced hiring by race and gender only because of race and gender, not because of ability. In Chapter 2, we saw that one group of students was willing to pay different amounts for men's and women's sports. Because that observation held across exactly the same set of people, the difference in willingness to pay has to be based on preferences.

Some preferences are not subjected to social scrutiny. For example, preferences toward absolute competition can vary between people. If the same set of fans feels there is a higher level of absolute competition in men's sports and higher levels of competition are more satisfying to them, then they will be willing to pay more as the level of absolute competition rises. This really is no different from the observation that people pay more for major league sports than for minor league sports. Few would think that this type of preference is illegitimate.

However, some preferences are the objects of society's scrutiny. If some fans like men's basketball over women's basketball only because women play the latter, then those fans are sexist (by definition). Sexist preferences have become so unpopular that many manifestations of them are illegal (under the Civil Rights Acts of the 1960s and Title IX in 1972).

A Note of Caution How can an outside observer tell whether it is preferences for higher absolute levels of play or sexism? As with our earlier example of MLB prior to integration, discrimination can be difficult to identify. This is further confused by the fact that men never play against women. We simply cannot observe them in common competition and make any objective comparison of ability. For example, consider the so-called major tournament values for tennis and golf in Table 7.7. A number of interesting questions arise. Why is the total purse larger for men than women in two of the four tennis majors and in all of the golf majors? Why does the winner of the men's singles event at Wimbledon make so much more than the winner of the women's singles event? Why can't even one winner of a women's major golf tournament come close to making $1 million when all of the winners of men's majors earn over $1 million? The possibilities discussed in this section might explain why, but we will not ever be able to distinguish them because men have yet to play against women in singles competition.

Table 7.7 Purses and Shares in Tennis and Golf Majors

	MEN'S PURSE	MEN'S WINNER'S SHARE	WOMEN'S PURSE	WOMEN'S WINNER'S SHARE
Tennis 2004				
Australian Open	$19.0 million	$924,480	$19.0 million	$924,480
French Open	$8.3 million	$1.04 million	$7.56 million	$1.02 million
Wimbledon	$9.9 million	$1.10 million	$7.82 million	$1.02 million
U.S. Open	$17.8 million	$1 million	$17.8 million	$1 million
Golf 2003				
Masters	$6 million	$1.08 million	$2.1 million	$320,000
U.S. Open	$6 million	$1.08 million	$3.1 million	$560,000
British Open	$6.2 million	$1.1 million	$1.6 million	$240,000
PGA	$6 million	$1.08 million	$1.6 million	$240,000

Notes: Tennis purses for U.S. Open and Australian Open are the total for both men and women; separate amounts not reported. The French Open purses do not include mixed doubles, men's seniors, or per diem. Total: $17.6 million. Currency converted at current rates.

Source: Tennis amounts are from official tournament Web sites. Golf amounts are from www.golfweb.com.

When we turn to race or ethnicity and fan discrimination, things are greatly simplified. There is no basis for any variation in the level of absolute competition that can be attributed to race or ethnicity. Men may play at a different level than women, but people of different ethnic backgrounds compete in the same leagues and demonstrate comparable skill. Any detectable pay or hiring difference based on race and ethnicity must reflect preferences alone. The possible sources of this type of preference-driven discrimination are fans, owners, and teammates.

Graphical Analysis of Fan Discrimination   To isolate fan discrimination, let's assume that owners are not bigots. This assumption means that if owners maximize profits, then they will hire the players that fans want to see, regardless of race or ethnicity. Figure 7.9 depicts the fan discrimination situation. Actual MRP is shown, along with another willingness to pay construct, MRP + Race Premium. You should think of the actual MRP as the value of this type of talent to an owner with nonbigoted fans. In Figure 7.9, the race premium shifts MRP to the right because the owner values the players under analysis at a premium over their actual MRP. This is because fans are willing to pay more to see sports played by this type of player over others. At every price, the owner would hire more of the type of player that fans will pay more to see in order to collect this premium from fans.

We can find the pay and hiring outcome from fan discrimination from Figure 7.9. In a competitive setting, the result is the intersection of the supply and demand for talent. S_R and W_R are the amount of the preferred talent hired and its wage in a bigoted fan market, respectively. S_A and W_A are the amount of the preferred talent and its wage in a nonbigoted fan market, respectively. In the presence of fan discrimination, more talent of the race or gender that fans demand the most ($S_R > S_A$) will be hired, and it will be paid more ($W_R > W_A$) than would be the case in a market of nonbigoted fans. Any other choice would mean less profit for the owner than is

Figure 7.9   Fan Discrimination

Favored-race players have an MRP that includes the race premium put on them by fans. As a result, relative to their MRP in the absence of such favored status, more of their services are hired in the presence of fan discrimination, $S_R > S_A$, and they are paid more, $W_R > W_A$.

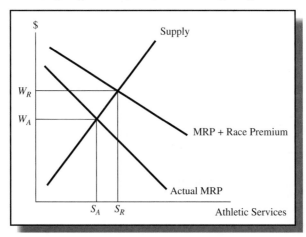

possible in this market. Fans are willing to pay more for every unit of talent between S_R and S_A than it costs to hire those units.

The Costs of Discrimination to Fans In a market with fan discrimination, the team owner either buys talent that wins less than a more integrated lineup could win or pays far more than the minimum amount possible for a given level of winning percent.

It seems reasonable that the first option is more likely. The **cost of fan discrimination** is that better players are forced out of particular locations in order to pack the lineup with the players of the preferred race or ethnicity. Therefore, bigoted fans pay a price for their preferences in terms of a lower winning percent than if they were not bigots. As long as the bigoted fans are willing to pay this price, their preferences can persist. Only circumstantial evidence on this point exists in real sports markets. The obvious example is the integration of MLB, beginning with Jackie Robinson joining the Brooklyn Dodgers in 1947. It took 12 years for MLB to become fully integrated, when Pumpsie Green joined the Boston Red Sox in 1959. Since black players demonstrated their equal talent immediately upon entering the league in the late 1940s, this very gradual integration indicates resistance that can be attributed at least in part to fan discrimination. There is also some indirect evidence of fan discrimination in the market for memorabilia and voting for hall of fame candidates, as covered in the Learning Highlight: Discrimination Is Where You Find It. But, as we will see shortly, teammate and owner discrimination also can play a role.

Ownership Implications What would happen if the owner were forced to integrate the lineup? Fewer fans would come to the games (those without racial or ethnic preferences), and the owner would suffer reduced revenues as demand shrank (shifted to the left). The owner would clearly pay a price for any policy move that forced integration. These owners are not bigots, by our earlier assumption, even though the pursuit of profits does lead them to cater to the preferences of bigoted fans.

Graphical Analysis of Owner and Teammate Discrimination

Figure 7.10 demonstrates **owner discrimination** and **teammate discrimination.** In this case, the premium placed on the particular group of players is due to preferences by the owner or teammates. If these preferences are satisfied, owners will hire more of this type of talent ($S_R > S_A$) and pay it more ($W_R > W_A$) than it really is worth in terms of contribution to winning percent.

However, unlike the case of fan discrimination, owner and teammate discrimination would not be expected to stand in a competitive league of profit-maximizing owners. This is because the owner, rather than the fans, pays the premium on preferential hiring. In this case, the team is less profitable than it could be due to the owner's choices. The shaded area in Figure 7.10 shows the cost of owner discrimination. On every unit hired beyond S_A, the payment by the owner, W_R, exceeds the benefits an owner could ever get from fans in terms of the talent's actual MRP. The owner wins less than is possible for the level of spending that occurs. This sort of profit wasting usually means that another potential owner can take over the team, integrate the lineup, and increase the value of the team as

LEARNING HIGHLIGHT
Discrimination Is Where You Find It: Baseball Cards and Hall of Fame Voting

As stated later in this chapter, the evidence suggests that racial and ethnic discrimination no longer plague salaries in professional team sports. But early in the chapter it was stressed that this is only one part of discrimination. Discrimination can still be active in other ways. For example, it appears that fan discrimination exists in two other places, baseball card markets and voting for members of the Baseball Hall of Fame.

In baseball cards, the evidence concerns the difference in card prices for white stars and others. Baseball cards for black and Latino players sell for about 10 percent less than cards for white players that have comparable historical playing statistics. It seems black sluggers are the particular target of this type of fan discrimination. The difference is 13 percent for the cards of pitchers of color but, interestingly, there is no difference for Latino pitchers. Of course, one would suspect that if all that mattered was performance there would be no difference in price for the cards of star hitters or pitchers based on race or ethnicity.

There is some limited evidence that both black and Latino retired players eligible for the National Baseball Hall of Fame also face fan discrimination. Members of the Baseball Writers Association of America cast the deciding votes. On the first ballot, darker-skinned Latino players receive fewer votes than other players with comparable lifetime statistics. This is an interesting switch from the baseball card outcome because there is no similar finding for eligible black players. The reason this voting evidence is limited is because this type of fan discrimination does not deny truly star players their place in the hall. Instead, Latino players who were eligible but probably would not have gained entry based purely on their statistics are the object of voting discrimination.

Fan discrimination analysis suggests that Sammy Sosa's baseball card will sell for less than the card of other sluggers and that he will receive fewer Hall of Fame votes than other sluggers.

Sources: Fort and Gill (2000); Jewell, Brown, and Miles (2002).

an economic asset. If competition were vigorous enough and profits were the object, owner or teammate discrimination would not be expected to survive.

There is some evidence that just such a situation occurred in the NBA. In the late 1980s, the league expanded and a new labor agreement was struck between owners and players. Bodvarsson and Brastow (1999) argue that these changes increased competition for players. In the face of this increased competition, the salary premium to white players over black players disappeared. Because nothing happened to change fan preferences and the composition of rosters remained unchanged, they concluded that employer discrimination had been in place and wilted with increased competition.

Figure 7.10 Employer/Teammate Discrimination

Favored-race players have an MRP that includes the race premium put on them by employers or teammates. As a result, relative to their MRP in the absence of such favored status, more of their services are hired in the presence of employer/teammate discrimination, $S_R > S_A$, and they are paid more, $W_R > W_A$. However, in this case, the employer bears the cost of the premium because fans do not share their preference and will only pay according to the actual MRP. In order to have favored-race players, the owner pays a wage, W_R, in excess of the value to fans given by actual MRP. The owner's excess payment is equal to the shaded area.

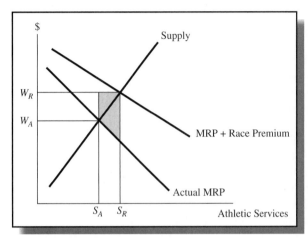

However, two factors might hinder elimination of discrimination by competition among owners for the best talent. First, entry into pro sports ownership is now pegged in the hundreds of millions of dollars. At any point in time, there may not be many takers at that price. So owner preferences could survive quite some time. Second, owners are wealthy individuals. If they care about their team's bottom line but value their own preferences highly, they may be perfectly happy to bear the cost of their choices. Therefore, from the economic perspective, if owner or teammate discrimination persists, all we can say is that competition among owners isn't brisk.

Talent Supply Issues

All of these issues stem from the demand side of the sports talent equation. However, supply issues also influence differential pay. Two of these issues are the opportunity cost of time spent on the job and preferences toward the job.

Opportunity Costs Other job and nonjob opportunities determine the **opportunity cost of time.** Investments in training and experience qualify a person for a variety of jobs. If the demand for one job changes, raising the return at another job, then people can switch jobs. Because the payoff may be distant in time, the expected value of nonsports jobs can be larger than for sports jobs. We will never know how many high-salary career people could have been professional soccer players, but you get the idea.

Another factor that determines the opportunity cost of time spent on the job is family commitments. The allocation of time to family, such as the role of primary care provider, may be a social convention that falls to one gender over another. Because being the primary care provider is an arduous and demanding task, the time remaining for participation in sports can vary by gender. Clearly, these attitudes shape the opportunity cost of time spent in sports pursuits for women in the United States.

Worker Job Preferences The other supply consideration is the preferences of those offering up talent in sports markets. **Worker job preferences** often lead athletes not to choose their highest possible earnings. They may choose a job based on nonwage factors. In the next chapter, there is a full discussion on how free agency altered many players' decisions about where to play. Suffice to say here that star free agents in all sports have joined teams at lower pay to avoid the hectic pace, lack of privacy, and press scrutiny of big cities, or because teams looked like they were building a winner. Nonwage factors may include what players perceive to be an owner's commitment to winning beyond what their market might bear in terms of revenue or a coach's style of play.

In terms of discrimination, preferences by one group of players may influence their choice of team. Rod Carew made his preferences quite clear in the wake of Twins' owner Griffith's statements. One wonders if other black players shunned the Twins as well. Although the racial climate may have changed over time in Minnesota, to this day, some cities have a better reputation for racial tolerance than others do. Black players may be willing to take less money in order to choose between cities based on their own preferences.

ECONOMIC FINDINGS ON PAY DISCRIMINATION

The primary objective in presenting the findings of economic analysis of discrimination in sports is not to pass judgment on the level of discrimination in pay and hiring in sports. Instead, the findings simply serve to reinforce the idea that examining race and gender outcomes is a difficult prospect.

Did You Know?
When MLB first became integrated, home attendance increased as the number of blacks in the league rose. However, during the 1960s, the opposite occurred, and a definite dampening on revenues accompanied black participation in the majors. Then, by the end of the 1970s, these effects disappeared. Analysts now find no pay differential between black and white players of equal ability.

Extensive data and analyses on pay discrimination are available. For our purposes we will follow the reviews of one of the most respected analysts of discrimination in sports, Lawrence Kahn (1991; 2000). This section presents a synthesis of Kahn's work, but interested readers are encouraged to read Kahn's reviews.

Kahn (1991) cites evidence of racial pay differences driven by fan discrimination in the NBA. Up until the late 1980s, researchers found an 11 to 25 percent shortfall for blacks of equal talent. Meanwhile, more limited evidence had been found on pay discrimination and fan discrimination against French-Canadian players in the NHL and fan discrimination favoring white MLB players. As we mentioned earlier, in Grand Slam tennis events prize money for women is lower despite the fact that they generate at least as much revenue as men.

Fan discrimination, then, at least for team sports, appears to be confined to the NBA and MLB. In MLB, initially after integration, blacks increased home attendance. By the 1960s, revenues for teams with more black players were lower than for teams with fewer. However, these effects disappeared by the 1970s. Kahn also cites some evidence that nonwhite players earn more in areas with large nonwhite populations, and vice versa for white players. Scully (1989), updating his original work on pay discrimination in MLB, flatly stated: "We can conclude that *holding performance constant, black and white players are paid the same on average*" (p. 178).

Did You Know?

A different type of pay discrimination appears to operate in hockey. Few players are black, but a substantial portion are French speaking. Some analysts have found pay discrimination against these French-speaking players relative to the rest of the players in the NHL.

Kahn (2000) concludes that by the mid-1990s, pay discrimination had pretty much disappeared from the NBA. The only remaining evidence of pay discrimination was a significant but very small white premium at the very top of the NBA pay scale. There was no evidence of any pay discrimination in the NFL or MLB by the mid-1990s. In hockey, there is still evidence that in the NHL, French-speaking hockey players are the victims of pay discrimination relative to other hockey players.

DISCRIMINATION IN HIRING

With the analysis of pay discrimination behind us, the analysis of hiring discrimination is straightforward. Somewhat ironically, given his quote at the beginning of this chapter, Frank Robinson did become an MLB manager for 9 years (Cleveland, 1975–1977; San Francisco, 1981–1984; Baltimore, 1988–1989), and he currently manages the new Washington Nationals, but he was the first and only black manager for quite some time. The lack of minority hiring in the head coaching ranks of the NFL is viewed by many to be such a problem that there is a league policy, the "Rooney Rule," that requires candidates of color to be considered whenever there is a head coach opening. Detroit Lions president Matt Millen was fined $200,000 for failing to interview any black candidates when he hired Steve Mariuchi in 2003 (cbs.sportsline.com, July 25, 2003).

The outcome of simple hiring discrimination is underrepresentation of those equally qualified but denied hiring on the basis of race, ethnicity, or gender. However, there is another subtle form of hiring discrimination called **stacking**. Stacking refers to the hiring outcome on the field. Stacking occurs when nonwhite players are put in less conspicuous positions, such as outfielder as opposed to pitcher in baseball or wide receiver as opposed to quarterback in football. Although it is clear on the field, stacking is difficult to analyze off the field. For example, suppose nonwhites were disproportionately represented in less-visible front-office activities. That would be similar to stacking. However, the term *stacking* is reserved for on-field outcomes.

Economic Explanations for Hiring Discrimination

Economics would suggest one of three things about hiring discrimination. First, members of the group facing discrimination may possess different bundles of skills. Second, workers' preferences vary by group so that minorities and women choose not to take these jobs. Third, hiring discrimination continues based on current discrimination and the legacy of past discrimination, that is, based on statistical discrimination. The first idea leads us right back down the path of statistical discrimination. If there are skill differences, what is it about obtaining skills (through training and experience) that has precluded their acquisition by one group but not another? Given the payoff, it seems unlikely that individuals would choose not to train or gain experience that would open doors to employment in higher-paying jobs.

The second explanation of hiring discrimination concerns worker preferences. For this explanation to carry any weight in explaining hiring discrimination economically, it would have to be the case that minorities and women choose not to engage in particular sports jobs. This is pretty difficult to swallow. For example, society might once have dictated that coaching or top-level management was not "women's work." But that time is long past. Certainly no similar societal explanation seems valid in the case of blacks and Hispanics.

That leaves an explanation of hiring discrimination based on current discrimination and the legacy of past discrimination (i.e., statistical discrimination). Stacking may occur, and discrimination may preclude the participation of women and minorities at the top executive level because employers have developed rules of thumb based on the unobservable productivity characteristics of these groups. These rules discount the human capital of current minority and women candidates; these perception barriers will have to be breached in order to eliminate such rules of thumb. In the rest of this section, we will look at specific data regarding hiring discrimination.

Findings on Hiring Discrimination

Almost all formal economic analysis of hiring discrimination concerns players. The formal analysis concerning baseball managers and football head coaches is sparse, but interesting, and reserved for the Learning Highlight: Why Are There So Few Black MLB Managers and NFL Head Coaches? Kahn's (1991) review of hiring discrimination points out the obvious absence of black players in all major league sports prior to the end of World War II. Since then, there is no evidence of reduced hiring in the NBA, but there is some evidence that black players exit the league earlier and at higher rates than whites, performance held constant (Kahn, 1991). Similar evidence has been found in MLB (Kahn, 1991). Kahn (2000) cites evidence of hiring discrimination in the NFL draft. Equal-quality black college players are chosen later in the NFL draft than whites. The opposite has been shown to be true in the NBA draft, but just barely.

The Racial and Gender Report Card

The Racial and Gender Report Card (RGRC), published annually by the Institute for Diversity and Ethics at the University of Central Florida, is a periodic summary of the status of minorities and women in sports. It offers little in the way of analysis of discrimination, but it does report current statistics. The RGRC (2003), abstracted in Table 7.8, lists the percentage of minority and women participants in various capacities in MLB, the NBA, the NFL, and the NHL (the RGRC also reports on Major League Soccer, the WNBA, and college sports, but we'll maintain our focus on the four major pro sports here and leave college to Chapter 13).

Turning first to race, the RGRC clearly shows that only MLB hires managers and coaches in proportion to the racial composition of players (we'll omit the NHL from

LEARNING HIGHLIGHT
Why Are There So Few Black MLB Managers and NFL Head Coaches?

Sports economist Gerald Scully (1989) analyzed just why discriminatory hiring occurs at the MLB-manager level. Writing in 1989, when Frank Robinson was the only black manager in MLB and there were only a few black coaches, Scully noted that baseball managers' positions during their playing days were a major determinant in becoming a manager—nearly 90 percent of MLB managers were infielders during their playing days.

Scully made the simple observation that black players had different access to infield positions and, as a result, were destined to be the object of statistical discrimination. When he was writing, blacks predominated in the outfield and were badly outnumbered in the infield by white players. Further, most managers were previously coaches. Infield coaches, formerly infielders themselves, dominated the coaching ranks. In the chain of events that generates an MLB manager, blacks were outnumbered every step along the way.

Scully concluded that the lack of black managers appeared to be a supply-side problem. It is a statistical discrimination problem stemming from the fact that black players are usually outfielders and miss out on the background that leads to big league manager positions. Interestingly, Frank Robinson was an outfielder until very late in his career. As the first black manager, and an outfielder to boot, he began the long process of dispelling beliefs about the lack of training for blacks and for outfielders.

Recent work by Janice Madden (2004) finds quite a different reason for the lack of black head coaches in the NFL. Looking at the regular season and whether their teams make it to the playoffs, Madden finds significantly higher success rates among black head coaches

than their white counterparts. She also finds some evidence that black head coaches are hired by better teams in the first place. But even holding this fact constant, teams with black head coaches outperform teams with white head coaches. Finally, Madden rejects the Scully-type argument of "pipeline" effects by examining the playing positions of coaches. Overall, Madden concludes that this evidence is consistent with black head coaches' being held to higher standards to get their jobs in the NFL, clearly an earmark of discriminatory hiring.

Frank Robinson once asked, "Why don't we have black managers . . . in baseball?" Then he became the first.

Sources: Scully (1989) and Madden (2004).

Table 7.8 2003 Racial and Gender Report Card

	MLB			NBA			NFL			NHL		
	Black	Other	Female	Black	Other	Female	Black	Other	Female	Black	Other	Female
Players	10	30		78	2		65	2		1	0	
League office professionals	13	20	46	17	11	40	14	12	26	4	12	39
League office support staff	—	—	—	36	20	67	25	24	54	0	6	9
Team majority owners	0	0	0	0	0	0	0	0	9	0	0	0
Team coaches/managers	26	6		48	0		6	0		1	0	
Team assistant coaches	16	12		33	0		28	1		0	0	
Team COBs/presidents	0	0	3	4	0	4	3	0	3	0	0	0
Team GMs/dirs. player personnel	3	3	0	17	0	0	6	0	0	3	1	0
Team VPs	5	6	12	7	3	15	7	1	9	1	2	9
Team senior administrators	10	4	24	14	5	29	15	2	15	0	0	19
Team public relations directors	0	0	7	14	10	31	19	0	0	3	3	13
Team directors of community relations	33	3	67	36	0	55	19	4	65	3	0	79
Team chief financial officers	3	10	7	4	4	3	4	4	13	5	4	3
Team professional administration	7	6	22	13	8	48	10	3	29	1	3	40
Team medical staff	1	3	6	0	2	0	1	3	2	0	3	1
Team head trainers	0	3	0	11	4	0	15	0	0	0	0	0
Radio/TV announcers	4	13	1	16	7	3	10	3	2	0	3	1
Officials/referees				30	3	3	17	1	0	0	0	0
Team support staff				23	11	83	10	4	83	5	4	98
Players' association exec. coms.				89	0		64	2				

Note: Most entries are for 2002.
Source: Race and Gender Report Card, 2003, Institute for Diversity and Ethics, University of Central Florida.

further consideration because our conclusion will always be the same—no women or minorities coach or are in the front office). Although there are very few board chairs, presidents, general managers, and player development directors of color, nearly no majority owners of teams are of racial or ethnic minorities. Too late to be included in the RGRC tables, Robert Johnson bought the NBA's Hornets in 2003 and Arturo Moreno bought MLB's Anaheim Angels in 2004. Prior to that, only the majority owners of the NHL's Islanders, Charles Wang and Sanjay Kumar, were people of color. Radio and TV personalities are almost all white. One of the few categories reasonably represented by minorities is directors of community relations, a figurehead position occupied primarily by previous players loved by fans. Finally, as one would expect because they almost always are previous players, the racial composition of players' association officers mirrors the composition of players themselves.

Fewer data are available on women in pro sports, but Table 7.8 also lists what the RGRC has to offer. Women participate at their highest levels as team directors of community relations, league office professionals, and team senior and professional administrators. Compared to minorities, women are much more likely to be league professional and support staff and directors of community relations. Women owners and GMs for all practical purposes do not exist except in the NBA. Even fewer women than black men are broadcasters. In the WNBA, only 41 percent of head coaches are women. As the RGRC itself acknowledges, "As in society itself, we have a long way to go to achieve equality in sport" (p. 61).

Findings on Stacking

Kahn (1991, 2000) found clear evidence of stacking in MLB, the NFL, and the NHL but no significant stacking in the NBA. Blacks were underrepresented as pitchers, catchers, and infielders in MLB. In the NFL, blacks were underrepresented as quarterbacks, kickers, and linebackers. In the NHL, French-Canadian players were underrepresented as defensemen and overrepresented as goalies. Kahn points out that it is only speculation as to whether stacking is caused by co-worker discrimination or by statistical discrimination based on lack of access to equivalent training.

Did You Know?
In the NFL, 65 percent of the players are black; 24 percent of quarterbacks are black; and blacks predominate at the so-called speed positions of running back, wide receiver, and defensive back. In MLB, 10 percent of the players are black, but 31 percent of the outfielders are black and only 3 percent of the pitchers are. The racial distribution of players is much more proportional for the 30 percent of players that are Latino.

Table 7.9 lists the RGRC tally on race and position in the NFL and MLB for 2002. In the NFL, there are some clear differences compared to the earlier findings by Kahn. Relative to their overall player proportion of 65 percent, blacks are underrepresented everywhere on the offensive side of the ball except running back and wide receiver (the so-called speed positions). Blacks clearly predominate on defense, especially the defensive backfield, including linebacker (nearly 100% of the pass coverage defense is black). In MLB, it doesn't appear that there has been much progress compared to Kahn's earlier findings—nearly no pitchers, catchers, or third basemen are black, whereas over 30 percent of the outfielders are (remember, blacks are 10% of all ballplayers). The RGRC reports that stacking does not appear to plague Latino players (30% of major leaguers).

Table 7.9 Stacking in the NFL and MLB, 2002

NFL Position	%Black	MLB Position	%Black	%Latino
QB	24	P	3	22
RB	82	C	1	37
WR	88	1B	14	23
TE	41	2B	21	43
OT	53	3B	0	29
OG	41	SS	11	60
C	14	OF	31	25
CB	98	Overall	10	30
S	87			
LB	78			
DE	78			
DT	78			
Overall	65			

Source: Race and Gender Report Card, 2003, Institute for Diversity and Ethics, University of Central Florida.

CHAPTER RECAP

Players are fabulously compensated for their efforts, but sports stars do not make as much as entertainment stars in general. Over time, sports salaries have increased dramatically, and always in favor of superstars. NBA players are the most highly compensated, followed by NHL, MLB, and NFL players.

Marginal revenue product (MRP) offers the strongest explanation of pay in sports. Essentially, in a competitive talent market, players will earn somewhere between their highest and second-highest MRP in the league. That is, players will earn pretty close to their highest revenue contribution across all the teams in the league. Player earnings over time also follow the usual experience–earnings profile, and the explanation extends quite nicely to coaches and managers.

The graphical analysis of the talent market reveals three important things. First, marginal revenues are equal across all teams at the equilibrium in the talent market. Second, large-revenue market teams spend more on talent than small-revenue market teams do. Finally, in a competitive situation, large-revenue market teams will choose to win more than small-revenue market teams. We should expect competitive imbalance as long as there is revenue imbalance. Long-term contracts exist so that owners and players can cope with risk and so that owners can give players incentives to continue high-quality effort throughout their careers.

The MRP theory also sheds light on some confusing sports outcomes. The theory helps show that while there will be busts and bargains for any particular team at any particular time, the market sends talent to its highest valued use over time. Owners and their personnel directors do not make systematic mistakes in the hiring market. MRP theory also helps to show that rising player salaries do not drive up ticket prices. Instead, salaries rise because fans' willingness to pay increases. The theory also shows how we can value sports stars' services less than other types of labor and still pay them more.

The fantastic payment to players has led some economists to produce explanations of player pay and hiring not based on MRP. However, these special explanations for such high pay typically only apply in special situations, if at all. The setting is not right for the winner's curse; bidding wars only make sense for a few teams and only as they approach the playoffs; and the winner-take-all logic, although a possibility for individual sports, does not apply to team sports.

Economics can offer limited but occasionally strong insights into gender, race, and ethnic discrimination in sports. Again, based primarily on the MRP concept, the insights are in the areas of pay and hiring differentials based on gender, race, and ethnicity. Pay differentials are mostly a thing of the past, but hiring variation and stacking still remain. Although economics can help to identify discrimination, it can contribute little to the debate on what should be done about it, as that is not an economic question.

KEY TERMS AND CONCEPTS

- Marginal revenue product (MRP)
- Competitive talent market
- Free agents
- Experience–earnings relationship
- Experience–earnings profile
- Arbitration
- Talent market equilibrium

- Payroll imbalance
- Competitive imbalance
- Revenue imbalance
- Expected MRP
- Unbiased expectations
- Winner's curse
- Bidding war
- Winner-take-all explanation
- Discrimination in pay and hiring

- Statistical discrimination
- Fan discrimination
- Cost of fan discrimination
- Owner discrimination
- Teammate discrimination
- Cost of owner discrimination
- Opportunity cost of time
- Worker job preferences
- Stacking

REVIEW QUESTIONS

1. Why are a league's average and median salaries both important when comparing salaries at the top and bottom of the league for a given year? What is the implication for the growth of salaries over time when the average salary dwarfs the median salary?

2. What is endorsement income? In percentage terms, who increases their incomes more with endorsements, male or female athletes? Why?

3. Define marginal revenue product (MRP). Carefully explain both elements of MRP (*MR* and *MP*). What happens to MRP as winning percent increases? Explain the impact on both *MR* and *MP*.

4. What is the age–earnings relationship? Draw a quick graph of what it looks like for a pro athlete. Is this shape any different than would be expected for any other job?

5. Define the competitive equilibrium in the market for talent. What are the two main characteristics of this equilibrium? What is the relationship between revenue imbalance, payroll imbalance, and competitive imbalance on the field?

6. Explain the idea of expected MRP. What does it mean if owners have unbiased expectations about player performance? If owners do have unbiased expectations about player performance, can there be bargains and busts?
7. What is the MRP explanation of the relationship between ticket prices and player salaries? According to MRP theory, which causes which? Why did salaries rise so significantly during the 1980s even though ticket prices typically fell over the same period in real terms?
8. What are the special circumstances that must hold for a winner's curse explanation of player pay? Would you expect this explanation to hold over an extended period of time?
9. What special circumstances must hold for each of the following to explain player pay? When would you expect to observe these special circumstances?
   a. A bidding war
   b. A winner-take-all outcome
10. How might one confuse a winner-take-all outcome with one that is simply designed to give players in a tournament the incentive to show up and play as well as possible?
11. What are the explanations based on the marginal product, or *MP*, part of MRP for economic discrimination against women and minorities? How does statistical discrimination follow from this explanation?
12. What are the explanations based on the marginal revenue, or *MR*, part of MRP for economics discrimination against women and minorities? Name the two types of discrimination that follow from this explanation.
13. What happens to an owner in a market with bigoted fans if talent is hired purely on the grounds of ability and not race? Explain why owner discrimination will not survive in the face of vigorous competition over players.
14. State the three reasons for an observed deficiency of hiring one race or gender relative to another.
15. Summarize the economic findings on pay discrimination and hiring discrimination. What are the findings on black/white pay differences? Racial stacking?

THOUGHT PROBLEMS

1. Using MRP theory, explain why NBA players make more than other sports players. Using MRP theory, explain why Mel Gibson makes more than any pro athlete in Table 7.3.
2. Suppose winning one more game increases revenues by $500,000. A solid slugger adds 55 winning percent points. Rounding all of your calculations to the nearest whole number, show that adding a solid slugger is worth $4.5 million to the team owner in terms of marginal revenue.
3. Mark McGwire held the homerun record prior to Barry Bonds. During the 1998 season when he earned the record, compared to his career average McGwire played in 49 more games (career average 106), had 153 more at bats (career average 356), and 60 more hits (career average 92), and of course, hit 40 more home runs (career average 30). Because he earned $8.9 million but had a career year, sports writers would have called him a bargain. How would you evaluate this claim?

4. In our example in Table 7.4 and Figure 7.1, Randy Johnson won 20 games with a terrific earned run average in 1997. He was paid about $7.5 million. In 2001, he had nearly an identical season to 1997 but earned almost twice as much. Does this violate MRP theory? Why or why not?

5. Observers of pro sports leagues have lamented over competitive imbalance in one league or another at different points in time. Without exception, these observers point to payroll imbalance as the culprit. Correct them or agree with them, and justify your correction or agreement.

6. The examples in Figures 7.4 through 7.6 are only that. How would you perform a more thorough investigation of the relationship between ticket prices and salaries? Fully explain your method and the data you would need.

7. How can society value teachers more than ballplayers but end up paying ballplayers more? Explain using a graph like the one in Figure 7.7.

8. If the problem with Canadian teams is that they cannot compete in Canadian dollars, why don't they just write the contract in U.S. dollars and pay players that way?

9. Looking at the outcome of overinvestment in a pro career by some youths, it would be easy to identify it as a winner-take-all outcome. But what is the argument against it? How do you come down on the issue?

10. Explain the limits of any economic analysis of player pay and hiring discrimination.

11. In the case of fan discrimination, depicted in Figure 7.8, show what happens if fans learn over time and the level of discrimination falls by half in 1 year. What if it falls by half again the following year?

12. How would you design a test that would allow you to tell whether some observed pay differential between genders was due to statistical discrimination?

13. Now that salaries in all major pro sports are equal by race, does that mean that discrimination is no longer an economic problem in sports? What other indicator of discrimination suggests that it remains an economic problem?

14. Only 41 percent of the head coaches in the WNBA were women as of the 2003 data reported in Table 7.8. Does this mean that there is hiring discrimination against women at that position? State the arguments for and against that position. Can you draw any conclusions?

15. Scully (1989) suggests that stacking is behind the absence of managers of color in MLB, according to the Learning Highlight: Why Are There So Few Black MLB Managers and NFL Head Coaches? But what lies behind the stacking outcome in the first place? Explain your answer fully.

ADVANCED PROBLEMS

1. What would the impact on player salaries be if a professional sports league with free-agent players decided to relocate one of its teams? Think in terms of MRP and explain your answer fully.

2. For the MLB 1999 season, Kevin Brown signed for $105 million with the Dodgers, causing a huge stir. Just 2 years later, Alex Rodriguez moved to the Rangers for the MLB 2001 season for $252 million. Do you think that player salaries can rise forever? Why or why not?

3. Starting from a separate graph of the talent market equilibrium in Figure 7.2 for each case, show what happens to the price of talent and the amount of talent hired by two teams if
   a. Fan demand in both cities increases willingness to pay at the margin by 20 percent in both locations.
   b. Economic hard times befall the fans in the larger-revenue market location and incomes fall.
   c. Foreign demand for American sports on TV increases, and those fans always root for the underdog.
4. Take a two-team league as in Figure 7.2 and let the larger-revenue team's marginal revenue function be $MR_L(W) = 90 - 90W_L$ and the smaller-revenue market team's marginal revenue function be $MR_S(W) = 60 - 60W_S$, where L denotes the large-revenue team, S denotes the small-revenue team, and W is winning percent.
   a. Graph the MR functions.
   b. Show the clearing talent price.
   c. Determine what the W will be for each at the clearing price.
   d. Determine what the total talent bill will be for each.
5. Find MLB revenue data and team payrolls for 1994. Graph payroll against revenue and calculate the correlation between them. What did you find? What does that do for your thoughts about MRP theory?
6. How would you determine whether owners consistently pay more for free agents or rookies than they are worth? Describe:
   a. The hypothesis you would test
   b. The calculations you would do to perform your test
   c. The data you would need in order to do the calculations and perform the test
7. Suppose an NBA rookie will generate $5 million per year in combined TV and gate revenue for an expected 8-year career. At 6 percent, show that the discounted present value of the most that an owner would pay over those 8 years for the player's services is $31 million. If the rookie would agree to $2 million per year for an 8-year contract, show that the largest bonus that the owner would pay to sign him is $18.6 million.
8. Why did it take so long for MLB to fully integrate after Jackie Robinson joined the league in 1947? Did economic discrimination end once the league was fully integrated? What is the evidence that economic discrimination continued even after that?
9. How would you design a test that would allow you to tell whether some observed pay differential between races was due to statistical discrimination? Fan discrimination? Owner/teammate discrimination?
10. The following are the minimum, maximum, and average purses and first-place prizes for men's and women's pro golf tournaments in the year 2000 (extracted from *Sports Business Journal*, April 2, 2001, pp. 29–33). Explain the age and gender pay outcomes from the MRP perspective. Explain the outcome from an age and gender discrimination perspective.

	PGA		SPGA		LPGA	
	First Place ($Million)	Purse ($Million)	First Place ($Million)	Purse ($Million)	First Place ($Million)	Purse ($Million)
Purse						
Minimum	$2.0	$0.4	$1.2	$0.2	$0.8	$0.1
Maximum	$6.0	$1.1	$2.4	$0.4	$2.8	$0.2
Average	$3.6	$0.7	$1.5	$0.2	$1	$0.1

INTERNET RESOURCES

For a host of additional material and questions for thought, visit this book's Web site at www.prenhall.com/fort.

DATA NOTES

The average and median salaries in Table 7.2 were found in a variety of different sources. Recently, USAToday.com has begun a salaries database for each of the four major pro sports. Only median and total salaries are reported there and for different time periods for each sport. Sometimes the data have appeared in individual articles at ESPN.com, USAToday.com, SFAWeb.com, ProIceHockey.miningco.com, and other newspaper Web sites. These are found through Web searches. Others who watch averages, medians, and totals include:

Patricia's Various Basketball Stuff: www.dfw.net/~patricia/.

Andrew's Dallas Stars Page: www.andrewsstarspage.com/NHL-Business/.

In chronological order, traditionally published sources are:

U.S. House of Representatives, Committee on the Judiciary, Subcommittee on the Study of Monopoly Power, 1951, 82d Congress, 1st Session Series No. 1, Pt. 6, Organized Baseball.

Committee on the Judiciary. House of Representatives. The Antitrust Laws and Organized Professional Team Sports Including Consideration of the Proposed Merger of the American and National Basketball Associations. Serial No. 38. 1972.

Dworkin, James, "Balancing the Rights of Professional Athletes and Team Owners: The Proper Role of Government," in A. Johnson and J. Frey, eds., *Government and Sport*. Totowa, NJ: Rowman & Littlefield Publishing, 1985.

Berry, R. C., et al., *Labor Relations in Professional Sports*. Dover, MA: Auburn House Publishing, 1986, pp. 13, 221.

Staudohar, P. *The Sports Industry and Collective Bargaining*, 2d ed. Ithaca, NY: ILR Press, 1989.

Spokane Spokesman-Review/Chronicle, July 7, 1993, p. C5.

USA Today, December 16, 1993, p. 2C.

The Sporting News, October 17, 1994, p. 54.

Financial World, February 14, 1995, p. 46.

National Football Players Association Report, June 13, 2000.

REFERENCES

Bodvarsson, Orn B., and Raymond T. Brastow. "A Test of Employer Discrimination in the NBA," *Contemporary Economic Policy* 17 (1999): 243–255.

Cassing, James, and Richard W. Douglas. "Implications of the Auction Mechanism in Baseball's Free Agent Draft," *Southern Economic Journal* 47 (1980): 110–121.

Ehrenberg, Ronald G., and Michael L. Bognano. "Do Tournaments Have Incentive Effects?" *Journal of Political Economy* 98 (1990a): 1307–1324.

Ehrenberg, Ronald G., and Michael L. Bognano. "The Incentive Effects of Tournaments Revisited: Evidence from the European PGA Tour," *Industrial and Labor Relations Review* 43 (1990b): 74S–88S.

Fort, Rodney, and Andrew Gill. "Race and Ethnicity Assessment in Baseball Card Markets," *Journal of Sports Economics* 1 (2000): 21–38.

Frank, Robert H., and Philip J. Cook. *The Winner-Take-All Society*. New York: The Free Press, 1995.

Jewell, R. Todd, Robert W. Brown, and Scott E. Miles. "Measuring Discrimination in Major League Baseball: Evidence from the Baseball Hall of Fame," *Applied Economics* 34 (2002): 167–177.

Kahn, Lawrence M. "Discrimination in Professional Sports: A Survey of the Literature," *Industrial and Labor Relations Review* 44 (1991): 395–418.

Kahn, Lawrence M. "The Sports Business as a Labor Market Laboratory," *Journal of Economic Perspectives* (2000): 75–94.

Lehn, Kenneth. "Information Asymmetries in Baseball's Free Agent Market," *Economic Inquiry* 22 (1984): 37–44.

Madden, Janice F. "Differences in the Success of NFL Coaches by Race, 1990–2002: Evidence of Last Hire, First Fire," *Journal of Sports Economics* 5 (2004): 6–19.

Nelson, Kevin. *Baseball's Greatest Insults: A Humorous Collection of the Game's Most Outrageous, Abusive and Irreverent Remarks*. New York: Simon and Schuster, 1984.

Noll, Roger G. "Economic Perspectives on the Athlete's Body," *Stanford Humanities Review* 6.2 (1998). www.stanford.edu/group/SHR/6–2/html/noll.html.

Peterson, Robert. *Only the Ball Was White*. New York: Gramercy Books, 1970.

Porter, Philip K., and Gerald W. Scully. "Measuring Managerial Efficiency: The Case of Baseball," *Southern Economic Journal* 48 (1982): 642–650.

Scully, Gerald W. "Economic Discrimination in Professional Sports," *Law and Contemporary Problems* 38 (1973): 67–84.

Scully, Gerald W. "Pay and Performance in Major League Baseball," *American Economic Review* 64 (1974): 915–930.

Scully, Gerald W. *The Business of Major League Baseball*. Chicago, IL: University of Chicago Press, 1989.

Chapter 8

The History of Player Pay

Chapter Objectives

After reading this chapter, you should be able to:

■ *Graphically demonstrate in general terms the value to owners of reducing competition over player talent.*

■ *Understand both the theoretical reason that player drafts reduce competition over player talent and the particular ways the drafts have been implemented in pro sports leagues.*

■ *Understand the theoretical reason that the reserve clause reduces competition over player talent and know the history of the evolution and demise of the reserve clause in pro team sports.*

■ *Describe the data that show how much reduced competition over player talent has been worth to owners, especially the value of the reserve clause while it was in effect.*

■ *Understand the invariance principle and its implications for competitive balance.*

> *No one foresaw what was coming in salaries. Not the players. Not the management. I always had thought I'd be an Oakland A for my whole career, that I'd end like Al Kaline or Brooks Robinson. That just isn't going to happen anymore. It's sad, bad for baseball, but it is the truth.*

—REGGIE JACKSON, THE HIGHEST PAID OF THE FIRST CROP OF 1976 FREE AGENTS AT $3 MILLION OVER 5 YEARS, ON FREE AGENCY

*A*fter a 12-year career with the St. Louis Cardinals, Curt Flood was traded to Philadelphia. Under the legal relationship in force between players and owners at that time, he was obligated by his contract to go. Flood, however, had established his life and business in St. Louis and did not want to move it all to Philadelphia. In his appeal to Commissioner Bowie Kuhn to be exempted from this trade, he said, "After 12 years of being in the majors, I do not feel I am a piece of property to be bought and sold irrespective of my wishes." Commissioner Kuhn replied, "I certainly agree with you that you, as a human being, are not a piece of property to be bought and sold. This is fundamental to our society and, I think, obvious . . . [but] I cannot see its applicability to the situation at hand" (Helyar, 1994, p. 108). The contradiction was obvious to Flood, and he left baseball to sue MLB under the antitrust laws. He lost, but helped set the stage for players to win freedom over where they would play in the future.

In this chapter, we will examine the history of owners' attempts to keep as much of the value created by players as possible. The dramatic rise in salaries after free agency indicates just how much owner restrictions on players were worth. Perhaps the most important insight in sports economics is the invariance principle—regardless of whether it is owners or players who get to keep the value created by players, competitive balance remains unchanged. As you will see, the draft and free agency do not affect competitive balance. Some of the same arguments about restricting competition for players made before free agency are surfacing again, including the opinion voiced by Reggie Jackson in the introductory quote for this chapter, and they are just as incorrect now as they were then.

RESTRICTING COMPETITION OVER TALENT

Thus far, our presentation of player pay has been in the context of competition over player services. MRP is the most that can be paid to athletes, and they receive close to their MRP as long as competition prevails. However, pro owners would certainly pay less if they could and pocket the extra revenue. This would require making the market for player services less competitive.

In this section, we will analyze why owners would reduce player payments below their MRP. We will also present an "owners'-eye" view of how competition in the talent market could be reduced at the entry level and after players have entered a given league.

The Value of Reducing Competition over Talent: Graphical Analysis

Figure 8.1 uses the graphical analysis of the labor market from Chapter 7 to analyze the value of restricting competition over players. The figure shows the competitive outcome for a two-team league where the price of talent is P^* and the level of

Figure 8.1 The Value of Immobilizing Talent

In equilibrium, $P = MR_S = MR_L$. and winning percents are $W_L^* = 1 - W_S^*$. The value of immobilizing talent comes from reducing alternatives and lowering the going price of talent to N. Each owner then reduces spending on talent. The reduction for the smaller market owner is $(P - N)W_S^*$.

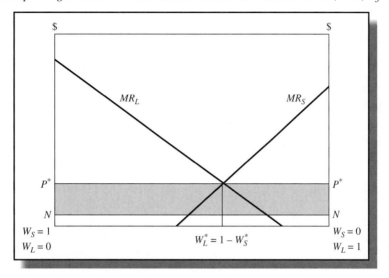

winning percent is $W_L^* = 1 - W_S^*$. The shaded rectangles in Figure 8.1 are prizes that can be won if employers can figure out how to stop talent from collecting its MRP. With this analysis, we need to recognize that there is a next-best opportunity available to talent providers. Suppose the opportunity cost outside the sport is N. If teams acting together as a league can reduce the price paid to talent away from P^* and closer to N, they get to keep the difference. Talent bills are reduced to the much smaller shaded areas, and the league keeps the amount shown by the top shaded rectangle, namely, $(P^* - N) \times (W_L^* + W_S^*)$. (Note that this saving is actually $P^* - N$, because the summed winning percents are equal to one for a two-team league.) So far, the gains to owners are just rectangles in a graph, but shortly we will see just how valuable these gains may be to a league.

The Two-Step Plan to Reduce Pay

Put yourself in the place of owners. You have an organization that allows you to act together with other owners to make decisions jointly, namely, your league. If the league were to design a system that reduced payment to talent to the lowest possible level, you would be sure to start at the point where talent entered the league. Then the league would think about reducing competition for talent once it was in the league. Of course, players would have to make enough to keep them in their sport, and many intangibles would have to be covered in order to keep players happy. But the bottom line is that payment to players would be reduced and owners would keep the difference. In the following sections we will present a simple, two-step plan that owners have used to reduce competition over talent and maximize their share of players' MRP.

RESTRICTING COMPETITION OVER INCOMING PLAYERS: THE DRAFT

The first step to reducing pay involves the entry of new talent into the pro ranks. Under a competitive structure, all of the pro teams would scout the country at the same time and in the same places to turn up their own talent. Scouts from each team would outrace and outbid each other to sign that new talent. This type of competition drives up signing bonuses and initial contract values to players. Think how much could be saved if all of the league members agreed not to do that. Spending in the pursuit of talent and payments to players could be reduced. Note that the money does not go away but is preserved for whomever gains rights to the player entering the pro ranks. Somebody gets to keep the money, but not the player. Just who gets to keep it depends on the method devised for distributing the savings.

The Original Imposition of the Draft: The NFL

The NFL set the ball rolling. In 1936, NFL owners instituted a college draft. This followed on the heels of two interesting episodes. First, the Chicago Bears signed Red Grange immediately after the 1925 college football season ended. School was still in session, but Grange left and joined the Bears for their last two regular-season games. College coaches screamed bloody murder, fearing that the pros would start raiding their rosters even before the season ended. In 1926, the NFL agreed not to pursue college players until their class had graduated. This type of hands-off policy survived until just recently.

The second episode that led to the imposition of a college draft was the signing of Stan Kostas prior to the 1935 season. Up to that time, any team could pursue any college player, and competition could be brutal. In the Kostas episode, the Brooklyn (football) Dodgers and Philadelphia Eagles bid up his services to a $5,000 starting salary. This was as much as the premiere players in the league earned, and owners saw the writing on the wall. At the very next league meeting, the **reverse-order-of-finish draft** was established. With this system, the weakest teams draft first, enabling them to have first shot at signing the best talent or (in some leagues) trade the rights to draft the best talent to other teams. The drafted players must play for the teams that draft them or not play at all. The NFL did have a draft in the days before the Kostas incident, but it was geographical rather than reverse order of finish.

General Impacts of the Draft

Today, the reverse-order draft is the standard in all pro sports leagues (although the NBA decides draft order in early rounds using a lottery system). Under the draft, part of the value of talent that would have gone to recruiting and signing compensation is preserved for the league and distributed to the weakest teams in the league. If the weak teams keep their high draft picks, they get to enjoy a higher level of talent. If the team's fans get excited about the new level of talent, then revenues respond so that the weaker teams can later hold on to that talent by increasing its pay. This is better for the league as a whole in terms of competitive-balance. In addition, league revenues rise and all teams share in that success through gate-revenue-sharing and TV-revenue-sharing arrangements.

However, if the fans of weak teams do not respond, then the stronger teams will place a higher value on that talent and obtain it from the weaker teams that drafted ahead of them. In this case, weaker teams enjoy better talent for a short time and earn some return when players move on to stronger teams through trades and sales. The league also keeps that part of talent's value that would have been earned by incoming players if teams competed for new talent. For this to happen the teams must be able to trade or sell player contracts and players must be bound to follow their contract wherever it goes.

Owners defend the draft as a financial sanity measure and as a tool for weak teams to get talent they otherwise would be unable to sign. Owners stress that careful drafting and good player development can turn losing teams into winners. We will explore this idea in detail later in this chapter.

Drafts in the Rest of the Pro Sports Leagues

Whatever its merits in terms of team survival, the college draft certainly acted to lower bonuses and salaries paid to players entering the NFL. It should come as no surprise that all of the other pro leagues also adopted a draft. The NBA college draft has existed since the formation of the league for the 1949–1950 season, and it has undergone many changes. Today, it consists of two rounds. In the first round, the order of the draft for the first eight picks is determined by lottery. After that, it is by reverse order of finish.

In MLB and the NHL, the draft started much later. Both leagues originally developed their talent primarily through their own minor league systems rather than by recruiting college players. In MLB, the draft started in 1965, and it continues today with each team drafting approximately 30 new players each year. The NHL draft started in 1963.

RESTRICTING COMPETITION OVER LEAGUE PLAYERS: THE RESERVE CLAUSE

The second step to reducing pay is the reduction of competition over talent after it has been drafted. Suppose the pro teams all agree that players must play for the team that obtained them, unless that team chooses to send the player, by either trading or selling their contract, to another team. The same rule holds for the next team that obtains the rights to a player, and so on. This would eliminate competition and pretty much force the players to live with the amount offered by their current team. In the context of Figure 8.1, N would be the best that the players could hope to do outside of their sport, and the amount that owners would keep would be as large as possible.

Attempts to eliminate competition over player talent are practically as old as professional sports. James Quirk and I (1992) trace it back to pro baseball. At its inception in 1876, the National League had no rules governing competition over talent. Owners and players operated in a truly free market. Of course, team costs reflected this fact, and owners were constantly bickering about talent raiding by their fellow league members. Owners realized that steps had to be taken to reduce that competition and raise owner profits at the expense of players.

The first thing the National League did was to close the market to talent raiding during the season. No contracts could be written until well after the season was over. But this was just one step in reducing competition over players. In 1879, one of the Boston owners, Arthur Soden, suggested that all teams recognize a list of five players that every other team would hold off the market at the end of the season. Salaries were cut in 1880, and more teams were profitable than ever before.

Player contracts specified that they would obey the league's constitution and bylaws that included this reservation system, so players had to live with it. Even though this was just the beginning of such owner actions, John Montgomery Ward, one of the chief architects of baseball's first labor organization, the Brotherhood of Baseball Players, recognized the reservation system for what it was in 1890:

> "The reserve rule and the provisions of the National Agreement gave the managers unlimited power, and they have not hesitated to use this in the most arbitrary and mercenary way. . . . Players have been bought and sold as though they were sheep instead of American citizens. 'Reservation' for them became for them another name for property right in the player.' —John Montgomery Ward, 1890

The reserve rule and the provisions of the National Agreement gave the managers unlimited power, and they have not hesitated to use this in the most arbitrary and mercenary way. . . . Players have been bought and sold as though they were sheep instead of American citizens. "Reservation" for them became for them another name for property right in the player. (Lewis, 2001)

Ironically, Ward ended up as a lawyer for the National League, primarily charged with enforcing the reserve system.

The Original Reserve Clause: MLB

By 1889, owners had inserted a **reserve clause** into player contracts. It read:

> It is further understood and agreed that the party of the first part [the team] shall have the right to "reserve" the said party of the second part [the player] for the season next ensuing . . . [subject to the condition that] the said party of the second part shall not be reserved at a salary less than that [paid in the present season]. . . . (Quirk and Fort, 1992, p. 182)

Owners interpreted this clause to mean that they had a perpetual option on the player. All they had to do was invoke the reserve clause and extend the contract at its stated price every year. Contract prices could only change if the player bargained during the regular season. The only bargaining tool players had was to threaten not to play at all for any team. This particular version of the reserve clause did not stand court tests, but the owners kept searching for language that would stand. In the meantime, they kept the reservation system in place.

In 1901, the new American League was formed. It raided talent mercilessly from the older National League. Owners in each league could see that the bidding up of talent in this fashion meant lower profits for all. In 1903, they reached a "peace settlement." One of the primary terms of peace was the observance of all teams' reserve clauses by all owners in both leagues. However, players challenged the reserve clause for another 20 years.

The Federal Baseball Decision Not until the monumental *Federal Baseball* decision of 1922 was the issue of the reserve clause settled (*Federal Baseball Club of Baltimore v. National League of Professional Baseball Clubs*, 259 U.S. 200 [1922]). In *Federal Baseball*, a team in a rival league sued the National League over its reserve clause. The rival league sued under the relatively new antitrust law, the Sherman Act of 1890, arguing that the reserve clause was a restraint of interstate trade. The case made its way to the Supreme Court. Justice Oliver Wendell Holmes ruled for the majority:

> The business is giving exhibitions of baseball, which are purely *state affairs* [italics added] . . . the fact that in order to give exhibitions the Leagues must induce free persons to cross state lines . . . is not enough to change the character of the business. . . . That which in its consummation is not commerce does not become commerce among the States because the transportation that we have mentioned takes place. . . . If we are right . . . the restrictions by contract that prevented the plaintiff [the rival league] from getting players to break their bargains and the other conduct charged against the defendants were not an interference with commerce among the States. (Quirk and Fort, 1992, p. 185)

Essentially, the court majority argued that baseball was not interstate commerce and, as a result, did not fall under the federal antitrust laws. The plaintiff rival league lost, and this court decision created what has come to be known as MLB's antitrust exemption. The *Federal Baseball* decision simply meant that it would be nearly impossible to challenge the reserve clause because the Supreme Court had failed to rule against it.

Immediately, the owners inserted a binding (by Supreme Court decision) reserve clause into every player contract. Because player contracts are personal agreements between parties, the precise wording of the clause may vary. However, the reserve clause, unchanged from the *Federal Baseball* decision until the 1950s, reads:

> [I]f prior to March 1, . . . the player and the club have not agreed upon the terms of such contract [for the next playing season], then on or before ten days after said March 1, the club shall have the right to renew this contract for the period of one year on the same terms, except that the amount payable to the player shall be such as the club shall fix in said notice. . . . (Quirk and Fort, 1992, p. 185)

Thus, owners went back to interpreting the clause to mean that contracts never expired. When a player signed a contract with either the American League or the National League, he accepted the entire contract, including the reserve clause. Doing so bound the player to that club as long as the owner submitted a new contract to the player before March 1, whether the player signed that contract or not. The clause also was included in the new contract as well.

Because the contract never expired, players were bound to the team holding their contract. Further, the players could never let their current contract expire and seek higher compensation in any competitive bidding process. Under this regime, as long as contracts could be traded, owners were in control of the value of players over their entire career.

Owner Arguments in Favor of the Reserve Clause

For decades, all contracts in every pro sport contained a version of the reserve clause. The owners in the other sports essentially lifted the idea from MLB and imposed it on their players to keep costs down and profits up. If a team sold or traded the contract to another team, players had no choice but to move, break the contract and face the legal repercussions, or quit their sport. Competition over players was reduced, and owners maximized their share of the players' MRP.

Owners, of course, used noneconomic arguments in favor of the reserve clause. First, they argued that it enhanced fan confidence in the integrity of the outcome on the field. How could fans believe that players were doing their best against a team that might be their employer in the next season? By binding players under the reserve clause, the fans could be sure that the players were doing their best. Further, with players changing teams at the will of competition, fans would lose identity with teams if rosters changed annually.

Owners went so far as to argue that abolishing the reserve clause so that free agency ruled would be the end of sports. They argued that in such a competitive regime the rich teams would buy all of the good talent. Eventually, the leagues would fall apart because the large-revenue market teams would be unbeatable. Fans would end up watching the same few teams in the championship every year. In time, fans would lose interest and the smaller-revenue teams would fold. According to this argument, echoing the uncertainty of outcome hypothesis, the reserve clause preserved teams for fans and cities that would otherwise not have a team. The same idea fueled the argument in the last league to end its player reservation system, the NFL. In discussions about eliminating the last impediments to complete player mobility in his league, NFL Commissioner Paul Tagliabue echoed arguments that were about 100 years old: "Total free agency would destroy the National Football League" (*Sports Illustrated*, September 10, 1990, p. 42).

"Total free agency would destroy the National Football League." —NFL Commissioner Paul Tagliabue, 1990

The End of the Reserve Clause in MLB

In MLB, the reserve clause existed until 1975. There were court challenges galore, but the courts' answers always went straight back to the *Federal Baseball* decision. The reserve clause in baseball was specifically exempted from such challenges. In 1974, MLB players finally started to overcome the reserve clause. Under labor law, arbitrator Peter Seitz decided that Oakland Athletics pitcher Catfish Hunter was a free agent at the end of the 1974 season. Seitz agreed that A's owner Charley O. Finley had violated a clause in Hunter's contract concerning contributions to Hunter's retirement fund. With the contract violated, it was null and void, and Hunter was free to sell his services to the highest bidder. He ended up with the New York Yankees and became baseball's first millionaire player.

Almost immediately after that, pitchers Dave McNally and Andy Messersmith let their contracts expire, played out the 1975 season without a contract, and sought arbitration when their team owners invoked the reserve clause. Once again, arbitrator Peter Seitz decided they also were free agents, reversing the reserve clause that had existed in MLB since 1901 and that had withstood all legal challenges since 1922. The floodgates were open.

The Reserve Clause in Other Leagues

Interestingly, the courts were unwilling to extend the same exemption to other sports. Reserve clauses began dropping from NFL, NHL, and NBA contracts beginning in the 1950s. But full competition for player services in these leagues did not come until much later. In the NBA, players were free to seek their highest payment, relatively unfettered, beginning in 1981. The NFL and NHL had the longest tenure of reserve clause restrictions. Free agency was not fully established until 1993 in the NHL and 1994 in the NFL.

Reserve Clause Remnants

Free agency remains in limited forms in all sports. Continuing with the baseball example, free agency occurs after only 6 years in the league (or in the sixth year for the very top players). According to the 2002–2006 Basic Agreement negotiated between owners and players, the reserve clause for players with less than 6 years' experience reads:

> 10.(a) Unless the Player has exercised his right to become a free agent as set forth in the Basic Agreement, the Club may retain reservation rights over the Player by instructing the Office of the Commissioner to tender to the Player a contract for the term of the next year by including the Player on the Central Tender Letter that the Office of the Commissioner submits to the Players Association on or before December 20 (or if a Sunday, then on or before December 18) in the year of the last playing season covered by this contract. (See Article XX(A) of and Attachment 12 to the Basic Agreement.) If prior to the March 1 next succeeding said December 20, the Player and the Club have not agreed upon the terms of such contract, then on or before ten (10) days after said March 1, the Club shall have the right by written notice to the Player at his address following his signature hereto, or if none be given, then at his last address of record with the Club, to renew this contract for the period of one year on the same terms, except that the amount payable to the Player shall be such as the Club shall fix in said notice; provided, however, that said amount, if fixed by a Major League Club, shall be in an amount payable at a rate not less than as specified in Article VI, Section D, of the Basic Agreement. Subject to the Player's rights as set forth in the Basic Agreement, the Club may renew this contract from year to year.

THE VALUE OF REDUCED COMPETITION OVER PLAYERS

In this section we will examine just how much the reserve clause was worth to owners. Three different analyses will be presented. One estimates how much players should have been worth under competitive salary determination and compares it to their actual pay. The second analysis looks at what happened to the salaries of that first crop of free agents in MLB. Finally, we will examine how salaries changed in the aggregate for all four major sports with the end of their respective reserve clauses. At the end of the section we will discuss an important outcome of free agency—long-term contracts.

Estimates of the Value to Owners of the Reserve Clause

We will begin our examination of the value of the reserve clause by reviewing more of the work of Gerald Scully (1974). One measure of the amount of player MRP that was kept by owners when the reserve clause was in force is called **player exploitation**. Player exploitation is simply the percentage of money employers keep over and above the amount actually paid to players. Scully's approach was to estimate how much players would be worth in a competitive market, that is, their MRP, and compare that with the actual salary paid. Because salaries are less than MRP under the reserve clause, the following simple ratio measures player exploitation: (MRP – Actual Salary)/MRP. On average, for hitters, Scully estimated that owners kept 79 to 88 percent of MRP, depending on hitter quality. For pitchers, on average, owners kept 80 to 90 percent of MRP. Let's keep these percentages in mind as we look at what happened to salaries with the advent of free agency. The salaries that might have been for one MLB legend and member of the Hall of Fame, Willie Mays, are in the Learning Highlight: Say Hey! The Reserve Clause and Willie Mays.

The First Crop of Free Agents   Sommers and Quinton (1982) looked for evidence of the value of the reserve clause to owners in the salary data on the first crop of free agents, shown in Table 8.2. Except for one player, most earned two to three times their previous salary once they became free agents in 1976. Interestingly, and quite in accord with the MRP explanation of player pay from Chapter 7, there was one real "bust" in this first crop of free agents. Look at pitcher Wayne Garland in Table 8.2. His salary increased over eight times its previous level after only 4 years in the major leagues. He pitched five more uneventful seasons as a spot starter. This first crop also had some bargains. Gary Matthews, also in the league only 4 years when signing as a free agent with San Francisco, eventually played 16 years and made the National League championship series twice and the World Series once with the Phillies in the early 1980s. On average, this first crop of free agents included solid stars; Rollie Fingers and Reggie Jackson were inducted into the Hall of Fame in 1992 and 1993, respectively.

The salary increases in Table 8.2 are typically less than Scully's estimates. For superstar hitters and pitchers, Scully estimated that owners were keeping about eight times the salary. Therefore, Scully's estimates were close only for pitchers Wayne Garland and Bill Campbell. However, the years shown in Table 8.2 were adjustment years, and salaries continued their upward adjustment to free agency for

LEARNING HIGHLIGHT
Say Hey! The Reserve Clause and Willie Mays

Willie Mays's career ended just about the time that the reserve clause was dying, so he missed out on free agency. His salary history is shown in Table 8.1. It is clear that Mays was a star player. For example, in 1971, the minimum salary was $51,982; the average was $82,305; and Mays earned $779,727 (all in 2004 dollars). Earning nine times the average isn't bad, but what was he really worth to his teams?

In 2004 dollars, Mays earned about $12.3 million over his career. Scully (1974) estimated that owners kept about 89 percent of a star hitter's contribution to revenues prior to free agency. This means that owners made about 8.1 times what they actually paid a star hitter. For Mays, that would have been a cool $99.5 million that owners were able to keep due primarily to the reserve clause. Although $12.3 million is a lot, another $99.5 million is a lot more, and that does not even include any interest that would have been earned on portions invested over the nearly 50 intervening years.

Willie Mays earned $12.4 million over his career, but could have made $100 million more as a free agent.

Source: U.S. News and World Report, April 19, 1985, p. 23; *Spokane Spokesman-Review*, April 29, 1991, p. C2; and *Business Week*, August 12, 1985, p. 44.

Table 8.1 Salary History of Willie Mays[a]

YEAR	TEAM	SALARY	2004 DOLLARS
1951	New York Giants	$5,000	$36,327
1952	New York Giants	$7,500	$53,462
1954	New York Giants	$12,500	$87,779
1955	New York Giants	$30,000	$211,455
1958	San Francisco Giants	$100,000	$653,633
1959	San Francisco Giants	$80,000	$519,313
1971	San Francisco Giants	$180,000	$839,556
1972	San Francisco Giants	$180,000	$813,445
1972	New York Mets	$170,000	$768,254
1973	New York Mets	$170,000	$723,266

[a]Some values interpolated.

Source: Spokane Spokesman-Review, April 29, 1991, p. C2; *U.S. News and World Report*, April 19, 1985, p. 22; *Business Week*, August 12, 1985, p. 44.

Table 8.2 MLB's First Crop of Free Agents

Player	1975 Salary	1976 Salary	1977 Salary	% Change[a]
Hitters				
Reggie Jackson	$135,000	$185,000	$400,000	196.3
Joe Rudi	$50,000	$67,200	$200,000	300
Gary Matthews		$42,000	$100,000	138.1
Don Baylor		$40,000	$170,000	325
Bobby Grich	$46,000	$65,000	$190,000	313
Gene Tenace	$45,000	$40,800	$155,000	244.4
Norm Cash		$105,000	$200,000	190
Sal Bando	$100,000	$80,000	$250,000	150
Bert Campaneris		$72,000	$190,000	163.9
Pitchers				
Wayne Garland		$23,000	$215,000	834.8
Don Gullett		$58,400	$150,000	156.8
Rollie Fingers	$65,000	$71,200	$200,000	207.7
Bill Campbell		$22,000	$160,000	627.3
Doyle Alexander		$28,400	$150,000	428.2

[a]The percentage change is for 1975 to 1977, unless player had no observed 1975 salary, in which case the percentage change was for 1976 to 1977.

Source: Adapted from Sommers and Quinton (1982).

a few years after 1976. We can see this best by turning to the aggregate data for all the pro leagues over time. In addition, turning to the aggregate data allows us to look at the impact of free agency in the other three major sports.

Salary Growth over Time Table 8.3 shows average salaries 5 years before and after free agency in each of the four major pro sports leagues. Baseball and hockey had no other salary restrictions, whereas basketball implemented a salary cap two years after free agency was put in place. Free agency and a salary cap both were implemented at the same time in football. This variation reveals interesting differences in the impact of free agency that have yet to be examined in any detail.

In MLB, there was an immediate increase of 38.7 percent in real salaries. The real growth rate in salaries from 1971 to 1975, the 5 years prior to free agency, averaged 1.6 percent annually. After free agency, with **competitively determined salaries**, the average annual real growth rate jumped to 17.8 percent. Clearly, the advent of free agency cost MLB owners dearly. In the NHL, there was a similar 32.2 percent immediate increase in real salaries. Interestingly, however, the real annual rate of growth did not change after free agency in 1993. The reason for this difference awaits further analysis, but a reasonable idea is that revenues simply grew larger and faster in baseball than in hockey.

The impacts in the two leagues without salary caps are different in every way from each other and differ a bit from the leagues without caps. True free agency in the NBA began in 1981, and a salary cap was put in place in 1983. Free agency and a salary cap

Table 8.3
Average Salaries in Pro Sports Centered Around Free Agency (All Values in $2004)

YEAR	MLB	NBA	YEAR	NHL	NFL
1971	$158,501		1988	$300,482	
1972	$165,981		1989	$336,389	$483,374
1973	$167,601		1990	$417,343	$525,142
1974	$168,582		1991	$530,060	$588,619
1975	$168,995		1992	$537,440	$660,365
1976	$184,199	$431,993	1993	$710,562	$867,544
1977	$255,447	$433,698	1994	$714,472	$799,954
1978	$311,743	$429,200	1995	$938,760	$903,217
1979	$318,320	$442,749	1996	$1,084,766	$970,105
1980	$355,044	$392,387	1997	$1,264,857	$868,237
1981		$440,979	1998		$1,093,880
1982		$487,885			
1983		$522,058			
1984		$591,444			
1985		$658,968			
1986					
1987					
Immediate % Change	38.7%	12.4%		32.2%	−7.8%
Growth Before	1.6%	−2.4%		15.6%	15.7%
Growth After	17.8%	10.6%		15.5%	8.1%

Source: Averages from Table 7.2.

simultaneously occurred in the NFL in 1994. The immediate increase in the NBA was much smaller than in the non-cap leagues, and there actually was a decline in salaries in the NFL in 1994. The growth rate in salaries increased dramatically in the NBA, reversing declines in the previous five years, whereas the growth rate in NFL salaries fell to almost half its pre-free-agency rate. Again, just why these differences occur remains unknown, but it is clear that the impact of the salary cap in the NFL reduced player salaries and dramatically reduced their rate of growth. This lends some support to the view that the NFL cap was more tightly defined and enforced than the cap in the NBA had been following along with our discussion in Chapter 6.

Special Issue: Long-Term Contracts

Prior to free agency, there was no need for **long-term contracts**; players might have wished for them, but owners already had them in the form of the reserve clause. After free agency hit pro sports, the long-term contract became important to both owners and players. With the dramatic escalation in salaries brought by free agency, risk drove owners and players to long-term contracts. However, the downside to long-term contracts is the possibility that players will conserve effort for strategic contract years. Let's examine each of these outcomes in turn.

Risk and Long-Term Contracts In sports, risk is a double-edged sword. On the one hand, owners would rather not undergo the expensive negotiation process associated with annual hiring, especially for established players who have strong bargaining power under free agency. There is some economy to be gained by owners if they can assure themselves a steady supply of a player's services and avoid **annual hiring risk**. On the other hand, players face the **risk of performance** ups and downs and the **risk of injury**. Players would like to ensure payment in the face of these performance and injury risks. Long-term contracts thus serve the needs of both sides of the talent market.

For quite some time now, the price of talent has risen, and it would be rational for owners to expect the price of talent to continue to rise. Long-term contracts allow owners to play off the injury risk faced by players against their own expectation that the price of talent will continue to rise. Many players would be willing to give up some expected salary against the assurance that they will be paid something even in the event of poor performance or injury. Some owners will be willing to offer such a contract if it reduces current payments to talent by a large enough amount. As a result, players take a lower price per year and avoid the risk of variable earnings. Owners reduce talent costs and take a chance on injury. The length and payment sequence depends on expectations and the way the players and owners feel about risk. Further, detailed in Chapter 9, long-term contracts are guaranteed only in MLB. In other leagues, injury contingencies and other forms of performance clauses are contract-specific.

The Downside to Long-Term Contracts: Shirking and Strategic Effort

On the topic of effort by players, former Pirates manager, Jim Leyland, once said:

> I have never seen any correlation between what a player makes and his desire to do well. I disagree with anyone who makes those kinds of charges. If a guy dogs it when he's making $200,000, he's going to dog it when he's making $4 million. If he hustles when he's making $600,000, he's going to hustle when he makes $6 million. (*Sporting News*, September 5, 1994, p. 14)

Sports history, however, is replete with examples of **shirking**, the expending of effort at a rate below a player's potential. Athletes are not necessarily any different from others who would rather exert less effort for the same salary. These episodes can be extremely expensive for team owners. At the same time, shirking can be very difficult to detect.

The Difficulty in Detecting Shirking: An Example In 1998, Washington State University quarterback Ryan Leaf was the second player selected in the NFL draft. The San Diego Chargers signed Leaf to a 5-year deal worth at least $25 million that could have topped out at $31.25 million. His signing bonus was $11.25 million. Leaf subsequently became the worst quarterback in the league, and his workout schedule was what can only be described as "light." The press had a field day calling into question his determination and work ethic.

Only Leaf knows the answers, but if effort is the issue, this is precisely the kind of problem that long-term contracts might breed. As a 23-year-old with $11.25 million in his pocket and a hefty payday just for showing up, the question was whether he had decided that he had worked hard and long enough. Of course, owners want players at top performance at all times, and effort can be tough for an owner to monitor. So what are owners to do?

Economic Remedies for Shirking   Shirking actually is an old economic issue falling under the heading of **principal-agent problems**. How do the principals of any firm protect themselves against workers who do not have the same interests? One answer is to expend resources on **monitoring effort**. In sports, entire staffs, from personnel management to on-field coaches, are devoted to overseeing talent and its performance.

The sports world has monitoring tools not found in the usual firm oversight processes. First, all players are pulled through a grueling selection process from the time they reveal any talent as children. Talented players who put forth great effort are selected for higher levels of play, from youth sports on into select teams and high school, college (for all four major sports), and the minor leagues (for baseball and hockey). Players that fail to pass this scrutiny fall by the wayside. Direct oversight by parents, coaches, on-field managers, general managers, owners, teammates, sports writers, gamblers, and fans puts players under the microscope through their entire career.

In addition, although observers may never know the greatest potential performance of any given player, many other players have approximately the same bundle of talent. Comparisons between players always are possible. For example, players' agents and their ownership adversaries bring a long list of comparable players to the table in order to determine the value of any given player during arbitration and salary negotiations. The observations of players who do work hard at least allow effort to be compared.

Strategic Effort   A related, stickier issue remains. Players may work reasonably hard all of the time but only perform at their absolute top levels at specific, economically strategic times prior to arbitration or contract negotiation. This is called **strategic player effort**. In the unpredictable world of sports, it can be difficult to tell whether performance patterns are due to strategic player effort or uncertainty. Players can always say that they just had a bad year or a nagging injury.

This type of problem is not new to those studying economics. All types of firms have to deal with the problem of obtaining high levels of effort from salaried employees and contract consultants. The tried and true approach is to devise **incentive-compatible mechanisms** that tie rewards to outcomes.

Performance Incentives and Contingency Payments   In sports, incentive-compatible mechanisms are either actual performance incentives or contingencies that are paid only if the outcome is consistent with a high level of effort. Actual performance incentives in contracts make up only a small share of overall compensation due to union preferences in the collective bargaining arena, but they do exist. Typically, they are in the form of bonuses for playing time or for making the postseason.

Contract contingency payments are much more common. For example, take Peyton Manning's original contract with the Indianapolis Colts. If Manning played a significant proportion of the season, he earned a shot at early free agency. But if he did, the team could take advantage of that outcome and preclude his free agency pursuit with an agreed-upon bump in annual salary. Either way, Manning was best off if he exerted top effort. In addition, long-term contract payments increase over the duration of the contract. Barry Sanders signed a $34.56 million, 6-year contract in 1997 with the Detroit Lions. The signing bonus was $11.75 million. His salary increased each year from 1997 to 2002, beginning at $1.4 million and ending at $6 million.

Signing bonuses are also contingency payments. In the case of Ryan Leaf, the San Diego Chargers were constantly threatening to revoke signing bonus payments without a substantial increase in effort by Leaf. Similarly, when Barry Sanders retired prematurely, the Lions owners went after a prorated share of the signing bonus. These types of contingency payments are very common effort-inducing mechanisms as detailed in the Learning Highlight: A-Rod's $252 Million, or Is It $69.5 Million?

Evidence on the Downside of Long-Term Contracts   Despite all of these mechanisms to overcome the downside to long-term contracts, work by economists suggests that shirking and strategic effort still persist. For example, Lehn (1982) found that time spent on the MLB disabled list increased with the rise of long-term contracting in the league. If players were not getting injured at a higher rate, then they must have been choosing to go on the disabled list. Other analysts have examined strategic performance behavior and long-term contracts, finding mixed results. Some have found that it occurs (Scoggins, 1993; Sommers, 1993), whereas others do not (Krautmann, 1990; Maxcy, 1997).

LEARNING HIGHLIGHT
A-Rod's $252 Million, or Is It $69.5 Million?

At this writing, an important caveat given the incredible increases in sports star salaries, the most famous contract in sports history belongs to Alex Rodriguez of the New York Yankees. "A-Rod" signed a contract touted at $252 million over 10 years, leaving the Seattle Mariners for the Texas Rangers in 2001. But before that contract ran out, he moved on to the New York Yankees after the 2003 season. Details of the contract are in Table 8.4.

Table 8.4 A-Rod's Contract

YEAR	SALARY ($MILLIONS)	DEFERRED PAY ($MILLIONS) (W/O 3% INTEREST)	SIGNING BONUS ($MILLIONS)
2001	$16	$5	$2
2002	$17	$4	$2
2003	$18	$3	$2
2004	$18	$3	$2
2005	$21	$4	$2
2006	$21	$4	
2007	$23	$4	
2008	$24	$3	
2009	$24	$3	
2010	$24	$3	

Source: Table used with permission of Street & Smiths *Sports Business Journal,* December 18, 2000, p. 1. Additional information from cbs.sportsline.com, February 15, 2004.

Contrary to the common observation that Rodriguez would make $25 million per year with the Rangers, team owner Tom Hicks claimed that the discounted present value of the total contract is closer to $180 million. First, the contract stipulated that portions of the payments were deferred to the 10 years after the contract expires (and interest on the deferred pay is set at 3%), and the entire 10 years might never come to pass. First, after 7 years (end of the 2007 season), the Rangers agreed to increase A-Rod's salary by either $5 million or $1 million more than the league's highest paid player for the final 2 contract years. That made the 2009 and 2010 earnings a minimum of $32 million each year. If the Rangers decided not to meet this requirement, Rodriguez would become a free agent.

A much more important reason why the entire 10 years would be irrelevant was if A-Rod moved to another team. That came to pass at the end of the 2003 season when a deal was worked out between the Rangers and the New York Yankees. The Rangers agreed to pay $67 million over the remaining years of the contract to the Yankees (the details of this payment were not released to the public). So, at present, the contract is a $179 million contract with the Yankees (contract value from 2004 on, in Table 8.4), with the Rangers paying $67 million of it.

In return, the Rangers received the Yankees' more than adequate second baseman, Alfonso Soriano and minor leaguers. In addition the Rangers escaped both the remaining $112 million in salary payments and around $13 million in interest on deferred payments. So in the end, A-Rod's $252 million contract with the Rangers ended up to be "only" $51 million in salary, $12 million in deferred compensation plus 3 percent interest, and $6 million in signing bonuses. And that total of $69.5 million is a lot less than $252 million!

Alex Rodriguez signed a multiyear contract with the Texas Rangers touted at $252 million. Contingency clauses may put the actual value closer to only $180 million and the Rangers actually ended up paying Rodriguez around $69.5 million in total.

Source: Street & Smith's *Sports Business Journal*, December 18, 2000, p. 1.

WHAT ABOUT COMPETITIVE BALANCE?

Players made out quite nicely after free agency, as one would expect if their earnings during the reserve clause period were depressed as much as 90 percent. Earlier we discussed how owners argued that a host of problems would accompany any interference with the reserve clause. In the rest of this section, we will explore these competitive balance claims in detail.

Rottenberg's Invariance Principle

As you recall from Chapter 7, payments to players are at their maximum in a competitive talent market when marginal revenues are equal. In a two-team league model, this would mean that $MR_L^* = MR_S^*$, where L and S denote the larger- and smaller-market teams, respectively. This also means that the largest possible amount that owners can keep when competition for players is restricted also occurs when $MR_L^* = MR_S^*$, because it is at that equilibrium where the profits earned from player talent are as large as possible.

Therefore, each owner wants to hire their profit-maximizing level of talent and keep the largest possible amount that can be generated by that level of hired talent. This means that in either the competitive case, where players earn their MRP, or the reserve clause case, where owners keep as much of player MRP as possible, the same amount of talent is hired by team owners. That is, talent is hired until $MR_L^* = MR_S^*$ in either case. Remember that larger-market owners hire more talent than smaller-market owners when this condition holds, so there will be the same level of competitive imbalance in either case as well.

This was one of the most important findings in sports economics. Economist Simon Rottenberg (1956) was the first to discover this outcome, and it has come to be called the **invariance principle**. Essentially, it is defined as follows:

> The distribution of talent in a league is invariant to who gets the revenues generated by players; talent moves to its highest valued use in the league whether players or owners receive players' MRPs.

The invariance principle predicts that competitive balance is the same whether the talent market is competitive or governed by the reserve clause. If the league is imbalanced to start with, it will be equally imbalanced in either case. This is directly the opposite of what owners predicted would happen.

Here is an intuitive description of the invariance principle. Suppose the talent market is competitive; that is, there is no reserve clause. Players, by and large, shop for the owner that offers the highest salary and go there. The large-revenue owners buy the most talent. Thus, the free agency distribution of talent has larger-revenue market owners with a higher level of talent than smaller-revenue market owners. If competition over players is restricted—that is, there is a reserve clause in place—the only difference is that players will do short stints at teams where their value is lower. Eventually, larger-revenue market owners will want to buy the better players, and better players will move to the teams with the highest valued league-wide use. In this case, larger-revenue market owners just pay smaller-revenue market owners to get the talent rather than paying the talent itself. The same competitive balance result occurs in the reserve clause case as in the competitive case.

Restrictions on competition for players do not cause any change in competitive balance. This is the crucial invariance principle result. However, restrictions on competition do reallocate payments away from players toward smaller-revenue market owners.

The invariance principle also suggests another explanation for owner enthusiasm for restrictions on competition for players. Both the draft and the reserve clause reallocate portions of MRP from players to owners. Even though owners might hoist the banner of competitive balance to support their pleas for restrictions on competition over players, they simply are better off, financially, with the draft and reserve clause in place.

The Invariance Principle and the Draft

Owners argue that the draft equalizes talent in the league, enhancing competitive balance. According to the owners' argument, weak teams draft the better players, strengthen themselves, and become more economically viable. Additionally, fans get to enjoy the stability of team rosters over time. Better players that would have been scooped up by larger-revenue market owners in a competitive hunt for talent now play for the owners of smaller-revenue market teams.

The invariance principle suggests other results. The invariance principle predicts that the better players will move to better teams, even if a draft is installed. Larger-revenue market owners will compensate smaller-revenue market owners for talent rather than find the talent on their own. If there were no draft, the players would get the money because they would simply go directly to the teams in higher-revenue markets and collect the returns in terms of higher starting salaries and signing bonuses. What do the data say?

Players Actually Move Before They Are Drafted! In leagues like the NHL and NFL, where draft picks can be traded before the draft even occurs, the usual perception is that teams are trying to trade for higher draft picks. Sometimes this does occur, but it also can make perfectly good sense to trade higher draft picks for lower ones. On this outcome, Carolina Panthers General Manager Bill Polian once said, "The economics, and the price you have to pay for these rookies, has certainly affected how you draft. You begin to erode the real purpose of the draft—which is to equalize talent" (*Wall Street Journal*, April 18, 1997, p. B9). Polian is lamenting what has come to be called **trading down draft picks**. Trading down means that a team actually trades higher draft picks for lower draft picks (in leagues where trading draft picks is allowed). By the way, notice that Polian's claim about the "real purpose" of the draft (to equalize talent) is counter to the invariance principle.

"The economics, and the price you have to pay for these rookies, has certainly affected how you begin to erode the real purpose of the draft—which is to equalize talent." —Bill Polian, general manager of the Carolina Panthers, 1997

The reason that it can make perfectly good sense to trade higher-valued draft picks for lower-valued ones is that an owner may not be able to afford to pay the signing bonuses. Even though there is a reverse-order-of-finish draft, owners of weaker teams often cannot take advantage of it. Rookie bonuses have been driven so high that smaller-revenue owners cannot afford to sign high draft picks. Because they never get these better players, they also never get to enjoy the compensation from selling the high-value talent to larger-revenue teams. Players benefit by getting more of their entering MRP because they are drafted by owners of better teams at higher bonuses. But trading down at least allows smaller-revenue owners to get something for their draft pick.

In any event, regardless of whether owners trade draft picks up or down, talent moves to higher-valued uses (presumably to larger-revenue market owners) before the draft even occurs. Certainly, in these cases, the draft simply transfers wealth without impacting the eventual distribution of talent in the league.

Players Do Not Stay Put Once They Are Drafted   Consistent with the invariance principle, but contrary to the owners' justification for the draft, better players do move to larger-revenue market teams after they are drafted. For years, owners of the Seattle Mariners drafted terrific pitching. However, their revenue position did not allow them to hold onto those pitchers. The Mariners simply became a training team for the rest of the pitching rosters in MLB. The reward for finishing low in the standings was a continual replenishment, through trades and high draft picks, of a roster full of good minor league talent. And the Mariners then developed that talent for the rest of the league owners.

A recent example from the NBA also points out that strong talent does not necessarily stay with the owners who drafted it. According to *Sports Illustrated* (June 23, 1997), only 3 of the 10 players drafted first in the 1987–1996 drafts remained with their original team—David Robinson of the San Antonio Spurs, Glenn Robinson of the Milwaukee Bucks, and Allen Iverson of the Philadelphia 76ers. Only one of the remaining seven ended up at a smaller-market team—Joe Smith. The draft simply does not keep players on smaller-revenue market teams.

Evidence on the Dispersion of Winning Percent   According to owners' arguments, the draft should enhance competitive balance. The invariance principle states that competitive balance will not change with a draft. One way to measure competitive balance is with the ratio of the actual standard deviation of winning percents to the idealized standard deviation, introduced in Chapter 6. The closer the ratio is to one, the more balanced the league is in terms of talent. If the owners are correct, then the ratio should have fallen after the draft was put in place. Which view do the data on winning percent support?

Table 8.5 shows the standard deviation ratio in the NFL and MLB in the years before and after their drafts were implemented. The ratio rose in the NFL and fell in both leagues in MLB. In this type of analysis, the question becomes whether the changes were statistically significant. In this case they are not statistically significant. Statistically speaking, the difference before and after the draft in both the NFL and the NL in MLB is probably equal to zero. But it does appear that competitive balance improved in the AL.

Whether it was the draft that led to improved balance in the AL is open to question. Recall from Chapter 3 that CBS owned the New York Yankees from 1964 to 1973. While the Yankees won ten of twelve AL pennants from 1953 to 1964, the year that CBS took over, the team only won one pennant in the period after the draft, 1965 to 1976. That was in 1976, after the group headed by George Steinbrenner bought the club. So was it the draft, or was it a failed experiment by CBS aimed at reducing the competitive power of the Yankees? Because Baltimore won seven of the twelve pennants after the draft, season outcomes were closer, but the title was still pretty concentrated, which supports the failed experiment explanation. Essentially, Baltimore just took over the Yankees' spot during the CBS ownership period.

Did You Know?
There is nearly no evidence that the reverse-order-of-finish draft used in all pro sports has improved competitive balance in any sport.

The data reject the owners' argument that the draft equalizes talent in the NFL and in the NL in MLB because the standard deviations do not fall significantly. The distribution of talent and, subsequently, team winning percents are mostly invariant to the existence of a reverse-order-of-finish draft, as predicted by the invariance principle.

Table 8.5

Standard Deviation of Winning Percent Imbalance, Pre- and Postdraft

	NFL		
YEAR	PREDRAFT	YEAR	POSTDRAFT
1930	1.68	1936	1.81
1931	1.75	1937	1.70
1932	1.83	1938	1.42
1933	1.45	1939	2.10
1934	1.79	1940	1.65
1935	1.49	1941	1.99
Average	1.67	Average	1.78

MLB

PREDRAFT			POSTDRAFT		
YEAR	AL	NL	YEAR	AL	NL
1953	2.82	2.78	1965	2.30	2.31
1954	3.65	2.40	1966	1.39	1.91
1955	2.75	1.86	1967	1.57	1.84
1956	2.49	2.12	1968	1.88	1.19
1957	2.30	1.92	1969	2.26	2.54
1958	1.41	1.27	1970	2.40	1.56
1959	1.69	1.25	1971	2.12	1.62
1960	2.11	2.17	1972	1.73	2.08
1961	2.51	2.42	1973	1.71	1.62
1962	1.59	3.16	1974	1.14	1.96
1963	2.16	2.20	1975	1.87	1.88
1964	2.29	2.06	1976	1.57	2.19
Average	2.34	2.13	Average	1.83	1.89

Note: Author's calculations.

History Repeats Itself: The Blue Ribbon Panel Report, 2000 Many observers worry that the level of competitive imbalance has become a problem in MLB. Competitive imbalance has always existed in baseball, but some think it has become worse. Perhaps in response to these worries, MLB commissioned a special highly respected panel to analyze baseball's competitive balance and make any recommendations it saw fit to make. The "Blue Ribbon Panel" was composed of

- Richard C. Levin, president of Yale University (and professor of economics)
- George J. Mitchell, former senator and peace negotiator in Northern Ireland
- Paul A. Volcker, previous chairman of the Federal Reserve Board
- George F. Will, noted wit, syndicated columnist, baseball expert, and member of the board of directors of a few baseball teams

The *Blue Ribbon Panel Report, 2000* (Levin, Mitchell, Volcker, and Will, 2000), came down squarely that MLB had significant competitive balance problems. It suggested (among other things) a number of alterations in MLB's draft system. Our guiding light in the analysis of the *Blue Ribbon Panel Report* recommendations for the player draft is the invariance principle. The principle suggests that the draft has no impact on competitive balance, and the evidence we have examined tends to support this conclusion. Let's examine the *Blue Ribbon Panel Report*'s suggestions to see the invariance principle in action.

A Proposed Competitive-Balance Draft   The report suggests a "competitive-balance draft" that would let teams at the bottom choose players from teams at the top but not from the 40-man (major league) roster. The worst eight teams would get to draft from the minor league rosters of the eight teams that made it to the playoffs the year before. Actually, this is a variant of a type of draft that existed in baseball just prior to the imposition of the current draft in 1965, and Rottenberg (1956) addressed this very issue!

These players will eventually end up at their highest-valued location. If that location is not with their current team, it may not be with a weaker franchise either. If the weaker team that participates in the competitive balance draft would have been the eventual home of players chosen in a competitive balance draft anyway, then that special draft would not alter competitive balance. If it would not, then players who are drafted by weak teams in the competitive balance draft would eventually end up where they would have gone anyway. All that happens is that the competitive-balance-drafting team gets the reward rather than the original drafting team. Indeed, if the talent market is sending players to their highest league value, in all likelihood, the players going to weaker teams in the competitive-balance draft will just turn around and head back to where they came from. Weaker teams will be compensated by those receiving teams. Again, nothing happens to competitive balance.

Extending the Draft to International Players   Another reform would extend the draft to include international players. This would end the current "who finds them first" approach, which sounds like MLB's mode of domestic operations prior to the draft in 1965. However, this simple extension will have the same impacts as the original imposition of the draft back in 1965: Owners get to keep the money with no impact on competitive balance.

Eliminating Compensation Draft Picks   Currently, MLB draft picks go to team owners who lose players to free agency. The idea is that better teams will have more top draft picks after they lose free agents. As a result, they can draft sets of players to their advantage rather than just individual players. The report calls for elimination of this practice. But at the risk of sounding like a broken record, the players they draft would eventually end up with that team anyway. Therefore, competitive balance should not change if these picks are eliminated. Besides, it is typically smaller-revenue market teams that lose the bulk of the free agents in MLB.

Ending the Remaining Eligibility of College Players Entering the Draft   Under another draft remedy for imbalance, amateurs entering the draft would lose their remaining college eligibility, as they currently do in basketball and football. The report notes that if the NCAA were to adopt this position, bargaining leverage would be altered because players would not be able to fall back on college ball if they were unhappy with their bonus offer. This is good for MLB owners, but it is unlikely that incoming college players would agree with them. Again, this does not change who gets the players; it just changes the balance of bargaining over the amount. It would have no impact on competitive balance.

Creating Imbalance in the Number of Draft Picks Another idea in the report would have weak teams draft more players than strong teams. Playoff teams from the preceding year would not be allowed to draft until the second round. Here, the impacts are the same as under the current system; it is just that more of the value goes to weaker teams than before. Eventually, talent ends up in the same place, and there is no impact on competitive balance.

Allowing Trading of Draft Picks Finally, like other sports, the panel suggests that MLB teams ought to be allowed to trade draft picks. All draft pick trading does is move players more efficiently to the larger-revenue market teams and provide yet another way for larger-revenue market owners to compensate smaller-market owners at the outset rather than after drafting has occurred. This occurs through trading up or trading down, discussed just above. Talent will still end up where it is most valuable. Again, this will have no impact on competitive balance.

In summary, none of these draft changes will do anything except redistribute even more money away from incoming players and owners of larger-revenue market teams to owners of lower-revenue teams than currently occurs. It seems that the invariance principle, a concept that has been around for nearly 50 years and empirically verified over and over again, has been conveniently forgotten when MLB owners assess their financial welfare.

The Invariance Principle and the Reserve Clause

Owners had long argued that the reserve clause was essential to competitive balance: If players moved according to the dictates of competition, then the rich teams would buy all of the good players. The invariance principle suggests otherwise. As you now know, larger-revenue market owners value players more than other owners, and they will buy talent from smaller-revenue market owners. All the reserve clause does is transfer the value of the players to owners holding those players' contracts, but the players move to their highest-valued use to the league, nonetheless. Under a reserve clause, the owner trades or sells the contract and gets the value of the move. If the talent market is competitive and players are free agents, the players run out their current contracts, move to that location, and collect the higher value for themselves. But here is the important point: The players move to the larger-revenue market team with or without the reserve clause.

Do Players Really Move More Without a Reserve Clause? Let's look first at the movement of players under free agency. Owners raised concerns about roster stability in the absence of the reserve clause. However, there is little evidence to suggest that free agency had much effect on player movement. Perhaps the most comprehensive analysis of player movement is by Tom Ruane (1998). According to Ruane, player movement is actually quite consistent decade-by-decade from 1900 to 1995. About 22 percent of players stay put and 57 percent change teams, and there was a 1 percent decrease in players moving after free agency.

However, movement does not capture everything. Maybe better players are moving more often. That is, one might compare **player moves versus performance moves**. Controlling for playing-time variables (at bats for hitters and innings pitched for pitchers), Ruane finds that the story is only a little different. The same consistent outcome over the decades occurs in terms of the *playing-time variables* represented by player movement. But a look across decades finds a 5 percent increase in the movement of playing time after free agency. Therefore, although the amount of movement did not change, the players who were moving were a little better after free agency than before. This 5 percent difference is quite small. Essentially, the owners overstated the actual consequences of free agency on player movement. But even to this day, owners, fans, and sportswriters often lament the end of the golden age when star players finished their careers with their original teams. Whether this ever really was true is the topic of the Learning Highlight: Was There Ever a Golden Age of Player Loyalty?

LEARNING HIGHLIGHT
Was There Ever a Golden Age of Player Loyalty?

Some fans lament the instability of team rosters. Many wax nostalgic for the days of flannel uniforms and high socks when baseball was "just a game" and icon players ended their careers with the team that brought them into the league. More often than not, they blame it on free agency. Commissioner Bud Selig echoes these laments (Stark, 2004), "You worry sometimes that franchises won't be identified anymore with certain players. You hope, as a sport, to have as much of that (player identification) as possible."

Analysis in the economics literature suggests a detectable increase in attendance associated with roster stability (Kahane and Shmanske, 1997). But to the extent that we see roster stability, it occurs because it makes some contribution to higher winning percents and higher attendance. Once that contribution is gone, owners alter lineups to regain their targeted winning percent level. So there is a trade-off between a stable roster that fans like and eventual declines in winning percents that fans won't stand for. All this really means is that there is a profit-maximizing level of roster stability.

All well and good, one might say, but has the duration of roster stability, especially as it pertains to beloved star players, changed since free agency? The evidence suggests that it has not. The first piece of evidence is already cited in the text; players move at about the same rate with just a slight increase in the quality of players who do move.

The second piece of evidence concerns the rate at which players end up with the teams they started with. In 1934, 12 players on starting rosters had been with their teams for at least ten years. There were sixteen teams in the league with roughly 400 players on major league rosters. That means that those 12 represent only 3 percent of the total. Similar extremely small percentages from 2 percent to 5 percent have been found for 1964 (23 players), 1975 (15 players), 1994 (17 players), and 2000 (15 players). Interestingly, Hall of Fame players average three different teams during their career. Even Ty Cobb spent his last two seasons with the Philadelphia Athletics after 22 seasons with Detroit. These results suggest that long tenure on a given team may be a matter of sheer chance.

It makes sense that this would be so, both before free agency and after. Let's think about baseball only after the institution of the draft in 1965. Players are distributed through the league, typically to teams that they eventually will leave. It takes time for that to occur, easily three to six years just to make the majors and as much as ten years for some. As their skills develop over time and are revealed, their value changes over time and they move to those teams that value them the most. According to Rottenberg's invariance principle and the evidence in this chapter this was just as true before free agency as after. The only difference was in whose choice it was. And that brings us to the loyalty issue.

Prior to free agency, the period fans ironically refer to as the golden age of roster stability, there was no such thing as player loyalty because it was impossible for players to exercise loyalty at all. Players simply went wherever their contract was traded or sold. Apparently, only in very few cases did a player's contract remain most valuable to the team where he started his career. After free agency, just as ironically, is the only time that player loyalty can even enter into the picture. Even then most free agents move strictly involuntarily. Players with fewer than 10 years with the same club do not typically have any control over being traded once they sign a free agent contract. Involuntary free agency is especially acute among the oldest players (in the economics literature, Horowitz and Zappe, 1998, document the impact of this treatment on players at the end of their careers). Long-time player agent Tom Reich puts it this way): "And even with free agency, go through this year's list of free agents. What you'll find is that the vast majority are involuntary free agents. They're not free by their own choice. They're free because their team doesn't want them anymore. And there's a tremendous difference between voluntary free agency and involuntary free agency"

(Stark, 2004). Precisely so: Those involuntary free agents who may have wished to remain loyal actually have no chance to reveal any loyalty at all.

So it is only the very few superstar free agents who have any chance to exhibit what fans think of as loyalty to their team. From this perspective, it simply is misplaced anger that blames free agency for the lack of roster stability. Blaming player mobility on a lack of loyalty reveals a misunderstanding about who can exercise loyalty and when (historically). The text suggests that player preferences for loyalty have been exercised in many cases, a recent example being Barry Bonds's love affair with San Francisco.

One last pair of historical comparisons serves to emphasize that roster stability has nothing to do with free agency. While Lou Gehrig and Joe DiMaggio spent their entire MLB careers with the Yankees, Babe Ruth came from Boston and ended his career there again with the Braves. A later Yankee, Roger Maris, played his entire career prior to free agency. But he played for twice as many teams (Cleveland, Kansas City, New York, and St. Louis) as the player who eventually broke his single-season home run record well after free agency, Mark McGwire (Oakland and St. Louis).

Ultimately, there is a question of fairness here. Baseball is a business. Why should there be more loyalty in the baseball business than in any other? Gene Orza, chief operating officer for the Major League Baseball Players Association, puts it this way: "If you're a Minnesota fan and I said, 'You have to stay in Minnesota for six years,' most people would say, 'No, I've got an obligation to my family. If I get a better job somewhere else, I'd have to take it.' And that's the American way. Loyalty has to take second place to freedom" (Stark, 2004).

Sources: Canham-Clyne (1994); Oberman (1998); Caple (2004); Stark (2004); Kahane and Shmanske, "Team Roster Turnover and Attendance in Major League Baseball," *Applied Economics* 29 (April 1997); Horowitz and Zappe (1998).

Evidence on the Relationship Between Market Size and Winning   If the owners are right, the shift to free agency in 1976 should be accompanied by an increase in the dominance of larger-revenue markets. Fizel (1997) reviewed the literature on this topic and found little support for increased dominance based on market size. Large-market teams do not consistently win more than small-market teams after free agency. By this measure, competitive balance survived free agency unchanged, as the invariance principle predicts.

Evidence on the Dispersion of Winning Percent   Table 8.6 shows the standard deviation of winning percents before and after the demise of the reserve clause in MLB (you should be able to state why it is appropriate to use the actual standard deviations rather than the ratio measure used in Table 8.5). Owners' claims would have it that the standard deviation of winning percents should increase after the demise of the reserve clause. A look at the post-free-agency years of 1976 to 1985 shows that the standard deviation did not change in any statistically significant degree for the National League. This means that, as best as can be tested, free agency had no impact on competitive balance at all in that league. This is the invariance principle in operation.

The story in the American League is a bit different, as it was with the draft. Here, the increase in the standard deviation is probably statistically significant. This decrease in competitive balance in the American League rejects the invariance principle. But again, as with the draft, was the decrease in balance the result of free agency, or was it the result of the resurgence of the Yankees as they returned to private ownership under Steinbrenner's group? Evidence in support of the latter explanation was found in Chapter 6. The standard deviation of winning percent fell on average in the 1970s and 1980s, lending more evidence against the owners' view. But strictly speaking, the invariance principle would not predict a decline in balance with free agency, a subject to which we will turn after we have a look at championships.

Table 8.6
Competitive Balance and the Reserve Clause Before and After Free Agency in MLB (Adjusted for Expansion)

RESERVE CLAUSE			FREE AGENCY		
YEAR	NL	AL	YEAR	NL	AL
1966	0.064	0.051	1976	0.086	0.062
1967	0.071	0.059	1977	0.081	0.099
1968	0.058	0.069	1978	0.063	0.087
1969	0.092	0.083	1979	0.072	0.091
1970	0.049	0.088	1980	0.062	0.080
1971	0.060	0.080	1981	0.085	0.076
1972	0.078	0.067	1982	0.062	0.069
1973	0.062	0.067	1983	0.045	0.073
1974	0.075	0.042	1984	0.054	0.058
1975	0.067	0.072	1985	0.074	0.055
Average	0.068	0.068	Average	0.068	0.075

Source: Fort and Quirk (1995). Used with permission.

Evidence on Championships The **distribution of league championships** provides a different view of competitive balance. The owners' view would be that free agency would result in a higher concentration of championships in the hands of larger-revenue market team owners.

Fizel (1997) analyzed the number of contenders for division championships within seasons. If balance were harmed by free agency, there should be fewer contenders after the demise of the reserve clause. Fizel also analyzed the number of different teams winning division championships across seasons. A decline in the number of different teams winning championships would indicate less competitive balance. The result of free agency is that pennant races have become furious battles with multiple contenders, and the chance to build dynasties has declined because the number of teams winning championships has increased. These results are consistent with the invariance principle but not with the owners' claims about free agency.

The Gini coefficient is another way to examine the distribution of championships. If the Gini coefficient rose after free agency, then championships were concentrated on fewer teams. Such a result would be consistent with owners' views that competitive balance is harmed by free agency. Again, the evidence presented is from MLB (Fort and Quirk, 1995). In the National League, the Gini coefficient fell by 2 percent after free agency, from 0.400 to about 0.392. In the American League, there is a larger fall of about 10 percent, from 0.415 to 0.372. These decreases in the Gini coefficient on championships certainly do not support the owners' claims against free agency on competitive balance grounds.

Did You Know?
There is no evidence that free agency in any sport reduced the level of competitive balance.

Another Twist: Player Preferences Under Free Agency The fall in the concentration of championships for the National League, along with the earlier report that the standard deviation of winning percent also fell in MLB generally in the 1970s and 1980s, does not support the invariance principle either. Under the invariance principle, there should have been no change in the concentration of championships.

The invariance principle requires that owners and players care only about profit and income. But players also care about other things. As we mentioned in Chapter 7, player preferences may also involve winning, locations, and press pressure. Perhaps some of the nonmonetary elements of talent supply are responsible for these findings. For example, Ken Griffey, Jr., asked the Seattle Mariners for a trade in 1999 despite efforts by Mariners owners to make him the highest-paid player in the history of MLB. He claimed that he wanted to be closer to his family and reduce their travel. He also claimed that he would take less money in order to satisfy these other goals.

If nonmonetary preferences are prevalent, then some players may not move to their highest financial value to the league. They may stay with teams that do not pay as much as the teams that owners would have sent them to under the reserve clause. This type of behavior might actually enhance competitive balance; some better players will stick with some smaller-revenue market teams.

The Yankees always get all the best talent, right? Well, think again. It's really the case that they do not get all the players they seek. The reason, of course, is the same as in all job markets. There are nonwork aspects to every job. In 1993, for example, the Yanks offered $10.4 million more for six free agents—Barry Bonds, Greg Maddux, Doug Drabek, David Cone, Terry Steinbach, and Jose Guzman—than those players eventually accepted with other teams (*Sporting News*, March 8, 1993, p. 13). The duration of contracts was the same and the Yankees offered an average of $400,000 more per player. Only Bonds actually took a higher paying contract with the San Francisco Giants, but all went elsewhere. Bonds had this to say after signing his subsequent $90 million, 5-year contract that placed him only fifth among other players in 2002: "My heart has always been here," Bonds said. "No amount of money would make me leave San Francisco, to be honest with you. I always wanted to stay a San Francisco Giant. Unless there was a blockbuster, out-of-the world offer, I wasn't going to leave. All I want now is a World Series ring" (espn.go.com, January 14, 2002). Bonds sounds like he is singing that old Beatles tune with the famous line "money can't buy me love."

We also have more on Greg Maddux's choice. Yankees GM Gene Michael had this to say after losing Maddux to the Braves: "Salaries throughout the industry have outgrown a player's financial need to come to New York—and Maddux is a perfect example" (*Sporting News*, March 8, 1993, p. 13). The same article quoted Maddux as saying, "I felt the Yankees were in a rebuilding process; that Atlanta's ability to win was better than New York's. The decision was not hard at all. Atlanta was where I wanted to go and as soon as the Braves made room for me, the decision was over." At the margin, it appears that winning mattered a bit more to Maddux than money. The Yankees offered him $32.5 million for five years while the Braves got him for $28 million for five years, about a 14 percent sacrifice.

One of the all-time great examples of players taking less than they could get is the Minnesota Twins in the 1990s (*Sports Illustrated*, January 27, 1997, p. 58). Five free agents collectively took $25.5 million less to play in Minnesota rather than play for more elsewhere. Two more didn't even bother to wait for another offer before sticking with the Twins. Indeed, one of these two, Paul Molitor, took a $1.5 million pay cut to play for the Twins.

Yearning for the Good Old Days: MLB Owner Collusion, 1985–1987

By and large, free agency was the order of things in MLB by the end of the 1970s. The astronomical increases in salaries demonstrated earlier in this chapter were previously the portion of player MRP kept by owners. The result, of course, was that player costs increased and revenues did not. Owners were not in danger of going out of business, but they were making less on net than they had during the reserve clause era. It appears that old habits die hard because during the mid-1980s two different arbitrators found the owners guilty of colluding to suppress pay to free agents. The episodes came to be called **Collusion I, II, and III** by the press, denoting the sequence of the findings over the years 1985, 1986, and 1987. The presentation here relies heavily on Scully (1989) and Staudohar (1996).

Collusion I   In Collusion I, outsiders could make the following observations. At the end of the 1985 season, 62 players became free agents. Of those, 57 ended up signing with their previous clubs because they got no serious offers; that is, if they got an offer it was only from a smaller-market team. The top free agents literally received no offers.

The players' union filed a grievance claiming collusion by the owners. The agreement between players and owners in force at the time stated quite explicitly, "Players shall not act in concert with other Players and Clubs shall not act in concert with other Clubs" (Staudohar, 1996, p. 38). The players' side made the easy case first. They argued that no single team would turn away from the best available players in the league unless all teams did the same. Otherwise, they risked becoming less competitive. Then the players' side noted that Commissioner Peter Ueberroth had scolded teams about bidding up free agent prices at meetings when there were ongoing negotiations with some free agents. Finally, the players' side noted that advisors had told owners that free agents typically signed to long-term contracts showed a decline in performance (see the discussion of shirking earlier in this chapter). Owners replied that there was no collusion, just a natural slowdown to a stable market after the advent of free agency.

Arbitrator Tom Roberts sided with the players. The linchpin of his decision was that the free agent market appeared to be in full swing with the usual type of negotiations with free agents until the meetings where Ueberroth scolded the owners. The free agents were set loose again in an extraordinary measure.

Collusion II and III   This was not the end of it. Arbitrator George Nicolau presided over the cases of both Collusion II and III concerning the 1986 and 1987 seasons, respectively. The players won both cases. Every step along the way, Nicolau stated careful comparisons between the language of the agreement between players and owners and the actions of owners.

As a result, the owners' "information bank," used to share free agent offer information, was revoked as a collusive activity. The owners were also hit in the wallet. Although 843 players made claims (most were tossed and received nothing), some players received settlements as high as $2 million. Eventually, the owners paid $280 million, including interest and lost salary, to players. After the decision, salaries resumed their upward climb.

The owners continued to deny they colluded after the proceedings ended. Sports economist Scully (1989) looked for economic evidence of collusion. First, Scully compared the 1987 salaries of players who entered the free agent market in 1986 to those of players who did not enter that market. He found that the salaries of hitters who entered the free agent market in 1986 were $260,000 lower than the salaries of hitters who did not enter that market at that time. For pitchers who entered the free agent market, the difference was $259,000. Scully could not attribute this outcome to performance declines across years. Strike one against the owners' claims of innocence on the collusion charge.

Second, using the approach described in Chapter 7, Scully calculated the MRP of free agents and nonfree agents in 1986. He discovered that the ratio of free agent salaries and their estimated MRP was lower than the same measure for nonfree agents. One would expect that the ratio should be higher. Strike two against the owners.

Finally, the ratio of player salary to league total revenue fell in 1987. It had remained constant or grown for many years. But it would have required an additional $100 million to make the 1987 ratio of salaries to total revenue equal to its 1982 level. Strike three against the owners. Scully comes down squarely that owners colluded.

CHAPTER RECAP

Graphical analysis shows that if ways can be found to reduce competition over player services, owners get to keep the difference between the higher competitive payment and the lower, less competitive payment. The next best option for players is not their second-highest value to the league but their highest-valued opportunity outside of their sport.

The draft and reserve clause transferred player MRP to owners. The draft removed competition over entering talent, reducing recruiting costs and signing amounts. The reserve clause effectively ended the ability of players to capture the benefits of competition for their services once in the league. Instead, owners earned the value of players moving from one team to another.

It has been estimated that 80 to 90 percent of player MRP was transferred from players to owners. This is undeniably a large amount of money. The first crop of free agents in baseball, for example, typically enjoyed double or triple their previous salaries, and a few as much as eight times their previous salaries. It is clear how salaries in all sports jumped at the time of the death of the reserve clause in each league, except for the NFL, especially for superstar players. With more on the line after free agency, owners facing the risk of annual contracting and players facing both performance and injury risks have come to rely upon long-term contracts. There is a downside to long-term contracts, but both monitoring of players and incentive arrangements counteract it.

The invariance principle states that players go to the same teams whether they are paid their MRP or owners are able to extract portions of it. The implication of the invariance principle is that competitive balance will be the same whether players earn their MRP or not. The evidence pretty much favors the principle. Competitive balance was for the most part unchanged with the imposition of drafts, and it did not go to ruin with free agency. This outcome suggests that arguments in favor of the draft or against paying pro players their MRP really were self-interested on the part of owners.

KEY TERMS AND CONCEPTS

- Reverse-order-of-finish draft
- Reserve clause
- Player exploitation
- Competitively determined salaries
- Long-term contract
- Annual hiring risk

- Risk of performance
- Risk of injury
- Shirking
- Principal-agent problems
- Monitoring effort
- Strategic player effort
- Incentive-compatible mechanisms

- Invariance principle
- Trading down draft picks
- Player moves versus performance moves
- Distribution of league championships
- Collusion I, II, and III

1. What is a player draft? Give the usual owner arguments in support of the reverse-order-of-finish draft.
2. Describe the original hands-off policy of the NFL toward college football in 1926. What was the goal of this policy?
3. Describe the original reserve system invented by Arthur Soden. How did this system generate downward pressure on player salaries?
4. What is the reserve clause? How was it used to end player freedom of movement between teams?
5. What was the *Federal Baseball* decision? What effect did it have on competition over players in MLB?
6. Give the usual owner argument in support of the reserve clause.
7. How did players overcome reserve clauses in sports beside baseball? How did baseball players eventually overcome the reserve clause?
8. Define player exploitation. According to the percentage estimates of Gerald Scully, how large was player exploitation during the reserve clause era?
9. What is a long-term contract? Why did long-term contracts evolve after free agency?
10. Describe annual hiring risk and risk of performance. How do long-term contracts protect players and owners against these risks?
11. What is shirking? What is strategic effort? What effect does each have on long-term contracts?
12. State Rottenberg's invariance principle.
13. What is trading down draft picks? Why does it occur?
14. What is the difference between player moves and performance moves? Why does this distinction matter in analyzing the impacts of free agency?
15. What do player preferences have to do with the impact of free agency on the distribution of winning percents or championships?

THOUGHT PROBLEMS

1. Using Figure 8.1, show graphically what happens to the value of reducing competition over players when:
   a. Fan willingness to pay increases
   b. The opportunity cost outside of the sport falls
   c. A rival league forms
2. Why did MLB and the NHL institute their drafts so much later than the NFL and the NBA?
3. Why didn't all players just let their current contract run out and refuse to play until the owners gave in and removed reserve clauses from all contracts?
4. Remnants of the reserve clause linger for the youngest players in all leagues. What impact does it have on the earnings of these young players?
5. Summarize the data on the value of reduced competition over player talent. Be sure to include the Willie Mays example, the first crop of free agents, and salary growth over time.

6. Why did salaries grow at such a larger rate after free agency in MLB and the NBA relative to the NFL and NHL?
7. Why were long-term contracts nearly nonexistent prior to free agency?
8. How do owners protect themselves against shirking in long-term contractual arrangements with players? How do owners protect themselves against strategic effort by players with long-term contracts?
9. Despite how closely players are watched throughout their careers, what evidence do we find in actual contracts that shirking and strategic effort can still be problems for owners?
10. If information about players is expensive, some players may not find their way to their highest valued league use. The same might be true if the transactions costs (e.g., legal costs) of moving players between teams are high. How do these factors temper the idea of the invariance principle?
11. Using the invariance principle:
    a. Evaluate owner arguments in favor of the draft
    b. Evaluate owner arguments in favor of the reserve clause
12. Does the income increase that happens for weaker teams under the reverse-order-of-finish draft come from larger-market owners? Players? Both? Explain fully.
13. How can trading down draft picks possibly make any sense? What is the main factor in the market for player talent that forces this outcome on weaker teams?
14. Suppose that player preferences are responsible for the increase in competitive balance after free agency in MLB. Does this negate the invariance principle?
15. What possible reason is there to care whether owners or players get to keep the majority of player MRP?

ADVANCED PROBLEMS

1. The WNBA once drafted players and assigned them geographically to teams. What did they hope is true about fan demand? Compare and contrast this to what the men's pro sports leagues believe about talent and fans.
2. The text of this chapter states a condition where the draft actually will level the playing field. If this condition occurs, is the invariance principle violated?
3. Explain fully what would happen to the following if the draft were abolished:
    a. Rookie player salaries and bonuses
    b. Team profits
    c. Competitive balance in the league
4. Explain fully what would happen to the following if free agency were abolished and we went back to the reserve clause:
    a. Individual player salaries
    b. Team profits
    c. Competitive balance in the league
    d. The length of player contracts
5. How would you be able to tell whether Ryan Leaf's performance problems were shirking or just due to a bad rookie year? Explain fully the data you would need in order to tell. What are the chances that you will ever have these data? What are the impacts for long-term contracts?

6. Suppose you took players who were up for a new contract and then compared their efforts before and after their new contract. Further, suppose their performance fell after their new contract. Would you be able to tell from this outcome whether these players were strategic in their effort? If so, explain. If not, what additional data would you need?

7. Why is it important to owners that the competitive equilibrium level of talent on all teams be maintained when measures to reduce competition over player talent are implemented?

8. Summarize the evidence on the impact of the draft in light of the invariance principle. Be sure to include what happens to players before the draft, after the draft, and the dispersion of winning percents.

9. Suppose that the NCAA followed the Blue Ribbon Panel, 2000, suggestion and ended eligibility for college players entering the draft. Would teams in MLB be better off? Why? Would college players be better off? Why? Would there be any impact at all on competitive balance? Explain fully.

10. Summarize the evidence on the reserve clause in light of the invariance principle. Be sure to include whether players really do move more, whether the relationship between market size and winning changed after free agency, winning percent evidence, and championship participation evidence.

INTERNET RESOURCES

For a host of additional material and questions for thought, visit this book's Web site at www.prenhall.com/fort.

REFERENCES

Canham-Clyne, John. "Loyalty Griping Ignores Simple Truth." *Baseball America*, August 8, 1994, p. 10.

Caple, Jim. "Free Agency Simply Great for Baseball." ESPN.com, November 26, 2004.

Fizel, John L. "Free Agency and Competitive Balance." In *Stee-Rike Four! What's Wrong with the Business of Baseball?* D. R. Marburger, ed. Westport, CT: Praeger, 1997.

Fort, Rodney, and James Quirk. "Cross-Subsidization, Incentives, and Outcomes in Professional Team Sports Leagues." *Journal of Economic Literature* 23 (1995): 1265–1299.

Helyar, John. *Lords of the Realm: The Real History of Baseball.* New York: Willard Books, 1994.

Horowitz, Ira, and Christopher Zappe. "Thanks for the Memories: Baseball Veterans' End-of-Career Salaries." *Managerial and Decision Economics* 19 (September 1998): 377–382.

Kahane, Leo, and Stephen Shmanske. "Team Roster Turnover and Attendance in Major League Baseball." *Applied Economics* 29 (April 1997): 425–431.

Krautmann, Anthony C. "Shirking or Stochastic Productivity in Major League Baseball." *Southern Economic Journal* 56 (1990): 961–968.

Lehn, Kenneth. "Property Rights, Risk Sharing, and Player Disability in Major League Baseball." *Journal of Law and Economics* 25 (1982): 343–366.

Levin, Richard C. et al. *The Report of the Independent Members of the Commissioner's*

Blue Ribbon Panel on Baseball Economics. New York: Major League Baseball, July 2000.

Lewis, Ethan L. "A Structure to Last Forever: The Players' League and the Brotherhood War of 1890." Master's thesis (www. ethanlewis.org), Purdue University, 2001.

Maxcy, Joel. "Do Long-Term Contracts Influence Performance in Major League Baseball?" In *Advances in the Economics of Sport.* W. Hendricks, ed. Greenwich, CT: JAI Press Inc., 1997.

Oberman, Keith. "Hall of Famers on the Hoof." *Sports Illustrated*, June 8, 1998, p. 74.

Quirk, James P., and Rodney D. Fort. *Pay Dirt: The Business of Professional Team Sports.* Princeton, NJ: Princeton University Press, 1992.

Rottenberg, Simon. "The Baseball Players' Labor Market." *Journal of Political Economy* 64 (1956): 242–258.

Ruane, Tom. "Player Movement." Baseball Think Factory, www.baseballstuff.com/btff/scholars/ruane/articles/player_movement.htm.

Scoggins, John F. "Shirking or Stochastic Productivity in Major League Baseball: Comment." *Southern Economic Journal* 60 (1993): 239–240.

Scully, Gerald W. *The Business of Major League Baseball.* Chicago, IL: University of Chicago Press, 1989.

Scully, Gerald W. "Pay and Performance in Major League Baseball." *American Economic Review* 64 (1974): 915–930.

Sommers, Paul M. "The Influence of Salary Arbitration on Player Performance." *Social Science Quarterly* 74 (1993): 439–443.

Sommers, Paul M., and Noel Quinton. "Pay and Performance in Major League Baseball: The Case of the First Family of Free Agents." *Journal of Human Resources* 17 (1982): 426–436.

Stark, Jayson. "The Decision That Changed the Game, Part 3: Player Movement a Fact of Life." ESPN.com, November 23, 2004.

Staudohar P. D. *Playing for Dollars: Labor Relations and the Sports Business.* New York: Cornell University Press, 1996.

Chapter 9

Labor Relations in Pro Sports

Chapter Objectives

After reading this chapter, you should be able to:

- *Discuss the major elements of the modern labor relations process, including the legal setting, how owners and players are organized, and how they interact to produce collective bargaining outcomes.*

- *Explain why unions organize and what organizational problems union organizers must overcome.*

- *Understand that basic bargaining is the process of looking forward and working back. The basic 50–50 outcome is adjusted by the alternatives that are available to each side of collective bargaining negotiations.*

- *Explain how work stoppages happen.*

- *Understand the history of labor relations in each of the four major pro team sports.*

> *Players say the owners are stupid, owners say the players are greedy, and both sides are right; they make one pine for simpler days when the owners were greedy and the players were stupid.*

—RICHARD CORLISS ON THE INABILITY OF OWNERS
AND PLAYERS TO AVOID THE MLB STRIKE OF 1994
Time, August 8, 1994, p. 65

$\mathcal{J}$n his book *Instant Replay* (1968), author Jerry Kramer tells the story of star center Jim Ringo meeting with Packers coach Vince Lombardi to discuss his 1964 contract. According to Kramer, at the meeting Ringo told Lombardi that his agent would be handling all of his contract negotiations. Lombardi asked Ringo and his agent to wait outside while he went in his office. When Lombardi came back out, he announced that Ringo would not need his agent to deal with the Packers—he had just been traded to the Philadelphia Eagles. Although Ringo has denied the story, in any case, he was traded to the Eagles immediately after he asked Lombardi for a raise in 1964 (Quirk and Fort, 1992, p. 179).

Labor relations, the subject of this chapter, have come a long way since 1964. Modern labor relations occur in an environment governed by federal labor law that specifies the rights of players to organize and the process of interaction between unions and leagues. We can begin to understand labor relations by recognizing unions for what they are, namely, small democracies. As such, we should expect them to pursue policies most valued by the subset of players who are politically powerful within the union. We will also develop in this chapter the rudimentary game theory behind bargaining. Although work stoppages (strikes by players and lockouts by owners) nearly never happen, they are significant events, and we will examine how they may occur. Finally, we will cover labor relations in each major sport separately.

MODERN SPORTS LABOR RELATIONS

Labor relations—the interactions between players and owners concerning employment, pay, and the negotiating environment—were not a big deal in pro sports until the early 1970s (Staudohar, 1996; Koppett, 1991; Voigt, 1991). But by the 1970s, revenues were growing at an astonishing rate in all pro sports. The trade union movement in sports grew slowly and surely as the value of organizing rose. As sports evolved into a large-scale entertainment industry, players began looking more and more like entertainment stars. They employed agents to negotiate contracts, and they got behind their organized labor associations in the face of the restrictions in place against their earnings. All major leagues have unions in the era of modern labor relations.

Exclusion and Counteracting Management Power

Going back to the original trade guilds of Europe, labor was organized in order to assure the progression from apprentice to journeyman to master. Trade guilds served to train individuals, but they also greatly limited competition. Later, labor organized in order to counteract the power that firms often have over worker earnings by reducing competition for jobs and raising wages.

Early on, when no formal agreement existed among owners in various leagues, pro sports players did well, jumping from one team to another at the drop of a hat. However, owners did not like this competition because it made it difficult to build winning teams and pushed wages to competitive levels. Out of this horrible situation (from management's perspective) came the controls covered in Chapter 8, most notably the draft and reserve clause. Before the era of modern pro sports labor relations, owners simply imposed drafts and reserve clauses on players. Players confronted this power by organizing into player associations and, eventually, legally recognized collective bargaining units usually called unions.

In the mature stages of sports labor relations, players have responded to management power by organizing into unions. Although owners may wish otherwise, this type of cooperative action is legal under labor law. But let's not operate under any illusions. The essence of modern sports labor relations is power—organized owners against organized players. The Learning Highlight: Champions of the "Free" Market for Players? Not Who You Might Think discusses the impacts of this power in more detail. In the rest of this section, we will examine the legal setting and the major actors in owner-player negotiations.

Modern Labor Relations: The Law

The modern, mature structure of labor relations in sports is shown in Figure 9.1. Owners acting through leagues and players acting through unions interact with each other under the legal structure that governs the collective bargaining process. **Collective bargaining** just means that players are allowed to act as a unit and owners are obligated by law to recognize that right. The legal setting and major actors depicted in Figure 9.1 are worth addressing individually.

The National Labor Relations Act   State and federal labor laws comprise the legal structure that governs collective bargaining. Most important in this regard is the 1935 **National Labor Relations Act** (NLRA) and the **National Labor Relations Board** (NLRB) it created to oversee the formation of unions and the process of collective bargaining. The NLRA broadly covers workers involved in interstate commerce and defines the criteria under which a group of employees can act collectively through union representation. It guarantees three essential rights for labor:

1. The right of labor to organize and form unions
2. The right of labor to bargain collectively through representatives of their own choosing
3. The right of labor to use pressure tactics such as strikes and picketing

Modern labor relations have evolved under the NLRA and the decisions of the NLRB and the federal courts. Hundreds of decisions have helped define the collective bargaining relationship in all industries. A few of the more important decisions in sports are discussed in this chapter.

The National Labor Relations Board   The NLRB enforces the NLRA by deciding grievances brought either by labor or management. Appeals of unfair labor practices go to the NLRB for a ruling. If the NLRB finds a problem, NLRB decisions are

LEARNING HIGHLIGHT
Champions of the "Free" Market for Players? Not Who You Might Think

Sports economist Allen Sanderson of the University of Chicago has long pointed out that unions have acted just as purposefully as owners have in their pursuit of power over players' earnings (*Sporting News*, September 9, 1995, p. 38). Players do not want real economic competition any more than owners do. For example, unions have never supported completely unrestricted free agency. All restricted versions of free agency restrict supply and raise the prices of experienced players relative to complete free agency. Sanderson puts it this way:

> The reason we have one league and 28 teams [in 1995] is not because of economy of scale or because there's not enough player talent. It's because 28 owners and 700 players can benefit handsomely from restricting the market. The owners have a monopoly over franchises. The union has a monopoly over the labor market. This is an intrafamily squabble over who gets monopoly profits. The players share in those monopoly profits. They make substantially more money than they would in a competitive market. (*Sporting News*, September 9, 1995, p. 38)

The executive director of the Major League Baseball Players Association (MLBPA), Donald Fehr, responded to Sanderson's assertion as follows:

> He's talking philosophy. In order to have perfect freedom, you'd have to have no draft, no trade rules, no minor league reserve system. We come from a different perspective. Total freedom in the abstract is destructive of everything desirable. We're realistic. Our goal is to negotiate minimum standards that allow you to then get whatever freedom you can. (*Sporting News*, September 9, 1995, p. 38)

Player union leaders recognized almost immediately that complete free agency was not in their best interest, and so did one owner. When free agency was on the horizon in MLB in the mid-1970s, the then-owner of the Oakland A's, Charley O. Finley, saw a chance for owners to salvage something from free agency. If free agency was inevitable, then Finley's plan was to have as many players competing for each open spot as possible, every year, which would bring salaries down. Apparently, the then-executive director of the MLBPA, Marvin Miller (1991), heard of this and held his breath:

> In the wake of the Messersmith decision [which created the free agency era] it dawned on me, as a terrifying possibility, that the owners might suddenly wake up one day and realize that yearly free agency was the best possible thing for them; that is, if all players became free agents at the end of each year, the market would be flooded, and salaries would be held down. . . . In the midst of all the panic in the owners' ranks after the arbitration decision . . . there was Finley, maybe the only original thinker in the group, saying, "Hey, what's the problem? Let them be free agents every year. It'll flood the market with players; it'll keep salaries down." It was so logical, so obvious, that to this day I cannot understand why other owners did not think of it. (p. 370)

Miller meant that restricted free agency was a limitation on freedom but one that raised the salaries of experienced players more relative to truly unfettered free agency. Miller and Finley both knew that annual free agency for all players would increase the supply of labor and push wages down relative to a version of free agency that would restrict supply and raise the prices of experienced players. Finley simply wanted to dance with his own devil—unlimited free agency—rather than the one preferred by the players. Miller used the remaining owner sentiment to negotiate limited free agency that kept the labor market orderly because owners could only bid up the price of the top players without setting so many players free that salaries would fall.

Sources: Sporting News, September 9, 1995, p. 38; Miller (1991).

Figure 9.1 Modern Sports Relations

Modern labor relations are a complex process. Government, leagues and owners, and players and union are the central actors. The commissioner of the league also acts, ostensibly independently. All come together in the collective bargaining process. Agents have input into the deliberations of leagues and unions but no legal role in the negotiations. Special instances lead to mediation and arbitration.

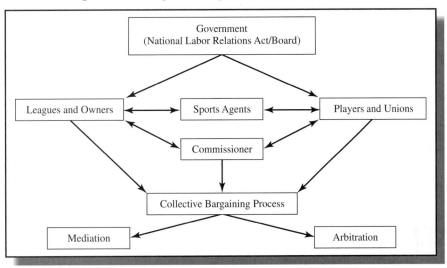

Source: Staudohar, Paul D., *Playing for Dollars: Labor Relations and the Sports Business* (Ithaca, NY: ILR Press, 1966), p. 7.

Did You Know?
Under federal labor law, owners must provide information about their team finances to player unions to establish a basis for negotiation.

enforced through motions filed in the federal courts. In sports, both unions and owners often bring actions to the NLRB that involve violations of good-faith bargaining on the part of the other side. **Bargaining in good faith** means that opponents must be striving to reach an agreement rather than striving to drive a wedge in negotiations. For example, owners are required to provide information about team finances to the unions so that the unions can establish a basis for negotiation. Further, the NLRB helps leagues and unions determine the scope of bargaining, that is, what lies within the law and what does not.

Owners, Their Leagues, and the Commissioner

Owners, acting through leagues, are on one side of the process in Figure 9.1. Remember from Chapter 5 that owners deal with players' associations as a league joint venture activity. However, owners do not have to negotiate as a group with their respective player associations (unions). For example, Ford, GM, Chrysler, and American Motors choose not to join forces in dealing with the United Auto Workers. Our conclusion in Chapter 5 was that team owners must simply be better off acting together to confront player associations.

Occasionally, league commissioners play a role in collective bargaining. Technically, every commissioner is hired by the owners, acting through their leagues, and serving at their discretion. As such, it would be wrong to say that the commissioners act autonomously in the best interests of their respective sports. Even though they portray themselves that way, if they cross the owners, they can be fired. However, commissioners do have some autonomy. For example, they act as public spokespersons and buffers between collective bargaining adversaries. They also have participated in labor negotiations under the "best interests of the sport" banner.

Players, Unions, and Agents

Unions represent players in the collective bargaining process. Unions are governed by the very strict rules set forth in the NLRA. All unions are organized as representative democracies of players. Typically, the equivalent of the trade union local chapter is the individual sports team, with each team electing a **player representative**. The representatives meet to conduct the union's business. All unions have elected officers, including a president. In addition, hired executive directors play an important role as professional negotiators.

Under the NLRA, once the players have ratified a union, it has the right to represent them in all negotiations. Union platforms are generated by the team representatives. All actions by the representatives, especially work stoppages, are voted on by the membership.

The role of agents in collective bargaining often is misunderstood. **Player agents** represent players seeking their highest financial reward in individual negotiations with teams. However, as indicated in Figure 9.1, their access to the collective bargaining process is limited. Agents are not included in the collective bargaining process. Legally, they do not have a place at the table. However, some unions have taken a particular interest in player agents and have included agent regulation in their agreements with owners. This is only natural because players have agreed to allow unions to be their sole bargaining authority under the NLRA.

The Major League Baseball Players Association (MLBPA), National Football League Players Association (NFLPA), and the National Basketball Players Association (NBPA) have negotiated union-certification restrictions on agents in their respective collective bargaining agreements. Owners have agreed that they will deal only with agents certified by unions. The certification process requires applicants to reveal any criminal past, detail their sports experience, reveal any conflict of interest, and specify their fees. Unions also typically require a standard contract between agents and players that includes arbitration of any disagreement. Only the National Hockey League Players' Association (NHLPA) has chosen to stay out of the agent issue completely. Agents do represent hockey players, but they are not regulated in any way by the NHL.

Did You Know?
All players associations, except the NHL, have negotiated restrictions on player agents requiring them to reveal their past, their experience, any conflict of interest, and their fees.

Collective Bargaining Agreements The essence of collective bargaining is that both owners and players have relinquished some of their individual bargaining rights to their representatives, leagues, and unions. Thus, leagues and unions negotiate **collective bargaining agreements**, which represent a clear specification of the rights of owners and players in the process as well as the items that result from the process. Collective bargaining agreements typically include:

- The duration of the agreement (3 years is the most common)
- So-called reopening clauses under which new negotiations can occur before the expiration date of the agreement
- The rules and procedures governing the draft
- Pay issues common to all players, such as free agency, minimum salaries, meal money, playoff pay, sharing percentages under salary caps, and retirement funds
- Player location issues (such as the ability by veteran players to have a say in where they will and will not play)
- Channels for addressing grievances, primarily arbitration and mediation

Within the setting created through collective bargaining, owners and players do retain some **individual bargaining rights**. Owners and players each retain the right to negotiate individual salaries. In addition, owners also retain the right to sell and trade player contracts. However, this usually is limited to younger players, because older players have refusal rights specified in the collective bargaining agreements in each league. For example, MLB has the "10-and-5" rule. Players with 10 years in the league and 5 years for a given team have refusal rights over any trade. In essence, this means that 10-and-5 players can dictate the next team for which they will play.

Standard Contract Elements Player contracts have many elements that are subject to collective bargaining. All contracts within a league include standard sections, but those standard sections vary quite a bit across leagues. Most contracts typically limit player participation in other sports. Standard language appears in all contracts covering breach of contract. This language is very specific on redress to both parties in the event of a breach. All contracts include standard language specifying grounds for termination by the club—personal conduct, physical fitness, declining skills, or failure to render services to the club. Injury is not grounds for release. All standard contracts contain language containing player rights to redress of grievances. Disciplinary rules and filing deadlines, along with player shares of group licensing and promotion, also are specified. Most importantly, trades also are governed by standard contracts. Typically, the teams have full control over trades; however no-trade clauses and items like the 10-and-5 rule in MLB do exist.

Special Labor Relations Topic: Salary Arbitration

Collective bargaining agreements in the NHL and MLB explicitly cover the situation where a player and owner cannot agree to a contract. In these situations, individual players can exercise their collective bargaining rights to have an independent third party decide the issue. This is commonly referred to as salary arbitration, and the independent third party is called the arbitrator. If a dispute reaches arbitration, both sides must agree to abide by the arbitrator's decision.

In the arbitration process, players try to maximize the expected value of the outcome. They choose the highest possible defensible salary and defend it by providing information on other comparable players in the league, free agents included, based on performance. The question then confronting the arbitrator is "How can a player be paid less than comparable players?" Owners counter with a defensible lower offer based on their evaluation of the player in question.

Arbitrators are the essential element in this process. They are professionals serving at the discretion of both the players associations and the leagues. Presumably, arbitrators wish to keep their jobs. They must, therefore, decide between owners and players in a way that both perceive to be fair. All things considered, arbitrators strive to determine the value of a player and then find in favor of the side that is closest to that value assessment.

Technical Arbitration Issues: Eligibility and Final Offers

Two types of players are eligible for arbitration: free agents at the end of their contract and non-free agents who can file for arbitration according to the rules for that procedure in collective bargaining agreements. Free agent players at the end of their contracts enter into negotiations with their team owner. At any time during the process, these players can file for arbitration. If an impasse is reached, the player must decide whether to begin arbitration proceedings or enter the free agent market. Some non-free agents also are eligible for arbitration (e.g., in MLB, players are eligible for arbitration after 3 years in the league but are not free agents until their sixth year). If non-free agents fail to exercise arbitration, they simply accept the owner's pay offer.

In the NHL, arbitrators may choose any number they deem fair between the owner's offer and the player's demand, but MLB uses **final offer salary arbitration (FOSA)**. This means that the independent arbitrator cannot choose a fair difference between the team's offer and the player's request. Arbitrators must choose one or the other. Uncertainty about the arbitrator's choice actually gives both parties an incentive to reach an agreement on their own before turning to arbitration. Economically speaking, in order to let an independent third party make the decision for them, parties to a negotiation must be willing to live with the expected outcome. If not, then the parties should work harder on reaching an agreement prior to arbitration. As you might expect, this contentious FOSA process is destined to create hard feelings between owners and players.

Did You Know?
MLB uses final offer salary arbitration; the arbitrator must choose either the player's demand or the owner's offer.

FOSA Outcomes in General

FOSA should lead to earnest and sincere salary negotiations. Owners fear lavish decisions in favor of players, and players fear that pushing owners beyond their ability to pay may shorten their tenure with that team. As owners and players fear the unknown, they should strive harder to reach an agreement rather than face FOSA. Generally, this is the case. Few players actually exercise their arbitration rights each year, indicating that the salary determination process generates satisfied owners and players in the vast majority of cases.

Arbitration produces two interesting outcomes. First, owners typically win more cases than the players. However, simple tallies do not tell the whole story about arbitration. This leads to the second outcome: Salaries are higher in the presence of FOSA than they would be otherwise. As we just saw, owners negotiate sincerely with players who do not enter arbitration. The threat of losing arbitration cases can lead owners to raise salaries to avoid arbitration.

But FOSA, once invoked, also raises salaries whether players win or lose their case. If the players win, their salaries rise dramatically. If the arbitrator finds against a player, the owner's offer still is well above what the player made previously because owners try to appear fair to the arbitrator. Either way, the player earns more. For the players, it is a matter of getting rich (if they lose) or richer (if they win).

Although players like this outcome, owners do not. They dislike it because it allows players to move up the salary distribution at a faster pace than would happen in the absence of arbitration. Remember that arbitration is the result of negotiation, and there is no reason to think that the system in place before arbitration was either fair or efficient. Owners prefer anticompetitive outcomes because they are able to keep more money than they are able to keep under arbitration.

Special Labor Relations Topic: Union Decertification

Union members forfeit their rights to individual legal action when they vote for a union to represent them in collective bargaining. For example, the antitrust laws protect all individuals from the exercise of market power by firms in the American economy. However, players organized as unions cannot sue owners under these laws because they have voted to deal with owners through collective bargaining. The ultimate aim of players is to hold onto gains against owners and, if possible, gain further concessions that enhance their wealth and happiness. Almost always, these gains are made through collective bargaining, but in very special situations individual action may further these goals better than collective bargaining.

In these very special cases, players may decide on **union decertification** to pursue gains against owners. Under decertification, players simply vote to cancel collective representation by their union. Such an approach is allowed under the NLRA and has been used to great effect by football and basketball players.

UNION GOALS, ORGANIZATIONAL PROBLEMS, AND GOVERNANCE

Players formed unions to counter the market power that team owners exercised over them and to limit competition over their jobs. Thus, the goal of unions is to move players economically forward against owners. However, obstacles must be surmounted before unions can form. Once a union is formed, its governance can lead to some surprising insights into collective bargaining outcomes. Let's first start with the economic battle to be fought because it is those gains against owners that fuel union organizations in the first place.

The Role of Marginal Revenue Product

The economic struggle between owners and players is over player marginal revenue product (our old friend MRP), the contribution that players make to the value of team revenues. At the time that unions formed in pro sports, players all suffered from the exercise of owner power over player MRP, a power derived from the reserve clause and player drafts. These owner-imposed restrictions on players reduced competition in the player market. In the presence of these restrictions, players' alternatives were limited to earnings outside of their sport. As these outside earnings were typically lower than player sport MRP, owners could keep the difference between MRP and the next-best player opportunity. In theory, owners would pay just enough to keep players in their sport, and little more.

MRP is composed of two components: marginal product and marginal revenue. Because team owners enjoy market power, player contributions to team revenues are larger than they would be in a competitive situation. The monopoly profits are included in the evaluation of player contribution to revenues. This makes the prize for union organization just that much larger.

In a nutshell, the goal of unionization is to offset owner power over MRP in order to drive payment closer to the level that would be determined under a competitive pay structure. This is the value to individual players of forming a union. In percentage terms, the value that can be earned by individual players is the level of salary exploitation discussed in Chapter 8:

$$\text{Salary Exploitation} = \frac{\text{MRP} - \text{Salary}}{\text{MRP}}$$

The total value of forming the union will be the sum of these values across all players. As noted in Chapter 8, estimates of exploitation were in the 80–90 percent range. The value of unionization is clearly in the hundreds of millions of dollars, annually.

Obstacles to Organization

With that type of money at stake, it would seem a simple matter to form a union. The players would just get together, add up these values, recognize that hundreds of millions of dollars are at stake, and set up a union structure. However, there are quite a few obstacles in the way.

Education Costs   Although some players may immediately recognize the value of organization, not all will. Therefore, the potential union incurs start-up **education costs**. From the very start of player associations, players had to be educated about the salary exploitation practices of owners and how they could be fought through organized action. Because players are located across the country, the costs of flying union leaders around the country were large. Further, players had to meet in order to hear the message, and their time was especially valuable during the season. Collecting players and their leaders in central places was costly.

The education task proved a formidable one for fledgling unions. Players were distrustful of the motivations of union enthusiasts and had a low level of understanding of their actual value to owners. For example, as shown in the Learning Highlight: Pro Athletes as "Company Men," most players in early testimony before Congressional subcommittees revealed very

"Yes, sir. I think if professional baseball owners themselves are in favor of it, we are, because I believe—I would say this: I think anything that is good for them in this particular line is definitely going to be good for us."
—Robin Roberts, MLBPA President, 1958

It took players an extraordinary amount of time to figure out the power that owners had over MRP, let alone how much it was costing them. Nothing speaks more clearly than the players' own words. The following are some excerpts from Congressional testimony in the 1950s. Much of the testimony concerned the reserve clause that essentially bound players to their team for life, greatly reducing their bargaining power in salary negotiations. Listen for the owners' arguments that you have studied in Chapter 8 and remember that these are players talking. (Only player representatives are included here, but other notables toeing the party line in these hearings included Ty Cobb, Pee Wee Reese, Lou Boudreau, Stan Musial, Mickey Mantle, and Ted Williams in baseball; Chuck Bednarik and Red Grange in football; and Bob Pettit in basketball.) The others mentioned in examples are members of Congress or their staff.

As a player representative, Robin Roberts once said of owners, "I think anything that is good for them in this particular line is definitely going to be good for us." Jackie Robinson, on the other hand, argued forcefully for player economic freedom.

BASEBALL

Fred Hutchinson of the Detroit Tigers and chair of the American League players' representatives:

MR. HUTCHINSON: In my opinion the players as a rule have been treated fairly by the clubs and have generally been paid in accordance with their value to the clubs.

Mr. Lane: As the players' representative, in handling all their grievances and complaints and being in constant touch with them day in and day out, do you feel, in your own mind, that the players wish to retain the reserve clause, as a whole?

Mr. Hutchinson: Yes, sir.

Eddie Yost of the Washington Senators and chair of the American League players' representatives; Robin Roberts of the Philadelphia Phillies and chair of the National League players' representatives; and Jerry Coleman of the New York Yankees and players' representative:

MR. SINGMAN: Do you think, then, the players are generally satisfied with the reserve clause?
MR. YOST: Yes, I do.
MR. ROBERTS: I think most of them are and those that aren't feel there isn't anything they can do with it.
MR. COLEMAN: I have had no complaints administered to as far as the reserve clause.

FOOTBALL

Jack Jennings of the Chicago Cardinals and players' representative:

MR. HARKINS: You are aware in your contract there is a method by which you can become a free agent, and, after that, presumably, any member club in the league is in a position to hire you?
MR. JENNINGS: That is right.
MR. HARKINS: That has never happened in the league?
MR. JENNINGS: That is right.
MR. PIERCE: What you are saying is, no matter how we slice this, in the long run the draft helps the club and helps the player?
MR. JENNINGS: That's right.

Bill Howton of the Green Bay Packers and players' representative:

MR. DIXON: How do the players feel about this limited reserve clause?

(Continued)

(Continued)

MR. HOWTON: As we stated, it appears that it is necessary in the livelihood of professional football, in the event the reserve clause were dropped, the teams with the wealth would naturally buy the best ballplayers. The teams with smaller wealth would obviously fall in rank and eventually die off. So the stronger teams would dominate the game, and it seems as though it is a strong stabilizer for the game although it puts the players in a bad bargaining position.

A couple of voices sounded more like what one would have expected from players who truly understood what was going on. Here are two.

Kyle Rote of the NFL's New York Giants and union organizer:

MR. ROTE: As far as the player is concerned, there is, at present, no check over the activities of the NFL as relates to the player. The draft and reserve clause are necessary to the pro game. But they are not necessary when given free rein and result in abuses of the players' rights.

Jackie Robinson of MLB's Brooklyn Dodgers:

MR. ROBINSON: ... So I sometimes feel, myself, that when we see the Ted Williamses and the Mickey Mantles, and the Stan Musials down here testifying, that perhaps when they say they like things as they are, I would certainly have to agree because of the tremendous salaries that they get. But I wonder whether or not the 8 or 9 or 10 men on the ball club would agree to what is happening today as the right thing so far as the baseball player is concerned. ...

SENATOR KEFAUVER: Let me ask you, first, do you think there should be some limit on the length of time of a reserve contract?

MR. ROBINSON: Yes; I do, sir.

Senator Kefauver: What do you think about the draft system? Do you recommend an unrestricted draft?

MR. ROBINSON: ... If a ballplayer so desires, I think a ballplayer should have a say as to whether or not he should be subject to draft or not. In other words, I feel that a ballplayer should have some say personally in his baseball future.

Sources: Hearings before the Subcommittee on Market Power, Committee on the Judiciary, House of Representatives, 82nd Congress, 1st Session, Part 6, Serial No. 1, various dates in July, August, and October 1951. Hearings before the Antitrust Subcommittee, Committee on the Judiciary, House of Representatives, 85th Congress, 1st Session, Parts 1, 2 and 3, Serial No. 8, various dates in June, July, and August 1957. Hearings before the Subcommittee on Antitrust and Monopoly, Committee on the Judiciary, U.S. Senate, 85th Congress, 2nd Session, July 1958.

little opposition to the reserve clause and the draft. In Congressional testimony in 1958, when asked if he favored legislation that would officially exempt owners from the antitrust laws, Robin Roberts (president of the MLBPA at the time) actually said, "Yes, sir. I think if professional baseball owners themselves are in favor of it, we are, because I believe—I would say this: I think anything that is good for them in this particular line is definitely going to be good for us." Early on, players and their representatives did not realize how much owner control over MRP was costing them, and they would not find out for almost 20 years. The players simply trusted that baseball owners would look out for them.

This type of sentiment was difficult to overcome. Even years later, when Curt Flood was battling MLB for free agency in the courts, Marvin Miller (1991) noted this about the unwillingness of stars to show support:

> They may have wanted Flood to win, but they felt that they had their careers to be concerned with, and that was that. Even though I had explained the importance of modifying the reserve clause, many of the players remained in the dark about what the case might mean. (p. 197)

Free Riding Perhaps the most important problem facing all volunteer organizations (unions, political action groups, and philanthropic organizations alike) is **free-riding behavior** by members. If you have ever felt cheated in a study group because some members of the group did not carry their weight, then you know all about free riding. Now, imagine you are a players' association organizer. You have done your job educating players, and they now understand the exploitation that they want reduced. Now is the time to generate official membership and a budget so that you can carry forward the association's agenda. You appeal to the players for a dues structure so that you can start your work.

Think about your request from the perspective of any given player. The value of membership equals the difference between that player's MRP and actual salary. Union leaders want part of that difference to go to union dues. However, here is how a player might see the situation. If the rest of the players pay their dues and one particular player does not, then that player gets the benefits of the union activity (namely, MRP – Wage) without paying anything. The rest of the players pay their dues, the union carries the battle and, if it succeeds, generates salaries closer to MRP. Players who do not contribute keep all of the gain without any of the pain of union dues.

Therein lies the problem from the organizer's perspective and, ultimately, from the perspective of individual players. If all players free ride, then no dues will be collected. The union leadership will never be able to start their activities to wrestle salaries closer to MRP. Free-riding behavior that seems such a wise move from the individual perspective leads to collective ruin when all practice it.

Unions overcome free-riding behavior in a number of ways. First, once players get behind the union idea, there appears to be a strong sense of solidarity. This greatly reduces free-riding behavior. Second, there is the aspect of enforcement on the field. An "errant" major league fastball, missed blocks on massive defensive linemen, flagrant basketball fouls, and menacing hockey sticks provide ample incentive against free riding.

Did You Know?
When some prominent MLB stars jumped their reserve clause and joined the Mexican League, the commissioner banned them for 5 years. When the players returned, the ban was reduced to 3 years.

Owner Retaliation **Owner retaliation** in the form of blacklisting union activists or interfering with their professional development might also hinder players' union participation. Blacklisting has occurred in the past. Shortly after World War II, Jorge Pasquel took a shot at promoting his Mexican League to major league status. He lured a few true stars—Mickey Owen, Luis Olmo, Danny Gardella, Tommy DeLaCruz, and Sal Maglie—into jumping their MLB reserve clauses for a chance at promised big money. Owners feared the worst as this rival league reared its ugly head.

In 1946, Commissioner Happy Chandler announced that players who jumped would be banished from MLB for 5 years.

In the end, Pasquel's dreams were bigger than both his fan base and his checkbook. The league folded after just a year. When players returned with their hats in their hands, owners did not go after them in the usual way with lawsuits over contract disputes. Instead, the disloyal players were punished for jumping ship by the league. The banishment was reduced to 3 years, and Owen and Olmo rejoined the Dodgers in 1949. (Ironically, Pasquel sued Owen for jumping back to MLB!)

Penalties for jumping leagues are not technically retaliation against union activity, but they do set the tone for relationships between owners and players. Reports of retaliation against player representatives were numerous during the rise of the MLBPA under Marvin Miller's firm hand in the early 1960s. However, note that a statistical treatment by Coffin (1999) did not find any difference between player representatives and other players in time spent on a team, the number of trades, or career length. Specific well-known instances of retaliation are still worth exploring because their impact on player willingness to participate in union activity can be significant, even if the impact of occurrences on player representatives, themselves, is not.

"I don't know how many times pitchers with a 2.29 ERA have been traded, but I'd bet it happens much more often among pitchers who are player reps." —Marvin Miller, MLBPA Executive Director

Owners also have interfered with the career development of union activists. When the MLBPA's executive counsel returned from its meetings in Mexico City in 1967, union activist and counsel member Jim Bunning found he had been traded from the Phillies to the Pirates. Bunning's pitching statistics had been top-notch, leading Marvin Miller to wonder, "I do not know how many times pitchers with a 2.29 ERA have been traded, but I'd bet it happens much more often among pitchers who are player reps" (1991, p. 163).

Later, in 1968, pitcher Milt Pappas informed the MLBPA that the Reds were not living up to collective bargaining requirements on travel accommodations. Miller intervened, suggesting that the team live up to its agreement or suffer the consequences. Pappas was traded to Atlanta in the same season.

Miller did not encourage marginal players to support Curt Flood in his antitrust action against the owners in 1968. The trial was during the season, and they had their careers to work on. But Miller also noted:

> Further, it was in the back of my mind that a great many marginal players might be the targets of owner revenge if Flood lost: A utility infielder who was active in the union and made a public show of support for Flood might find himself losing a job to a utility infielder who wasn't active in the union. Union reps had a tough time as it was; they tended to be traded more often than players who were less active in the union. (1991, p. 196)

"These people aren't very big on player reps." —Gene Mauch, manager of the Twins, to newly acquired pitcher and union activist, Mike Marshall, 1978

Ten years later, the Twins signed relief pitcher and union activist Mike Marshall as a free agent in 1978. Manager Gene Mauch said to Marshall, "Of course, you're not going to do any of that Player Association stuff, are you? These people aren't very big on player reps" (Miller, 1991, p. 304). Marshall remained active, especially during the events leading up to the strike of 1981. Marshall was hardly used by the Twins during these activities. In June 1980, after he allowed one run in five consecutive appearances, the Twins released him for poor performance. The MLBPA brought a grievance and the Twins settled, agreeing to pay the remainder of his contract.

Again, these incidents do not prove owner retaliation. They merely suggest that a very small group of players may have suffered for their union involvement. Nonetheless, these examples could very well sour some players on union participation.

Political Sentiment and Illegal League Behavior Still other factors can affect the ability of a union to form and perform. First, hostile political environments can undo union efforts. It was years before player trade unions even were an imaginable concept in the United States. Second, there are examples of **illegal owner behavior**. At the outset, MLB owners controlled the operating budget of the MLBPA. This practice was not only an obvious conflict of interest (how would the union survive if it pushed the owners too hard?), but also an illegal act under federal labor law. It had been common practice for years before Marvin Miller took over the union in 1966.

Union Democracy and Expected Union Outcomes

What should we expect from union leadership in the collective bargaining process? According to our basic idea of union formation, the idea would be to push player salaries closer to MRP. In addition, other compensation issues (like pension plans) and workplace safety issues also are the objects of collective bargaining. The form that this pursuit takes is dependent on the fact that unions are democracies, warts and all.

For example, why in the world would a union agree to a salary cap? We have already seen that caps reduce payments to talent if they are effective. A simple explanation is that a cap represents a trade-off between higher employment and higher wages. Indeed, in the NBA where it was first introduced, the cap came during the merger of the NBA and ABA, when a small number of teams in each league were failing. At that time it did look like players needed to take a pay cut in order to ensure survival of teams and a number of jobs. However, the merger between the NBA and the ABA ended up reducing the number of teams dramatically. Either the NBPA made a crucial error or there must be a better explanation of union behavior.

The Logic of Collective Action A more complicated model of union behavior solves this puzzle. Political scientist Mancur Olson (1965) took the approach that unions are small democracies. The rank-and-file members elect representatives and a leadership that participates in the formation of union policy. The leadership then interacts with union executive directors, primarily lawyers, and collective bargaining professionals in carrying out the will of the membership. As in any democracy, only certain parts of union policy ever actually go to a vote by the rank and file. The rest of the policies are decided by union representatives and apply to all union members. This means that representatives, leaders, and directors have substantial discretion in the formation of union policy.

What should we expect from such discretion? First, let's think about the rank-and-file players. On any given policy issue, details are left to team representatives and leadership. As a result, any given player knows nearly nothing about almost everything that the union does. This is called **rational ignorance.** Rational ignorance is fueled by the fact that it is difficult for individual players to tell how any given choice will impact them. It is also expensive to discover any particular representative's role in any given policy. Every hour spent on union matters is an hour lost trying to keep up with the players' opponents on the field. That is expensive time, indeed, in a business of very short average careers (especially for younger aspiring players). As a result, it is rational for players to be ignorant about union policy because it is expensive to be informed. Rational ignorance reduces the incentive to compete in the union process. The rank-and-file players really do rely almost completely on their elected union representatives and leaders. A perfect example is the NFL strike of 1987, detailed later in the section on NFL labor relations.

Rational ignorance is, by definition, a matter of degree. The higher the value of being informed and participating, the more players will strive to do so. The players who are not rationally ignorant are those who stand to gain or lose the most from union choices and have lower participation costs—a characterization of established veteran stars. Their economic stake in the outcome is large, and they already are established stars, reducing their costs of participating; they do not lose ground against the competition because they are at the top of their game. Indeed, it is these players who dominate union activity.

The one thing we know about union leaders is that they want to be union leaders. This means that they constantly weigh the impacts of their policy decisions and negotiations in terms of the impacts on their chances to continue as union leaders. They cannot please all of the players all of the time, and they do not have to. All they have to do is please the members of the group of players that actually determines their reelection. Because rational ignorance prevails, nearly none of the rank and file knows what goes on anyway. As long as union leaders keep enough of the players happy enough, then they gain reelection. The players we would expect to be the most influential are the league's stars. The individual league histories later in the chapter show that this is indeed what typically happens.

Olson's framework (1965) suggests that union leadership will produce **concentrated benefits** (concentrated in the sense that they are large relative to the small group of star players who receive them) and **dispersed costs** (dispersed over the majority of nonstar players in the league). This outcome may not be anything close to the will of the majority of the union rank and file, but the majority of the rank and file remains rationally ignorant. They have bigger fish to fry—most are struggling just to keep their jobs in an extremely competitive environment. In this way, the concentrated group of stars gets its way, and the costs are spread over the rationally ignorant rank-and-file union membership.

This idea is portrayed in Figure 9.2. Powerful players control the fate of union officials. Their preferences are made clear to the leadership that chooses union policies (the path of preferences points from powerful members to union officials and not in the other direction). The policies then feed back to powerful union members. If they are happy on net with these policy choices, then the current union leadership gets to continue in that role. If not, then others can be chosen who will implement the preferences of the powerful members. The rank-and-file players are left pretty much on the periphery, with little impact on union outcomes.

Figure 9.2 The Labor Union Triangle
The outcomes from players' unions have been analyzed under the logic of collective action. Powerful union members are in control of the electoral chances of union officials. Those officials choose policies that powerful union members evaluate in terms of their own economic welfare. If the policies benefit the powerful union members, union officials get reelected. The rank-and-file members are relegated to the sidelines.

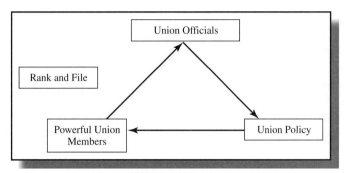

Collective Action and the Salary Cap   With this somewhat more complex view of union governance, let's revisit the issue of salary caps. Caps are really just revenue sharing between owners and players. Thus, caps only establish a ceiling (and floor, in practice) on team spending on talent. Therefore, players might find that they are able to bargain a larger share of league revenues in the form of defined gross revenues from owners during collective bargaining than they would otherwise get competitively. If so, then a cap makes sense because owners make the mistake of giving a larger percent of revenues to players than competition would generate. Alternatively, bargaining power may put the union in a position to do the same thing, that is, generate a larger than competitive share of the total revenue pie.

However, the failure of democracy is that it sometimes redistributes wealth away from the less wealthy majority toward a wealthier minority. The particular way that a cap is implemented with exemptions and special clauses may bring about redistribution in the direction of the politically powerful players. That is, even though there is a cap, the players at the top of the pay scale may do just fine under the cap, even relative to the alternative without the cap.

This is especially true in the world of pro sports, where career lengths are short and the winners do not have to confront those who bear the costs of their actions. If the current powerful player group is comprised of veterans, by the time the rank-and-file players move into that same position, the previous veterans are long gone into retirement. This is especially likely in the NBA, where just a few players run the union under the threat of either forming another union on their own or even forming their own league.

The logic of concentrated benefits and dispersed costs takes an interesting twist in a league with many players, such as the NFL. With so many more players, there is some evidence that the NFLPA democracy may work differently than the NBPA (Bishop, Finch, and Formby, 1990). With so many more players, owners appear to have found an ally in the NFLPA in taking money away from the top salary earners.

In this case, the union does not appear to benefit the narrowly defined top players. The top players simply do not have the same power over the NFLPA that they have in the NBA. In addition, rookies may have voted for the cap because they liked its minimum-spending requirement!

BASIC BARGAINING: GAME THEORY

When we enter into a discussion of bargaining, we are in the realm of game theory. Here, we will use the simplest of all game explanations to gain insights into unions. More sophisticated approaches are available, along with a complete set of jargon, and your instructor may choose to show them to you. However, in our discussion, the aim is to introduce you to the basics of strategic behavior.

The Simplest Bargaining Outcome

If you have ever shared a Popsicle with a friend, you have a pretty good idea of the simplest bargaining setting. You both know that the ultimate outcome without a sharing agreement is a melted puddle. You both know that the longer you wait, the less there is to enjoy. Thinking about what happens at the very end of your bargaining period and the effects of the passage of time, both of you reason your way to the up-front **50–50 split**. Every step along the way, thinking back from the end to the present, you both considered the best you could do, given the outcome that would result without an agreement. Choosing rationally each step along the way, both of you reached the conclusion that the 50–50 split is best. This "**look forward, work back**" approach is basic to analyzing bargaining.

This simple Popsicle game is insightful, even for something as complicated as sports bargaining. Here we present a straightforward adaptation of a simple example found in Dixit and Nalebuff (1993). Suppose you have a finite sports season of 151 days (about 5 months). Agreement between the players and owners is required before there can be any play. Unions act on behalf of players, and the league acts on behalf of owners. Further suppose the union makes its final demand on day 150, with one day left in the season. Offers are made in turns on daily intervals. Play on any given day is worth $13 million, for a total season revenue value of about $2 billion (not far off from most pro sports). In this type of situation, if both parties wish to do as well as they can, they would try to structure their thinking about the problem just like the Popsicle game—determine what would happen at their very last chance to strike a bargain at the end of the season; estimate the payoffs every step along the way, including the choice that the other party would make; and then calculate the most profitable choice of all. Table 9.1 shows this simple bargaining scenario.

Both the union and the league know what will happen if no agreement is reached until the last bargaining day (1 day left in Table 9.1). On that 150th day, it is the union's turn to make an offer. There is $13 million on the table because there will be a 1-day season if an agreement is reached. The union offers the league $0 and

Table 9.1 A Simple Bargaining Scenario

Days Left	On the Table	Turn	Union's Share ($Millions) Total	Union's Share ($Millions) Daily	Management's Share ($Millions) Total	Management's Share ($Millions) Daily
1	$13 million	Union	$13	$13	$0	$0
2	$26 million	League	$13	$6.5	$13	$6.5
3	$39 million	Union	$26	$8.67	$13	$4.33
4	$52 million	League	$26	$6.5	$26	$6.5
5	$65 million	Union	$39	$7.8	$26	$5.2
150	$1.95 billion	League	$975	$6.50	$975	$6.5
151	$1.9563 billion	Union	$988	$6.54	$975	$6.46

keeps $13 million. Why is the league forced into this corner? The union knows that if the league says no, owners get zero anyway because the season is over and no bargain has been reached. The union will earn a 100–0 split if no agreement is reached until there is only one day left before the end of the season.

With this knowledge, consider the situation with 2 days left in the season. It is the league's turn to make an offer. The league knows that if no agreement is reached, they will move into the 1-day-left situation where the union will get $13 million and the owners get $0. But with 2 days left, there is $26 million on the table. The league knows that a $13 million offer to the union, with the remaining $13 million going to the league, will be an acceptable bargain. After all, $13 million is the best the union can do by saying no and moving to the one day left situation. The league sees right away that it can obtain a 50–50 split.

The logic of working back from 3 days left all the way to 151 days left is summarized in Table 9.1. For example, with 3 days left, there is $39 million on the table (3 days at $13 million each). If the league says no to the union offer, the best it can do is to earn $13 million by moving into the 2 days left situation. Therefore, the union offers the league the $13 million and keeps $26 million for a 67–33 split. Note that this is much closer to 50–50 than the next move that the union can make on the last day of bargaining. A quick check of Table 9.1 shows that the league constantly is reminded that the best it can hope for is a 50–50 split.

Tracking the situation for the union in Table 9.1 shows that ultimately the players come to realize that the 50–50 split is the best they can do. It is better to split 50–50 on the very first chance they get to make an offer than to lose even a single day's worth of $13 million per day. The league recognized this almost immediately in its calculations. It is the Popsicle game all over again. The payoff from a 50–50 split, reached before the season even begins (i.e., with 151 days left), provides the highest payoff to each party among all the alternatives. Just like kids with a Popsicle, the union and league strike their 50–50 bargains before the season even begins. Work stoppage never enters the consideration.

One Step Toward Reality: Differential Alternatives

The real-world splits are seldom 50–50 between players and owners. Estimates of the actual splits in the major sports leagues are shown in Table 9.2. First of all, players have managed to increase their share of total revenue in all leagues except the NFL. On average, over the tabulated years, players have managed to obtain 61–39 and 60–40 splits in MLB and the NBA, respectively. The NHL also is in the same neighborhood with a 62–38 split. However, NFL players have managed only a 56–44 split. Thus, we do not observe the equal sharing outcome in any given league. It looks like we need to expand our basic bargaining logic just a bit to gain some realism.

In the basic bargaining outcome, owners and players earned nothing on any day that no agreement was reached. But in most cases, even if there is no season, players and owners still have profitable options. On the player side, one famous example is the holdout by Los Angeles Dodgers pitchers Don Drysdale and Sandy Koufax prior to the 1966 season. In 1965, the two players combined to win 49 games while losing only 20. Through the 1960s they simply dominated the entire league. Drysdale led the National League in wins in 1962, Koufax in 1963 and 1965 (and Koufax won the Cy Young Award in each of those seasons as well as the league MVP for 1963). Koufax led the league in ERA over the period 1962–1965 and was the strikeout leader in 1961, 1963, and 1965. Drysdale was an All-Star selection in 1959, and both were All-Stars over the 1961–1965 period.

Table 9.2 Player Costs as a Share of Total Revenue in Pro Team Sports

YEAR	MLB	NBA	NFL	NHL
1991	45	39	47	33
1992	58	44	60	39
1993	57	48	64	41
1994	63	40	64	41
1995	62	46	68	38
1996	54	47	67	51
Earlier Average	57	44	62	41
1999		60		57
2000	58	62	61	57
2001	57	57	56	
2002	67	62	51	66
2003	66	59	55	66
2004	59			
Recent Average	61	60	56	62

Note: Missing values reflect no data. Player costs include deferred payments, bonuses, insurance, workers' compensation, and pensions.

Sources: Financial World, July 7, 1992, pp. 50–51; May 25, 1993, pp. 26–30; May 10, 1994, pp. 50–59; May 9, 1995, pp. 42–56; May 20, 1996, pp. 52–68; June 17, 1997. All data from 1999 on are from forbes.com annual team valuation surveys, except 2001, MLB report is from Commissioner Selig's office.

Did You Know?
Don Drysdale and Sandy Koufax signed movie contracts and threatened to retire from baseball in order to show that their next-best alternative was highly valuable.

Did You Know?
Owners have used replacement players, bought strike insurance, and taken out lines of credit with work stoppages brewing in order to show that the cost of waiting out the stoppage is inconsequential.

According to Drysdale (Drysdale with Verdi, 1990), he and Koufax each earned $80,000 in 1965. The two joined forces in February 1966 after Dodger general manager Buzzie Bavasi tried to play them off against each other. They began their holdout by asking for $1.05 million for the next 3 years to be split evenly between them (about $175,000 each, per year). When Bavasi balked, they threatened retirement. Both signed movie contracts (Drysdale would later become a regular celebrity TV show guest), clearly indicating their intention to enjoy some returns to their sports stardom. Bavasi handed negotiations over to owner Walter O'Malley, who caved on March 30, 1966, giving $130,000 per year to Koufax and $105,000 per year to Drysdale for 3 years.

Actions taken by owners in the 1987 NFL strike and the 1994 MLB strike show that they also have options. During those work stoppages, owners fielded replacement players. It was not pretty on the field (owners did not even buy fitted caps for the replacement baseball players!), but with labor costs way down, profits were earned (at least for a short period). The owners still claimed TV revenues plus what little gate revenue there was. In addition, owners may purchase insurance against revenues lost to a work stoppage or take out a line of credit to indicate their staying power.

A Hypothetical Example of Differential Alternatives Let's suppose that owners have a $5 million per day alternative in the event that no agreement is reached. (They might be able to sell televised music concerts, for example.) We will leave the players' alternative at $0 for now. What happens to the split between the players and the owners? Table 9.3 shows how the logic of thinking about the result on the final day of bargaining and working back toward the present must be altered in the presence of this alternative. With one day left, the union knows that the league can make $5 million even if no agreement is reached. They offer just that amount to

Table 9.3 A Bargaining Scenario When Owners Have a $5 Million Alternative

Days Left	On the Table	Turn	Union's Share ($Millions)		Management's Share ($Millions)	
			Total	Daily	Total	Daily
1	$13 million	Union	$8	$8	$5	$5
2	$26 million	League	$8	$4	$18	$9
3	$39 million	Union	$16	$5.33	$23	$7.67
4	$52 million	League	$16	$4	$36	$9
5	$65 million	Union	$24	$4.8	$41	$8.2
150	$1.95 billion	League	$600 million	$4	$1.35 billion	$9
151	$1.963 billion	Union	$604 million	$4.00	$1.359 billion	$9.00

the owners and keep the rest for a 62–38 split. Comparing the same point in the decision process in Table 9.1, this is a decidedly lower split than the 100–0 split they enjoyed when the owners had no alternative.

With two days left and $26 million on the table, the league must cover the $8 million that the union will make if no agreement is reached and bargaining moves to one day left. They keep the remaining $18 million, a 69–31 split in the league's favor. As happened in Table 9.1, this same 69–31 split confronts the owners whenever it is their turn. Finally, as before, the union realizes that the same 69–31 split is in the offing as it works its way back to the decision period just before the season starts. Therefore, both parties realize that they should go straight to the 69–31 split in favor of the owners and waste nothing in the process. Referring to the Popsicle scenario, with a candy bar to enjoy in the event that your Popsicle negotiation breaks down, your friend would actually be able to parlay that into a larger portion of the Popsicle. Your friend would munch away happily on the alternative goody while you watched the Popsicle melt.

A general observation can be made about this outcome. Owners earned their next-best alternative, plus half of whatever is left. Refer to the outcome in Table 9.3. With $1.963 billion, the total for the season (151 days at $13 million), how does the split work out? Over that same period, the total value of the owners' next-best alternative is $755 million (151 days at $5 million). The total, $1.963 billion, minus $755 million equals $1.208 billion. Splitting that in half equals $604 million. Owners earn $755 million to cover their alternatives and half of the rest, or another $604 million. Their share is 69 percent [(755 + 604)/1963]. Players get the remaining $604 million, for 31 percent.

Of course, players also will have alternative earning possibilities in the event there is no season, and we could go through the same exercise with this factor added. However, there is no need. The same logic extends to cover this additional factor. These **differential alternatives**, where one party to the negotiation is in a better situation than the other if no agreement is reached, must come out of the total. Then the balance is split 50–50. Let X be the amount on the table. U and L are the next-best alternatives for the union and league, respectively. The outcome is that each earns its next-best alternative, plus half of whatever is left after covering both union and league alternatives:

$$\text{Union: } U + 0.5 \times (X - U - L)$$
$$\text{League: } L + 0.5 \times (X - U - L)$$

Each participant earns its respective next-best alternative, U for the union and L for the league. The terms in parentheses equal the amount on the table minus the sum of the parties' next-best alternatives, and each party splits that amount equally. Of course, if $U + L > X$, then both the union and the league are better off pursuing their other alternatives. The opportunity cost of any season at all is too high in this case.

The Simplest Strategy

These expressions prove useful in thinking about strategies that might occur to either party. First, you can see that it pays to get the other side to believe that the value of your next-best alternative is high. If the other side builds in a higher next-best alternative for you, your share rises. Strategically, then, in a world of uncertainty about alternatives, it can pay to convince the other side that your alternatives are great even if they are not. Second, it can be valuable to take actions that affect the size of your opponent's alternatives.

Suppose that the league can take an action that reduces the union's next-best alternative by an amount equal to A. The union result is now:

$$\text{Union: } U + 0.5 \times [X - (U - A) - L] - A$$
$$= U + 0.5 \times (X - U - L) - A + 0.5A$$
$$= U + 0.5 \times (X - U - L) - 0.5A$$

Thus, when the league is able to take such an action, it drives the union's share down by half the amount of the fall in the union's next-highest-valued alternative. Where did that half go? You probably already guessed it, but let's look at the league's result:

$$\text{League: } L + 0.5 \times [X - (U - A) - L]$$
$$= L + 0.5 \times (X - U - L) + 0.5A$$

The league gains exactly half of the decrease in the next-best union alternative. This type of strategic behavior alters shares, but it also helps parties in a bargaining situation determine just how much they are willing to spend in order to alter the next-best alternative of their opponent. The answer is half of the expected decline in the opponent's next-best alternative. Leagues and unions might try to impact each other's alternatives through public relations. They could try placing blame in media statements, ads, and other testimony. The calculation shows that neither party would spend any more than half of the damage they hope to cause with the ads.

WORK STOPPAGES

If both sides have bargained faithfully but still reach an impasse, two types of work stoppages are allowable under the NLRA. Players can **strike**, withholding their services from owners, or owners can confront players with a **lockout**, refusing to allow them to play. Fortunately for fans, despite a rise in frequency lately, the most obvious historical observation is that work stoppages rarely happen in sports. The entire history of work stoppages in all sports, shown in Table 9.4, includes only 16 total occurrences. All but four of these were in baseball and football. Only seven stoppages were of any real duration where games were actually lost to fans. To get a feel for the infrequency of work stoppages, player associations in sports have existed since the mid- to late-1950s—roughly 45 years. With four leagues, that's 180 total years, but collective bargaining agreements have typically been three years in length, leaving 60 total chances for a stoppage. So negotiations precluded a significant work stoppage 53 of 60 times, an 88 percent "success" rate.

The basic bargaining model does not explain why strikes and lockouts occur. We will have to look for additional elements in the bargaining process to find the causes.

Strikes and lockouts happen for basically two reasons. First, even though they sincerely wish for no work stoppage, one side or the other may miscalculate amounts

Table 9.4 The History of Work Stoppages in Professional Sports

Year	Episode
MLB	
1969	Spring training delay/strike
1972	2-week player walkout
1976	Spring training lockout
1981	3-month strike (season shortened to fewer than 60 game "first half" and fewer than 55 game "second half")
1985	2-day strike
1990	1-month lockout
1994–1995	Partial season 2004 (ends after about 114 games), League Championship Series 2004, World Series 2004, and Partial Season 2005 (reduced to 149 games) strike
NBA	
1998	Partial season lockout (50 game season played)
NFL	
1968	10-day training camp lockout
1970	20-day training camp lockout
1974	42-day training camp strike
1982	2-month strike (9 game season played)
1987	1-month strike (15 game season played)
NHL	
1992	10-day player walkout
1994	103-day lockout (about 45 game season played)
2004	Full season and playoff lockout (in progress at press)

on the table or the value of their opponent's next-best alternative. The second reason for a work stoppage is that it simply can be worth it, in terms of expected value, to force such a stoppage.

Sincerity, Asymmetric Information, and Misrepresentation

To see how a work stoppage can occur due to miscalculation, suppose the true amount on the table really is $13 million per day, as in the hypothetical example we used earlier in this chapter. However, if only the league knows this amount with certainty, then the union can only offer and respond based on its estimate of that amount. This is a classic case of **asymmetric information**, where one side of the negotiations knows something that the other does not. In this case of asymmetric information on the part of the league, if the union estimates were wrong, the league would refuse union offers, not because the union or league is trying to pull a fast one but because the union simply lacks information. Work stops, not because that was the intent of either party but because of the uncertainty inherent in the process.

This type of miscalculation is further complicated when negotiators use **strategic misrepresentation** of their next-best alternatives. Strategic misrepresentation means that each side will try to make the other side believe that they will enjoy the better situation in the event no agreement is reached. Suppose the league's next-best alternative really is $5 million, as portrayed in the last section. However, the union knows that the league has every incentive to overstate its next-best alternative. Thus, the union discounts the league's claim, estimating it at $2 million instead. The union makes an offer that covers their estimate of the league's next-best alternative, but the league refuses to accept the offer. The $2 million is not enough to cover the league's next-best alternative. However, the union thinks the league is just posturing and sticks to its guns. Work stops. Again, uncertainty plays a role with the added complexity of strategic posturing of alternatives.

The Expected Value of a Work Stoppage

The second reason for a strike or lockout is that the expected value of such a work stoppage may simply be worth it to one side or the other. In this case, one side of the negotiations really does want a work stoppage, not because of information differences, miscalculation, or strategic posturing but because it will be a **profitable work stoppage**.

For reasons that will become apparent shortly, let's index time during the stoppage as $t = 0, 1, 2, \ldots, S$. After the stoppage, time runs from $t = S + 1, S + 2, \ldots, T$, so that T is the end of the planning horizon. Because a time element is involved, we will need to have r_t as the interest rate at time t during and after the stoppage. Finally, let P equal the probability that the stoppage is successful and $1 - P$ the probability that it is not.

Values and Costs of a Work Stoppage Four elements must be considered here. First, A is the alternative value open to the decision maker. Owners might be able to play games using replacement players or rent out their facilities. Players may be able to capitalize for a while on their fame through more guest appearances and endorsement activity. Because these alternatives are earned during the stoppage, from $t = 0, \ldots, S$, we write:

$$A = \sum_{t=0}^{S} \frac{A_t}{(1 + r_t)^t}$$

Second, M is the up-front money cost borne by the side declaring the work stoppage. This could be lost income to players or lost revenues to owners because no games are played during the stoppage. These losses also are borne during the stoppage, $t = 0, \ldots, S$. Therefore, we would write:

$$M = \sum_{t=0}^{S} \frac{M_t}{(1 + r_t)^t}$$

The third element, G, is the possible gain from the stoppage. For players, it may be a reduction in the number of years to free agency or a larger percentage of revenue in a salary cap situation. For owners, just the opposite would be gains. Gains come from concessions by the other side after the stoppage is over, $t = S, \ldots, T$. Therefore, we would write:

$$G = \sum_{t=0}^{T} \frac{G_t}{(1 + r_t)^t}$$

Last, F is losses at time t due to fan repercussions after the stoppage. With any extended stoppage, fans may hold it against leagues and players that interrupt play. It was widely hypothesized that MLB suffered dramatically at the gate after its strike cost fans part of the 1994 season, all of the 1994 League Championship Series, and the 1994 World Series. *Time* (August 22, 1994, p. 71) reported a survey showing that fans blame owners and players about equally and believe that owners' profits are too high and players make too much money. A *Baseball America* (December 23, 1996–January 5, 1997, p. 26) survey reported the same blame routine, as well as a drop from 9.5 to 8.1 on the "1–10 scale of interest in baseball." These costs are only lately the point of economic analysis. For example, Schmidt and Berri (2004) find that the attendance impacts of work stoppages in pro sports are only temporary at best. But in our formulation, we'll allow that fans may not happy when their sport is withheld from them, and they may exercise their wrath after the stoppage is over, $t = S, \ldots, T$. For these losses, we write:

$$F = \sum_{t=S}^{T} \frac{F_t}{(1 + r_t)}$$

Now let's look at the state of things in the event that the stoppage is successful. If successful, then the winner earns $A - M + G - F$, but this only happens with probability P. In the event the stoppage is unsuccessful, the loser nets $A - (M + F)$. This gives the following expected value of a work stoppage EV_S:

$$EV_S = P(A - M + G - F) + (1 - P)[A - (M + F)]$$

If we combine like terms and simplify, we get a simple expression full of insight:

$$EV_S = (P \times G - M) + (A - F)$$

The expected value of a work stoppage is determined by the expected net gain $(P \times G - M)$, adjusted by the balance of the next best alternative and fan costs. Figure 9.3 depicts the relationship graphically. Note that the y-intercept for our expected value is negative; if the alternative, net of fan costs, exceeded the value of running the season, then the owners should pursue the alternative. Note also that a particularly interesting interpretation can be attached to the point where the EV_S function crosses the x-axis. That point is labeled P_{BE}, for the breakeven probability. At this breakeven probability, the expected value of the work stoppage is zero. But this also serves to highlight that any probability greater than P_{BE} generates a positive expected value. Put another way, if the chances of winning are less than P_{BE}, then the work stoppage isn't worth it. Let's turn to a numerical example.

Suppose $G = \$500$ million, $M = \$200$ million, $A = \$100$ million, and $F = \$100$ million. We can actually solve for the breakeven probability in this case. If

Figure 9.3 The Expected Value of a Work Stoppage

The expected value of a work stoppage, EV_S, depends on the probability of winning, P. For $P > P_{BE}$, $EV_S > 0$. But if $P < P_{BE}$, the chances of winning are such that $EV_S < 0$, and forcing a work stoppage simply will not pay. If the lost value, M, declines, or the next best alternative, A, increases relative to later fan costs, F, then EV_S shifts upward. The same will happen if the length of the stoppage declines or interest rates decline.

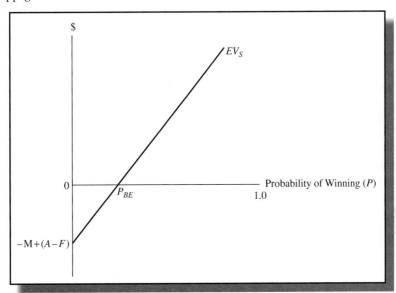

we just remember from Figure 9.3 that $EV_S = 0$ when $P = P_{BE}$, we can rearrange and get:

$$P_{BE} = [M - (A - F)]/G$$

Now just plug in the example values and see that $P_{BE} = 0.40$. Thus, if the chance of winning is less than 40 percent, it is not in this decision maker's best financial interest to force the stoppage. The possible gains, net of the up-front costs and any future losses due to fan irritation, just are not worth it.

Did You Know?
Work stoppages may happen due to misjudgments by players or owners. They may also happen just because one side or the other calculates that it would be profitable to force a stoppage.

But what determines whether the chances of winning the work stoppage are greater than P_{BE}? From the economic perspective, it all depends upon the ability to weather a stoppage. This single factor has the greatest impact on the eventual outcome. It is sort of like a medieval castle siege. Each side measures the other's ability to withstand the siege. The victor will be the one that lasts the longest, and the other side will be out a tremendous amount of resources.

Finally, using Figure 9.3, we can assess how changes in expected gains, costs, and some underlying parameters will alter EV_S. First, if the gain increases, our function pivots to the left, raising EV_S for all values of P. If $A - F$ increases relative to M, the function shifts up in a parallel fashion, raising EV_S. Clearly, if M increases relative to $A - F$, then EV_S shifts down. Turning to the other parameters in the explicitly discounted future values listed above, if the duration of the stoppage, S, rises or the interest rate, r, rises, all else constant, current costs become more important relative to future net gains, and the expected value falls.

We'll use this logic to get a handle on the NBA lockout of 1998. In addition, we'll use it to gain insight about the work stoppage in the NHL, that began in late 2004. But let's approach these recent episodes from within the context of the overall history of labor relations in pro sports, beginning with MLB.

LABOR RELATIONS IN MLB

In MLB, once the reserve clause was firmly entrenched in the late 1800s, players could be sold, traded, and released as management saw fit. Because players' next-best choices were outside their sport in the presence of the reserve clause, owners had the upper hand. Players had to be paid enough to keep them in their sport, but not much more than that.

John Montgomery Ward formed the Brotherhood of Professional Baseball Players around 1885 and the Players League in 1890. This "Brotherhood Revolt" involved about 200 of the greatest players of their time. But, as we saw in Chapter 8, ideals do not stand much of a chance against the concerted economic forces of owners acting together through sports leagues. The Players League lasted only a year.

Did You Know?

One of the earliest job actions in sports occurred when Detroit Tigers players struck in support of their teammate Ty Cobb, who had been suspended for one of his infamous acts of temper.

There were other early attempts at player organization, but labor strife in MLB was pretty much confined to infrequent confrontations between individual players and particular team owners. One early attempt at organized player labor action in baseball centered on the legendary Ty Cobb. For an act of temper (Cobb entered the stands attempting to beat up a heckler), Cobb was suspended 10 days in 1912. In baseball's first organized work stoppage, the Detroit players struck in support of Cobb, and union sentiment spread among other American League teams. However, the resulting Baseball Players Fraternity failed 5 years later because it could not produce any economic gains from owners for players.

After a long organized labor hiatus, the American Baseball Guild formed in 1946 out of the turmoil caused by the one-year stint of the Mexican League. Players were jumping to the Mexican League, breaking their current MLB contracts despite a promised 5-year banishment. As players jumped, MLB grew cautious and actually began to talk to the guild. As a result, it was recognized as an official bargaining unit under federal law and negotiated minimum salaries and a pension plan. The guild was also instrumental in negotiating the return of former MLB players after the demise of the Mexican League.

Did You Know?

In its infancy, MLBPA meeting expenses and executive director expenses were paid by MLB in direct violation of federal labor law.

The modern MLBPA began in 1954. It was not an official federally recognized bargaining unit but continued the pursuit of a better player pension plan funded out of All-Star Game and World Series revenues. However, the organization was impotent on the main issues confronting players, namely the reserve clause and player grievances. Further, the original MLBPA was dominated so much by owners that they appointed the director and paid the association's bills, which was patently illegal under labor law.

All of this changed with the hiring of Marvin Miller in 1966. He immediately ended the illegal funding by owners and quickly got to work reforming the pension system. The player pension system is now funded by a negotiated contribution from owners. In a second important stride forward for MLB players, the formal grievance procedure was instituted in the first real Basic Agreement in 1968. The 1970 agreement allowed for a three-person review of grievances, one each from MLB and MLBPA plus a permanent independent chair. MLB has no salary cap, but currently employs the rest of the items used across other leagues under collective bargaining.

Arbitration

Owners hate arbitration. Owners gave it to the players in 1974 because they were afraid of all-out free agency. After the famous court case that denied Curt Flood free agency in 1972, owners feared the worst in the subsequent collective bargaining process. In gaining arbitration, the players, in turn, agreed to put off free agency to a study group. However, the owners opened the equivalent of Pandora's Box with arbitration.

Did You Know?
Although there are legitimate reasons for owners to hate the arbitration process, they do end up winning the majority of arbitration decisions.

Few players actually exercise their arbitration rights, and owners typically win more cases than the players. According to James Dworkin (1997), over the 20-year period of 1974 to 1994, only 375 cases went before arbitrators (just under 19 cases per year, on average). In 1994, of 16 arbitration cases 10 ended in the owners' favor and six in the players' favor. These 16 cases represented only 10 percent of all players eligible for arbitration. The largest number in any year was 35 in 1986, but there were only nine in 1978. Through 1994, clubs won 209 times and players only 166. That is a 56 percent advantage in the favor of owners.

Just keeping a tally misses the point about the winners in arbitration. Players win just because arbitration is available to them. Data on salaries show that, relative to years prior to arbitration, just filing has resulted in a doubling of salary even for those players who never go to arbitration. The threat of arbitration has revealed that owners fear those 44 percent of the outcomes that they lose. Thus, they raise salaries to avoid arbitration. It is precisely because arbitration does what it is designed to do (force bargaining in earnest prior to any filing for arbitration) that owners hate it.

The MLB Draft/Entry System

All leagues have drafts subject to collective bargaining. MLB's draft began in 1965. The main difference in drafts across leagues is in the number of rounds. In MLB, each team drafts approximately 30 players. There are no supplemental rounds. Baseball allows players to be drafted after they finish high school. Unlike other sports, college players can return to their university teams even if they enter the draft. No eligibility is forfeited. There is no draft for international players, who are scouted and signed subject to age restrictions, just as U.S. players were before 1965. There are no restrictions on entry-level pay, in stark contrast to the other three leagues, as we shall soon see.

Free Agency

As we saw in Chapter 8, the arbitration procedure eventually led to the end of the reserve clause. Free agency clearly has been the major win for any players' union.

Did You Know?
It took three rounds of collective bargaining, covering 1976–1984, before owners and players in MLB settled on a stable system of free agency.

Interestingly, it took quite a bit of trial and error to get to the modern version of free agency. During the lockout of 1976, owners and players designed the first among many versions of free agency through collective bargaining. In the 1976 Basic Agreement, players with 6 years of experience were free agents but had to wait 5 years to become free agents a second time. Further, teams gaining a free agent compensated the team losing the player with a draft pick.

In the next go-round, disagreement over free agency and compensation led to the strike of 1981. The compromise for the 1981 Basic Agreement defined a Type A free agent as a player in the top 20 percent of performance at his position. Any team gaining a Type A free agent had to put all but 24 of its own players into a pool from which teams losing a Type A free agent would draw their compensation (not necessarily from the team signing the free agent). Teams not gaining a Type A free agent could protect 26 players. An exemption could be issued if a team promised not to chase Type A free agents for 3 years. The 6-year rule and draft choice compensation also remained.

For the 1984 Basic Agreement, all compensation was eliminated, except for the draft pick for Type A free agents. For Type B free agents (the next 10 percent of players by performance at their position), an extra pick was sandwiched between the first and second rounds of the next draft. This is where the situation now stands. Players with fewer than 4 years in the league are completely restricted, without free agency or arbitration. Their situation is the same as under the reserve clause of old.

Guaranteed Contracts

Player contracts in MLB are guaranteed. This means that even if players are injured and cannot continue to play, they still are paid the remaining obligation in their contract. Again, this isn't true in all pro sports leagues, as we will see shortly.

The "Luxury" Tax

MLB actually names their "luxury tax" the Competitive Balance Tax. Owners who spend more than $128 million on payroll in 2005 will pay a tax rate of 22.5 percent. For 2006, the last year of the current agreement, the threshold is $136.5 million, but no tax is paid if surpassing it is a first offense. All second offenders pay 30 percent and third-time offenders pay 40 percent.

Revenue Sharing

Thirty-four percent of each team's locally generated revenue, including gate receipts and local TV revenue, goes into a central fund. The amount is net of stadium costs, either direct or in terms of interest payments. The money is split equally among all

30 teams. In 2004, it was expected that $280 million would be redistributed from large-revenue to small-revenue teams.

Work Stoppages At the 2001 Washington University conference on the business of baseball, current executive director of the MLBPA, Donald Fehr, repeated a statement I had heard from him before: "Owners have always said two things about baseball; there is never enough pitching and no owner ever made any money." As we have seen in other chapters in this book, owners always plead poor in negotiations with players, especially those that have ultimately ended in work stoppages.

As shown in Table 9.4, early work stoppages in MLB were short and of literally no consequence to fans. In 1969, a spring training delay strike preceded the players obtaining a grievance panel. The 10-day season delay strike in 1972 over a pension dispute preceded the players gaining arbitration. Owners locked players out in 1976 in the dispute over free agency, but it ended up that nothing could stop the demise of the reserve clause.

Did You Know?
The 1981 MLBPA strike lasted long enough to cause MLB to devise a split-season playoff system wherein the first-half winners met the second-half winners to determine the eventual postseason matchups.

Things got much uglier from the fan perspective with the 1981 strike. The issue was still free agency—owners wanted compensation for lost free agents. Owners hunkered down for the long haul, buying $50 million in strike insurance to add to a $15 million strike fund from owner contributions over the preceding 2 years. Players lived on solidarity. The strike lasted 50 days. By all accounts, the players won, yielding little on compensation for lost free agents. The result of so many lost games was the infamous split-season playoff system. The winners of the "first half" of the season (before the strike) played the winners of the "second half" (after the strike) to determine the overall postseason setup.

In 1985, the list of contentious issues included contributions to the players' pension fund from TV revenue (the national contract had exploded to over $1 billion, and owners were balking at their then existing 33 percent contribution), compensation requirements for lost free agents, and minimum salary increases. The result was a 2-day strike that had nearly no impact on fans. Owner contributions to the pension fund doubled (even though percentage decreased); players won arbitration after 3 years; and the minimum salary was increased from $40,000 to $60,000. Owners also gained further redefinition of free agents that continued the practice of compensating owners who lost free agents to other teams.

The lockout in 1990 was over the maximum share of league revenues that could go to players (owners offered 48 percent of ticket and national and local TV revenues), a seniority pay scale, and a salary cap. Players responded with 2 years to arbitration, double the minimum salary, continuation of the owners' fixed contribution to the players' pension plan, collusion protection language, and an increase to 25 players on the roster. The players won, hands down, and got nearly everything they wanted. The season was just pushed back to make up for the lost start time, so nothing was lost in the eyes of fans.

The **MLBPA strike of 1994** was the "mother of all strikes." Using a reopener clause from earlier negotiations, owners wanted broader revenue sharing among themselves but only if the players accepted a cap of the NBA variety. The owners also wanted the end of arbitration, offering a reduction to 4 years for free agency eligibility in return. Players struck in August, when it was best for them. They had nearly all of their annual salary while the owners were looking forward to the playoffs. The playoffs and World Series were lost, and no end was in sight even after the scheduled start of the 1995 season.

The owners could see they were getting nowhere and changed their demands. The union would go along with the revenue-sharing idea, but not the cap. Owners withdrew the cap demand, substituting a luxury tax plan. Players countered with a different luxury tax that reduced player salaries by less. Owners countered that they would continue the season with replacement players.

In the meantime, the MLBPA filed a grievance with the NLRB claiming that the owners had blocked arbitration and free agency. MLBPA Executive Director Donald Fehr said players would return if the courts issued an injunction against these owner actions. The NLRB agreed and the District Court issued the injunction. Fehr announced the end of the strike. The owners could have continued the stoppage with a lockout but chose not to do so. Only 144 games were played in the 1995 season, rather than the usual 162.

LABOR RELATIONS IN THE NBA

In basketball, eventual Hall of Famer Bob Cousy was instrumental in the 1954 formation of the NBPA. As was the case in football, NBA owners simply ignored the NBPA at first. Nevertheless, the NBPA gained momentum under Lawrence Fleisher, beginning in 1962. Solidarity rose and the players gained some ground with a pension fund in 1964. In 1967, the NBPA threatened to seek official federal government recognition as a bargaining unit if the pension plan was not bolstered. Under that threat, the league agreed to the NBPA's demands. The collective bargaining agreement signed that year was the first in all of pro sports. In 1970, minimum salaries were established. The NBA has no arbitration, and all player contracts are guaranteed regardless of injury. In addition, only the national TV contract proceeds are shared; there is no other revenue sharing in the NBA.

The Draft/Entry Restrictions

The NBA has two draft rounds, usually drafting 58 players. Since 1985, the first important picks have been determined by a lottery, with the number of chances based on a team's past performance. For example, the first 14 picks in the 2004 NBA draft were determined by the lottery, and the Orlando Magic had the first pick. The remaining draft order was based on the previous year's standings. The NBA has no special relations with other entities concerning restrictions on draft eligibility. Players can be drafted after they finish high school, and all college players are considered fair game.

There also are other entry restrictions on contract length and pay for new players. For example, there are fixed 3-year contracts, plus an option year, for first-round draft picks based on the rank of their selection. Rookie salaries also are controlled under a rookie wage.

Free Agency

In 1970, thanks to a lawsuit by legend Oscar Robertson, NBA players won free agency. In 1981, all compensation to teams losing free agents ended. Unrestricted free agency began in 1988 for players who had played in the league for more than 4 years. Earlier, players with more than 4 years were restricted free agents. The restriction was that the team could match an outside offer and retain the player. In addition, no compensation was required if the team chose not to exercise this right of first refusal. Currently, even the right of first refusal is gone; players simply are free to sell their services to the highest bidder after 4 years.

The "Luxury" Tax

The NBA has an interesting variation on prohibitions of spending on players. Teams are taxed dollar-for-dollar at payrolls above a threshold level that changes over the course of the collective bargaining agreement. But the tax kicks in only if *league-wide* player salaries exceed a specified percentage of NBA revenue. Some of the onus is on the players to keep salaries down. Portions of their salary are held in an account that is returned to owners to help them pay if the league exceeds the tax threshold.

Payroll Cap

The NBA salary cap is the longest standing cap in pro sports, firmly entrenched since the 1982–1983 season. The NBA cap until very recently was referred to as a soft cap. It had built-in exceptions, such as the famous "Larry Bird rule." These exceptions allowed teams to keep their own free agents regardless of their impact on team salary relative to the cap. As you saw in Chapter 6, NBA teams rarely were anywhere near the cap amount. The cap was toughened significantly in 1998. However, as you also saw in Chapter 6, it still is not working. The Learning Highlight: Another Kind of Cap Cheating shows yet another way that the cap poses problems for all involved.

Work Stoppages

The NBA was always held up as the only league without a stoppage. But there has been labor unrest. Basketball decertified its NBPA in 1995; however, the NBPA leadership was none too happy about it. Although the NFLPA had been instrumental in decertifying itself, as we will see, the leaders of the NBPA fought tooth and nail to hold onto their power. Important players like Michael Jordan and Patrick Ewing collected petitions from a majority of players, decertifying the union in 1995. They then brought suit against the NBA alleging that any joint action over NBA players by NBA owners—be it a lockout or a continuation of the salary cap—violated antitrust laws.

LEARNING HIGHLIGHT
Another Kind of Cap Cheating

We saw in Chapter 6 that the cap is fairly ineffective in both the NBA and the NFL. Here we present another way owners circumvent the cap. Remember that the cap is determined relative to defined gross revenue. It ends up that in the NBA, the owners were caught understating these shared revenues by the players.

In 1991, independent auditor Charles Bennett discovered a problem. He was poring over trial documents from a 1990 antitrust suit brought by Chicago Bulls owner Jerry Reinsdorf against the league, challenging its local TV rules. Reinsdorf wanted his Bulls to be on TV more than league agreements allowed. In the documents, Bennett discovered that the owners had underreported defined gross revenues by nearly $100 million, thereby short-changing players in salary cap determinations.

The league contended that it was not *defined* gross revenue and, therefore, did not need to be reported. However, the league

settled with the players in 1992 for a sum reported around the missing $100 million. Bennett was immediately hired by the NFLPA and, according to one NFLPA official, helped push up the 1994 cap by nearly $1 million per team.

By suing his own league, Chicago Bulls owner Jerry Reinsdorf unwittingly revealed that the league had shortchanged players in salary cap determinations.

Source: Sports Illustrated, April 28, 1994, p. 10.

Did You Know?
Despite being decertified by its membership in 1995, the leaders of the NBPA refused to step down. The NLRB had to step in and call for a new election to decertify the union, and the majority of players voted to retain the union.

However, the NBPA did not step down after decertification. It continued negotiating with the owners as if the petitions decertifying the union had never been circulated or collected. In these wacky proceedings, you had the majority of NBA players who supported the suit and decertifying the NBPA on one side, and on the other side, you had the never-say-die NBPA and the owners negotiating with each other! The NLRB called for a new election. The NBA openly announced that decertifying the union would lead to an immediate lockout. Apparently this changed the minds of many players, and the majority voted to retain the union. A new collective bargaining agreement was reached in 1996.

The long-standing absence of work stoppages in the NBA ended as the 1998–1999 season was about to begin. Claiming that players received 57 percent of total revenues in the 1997–1998 season, the owners exercised a clause in the NBA basic agreement that allowed renewed negotiations if the players' share reached these levels. Negotiations were opened but ended in disaster.

The NBA owners announced there would be no 1998–1999 season unless some new agreement was reached that tightened the cap. They would lock the players out. The players did not budge.

Based on our discussion earlier in this chapter, it can be shown that the owners may have locked out the players in a move to increase profits. (The following example, attributable to Roger Noll, first appeared in Quirk and Fort [1999]). Let's think about the revenues lost from a lockout, denoted M in our earlier analysis. First, suppose an entire season were lost, that is, S = one season. The NBA was a $1.7 billion industry just prior to the 1998 dispute. There was $700 million at the gate, $637 million from TV contracts, $225 in venue revenues, and $160 million in other revenues. The 57 percent going to players would amount to $969 million. That leaves $731 million for owners. About 30 percent, or $510 million, would typically go to other expenses, leaving the owners 13 percent, or $221 million. Thinking in terms of a one-season stoppage, M = $221 million.

What about the cost of fan irritation? This cost would have to be figured into the arithmetic of a lockout, and we do not know this value. Therefore, the losses of a one-year stoppage are $221 million, plus the losses that would be caused by hard feelings on the part of fans.

What about the gains? Suppose that the owners are shooting for a 50–50 split. A reduction in the players' share from 57 to 50 percent is worth $119 million per year. Although we have to guess about the planning horizon, let's suppose it is 10 years, that is, T = 10. This amounts to $1.19 billion, but we must discount those dollars to present value. At 6 percent, the discounted present value is G = $876 million. Further, even though the alternatives might be small, there is no reason to suspect that owners would not take their resources to a next-best use. The value of these alternative uses would offset the losses. However, data on these alternative values are unavailable.

Without knowledge of fan irritation costs or alternative opportunity values, the expected value of a lockout boils down to a pretty simple comparison. The owners had to consider whether it was worth it to risk $221 million in hopes of gaining $876 million. That expected value would be written:

$$EV_S = (P \times 876 - 221) + (A - F)$$

Now we reach the point where P looms large in the decision. Although owners might have their own idea of the probability of winning from a work stoppage, let's have a quick look at the breakeven probability of winning the lockout. Setting EV_S = 0, the breakeven probability is:

$$P_{BE} = M/G - (A - F)/G = 0.25 - (A - F)/876$$

We can see that owners will consider the breakeven probability of 25 percent, give or take the net of the next best alternative over fan costs, divided by the gain. For every dollar that the next best alternative exceeds fan costs, the breakeven probability falls by 1/876, or 0.11 percent. If the owners think there is less than this breakeven chance that the players will fold, then the expected value of a lockout is less than zero and clearly not worth it.

Did You Know?
Reasonable calculations
support the idea that the
NBA lockout of its players
in 1998 was a rational
move based strictly on
the profitability of the
gains that owners could
get from players.

Let's suppose that the owners believe it is a coin toss, that is, a 50–50 chance that the union will fold. In this case, the expected value becomes $217 million, plus $(A - F)$. Quite plainly, even if owners had no next best alternative, fan costs would have to be nearly the entire value of a complete season in order to drive EV_S to zero. We are left to suspect that NBA owners felt that at least a couple of hundred million dollars could be won from players with an effective lockout. In any event, the owners did lock out the players for a portion of the 1998 season.

Much was made of the idea that owners needed to harden the salary cap in order to obtain some degree of cost predictability. However, it is difficult to justify that the owners needed any change in the cap at all. In 1998, there were 29 NBA team owners. Suppose that the owners shared all of the league revenue equally. That would have been about $58.6 million per team ($1.7 billion/29). Even if nothing were done to enforce the cap and players continued to receive 57 percent of total revenue, that still would leave each team with $25.2 million on average ($58.6 million − $33.4 million). Even after the 30 percent or so that goes to other nonplayer costs, $7.6 million per team remains ($25.2 million − $17.6 million). Thus, an alternative to hardening the cap would be to share revenues.

But why should they share revenues if they can reduce costs by reducing the players' share of revenues? Beside, the New York Knicks, Chicago Bulls, Los Angeles Lakers, Detroit Pistons, Portland Trailblazers, and Boston Celtics all were making more than $7.6 million. The chance that these dominant teams would share the wealth with their weaker cohorts is pretty slim. It would make more sense, economically, for these large-revenue market mainstays just to form a separate league. And so the result was the **NBA lockout of 1998**.

How did the lockout go? Owners demanded a hard cap, doing away with the Larry Bird exemption that allowed a team to exceed the cap in order to retain its own free agents (that is how Michael Jordan could earn $33 million in his last year when the cap was only $26.9 million). In essence, the owners wanted no deviation at all from the agreed upon 52 percent to players. Owners also wanted to lengthen rookie contracts from 3 to 5 years, with only the first 3 guaranteed unconditionally.

The NBPA wanted no change in either the soft cap or rookie contracts. It also wanted to increase the minimum salary for veteran players to $272,250. Finally, the NBPA wanted to change the so-called team exception. The exception enabled a team to sign one free agent for $1 million every 2 years. The NBPA wanted to alter the exception to an annual signing at $2 million to $3 million.

Talks began in earnest in April 1998. By the end of June, negotiations were still going nowhere, and the NBA announced its lockout. Toward the end of August, arbitration hearings began on whether owners had to pay guaranteed contracts, totaling about $800 million, during the lockout. This would have changed the alternatives available to players and altered the balance of power during the lockout. By October, the NBA announced that there would be no exhibition season. On October 13, bargaining resumed but lasted only a few hours. The NBA announced cancellation of 99 regular season games, lost to all teams in the first 2 weeks of the season. Shortly thereafter, the NBPA capitulated and the owners pretty much got their way.

Labor Relations in the NFL

The first football union, the NFLPA, was formed in 1956. Owners were reluctant to even recognize the NFLPA, a typical response by owners at the inception of player organizations. However, the threat of antitrust suits brought football owners around pretty quickly. Minimum salaries were established in 1957, and a pension plan funded by owners began in 1959. Interestingly, the union did not achieve official federal bargaining unit recognition from the NLRB until 1968. It was a short-time affiliate of the AFL-CIO in 1979.

The NFLPA did not really flex its muscle until it shut down training camps in 1974. Player safety was always of primary concern to the NFLPA, and it made the use of artificial turf an element of the bargaining process (turf-related injuries had to be covered in health care plans).

The NFLPA has never relinquished its rights to negotiate individual salaries. It has never exercised those rights, however, choosing instead to allow football players and their agents to handle this task. The NFL has no salary arbitration, and unlike either MLB or the NBA, player contracts are not guaranteed. Teams can cut players at any time with no future obligations except to cover any remaining signing bonuses. There also is no luxury tax approach in the NFL.

The Draft/Entry Restrictions

The NFL draft has been in existence since the 1930s. The 2001 NFL draft had seven rounds with 246 players total. After the draft, the remaining new players enter the league as free agents. The NFL draft is restricted to college juniors and older, provided they renounce their remaining college eligibility. The league argues that drafting only upperclassmen protects players from tragic career mistakes. However, NFL owners really are protecting themselves from the wrath of colleges that could sue or adopt their own rules that would be worse. Previous NFL rules against drafting any but those who had finished their college eligibility were struck down by the courts.

NFL rookie salaries also are limited. Under collective bargaining agreements, rookies are subject to a cap within a cap. About 3.5 percent of defined gross revenues make up the "entering player pool." Unlike the share of defined gross revenue that goes to the rest of the players, the entering player pool is allocated across teams according to the level of their draft picks. Teams with higher draft picks can allocate a larger share of the pool than teams with lower picks. However, because the amount is restricted, it is less than otherwise would be spent on new players.

Free Agency

The NFL had a completely hamstrung form of free agency beginning in the late 1950s. Players were free agents at the end of their contract, plus 1 option year. However, no player ever changed teams under this arrangement. Owners simply did not sign free agents. Later, free agents sued the league for this behavior and won in the courts. In response, NFL Commissioner Pete Rozelle designed a system of compensation to teams losing free agents. This compensation, coined the **Rozelle Rule** in honor of its inventor, effectively stymied free agent movement. The level of required compensation was simply larger than the value of acquiring a free agent.

NFL players eventually won free agency by suing as individuals under the antitrust laws. Because individual players forfeit their individual rights to sue when they choose leagues as collective bargaining agents, the only way this could happen was if the union no longer represented players. The NFLPA was decertified in the battle for unrestricted free agency so that players could pursue better legal chances under the antitrust laws.

In the late 1980s and early 1990s, labor relations were going nowhere for the NFLPA. They lost in 1987 when the owners used replacement players to break a strike. The NFLPA also lost important court cases aimed at free agency. In 1989, the union decertified and became a trade association rather than a legally recognized union. The union did this by petition. A majority of NFL players agreed to withdraw the NFLPA's authority as a collective bargaining unit. This move allowed the trade association to support individual players trying to use all means possible to gain free agency. Of course, these means could not include collective bargaining because the union had been decertified. However, they could include antitrust suits, and one such suit eventually prevailed for players. The union then certified again and bargained for free agency and the salary cap.

The lawsuit that eventually forced the NFL owners to free agency is the now-famous 1992 case *McNeil v. NFL.* The bone of contention at that time was Plan B. Under Plan B, instituted some years earlier by the NFL owners in the absence of collective bargaining, teams could protect up to 37 players from free agency. Only the remaining, weaker players then entered free agency. If another team reached an agreement with a protected player, the team could offer that player the same salary and keep the player. If it did not match the offer, then the receiving team paid the losing team compensation for the lost player (two first-round draft picks). Needless to say, players argued that Plan B had a stifling effect on salaries, especially the salaries of the top players protected under Plan B. You can probably guess how the owners justified Plan B. That's right. It was essential to maintaining competitive balance in the league and it enhanced fan welfare.

Individual players, including New York Jets running back Freeman McNeil, argued that even if Plan B did help competitive balance, a less restrictive approach would accomplish the same ends. The players successfully showed that even run-of-the-mill players achieved restricted status, proving the plan was too restrictive. Further, the players showed that unrestricted players often received greater salary increases than players who were identified as better by being protected. Among other evidence, the players also noted that no such restrictions on coaches and administrators appeared necessary to preserve competitive balance.

The jury sided with the players. The jury found that Plan B harmed competition for player services. It also found that Plan B was too restrictive even though it aided competitive balance. The jury suggested that a less restrictive approach would produce the same balance results. Freeman McNeil and the rest of the players named in the suit won compensation. This case brought negotiations back into the realm of collective bargaining.

The amount of time required for unrestricted free agency was set to slide with the amount of time left on the collective bargaining agreement reached the next year, 1993. Early in the agreement, unrestricted free agency happened after 4 years. As the agreement has aged, the amount of time to unrestricted free agency has increased to 5 years. Players in year 4 of their contract are restricted free agents. Teams can meet outside offers, and draft choice compensation is required if one of these restricted free agents is lost to another team.

The Payroll Cap

The NFL salary cap also came out of the 1993 agreement between players and owners. After the lawsuit over free agency, the cap details were worked out through collective bargaining. With this agreement, a negotiated share of defined gross revenues goes toward player salaries. Those shared revenues are then divided evenly among all teams, yielding a maximum amount a team can spend on its players. Rules determine how the amount spent on each player counts against this cap amount; some elements of player compensation, such as signing bonuses and deferred payments, receive special treatment in the accounting process. In addition, the cap establishes a minimum amount of spending. Otherwise, spending could not be equalized across teams and the point of the cap would be undone.

If a team is over the cap, the commissioner steps in and enforces it. If a team falls below the minimum, the commissioner steps in, and players on that team are compensated at the end of the season. If the commissioner and the teams cannot resolve these issues, they move to mediation and the courts.

The NFL cap supposedly was a hard cap, but loopholes such as signing bonuses and deferred compensation have led to routine spending in excess of the calculated cap amount. According to cap rules, only salary counted. Bonuses and deferrals did not. The incentive was for players take their compensation as bonuses, and teams could then spread their cap spending farther. Furthermore, compensation could come in so many ways that it was difficult to track.

For example, in 1995, Miami Dolphins' quarterback Dan Marino purchased stock in Republic Waste Industries on the advice of Dolphins owner Wayne Huizenga. So did head coach Don Shula and general manager Eddie Jones. Huizenga then bought the company, and the stock value increased dramatically. Marino invested $390,000 at the starting price of $4.50 per share. After the purchase by Huizenga, the price rose to around $21.75 per share. Marino's gain was a cool $1.5 million (News and Observer Publication Co. Web site, www.newsobserver.com, August 31, 1995).

This transaction was possibly a violation of the cap rules. All payments, direct and indirect, by the team owner to players count under the NFL's salary cap. Commissioner Paul Tagliabue vowed there would be a "thorough look" into any possibility of cap violations in this transaction. If this was a compensation payment, the risks were large. Marino's contract could have been voided and a $2 million fine levied against the owner of the Dolphins.

Subsequent adjustments to the cap language removed some of these issues. Owners now are responsible for prorated portions of bonuses under the cap. In addition, the remaining portions of prorated bonuses still count against the original owner's cap amounts.

Revenue Sharing

The NFL's revenue sharing plan, covered in Chapter 6, is the most extensive in all sports. All TV revenues come from the national-level sale of rights and are equally shared among all owners, and 60 percent of local revenue is shared in a straight-pool plan similar to that of MLB.

Work Stoppages

Early disagreements between NFL owners and players were of little consequence. The complete list of stoppages is in Table 9.4. The 1968 strike was over pension fund contributions. Players boycotted training camps and owners locked them out, but these events ended after an agreement in 10 days. In 1970, a lockout ensued while pensions, postseason compensation, and grievance procedures were worked out. This lockout occurred during training camp and did not significantly affect fans.

Important labor-management disagreements have occurred in the NFL, beginning with the strike of 1974. The 42-day dispute was mainly over the Rozelle Rule, which was so strict in its compensation requirements for teams losing free agents that it essentially drove player movement to zero. However, veteran players crossed picket lines and the owners won.

During the strike of 1982, players proposed that 55 percent of league total revenues go to them as salaries and pensions. They also demanded a wage scale based on seniority. Owners did not budge and arranged for a $155 million line of credit after the players threatened to strike once the season started. Despite this significant display, the players did strike. The owners offered a modified version of revenue sharing, guaranteeing substantially less than 55 percent. Players went along with this offer, but they continued to argue over the dispensation of the funds. Players threatened to form a new league and even staged all-star games. The strike ended with owners getting pretty much what they wanted when it looked like the entire season would have to be cancelled.

The strike of 1987 was the most wishy-washy player action ever in any pro sport. Ostensibly, the strike was over free agency, but most observers note that it was actually caused by a management foul-up in the NFLPA. Executive Director Gene Upshaw was rallying the players over free agency, to which they were lukewarm, and simply neglected negotiations until time ran out. A strike was announced, but the players were not behind it. Owners put replacement players on the field and the striking players capitulated.

LABOR RELATIONS IN THE NHL

The NHLPA was formed in 1957. This was well after the NHL owners on their own had established minimum salaries and a pension plan for players. The only early confrontation over a nonshared TV contract was resolved without much fuss. During competition over talent from the World Hockey Association (recall the discussion of rival leagues in Chapter 5), hockey felt the pressure of free agency in that rival league. Later, the NHLPA made great strides earning free agency in 1995 with significant increases in player salaries. Player contracts are guaranteed but with a twist—contracts can be bought out at two-thirds of their value. There is no luxury tax approach in the NHL and (although this may change under a new collective bargaining agreement) no payroll cap. Just like the NBA, the NHL only shares its national TV contract revenues.

Arbitration

Players who are not yet full free agents (referred to as restricted free agents) are eligible for salary arbitration. But they must have been in the league for 5 years or be at least 24 years old. Unlike MLB, when players file for arbitration the case moves forward regardless of whether the owner agrees. This difference would suggest that players have even more of an upper hand than in MLB.

The Draft/Entry Restrictions

In 2004, the NHL draft had nine rounds, with 291 players chosen. However, there is some variation; 292 players were drafted the year before. The draft began in 1963. Players must be at least 18 years of age, and if they are drafted but not signed, they can reenter after a year's wait. If players are drafted a second time after waiting to reenter and still go unsigned, they do not have to sit out another year. These players are then free agents. In the modern version of the draft, the first 14 picks are determined by lottery; only teams that do not make the playoffs are able to participate. Only the four clubs with the lowest regular season points have a shot at the number one pick.

In the NHL, rookie salaries are limited under the collective bargaining agreement. The NHL has an age-based rookie wage scale. Players younger than 21 years of age (the vast majority) must sign contracts that last at least 3 years.

Free Agency

In the NHL, free agency is subject to the most complex set of rules of all sports. Players are divided into different groups based on age and experience. Most are restricted free agents, so that owners have the right of first refusal and receive draft-pick compensation in the event that they lose a free agent. Thus, most players in hockey are just like restricted free agents in the NFL. At the unrestricted end are 32-year-old players with four or more seasons in the league. For some of the remaining players, there is arbitration. At the other end of the spectrum, players with fewer than 3 years have no free agency rights.

Work Stoppages

As shown in Table 9.4, work stoppages have been rare in the NHL. The issues in the 1992 stoppage were a reduction in the number of draft rounds from 12 to 6; if fewer players are drafted, the remainder can sign as free agents, driving up salaries. The second issue is familiar—compensation requirements for teams obtaining free agents to pay the teams losing them. Other issues were increases in the playoff share for players and rights to likenesses on trading cards. The strike lasted 10 days and had no impact on fans. On balance, it appears the players won because the age requirement for free agency was dropped from 31 years to 30. However, the draft was reduced by only one round, and the season's length was increased from 80 to 84 games.

The **NHL lockout of 1994** lasted 103 days, and 468 games were lost. The owners were worried that the players' share of league revenues had reached 61 percent. They argued for a tax on payrolls, with the revenues going to smaller-market teams. Players countered with their own tax plan. They got nowhere until the season was about to be lost completely. It looks like owners won this round. The salaries of players under age 25 were capped so that they increase by small increments over 5 years, and eligibility for arbitration and free agency were restricted for all players.

One view has it that the owners have stronger alternatives than the players in the event of a work stoppage. Beamish (1991) contends that because hockey ownership is actually corporate ownership players have far to go before they can muster the resources to match owners. For example, Molson Companies, Ltd., owned the Montreal Canadiens. The team was at the fourth level of their corporate organization chart, a wholly owned and very subsidiary part of the parent company. Because of their greater resources, it seems extremely unlikely that owners will ever find a player association threat in hockey believable. Of course, a mitigating factor is that corporations seldom find it worthwhile to transfer funds from one division to another to cover losses unless that division is contributing at the margin to the overall value of the combined activity in some way. This would limit the willingness of the Molson company to ride out the losses incurred by their hockey team during a work stoppage.

As this is being written, a lockout begun in late 2004 is still ongoing. The entire NHL season, including Stanley Cup, will be lost. This will be the most significant work stoppage in the history of all pro sports in North America. It has all the earmarks of the NBA lockout of 1998. The owners demand "cost certainty" that they feel can be had only through the imposition of a salary cap. The players originally refused, but it appears they will reach agreement based on the imposition of a cap and a luxury tax. Once all of the final details are known, analysis of this hockey example can take its place next to our analysis of the NBA lockout of 1998 from the perspective of the expected value of work stoppages.

In the early years of professional sports, competition between leagues and owners kept player earnings at competitive levels. Eventually, owners devised methods, such as reserve clauses, to reduce player earnings below their MRP. To offset the power of owners over player salaries, players organized professional associations and unions.

With the National Labor Relations Act of 1935, players gained the right to collective bargaining through associations of their own choosing, and owners are bound to recognize those associations. The laws set forth by the NLRA are administered by the NLRB and enforced by the federal courts.

In professional sports, owners acting through leagues and players acting through unions negotiate collective bargaining agreements that determine the economic relationship between owners and players.

The NHL and MLB both have final offer salary arbitration (FOSA). If an owner and player are unable to reach a salary agreement, the player can have an independent arbitrator choose either the player's demand or the owner's offer. If the player loses, the player still gets the salary offered by the owner. Regardless of which salary the arbitrator picks, the player gets a salary increase. Fear of arbitration causes owners to offer most players substantial salary increases, so that arbitration never becomes an issue in most cases.

If a union is decertified, players can sue owners under the antitrust laws, an option unavailable under collective bargaining. In 1992, NFL players decertified their union and sued under antitrust laws to win unrestricted free agency.

In order for a union to be successful, unions must overcome the high costs of educating members and limit free-riding behavior. In addition, unions may face hostile political environments and illegal actions by owners. Once a union is formed, it acts like a small democracy. Elected union officials serve the needs of those who control their reelection. Because many rank-and-file members remain rationally ignorant of union leader choices, many union leaders are able to establish policies that favor a minority of players.

The first important observation about bargaining between unions and leagues is that work stoppages rarely occur. Game theory analysis of bargaining uses the idea that leagues and unions consider the consequences of each decision in the bargaining process, looking forward and working their way back to the present, to make themselves as well off as possible. Assuming full information and no alternatives in the event a deal is not possible, the result is a 50–50 split. When alternatives are available, the split covers the alternatives of both sides and divides the remainder of the value equally. This may cause one party to try to alter the opponent's alternatives. The value of this strategy is half the amount of the change in the value of the alternative. Given this analysis, there is no room for work stoppages.

Work stoppages occur (1) because of miscalculations due to lack of information or (2) because it is worth it for one side to bring a work stoppage. For the latter, the value of alternatives, gains to be had after the stoppage, the economic costs, and costs of lost fan enthusiasm must be considered. Perhaps most important is the estimation of the probability of a successful stoppage.

The current status of collective bargaining agreements varies across leagues. Both the NFL and NBA have salary caps and restrictions on rookie earnings. All leagues have free agency, but eligibility for free agency varies across leagues. All leagues have entry drafts. The history of strikes and lockouts offers many examples of the theoretical issues presented in this chapter.

KEY TERMS AND CONCEPTS

- Labor relations
- Collective bargaining
- National Labor Relations Act (NLRA)
- National Labor Relations Board (NLRB)
- Bargaining in good faith
- Player representative
- Player agents
- Collective bargaining agreements
- Individual bargaining rights

- Final offer salary arbitration (FOSA)
- Union decertification
- Education costs
- Free-riding behavior
- Owner retaliation
- Illegal owner behavior
- Rational ignorance
- Concentrated benefits
- Dispersed costs
- 50–50 split
- Look forward, work back

- Differential alternatives
- Strike
- Lockout
- Asymmetric information
- Strategic misrepresentation
- Profitable work stoppage
- MLBPA strike of 1994
- Rozelle Rule
- *McNeil v. NFL*
- NHL lockout of 1994
- NBA lockout of 1998

REVIEW QUESTIONS

1. Explain how organizing limits competition for player jobs. How do organized player associations counteract owner power?
2. What act created the right of collective bargaining? What are the three key features to that act? How is the act enforced? What federal agency has jurisdiction over enforcement?
3. Explain how a modern players' union is like a small democracy.
4. What is a collective bargaining agreement? How is one formed? What are the key features of such an agreement?
5. What is salary arbitration? What is meant by final offer salary arbitration? How is eligibility for arbitration determined?
6. What rights do players forfeit when they choose a collective bargaining agent? Why might players in a given league decertify their union?
7. What are the goals of a union? What role does player marginal revenue product play?
8. Define each of the following: education costs, free riding, owner retaliation, and political sentiment.
9. What is rational ignorance? Explain what is meant by concentrated benefits and dispersed costs in decisions made by union leaders. What does rational ignorance have to do with these decisions?
10. What is meant by "look forward, work back" in bargaining situations? Explain the basic 50–50 split outcome in simple bargaining. What are the crucial assumptions in such an outcome?
11. Explain the role of differential alternatives in determining the split in a simple bargaining game.
12. What is the difference between a strike and a lockout?

13. What is asymmetric information in a bargaining setting? How does it relate to strategic misrepresentation?

14. What is meant by a profitable work stoppage? What costs do owners or players incur during a work stoppage? After the stoppage is over?

15. What is the definition of the breakeven probability? Why is this concept important in determining whether to force a work stoppage?

THOUGHT PROBLEMS

1. Refer to the Learning Highlight: Champions of the "Free" Market for Players? Not Who You Might Think. Why did Charley O. Finley argue that if there was going to be free agency, then all players should be free agents every season? Why did Marvin Miller fear that type of outcome?

2. Is joint action by owners required to carry out collective bargaining with players? Does labor law require it? If so, what is the legal justification? If not, why does it happen anyway?

3. How does final offer salary arbitration lead owners and players to bargain more earnestly than they might without it? Explain why arbitration would still be good for players even if individual arbitration cases were lost more often.

4. Suppose players in a given sport decertify their union. What risks do they run in doing so? The NBA decertification episode might be helpful in determining your answer.

5. Carefully explain the role of each of the following in the formation of a union: education costs, free riding, owner retaliation, and political sentiment.

6. In the Learning Highlight: Pro Athletes as Company Men, why do you think players so perfectly echoed owners in their opinions on the reserve clause and the draft?

7. What happens in the simplest bargaining outcome with differential alternatives if $U + L > X$? Why?

8. Why is there no room in the simplest bargaining game for work stoppages?

9. Explain how a work stoppage can happen despite the wishes of both parties to avoid one.

10. Write the general formula for the expected value of a work stoppage. Carefully describe each element. Suppose that each element were to increase, one at a time. What happens to the expected value of the stoppage in each case? What happens to the expected value of the stoppage if the interest rate increases? If the length of the stoppage increases?

11. What role did signing movie contracts play in the Koufax-Drysdale holdout of 1966? What were they trying to demonstrate to Dodger owner Walter O'Malley by signing them?

12. What did Marvin Miller mean when he said that the growth in salaries attributable to arbitration was the result of "the unconscionable exploitation of players in the earlier years"? (1983, p. 33). What exploitation did he mean, and how did arbitration help solve it?

13. What is the impact on player movement of the requirement that compensation be paid to teams losing free agents to other teams? Why would the commissioner

of the NFL, Pete Rozelle, impose such restrictions? (*Hint:* Who hires the commissioner?)

14. What role did union decertification play in the advent of free agency in the NFL? Why was it essential to those pursuits? What happened when the NBA players tried the same approach? Why?

15. Does there appear to be enough revenue to go around to keep all teams in good financial shape in the NBA? Even though simply sharing these revenues would bolster the financial fortunes of smaller-revenue market teams, explain why it is unlikely to happen.

ADVANCED PROBLEMS

1. In Figure 9.2, suppose that another powerful group of players were to appear. Diagram how this group would enter the picture. What would have to happen for this new group of players to have any impact on union leaders' choices? How do you rate the chances of any such alteration in the status quo in sports unions?

2. For years, the NBA had what was called a soft cap. The NFL had a hard cap. What is the difference between a soft and a hard cap? Explain how differences in the union dynamic between the two leagues might produce such a difference.

3. Table 9.1 has many blanks. Fill in the blanks and prove that each party will independently determine that the best they can hope to do is to split the pot 50–50 without any work stoppage.

4. Table 9.3 has many blanks. Fill in the blanks and prove that each party will independently determine that the best they can hope to do is to split the pot 69–31 in favor of owners without any work stoppage. Demonstrate that this outcome fits the idea that, of what is on the table, both alternatives must be covered and then the balance split 50–50.

5. Suppose total revenue for the NBA is $4 billion. Without an agreement to work in a given year, players could make $200 million. Replacement players would generate $400 million for owners. What share of league total revenue will go to players? Now suppose owners know that if there is a work stoppage, picketing reduces their alternative to $300 million. If the threat of a picket is believable, what share of league revenue will go to players? How much would players spend to make picketing legal?

6. Using the general formula for the expected value of a work stoppage, identify which elements are affected when owners buy strike insurance or take out a line of credit to be used in the event of a strike.

7. Suppose owners in the NFL are considering a lockout. It will last 1 year. Owners usually make $300 million, net, in a given year. If the lockout is successful, owners will make $900 million the year after the lockout but only $100 million during the lockout year. If the lockout is not successful, owners will make $100 million during the lockout plus the usual $300 million the next year. If the chances of winning are 30 percent, what is the expected value of the lockout? Should they do it? (*Hint:* Be careful to consider the possible costs of fan ire in the year after the lockout.)

8. Why do you think the MLBPA always comes out on top in work stoppages in baseball? (That owners are inept is not an acceptable answer.)

9. Under a salary cap system, who benefits from a lid on rookie compensation? Given this, when would you expect union leaders to agree to rookie compensation lids in collective bargaining? Is your explanation consistent with the idea that union leaders concentrate benefits on politically powerful union members and disperse the cost over the rest of the rank and file? Explain.

10. In the expected-value logic of the NBA lockout, how large would the financial costs of fan ire, minus the league's alternative values, have to be to reduce the expected value to zero if the probability of winning the lockout were 30 percent? As a percentage of owner profit (given in the example), is this net cost of fan ire enough to cancel plans for a lockout? Why or why not?

INTERNET RESOURCES

For a host of additional material and questions for thought, visit this book's Web site at www.prenhall.com/fort.

REFERENCES

Beamish, Rob B. "The Impact of Corporate Ownership on Labor-Management Relations in Hockey," in *The Business of Professional Sports*. Paul D. Staudohar and James B. Mangan, eds. Urbana, IL: University of Illinois Press, 1991.

Bishop, John A., J. Howard Finch, and John P. Formby. "Risk Aversion and Rent-Seeking Redistributions: Free Agency in the National Football League," *Southern Economic Journal* 57 (1990): 114–124.

Coffin, Donald A. "'These People Aren't Real Big on Player Reps': Career Length, Mobility, and Union Activism in Major League Baseball," in *Sports Economics: Current Research*. John Fizel, Elizabeth Gustafson, and Laurence Hadley, eds. Westport, CT: Praeger Publishers, 1999.

Dixit, Avinash K. and Barry J. Nalebuff. *Thinking Strategically: The Competitive Edge in Business, Politics, and Everyday Life*. New York: W.W. Norton and Company, 1993.

Drysdale, Don with Bob Verdi. *Once a Bum, Always a Dodger: My Life in Baseball from Brooklyn to Los Angeles*. New York: St. Martin's Press, 1990.

Dworkin, James B. "Final Offer Salary Arbitration (FOSA)–a.k.a. Franchise Owners' Self Annihilation," in *Stee-rike Four! What's Wrong with the Business of Baseball?* Daniel R. Marburger, ed. Westport, CT: Praeger, 1997.

Koppett, Leonard. *The New Thinking Fan's Guide to Baseball*. New York: Fireside, 1991.

Kramer, Jerry. *Instant Replay*. Cleveland: World Publishing, 1968.

Miller, Marvin. *A Whole Different Ball Game: The Sport and Business of Baseball*. New York: Simon and Schuster, 1991.

Miller, Marvin. "Arbitration of Baseball Salaries: Impartial Adjudication in Place of Management Fiat," *Arbitration Journal* 38 (1983): 31–35.

Olson, Mancur. *The Logic of Collective Action: Public Goods and the Theory of Groups*. Cambridge, MA: Harvard University Press, 1965.

Quirk, James and Rodney D. Fort. *Pay Dirt: The Business of Professional Team Sports*. Princeton, NJ: Princeton University Press, 1992.

Quirk, James and Rodney D. Fort. *Hard Ball: The Abuse of Power in Pro Team Sports*. Princeton, NJ: Princeton University Press, 1999.

Schmidt, Martin B. and David J. Berri. "The Impact of Labor Strikes on Consumer Demand: An Application to Professional Sports," *American Economic Review* 94 (2004): 344–357.

Staudohar, Paul D. *Playing for Dollars: Labor Relations and the Sports Business*. Ithaca, NY: ILR Press, 1996.

Voigt, David Q. "Serfs versus Magnates: A Century of Labor Strife in Major League Baseball," in *The Business of Professional Sports*. Paul D. Staudohar and James B. Mangan, eds. Urbana, IL: University of Illinois Press, 1991.

Chapter

10

Subsidies and Economic Impact Analysis

Chapter Objectives

After reading this chapter, you should be able to:

- *Explain how sports teams provide external benefits that can justify a subsidy to team owners.*

- *Understand that it can make economic sense to subsidize a money-losing owner as long as buyers' surpluses are large enough.*

- *Appreciate that cost-benefit analysis provides a useful framework for analyzing subsidies to sports team owners.*

- *Understand that sports team subsidies do not appear to generate new economic impacts or enough development value to justify subsidies.*

- *See that some estimates of buyers' surpluses and external benefits indicate that sports owner subsidies may be worth the cost but that other estimates do not support that conclusion.*

Having a football team back in Houston will bring thousands of visitors to our city, and it will generate millions of dollars in our city. I'm excited about our new stadium with a retractable roof. And we're also very happy about getting a Super Bowl, and as you know that's very important economically to the city. It will generate probably $300 or $400 million into our economy. But more importantly, it focuses attention on a city that people do not know enough about.

—HOUSTON MAYOR LEE BROWN
NFL Report, Winter 1999, p. 7

Prior to the 1950s, most stadiums were privately owned and financed. The public share for such projects was just under 30 percent. However, this was soon to change. Shortly after his appointment in 1951, MLB Commissioner Ford Frick announced that cities were going to have to start directly supporting their teams through publicly owned and maintained stadiums. His statements were based on the observation that MLB teams were generating value to other businesses near privately owned stadiums that owners were unable to collect at the gate or through stadium advertising (Miller, 1990, p. 71). Frick knew that state and local politicians could collect taxes and provide stadiums for owners. However, he could not possibly have foreseen the modern consequences of his original announcement. The total bill for 25 pro sports facilities opening over the period 2000 to 2006 will be around $8.8 billion in 2004 dollars. The public share will average about 63 percent, or roughly $5.5 billion.

Did You Know?
The first official league policy demanding that local governments subsidize pro sports owners came clear back in 1951 from then MLB Commissioner Ford Frick.

In this chapter, we will see that sports owner subsidies can be justified, but that this does not mean that any size subsidy is justified. We will discuss how judging whether subsidies are worth it or not is a question of costs and benefits and that, although costs are difficult to ascertain, ongoing subsidies can be calculated. On the benefit side, we will see that direct and indirect economic activity is often highly touted in subsidy debates. However, as we will discuss, these benefits are small, at best, and empirical analysis finds that there is nearly no additional development value associated with pro sports teams. We will see how this leaves buyers' surpluses and external benefits to cover the cost of the bulk of sports subsidies and discuss how the jury is still out on the size of these types of benefits.

Did You Know?
Over the period 2000 to 2006, around $8.8 billion will be spent on pro sports facilities and 63 percent of it will come from public sources.

THE LOGIC OF SPORTS TEAM SUBSIDIES

According to Mayor Lee Brown of Houston (see the opening quote), it would seem that the value of a sports team to its host city is so large that careful analysis of exactly how much it is worth would be beside the point. A new stadium brings thousands of visitors! Millions of dollars during the regular season! Hundreds of millions of dollars for championship games! However, let's not forget that in raving about the benefits of having a football team in Houston, the mayor was trying to convince state and/or local taxpayers to provide millions of dollars in subsidies in the form of a new football stadium to the owners of the Houston Texans. Houston's mayor was not alone in making such a plea. Indeed, it has been fairly commonplace, especially since the early 1970s, for a city, county, or state to subsidize sports team owners. Table 10.1 shows stadiums and arenas either completed or forthcoming over the period 2000 to 2006 (Keating [1999] offers a complete list back to the 1920s).

Subsidies are not just limited to stadium construction. Some host states and cities subsidize streets near the stadium, water and sewer services, and game-day safety and crowd control services. In addition, the stadium and its operations are often exempt from property taxes, representing another source of public subsidy. Similarly, stadium leases typically grant generous revenues and low rent to team owners as a subsidy. Many question these subsidies in light of their size and the fact that they provide benefits for very few taxpayers.

Economic arguments and other rationales have been used to defend subsidies. The economic arguments are based on the external benefits created by sports teams and the idea that subsidizing a money-losing owner may be worth it to fans. The other arguments for subsidies have to do with politics and equity. Economists can only point out that equity pursuits are not without costs of their own to taxpayers.

Equity/Political Arguments for Subsidies

If judging whether subsidies to owners are worth it were such a no-brainer, there would not be any debate over subsidies. Subsidy foes argue that the subsidy money could be better spent on some other, worthier endeavor. From an economic perspective, the costs of any given expenditure are the other values that could be had with the same money. However, claims that education or some other social service would be a better way to spend the money may miss the mark. If people are willing to put more money into sports but would not put any more into other endeavors, then this is a vacuous argument. However, if it really is the case that money already spent on other activities is being diverted to sports, then their claims are correct.

Another argument regarding subsidies concerns the idea that subsidies go to billionaire team owners to enhance the incomes of millionaire players. Locally, this benefits very few taxpayers except for those who are fans. Many local residents find this to be unfair and believe that rich people should not be subsidized. An economic explanation of this issue will not satisfy anybody interested in the fairness of the subsidies. Let's suppose that a subsidy to a rich person generates more wealth for

Table 10.1
Recent and
Upcoming Stadium
and Arena Openings
($2004)

Team/City	Total ($Millions)	Public Funds ($Millions)	% Public Funds	Opening Year
Cincinnati Bengals	$444	$444	100	2000
Columbus Blue Jackets	$138	$0	0	2000
Houston Astros	$293	$199	68	2000
Milwaukee Brewers	$429	$303	71	2000
Minnesota Wild	$143	$105	73	2000
San Francisco Giants	$337	$29	9	2000
Dallas Mavericks/Stars	$449	$134	30	2001
Denver Broncos	$429	$322	75	2001
Pittsburgh Pirates	$244	$201	82	2001
Pittsburgh Steelers	$270	$188	70	2001
Detroit Lions	$315	$131	42	2002
Houston Texans	$422	$341	81	2002
New England Patriots	$433	$76	18	2002
New York Mets	$525	$410	78	2002
San Antonio Spurs	$184	$153	18	2002
Seattle Seahawks	$452	$315	70	2002
Chicago Bears	$624	$418	67	2003
Cincinnati Reds	$288	$288	100	2003
Green Bay Packers	$304	$174	57	2003
Philadelphia Eagles	$309	$185	60	2003
Memphis Grizzlies	$250	$207	57	2004
Philadelphia Phillies	$458	$231	50	2004
San Diego Padres	$449	$303	67	2004
Charlotte Bobcats/Sting	$257	$113	44	2005
Arizona Cardinals	$334	$237	67	2006
Totals	$8,778	$5,508	63%	

Sources: Adapted from Raymond Keating, "Sports Park: The Costly Relationship Between Major League Sports and Government," *Policy Analysis*, no. 339 (April 5, 1999), Table 2; *Sports Business Journal*, July 30, 2001, pp. 26–29; and *Sports Business Journal*, December 29, 2003 (By the Numbers), pp. 52–58, 72. 2004 values extrapolated for 2005 and 2006 by the author.

society than any other possible use of the funds. The world is still a better place with more wealth rather than less. However, this does not mean that such subsidies are fair.

Economics has more to say about the argument that subsidies are needed to keep a team competitive. For example, an owner may argue that a new stadium is needed in order to generate the revenue required to keep up with other owners who have new stadiums. This would be true if the increased revenues from the stadium were spent on better talent to field winning teams. The increase in quality associated with greater spending may cause fans to spend more on the team in terms of tickets and merchandise. This sort of contagious quality enjoyment might actually elevate the fortunes of the team and the owner in the long run. On the other hand, if the owner already knows the market and is already putting out the talent level that fans will pay the most to see, then this plea is without merit in terms of increasing quality. In this case, if fans give the owner a new stadium, team quality would not increase, and the owner will keep the money generated over a few short seasons.

A final argument against subsidies is that if having a new stadium is so important then team owners or their leagues should foot the bill to build stadiums. Economics has quite a bit more to offer on this point than the others. In some cases, it may well be true that the value sought would be produced in the absence of the subsidy. It could be a case of someone trying to get somebody else to pay for what others want. However, in other cases, the absence of the subsidy actually harms society even if the money goes to rich people.

Economics and Subsidies

There are two economic explanations for how the absence of a subsidy may hurt society. First, if owners cannot collect all of the value their team generates, they will choose a level of quality and attendance that does not reflect the true net value of those commodities to society. If owners could collect the true value to society, they would choose higher quality and greater attendance levels. Second, it can make sense to subsidize an owner who is losing money and who would rationally choose to move the team. In some cases, fans may be better off subsidizing the owner than losing the team altogether.

External Benefits from Sports Teams On some important dimensions, a sports team bears a striking resemblance to beekeeping. Both produce values that can be captured by owners. Fans pay at the gate and purchase advertised products, and the beekeeper's customers buy honey. Both produce benefits that their owners cannot capture. Bees pollinate nearby orchards, clearly of value to the orchard owners, but there is no way for the beekeeper to charge them for this service. In economics, this pollination service for the orchard owner is called an **external benefit** to beekeeping. Of course, the beekeeper does not pay the orchard owner for the pollen that the bees bring back to produce honey, either.

In sports, external benefits occur in two ways. First, there can be measurable economic activity that occurs in relation to the existence of the team. Newspapers and their writers report on sports outcomes and make money, but they pay no fee to sports team owners. TV sports channel news shows do the same, and are therefore nonpaying beneficiaries. Other independent writers and analysts (like yours truly) earn extra income from their proximity to sports teams and also pay nothing. TV is another external benefit generator. Once a game is aired, anybody with a television can enjoy it regardless of whether they help cover the costs. Teams capture some of these values through advertising revenue, but many fans who never pay a penny to teams or their advertisers enjoy televised games.

A second type of externality concerns one of the scarce factors mentioned in Chapter 2 , namely, the commonality provided to fans of a given team. Call it what you will—local unity, fan loyalty, civic pride—sports teams produce a broad array of external benefits that can be categorized under the heading of quality of life. Parents play catch with their kids because the latter wish to emulate sports stars. We talk about our teams around the water cooler at work. We experience collective joy when our team does well and we mope collectively when it does not. All of these benefits have two things in common: No price can be charged, and no one is excluded from this type of enjoyment when somebody else enjoys it at the same time.

Although external benefits are enjoyed by some fans, they create a very real problem for society. The level of sports team quality and the level of attendance do not reflect the true value that fans place on these sports outputs. Fans place a high enough value on additional quality and attendance to cover the costs of providing more. However, the owner can only collect a lower value than fans are willing to pay, so owners stop short of the quality level and attendance fans actually would pay to see. This is the **external benefit inefficiency.** Let's look at a graphical analysis of this phenomenon.

Graphical Analysis of External Benefits   Our analysis of external benefits follows Figure 10.1. The figure shows a short-run situation where the graph of attendance demand assumes that a particular level of quality has been chosen by the owner. (We will examine the long-run quality decision later.)

In Figure 10.1, D_C is the usual portrayal of the demand function. The owner can only collect the value of attendance by choosing ticket prices along this function. The second demand function, D_S, shows the willingness to pay both by fans and those enjoying external benefits. D_S is derived as follows. The *MEB* function represents marginal external benefits that cannot be collected by the team owner. The *MEB* function slopes downward, indicating diminishing utility from external benefits (it could lie anywhere; there is nothing special about the particular location of *MEB* shown in Figure 10.1). The vertical sum of *MEB* and D_C gives the demand function D_S. If the owner could actually collect along this true willingness to pay function, prices would be set along D_S, rather than D_C.

Figure 10.1   Positive Sports Externalities

Positive externalities are present when owners cannot collect the full value of attendance. The demand function, D_C, is the value that the owner can collect for different levels of attendance. For example, if attendance is A_1, the owner charges V_1. However, other benefits can exist that the owner does not capture, labeled *MEB*. At A_1, these external benefits are MEB_1. The vertical sum of captured and external benefits equals the true value that society places on attendance. At A_1, the sum is *MEB* + V_1. The function D_S shows the true value that society places on all levels of attendance.

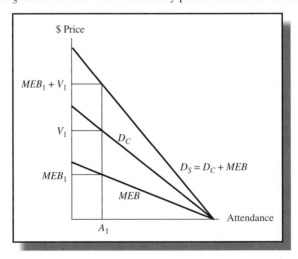

This idea may be better expressed by thinking about what happens in the presence of a positive externality at some particular level of attendance, such as A_1 in Figure 10.1. At output level A_1, the marginal external benefit enjoyed by nonbuyers would be MEB_1; the value that the owner can collect would be V_1; and the sum would be $MEB_1 + V_1$ on D_S. In the presence of external benefits, the full value of attendance is the vertical summation of MEB and D_C.

The Problem with External Benefits From bees to flu shots to lighthouses and national defense, a competitive market in the presence of external benefits produces a level of output that is inefficiently small. If the producers could collect from those nonpayers enjoying external benefits, they would increase output. The same is true for attendance in the short run (and quality in the long run). Although many observers think that we are wallowing in sports, the presence of external benefits means that attendance and attendance-related sales—plus televised games—are lower than they should be given the true value that fans place on them.

This problem is demonstrated in Figure 10.2. The short-run total revenue function TR_C is derived from the demand function D_C. The short-run total revenue function TR_S is derived from the demand function D_S. Remember that a higher demand function would be associated with greater team quality. In addition, short-run total costs will be greater in the higher-quality situation, so that TC_S is greater than TC_C. If the owner cannot capture external benefits, the profit-maximizing level of attendance is A_C^*. If those benefits can be captured, the profit-maximizing level of attendance is A_S^*. The problem is that $A_S^* > A_C^*$. If the owners could collect from those enjoying external benefits, their profit-maximizing level of attendance would increase. However, because owners are unable to collect, they make less, and fans get less than they are willing to pay for.

Figure 10.2 The Problem with Positive Externalities
The problem with positive externalities is that attendance is too low relative to the value that society actually places on it. If the owner cannot collect on externalities, total revenues are TR_C. Profits are maximized at attendance level A_C^*, where $TR_C^* - TR_C^*$ is maximum profit. If the owner could collect on externalities, total revenues would be higher, TR_S. The profit-maximizing level of attendance is A_S^*, where maximum profit is $TR_S^* - TC_S^*$. Therefore, if the owner can collect on externalities, attendance increases.

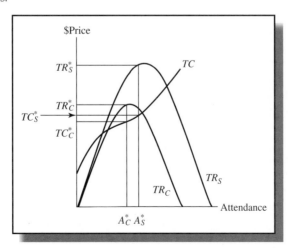

External benefits have the same impact on the long-run level of team quality. Because the externality is present for every possible quality owners might choose, whenever the owners consider profits for any level of quality, they will be smaller than if the owner could collect along the true social value of that quality. Therefore, owners choose a lower level of quality relative to the true underlying social value fans place on quality.

External Benefit Remedies   Both taxes and subsidies can allow the owner to achieve the output level A_S^*. For example, local government officials could inform the owners that they must increase team quality by hiring better players, and if the owners did not respond, a tax could be levied in such a way that the owners would choose to increase quality rather than pay the tax. However, in sports, this approach is not used. Instead, subsidies are paid, typically for stadium construction and operations. In the presence of external benefits, these subsidies must be paid to owners in a way that gets them to buy better talent. If the form of the subsidy is not tied to increases in team quality, then taxpayers run the risk of subsidizing owners and getting no increase in quality in return.

Subsidizing Owner Losses   Owners may lose money on their teams despite their market power position. We can envision two contributing factors in this case. First, it could be that even though the owner has adjusted quality in the long run to earn the highest possible return, that return is negative because actual costs of operation are not covered by revenues. If this is the deciding factor, the best such an owner could hope to do is drop down to minor league status; fans simply are not willing to pay for true major league production. But let's not forget the second contributing factor. Remember that economic costs include the opportunity cost confronting owners. Their next best option may be running their major league franchise in a different location that offers higher profits. These opportunity profits are imputed into the owner's cost functions at their current location. If this second is the deciding factor, we might well see an owner argue that they are losing money even though they may show positive accounting profits on an annual basis. The best thing for this owner to do is to move to the new location.

Of course, determining which mix of these two contributing factors actually is in operation in any particular case is complex. Our analysis in Chapter 2 casts serious doubt on the general poverty claims of owners, but that does not mean specific owners cannot on occasion lose money. It can be difficult to distinguish a long-term change in an owner's fortunes with a short-term fluctuation in the determinants of demand. Moreover, even if an owner's situation worsens, that does not mean the owner is losing money in the accounting sense. Profits could fall but still be positive, and given the difficulty of discerning profits by outsiders, one would be suspicious that owners would claim they are losing money just so that they can get a subsidy. And the final complication we have already seen— owners acting as a league actually act to keep viable threat locations open so that potentially profitable other locations are almost always available. This makes it easy for any current owner to claim they could be making more money someplace else, whether it is actually true or not. We'll say more about this last complicating issue in Chapter 11.

Let's suppose that the local sports team owner actually is confronting long-run losses. In addition, let's suppose that there are no external benefit problems so that we can focus on the issue of an owner losing money. In this case, collections at the gate, from TV contracts, and from concessions, parking, and memorabilia sales are not covering the owner's cost (which always includes the opportunity profit at another location), and the owner is losing money in the long run. We would expect that the owner would move the team elsewhere or sell it to someone who would do the same. In some cases, the buyers' surpluses enjoyed by fans (the excess of willingness to pay over the actual price paid) might be large enough to cover the owner's losses at the current location, and then there would be no reason to move the team. If some means of collecting the surplus from fans can be found, and the subsidy sufficient to cover losses is actually given to the owner, then the owner will stay put. We can gain significant insight with a more in-depth look at this situation.

Graphical Analysis of Subsidies from Buyers' Surpluses   We begin with a team owner who has chosen the long-run profit-maximizing level of quality, leading to the short-run costs and demand for attendance shown in Figure 10.3. For this owner, the long-run prospect is losing money at the profit-maximizing combination (A_m, P_m). The loss per unit of attendance is the deficiency of price (revenue per unit of attendance) below average cost (per unit of attendance) shown by line segment E_C in Figure 10.3. Total losses are calculated by multiplying average losses (per unit of attendance) by the number of fans through the gate. At the profit-maximizing level of output, total losses are the rectangle $DECP_m$. In this situation, we would expect the team to fold in its current location and either shut down or move to a more profitable location.

However, hope remains for fans based on the following important observation. Because the demand function already accounts for all of the consumption trade-offs

Figure 10.3   Money-Losing Monopoly

In this figure a monopolist loses money, but a subsidy exists that can cover losses and keep the monopoly team owner in business. The owner sets attendance at A_m, where $M_R = M_C$. The profit-maximizing price P_m is less than average cost by the distance EC. Losses incurred by the owner are the area $DECP_m$. Buyers' surpluses, the triangle AP_mC, which includes part of the loss, area $DBCP_m$, are more than large enough to cover these losses. The area of triangle ADB exceeds the remaining loss triangle BEC, and because the distance AD is greater than EC, the subsidy from the surpluses can cover the owner's losses.

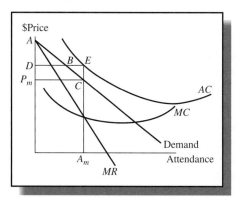

facing fans (and it already has external benefits included by assumption), then buyers are better off with this team than without it. In addition, if they gain enough satisfaction over and above their other payments to the team, then a subsidy may exist that would keep the team in its current location. Let's examine this possibility using Figure 10.3.

Again, the team's losses are rectangle $DECP_m$, and fans enjoy buyers' surpluses equal to the triangle AP_mC at the profit-maximizing level of attendance A_m. If buyers' surpluses exceed the losses and a portion of the surpluses sufficient to cover the losses can be collected from fans, then a subsidy exists that would keep the team in town. For the particular situation depicted in Figure 10.3, part of the buyers' surpluses triangle AP_mC already covers part of the loss, namely, area $DBCP_m$. With that area out of the way, the comparison boils down to the remaining buyers' surpluses, triangle ADB, and the remaining losses, triangle BEC. If the area of triangle ADB exceeds the area of triangle BEC, then buyers' surpluses exceed the team's losses. Because the line segment AD is longer than line segment EC, simple geometry dictates that the area of triangle ADB does, indeed, exceed the area of triangle BEC.

Thus, in the case shown in Figure 10.3, a subsidy does exist that allows two things:

1. The team would continue to operate at this location because losses are covered by the subsidy. Remember, the cost function already includes the value of the next-highest use of the resources going into team production. Therefore, the **minimum subsidy** just equal to rectangle $DECP_m$ is all that is required to keep the team in town.
2. Fans would be happier with the team, even though they would have to pay the subsidy, than they would be without the team. After all, at the minimum subsidy, some buyers' surpluses remain that are equal to the area of triangle ADB minus the area of triangle BEC.

Important Considerations and Cautions   The theory is sound, but a number of other factors must be considered. The most obvious follows from the discussion of subsidizing a money-losing owner. Just because a particular subsidy can be identified that will cover externalities and possible losses does not imply that a subsidy would exist in every case that might be analyzed. Sometimes, economically speaking, a team just has to go. It all boils down to whether line segment AD is longer than line segment EC in Figure 10.3. If it is not, then no subsidy exists that would keep the team in town and satisfy fans. The subsidy required to cover losses would exceed buyers' surpluses. Furthermore, over time, the subsidy issue would need to be revisited because cost and demand functions can shift.

Not Just Any Old Subsidy Level   For both the external benefit and money-losing owner cases, our analysis suggests that there is a minimum level of subsidy that will do the job. Just because a particular subsidy can be identified in each case does not mean that any sized subsidy would be justified. The minimum subsidy does two things:

1. It gives the owner the incentive to produce the efficient level of winning in the face of external benefits. The minimum subsidy increases attendance from A_C^* to A_S^* in Figure 10.2.
2. In the event of any losses, the minimum subsidy covers the area of rectangle $DECP_m$ in Figure 10.3.

The minimum subsidy is all that is required to keep the team in town. The owner may wish to obtain more, but no addition to the minimum subsidy is required to entice the owner to keep the team at its current location.

Collection Issues   Collection issues also exist, all of which are based on fairness. Let's define fairness as collecting from those who enjoy the benefits of the team. For example, in the case of external benefits, this idea of fairness would dictate that the subsidy is collected from those enjoying the externality. However, how do you find these people, and how much do you charge? It would be impractical to drive around and tax people playing catch with their children. Even if you tried, how would you decide the level of their enjoyment in order to levy an appropriate tax? These are classic issues in public finance that are not easy to overcome. Typically, governments resort to clumsy instruments that neither set taxes proportional to benefits nor collect just from those who enjoy the benefits.

In the case of trying to collect buyers' surpluses, the target would be fans who buy the team's outputs at the gate or purchase goods advertised during TV broadcasts. Ticket surcharges are one way to collect from fans who buy tickets and enjoy buyers' surpluses.

However, government choices are not always so precise. A tax on hotels and rental cars is another common device aimed at collecting buyers' surpluses from out-of-town fans. Although some hotel and rental car users may be fans from out of town, most are not. In this case, many who are not fans also are charged a portion of the subsidy. This is just as true of tax schemes covering all local taxpayers; not all residents are sports fans enjoying buyers' surpluses or external benefits, but they pay just the same. In this case, all the money does not come from fans, and there is no reason to expect these nonfans to be very happy about their forced contribution.

The Political Process   Finally, buyers' surpluses exist for team owners who are not losing money. Profitable owners may push for state and local governments to provide subsidies. Owners actually earning profits can use the accounting tricks discussed in Chapter 2 to argue that they are losing money and deserve such subsidies. Although subsidies are sometimes required for team owners who lose money in the long run, the political process can end up providing subsidies for a team that is doing just fine.

COST-BENEFIT ANALYSIS CONCEPTS IN SPORTS

As the preceding section points out, a particular subsidy is not the same as any subsidy somebody might want. **Cost-benefit analysis** offers a way to analyze whether a particular subsidy is worth it. In a nutshell, the analyst lines up all of the costs and all of the benefits of a subsidy. If the benefits exceed the costs, then the project at least is worthy of consideration. The analyst's next step would be to compare the net value of the project to other possible projects before committing public funds to any project at all. A cost-benefit analysis identifies which project has the larger net benefit.

Cost-benefit analysis proceeds on the basis of the project in question. If it is a large project, costs and benefits will be large. If it is a smaller project, costs and benefits will be smaller. A cost-benefit analysis cannot tell a person what size project to choose. Why build a stadium for $400 million? Why not $250 million, instead? Cost-benefit analysis is no help on that question. All it can do is compare costs and benefits of projects of different size.

For now, suppose we already have a project and we want to assess its benefits and costs in order to determine whether a positive net benefit exists. Comparing benefits and costs is fundamental to any economic decision. If such a comparison is not done or is done poorly, you cannot make yourself as well off as possible. Overvaluing benefits or undervaluing costs leads to decisions that waste resources. We all do cost and benefit comparisons—it is actually pretty easy to conceptualize. However, the actual analysis presents difficulties. For the rest of this section, let's look at the cost-benefit approach in general terms and the difficulties of actually performing one.

Sports Subsidy Costs

The first step in a cost-benefit analysis is to identify the costs. State and local government can subsidize sports by providing public infrastructure for the owner, subsidizing team operations at the stadium, and building or renovating stadiums. All of these are subsidy costs.

Infrastructure Subsidies   Infrastructure is a catchall name for the public services provided to the facility where the owner's team plays. These include public services, such as water, electricity, and streets, and safety services, such as police (both for security and for traffic management), fire, and ambulance services. State and local government may foot part of the bill for these types of services. **Infrastructure subsidies** are payments by cities and states to owners to pay for infrastructure costs.

Operating Subsidies   A second type of subsidy goes to owners through leases. Few owners actually own their own venue. Most owners lease facilities from the city or state. Clauses in the lease contract between team owners and the government often include subsidies to ongoing team operations called **operating subsidies**. For example, some owners pay no rent, others pay large rent, and rent can be a flat fee or based on the level of attendance.

Subsidies based on attendance can overcome external benefit problems associated with sports teams. However, rent is typically graduated so that it increases with attendance. This graduated increase does not give an owner incentive to increase attendance to overcome external benefits problems. Thus, the overall level of the subsidy, plus monitoring by government officials, will have to generate increased quality and attendance to take care of external benefit inefficiencies.

The rest of the overall operating subsidy includes all of the remaining revenues and costs at the stadium. Some owners get all of the concession and parking revenue, whereas others get none. Some owners get all of the nonsports revenue. Some owners are responsible for maintenance and upkeep. Similar variations in lease outcomes exist for signage and advertising revenues, as discussed in the Learning Highlight: "Subsidese," the Language of Lease Contracts.

Some lease outcomes might make for very interesting questions on an accounting quiz. For example, owners of the Colorado Rockies keep all revenues from the stadium except parking revenues. The owners also are responsible for maintenance and operations. However, if the partners take a cash return in any lease year equal to 5 percent of the original amount of capital they paid to become part owners, then they pay 2.5 percent of the team's net taxable income (after reduction by the 5 percent return) to the Denver Stadium Authority.

Some operating subsidies in leases are difficult to calculate. For example, Tampa Bay Buccaneers owner Malcolm Glazer also owns 70 percent of the Houlihan's restaurant chain. In the Buccaneers' lease, the Houlihan's chain pays $10 million annually for naming rights at Raymond James Stadium. However, under terms of the lease, all naming rights revenue goes back to the team owner, Glazer. Because he could simply give the money back to the restaurant chain, sponsorship could effectively cost Houlihan's nothing. Meanwhile, approximately 70 percent of any increase in Houlihan's profits as a result of this savings goes back to Glazer personally because he owns 70 percent of Houlihan's.

Leases also contain very interesting "nuts and bolts" clauses. Typically, teams receive all of the revenue from signage advertising. Few owners get none of these revenues. Most owners get at least a portion of signage revenue. In baseball, the Twins get all of the signage revenue, but no advertising is permitted on the scoreboard. The Yankees get 100 percent of signage revenue, except for signage on the exterior of the stadium. The Pirates get 33 percent of revenues from the concourse only. The Mariners pay $318,000 for signage rights and get to keep 75 percent of signage revenues, except they only get to keep 50 percent of revenues from the DiamondVision scoreboard in Safeco Field.

In basketball, the Mavericks get 50 percent of signage from static advertising and 100 percent from nonstatic advertising (all ads that are in animated or video form). The Nuggets get 70 percent of signage up to $200,000 and 100 percent thereafter. The Clippers get 100 percent of signage from basketball but only 50 percent from nonbasketball events. The Heat pays $275,000 for 100 percent of signage. The Spurs get 100 percent of arena and concourse signage but only 40 percent of any other signage. The Supersonics must pay $750,000 over 15 years for all of the signage.

In football, the Cardinals keep 100 percent of the revenue from message board and video display advertising. The Giants and the Jets occupy the same stadium, and each keeps 50 percent of net signage except from the scoreboard. The Rams get 75 percent of signage up to $6 million but only 90 percent after that.

Finally, in hockey, the Ducks get 100 percent of hockey-related advertising and 50 percent of the rest. The Sharks get 100 percent of hockey-related advertising and 50 percent of fixed signage.

Meanwhile, just figuring out occupancy charges (the aggregate of rent and any other charges) can be quite a chore. Because everything else (sponsorship, signage, other ads, concessions, and parking) are shared benefits, we will stick with any ticket or seat-based payments that owners must make and any amount of team profits that go to the stadium authority. The following are just a few examples. The only way to know how much Safeco

(Continued)

(Continued)

Field is worth to the Seattle Mariners is to understand the details of their lease.

In baseball, the Mariners pay 7 percent of revenue on the first million tickets sold or $160,000 plus 5 percent of revenue on the first million tickets sold, whichever is greater; 60 percent of net suite rental revenue on 48 of 77 suites; $9,750 for 1996 game-day expenses; and 5 percent of reported net operating profits.

It does not get any simpler in basketball. The Mavericks pay $10,000 or 7 percent, whichever is less if per game receipts are less than $324,000, and $10,000 plus 5 percent of excess of per game receipts over $324,000.

From football, the Jaguars pay $250,000 per year through 2000; $500,000 through 2005; $1 million through 2015; $1.25 million through 2025; $2.50 per ticket surcharge; and $2 per car surcharge.

Finally, as you might suspect from the complications for their cotenants, the NBA's Mavericks, the hockey Stars pay the lesser of 7 percent or $10,000 on gate receipts up to $324,000; $10,000 plus 5 percent on gate receipts over $324,000.

Sources: Sports Leases on CD-ROM, Major League Facilities, vols. 1 & 2 (Chicago, IL: Team Marketing Reports, 1998); Roger Noll and Andrew Zimbalist, "Build the Stadium—Create the Jobs!" in *Sports, Jobs and Taxes: The Economic Impact of Sports Teams and Stadiums*, Roger Noll and Andrew Zimbalist, eds. (Washington, D.C.: Brookings Institution, 1997).

Property tax treatment also can enter into operating subsidies. All property owners pay property taxes. The chance for a subsidy here lies primarily with the case of publicly owned facilities. Sports team owners may not pay any property tax outright, or they may pay it through their rent payment. Indeed, local authorities do not impute forgone property taxes into the cost of stadiums and arenas. However, if the property were leased or sold outright to another type of business, property taxes would be included. This special treatment of sports team owners is another element of the operating subsidy.

Stadium Construction Subsidies   The most talked about of all subsidies are **stadium subsidies** payments by taxpayers to team owners to support the construction and operation of a stadium for the owners' team. Construction costs are usually publicly stated, as we saw in Table 10.1. These amounts are so large that construction is financed through borrowing, either directly with loans or by issuing public bonds.

Revenue bonds must be paid off strictly from revenues generated by the facility. However, this dramatically limits the subsidy aspect of construction and renovation; therefore, this type of bond is very seldom used. General obligation bonds can be paid off through a wide variety of sources, which broadens the ability to subsidize owners considerably. Ticket surcharges and rent can be used to pay on these bonds, but other methods that fall less on fans also are popular. Taxes on goods and services like hotels and rental cars can also be used to pay bonds. This method is politically popular because out-of-towners typically pay the tax. Another popular method is to increase state and local sales taxes by a small amount. Sometimes a local government is granted sales tax forgiveness for a specified time period by its state in order to use those funds to make bond payments. In addition, this method of bond financing may put other costs off on taxpayers in a larger jurisdiction. Zimmerman (1997) points out that the use of tax-exempt bonds puts costs onto federal taxpayers, who must make up the difference.

Why Stadiums Rather Than a Cash Payment?   Siegfried and Zimbalist (2000) pose and then answer the question, "Why subsidize a stadium rather than just make a cash payment to the owner?" The authors give the following reasons why a stadium subsidy might be chosen over giving money directly to an owner:

1. There will be political support from local contractors and property owners at and around the site. Construction certainly will make contractors who do construction better off, and property owners near the site may see their property values increase (whether this is a true increase in value to the entire paying jurisdiction is another matter).
2. Stadium subsidies can tie the team to the city through the lease. Some lease clauses impose dramatic penalties on teams that try to leave the city, including repayment of the stadium subsidy.
3. The enhanced revenue stream that a stadium subsidy represents must be collected over time and through good team management. A single lump-sum cash payment does not provide the team owner with any incentive to manage well in order to obtain the payment.
4. Cash payments to the owner may draw other parties to demand cash payments as well.
5. Stadium subsidies are more politically palatable than cash grants to wealthy people.

Analytical Difficulties in Evaluating Subsidies

To avoid waste, subsidies must be evaluated relative to all the costs. In economics, opportunity cost is the guiding principle, and careful attention to opportunity cost leads us to consider secondary costs. Dollar costs, such as the amount of money that must be borrowed in order to build the stadium, may be very well known. For example, in Table 10.1, people in the Milwaukee area were asked to pay a subsidy of $303 million 2004 dollars as their share of the total for a new ballpark. However, a full evaluation of the opportunity costs may go beyond just the dollars cited. For example, the $303 million may not include property taxes forgone for a publicly owned stadium. In addition, the full implications of the costs imposed by the subsidy funding method must be considered. Further, because loan or bond payments are made over time, uncertainty also is an important cost factor. Future inflation and interest rate behavior are also important cost-determination factors.

We should not be naïve about the stadium funding process. Stadium supporters will overstate the benefits and understate the costs. Detractors will pursue an offsetting strategy. Cost overruns will occur. Intuition suggests that cost overruns are systematically understated in all subsidy considerations. If waste is to be avoided, all costs must be included and distortions of this type must be recognized in the analysis.

A Basic Formula for Calculating Subsidies

A straightforward way to calculate the annual costs of stadium subsidies is available (Okner, 1974; Quirk and Fort, 1992; Long, 2005). Once the actual amount of public spending is known, then the annual costs are depreciation, the opportunity cost of funds, and property taxes forgone. Thus, on an annual basis, if we cast operating benefits as net operating revenues from the facility to local government (the net revenue specified in the lease), then the **annual subsidy formula** is:

$$Annual\ Subsidy = Net\ Operating\ Revenue - (Depreciation + Opportunity\ Cost\ of\ Funds + Forgone\ Taxes)$$

As we will see, benefits can also be difficult to calculate. However, if the subsidy is known, we can at least ask if the benefits are worth at least that much.

Sports Subsidy Benefits

Having dealt with cost concepts, let's turn to the benefit side of the evaluation. Analysts have broken the types of subsidy benefits into four categories: economic activity benefits (direct and indirect), development value, buyers' surpluses, and external benefits. In the following discussion, all of these benefits are considered in the context of either having a team or losing that team altogether in the absence of a subsidy.

Economic Activity Benefits Economic activity concerns the measurement of wages, jobs, and taxes created by a team and its stadium both during the construction phase and after the stadium is completed and occupied by the team.

Direct and Indirect Economic Activity **Direct economic activity** is economic activity that occurs at the stadium. During the construction phase, all site planning, preparation, and construction are direct economic activities. After construction is completed, all activity that is generated by stadium and team operations and the support businesses that serve the team is direct economic activity. An easy measure of direct economic activity after construction would be team total revenues.

Indirect economic activity describes the benefits accruing to other businesses that do not pay anything to the team for those benefits. Some of these can be measured or estimated, such as peripheral economic activity near the stadium. Proximate businesses are the most obvious indirect economic activity. They do not deal directly with the team, but they do rely on fan traffic for part of their income. Nearby restaurants and retail outlets are good examples of proximate businesses. Be careful not to confuse indirect economic activity with external benefits. Remember, external benefits cannot be charged a price, and one person's enjoyment of the benefits does not interfere with another person's enjoying them at the same time. In comparison, indirect economic activity produces benefits, such as income, that can only be enjoyed by the individuals who receive them.

Did You Know?
The Atlanta Sports Commission estimated in 2000 that around $4.9 billion (2004 dollars) would flow into the city from scheduled athletic events and pro team sports over the next three years.

Some businesses are not close to the team in location but depend on game outcomes for a portion of their income. Take newspapers, for example. Suppose a city failed to provide a subsidy and lost its NFL team. How would a newspaper fare without a home team on the sports pages? Circulation and ad revenues would probably decline. The same goes for local TV broadcasts. One would expect that the advertising slot value of the sports segment of the local news would decline in value if the city lost its team.

Table 10.2 Atlanta Economic Activity Value 1999–2003 ($2004 Millions)

EVENT	YEAR(S)	ESTIMATED VALUE ($2004 MILLIONS)
Major League Baseball All-Star Game	2000	$54.4
NFL Super Bowl	2000	$272.0
Southeast Conference Football Championship	1999–2003	$244.8
Chick-Fil-A Peach Bowl	1999–2003	$244.8
McDonald's Heritage Bowl	1999–2003	$408.0
Atlanta Football Classic	1999–2003	$81.6
Delta Air Lines Classic	2000	$5.4
Southeast Conference Men's Basketball Tournament	2000, 2002	$54.4
Atlantic Coast Conference Men's Basketball Tournament	2001	$27.2
NCAA Men's Basketball Tournament	2001	$15.2
NCAA Men's Final Four	2002	$54.4
NCAA Women's Basketball Final Four	2003	$27.2
Atlanta Motor Speedway	1999–2003	$2,475.2
Peitie LeMans	1999–2003	$54.4
Atlanta Dragway	1999–2003	$213.2
USATF Indoor Track and Field Championships	1999–2003	$8.2
Peachtree 10K	1999–2003	$38.1
BellSouth (PGA) Classic	1999–2003	$16.3
Chick-Fil-A (LPGA) Charity Championship	1999–2003	$19.7
Nationwide Senior Tour	1999–2003	$19.0
The Tour Championship	2000	$30.5
PGA Championship	2001	$32.6
USGA Amateur Championship	2001	$0.8
AT&T (Tennis) Challenge	1999–2003	$6.8
Foxhall Cup (Equestrian)	2000–2003	$24.4
Pro Sports Teams		$0.0
Atlanta Braves	1999–2003	$572.8
Atlanta Hawks	1999–2003	$177.9
Atlanta Falcons	1999–2003	$52.2
Atlanta Silverbacks (United Soccer League)	1999–2003	$10.9
Atlanta Classics (United Soccer League, Women's)	1999–2003	$1.4
Total Revenue		$5,243.8

Source: Author's calculations from reports in *Sports Business Journal*, January 24, 2000, p. 51. Used with permission of *Sports Business Journal*.

Table 10.2 lists some economic activity values that were calculated by analysts in Atlanta. The sum total is impressive. But is the host city's economic activity value really this large? And where does the value go? Attempts to assess this value fall under the general heading of **economic impact analysis,** which we will shorten to EIA. A number of guiding principles determine correct EIA.

New Economic Activity   First and foremost, only **new economic activity** matters in EIA. New economic activity is any economic activity created by the subsidy that did not exist before the subsidy. This definition is nothing more than the marginal distinction common to all economic decisions. In a given jurisdiction, the opportunity cost of the subsidy (including all secondary effects on other programs) is the additional, or marginal, cost to taxpayers. The proper comparison is to the additional, or marginal, benefits that will flow from the subsidy. New economic activity commonly is referred to as economic growth. Therefore, only if new economic growth attributable to the subsidy exceeds the value of the subsidy is the subsidy worth considering.

This seems straightforward, but it is the most common cause of confusion in EIA. Let's remember how growth happens. A new firm might enter a jurisdiction. It raises wages by competing for labor. Rising wages represent increased income for the existing labor pool. As income rises, new economic impacts occur that can be measured through spending. Thus, in this case, observed increases in spending are due to growth. Other factors that result in growth are an increase in demand for things produced by people in the jurisdiction or enhanced training that raises productivity. Note that all of these result in greater income than previously was observed in the jurisdiction.

However, government subsidies that alter the flow of spending in a given jurisdiction need not create any growth at all. If the subsidy comes from rearranging taxes, then taxes that would have been spent somewhere else are now spent on the subsidy. Unless growth happens as a result of this rearrangement, all subsequent measurable spending will just be rearrangements that have nothing to do with growth. If government borrows to provide the subsidy, the same logic holds but the opportunity costs are borne over time. If there is no new growth, then the spending is just a transfer (over time), and observed changes in spending patterns are just rearrangements of economic activity that would have occurred anyway. No new income is created.

The question boils down to the likelihood that stadium construction and operations subsidies will create economic growth. Compare these types of subsidies to spending on education. The increased productive capacity provided by education leads to higher incomes, higher spending, and economic growth. However, what enhancement to productivity follows the construction of a ballpark or a more favorable lease? There may be a flurry of activity, but unless that flurry of activity generates new income, it is all rearranged spending that would have happened anyway. If there is no new income, no new economic impact is generated.

Consider fans and a direct economic activity—attending a game. At the ballpark, fans buy tickets, pay for their parking, and buy souvenirs and food. If there were no team and no ballpark, the same fans might go to the movies or to a play. Once again, tickets would be purchased, parking would be paid, and food would be bought. Admittedly, more movies might be attended, but spending on the part of fans is just rearranged. No new income is created.

Let's look at an example concerning indirect economic activity. Suppose a restaurant moves from a neighboring city to enjoy the crowds created by a new ballpark. This is a new economic impact only if growth occurs. That is, the move represents a new economic impact if the restaurant bids up the price of labor in the city so that incomes rise. Otherwise, employment just moves from other restaurants or elsewhere in the service sector, and the net impact of the restaurant is zero. Even increased revenue enjoyed by the relocated restaurant owner will not be new spending if it is simply rearranged from another activity in the city. This would be even more likely for a restaurant that moved from one part of the same city to be closer to the ballpark. Again, there is no growth. In this case, it would be incorrect to count the entire value of a restaurant that moved close to the stadium, even if from another city entirely. If all of this activity were counted as a value flowing from the subsidy, the analyst would be guilty of double counting. Rearranged spending simply is not new activity.

The same goes for more distant types of indirect economic activity. Again, only new benefits should be included in the EIA. Without a team, newspapers would still have sports sections, but they would be limited to reporting the scores of other teams. The same goes for local TV news broadcasts. The measure of indirect economic activity is how much income these beneficiaries would lose in the absence of a team.

By the same analysis, subsidies will not generate growth if all they do is keep an existing team from moving. In this case, substantial alterations in business patterns will not occur because business patterns already were established around the existing stadium. Therefore, any new economic impact is unlikely if the subsidy is to keep an existing team rather than to entice a new one. The only chance for growth if a team already is in the area is any increased value that fans put on the stadium and team. The resulting increased spending must come from new income rather than from other spending.

Careful Boundary Definitions for Correct EIA   EIA must assess the benefits of a subsidy using the same political boundaries of the party that provides the subsidy. For example, suppose a city government is considering a stadium subsidy for its NFL team. Benefits that would occur outside the city limits would be irrelevant to the city decision makers. On the other hand, if the state government is providing the subsidy in question, statewide estimates of the benefits would be the focus of EIA. It is easy to see why proponents of a subsidy would like the jurisdiction of EIA to be larger than the spending jurisdiction. If benefits outside of the jurisdiction of interest are included but not identified as lying beyond the spending jurisdiction, it certainly would make a subsidy look more valuable relative to the costs. EIA practitioners must be ever vigilant on this issue, or they may dramatically overstate the benefits of a subsidy.

The Use and Abuse of Multipliers in EIA   Whenever a dollar of new income is created, it changes hands many times, creating income along the way. The **spending multiplier** shows how many times a new dollar changes hands, generating multiple impacts on incomes and spending. The idea of the multiplier is an important one in EIA. The dollars enter the economy directly (e.g., at the ballpark) or indirectly (e.g., at a hotel or restaurant). The bank balances of firms receiving these dollars rise. However, the dollars begin to move out of these firms' accounts. Some dollars go to local, state, and federal governments. Some go to business purchases. Some go to wages. Some "leak," or move outside of the jurisdiction. Then, another round occurs. Governments send the dollars to other businesses and households through investments and transfer payments. Households send the payments they receive into savings and local and nonlocal purchases. The cycle then repeats.

A multiplier is an important element in the determination of the value of a team to a city, county, state, or region, but extreme care must be exercised in applying a multiplier. First, a multiplier must only be applied to new value added. Our most important guiding principle cannot be avoided. If there is no new income, then there is no new spending, and the multiplier cannot be applied.

Second, care must be exercised to evaluate the multiplier from the original injection of a dollar to the end of the line. Dollars might be observed at different points along the spending trail, and different multipliers are appropriate at different points. Typically, there are two types of multipliers measured in terms of dollars: sales multipliers and household income multipliers. The first applies to an added dollar of economic activity, such as the dollar that comes into a hotel or ballpark. The second applies only once the dollars have reached household bank accounts. Because a dollar has much farther to travel for the former, sales multipliers are larger than household income multipliers.

Which of these multipliers is most relevant depends on your purpose. If you want to know how sales dollars multiply, then use the sales multiplier. If you want to know the impact on household incomes, then use the income multiplier. It is tempting to say that it is the latter that matters in EIA because households will fund the subsidy and enjoy the benefits. But that idea shows just how difficult a concept EIA really is. Most income that would be calculated in the case of stadium subsidies actually comes in the form of wages. But wages are a cost of providing the stadium, not a benefit. To use the income multiplier at the level of wages to stadium workers would be inappropriate in the case of stadium subsidies and would overstate the costs. (Crompton [1995] is a good source for more on the use of multipliers in EIA.) In the best of all possible worlds, one would have data on all sales and use the sales multiplier only on added sales.

Third, multipliers depend on the complex interactions of businesses, consumers, and governments. A multiplier that works in one geographic location will not necessarily hold in another, and a multiplier that works for one sector of a defined economic area may not work for another. For example, a retail clothing sector multiplier will not be the same as an entertainment sector multiplier, and entertainment industry multipliers in, for example, Seattle and Baltimore need not be the same either.

Finally, it can take quite some time before all of the rounds are complete in the calculation of a multiplier. This brings time into consideration and, along with it, discounting considerations. As future dollars are worth less than current dollars, later dollars must be discounted. As a result, the longer it takes a dollar to work its way through the spending jurisdiction, the smaller is the multiplier.

Did You Know?
Changing the spending multiplier from 1.9 to 2.0 increases a $100 million benefit estimate by $5.3 million!

The multiplier concept can be abused. Proponents of a stadium can just use the highest multiplier that can be found and apply it to all of the dollars in the stream. Opponents can do the opposite. Each strategy is unsupportable and incorrect from an accounting perspective. A correct EIA will use the appropriate multiplier and only apply it to new economic impacts.

Development Value   Some believe that cities with sports teams have higher economic growth rates than cities that do not and that part of that difference comes from the presence of the teams. This **development value** is a highly touted form of benefit. The idea behind development value is that cities with a pro sports team will have higher growth rates than cities without them. In a sense, sports teams are a "big-league city" viability indicator for the purposes of attracting and keeping business. As former Kansas City mayor Emanuel Cleaver once said, "Without the Chiefs and the Royals, Kansas City would be nothing but another Wichita . . . or Des Moines . . . or Omaha" (*Sporting News*, August 11, 1997, p. 38). Note that this type of big-league city growth would be over and above any that would occur due to actual construction and recurring economic activity associated directly with the team or indirectly with business relying on fan traffic or game outcomes.

> "Without the Chiefs and the Royals, Kansas City would be nothing but another Wichita . . . or Des Moines . . . or Omaha." —Kansas City Mayor Emanuel Cleaver

Consider the following example of development value. Suppose that IBM is relocating its corporate headquarters. Further, suppose that both Portland, Oregon, and Seattle, Washington, have put together the same set of location incentives for IBM. That is, just based on the incentives, IBM is indifferent between the two Pacific Northwest cities. But Seattle has the MLB Mariners, NFL Seahawks, and NBA Supersonics, whereas Portland has only the NBA Trailblazers. If there is any development value inherent in the presence of sports teams, or the number of them, IBM should choose Seattle over Portland because two more major league teams are in that city.

In addressing development value, let's be sure to remember one of the most important general principles of benefit analysis: Only new value matters. New development value would be relative to the next-best development that could be obtained. If not a sports team, then some other type of development could be subsidized. In addition, if the subsidy just keeps existing teams in town rather than drawing new teams, the chance for new value is slim. Further, as noted in an earlier section, uncertainty plays a role in subsidizing stadiums. The Learning Highlight: Build It and They Will Come? shows examples where subsidized facilities were built to try to entice teams but failed to do so.

Did You Know?
The original Tampa Bay Suncoast Dome (eventually Tropicana Field) sat empty for 6 of its first 10 years at a cost of around $247.1 million (2004 dollars).

Buyers' Surpluses and External Benefits The last type of benefit from a subsidy concerns the question, How much would you pay to keep your sports team around, over and above costs of attendance and spending on advertised products, and over and above any income you earn due to the presence of the team? Any answer greater than zero means that you enjoy either buyers' surpluses or external benefits or both. We have already addressed buyers' surpluses and sports teams in the case of subsidizing a money-losing owner. But it is important to point out that buyers' surpluses comprise part of the benefits received by those subsidizing pro team owners.

We also discussed external benefits in earlier sections of this chapter. However, we should be cautious in adding them to our list of benefits. Indirect economic activity is a benefit created by the presence of a sports team that owners cannot capture. However, for the most part, an outside analyst can find indirect economic activity just by identifying those sectors of the economy that should enjoy it. Then, if there is any increase in the revenues in that sector that is greater than reductions somewhere else in the jurisdiction, those benefits count as indirect benefits. Therefore, indirect activity can be measured fairly simply.

LEARNING HIGHLIGHT
Build It and They Will Come?

There is a famous line from the movie *Field of Dreams*: "Build it and they will come." Although this proved to be true in the movie—Kevin Costner's character built a stadium and players from the past came to play in it—it does not always happen this way in real life. A prime example is the Suncoast Dome, completed in 1990, in St. Petersburg/Tampa Bay, Florida.

The Suncoast Dome was built for $138 million ($197.3 million 2004 dollars) with public money in order to draw an MLB team or gain an expansion team in 1992. However, neither happened (recall their successive disappointment with the White Sox, Mariners, and Giants detailed in Chapter 5). The Suncoast Dome stood empty until the NHL expansion Tampa Bay Lightning appeared for their 1992–1993 season. The Lightning used the stadium, renamed the Thunderdome, as a temporary home until the Ice Palace was completed in 1996. Eventually, in 1998, Tampa Bay did get the MLB expansion team the Devil Rays. The Thunderdome was refurbished for baseball-only use for another $70 million ($62 million of which was publicly funded, about $71.3 million 2004 dollars). Renamed Tropicana Field, it opened in time for the 2000 baseball season.

Let's think about the costs incurred in this episode. Including the 2 years to build the original Suncoast Dome, it was 10 years before MLB came to Tampa Bay. In the meantime, the facility stood empty from 1988 to 1991, was partially occupied from 1992 to 1995 by the NHL Lightning, and was empty again from 1996 to 1997. Had the $138 million original construction cost been put in the bank at 6 percent interest, it would have grown to about $247.1 million by the year 2000, when a team actually occupied the stadium. And the additional $62 million would have grown to $69.7 million by 2000. Therefore, just the funding cost of building the facility in anticipation of a team would be $316.8 million in public money ($344.7 million 2004 dollars), minus miscellaneous revenues (concerts and the like) and revenue from the Tampa Bay Lightning lease (if any). The moral of this episode appears to be that it would be better to have a team, then promise to build it a stadium, than to not have a team and incur empty stadium costs.

The Suncoast Dome was built in 1990 to attract major league baseball to Tampa Bay, but it wasn't until 1998, reborn as Tropicana Field, that the facility hosted the MLB Tampa Bay Devil Rays.

Source: Devil Rays Web page, www.devilrays.com.

This still leaves external benefits that cannot be added up because no market creates any price for them. Remember that the crucial distinguishing feature of external benefits was that no price could be charged and enjoyment by one did not preclude enjoyment by any other person at the same time.

Although for many these external benefits are small, for others they can be quite large. Summed across an entire jurisdiction that might be considering a subsidy for the local pro sports team owner, the total can be huge. Returning to the case of Kansas City, columnist Jason Whitlock put it this way: "The only self-esteem this city gets is from its sports franchises" (*Sporting News*, August 11, 1997, p. 39). As a sports writer, Whitlock has some self-interest tied up in that claim, but I think you get the idea.

ESTIMATES OF SUBSIDY COSTS

We have laid out the conceptual approach to costs. The sizes of the obligations cities and states assume are shown in Table 10.1. Monthly payments are easy to determine once the bond issue and loans are signed. But then cost measurements become difficult. The sources used to make the monthly payments, detailed in earlier sections, carry a host of additional considerations. When all of these are considered, the basic formula gives a close assessment of the size of the subsidy. The subsidy is the excess of depreciation, opportunity cost of funds, and forgone taxes over net operating revenue from the stadium that actually goes to state or local government. In this section, we will examine subsidy costs in detail.

Early Subsidy Estimates

Benjamin Okner (1974) was the first to consider stadium subsidies under the basic subsidy formula. He compiled a survey that produced data on gains and losses of 30 publicly owned stadiums. A summary of his data is shown in Table 10.3. Only five of the 30 stadiums showed any net gain. The rest lost money. Converting Okner's 1970–1971 findings in Table 10.3 to 2004 dollars, fully 20 percent of the stadiums had losses in excess of $4.7 million. Okner found that the total subsidy for stadiums showing losses was about $23 million in 1970–1971, or about $108.1 million 2004 dollars. The average loss was about $3.9 million 2004 dollars per year for each of the 25 stadiums in the red.

Table 10.3
Early Subsidies
Circa 1970–1971

GAIN OR LOSS AMOUNT	# STADIUMS WITH GAIN OR LOSS	% STADIUMS WITH GAIN OR LOSS
Net gain	5	17
Net loss	25	83
Loss under $50,000	2	7
Loss $50,000 to $100,000	3	10
Loss $100,000 to $500,000	9	30
Loss $500,000 to $1 million	5	17
Loss over $1 million	6	20

Source: Benjamin Okner, "Subsidies of Stadiums and Arenas," in *Government and the Sports Business*, Roger Noll, ed. (Washington, D.C.: Brookings Institution, 1974), p. 347.

More Recent Subsidy Estimates

James Quirk and I (1992) report the results of a similar analysis on a more modern set of stadiums. The subsidies to 25 publicly owned stadiums and arenas were around $187.4 in 1989 dollars, or about $283 million 2004 dollars, for an average of $11.3 million per facility. This represents about a threefold increase in the average subsidy per facility per year over the earlier findings by Okner.

A few of the highlights of our calculations are shown in Table 10.4 For the discussion here, all values are converted to 2004 dollars. The minimum subsidy was for Green Bay's Lambeau Field at about $285,390 (Lambeau underwent a $304 million renovation in 2003, Table 10.1). The one closest to the average subsidy was Atlanta-Fulton County Stadium (the previous home of the Atlanta Braves and Atlanta Falcons), at about $11.4 million dollars. (The Braves moved into Turner Field in 1997; construction cost was $274.2 million. The Falcons moved into the Georgia Dome in 1992; construction cost was $280.4 million.) The real white elephant is the Superdome in New Orleans with an annual subsidy of about $63.7 million dollars (still the home of the New Orleans Saints).

In the most recent (and exhaustive) assessment of public subsidies, Long (2005) develops an extensive data set on all 99 facilities in use in the four major leagues as of 2001. Her data allow an in-depth examination of the basic formula for calculating subsidies. The data on the opportunity cost of public funds include not just building costs but public land and infrastructure costs as well. She also has extensive data on lease arrangements that allow a more precise assessment of the net operations portion of the subsidy calculation. In 2001 dollars, the total subsidy is about $17.3 billion across all 99 major-league facilities, or $18.5 billion 2004 dollars. Long concludes that a much larger share of the total cost has been borne by the public than previously realized:

> Overall, the findings refute the much-touted claim that during the 1990s, team owners and other private entities were "partners" in sharing the burden of facility financing with taxpayers. Instead, the analysis shows that upfront private contributions are often substantially recouped through lease-based subsidies and exemptions from property taxes. Although industry sources estimate that the average public share of

Table 10.4 Subsidies According to the Annual Subsidy Formula ($1989 Thousands)

FACILITY	NET OPERATING REVENUE (1)	DEPRECIATION (2)	COST OF FUNDS (3)	FORGONE PROPERTY TAX (4)	SUBSIDY 1 − (2 + 3 + 4)
Green Bay's Lambeau Field (Minimum)	$150	$153	$155	$31	$189
Atlanta-Fulton County's Stadium (Average)	−$1,478	$2,160	$3,243	$649	$7,530
New Orleans' Superdome (Maximum)	−$7,922	$8,572	$21,400	$4,280	$42,174

Source: James Quirk and Rodney D. Fort, *Pay Dirt: The Business of Professional Team Sports* (Princeton, NJ: Princeton University Press, 1992, p. 170).

costs for a new sports facility is 56%, my findings show that after adjusting for omitted subsidies, the average public share is 79%—an increase of 23 percentage points. (p. 139)

So we have the following comparison spanning Okner's original work for 1970–1971 to my work with Quirk for 1989 and on to Long's findings for 2001. All measured in 2004 dollars, the average subsidy grew from $3.9 million in 1970–1971, to $11.3 million in 1989 and on to $18.7 million in 2001. That's a real annual rate of growth of 5.2 percent, or about 73 percent greater than the 3 percent typical real growth rate in the economy at large. This is compelling evidence that the process generating stadium and arena subsidies deserves scrutiny, and we will move on to that in the next chapter.

Subsidies may also include a **federal subsidy component**. When stadiums are subsidized with tax-exempt bonds, taxes that otherwise would have been collected for the federal treasury must be made up by all federal taxpayers. On the same sample of stadiums used in Quirk and Fort (1992), Zimmerman (1997) calculates the maximum federal subsidy total to be another $24.3 million, or about $36.7 million 2004 dollars, over the life of those 25 stadiums.

ESTIMATES OF SUBSIDY BENEFITS

In this section, we will review the findings on the benefits of subsidies to pro team owners. EIAs play an important role in determining these benefits, but as we will see, they typically do not follow the conceptual guidelines outlined in previous sections, and they do not cover development value, buyers' surpluses, or external benefits. We will see this as we look at EIAs done for subsidies in Baltimore and Seattle.

Measuring the Benefit of Subsidies in Baltimore

Tables 10.5 and 10.6 show an EIA done in 1987 on subsidies proposed for the Camden Yards baseball and football complex in Baltimore. EIAs are often commissioned by local governments; sometimes they are commissioned by team owners. Let's see if any insights can be gained from this Baltimore example based on the guiding principles presented thus far.

Note that the jurisdiction issue was unresolved at the time of the EIA. Therefore, the analysts offered an array of possible jurisdictions, including the city, a five-county area, and the entire state. The issue was eventually put to a vote at the state level, so we will pay attention to the state specifications in Tables 10.5 and 10.6 for the remainder of this section. Further, the EIA reports both impacts for the construction phase and those that would recur annually after construction was completed. Also, keep in mind that no other types of values are included in either of the tables. We will examine development value, buyers' surpluses, and external benefits later in this section.

The EIA is careful to derive new economic impact. Indeed, only new value, the category "new value added," is reported. **New value added** equals new value minus

Table 10.5 Camden Yards Baseball New Value[a]

IMPACT CATEGORY	CONSTRUCTION ($MILLIONS)			RECURRING ($MILLIONS)		
	STATE	FIVE-COUNTY	CITY	STATE	FIVE-COUNTY	CITY
Total impact	$137.60	$30.30	$103.70	$44.00	$3.60	$39.90
Wages	$48.7	$9.9	$38.4	$5.8	$1.1	$4.7
New value added	$91.8	$18.3	$71.5	$30.2	$2	$28.4
Jobs	2,560	801	1,721	382	76	306
Taxes	$10.1	$1.3	$5.2	$3.5	$0.145	$20.048

[a]Site preparation results for each category have been divided equally between baseball (this table) and football (Table 10.6). The same is true of expenditures outside the stadium.

Source: Regional Science Research Institute, Camden Yards Studies, Philadelphia, PA, 1987.

Table 10.6 Camden Yards Football New Value[a]

IMPACT CATEGORY	CONSTRUCTION ($MILLIONS)			RECURRING ($MILLIONS)		
	STATE	FIVE-COUNTY	CITY	STATE	FIVE-COUNTY	CITY
Total impact	$121.10	$20.80	$98.00	$34.60	$6.20	$27.90
Wages	$36.2	$6.8	$29.2	$18.8	$2.1	$16.8
New value added	$81.9	$12.2	$67.6	$26.7	$3.8	$23.2
Jobs	1,839	464	1,324	566	145	421
Taxes	$8.1	$0.902	$4.4	$3.4	$0.272	$1.7

[a]Site preparation results for each category have been divided equally between baseball (Table 10.5) and football (this table). The same is true of expenditures outside the stadium.

Source: Regional Science Research Institute, Camden Yards Studies, Philadelphia, PA, 1987.

wages, a cost to the project under consideration. Unfortunately, the method of estimating new impacts is not reported. Again, for this discussion, all values are adjusted to 2004 dollars. However, from Tables 10.5 and 10.6, the state-level estimates of new economic impacts from baseball and football construction were reported at $151.4 million and $135.1 million, respectively. Recurring new state-level economic impact, net of wages, was estimated at $49.8 million for baseball and $44.0 million for football.

An extremely important issue was whether the proposed subsidy would keep current teams in town or draw new teams. At the time, the answer was mixed. The MLB Orioles already called Baltimore home, but the football spending would have been used to draw a new NFL team. Baltimore lost its NFL Colts in 1984 when owner Robert Irsay moved them to Indianapolis. Thus, it would seem much more likely that any new economic impact would be attached to the football stadium spending rather than the baseball stadium spending. However, the reported totals for both construction and recurring impacts are larger for the baseball portion of the proposed stadium subsidies.

The basic issue remains to be considered, even for the football spending. How much actual growth can stadium spending create? Would people in Maryland work harder, creating new income growth, in order to enjoy these amenities? Or is it more likely that these estimates include rearranged spending that would have happened anyway? Fortunately, other investigators have supplied some answers to these questions.

The Hamilton and Kahn Review   Hamilton and Kahn (1997) review the actual Camden Yards outcome and suggest that it fell far short of the projected net economic impact. The Orioles began play in their new Ballpark at Camden Yards in 1992. Hamilton and Kahn estimate that the state of Maryland loses about $9 million per year on the ballpark. The ballpark generates enough revenue to cover capital and operations, but the team owner keeps that revenue under the lease agreement. Therefore, the park is a loser in dollar terms to Maryland taxpayers. In addition, according to the authors of this critique, the national economy loses about $12 million per year because the ballpark was financed with tax-exempt bonds. It appears that the people of the state of Maryland paid around $200 million (original construction costs) in order to lose $9 million per year. Adjusted to 2004 dollars, that's $233.4 million in order to lose $10.5 million annually.

Hamilton and Kahn (1997) also show that a similar outcome can be expected for the NFL Ravens and their stadium at Camden Yards. They estimate losses of around $13 million per year. Because the Ravens were new to Baltimore and the stadium was nearly brand new at the time of the authors' critique, Hamilton and Kahn conceded that potential offsets might remain to be seen. For example, any new non-NFL activity occurring in the stadium would offset the losses. Losses to the national economy generated by the subsidy for football are about the same amount as for the Orioles' ballpark, $12 million. The expected cost of the Ravens stadium also is around $200 million. At least in its early stages, the Ravens stadium was no bargain, financially speaking.

Hamilton and Kahn (1997) do note that no other values are in the original EIA such as external benefits or buyers' surpluses. But they also note that, at least in the case of the Orioles, there is no reason to suspect that this type of benefit will increase because the team gets a new stadium as opposed to playing in its old one.

Measuring the Benefit of Subsidies in Seattle

The EIA in our previous example of Camden Yards did not separate direct and indirect economic activity. In our next example, direct economic activity and indirect economic activity are broken out for separate treatment. However, as in the Baltimore example, neither buyers' surpluses nor external benefits are covered in the Seattle EIAs. Further, there is no published review of these EIAs, so we are on our own when it comes to a review.

Tables 10.7 and 10.8 show summaries of the EIAs produced during subsidy debates over new stadiums for two of Seattle's pro teams, the MLB Mariners and the NFL Seahawks. The analysts, Conway and Byers (1994; 1996), provided only recurring impacts. Further, they stress that indirect impacts are only for businesses relying on fan traffic. This means that the tables do not include other types of indirect monetary inputs.

Table 10.7 Mariners' Value 1993

IMPACT CATEGORY	STATE ($MILLIONS) TOTAL ACTIVITY	STATE ($MILLIONS) NEW ACTIVITY	COUNTY ($MILLIONS) TOTAL ACTIVITY	COUNTY ($MILLIONS) NEW ACTIVITY	CITY ($MILLIONS) TOTAL ACTIVITY	CITY ($MILLIONS) NEW ACTIVITY
Direct						
Spending	$91.10	$29.10	$91.10	$40.40	$91.10	$40.40
Jobs	936	198	936	456	936	456
Wages	$44	$20.1	$44	$25.8	$44	$25.8
Indirect						
Spending	$50.90	$13.80	$20.40	$12.90	$6.50	$7.30
Jobs	1,313	229	869	229	599	121
Wages	$26.1	$5.3	$16	$5.2	$10.7	$3.1
Direct + Indirect						
Spending	$142.00	$42.90	$111.50	$53.30	$97.60	$47.70
Jobs	2,249	427	1,805	685	1,535	577
Wages	$70.1	$25.4	$60	$31	$54.7	$28.9
Taxes	$7.2	$1.5	$0.1	$0.1	$1.4	$0.5

Source: Adapted from Richard Conway, Jr., and William B. Byers. *Seattle Seahawks Economic Impact*. Dick Conway and Associates and Department of Geography, University of Washington, Seattle, WA, March 1996.

Table 10.8 Seahawks' Value 1995

IMPACT CATEGORY	STATE ($MILLIONS) TOTAL ACTIVITY	STATE ($MILLIONS) NEW ACTIVITY	COUNTY ($MILLIONS) TOTAL ACTIVITY	COUNTY ($MILLIONS) NEW ACTIVITY	CITY ($MILLIONS) TOTAL ACTIVITY	CITY ($MILLIONS) NEW ACTIVITY
Direct						
Spending	$85.00	$45.70	$85.00	$63.10	$85.00	$63.10
Jobs	1,700	261	1,700	985	1,700	985
Wages	$44.3	$29.7	$44.3	$35.4	$44.3	$35.4
Indirect						
Spending	$44.20	$21	$17.50	$13.10	$6.80	$5.70
Jobs	992	363	623	403	442	279
Wages	$22.3	$8.7	$13.3	$8.7	$9.1	$5.8
Direct + Indirect						
Spending	$129.20	$66.70	$102.50	$76.20	$91.80	$68.80
Jobs	2,692	624	2,323	1,388	2,142	1,264
Wages	$66.6	$38.4	$57.6	$44.1	$53.4	$41.2
Taxes	$5.4	$2.4	$0.1	$0.1	$1.3	$0.8

Source: Adapted from Richard Conway, Jr., and William B. Byers. *Seattle Seahawks Economic Impact*. Dick Conway and Associates and Department of Geography, University of Washington, Seattle, WA, March 1996.

Unlike the Baltimore case, the jurisdiction of interest, the state of Washington, was known at the time the EIAs were provided. In both cases, the EIA appeared during the debate over statewide subsidy referenda put before Washington voters. The Mariners subsidy failed to garner a majority of votes (the stadium was subsidized anyway through alternative approaches), but the Seahawks subsidy was approved by the voters. For now, let's think like voters and pay attention only to the state columns in Tables 10.7 and 10.8.

Evaluation   Once again, our guiding principles provide insights into the Seattle EIAs. Both EIAs identify new economic activity. We can also bring the value-added notion into play, but unlike the Baltimore EIA, the Seattle EIAs do not calculate it for us. New value added is found by subtracting wages from spending. New value added at the state level for the Mariners is $42.9 million minus $25.4 million, or about $17.5 million annually. About $9 million of this new value added comes directly from team and stadium operations and supporting businesses, whereas $8.5 million comes indirectly from other businesses that rely on fan traffic. A similar line of reasoning yields about $28.3 million in new value added at the state level by the Seahawks. About $16 million of this new value added comes directly from team and stadium operations and supporting businesses, whereas $12.3 million comes from indirect business activity. In total, new state-level direct and indirect economic impacts from both facilities would be $45.8 million per year. In 2004 dollars, that would be about $59.4 million.

By way of comparison, the recurring new value added by the Camden Yards stadiums was about $49.8 million for baseball and $44.0 million for football, a total of $93.8 million in today's dollars. The Seattle estimates are about 63 percent of the Baltimore estimates. It does not seem unreasonable that Baltimore teams would be more valuable to their city than Seattle teams would be to Seattle. After all, the Orioles were an extremely successful franchise at the time, and Baltimore has a much longer football and baseball history than Seattle. In addition, other demand factors probably were higher in Baltimore.

The ultimate question always boils down to this: Regardless of the relative value to cities, will the subsidies under consideration add any income growth? If not, there can be no new economic impact of any sort. Would people in the state of Washington work harder in order to enjoy the amenities offered by new stadiums or just rearrange spending? It seems extremely unlikely that any of the results in Tables 10.7 and 10.8 actually pertain to new impact that would not have occurred anyway, despite the estimates in the EIAs.

The Verdict on Economic Activity Value

The general verdict on EIAs is that they overstate the value of economic activity. Baade and Dye (1988), the pioneers in reviewing EIAs, devised an interesting scenario to illustrate this point. First, they suppose that Cook County, Illinois (where the city of Chicago is located), might contribute $100 million to a stadium subsidy. For a 3-year period of construction, the $100 million would represent about 3.11 percent of the entire Cook County capital project expenditure budget. Even if all of commercial sports in the county were produced in this hypothetical stadium, the result would be about $50.4 million in personal income in the county. That ends up to be less than 0.5 percent of the county income. Strictly based on economic impacts, Baade and Dye determined that it would make little sense to commit so much of the county capital budget for so little in return.

The collection of work in Noll and Zimbalist (1997b), as well as the survey by Siegfried and Zimbalist (2000), offers nearly nothing in support of any positive economic activity from such subsidies. The upshot of all the works in the former volume is most likely that there are no new economic impacts from sports stadium subsidies and that this is especially true for subsidies aimed at keeping an existing team as opposed to drawing a new team to an area. Typically, EIA claims of new impacts are just rearrangements of activity that would have occurred anyway. The implication is that EIAs have been produced primarily by proponents to overstate the benefits of subsidies. In fact, Siegfried and Zimbalist (2000) put it this way:

> Few fields of empirical economic research offer virtual unanimity of findings. Yet, independent work on the economic impact of stadiums and arenas has uniformly found that there is no statistically significant positive correlation between sports facility construction and economic development. (p. 103)

The Verdict on Development Value

Economic activity arguments offer nearly no support for subsidies. However, other values not examined by EIAs should be considered when evaluating a subsidy. The first, development value, is always touted as an important but difficult-to-measure benefit. One way to assess development value is to find a sample of cities that are similar except for sports teams and see if the presence of sports teams coincides with higher economic growth rates. This is exactly the approach taken by Baade and Dye (1988). Their study found no difference in manufacturing activity attributable to the presence or number of major league sports teams in a city, but there remains some debate on the issue.

Baade (1996a) offers an updated evaluation that arrives at the same conclusion—that teams do not provide development value. The primary beneficiaries of stadiums are the owners and players, not the taxpayers. Chema (1996) says that stadiums are part of an integrated growth approach for cities. He argues that cities must create chances for interaction and socialization or they are doomed. In his opinion, stadiums generate these chances. Chema says we just have to look harder to find the benefits that everybody knows sway the decision in favor of subsidies. However, he offers no analysis to support his thoughts.

Baade (1996b) replies that Chema's argument must be discounted by the fact that no difference in growth rates can be found based on the presence of pro sports teams. Baade does agree that additional analysis of external benefits is necessary for a complete picture of the benefits of subsidies, but he suggests that additional analysis probably will not change the outcome. But as with Chema's original point, Baade offers no evidence. This interaction sets up a discussion of the other values involved in subsidy decisions, namely, buyers' surpluses and external benefits. We'll turn to those values after this.

The most recent academic examination of the growth issue is Coates and Humphreys (1999). They investigate whether cities with pro sports teams and facilities have higher real per capita income. Their data cover 1969–1994 for cities with MLB, NBA, and NFL teams. Coates and Humphreys find no evidence of higher income, and in fact, there is some evidence that some cities with pro sports franchises actually have lower per capita personal income. In addition, they find no effect on the *growth* of income at all. Their conclusion is clear—they find no evidence that new teams and facilities spur any economic growth.

Buyers' Surpluses and External Benefits

Researchers have begun to estimate the size of buyers' surpluses in sports. Irani (1997) analyzed buyers' surpluses enjoyed by fans at eight MLB stadiums. Using estimates of demand, he calculated the net present value of buyers' surpluses over a reasonable stadium life. The total of buyers' surpluses over a reasonable subsidy period averaged about $9 million, with a high of $61 million at Dodger Stadium in Los Angeles (a range of $10.5 million to $71.2 million 2004 dollars). Because these are totals over fairly long periods, the buyers' surpluses estimated are quite small.

Alexander, Kern, and Neill (2000) estimated buyers' surpluses for teams and compared them with stadium payments. They calculated buyers' surpluses from published reports of team total revenues. This makes their estimates dependent upon where buyers are on the demand curve, that is, the elasticity of demand. Their results are presented in Table 10.9. Remember from Chapter 2 that most estimates of the elasticity of demand are at or just below 1.0. For an elasticity of 0.75, buyers' surpluses are in the range of $15 million to $17 million (or $16.3 million to $18.5 million 2004 dollars) annually. These estimates dwarf those by Irani (1997) because they are annual estimates whereas Irani's covered the entire length of the project.

Turning to external benefits, Rosentraub (1996) stressed that the study of the "psychic values" of teams and stadiums has been neglected and that these values can be large. For example, after development that included a new baseball park, downtown Cleveland is now an exciting "hot spot." Similarly, the values behind the sentiment expressed in the earlier quote by Mayor Cleaver of Kansas City have not been

Table 10.9
Buyers' Surpluses and Pro Sports Teams

League	Elasticity of 0.75 ($Millions)	Elasticity of 0.50 ($Millions)	Annual Payment ($Millions)[a]
MLB	$17.2	$25.7	$21.8
NFL	$15.1	$22.6	$21.8
NBA	$15.5	$22.3	$14.5
NHL	$17.0	$25.6	$14.5

[a]Payments listed are from their case of $300 million for NFL and MLB and $200 million for NHL and NBA.
Source: Adapted from Donald L. Alexander, William Kern, and Jon Neill, "Valuing the Consumption Benefits from Sports Franchises and Facilities," *Journal of Urban Economics* 48 (2000): 321–337.

analyzed. It could be that sport as a cultural icon is valuable enough to sway the margin in subsidy assessments. Finally, Rosentraub echoes Chema on one of the other benefits. Sport has value as coalition glue; without sports in the mix, it can be difficult to get any agreement on any public spending plan.

Of course, Rosentraub's "psychic benefits," lately referred to as "quality of life" values, actually are the external benefits discussed and analyzed early in this chapter. As with buyers' surpluses, economists have also begun to estimate the external benefits associated with sports output. Johnson, Groothuis, and Whitehead (2001) estimated external benefits generated by the Pittsburgh Penguins using consumer valuation surveys. Their upper-bound estimate of external benefits for just one NHL team equals around $3.9 million per year ($4.1 million 2004 dollars).

Carlino and Coulson (2004) approach quality of life values by examining the difference in rental prices and wages in cities with NFL teams compared to similar cities that do not have teams, circa 1999. On the one hand, if quality of life is higher, then people should be willing to pay higher rents to enjoy it. On the other hand, people should be willing to accept relatively lower wages to live in a place with higher quality of life. Carlino and Coulson's strongest evidence concerns central cities where rental prices were 8 percent higher in NFL cities (they find only very weak evidence of a much smaller impact on wages). For an average rent of around $500 per month, an additional 8 percent added about $480 in additional value per year in 1999, or $540 additional 2004 dollars per renter. The level of this rental difference applied to the average size of the renting population in central cities yielded a possible amount near $139 million annually in 1999 ($156.2 million 2004 dollars). Carlino and Coulson compared this amount to the subsidies paid on stadiums that Quirk and I found earlier, and they conclude that stadiums are easily worth it to city residents. Indeed, comparing their finding to Long's more extensive treatment would produce the same conclusion— $156.2 million in added rental value swamps an average subsidy of $18.7 million.

On a related note regarding wages, Coates and Humphreys (1999, cited earlier) did find that per capita income was actually lower in some pro sports cities. Carlino and Coulson did not find this result, but Coates and Humphreys suggest that there are alternative explanations for lower wages. One is the Carlino and Coulson argument that quality of life is higher, so people take lower wages to enjoy it. But another explanation is that sports subsidies divert taxes from other spending so that tax bills in pro sports cities must be higher in order to cover the usual public offerings. In this case, the anticipation of lower net wages would reduce the supply of labor in pro sports cities.

All-in-all, the analysis of external benefits is in its infancy, and many questions remain. For example, while denizens of the city's central core may benefit, governments typically collect from a much broader population base (the collections issue raised earlier in this chapter). Because Coulson and Carlino also find that the rental value does not extend to these other payers, their conclusion is tied up with transfers from other residents to central city residents. In addition, work in the area has yet to test the competing explanations for lower wages and income in pro sports cities. Finally, none of the work in the area addresses the basic issue of just why public funds should be spent to raise private rental values in the first place. Clearly, more work on external benefits is needed, but the evidence is mounting that this type of value is real and should be counted in the assessment of public subsidies to sports team owners.

Events

Our same guidelines remain in operation for individual events. Just hearing how politicians describe pro sports events should clue us in to that idea. In reference to Super Bowl XXXVIII, Texas comptroller Carole Keeton Strayhorn said, "Texas will be a winner, no matter who wins the big game" (Window on State Government, news release from the Texas comptroller, Friday, October 31, 2003). The values to the state of Texas of Super Bowl XXXVIII played at Houston's Reliant Stadium in 2004 were estimated as follows by the comptroller:

- 87,700 visitors from outside the state (85% of total visitors)
- At least $8.7 million increased state tax revenue
- $165.5 million from all visitors
- 5,637, full-time jobs for the year
- $336 million total economic impact

"Texas will be a winner, no matter who wins the big game." —Texas Comptroller Carole Keeton Strayhorn, 2003, on Super Bowl XXXVIII in Houston

This litany of benefits is familiar, and the same careful EIA approach must be exercised in assessing the value of events. Economist Philip Porter (1999), in his in-depth study of the value of Super Bowls, provides some shocking revelations about the absence of Super Bowl value to host cities, as you can see in the Learning Highlight: Super Bowl? Super Dud!

LEARNING HIGHLIGHT
Super Bowl? Super Dud!

Economist Philip Porter has shown that Super Bowls are actually super duds when it comes to direct and indirect economic activity (1999). Income and taxes simply do not materialize as promised, even though they are used repeatedly as justifications for city—county subsidies in the pursuit of megaevents such as the Super Bowl, NCAA playoffs, or even the Olympic Games. An NFL study found that the value of the 1995 Super Bowl to Miami was $365 million. Porter found conceptual errors in that analysis and notes that the projected massive activity from such events simply does not occur.

When there are perfect complements to events, such as hotel rooms, that have capacity constraints, there is nearly no net increase in local incomes if local suppliers raise prices in the face of dramatic demand increases. If hotels already are at capacity, prices rise but the number of sales cannot. Prices rise for local purchasers of goods and services, as well. The net activity is certainly much smaller than touted by the NFL. The gains to hotel owners are lost through higher prices paid by other local residents. Apparently, the NFL missed Porter's analysis; their commissioned study estimated the expected benefits for the immediately following Miami Super Bowl in 1999 at $396 million in total economic impact, an additional $31 million in just four years rather than the downward adjustment suggested by Porter.

(Continued)

(*Continued*)

Another unexpected reduction in hotel-related spending may also occur with events. When Tampa, Florida, got the 2002 Super Bowl, 35,000 rooms were immediately reserved. Proprietors required a minimum 7-day reservation for Super Bowl weekend. This was great for hotel owners because they enjoyed greater paid occupancy rates. But their guests actually only stayed for the weekend, crowding out a few days' worth of other tourists who would have occupied the rooms and spent over the entire week. Occupancy at hotels was high, but spending was lower than it otherwise would have been in the absence of the Super Bowl. But true to form, the NFL had already estimated that Tampa Bay would enjoy $250 million in total economic impact hosting that Super Bowl. More recently, the NFL clearly has continued to turn a deaf ear. A study jointly funded with the San Diego Super Bowl Host Committee claims that the 2003 Super Bowl generated $367 million in total economic impact, up from the city's last Super Bowl in 1998 by $72 million.

Recently, the National Association of Sports Commissions provided guidelines for uniform study of these benefits. Essentially, they suggest ascertaining the number of visitors multiplied by their spending, plus administrative and operations spending. Then, a reasonable multiplier can be used for total impact. But this clearly misses the point: it is "new" spending that matters, not "total" spending. As Porter so aptly puts it, what matters is how much more an event brings to a location over and above what already would have occurred anyway. In the case of sports megaevents, other activity-generating alternatives would have occurred in their absence.

Source: Philip Porter, "Mega-Sports Events as Municipal Investments: A Critique of Impact Analysis," in *Sports Economics: Current Research*, John Fizel, Elizabeth Gustafson, and Laurence Hadley, eds. (Westport, CT: Praeger, 1999); *Sports Business Journal*, January 15, 2001; NFL.com (NFL News), May 13, 2003.

ARE THE COSTS OF SUBSIDIES WORTH IT?

Subsidized projects are in the $200 million range for arenas and $400 million for stadiums and ballparks. The most recent and comprehensive treatment on subsidies by Long (2005) suggests annual subsidies around $19 million in 2004 dollars. Are the benefits created by these projects—economic activity value, development value, and buyers' surpluses and external benefits—worth these costs?

In the previous sections we found that direct and indirect economic activity and development value alone do not provide a solid argument for subsidizing stadiums. Almost all measured value is simply value rearranged from other sources, and analysts can find no development value. The most recent estimates of buyers' surpluses range from $16.3 million to $18.5 million per year in 2004 dollars. Finally, external benefits for a hockey team have been estimated at $4.1 million 2004 dollars per year, whereas NFL teams could raise some rental rates in the central core of cities by as much as $156.2 million 2004 dollars annually. Even at the lower levels of the estimates, buyers' surpluses and external benefits appear to be about equal to the average subsidy.

However, we must be extremely careful in our evaluation. First, only a few studies have even examined the benefits or the costs of subsidies. Further, subsidy amounts vary considerably, so comparisons at the average will be misleading in many cases. Clearly, more analysis is needed before any definitive answer to the subsidy question can be obtained. In addition, just because we can identify subsidy benefits does not mean that collection of funds for subsidies will be easy or fair. And there will always be vigorous argument over whether government should be undertaking actions only because they generate benefits for some people in excess of the costs to others.

CHAPTER RECAP

It is possible to justify subsidies that benefit team owners and fans. The presence of external benefits is one justification for sports team subsidies. When teams produce benefits to nonpayers, team outputs are lower than society would prefer. Subsidies to sports team owners can lead owners to produce greater attendance and TV output until fans receive the level of quality and attendance for which they are willing to pay. A second justification occurs when a sports team owner has a money-losing team. In such a case, if buyers' surpluses are large enough, a subsidy that keeps the team in business is better for fans than losing the team.

Just because subsidies provide the benefits does not mean that any subsidy size is justified. Cost-benefit analysis is crucial in assessing the size of a subsidy. However, assessment of benefits and costs is a complex problem. Costs are in the form of infrastructure subsidies, operating subsidies, and stadium construction subsidies. Some costs can be estimated, whereas others can only be identified. Components affected by time require discounting. Although dollar costs can be obvious, opportunity costs require deeper inspection. Finally, disinformation for political purposes complicates the determination of subsidy costs.

Care must also be taken in evaluating subsidy benefits. Economic activity benefits (direct and indirect) occur during construction and after the team has moved into a facility. Only new economic activity counts in the analysis of benefits. Boundaries for the analysis of benefits must coincide with the spending jurisdiction. The correct spending multiplier should also be used. Development values, buyers' surpluses, and external benefits should also be considered when assessing subsidy benefits.

The cost of a subsidy is approximately the sum of depreciation, opportunity cost of funds, and forgone taxes, minus the net operating revenue from the stadium that actually goes to the state or local government. Subsidies at the state and local level average between $16 million and $18 million in 2004 dollars on publicly owned facilities, plus a small amount more in federal subsidy if the facility is funded through tax-exempt bonds.

The Baltimore Camden Yards and Seattle Mariners and Seahawks subsidy examples make it clear that the economic impacts of subsidies are close to zero. Nearly all of the economic activity from the sport is just rearranged from other spending that would have occurred anyway. The bulk of economic analysis supports this conclusion. In addition, so-called development values do not appear to exist, despite their intuitive appeal. This leaves buyers' surpluses and external benefits to make up the bulk of the subsidy. Few studies have examined these last two types of benefits, but buyers' surpluses may be as high as $18.5 million per year in 2004 dollars, and external benefits have been estimated for hockey at about $4.1 million per year while annual rental rates in cities with NFL teams, representing another take on quality-of-life values, may be as high as $156.2 million annually. The small number of studies and the variation in their outcomes makes it difficult to pass judgment on whether sports subsidies are worth it. They appear to be so on average, but averages can be misleading in many cases.

KEY TERMS AND CONCEPTS

- External benefit
- External benefit inefficiency
- Minimum subsidy
- Cost-benefit analysis
- Infrastructure subsidies

- Operating subsidies
- Stadium subsidies
- Annual subsidy formula
- Direct economic activity
- Indirect economic activity
- Economic impact analysis

- New economic activity
- Spending multiplier
- Development value
- Federal subsidy component
- New value added

REVIEW QUESTIONS

1. Define external benefit. What distinguishes the two types of external benefits that sports teams produce? Give examples of each.
2. Describe external benefit inefficiency. How can it be remedied?
3. Define the minimum subsidy. Remember to include both external benefits and money losses to owners in your definition.
4. What is cost-benefit analysis? Why is it a valuable tool?
5. Can cost-benefit analysis tell us how much to spend in subsidies to sports teams? Explain.
6. What are the three main types of sports subsidies? Give an example of each.
7. Define the following terms: *stadium rent, concessions, parking, signage,* and *nonsport revenue*?
8. What is the difference between a revenue bond and a general obligation bond? Which is most commonly used to finance sports stadium subsidies? Why?
9. State the annual subsidy formula. Carefully describe each element of the formula.
10. Define economic activity benefits. What is the distinction between direct and indirect economic activity benefits? Give examples of each.
11. What is economic impact analysis (EIA)?
12. What is the difference between total economic activity and new economic activity? Which is more important in a cost-benefit analysis? Why?
13. What is a spending multiplier? What is the difference between a sales multiplier and an income multiplier? Should they be applied to total or new economic activity? Why or why not?

14. What is meant by development value? Is there a distinction between "total" and "new" for this type of subsidy benefit? Explain.
15. What is new value added? How would you calculate it?

THOUGHT PROBLEMS

1. Is it efficient to subsidize team owners for the benefit of a small proportion of taxpayers who are sports fans? Is it fair?
2. Explain how a new stadium might enhance the competitiveness of a particular team. Be very careful to state the particulars of the situation where this can happen.
3. Graphically demonstrate the inefficiency that occurs when sports teams produce external benefits. How will a subsidy remedy this problem?
4. In Chapter 2, we downplayed the idea that owners lose money. Can owners actually lose money? If so, can it make sense to subsidize a money-losing owner? Graphically demonstrate this situation.
5. If a subsidy is justified on external benefit grounds, is any size subsidy justified? Discuss the size of a subsidy in terms of the definition of a minimum subsidy. Would you expect owners to try to obtain larger than minimum subsidies? Why? Why might they be successful?
6. List the problems that confront state and local governments if they are to collect portions of buyers' surpluses and external benefits to provide subsidies to team owners.
7. Under general obligation bonds, hotel and rental car taxes are sometimes used to generate revenue for the bond payments. With this method, who pays for the subsidy? Is this fair? Why are these types of taxes politically attractive?
8. Why doesn't an estimate of the original construction costs give a full accounting of the costs of a stadium subsidy? What other subsidy elements does this original construction cost miss?
9. Why do we resort to the annual subsidy formula in describing the costs of stadium subsidies? What is gained by using this formula? What is lost?
10. Do you think the economic activity values given in Table 10.2 for Atlanta refer to total economic activity or new economic activity? Why?
11. Under what circumstances would the movement of a restaurant from a more distant location to a location close to a new stadium be new economic activity? (*Hint:* There are two explanations.)
12. Why is it less likely that new economic activity will accompany a subsidy to keep a team that already exists compared with a subsidy used to lure a brand new team?
13. Why aren't wages a subsidy benefit?
14. Compare and contrast the two EIA examples for Baltimore and Seattle (e.g., which values are included in each, how were they determined). Which is more believable? Why? Does either prove conclusively that there are large economic activity benefits? The critique by Hamilton and Kahn (1997) and the evaluation

for Seattle suggest these benefits are very low. Does that mean the subsidies were not worth it?

15. Summarize the general verdict on economic activity values from sports owner subsidies. Do the same for development value. Why is the final evaluation of the net value of sports owner subsidies given in the text a qualified one? What additional work needs to be done to reach a more definitive conclusion on the value of subsidies?

ADVANCED PROBLEMS

1. How must rent and shared revenue be structured in a sports team lease in order to take care of external benefit problems? Are rents that increase with attendance consistent with this setup? How else should subsidies be structured to overcome external benefit problems?

2. Refer to the Learning Highlight: Build It and They Will Come? What was the cost of the stadium construction subsidy to the citizens of the Tampa Bay–St. Petersburg area? Show how the cost was calculated. Will the Devil Rays provide enough benefits to make up for this subsidy?

3. Why do you think that the average subsidy has grown threefold over the period from early estimates (the early 1970s) to the more recent estimates (late 1980s) discussed in the text? (Remember, the threefold statement already includes inflation.)

4. The *Sports Business Journal* (November 6, 2000, p. 15) reports that the *New York Times* stepped up its usual World Series coverage by 12 to 15 percent for the subway series. The *Daily News* had its largest Sunday edition ever for game one of the series and printed 1 million copies daily (from Saturday to the end of the series), when its regular subscriptions are only 730,000. What type of benefits are these? What were they worth to the *Daily News*? Relate your answer to arguments for sports subsidies.

5. Read the buyers' surpluses analyses of Irani (1997) and of Alexander, Kern, and Neill (2000). What were their assumptions? What were their statistical techniques? If they used surveys, how did they treat nonrespondents? Does this treatment of nonrespondents influence their results? Why do you think the average discovered by Alexander, Kern, and Neill (2000) is so much larger than the average discovered by Irani (1997)?

6. Read the external benefit analysis of Johnson, Groothuis, and Whitehead (2001). What were their assumptions? What were their statistical techniques? If they used surveys, how did they treat nonrespondents? Does this treatment of nonrespondents influence their results? What are the limitations of an analysis of one team in one league?

7. Write a brief response to the remarks by Texas comptroller Carole Keeton Strayhorn in the section on events. Be sure to use the ideas presented in the Learning Highlight: Super Bowl? Super Dud!

8. According to the *Sports Business Journal* (January 15, 2001, pp. 21–22), the National Association of Sports Commissions estimated the total economic

activity of a number of sports events. Total economic impact was calculated as follows:

$$V = \text{Number of out-of-town visitors}$$
$$S = \text{Average spending per day}$$
$$D = \text{Length of visit in days}$$
$$TVS = \text{Total visitor spending} = V \times S \times D$$
$$TAS = \text{Total administrative spending to make an event possible}$$
$$TDS = \text{Total direct spending} = TVS + TAS$$
$$M = \text{Regional spending multiplier}$$
$$TEA = \text{Total economic activity} = TDS \times M$$

Here are the results from the National Association of Sports Commissions for the top 10 professional events of 2000:

EVENT	LOCATION	TEA ($MILLIONS)
Indy 500	Indianapolis, IN	$336.60
Daytona 500	Daytona Beach, FL	$240
Brickyard 400	Indianapolis, IN	$219.5
Super Bowl XXXIV	Atlanta, GA	$215
SAP U.S. Grand Prix	Indianapolis, IN	$170.8
DirecTV 500	Ft. Worth, TX	$165.2
Goracing.com 500	Bristol, TN	$119.6
Food City 500	Bristol, TN	$80.5
Kentucky Derby	Louisville, KY	$60
Winston 500	Talladega, AL	$42.2

Source: Sports Business Journal, January 15, 2001. Used with permission of Sports Business Journal.

Suppose you are trying to figure out how much to subsidize these activities. Describe all of the possible problems with using these estimates to arrive at the value of a subsidy.

9. Which pro sport would produce the most positive economic impact for a community? Why?

10. The city of New Orleans recently renegotiated the Superdome lease of the New Orleans Saints (*Sports Business Journal*, July 16, 2001, p. 8). Prior to the renegotiation, the Saints were 25th in local revenue in 1999 ($35.2 million from tickets, special seat boxes, and concessions) and were expected to be last by 2003. Under the 2000 renegotiation, an additional $12.5 million goes to the team owner over the 2001 and 2002 seasons. The owner kept all concession revenue (previously, 40 percent) and occupancy was rent free (previously, rent was 5 percent of gross ticket revenue). If naming rights to the Superdome were sold, the Saints received all the revenue. In return, the owner agreed to stay in New Orleans for 2 more years while negotiations for a new football stadium were underway. If those negotiations failed, the team owner could buy out of the lease early at a greatly reduced amount. Does this renegotiation help overcome external benefit problems associated with the Saints? Does it fit the Siegfried and Zimbalist (2000) itemized list of reasons to give a subsidy rather than a cash payment to an owner? How?

INTERNET RESOURCES

For a host of additional material and questions for thought, visit this book's Web site at www.prenhall.com/fort.

REFERENCES

Alexander, Donald L., William Kern, and Jon Neill. "Valuing the Consumption Benefits from Sports Franchises and Facilities," *Journal of Urban Economics* 48 (2000): 321–337.

Baade, Robert. "Professional Sports as Catalysts for Metropolitan Economic Development," *Journal of Urban Affairs* 18 (1996a): 1–17.

Baade, Robert. "Stadium Subsidies Make Little Economic Sense for Cities, a Rejoinder," *Journal of Urban Affairs* 18 (1996b): 33–37.

Baade, Robert and Richard Dye. "An Analysis of the Economic Rationale for Public Subsidization of Sports Stadiums," *Annals of Regional Science* 22 (1988): 37–47.

Carlino, Gerald and N. Edward Coulson. "Compensating Differentials and the Social Benefits of the NFL," *Journal of Urban Economics* 56 (2004): 25–50.

Chema, Thomas. "When Professional Sports Justify the Subsidy, a Reply to Robert A. Baade," *Journal of Urban Affairs* 18 (1996): 19–22.

Coates, Dennis and Brad R. Humphreys. "The Growth Effects of Sports Franchises, Stadia, and Arenas," *Journal of Policy Analysis and Management* 18 (1999): 601–624.

Conway, Richard, Jr., and William B. Byers. *Seattle Mariners Baseball Club Economic Impact*. Dick Conway and Associates and Department of Geography, University of Washington, Seattle, WA, August 1994.

Conway, Richard, Jr., and William B. Byers. *Seattle Seahawks Economic Impact*. Dick Conway and Associates and Department of Geography, University of Washington, Seattle, WA, March 1996.

Crompton, John L. "Economic Impact Analysis of Sports Facilities and Events: Eleven Sources of Misapplication," *Journal of Sports Management* 9 (January 1995): 14–35.

Hamilton, Bruce and Peter Kahn. "Baltimore's Camden Yards Ballparks," in *Sports, Jobs, and Taxes: The Economic Impact of Sports Teams and Stadiums*. Roger Noll and Andrew Zimbalist, eds. Washington, D.C.: Brookings Institution, 1997.

Irani, Daraius. "Public Subsidies to Stadiums: Do the Costs Outweigh the Benefits?" *Public Finance Review* 25 (1997): 238–253.

Johnson, Bruce K., Peter A. Groothuis, and John C. Whitehead. "The Value of Public Goods Generated by a Major League Sports Team: The CVM Approach," *Journal of Sports Economics* 2 (2001): 6–21.

Keating, Raymond. "Sports Park: The Costly Relationship Between Major League Sports and Government," Policy Analysis No. 339. Washington, D.C.: The Cato Institute, April 5, 1999.

Long, Judith Grant. "Full Count: The Real Cost of Public Funding for Major League Sports Facilities," *Journal of Sports Economics* 6 (2005): 119–143.

Miller, James Edward. *The Baseball Business: Pursuing Pennants and Profits in Baltimore*. Chapel Hill, NC: University of North Carolina Press, 1990.

Noll, Roger and Andrew Zimbalist. "Build the Stadium—Create the Jobs!" in *Sports, Jobs, and Taxes: The Economic Impact of Sports Teams and Stadiums*. Roger Noll and Andrew Zimbalist, eds. Washington, D.C.: Brookings Institution, 1997a.

Noll, Roger and Andrew Zimbalist, eds. *Sports, Jobs, and Taxes: The Economic Impact of Sports Teams and Stadiums*. Washington, D.C.: Brookings Institution, 1997b.

Okner, Benjamin. "Subsidies of Stadiums and Arenas," in *Government and the Sports Business*. Roger Noll, ed. Washington, D.C.: Brookings Institution, 1974.

Porter, Philip. "Mega-Sports Events as Municipal Investments: A Critique of Impact Analysis," in *Sports Economics: Current Research*. John Fizel, Elizabeth Gustafson, and Laurence Hadley, eds. Westport, CT: Praeger, 1999.

Quirk, James and Rodney D. Fort. *Pay Dirt: The Business of Professional Team Sports*. Princeton, NJ: Princeton University Press, 1992.

Regional Science Research Institute. Camden Yards Studies. Philadelphia, PA, 1987.

Rosentraub, Mark. "Does the Emperor Have New Clothes? A Reply to Robert J. Baade," *Journal of Urban Affairs* 18 (1996): 23–31.

Siegfried, John and Andrew Zimbalist. "The Economics of Sports Facilities and Their Communities," *Journal of Economic Perspectives* 14 (2000): 95–114.

Sports Leases on CD-ROM, Major League Facilities. Vols. 1 & 2. Chicago, IL: Team Marketing Reports, Inc., 1998.

Zimmerman, Dennis. "Subsidizing Stadiums: Who Benefits, Who Pays?" in *Sports, Jobs, and Taxes: The Economic Impact of Sports Teams and Stadiums*. Roger Noll and Andrew Zimbalist, eds. Washington, D.C.: Brookings Institution, 1997.

The Stadium Mess

Chapter Objectives

After reading this chapter, you should be able to:

- Understand the basic concentrated benefits and dispersed costs prediction of the rational actor explanation of representative democracy outcomes.

- Explain how league control of team location gives team owners the upper hand in stadium negotiations.

- Argue that the concentrated benefits and dispersed costs explanation depicts the typical stadium subsidy outcome.

- Explain that direct democracy through referenda and initiatives has not curbed the stadium mess because it has both theoretical and practical limitations.

- Understand why the stadium mess realistically can be reversed only if consumer interest groups fight the current winners in the stadium subsidy process.

USA Today: The excitement from that playoff run (in 1997), and the excitement you provided as a young superstar, saved baseball in Seattle. Do you feel in some way that Safeco Field is the House That Junior Built?

Ken Griffey, Jr.: No. The people of Seattle built it. They're the ones who went out and said "yes" to keep this ballclub here. The 25 guys on the field helped, but it was eventually the people of Seattle who said they wanted the ballpark and wanted the team to stay. They could have said "no" and we would have ended up somewhere else.

www.usatoday.com, JULY 15, 1999

Sometimes it is simply amazing how history is rewritten by sentimentality and selective memory. The opening quote is a great example of this. At the time Ken Griffey, Jr., made his remarks, he was moving from the Seattle Mariners to the Cincinnati Reds. Apparently, his memory was short and a little bit fuzzy. It is true that there was a stadium vote in King County (not just in the city of Seattle) for a new ballpark for the Mariners, but the people did not say yes. The referendum failed by the narrowest of margins. The people actually said no. However, despite this defeat, the Mariners did get a new ballpark. The Washington state legislature developed a funding package for the ballpark that raised the price to taxpayers and spread the costs out over many more of them than was specified in the original referendum. If anything, the will of the people was not obeyed. Voters voted against the ballpark but they got one anyway. Astonishingly, it came at a greater cost than they refused in the referendum. Let's hope Griffey remembers his manager's signals better than he remembers the ballpark voting episode in Washington state.

In this chapter, we develop an explanation for why so many stadiums are built and at such extravagant costs. The important role of owners and leagues in what I call the "stadium mess" receives particular attention. In addition, the role of direct democracy (referendum and initiative votes) is presented. As we will see, theoretically, weaknesses in direct democracy reduce its ability to ameliorate the stadium mess. Examples of MLB and NFL stadium financing in Seattle are used to illustrate the points made throughout the chapter. Finally, because the outcome is political, we will see how an alteration in the power of interest groups is the only realistic hope of altering the stadium mess.

RATIONAL ACTOR EXPLANATIONS IN POLITICS: GENERAL INSIGHTS

As we saw in Chapter 10, sports team subsidies are large and can be justified in only a few cases. The highly touted increased economic activity and development value are not large enough to justify the large pervasive subsidies we observe. The most important subsidy to sports teams is the provision of public stadiums. In this section, we provide the general framework used by economists and other analysts to explain how stadium subsidies come about.

Social scientists have been examining the logic of collective action since the original works of Nobel Prize winner James Buchanan, his colleague Gordon Tullock, and Mancur Olson in the mid-1950s and early 1960s. We used a version of the logic of collective action when we analyzed union governance in Chapter 9. The **rational actor explanation** is their description of political outcomes.

The rational actor explanation assumes that people pursue their own self-interest in politics just as they do in private markets. Voters look to obtain benefits that they either cannot get from markets or can get more of from the political process. Politicians, for whatever reason, enjoy being politicians and pursue reelection in the political choices and legislation that they propose and support. The outcome of an election is determined by the relative political potency of groups. Those groups that provide the most effective political support for politicians tend to gain from the political process. The rational actor explanation makes a very special prediction: In the political process, for any particular special interest under consideration, benefits will tend to go to the politically powerful groups while costs are spread over those without power. In essence, if some group is not fighting for you on a particular issue, then you will tend to pay rather than receive.

Sources of Dissatisfaction with Market Outcomes: Turning to Government for Remedies

It is important to understand that government and markets are two different methods of satisfying people's desires. Before we turn to an explanation of government outcomes, let's recognize why groups turn from markets to governments in the first place. One reason is to remedy **market failures**. In sports, the failures are market power and external benefits. More generally, hospitals, electric utilities, and even tree surgeons are regulated for quality and market power in the name of consumer protection. Interestingly, despite their obvious positions of market power, sports leagues remain unregulated (see Chapter 12 for why this is the case).

The external benefit problem and how it relates to team production was presented in Chapter 10. The argument is that sports teams create value to fans that team owners cannot capture. As a result, attendance (in the short run) and quality (in the long run) are lower than they would be if owners could capture more of the value they create. These benefits are small, but that does not prevent owners from trying to make the most of them in arguments for stadium subsidies.

Finally, government has the power to redistribute wealth from some people to others. Sometimes such **wealth redistribution** occurs out of a sense of fairness. For example, all taxpayers help pay for programs that transfer purchasing power to those defined as poor. However, sometimes redistribution occurs just because a group has the power to get more of what it seeks through political approaches than through market approaches. As we will see, this last type of demand for redistribution can help explain the behavior of team owners as they pursue stadium subsidies.

Rational Actor Politics: An Overview

Rational actor politics predicts that powerful groups win in the political process. We can see how they get the upper hand by thinking about political participation, in general, using the following identity (note that everything cancels so that the left and right sides of the equation are identical):

$$\frac{V_m}{E} \equiv \left(\frac{R}{E}\right)\left(\frac{B}{R}\right)\left(\frac{V_m}{B}\right)$$

V_m is the number of people casting votes on a ballot measure identified by the subscript m. The measure could be a ballot for candidates to elective office, or it could be a direct democracy ballot (referendum or initiative) for a stadium subsidy. Note that there are E members in the eligible voting population. Clearly, then, the only time that the ratio on the left side of the identity equals one is when every member of the eligible voting population actually casts a vote on the particular measure. However, universal voting is far from the norm. If enough people do not vote on a particular issue or for a particular elected official, then the outcomes may favor special interests. We will examine how this occurs.

Costs of Registration   On the right-hand side of our identity, R voters register out of the eligible population, E. This first ratio on the right side is less than one for at least a couple of reasons. Voter registration is not free. It requires an eligible person to find a place to register, incur costs in getting there, and fill out paperwork. Given the costs, some people do not feel strongly enough about participation to register. Those interested in raising the registration rate often attack the problem by trying to lower the costs of voter registration. For example, so-called motor voter registration allows eligible individuals to register when they pay their vehicle license fees or renew their driver's license.

Costs of Turning Out to Vote   The second ratio on the right side of the identity indicates that B of the R registered voters actually make it to the booth. This is typically called turnout. Again, this ratio also is less than one. Even after a person has registered, the actual act of getting to the booth has a cost. The cost may include time away from work and fees for transportation and childcare. These costs may cause participation to wane. In some states, to overcome this, all ballots (not just absentee ballots) are actually mailed with return postage and mail-in voting across entire counties is becoming common.

Fall Off, Rational Ignorance, and Free Riding   Finally, only V_m votes are cast out of the B voters that actually turn out. This phenomenon is called fall off. One of the most compelling reasons for fall off in the booth is the idea of rational ignorance discussed in Chapter 9. Because information is expensive, it is rational for individuals to be ignorant about most things. Typically, individual voters overcome these costs by being informed only concerning those few issues about which they most care. The cost of becoming broadly informed is just too high. This is one of the reasons that voters typically receive a state-sponsored voter's pamphlet with balanced descriptions of the issues on the ballot.

Rational ignorance is the most compelling explanation of the fall off ratio on the far-right side of our voting identity. Why else would people fail to cast a vote on some particular issue once they have overcome all of the other costs? The only answer is that they have not taken the time to become informed on all of the issues and are unwilling to make an uninformed vote. Rational ignorance also plays a role in the other ratios on the right side. If voters remain rationally ignorant, they may never see the point in registering or turning out in the first place.

Another factor affecting the right side of the identity also was discussed in Chapter 9, namely, free riding. For example, if other voters are informed, and many of them are like me, then I might believe that the result will be the same regardless of whether or not I vote. The idea that follows this reasoning is that if there are others just like me and I think enough of them will vote, then why should I vote? This free riding contributes to fall off.

The Rational Level of Voting and the Behavior of Elected Officials

The **rational level of voting** is the total number of votes on any given issue or politician after people fail to register, do not turn out, and fall off on the given vote. Thus, the rational level of voting is lower than the total number of eligible voters. Here is the kicker: The more specialized the voting measure becomes, the lower the expected turnout and the number of votes cast on the particular measure. Indeed, it may well be that the rational level of voting has a distinct minority of the eligible voting population deciding many of the issues on a given ballot.

Perhaps the most important observation by rational actor theorists is that politicians understand the rational voting behavior of their constituents and, consequently, make choices based on this knowledge. Politicians seek to satisfy groups of constituents that play a prominent role in reelection. If V_m is a reelection vote for them, politicians know that the majority of their constituents never cast votes in the first place. Thus, whenever possible, in the bundle of choices politicians must make, many of the decisions will provide benefits to politically potent constituent groups and spread the costs out in small amounts onto others. This is the concentrated benefit and dispersed costs outcome we saw in Chapter 9 at work in unions, only here it occurs in the larger context of state and local government.

As those bearing the costs are, for the most part, rationally ignorant, they will never figure out what hit them, and even if they do, the per capita costs will be small. Those bearing the costs are unlikely to raise a politically potent response to special interest outcomes. Special interests, on the other hand, bring block votes from potent groups and campaign contributions from lobbyists that politicians require in order to gain reelection. Sports leagues have learned the lobbying lesson as well as any participant in the political process, as shown in the Learning Highlight: MLB Lobbying Efforts.

A Diagrammatic Model of Rational Actor Political Outcomes A useful diagram of rational actor political outcomes is shown in Figure 11.1, which presents a generalized version of the triangle describing union governance we saw in Chapter 9. The reelection constituency is at the top of the triangle. Members of this group are politically potent potential suppliers of votes and campaign contributions to elected officials. Elected officials make policy choices in a given policy area to keep their reelection constituency happy. That constituency then evaluates the outcome and decides whether to reelect the responsible elected officials. If the constituency is pleased, elected officials retain their seats. If they are not, a pool of potential elected officials always is waiting in the wings to give politically potent groups what they want. The general constituency sits by the sidelines, bearing the dispersed costs of policy choices because they are rationally ignorant and do not participate in this particular policy area. Figure 11.1 suggests that we look closely at politically potent participants if we want to explain stadium subsidy outcomes.

LEARNING HIGHLIGHT
MLB Lobbying Efforts

Lobbying is one way that politically potent groups influence the political process. That sports leagues lobby as heavily as many larger industry interests may come as a surprise. Indeed, some sports leagues, including MLB, have full-time offices staffed in Washington, D.C., devoted to lobbying efforts. In the first half of 1999, MLB spent $900,000 lobbying Congress on various issues. The MLBPA spent $200,000. Other leagues and unions spent less, but spend they did. The NFL spent $170,000, and the NFLPA spent another $45,000. The NBA spent $65,000, and the NHL spent $25,000. As Joe Browne, executive vice president for communications and public affairs of the NFL puts it, "The first amendment gives every individual and organization in this country the right to petition the government. We're there to let them know where we stand on issues, just like every other entity and industry in the country" (*Sports Business Journal*, January 12, 2004, p. 18). Compared to other industries, MLB's lobbying efforts are large. In fact, in 1999, MLB spent as much on lobbying as Ford Motor Co., RJR Nabisco, and Westinghouse. As is common with many lobbying efforts, MLB's lobbyists spent $400,000 of the $900,000 and contracted out the balance to other lobbying firms. In 2001, MLB was the first pro sports league to form its own political action committee. The PAC spent about $372,000 in 2004. The total spent through other lobbyists since 1997 is around $6 million.

MLB's main lobbying efforts were pushing legislation that fortified the league's antitrust exemption and fighting legislation aimed at reducing that exemption. For example, the Stadium Financing and Relocation Act, which would have forced baseball franchises to fund stadiums privately in order to keep their antitrust exemption, was introduced by Arlen Specter (R-PA). He made no bones about the fact that it was intended to curb the type of spending that had happened in Pennsylvania at the time. Pennsylvania state legislators had approved stadium funding for MLB's Pirates and Phillies and the NFL's Steelers and Eagles.

Other nuts-and-bolts issues also received MLB lobbying attention:

- Trade with Cuba (mainly clearance for the Baltimore Orioles to play exhibition games in that country)
- Communications (prohibiting Internet gambling and increasing satellite broadcast regulation)
- Copyright law (especially important to MLB broadcasts)
- Tax law (governing deductions when entertaining at sports events)

Alan Sobba, MLB director of government relations with offices in Washington, D.C., made it clear that MLB participates in the lobbying process with the same goals of any potent political participant, "We're up there [Capitol Hill] on a day-to-day basis to make sure we get a fair shake on these pieces of legislation." In Congressional hearings on steroid abuse in early 2005, oversight committee members had received $8,000 from MLB's PAC and faced the man in charge of those political contributions, Commissioner Bud Selig.

Sources: Sports Business Journal, October 11, 1999, p. 6, and January 12, 2004, p. 18; BostonHerald.com, March 17, 2005; DailyNews.com, March 20, 2005.

Figure 11.1 The Collective Action Triangle
The outcomes from collective action follow rational actor politics. A powerful reelection constituency is in control of the electoral chances of elected officials. Those officials choose policies that their reelection constituency evaluates in terms of their own economic welfare. If the policies are best for the reelection constituency, elected officials get reelected. The general constituency is relegated to the sidelines.

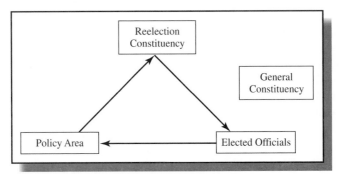

OWNERS AS BENEFICIARIES OF RATIONAL ACTOR SUBSIDY POLITICS

Team owners are an important reelection constituency for state and local politicians. Let's take a look at the value of the benefits owners seek from the political process. The size of those benefits should clue us in on how much owners will flex their political muscle in order to get stadium subsidies.

Two things are expected from a stadium subsidy. First, **subsidies raise owner profits**. Subsidies are expected to increase revenues at the gate and, in the event of a better lease, owners will receive a greater share of concessions and parking. In addition, under a better lease, costs such as rent and stadium maintenance could fall. Second, in the eyes of fans, the team should improve. However, the relationship between **subsidies and team quality** can be complicated. As we learned in earlier chapters, revenues can rise, but the team may not get any better. The owner will be better off in any case, but the profit-maximizing use of the subsidy may not be to increase the team's level of quality.

From Chapter 4, we know that owners are constantly striving to find that level of team quality that maximizes profits in the long run. From that perspective, here is how an injection of new revenue would not alter team quality. If the subsidy revenue comes in but the owner does not think that fans will support increased quality in the long run, then no more spending on talent will occur out of subsidy revenues. We should expect the owner to pocket the subsidy. However, if the owner perceives that fans will support a higher level of talent in the long run, then subsidy revenues will go to hire more talent and the team should improve.

It is difficult to know which will occur beforehand, and looking at revenues and team quality after the fact is not always enlightening. Suppose that both revenues and quality increase after a particular team owner obtains a stadium subsidy. Did the subsidy lead to the increase in quality? The answer can only be maybe. The team may have been improving prior to the subsidy and simply have continued a long-run plan that would have occurred without it. In this case, the team improved because the owner had made the decision prior to the subsidy that profits would improve with a higher quality team. Again, because the subsidy had nothing to do with the team's quality improvement, we would expect that the subsidy would just go in the owner's pocket and that no spending on talent beyond that already planned prior to the subsidy would occur.

Another explanation exists for an observation of improved quality prior to the subsidy. The owners could have been so sure that the subsidy was forthcoming that they went out on a limb and began hiring talent before receiving the subsidy. The owners may have forecast that their fans would pay more for higher quality and borrowed against the future subsidy in order to increase quality. As you can see, there are two explanations for the same outcome. One does not depend on the subsidy, the other does.

Let's keep all of these ideas in mind as we look at the evidence on revenues, spending on talent, and team quality after stadium subsidies. In addition, remember that owners will always be better off with a subsidy than without one. They will either spend the subsidy on higher quality and earn greater profits in the future or they will just pocket the subsidy. In our empirical analysis of subsidies and revenues, to which we now turn, we will focus mostly on MLB.

An Early Analysis of Subsidies, Revenues, and Winning

In our 1992 book *Pay Dirt: The Business of Professional Team Sports*, James Quirk and I detail the impact of new stadiums on attendance and performance in MLB over the period 1960–1982. Focusing on the 5-year average attendance before and after a new stadium, we found that MLB teams with new stadiums enjoyed an attendance increase of about 624,000 per year. A similar calculation for the remaining teams in the league (those without new stadiums) revealed only a 96,000 increase per year. Thus, teams with new stadiums enjoyed about 6.5 times the attendance increase of the rest of the league. New stadiums draw more people, just as we would expect from our analysis in Chapter 4, because the quality of the stadium experience has increased. The long-run stadium decisions of teams should lead to improved fan enjoyment.

Did You Know?
From 1960 to 1982, MLB teams with new stadiums enjoyed about 6.5 times the attendance increase of all the other teams in the league.

Quirk and I also show that the on-field performance of teams with new stadiums improved over that same period (1992). The same 5-year average comparison before and after a new stadium showed that teams with new stadiums enjoyed a 35-point winning percent increase. Each game won represents about 6.2 points (1,000 total possible points, divided by 162 possible wins, yields 6.2 points per win). So 35 points would be worth about 5.6 more games per year. From our analysis of winning percent increments and final league standings in Chapter 4, that is enough to move a team out of the cellar and is a goodly portion of the amount needed to move a team through the rest of the standings. At least on one sample, new stadiums improve attendance and revenues, and those improvements are parlayed into better teams on the field.

Did You Know?
From 1960 to 1982, MLB teams with new stadiums won about 5.6 more games per season than teams without new stadiums.

Quirk and I (1992) also noted that part of the overall increase for teams with new stadiums would be bound to occur because four of the twelve teams in the analysis were expansion teams. Expansion teams slowly improve over time. We offered the same explanation for our findings that you would offer from your understanding of owners' long-run profit pursuits:

> A new stadium will tend to improve the drawing potential of a team, for a given roster of players. As makes sense intuitively (and from economic theory . . .) the stronger the drawing potential of a team, the more a profit-maximizing team finds it worthwhile to spend in improving the caliber of the team. In effect, a new stadium converts a small-town market, such as Kansas City, into a market that is not quite so small as before, and the profit incentives this creates lead predictably to the team's acquiring higher quality players, producing a better performance on the playing field. . . . (Quirk and Fort 1992, p. 139)

This explanation is entirely consistent with our findings. However, team quality does not always increase following a move into a subsidized stadium.

Hamilton and Kahn (1997) note that attendance rose significantly for the Orioles after they moved to their new Camden Yards Ballpark for the 1992 season. In the 5 years before the Orioles began play in the new park, attendance averaged 29,459 per game per year. In the 5 years after, the average increased by 53 percent to 45,034. Further, they note that stadium revenues rose by $25.5 million after the Orioles paid about $1.8 million to the stadium authority. Thus, the owners acquired about 93 percent of the stadium revenue increase. This clearly indicates that the Orioles' owners benefited from a new park. How did the new park affect the quality of the Orioles? In the 5 years prior to the 1992 season, the Orioles' average winning percent was 0.434 (with a range from 0.335 to 0.537). For the 5 years from 1992 through 1996, their average winning percent was 0.534, a full 23 percent increase in quality. It does not appear that this dramatic improvement was by prior design, as the Orioles' winning percent had fallen steadily from 1989 to 1991.

Some evidence shows that the new stadium revenues went to talent, as the Orioles' team payroll jumped from $14 million in 1991 to $24 million in 1992 and continued to increase by about $8 million per year thereafter, whereas league-wide the average team payroll rose about $500,000 per year over the same period. Remember, we cannot know whether the subsidy drove the higher winning percent outcomes observed here, but in the Orioles' case, it appears that the stadium subsidy, in addition to making more money for the owner, did coincide with a better team.

Of course, we cannot know whether this increase in quality was planned regardless of whether a subsidy was obtained, and moreover, the possibility that the subsidy was just pocketed by the owner cannot be ruled out either. Interestingly, the team did not make it to the playoffs in the five years prior to moving into Camden Yards, and they did not improve enough to make it to the playoffs after that even with the revenue injection from their new stadium.

A More Recent Analysis of Stadiums, Revenues, and Winning

In my 1999 article "Stadium Votes, Market Power, and Politics," I took an updated look at team owner benefits from the most recent stadium subsidies where data were available. Looking at MLB, data availability narrowed the field to the White Sox (New Comiskey Park), Orioles (Camden Yards), Indians (Jacobs Field), and Rangers (Ballpark at Arlington). The data in Table 11.1 show the annual averages for the 5-year periods before and after the new stadiums. The impacts from the recent stadiums are huge. The smallest annual average attendance increase was 941,000 for the Sox, and the remaining teams enjoyed average increases of over 1 million fans at the gate per year.

Did You Know?
On average, for the 5 years after they moved into their new Comiskey Park in 1991, the White Sox enjoyed an annual attendance increase of 941,000. On average, for the 5 years after the Indians and Rangers moved into their new stadiums in 1994, they enjoyed an annual attendance increase of over 1 million.

Because we have already discussed the winning percent results for the Orioles, let's focus on the remaining teams. Winning percent increases were enough to move the White Sox and the Indians up an entire place in the standings, and this improvement was enough to push the Indians into pennant contention once they began play in their new Jacobs Field. Team salaries also followed a familiar pattern. For the White Sox, team payroll increased $7 million in 1991, $14 million in 1992, and another $12 million in 1993. In 1994, the Indians' team payroll went up $15 million, and then another $9 million in 1995 and $7.5 million in 1996. Success followed the revenue injection from a new stadium for these two teams. Again, whether these quality increases were planned with or without the subsidies from new stadiums cannot be known. However, it is clear that winning percent increased coincident with owners' receiving subsidies.

The Rangers illustrate the cautions discussed at the beginning of the section. First, to be sure, Table 11.1 shows that gate and venue revenues took a decided jump up. However, no increase in quality followed their movement into their new park in 1994. This should come as no surprise because the Rangers' owners spent hardly anything more on talent after the move. Team payroll fell $3.6 million in 1994 and increased just $3.5 million and $4.8 million in the next 2 years. It appears that the Rangers' owners did not put much, if any, of the increased gate and venue revenues toward talent. The theory in Chapter 4 would suggest that this was because the owners saw no gains in terms of fan willingness to pay for increased quality in the long run. We can reach no other conclusion except that the owners pocketed the subsidy.

Did You Know?
Despite attendance increases over 1 million, gate revenue increases of $9.9 million, and venue revenue increases of $328 million in 1994, team payroll fell $3.6 million and there was no difference in the Rangers' winning percent in the years following their move into the Ballpark at Arlington in 1994.

Quinn, Bursik, Borick, and Raethz (2003) extend the examination of the relationship between new stadiums and winning to all four major pro sports leagues. They take both 7-year and 3-year before-and-after looks at all teams in all four leagues. They find that there is no improvement in team quality measured by winning percent in any league except MLB. They also find that the magnitude of the impact of a new stadium on MLB on-field success is about what Quirk and Fort (1992) found, on the average nearly six more games per season.

Table 11.1 Value of New Stadiums to MLB Owners

TEAM	YEAR OPENED	ATTENDANCE (THOUSANDS)		WINNING PERCENT (POINTS)[a]		GATE REVENUE ($MILLIONS)[b]		VENUE REVENUE ($MILLIONS)[c]	
		DIFFERENCE[d]	% CHANGE	DIFFERENCE[e]	% CHANGE	DIFFERENCE[f]	% CHANGE	DIFFERENCE[g]	% CHANGE
White Sox	1991	941	69.3	51	10.4				
Orioles	1992	1,135	52.5	80	17.6				
Indians	1994	1,585	114	152	34.3	$21.7	147	$11.2	8.7
Rangers	1994	1,564	144	22	20.5	$9.9	53.9	$32.8	85.6

[a] One game won equals 6.2 points.
[b, c] Data are unavailable for White Sox and Orioles.
[d, e, f, g] The difference between the average for the 5 years before and the 5 years after the opening of the new stadium.

Source: Rodney Fort, "Stadium Votes, Market Power, and Politics," *University of Toledo Law Review* 30 (1999): 419–442. Reprinted by permission of the *University of Toledo Law Review.*

What to Expect from Owners

Although revenue injections from stadium subsidies appear to lead to higher team quality only in MLB, new stadiums do help owners by increasing revenues and possibly lowering costs; profits should, therefore, increase. Stadium revenues have always been important to all teams in all pro sports leagues. In Tables 11.2, 11.3, and 11.4, stadium revenues are shown both in real 2004 dollar values and as a percentage of total revenues for MLB, the NFL, and the NBA, respectively (alas, this is yet another case where only incomplete, and older, data exist for sports analysis). In

Table 11.2 MLB Stadium Revenues ($2004)

	LOW		HIGH		AVERAGE		
YEAR	($MILLIONS)	TEAM(S)	($MILLIONS)	TEAM(S)	($MILLIONS)	TEAM(S)	STANDARD DEVIATION
1990	$1.58	Detroit	$22.07	NY Mets	$ 8.60	White Sox, San Diego	$5.30
1991	$4.13	Milwaukee	$26.54	White Sox	$12.10	Houston	$6.74
1992	$0.00	St. Louis	$30.70	Los Angeles	$11.75	Oakland	$8.01
1993	$2.98	Pittsburgh	$28.26	White Sox	$11.67	Oakland	$5.70
1994	$3.16	Pittsburgh	$18.45	White Sox	$9.48	NY Mets, St. Louis	$3.92
1995	$1.84	Pittsburgh	$25.44	Texas Rangers	$12.54	San Francisco	$6.39
1996	$3.70	Toronto	$30.44	Texas Rangers	$15.04	San Diego	$8.00

As a Percent of Total Revenues

YEAR	LOW	TEAM(S)	HIGH	TEAM(S)	AVERAGE	TEAM(S)	STANDARD DEVIATION
1990	2	Detroit	30	Kansas City	11	California, NY Mets, Toronto	0.053
1991	7	Minnesota	26	Kansas City	14	Toronto	0.056
1992	0	St. Louis	27	Los Angeles	14	Cubs, Milwaukee, Oakland	0.066
1993	5	Pittsburgh Pittsburgh	28	White Sox	14	California, NY Mets	0.054
1994	9	Toronto	32	White Sox	19	St. Louis	0.059
1995	6	Pittsburgh	33	Texas Rangers	20	St. Louis, Florida Marlins, San Diego	0.068
1996	4	Toronto	30	White Sox	19	Boston, San Francisco, Pittsburgh	0.061

Sources: Calculated from data in the *Olympian*, June 21, 1991, p. B4; and *Financial World*, July 7, 1992, pp. 50–51; May 25, 1993, pp. 26–30; May 10, 1994, pp. 50–59; May 9, 1995, pp. 42–56; May 20, 1996, pp. 52–68; June 17, 1997.

Table 11.3 NFL Stadium Revenues

	LOW		HIGH		AVERAGE		STANDARD
YEAR	($MILLIONS)	TEAM(S)	($MILLIONS)	TEAM(S)	($MILLIONS)	TEAM(S)	DEVIATION
1990	$0.00	Denver	$25.37	Miami	$6.02	Minnesota, Seattle	$4.59
1991	$0.00	Denver	$24.75	Miami	$5.91	Phoenix	$4.95
1992	$0.00	Atlanta	$14.28	Philadelphia	$2.94	Chicago, Green Bay, St. Louis, San Diego	$2.94
1993	$0.00	Atlanta, Denver, Detroit	$38.89	Dallas	$5.96	Houston	$7.65
1994	$0.00	Atlanta, Denver, Detroit	$47.14	Dallas	$6.82	Phoenix	$8.97
1995	$0.00	Denver, Detroit	$48.91	Dallas	$7.62	Atlanta, Green Bay	$8.97
1996	$0.00	Denver	$49.54	Dallas	$9.07	Green Bay	$9.31

As a Percent of Total Revenues

							STANDARD
YEAR	LOW	TEAM(S)	HIGH	TEAM(S)	AVERAGE	TEAM(S)	DEVIATION
1990	0%	Denver	28%	Miami	9%	Minnesota, Giants, San Francisco, Seattle	0.052
1991	0	Denver	27	Miami	8	Houston, Indianapolis	0.054
1992	0	Atlanta, Denver, Detroit	17	Philadelphia	4	Chicago, Green Bay, Rams, Minnesota, Phoenix, San Diego	0.036
1993	0	Atlanta, Denver, Detroit	32	Dallas	7	Green Bay, Rams, Phoenix, Tampa Bay	0.068
1994	0	Atlanta, Denver, Detroit	37	Dallas	8	Tampa Bay	0.076
1995	0	Denver, Detroit	36	Dallas	8	New England, Kansas City, Chicago, Minnesota	0.071
1996	0	Denver	34	Dallas	9	New England, Minnesota	0.071

Sources: Calculated from data in the *Olympian*, June 21, 1991, p. B4; and *Financial World*, July 7, 1992, pp. 50–51; May 25, 1993, pp. 26–30; May 10, 1994, pp. 50–59; May 9, 1995, pp. 42–56; May 20, 1996, pp. 52–68; June 17, 1997.

Table 11.4 NBA Arena Revenues

	LOW		HIGH		AVERAGE		
YEAR	($MILLIONS)	TEAM(S)	($MILLIONS)	TEAM(S)	($MILLIONS)	TEAM(S)	STANDARD DEVIATION
1990	$0.00	Phoenix	$32.10	Lakers	$ 4.59	Cleveland	$6.59
1991	$0.72	Minnesota, Phoenix	$11.46	Cleveland	$ 3.58	Orlando	$2.58
1992	$0.00	Boston	$30.38	Lakers	$ 6.31	Denver	$7.45
1993	$0.72	Boston, New Jersey	$34.39	Lakers	$ 7.45	Denver	$7.45
1994	$0.72	New Jersey, Philadelphia	$28.37	Detroit	$ 7.60	Denver	$6.45
1995	$0.72	New Jersey	$28.23	Detroit	$ 8.60	Minnesota	$6.74
1996	$3.30	Dallas	$35.11	Detroit	$10.75	Boston	$7.60

As A Percent of Total Revenues

YEAR	LOW	TEAM(S)	HIGH	TEAM(S)	AVERAGE	TEAM(S)	STANDARD DEVIATION
1990	0%	Phoenix	36%	Lakers	12%	Denver	0.091
1991	2	Minnesota	22	Cleveland	8	Lakers, Sacramento, Seattle	0.044
1992	0	Boston	30	Detroit	11	Indiana, Orlando	0.086
1993	1	Boston	35	Lakers	12	Indiana	0.084
1994	1	Boston, New Jersey	29	Detroit	11	Indiana, Miami, Phoenix	0.073
1995	1	Nets	31	Detroit	11	Chicago, Golden State	0.074
1996	5	Philadelphia, Dallas	32	Detroit	20	Charlotte	0.058

Sources: Calculated from data in the *Olympian*, June 21, 1991, p. B4; and *Financial World*, July 7, 1992, pp. 50–51; May 25, 1993, pp. 26–30; May 10, 1994, pp. 50–59; May 9, 1995, pp. 42–56; May 20, 1996, pp. 52–68; June 17, 1997.

percentage terms, stadium revenues have become a much larger component of total revenue in MLB, doubling over the 1990s to about 20 percent of total revenue. In the NFL and NBA, the share has remained nearly constant, on average, but the amount has been growing in both leagues.

What we should expect from team owners is indicated by the large gap between the stadium haves and have nots. Revenue gaps have shown a tendency to increase over time. For example, in MLB and the NFL, the standard deviations approximately doubled for the tabled years. Although most of this difference is determined by whether a team is located in a large-revenue market, that will not deter owners who suffer a "stadium revenue disadvantage" from pushing their hosts for a larger subsidy. Owners will use the argument that such subsidies will help them stay competitive with teams with better stadiums and lease arrangements.

We have just seen that these arguments have dubious merit. But, we also know from Chapter 5 that team owners can point to other cities that may offer a large stadium subsidy as a potential place to move if their current hosts do not help them to keep up with the Joneses. Therefore, although all revenues are important in determining a team's competitiveness, getting a better stadium deal is important to any given team if for no other reason than that the money is nice to have.

Stadium Subsidies and the NFL Salary Cap NFL owners would like to pursue stadium subsidies like any other owners. But any argument they make that subsidies will increase quality faces a direct challenge. The NFL shares nearly all revenues and has a salary cap, ostensibly designed to equalize spending and level the league, competitively speaking. So where can there be any competitive advantage in a stadium subsidy? The answer lies in the fact that not all stadium revenues are shared with other teams, and these unshared revenues increase the salary cap. The cap goes up, but only some teams actually have the increased revenue to increase the quality of their team.

For example, stadium sponsorship and so-called luxury-box revenues are not shared with other teams in the NFL. Suppose the configuration of a new stadium includes more of these unshared revenues than the owner enjoyed in the old stadium. This NFL owner might be able to obtain a stadium-specific revenue advantage over the rest of the owners. The revenue from that owner's stadium advantage goes into defined gross revenue, raising the league-wide cap on salaries. Because the cap has increased, all teams are now supposed to spend more on talent, and the minimum-spending requirement has also increased. However, only the owner who gained the stadium advantage actually has the increased revenue to spend up to the new cap. The rest of the teams are left behind because they do not have any increased revenue to put toward talent.

Now, as we saw in Chapter 5, NFL owners typically spend more than the cap amount on players. However, this extra spending varies considerably. In general, the sort of one-upping behavior driven by stadium-specific revenue advantages will always leave some teams behind, competitively speaking, at any point in time. The result is that every time one owner gets a better stadium arrangement or a new stadium, demands by the rest of the owners without these revenues increase.

THE ROLE OF LEAGUES IN RATIONAL ACTOR SUBSIDY POLITICS

Leagues play an important behind-the-scenes role in the modern stadium mess. In fact, they always have played a role in stadium subsidy issues. As detailed in Chapter 5, it is clear that MLB chose not to expand westward until well into the 1950s, despite Congressional scrutiny and pressure from a potential rival, the Pacific Coast League. The result of keeping the West open was quite advantageous for the owner of the Brooklyn Dodgers, Walter O'Malley. O'Malley, increasingly vocal about needing a new stadium, could get nowhere with the New York City director of public parks in his pursuit of land for a new stadium. In the end, O'Malley moved the Dodgers to Los Angeles after the end of the 1956 season. The Dodgers went from being the most financially successful team in baseball, in Brooklyn, to being one of the most successful sports franchises in any league in history in their Los Angeles home. This happened because MLB had kept the West open.

Location Management by Leagues

Leagues facilitate the market power position of team owners by restricting the number of teams in the league. In the stadium subsidy context, this artificial restriction stacks the deck in favor of teams in their stadium negotiations with host cities. As long as leagues carefully manage team location, existing teams will always have a believable threat location in their negotiations with their current hosts. The relationship between **subsidies and believable threat locations** is clear. There has not been an MLB team move since the Senators left for Texas after the 1971 season. This is because nearly every team in baseball has gotten either a new stadium or a significantly renovated stadium in the meantime. The San Francisco Giants are a perfect case in point. After searching in vain for a new location willing to build a new stadium in the Bay Area and a bit inland through the early 1990s, the owner sold the team in 1992. Immediately new owner Peter McGowan said, "I think the people now know if we don't get a [new] stadium, the team will be forced to move" (*Sporting News*, November 23, 1992, p. 5). Shortly thereafter, the owner managed to get some infrastructure subsidy for the Giants' current home, SBC Park, completed in San Francisco in 2000. The most recent NFL expansion, when the league was deciding between Houston and Los Angeles, is instructive on this point. In general terms, the decision between the locations hinged on two considerations regarding the Houston and Los Angeles markets. First, the league considered the financial contribution that either location would make to the league. Second, the league considered the value of an open location and the negotiating advantages it provided to current league members. Keeping the best believable threat location helps owners in negotiations with their current host cities.

"I think the people now know if we don't get a [new] stadium, the team will be forced to move."
—New San Francisco Giants owner Peter Magowan in 1992 after the previous owner had failed to obtain a new stadium either in the Bay Area or inland

Special Problems for the NFL   In the NFL, through a combination of lawsuits and owner preferences, teams are able to move between cities much easier than in other leagues. This means that a given community might perceive that they actually have a good chance to replace their team if stadium subsidies lead their current owner to leave. Some evidence supports the view that alternative threat locations are less important to NFL owners than they are to, say, MLB owners. In every case, a city that lost their team got a new one within a few years (except for Los Angeles).

In the most famous case, the Oakland Raiders moved to Los Angeles and back to Oakland again within a few years. Baltimore lost their Colts to Indianapolis but landed the new Ravens within a few years. As detailed in the Learning Highlight: The Stadium That Didn't Get Built and Then Did, when St. Louis did not meet the stadium demands of Cardinals owner Bill Bidwell, he took his team to Arizona in 1988. St. Louis was without pro football until they built a new stadium, luring the Los Angeles Rams to St. Louis in 1995.

Thus, in the NFL, some cities have been able to cut demanding NFL owners loose and find another team. Los Angeles remains the only exception, but both the former Seahawks owner and the owners of the Buccaneers have shown an interest in filling the hole in Los Angeles. However, the league refused those moves. Perhaps the NFL has something greater in store for that city or perhaps they are just waiting for the right offer.

In contrast to the NFL, in MLB, with its antitrust exemption and owners unwilling to replace an owner who threatens to move, cities have paid dearly and more often to keep their teams. Former Washington, D.C., mayor Sharon Pratt Kelly put it this way:

> If no mayor succumbs to the demands of a franchise shopping for a new home then the teams will stay where they are. This, however, is unlikely to happen because if Mayor A is not willing to pay the price, Mayor B may think it is advantageous to open up the city's wallet. Then to protect his or her interest, Mayor A often ends up paying the demanded price. (Shropshire, 1995, p. xi)

Given that leagues manage locations to keep teams the only game in town, a local government must deal with its current tenant or lose a team and hope that it can woo an unhappy owner or gain a team in the next expansion round. Arguably, this single factor contributes more to the stadium mess than any other element in that process. Now that we understand the role of politics, owners, and leagues, we are ready to bring the rational actor explanation to bear on the stadium mess.

LEARNING HIGHLIGHT
The Stadium That Didn't Get Built and Then Did

The Cardinals are the oldest team in the NFL, their roots going back to Chicago in the 1890s. Owned by the Bidwell family since the 1930s, they moved from Chicago to St. Louis to play the 1960 season. The team sank into mediocrity in St. Louis. In 1985, owner Bill Bidwell announced that he was exploring alternatives for his team. The football and baseball Cardinals shared Busch Stadium, and average attendance had been the lowest in the NFL, at about 48,000 per game.

Bidwell had two alternatives in mind: St. Louis could build a new stadium for the Cardinals and Bidwell would stay in St. Louis, or St. Louis could refuse and he would move the team. He argued that Busch stadium was too small (even though the football Cardinals had never sold it out at its 56,000 football capacity) and objected to the sale of beer in the stadium (unlikely to change because the Busch family, of Anheuser-Busch fame, owned the stadium and the concession rights).

Two groups formed in response to Bidwell's demands. One group wanted a privately owned stadium well out of town. The idea that it would be privately owned was a stretch, because the proposal called for city and county bonds to finance $120 million out of the $150 million construction cost. The second group wanted a publicly owned stadium downtown. Both proposals included a domed stadium that would seat around 70,000.

Engineering estimates suggested that the out-of-town version would leave a $2 million annual operating surplus, whereas the downtown version would lose $5 million annually.

After an economic analysis of the situation by noted economist James Quirk, these estimates both were revised downward: $5 million in losses out of town and $10 million in losses downtown.

In the end, the mayor rejected both proposals in favor of a renovation project for Busch Stadium with luxury suites and added seating. Bidwell rejected it and in 1988 moved the team to Phoenix, where mediocrity continues to reign for the NFL Cardinals. Bidwell is finally going to get the new stadium he desired. The people of the state of Arizona voted for a new stadium in November 2000. The location was up in the air for years before settling on Glendale, Arizona. The $450 million facility, currently under construction, is scheduled to open in 2006. St. Louis ended up building a new stadium to attract an NFL team. In the early 1990s, the people of St. Louis approved a multimillion dollar bond issue for a downtown stadium. In 1995, when the TransWorld Dome (capacity 66,000) was nearing completion at a cost of about $290 million, a team finally committed to move to St. Louis. Georgia Frontiere, owner of the Rams, agreed to sell a portion of the team to local St. Louis interests, and the new owners of the St. Louis Rams moved the team in 1995 under the following agreement:

- A $30 million relocation fee was paid to the NFL stadium fund.

- The NFL would keep the Rams' $13.5 million share from the next expansion.
- A $12.5 million payment was made to cover the expected reduction in the FOX broadcast contract with the team in St. Louis rather than Los Angeles.
- A $17 million payment was made to a St. Louis group that raised enough money through PSLs to get the NFL's consent to move the team.

All things considered, that is about $73 million and a reduction in ownership rights as the cost of moving the team. Although nobody expects the Cardinals to ever improve, the move by the Rams eventually led to a Super Bowl title in 2000.

Previous St. Louis Cardinals owner Bill Bidwell could not get a new stadium and left St. Louis. The Los Angeles Rams moved into the new TransWorld Dome in 1995 and were Super Bowl champs in short order.

Sources: News & Observer online (www.newsobserver.com), 1995; James Quirk and Rodney D. Fort, *Pay Dirt: The Business of Professional Team Sports* (Princeton, NJ: Princeton University Press, 1992).

THE STADIUM MESS EXPLAINED

Elected officials make stadium decisions according to the rational actor logic just developed. That logic leaves us every reason to believe that subsidies will be too large and paid by many who couldn't care less about pro sports. Let's walk through the logic applied to the stadium mess, then turn to a real-world case in Seattle.

Rational Actor Politics and the Stadium Mess

Imagine that a stadium subsidy issue is brewing somewhere. Subsidy critics will deplore both the size and purpose of such spending. On the size dimension, opponents will push any and all estimates to the upper limit of belief (and possibly beyond), causing rationally ignorant voters to get an uneven portrayal of the costs. The voters will also be made to feel guilty about supporting the subsidy. Who can reasonably argue that stadiums and pro sports teams are more important than schools? Surely, say the critics, voters will not be able to look themselves in the mirror if they support such spending.

Stadium supporters will be quick to defend the subsidy. Supporters typically chalk up the entire amount of economic activity on the benefits side, dramatically overstating the benefits of the subsidy. Reports from consultants are presented that tout the massive economic benefits of the team's presence; payback periods are often shown to be less than 10 years. Once again, voters get a skewed perspective, but this time on the benefit side. Few form a reasonable view of the new net economic activity from a proposed subsidy.

Further, both sides argue about the "intangible" benefits of the stadium. Supporters overstate them and opponents minimize them. At the very least, there are comparable situations that could be examined but never are. The reasons for this are clear. Team owners employ a "short-fuse" ultimatum strategy; the pot may simmer for a year or two, but then state and local government officials are given a very short time to generate the subsidy or lose the team. Another reason solid analysis never comes into play could be that owners and their supporters already know that, in all likelihood, the net values will not justify the size of the subsidy they seek. Again, voters are left with nothing but rhetoric.

There is more. Remember from Chapter 10 that a minimum subsidy charges users the extra costs of operation, and government collects a tax that makes the stadium worth it. However, the actual type of tax mechanism chosen almost never matches this subsidy-minimum prescription. Tax collection options range from hotel taxes, which are paid by both fans and nonfans, to sales taxes, to bond issues guaranteed out of the general fund. A favorite is property tax relief for the stadium and/or sales tax relief for the local government. In each case, the amount available for other purposes, statewide, is reduced, and nonfans pay the vast majority of the price of keeping a team in town.

Nearly all of this is driven by the maintenance of believable threat locations by owners acting as leagues. Fans are confronted with an all-or-nothing alternative. If the state or local government fails to meet the owner's subsidy demands, then the team will move to one of the locations kept open by the league.

This sets the political stage. Detractors emphasize only the costs and supporters overstate the benefits. Little in the way of independent analysis is forthcoming. The poor taxpayers are left with only extreme information with which to weigh the situation, and that is if they are even paying attention in the first place. In such a setting, one would expect benefits to be concentrated in the hands of politically powerful stadium proponents and costs to be dispersed among the rest of the taxpayers.

A Diagrammatic Model of the Stadium Mess   The stadium mess can be portrayed as a triangle, as shown in Figure 11.2. Powerful local and state political interests make their demands known to local and state elected officials. These officials produce financing arrangements for a stadium subsidy (or take it directly to the people with a referendum). The demands of powerful groups are met, and these groups reward politicians with votes and election resources. The general taxpayer is left on the sidelines. New York City council-woman Letitia James, commenting on the move to use public money to build a Westside stadium said, "When I run for office, I knock on hundreds and hundreds of doors, and nobody ever says we need arenas or stadiums" (*Sports Business Journal*, December 27, 2004, p. 18). But she is just describing how the general taxpayer is left on the sidelines in this particular policy arena. As predicted, benefits are concentrated and costs dispersed, and the costs are likely to exceed the benefits.

> "When I run for office, I knock on hundreds and hundreds of doors, and nobody ever says we need arenas or stadiums."
> —New York City Councilwoman Letitia James on proposals to spend public money on a Westside stadium, 2004

The economic beneficiaries of a stadium subsidy usually are well organized and easy for politicians to recognize. The team, ardent fans, the press and TV media, members of the construction and concession industries, and businesses near the stadium stand to gain because the subsidy keeps the team in town. These interests have a very large stake in getting a stadium improved or approved. It is reasonable to expect that they will reward politicians who give them what they want with the resources that politicians need to campaign successfully.

Did You Know?
After changing his vote to favor the construction of Miller Park in Milwaukee in 1995, state senator George Petak from Racine was removed from office by recall vote.

On one occasion, the public did exact political punishment for a massive stadium subsidy. At first, Wisconsin state senator George Petak (from Racine) opposed a legislative financing scheme for a new MLB Brewers stadium in 1995. However, in short time and under heavy lobbying by the governor, he changed his vote. His constituency back in Racine was so enraged that he was recalled by

Figure 11.2 The Stadium Mess Triangle
The stadium mess follows rational actor politics. A powerful constituency of owners and support-ers influences the electoral chances of state and local elected officials. Those officials choose subsidy levels and methods that owners and supporters evaluate in terms of their own economic welfare. If the policies are best for the owners and supporters, elected officials get reelected. The general taxpayers are relegated to the sidelines but help pay the subsidies.

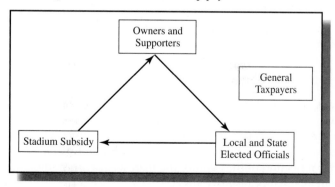

popular vote—but the rarity of this event makes it the exception that proves the rule. Politicians do not want to lose their team and the election support that would follow a team move. Even if the team really wouldn't move, special interest politics can still yield the same outcome.

What Are Taxpayers to Do?

There are two ways that taxpayers can affect the subsidy approval process, neither of which can be expected to slow the stadium juggernaut. One way is through direct democracy. We will look at this topic in detail in the next section. The other method is through the review of the choices made by elected officials the next time they are up for election. In this case, rational ignorance takes over with a vengeance. Even voters vehemently opposed to stadium construction will have a difficult time trying to hold local and state representatives accountable. Rationally ignorant voters will never really know the benefits that were provided and to whom, and the costs on a per voter basis will be quite small. As long as these elected officials provide benefits from other decisions that offset the very small costs borne by the general voter, they will be safe in their reelection pursuits. At least that is the outcome predicted by the rational actor explanation, what we have referred to here as the stadium mess. Some hold out the hope that direct democracy (referenda or initiatives) is a way out of the stadium mess.

DIRECT DEMOCRACY AND THE STADIUM MESS

One avenue of public participation in decisions about sports stadiums is direct democracy through referenda and initiatives. But can direct democracy help alleviate the stadium mess? Although uncommon, some subsidies have been voted on in referenda and initiatives. In this section, we will examine the relationship between **subsidies and direct democracy**.

Typically, when a stadium issue appears on the ballot, it is the culmination of a complex political process. In some cases, when taxes are changed or bonds are issued, a referendum may be required by the state constitution. In other cases, public officials can place a stadium measure on the ballot even though it is not required. In still other cases, citizens use the initiative process to force a public vote.

High Hopes for Direct Democracy

It is easy to see why subsidy opponents might think that direct democracy can save the public from stadium subsidies. The whole point of direct democracy is to allow voters a direct means of expression. In theory, a more "hands-on" decision process will produce outcomes that are (1) more legitimate in the eyes of participants and (2) a better reflection of the "will of the people." Direct democracy takes the decision away from elected representatives.

Direct democracy has other appealing characteristics. On stadium subsidy ballot issues, the choices confronting voters are quite simple and cover a single element, spending. The alternatives seem quite clear: the ballot choice versus the current situation. In addition, information presented by subsidy supporters and foes may generate well-reasoned debates prior to the vote so that voters are no longer rationally ignorant.

Weaknesses of Direct Democracy

Direct democracy, however, has some important weaknesses relative to representative democracy. The outcome of a democratic process depends on which voters turn out to vote. This, in turn, depends heavily on the amount and quality of information that is available to citizens. As we have seen in previous sections, both turnout and information can be biased, and the same holds true for public votes on stadium issues. In addition, elected officials may control the alternatives presented to voters, and these alternatives may actually force higher spending than would occur through a representative decision process.

Biased Turnout Turnout can be biased due to the registration and voting costs discussed earlier. Further, rational ignorance and free riding drive both turnout and fall off. The incentive to turn out and vote is dramatically less for the rationally ignorant voter who will eventually bear the dispersed costs of stadium subsidies. Those standing to gain typically have a much larger stake in the outcome and are more likely to vote. This is the **biased turnout** result for direct democracy.

Biased Information: The Seattle Seahawks Vote Let's turn to the **biased information** question. In most elections, the information that is offered to fuel "well-reasoned debate" is polarized. Proponents present information that overstates the benefits. Conversely, opponents present information that overstates the costs. Independent analysis is rarely offered. A recent example makes this very clear.

"Our Team Works" and the Seahawk Stadium Information Blitz Proposition 48, the referendum on a new stadium for the Seattle Seahawks, reached a vote in 1997. The information distortion surrounding Proposition 48 was incredible. Supporters of the new stadium funded a huge information blitz. Paul Allen alone spent around $3 million in advertising, whereas opponents spent only $160,000. A full-page newspaper advertisement that ran in one of the state's major newspapers (*Spokane Spokesman-Review*, May 12, 1997, p. C4) touted the benefits of Proposition 48. The article was paid for and presumably formulated by "Our Team Works" (henceforth, OTW), the publicity organization in support of the stadium. In this ad, OTW attacked the then-home of the Seahawks, Seattle's Kingdome:

> Remember the day the Kingdome roof fell in?
> The disaster left property taxpayers with a $70 million hangover. This adds up to $5 million per year in property tax debt for which our taxpayers receive no services. In fact, the Kingdome has cost taxpayers more in the

last 2.5 years for repairs than the original construction costs . . . and now $42 million more is needed for basic repairs.

The good news? The funding package for the new stadium and exhibition center [Proposition 48] will retire all Kingdome debt, and free the property taxes for better purposes. (*Spokane Spokesman-Review*, May 12, 1997, p. C4)

Picking apart this distortion is like shooting fish in a barrel. First, OTW forgot about inflation. It is invalid to compare the 1996 repair bill of $70 million to the $67 million original construction cost in 1976. That $67 million, adjusted for inflation, would have been worth about $187 million at the time of the vote in 1996. This changes the comparison considerably. Far from being over twice the original cost, the cost of repairing the Kingdome after 20 years of faithful service actually was less than half the original cost.

The second distortion also follows from the observation that the Kingdome was 20 years old by 1996. All capital equipment wears out eventually and requires upkeep in order to remain productive. The simple fact that repairs were needed is not damning criticism of the structure.

A third observation about the OTW's claims concerns the idea that no services were gained from the repair costs. Without the repairs, the Kingdome would have had to close quite some time before the election. In that case, the NFL and MLB teams would have been without a stadium, and non-sports-related functions would have been without a venue. Therefore, services certainly were obtained through maintenance and upkeep. The question is whether it is worth spending on maintenance relative to the alternatives, such as a new football stadium.

The question of whether repairs are worth it is just a version of the classic used car problem. Suppose you have $1,000 in cash plus an existing used car worth $1,000 to put toward a transportation upgrade. But then the car breaks down, requiring repairs of $1,000. Should you put $1,000 into a car that will have a market value of $1,000 after the repair? If your next-best alternative is to buy a car costing $1,700, but you only have $1,000 plus a broken-down trade-in, then putting the $1,000 into the broken-down car clearly is rational. Just because the Kingdome had broken down a bit does not mean that it was irrational to fix it.

As a fourth observation, the remaining debt on the Kingdome does not magically disappear just because it is "retired" under the new funding plan. Indeed, the balance was simply rolled over into the debt represented by Proposition 48. To return to the used car analogy, suppose you trade in your current used car for a price less than you owe on it. The remainder just rolls over into the new contract. The debt does not go away; it still has to be paid.

One final observation is critical. Tearing down the Kingdome makes the new stadium/exhibition center the only place in town that large non-NFL activities can take place. Because the lease arrangement with the Seahawks turns all nonfootball revenue over to the team's owner, the owner has a monopoly on the only venue in town for professional and amateur soccer, trade shows, community festivals, and other entertainment events. If the Kingdome were not torn down and remained as a viable alternative for these activities, price competition would increase the number of these types of events and lower the rental price charged. Therefore, the team owner benefits from removing a competing facility.

An Important but Technical Issue: The Alternatives Confronting Voters

In cases where the alternatives that actually confront voters are controlled by a few people, such as the mayor or city council, problems can arise if elected officials have a preference for high levels of stadium spending. If the alternative to the high spending proposal is complete loss of the team or if the current stadium really is decrepit, those in **control of ballot alternatives** on which the voters vote can actually force high spending levels even though the voters may favor a lower amount of spending. Those in control of the ballot alternatives have come to be called "the setters" and the following uses what has come to be called "the setter model" of referendum outcomes.

This possibility is shown in Figure 11.3, an example from my 1997 chapter "Direct Democracy and the Stadium Mess" (Noll and Zimbalist, 1997). In Figure 11.3, a one-dimensional line represents the level of possible stadium spending and four possible outcomes. The left-most outcome is no team and no spending. This is the preferred position of citizen A. To the right of this position is the current spending level. Citizen B prefers this outcome, with a team playing in a dilapidated, out-of-date facility. Next to the right is a new facility that would be an improvement over the existing obsolete stadium but without any frills. Both citizens C and D prefer this option. Finally, far to the right is an elaborate facility with luxury boxes, restaurants, lavish offices, and an internal shopping mall. Citizen E prefers this outcome.

If our five citizens could debate and consider all of the issues, the most likely winner is the no-frills stadium. It beats the no-team option hands down (B, C, D, and E defeat A). Similar thinking shows that the no-frills stadium beats the obsolete stadium option by a vote of three to two. The no-frills stadium also beats the elaborate stadium four to one. But suppose that the alternatives put before the voters are restricted so that this pair-wise comparison never occurs in the voting booth. This might occur because citizen E is the most powerful in terms of election resources, and the ballot issue is framed in citizen E's favor. In this case, "the setter" confronts voters with alternatives that move the outcome closer to citizen E's preferred stadium.

In this case, the most elaborate option would be offered on the ballot, and both elected officials and citizen E would try to convince voters that the no-team option

Figure 11.3 Setter Model of Voter Stadium Preferences

On a single dimension of stadium spending, voter A prefers none (and no team), voter B prefers the current, obsolete stadium (no spending increase), voters C and D most prefer a new modest stadium, and voter E prefers a new elaborate stadium. In a simple majority vote, voters C and D would get their way because their most preferred outcome is better for voter E than the obsolete stadium. But if the alternative is no team at all, voters C and D would join voter E in voting in favor of a new elaborate stadium because that is closer to their preference than the alternative.

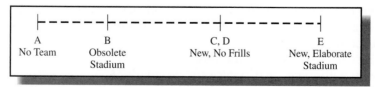

Source: Rodney Fort, "Direct Democracy and the Stadium Mess," in *Sports, Jobs, and Taxes: The Economic Impact of Sports Teams and Stadiums*, Roger Noll and Andrew Zimbalist, eds. (Washington, D.C.: Brookings Institution, 1997).

would occur if the election failed. Leagues reinforce the fear by keeping believable threat locations open for the owner of the team. The outcome in our case is as follows. Voters C and D, and maybe even voter B, might prefer the elaborate stadium to no team at all. So the vote is going to be at least 3–2 in favor of the elaborate stadium (and quite possibly 4 to 1), even though all voters but E would prefer the no-frills facility to the elaborate option. Even if voters believe that the team will stay and play in the obsolete stadium, the elaborate option is likely to win if voters C and D marginally prefer keeping the team and having a new stadium to keeping the team in a decrepit stadium.

Again, the role of leagues in maintaining believable threat locations open plays a crucial role. In a real-world example, Bob Lurie (chairman of the San Francisco Giants at the time) wrote a very forceful, thinly veiled all-or-nothing threat in the San Francisco ballot statement of 1987:

> The issue is not whether or not we should build a ballpark for Bob Lurie or for the Giants. This franchise will be around a lot longer than I, and they will always have a place to play. I just think it would be tragic if it is not in San Francisco.

The believable threat location in this case was Tampa Bay/St. Petersburg (detailed in Chapter 5 and a learning highlight in Chapter 10). If fans believe they will lose their team to another location, the spending level that may ultimately win support is higher.

Evidence from Referenda

Although there is ample theoretical reason to doubt that direct democracy will remedy the stadium mess, what do actual voting outcomes reveal? Table 11.5 shows the outcome of facility referenda since 1995. Prior to the 1990s, stadium votes typically did not pass (Fort, 1997), but what a turnaround from 1995 on! Eighty percent of the issues in Table 11.5 passed. Sports owners are having an amazing streak of stadium subsidy victories. Interestingly, these direct democracy votes occur predominantly in cities trying to keep their current teams.

Do Referenda Result in Lower Spending? The effects, if any, of direct democracy can be seen in two comparisons (Fort, 1999). First, we can compare the spending levels of all issues that passed with those that were funded without a vote. If direct democracy offers a remedy to the stadium mess, we would expect spending to be lower for facilities voted for by the public. The actual results are mixed, as shown in Table 11.6. Spending under direct democracy is about the same for MLB and much higher for the NFL. Spending is only lower for the single issue that occurred for an NHL/NBA arena.

Second, we can compare those votes that failed but were eventually funded anyway with issues that never came to a vote. Again, if direct democracy has an ameliorating effect, spending should be lower for those votes that failed but found some other funding path. Interestingly, of those that failed, half eventually were funded outside of the direct democracy process. This outcome echoes a sentiment

Table 11.5 Sports Facility Referenda Since 1995

MARKET	FACILITY (TEAMS)	YEAR	RESULT	OPEN
Cleveland	Browns Stadium (NFL Browns)	1995	Passed	1999
Milwaukee	Miller Park (MLB Brewers)	1995	Failed	2001
Cincinnati	Great American Ball Park (MLB Reds)			
	Paul Brown Stadium (NFL Bengals)	1996	Passed	2003
Detroit	Comerica Park (MLB Tigers)	1996	Passed	2001
Detroit	Ford Field (NFL Lions)	1996	Passed	2002
Houston	Enron Field (MLB Astros)	1996	Passed	2000
Miami	American Airlines Arena (NBA Heat)	1996	Passed	1999
Nashville	Adelphia Stadium (NFL Titans)	1996	Passed	1999
San Francisco	Pacific Bell Park (MLB Giants)	1996	Passed	2000
Tampa	Raymond James Stadium (NFL Buccaneers)	1996	Passed	1998
Pittsburgh	PNC Park (MLB Pirates) and Stadium (NFL Steelers)	1997	Failed	2001
San Francisco	Stadium (NFL 49ers)	1997	Passed	2004
Seattle	Stadium/Exhibition Center (NFL Seahawks and University of Washington)	1997	Passed	2003
Dallas	American Airlines Center (NBA Mavericks/NHL Stars)	1998	Passed	2001
Denver	Invesco Field (NFL Broncos and MLS Rapids)	1998	Passed	2001
San Diego	Stadium (MLB Padres)	1998	Passed	2003
Houston	Arena (NBA Rockets and WNBA Comets)	1999	Failed	N/A
San Antonio	SBC Arena (NBA Spurs)	1999	Passed	2002
Scottsdale	Arena (NHL Coyotes)	1999	Passed	2003
St. Paul	Stadium (MLB Twins)	1999	Failed	N/A
Green Bay	Lambeau Field renovations (NFL Packers)	2000	Passed	2003
Houston	Arena (NBA Rockets and WNBA Comets)	2000	Passed	2003
Phoenix	Stadium (NFL Cardinals)	2000	Passed	2004
Arlington	Stadium (NFL Cowboys)	2004	Passed	Pending
Kansas City	Arrowhead and Kauffman Improvements (NFL Chiefs and MLB Royals)	2004	Failed	N/A

Source: Sports Facility Reports, vol. 2, no. 2, Appendix 2 (Marquette Sports Law Institute, 2001); sportsbusinessnews.com, November 4, 2004.

Table 11.6
Average Public Spending for Stadiums and Arenas Where the Public Share Was at Least 50 Percent

LEAGUE	VOTES THAT PASSED ($MILLIONS)	NO VOTE ISSUES ($MILLIONS)	FAILED, EVENTUALLY
MLB	$264	$266	$301
NFL	273	266	
NHL/NBA	125	177	187
Total Cases	12	23	4

Source: Rodney Fort, "Stadiums and Public and Private Interests in Seattle," Marquette Sports Law Journal 10 (2000): 311–334.

of Chandler, Arizona, Mayor Jay Tibshraeny, who was in favor of upgrading a spring training facility, "I believe the citizens should have a say in this issue. If the voters pass this, we will move forward. If the voters don't pass this, we will still move forward" (*Phoenix Gazette*, October 13, 1995, p. A1).

Table 11.6 shows that for both MLB stadiums and NHL/NBA arenas, funding levels were dramatically higher for issues that failed but found eventual funding than for those that never went to a vote. Maybe proponents knew that voters wanted them to spend more. The alternative explanation is that direct democracy did not have any dampening effect on spending even when the vote failed. Voters said no, and some issues moved forward anyway at larger spending levels than would have occurred even if there had not been any referendum.

The Public-Private Spending Mix

More evidence of the impacts of direct democracy can be seen in patterns of public-private spending on stadiums and arenas shown in Table 11.7. In the 1970s, the public's share for such projects rose to a high of about 90 percent and fell back to around 60 percent through the 1980s and 1990s. The few available data on stadiums and arenas opening in the early 2000s show that the public's share is still around 60 per-

cent. If direct democracy reins in stadium spending, then the public share should be lower for those projects put to a vote. The data show that the lowest public shares occur when funding is determined outside of the direct democracy process (Fort, 1999). Further, if you look at the level of spending, public shares under direct democracy have more at the high end of the distribution than occurs for other types of issues. So public shares determined by election are higher, and higher on average, than occur for nonelection stadium subsidies.

Evidence on the Control of Alternatives Confronting Voters There is some evidence that "the setters" controlling the alternatives confronting voters are nudging spending upward (Fort, 1997). The implication from our simple theoretical depiction in Figure 11.3 is as follows. Suppose that the stadium that will exist if the vote fails is far below the preference of most citizens. If those in control of the ballot alternative present voters with the highest possible spending level that will pass, then the voting outcome should be barely enough to win. If there really is control over the alternatives and voters believe the worst in the event of failure, then votes should pass by the barest majority.

Now, among votes that passed, 70 percent of the stadium votes that received at least a majority were clustered around the bare majority for passage. This is not due to random chance; bare majorities are common in stadium elections. Therefore, when a referendum passes, cities are more likely to spend more on stadiums than the middle-ground preferences of most citizens. Not much can be said about referenda that failed. Perhaps those in charge of ballot alternatives either guessed wrong or the alternative in event of failure may not have been so bad in those cases.

Table 11.7
The Public-Private
Spending Mix

Decade Opened	Average Public Percent
1900–1939	28.6
1940–1959	70.0
1960–1969	78.6
1970–1979	90.0
1980–1989	60.0
1990–1999	61.9
2000–2003	61.9

Sources: David Swindell, "Public Financing of Sports Stadiums: How Cincinnati Compares," *Policy Solutions* (Dayton, OH: The Buckeye Institute for Public Policy Solutions, 1996); Rodney Fort, "Stadium Votes, Market Power, and Politics," *University of Toledo Law Review* 30 (1999): 419–442.; Raymond J. Keating, "Sports Pork: The Costly Relationship Between Major League Sports and Government," Policy Analysis No. 339 (Washington, D.C.: Cato Institute, April 5, 1999); *Sports Business Journal*, July 30, 2001, pp. 26–29.

FIRST DOWN AND $782 MILLION TO GO IN SEATTLE

In this section, we will look at the recent Mariners and Seahawks stadium outcomes in detail (the discussion here is from Fort [2000]). Many of the issues surrounding these stadiums were very similar to those encountered 25 years ago when the Kingdome was built. Speaking of the Kingdome, let's remember that it represents the alternative if the teams were to stay in Seattle. The ongoing subsidy from original construction, covered in the next sections of this chapter, was around $23 million annually, measured in 2004 dollars. In addition, there were $70 million in repairs in 1995, and another $42 million in repairs needed in 1997. That's a total of $135 million in 2004 dollars at about the time the Kingdome turned 20 years old. With that type of renovation, let's suppose the Kingdome would have lasted another 20 years. At 6 percent for 20 years, that raises the payment by about $11 million annually, for a total (including the ongoing subsidy) of about $33 million per year. We'll use this comparison value shortly.

As discussed earlier, Safeco Field for the MLB Mariners was denied public funding by referendum. However, a creative funding package was moved through the representative process. In contrast, spending on a stadium/exhibition center for the NFL Seahawks was approved by referendum. Therefore, the Seattle story offers an interesting example that includes nearly everything that can occur in stadium financing and construction: the intrigue of threats to move teams, public revelation of spending preferences through referenda, and the response by state and local politicians to rejection by voters.

The Mariners and Safeco Field

Previous Mariners owner Jeff Smulyan paid about $77 million for the team in 1989 ($116 million in 2004 dollars). The current owners bought him out for about $106 million in 1992 ($142 million in 2004 dollars). Although Smulyan cried poor, that was a 22 percent increase in real value in just four years. It did not take long before the Mariners' "stadium problem" surfaced. In the usual way, the new owners made it clear that they were losing millions of dollars on the team annually. Our look at paper profit reports in pro sports in Chapter 4, along with the return earned by Smulyan, would lead us to doubt these claims. Nonetheless, under this pressure, a stadium referendum issue went before state voters.

The People Say No but Spend $417 Million On September 19, 1995, in a special election, the stadium vote in King County failed by a narrow margin (50.1% to 49.9%). Voters were unwilling to raise the sales tax by half of a percent toward the projected $240 million cost of the new stadium plus repairs to the Kingdome. As would be expected when there are believable threat locations, team executive John Ellis announced that the Mariners would be sold. The Washington, D.C./Northern Virginia area seemed primed to receive the team.

In the end, the team did not move. A special funding package was passed in the state legislature. To see why this would happen, imagine the situation facing state and local politicians after such a close vote. If politicians let the vote stand, the politically potent groups in favor of the stadium in the more densely populated part of the state would feel abandoned. Remember, if state politicians irritate the politically less potent and help the politically powerful, election chances can be enhanced. As one would expect, the will of the people revealed through the referendum process was overridden by the representative government.

Senator Slade Gorton and Governor Gary Locke found state funds for the project and devised a way to ease a spending limitation in effect for King County at the time. Easing the limitation required the approval of the King County council, which was granted in early October. In 1997, $414 million in spending was authorized, to be funded through state bonds. The city also provided land worth $33 million. The team agreed to pay $45 million, plus any overruns beyond a specified buffer as their share of the spending. Thus, the intended total was $459 million.

However, as is usually the case with stadium issues and public funds, the total amount spent missed the planned budget of $459 million by a long shot. Safeco Field cost $517 million in total, 81 percent of which was paid for with public money (*Seattle Post-Intelligencer*, Web site [www.seattle-pi.com], April 13, 1999). Team owners increased their share to $100 million. The final public tab was so much larger than the initial authorization due to overruns beyond the buffer specified in the original plan. Most of these overruns were due to the relentless push by the Mariners' owners to meet the 1999 opening date. All-in-all then, the 1997 amount of $417 million for Safeco Field ended up at about $487 in 2004 dollars. Suppose Safeco lasts as long as our assumption about the renovated Kingdome, 20 years. Let's keep in mind that, at 6 percent for 20 years, that's about a $42 million annual payment just on the borrowing. Even though it appears that most of the added spending was paid by owners, a look at their lease shows otherwise.

The Mariners' Lease   The Mariners' Safeco Field lease is very generous to the Mariners' owners. Of the owners' promised share, $30 million came from naming rights (hence, Safeco Field) granted to the team in the lease. These are just stadium revenues collected for the stadium authority by the owners. The authority could certainly have just collected the revenues and kept the money. The Mariners also get all revenues generated by use of the stadium, including parking and concessions. The team gets all of this for $700,000 in rent, down from the $1.39 million it paid at the Kingdome. The lease also includes some profit-sharing arrangements that can only come to pass under extremely unlikely circumstances. At most, James Quirk and I (1999) calculated that the team might pay $2.6 million per year. The team also has agreed (so far) to pick up the $10 million in annual maintenance. The total amount the Mariners will pay each year to play in Safeco Field is between 12 and 14 percent of their 1998 total revenues of about $89.7 million.

The lease also obligates the Mariners to stay in Seattle until 2020. But who would not agree to that stipulation? Essentially, the state built the owners a premiere facility and turned the keys over to them for less than 10 percent of their upgraded total revenues. The stipulation that they must stay and enjoy this for 20 years actually is a subsidy guarantee. The result of the building of Safeco Field is a substantial injection of revenue into the Mariners at significant public expense. Fans kept their team, all taxpayers are footing the bill, and as detailed earlier, it was not clear at the time of the funding agreement whether the team would improve in the long run. As it turns out, the Mariners did end up a better team during the regular season. Their winning percent rose from 0.508 in the five years prior to moving into Safeco to 0.583 after they moved in 1999. However, the team was less successful in the post-season, appearing only once after moving into Safeco as compared to twice in the five years prior to the move.

The Seahawks' New Stadium/Exhibition Center

New stadium demands by the previous owner of the NFL Seahawks, Ken Behring, began in 1995. Behring claimed that his Kingdome lease had been invalidated using some trumped up geographical data showing the Kingdome's vulnerability to earthquakes. Behind the scenes, Behring had been negotiating a new stadium in the Los Angeles area. When Seattle officials refused to build a new stadium, he proceeded to load his Seahawks into moving vans, turned south on I-5, and headed for Hollywood Park, California. The action was stopped after the NFL stepped in to remind Behring that he could not make such a move without league approval.

During the subsequent "time out," billionaire Paul Allen purchased an option to buy the team. The option contract put conditions on his willingness to pay Behring's $250 million asking price for the team. The conditions were pretty predictable. Allen stated that the $250 million would be forthcoming only if the people of the state of Washington would cover the lion's share of a new stadium/exhibition center. If not, then Allen would just let the option expire. If Allen did not purchase the team, it was almost certain that the team would leave Seattle. Allen even offered to personally finance the cost of running a referendum election on the issue. The exhibition center component of the package that included demolition of the Kingdome was virtually ignored, but as noted in the earlier discussion on misinformation, it was an essential element of the deal.

Voting on a "Complex" Simple Referendum

On June 17, 1997, for the second time in 2 years, state voters were asked to vote on a stadium subsidy. The total cost of the facility was set at $425 million. The roughly $325 million public share was clearly stated, and the vote was a simple yes or no. But underlying this simple decision was a confusing hodgepodge of funding mechanisms:

- A sales tax credit of $101 million (an amount that usually would go to the state fund now stayed in King County to cover stadium costs)
- New lottery games expected to add $127 million
- A ticket tax of $52 million
- A room tax extension in King County of $40 million
- A stadium parking tax of $4 million
- A $27 million construction tax break
- $14 million in interest on a $50 million escrow account set up by Paul Allen (in essence, Allen just added the interest to his contribution)

The total of $365 million was more than the $325 million public share that appeared on the ballot because of a contingency reserve for cost overruns and money for ball fields around the state. The ball fields were viewed as a return to the eastern part of the state for supporting a stadium that pretty much benefited west-side residents.

In addition to the funding mechanisms, the Kingdome debt would be retired and that facility torn down. Remember that retiring the Kingdome debt and demolishing the structure did two things. First, all remaining Kingdome debt was rolled into the bill for the new stadium. Second, with the Kingdome gone, the new exhibition center was pretty much guaranteed monopoly status for a wide variety of local events.

Allen promised to pay the balance of $100 million on the $425 million facility and cover any cost overruns beyond a specified buffer. It is important to note that the anticipated lease (at the time) was as generous as the Safeco Field lease. For example, Allen would keep all sponsorship revenues. Again, because the stadium authority could just as easily collect and keep these revenues themselves, having Allen do it for them and pay the proceeds as part of his $100 million promise actually raised the public share.

Here is how the election played out. The issue passed 51.1 percent to 48.9 percent. Unlike the Mariners issue, which failed by about the same margin as this one passed, elected representatives took no further action behind the scenes. The Seahawks moved to their new stadium in 2002. The $425 million or so (76% public money) originally approved for the stadium has yet to be augmented by any cost overruns making the public share, evaluated starting in 1996 at the $365 million that includes other payments, about $436 million in 2004 dollars. The payment under the same 6 percent for 20 years would be about $37 million annually just on the borrowing.

Once again, it was unclear whether the Seahawks would improve with this revenue injection or not. And the result was marginally more success than in the Mariners case; the team averaged one more win per year in their new stadium compared to the three years before 2002 and raised their number of Wild Card appearances in the play-offs from one to two.

This summary of events brings us to a point of cost comparison between keeping the Kingdome and building both a new baseball park and a new football stadium. As noted at the outset, the annual cost in 2004 dollars of keeping the Kingdome in action would have been around $33 million per year for 20 years. The annual cost in 2004 dollars of just the borrowing on the two new facilities totals $77 million annually. In addition, the previous borrowing cost remaining on the Kingdome would be rolled into the new funding amount. At least some of the same subsidy also would be present since public property and forgone taxes also went along with the new spending arrangement. It's entirely possible that the new facilities have an annual cost of nearly $100 million in 2004 dollars, easily three times the annual cost of keeping the Kingdome in operation. Just because the new facilities cost dramatically more does not mean they should not have been built. From Chapter 10, we know that this amount would have to be covered by additional buyers' surpluses and positive externality values because economic activity and development values typically are quite small. Because surpluses and externalities are most likely in the tens of millions of dollars (again, from Chapter 10), it appears that the logic of the stadium mess struck again in Seattle.

They Should Have Known Better: The Kingdome

The Seattle example is clear testimony to the power of pro sports teams in the political process. After all is said and done, the people of Washington may end up kicking themselves, but it will be because they ignored their own history. The history of the Kingdome certainly was available to Seattle voters at the time they were voting on the roughly $850 million in stadium spending for baseball and football. It is a history of delays, frustrations, and cost overruns. Let's look at that history and then revisit the estimates of the subsidy to the quickly forgotten Kingdome.

The History of the Kingdome
In 1966, an election was held in King County for a $25 million (about $145 million 2004 dollars) domed multipurpose stadium to draw NFL and MLB expansion franchises to Seattle. That election failed, but just 2 years later, in 1968, a $40 million ($215 million 2004 dollars) referendum passed. No doubt, this change of heart followed the granting of the expansion MLB Pilots franchise to Seattle in 1968.

During the debate surrounding the 1968 election, the projected opening of the Kingdome was set at 1970, so the Pilots played the 1969 season in a dilapidated minor league park, old Sick's Seattle Stadium. After the election results were in, a revised opening date of 1972 was given. A delay of 2 years in just a few days! The Pilots went bankrupt after one season and left Seattle for Milwaukee to become the Brewers, beginning play there in 1970. A lawsuit by the city of Seattle forced MLB to promise the city an expansion franchise. However, a team was not yet committed, so the voters were facing the prospect of a wonderful new domed stadium with no pro team occupants.

And perhaps the timing of the arrival of their teams helps explain the ensuing delays in building the Kingdome. After rejecting one stadium site, the final site on the edge of downtown was approved in 1972. Ground had not even been broken by the revised date that the facility was supposed to open. This was not the end of the delays. By 1973, the revised opening date was pushed back to 1975. Eventually, the facility opened in 1976, in time for the first Seahawk season (the Mariners began play in the Kingdome the following year). If one had believed the original debate, this was a 6-year delay. In addition, by 1976, the final cost of the stadium had mounted to $67 million ($221 million 2004 dollars), about 3 percent more than the original referendum statement in 1968.

Did You Know?

Despite their history with the Kingdome (a 6-year delay, millions in cost overruns, and an ongoing subsidy of close to $20 million per year), Washington State taxpayers will have spent $782 million on stadiums since 1997.

The Ongoing Kingdome Subsidy The Kingdome is one of the stadiums included in the Quirk and Fort (1992) subsidy analysis cited in the preceding chapter. That Kingdome subsidy calculation is shown in Table 11.8, following the basic subsidy formula of Chapter 10. Circa 1989, the Kingdome was losing about $1.5 million just from operations. Depreciation, the opportunity cost of capital, and forgone property taxes totaled about $12.8 million. This all added up to an ongoing annual subsidy of about $14.3 million in 1989 ($22.6 million per year in 2004 dollars).

Measured in 2004 dollars, the Kingdome cost about $221 million. For that price, those paying the bill bought into a $22.6 million annual subsidy. Although not technically correct because the subsidy probably was larger early on, when the Kingdome was demolished at the ripe old age of 20 years, the subsidy total was something on the order of $452 million in 2004 dollars. Let's not forget the federal component. Zimmerman (1997) calculates the total Kingdome federal subsidy at an additional couple of million dollars. It seems a lesson should have been learned from the Kingdome, but it appears that it has to be learned anew every generation or so.

Table 11.8
Kingdome Subsidy Calculation

Category	Amount ($Millions)
Net operating revenue	−$1.5
Depreciation	$3.1
Opportunity cost of funds	$8.1
Taxes	$1.6
Subsidy ($1989)	$14.3
Subsidy ($Today)	$22.6

Source: James Quirk and Rodney D. Fort, *Pay Dirt: The Business of Professional Team Sports* (Princeton, NJ: Princeton University Press, 1992).

ALTERING THE POLITICS OF STADIUM SUBSIDIES

The stadium mess is a political outcome. Hopes that either review of elected officials by their constituents at reelection junctures or appeals to direct democracy will ameliorate the mess through the rational actor approach are unrealistic. But that same rational actor approach does give us some insight into how the stadium mess can be cleaned up in the future.

Because the stadium mess is a political outcome, only a political response can change it. This will require altering the political status quo that now favors lavish stadium and arena construction. According to the theory presented in this chapter, we see massive and repeated stadium subsidies because special interest politics dictates that outcome; it is in the best interest of elected officials to have it that way. Two things would have to change to alter the politicians' current perceptions.

First, a new group must enter the fray, become politically potent, and wrestle its way into the triangle portrayed in Figure 11.2. Fan and taxpayer advocates would have to displace the current team and press, construction, and business beneficiaries. Forming a coalition that could displace a politically powerful group is an expensive proposition, much like forming a players' union, as described in Chapter 9. A broadly distributed group of current losers would have to be educated about their losses. In addition, free-riding behavior would have to be overcome, and finally, the organization leaders would have to carry the fight and win a place in the stadium policy arena.

These types of changes do not happen often in politics, but they do happen. The environmental movement is one example of a group's gaining political power. Once a loose-knit group of outdoor enthusiasts, the environmental movement is now potent enough to have its own set of laws and policies under the National Environmental Policy Act and the Endangered Species Act. Lately, environmentalists have had impacts on global economic planning processes in the international arena.

The rise of fan organizations on the Web is a sign that such a fan/taxpayer movement might be underway. In recent testimony before Congress, Frank Stadilus, CEO of United Sports Fans of America (USFans), a Web-based fan interest group, was there with MLB Commissioner Bud Selig, former senator and Blue Ribbon Panel 2000 member George Mitchell, commentator Bob Costas, syndicated columnist and Blue Ribbon Panel 2000 member George F. Will, and (yours truly) the author of your textbook. That Stadilus was invited to testify reveals that some members of Congress recognize fan/taxpayer groups. However, it will take more than just testimony; political potency requires funding and action.

The second thing that would have to happen to tidy the subsidy mess follows from the first. An important step in the direction of ending the stadium mess would be reducing or eliminating the ability of owners, acting through leagues, to maintain believable threat locations. However, reducing the leagues' power over team locations would require changing the status quo in sports politics at the federal level, which is the topic of our next chapter.

CHAPTER RECAP

Stadium subsidy outcomes are politically determined. The rational actor explanation of political outcomes explains why this is so. Because voters are rationally ignorant and tend to free ride on the voting behavior of others, only those with the most to gain typically participate in politics. Elected officials know this, and the rational actor explanation predicts that politicians will concentrate benefits to politically potent groups and spread the costs out as thinly as possible over the rest of the taxpaying public.

Owners are especially important elements of this political process. Owners gain from new stadiums. Attendance, gate revenues, and venue revenues all increase with a new stadium. In addition, if the fans in a given team's market are willing to pay, then a new stadium also can raise a team's winning percent. It appears that increased revenues go hand in hand with increased team quality, but this does not happen for all teams that receive a stadium subsidy. Given that owners always benefit from subsidies, we should expect team owners to pursue them vigorously, whether they end up improving the quality of their team or not.

An especially important part of the stadium subsidy process is the careful control of believable threat locations by the leagues. If a given locality fails to meet the subsidy demands of a particular owner, other locations hungry for a team just might. Thus, team owners have the upper hand in the negotiations over stadium subsidies.

In this setting—political determination of subsidies and team owners with the upper hand in bargaining—the rational actor explanation makes a clear prediction. Powerful pro sports team supporters will obtain stadium subsidies for team owners that are paid for by nonsports fans. The bulk of the total cost is paid in small per capita amounts. This is precisely what we observe.

There is little hope that direct democracy can curb the stadium mess. Participation and information bias will plague direct democracy approaches, just as they do other political decisions. Those in control of the ballot alternatives can pose the issue to voters in such a way that preferences for a medium-level outcome can be overcome in favor of large-scale spending on elaborate facilities. The data show direct democracy neither reduces amounts spent nor the public share of spending. In addition, it appears that those in control of ballot alternatives also have nudged spending toward higher levels.

Seattle offers an example of nearly all of the ideas presented in this chapter. The MLB ballpark issue was denied public funding by referendum, but state legislators approved a funding package anyway. The NFL stadium/exhibition center was approved by referendum. The result is about $850 million (2004 dollars) in facility subsidies to extremely rich team owners with very little in return to those footing the majority of the bill. They should have known better because similar problems plagued the Kingdome 20 years earlier.

Because these outcomes are determined by special-interest politics, the only realistic hope of solving the stadium mess is a change in the balance of power toward taxpayers. Antisubsidy groups will have to become politically potent before changes will occur. This is unlikely to happen, but reversals of this type have occurred. An integral element in the reversal of fortunes for taxpayers would be in reducing the power of leagues over team location.

KEY TERMS AND CONCEPTS

- Rational actor explanation
- Market failures
- Wealth redistribution
- Rational level of voting

- Subsidies raise owner profits
- Subsidies and team quality
- Subsidies and believable threat locations

- Subsidies and direct democracy
- Biased turnout
- Biased information
- Control of ballot alternatives

REVIEW QUESTIONS

1. What is the rational actor explanation of political outcomes? What do voters seek? What do politicians pursue? What is the very special prediction from this explanation?
2. What types of market failures characterize sports markets?
3. Beside market failure remedies, what other economic remedy do people seek from government?
4. Why doesn't everybody register to vote?
5. Why doesn't everybody turn out to vote?
6. Why doesn't everybody who turns out necessarily cast a vote on every issue on the ballot?
7. Why is the rational level of voting less than the total number of eligible voters?
8. How does rational voting contribute to the concentrated benefits and dispersed cost outcome that characterize rational actor politics?
9. How do subsidies increase owner revenues? Give examples.
10. How do subsidies decrease owner costs? Give examples.
11. Are owners always better off with subsidies than without them? Explain.
12. Insofar as leagues do not negotiate directly with host cities, how do they contribute to stadium subsidy outcomes?
13. Why don't those paying the costs of the stadium mess vote the responsible politicians out of office at the next election?
14. What is direct democracy? What are the reasons behind the hopes that direct democracy will curb the stadium mess?
15. What is the source of turnout bias? What is the source of information bias? What does it mean to have control of the ballot alternatives that actually go before voters in direct democracy? How do turnout bias and information bias reduce the chances that direct democracy will curb the stadium mess?

THOUGHT PROBLEMS

1. Using Figure 11.1, explain why the general constituency, as opposed to special interests, is not connected to the triangle that determines policy outcomes.
2. How do subsidies increase owner profits? Remember, profits consist of both revenue and cost considerations.
3. Owners will always be better off with subsidies, but the quality of their team may not increase. Why?

4. Why will new stadiums increase attendance? In analyzing the impact of subsidies on team attendance, why is it important to compare attendance with those teams that do not have a new stadium?

5. In analyzing subsidies and winning percent outcomes, why is it not important to compare the winning percents of teams with a new stadium with those without one?

6. Why is it so hard to figure out whether increased revenues from subsidies cause team quality to improve? How would you be able to determine if subsidies improved a team's quality?

7. Walk through the evidence from the study by Hamilton and Kahn (1997) that proves the move into Camden Yards raised the quality of the Baltimore Orioles. Was it necessarily the move into the new stadium that caused this outcome? Why or why not?

8. Walk through the evidence from my study (1999) that shows the move into the Ballpark at Arlington did not raise the quality of the Texas Rangers. Why would the owner of the Rangers reduce spending on talent despite a fairly large revenue injection from moving into the new ballpark?

9. Why might an MLB team's local TV contract value be the leading indicator of whether team quality will improve after moving into a new stadium?

10. Explain the stadium revenue disadvantage logic behind small-revenue market owners' pleas for new stadiums. Is that argument believable? If so, under what circumstances?

11. How does the greater legal mobility of teams in the NFL dampen the propensity of local government hosts to provide subsidies to "their" NFL teams?

12. There are two reasons why tearing down the Kingdome might have been a bad idea, economically speaking. Provide these two reasons. Even if the value of using the Kingdome into the future was less than the cost of repairs, what is one reason it should have remained standing?

13. Why might those in control of the ballot alternatives that confront voters in direct democracy prefer to influence voters toward higher rather than lower spending on stadiums? Explain using Figure 11.2.

14. Explain how the data on spending on stadiums and arenas refute the idea that direct democracy curbs the stadium mess.

15. Explain how the data on public spending on stadiums and arenas support the idea that there is some control of the alternatives confronting voters under direct democracy by those who prefer higher rather than lower spending levels on stadiums and arenas.

ADVANCED PROBLEMS

1. Control of believable threat locations is an essential activity for pro sports leagues. If laws aimed at curtailing MLB's power over team location were passed, the losses to MLB from these laws could be dramatic. Suppose that the interest rate is 5 percent, the value of power over team locations is $30 million annually, and the planning horizon is 10 years. How can it make

sense for MLB to spend around $1.8 million lobbying against these laws for the year 1999?

2. What is the one piece of evidence suggesting that the improvement in the Baltimore Orioles' winning percent after moving into Camden Yards was not due to the extra revenue generated by the new stadium?

3. Why have stadium revenues, as a percent of all revenues, grown in importance in MLB but not in the NFL?

4. Explain how a new stadium can increase an NFL team's ability to compete on the field despite the presence of a salary cap and nearly complete revenue sharing in the NFL. Does the observation that teams all violate the cap anyway have any bearing on this explanation?

5. Using the rational actor politics model in Figure 11.2, explain failed attempts at obtaining stadium subsidies.

6. In the Learning Highlight: The Stadium That Didn't Get Built and Then Did, voters and politicians in the St. Louis area denied Bill Bidwell a new stadium and then turned right around and built the TransWorld Dome, luring the Rams to town. What special problem that plagues a league that shares revenues such as the NFL might have led to this interesting result?

7. Suppose there is going to be a stadium vote and the voter preferences are as shown in Figure 11.3. Further, suppose that voters believe that "no team" will occur if the election fails to pass. If the elaborate stadium option is put before the set of voters shown, why will the vote be 3–2 in favor of the subsidy? What will be the voting result if voters believe the team will stay and play in the "obsolete stadium"? Redraw the figure to show where voters C and D would have to be located along the line for the issue to fail. Given your answers, is it always the case that control of the ballot alternatives will lead to an elaborate new stadium? Explain.

8. Using Figure 11.2, explain the Safeco Field outcome in Seattle. Remember, in that case, the voters said no in a referendum, but the stadium was funded and built anyway at a higher level of spending than was originally refused in the referendum.

9. Even though the ballot issue was a simple yes or no to a new stadium/ exhibition center for the Seahawks, explain how the issue actually was much more complex than portrayed to the voters. Did this impact the perceptions of people voting on the issue? Did they even know how to figure out the costs? Why is this consistent with the idea that politicians know that taxpayers are rationally ignorant?

10. Suppose you were going to start a fan protection action group. Describe the difficulties you would confront in becoming a politically viable interest group using the diagram in Figure 11.2.

INTERNET RESOURCES

For a host of additional material and questions for thought, visit this book's Web site at www.prenhall.com/fort.

REFERENCES

Fort, Rodney. "Direct Democracy and the Stadium Mess," in *Sports, Jobs, and Taxes: The Economic Impact of Sports Teams and Stadiums*. Roger Noll and Andrew Zimbalist, eds. Washington, D.C.: The Brookings Institution, 1997.

Fort, Rodney. "Stadium Votes, Market Power, and Politics," *University of Toledo Law Review* 30 (1999): 419–442.

Fort, Rodney. "Stadiums and Public and Private Interests in Seattle." *Marquette Sports Law Journal* 10 (2000): 311–334.

Hamilton, Bruce and Peter Kahn. "Baltimore's Camden Yards Ballparks," in *Sports, Jobs, and Taxes: The Economic Impact of Sports Teams and Stadiums*. Roger Noll and Andrew Zimbalist, eds. Washington, D.C.: The Brookings Institution, 1997.

Keating, Raymond J. "Sports Pork: The Costly Relationship Between Major League Sports and Government," Policy Analysis No. 339. Washington, D.C.: Cato Institute, April 5, 1999.

Noll, Roger and Andrew Zimbalist (eds.) *Sports, Jobs, and Taxes: The Economic Impacts of Sports Teams and Stadiums.* Washington, D.C.: The Brookings Institution, 1997.

Quinn, Kevin G., Paul B. Bursik, Christopher P. Borick, and Lisa Raethz. "Do New Digs Mean More Wins? The Relationship Between a New Venue and a Professional Sports Team's Competitive Success," *Journal of Sports Economics* 4 (2003): 167–182.

Quirk, James and Rodney D. Fort. *Pay Dirt: The Business of Professional Team Sports.* Princeton, NJ: Princeton University Press, 1992.

Quirk, James and Rodney D. Fort. *Hard Ball: The Abuse of Power in Pro Team Sports.* Princeton, NJ: Princeton University Press, 1999.

Shropshire, Kenneth L. *The Sports Franchise Game: Cities in Pursuit of Sports Franchises, Events, Stadiums, and Arenas.* Philadelphia, PA: University of Pennsylvania Press, 1995.

Swindell, David. "Public Financing of Sports Stadiums: How Cincinnati Compares," *Policy Solutions.* Dayton, OH: The Buckeye Institute for Public Policy Solutions, 1996.

Zimmerman, Dennis. "Subsidizing Stadiums: Who Benefits, Who Pays?" in *Sports, Jobs, and Taxes: The Economic Impact of Sports Teams and Stadiums.* Roger Noll and Andrew Zimbalist, eds. Washington, D.C.: The Brookings Institution, 1997.

Chapter 12

Taxes, Antitrust, and Competition Policy

Chapter Objectives

After reading this chapter, you should be able to:

- *Know the special tax and antitrust advantages afforded to owners of sports teams.*

- *See the value of the special status afforded to owners of teams and their players and the costs of these benefits to fans and other taxpayers.*

- *Appreciate the rational actor model of politics explanation of why pro sports owners enjoy special tax and antitrust status.*

- *Understand the somewhat pessimistic view that extremely unlikely changes will have to occur before politicians see fit to alter these special advantages.*

- *Discuss the role that competition policy can play in fixing the ills attributed to sports market power.*

> *Anyone who quotes profits of a baseball club is missing the point. Under generally accepted accounting principles, I can turn a $4 million profit into a $2 million loss, and I can get every national accounting firm to agree with me.*

—PAUL BEESTON
Toronto Blue Jays Vice President (Zimbalist, 1994, p. 62)

The United States Football League (USFL) disbanded after the jury decision in its lawsuit against the NFL in 1986. The USFL alleged that the NFL had violated the antitrust laws by tampering with the USFL's network contract negotiations. The USFL sought $567 million in damages that would be trebled under the law to $1.8 billion. The jury found that the NFL had tampered with the negotiations, but then something interesting happened. The total value of the damages to the USFL was set at $1. How could these antitrust violations only be worth $1? The jury cited USFL mismanagement as the reason for their paltry award. However, another answer lies in the ability of dominant leagues to drive out rivals. It could be the case that after the USFL failed to compete against the existing dominant NFL that it was practically worthless for all intents and purposes.

In this final chapter on pro team sports (we turn to college sports in Chapter 13), we will extend our look at the relationship between local, state, and federal governments and the sports business. The chapter offers a three-step approach to understanding the special tax and antitrust status of pro sports. First, we will identify and describe these two situations. Second, we will see how they are valuable to team owners and players. Third, we will use the rational actor description of democracy we developed in the last chapter to gain some insight into why leagues are able to maintain these special benefits. We wrap up the chapter, and our look at pro sports, with a look at competition policy. As we will see, all of the evils commonly attributed to sports can be remedied with a stiff dose of competition, but our rational actor model suggests that dramatic reversals of sports policy in favor of fans and other taxpayers should not be expected without some very important changes to the system.

TAXES

Bill Veeck, the famous baseball business entrepreneur, was no fan of business income taxes. He felt that MLB deserved a tax break. In *The Hustler's Handbook* (1962), he says, "Look, we play the 'Star Spangled Banner' before every game—you want us to pay income taxes too?" In his efforts to avoid personal income taxes, he created a lucrative special tax situation for pro sports team owners. This raises the issue of sports accounting and tax implications (also touched on in Chapter 4). In this section, we will examine the special tax situation of pro sports. Later in the chapter, we will look into why pro sports enjoy special tax status in the first place.

"Look, we play the 'Star Spangled Banner' before every game—you want us to pay income taxes too?"
—Sports team owner and entrepreneur Bill Veeck

Player Roster Depreciation Revisited

When a team is purchased, the new owner reorganizes it as a new business enterprise. This accomplishes two things. First, the player roster and other assets like the value of broadcast contracts are depreciable under tax law. In Chapter 4, we discussed the validity of such an approach, noting that players do not depreciate and, even if they did, they already are on the expense side of the ledger for tax purposes. Player roster depreciation can easily erase any team taxable income for owners.

The second thing that reorganization accomplishes follows from the form of reorganization. As we saw in Chapter 4, because roster depreciation typically generates huge losses for the first few years of ownership, millions can be saved on owners' other Form 1040 earnings. However, the owners can only do this if they are able to pass losses straight through to their personal income tax forms. The form of reorganization must facilitate this pass-through, typically as a partnership or Subchapter S corporation. In the San Antonio Spurs example in Chapter 4, an old version of roster depreciation was in force. For the purposes of understanding the relationship between government and the sports business, it is informative to trace the historical development of this type of special tax treatment to the present.

In 1959, Bill Veeck bought the Chicago White Sox for the first time (he would own them again in the 1970s). Always an innovator on and off the field (recall the Chapter 2 *Learning Highlight: Bill and Mike Veeck*), he argued that players "waste away" like livestock, and because livestock could be depreciated, why not players? The IRS agreed and roster depreciation was born (Fort, 2006; Rovell, 2004).

Bud Selig, who owned the Milwaukee Brewers prior to his current reign as MLB Commissioner, played a role in the development of roster depreciation back in 1970. A group led by Selig bought the bankrupt Seattle Pilots in April of 1970 for $10.8 million and moved them to Milwaukee, the second incarnation of the Brewers. Selig attributed $10.2 million of the purchase price to the player roster, set up his depreciation schedule accordingly, and submitted his tax forms. The IRS challenged Selig's claim that 94 percent of the purchase prices could be attributed to the player roster and demanded a large tax adjustment. Selig sued (*Selig v. U.S.*, 565 F. Supp. 524) and eventually won the case.

After a few more IRS challenges of subsequent large roster depreciation claims by other owners, the Tax Reform Act of 1976 set the level of roster depreciation at 50 percent of the purchase price and a 5-year depreciation schedule. Any claims over these limits had to be justified by the taxpayer. This version of roster depreciation still was in force and applicable to the 1994–1995 San Antonio Spurs example in Chapter 4 and held until the Tax Act Amendments of 2004. Under these recent amendments, owners can depreciate 100 percent of the team sale price over no more than 15 years.

The IRS justified this change on two grounds (Wilson, 2004). First, the IRS would spend less taxpayer money litigating depreciation claims by owners. In addition, the IRS argued that owners would actually pay more taxes under the new rules. The first of these justifications is obvious, but let's investigate the second in some detail. In what follows, we'll look only at the tax shelter value of the pass-through because any reasonable amount of roster depreciation should push team taxable net revenue to zero.

As always, we need to make a few assumptions because this is a complex issue. We'll examine an MLB team without any regional television ownership or stadium. Further suppose net operating revenue, nonroster depreciation, and amortization remain constant over time. In addition, the team is organized as a pass-through for tax purposes (Subchapter S corporation or partnership); profit or loss is claimed on the owner's personal Form 1040 at the personal income tax rate. For now, also suppose that net revenue after subtracting nonroster depreciation and amortization are positive but less than the value of roster depreciation. Finally, we'll use simple straight-line depreciation.

A little notation and some algebra become extremely useful at this point. Under the old plan, roster depreciation is half the purchase price P over 5 years, that is, $D_{old} = \dfrac{0.5 \times P}{5}$. Under the new plan, roster depreciation is the entire price over 15 years, or $D_{new} = \dfrac{P}{15}$. Let G be the gain (or loss) under the new version of roster depreciation, compared to the old version:

$$G = \sum_{t=1}^{15} \frac{\tau(D_{new} - E)}{(1 + r)^t} - \sum_{t=1}^{5} \frac{\tau(D_{old} - E)}{(1 + r)^t}$$

where τ is the owner's personal income tax rate (also assumed constant over time), E is net revenue after nonroster depreciation and amortization, and r is the real rate of interest (because the gain covers discounted present values over different lengths of time). Clearly, the gain hinges upon the different paper loss pass-through amounts, $D_{old} - E$ and $D_{new} - E$, and the difference in the periods of time. Our earlier assumption guarantees that both of the pass-through values are greater than zero.

Because the numerator of each term on the right-hand side is constant with respect to time by virtue of our previous assumptions, we write G as:

$$G = \tau(D_{new} - E)\sum_{t=1}^{15} \frac{1}{(1 + r)^t} - \tau(D_{old} - E)\sum_{t=1}^{5} \frac{1}{(1 + r)^t}$$

Now, if $G < 0$, the IRS is correct—the tax shelter value of the new version is less than the old version, and owners will pay more taxes. Otherwise, owners will have greater shelters under the new version.

At this point, let's make the algebra really easy by assigning reasonable numerical values to some of the variables in G. First, let P be the average team sale price over the last decade or so, $355 million 2004 dollars (Fort, 2006). Further, let the real rate of interest be $r = 0.03$, the typical real rate of growth in the economy at large. Finally, any owner almost certainly faces $\tau = 0.35$, the highest marginal income tax rate. These choices yield the following: $D_{old} = \dfrac{.5 \times 355}{5} = 35.5$; $D_{new} = \dfrac{355}{15} = 23.7$; $\displaystyle\sum_{t=1}^{15} \frac{1}{(1 + r)^t} = 11.9$; $\displaystyle\sum_{t=1}^{5} \frac{1}{(1 + r)^t} = 4.6$. Substituting these values into G, along with $\tau = 0.35$, yields the following:

$$G = 0.35\,(23.7 - E)\,11.9 - 0.35\,(35.5 - E)\,4.6 = 41.5 - 2.6E$$

The graph of $G = 41.5 - 2.6E$ in Figure 12.1 shows that the IRS could possibly be right. If net operating revenue after nonroster depreciation and amortization but

Figure 12.1 Roster Depreciation Gain under the 2004 Amendments for the Purchase of an Average Priced Team

Purchasing an average priced team for $355 million that is organized as a pass-through for tax purposes: If the real rate of interest is 3 percent and the owner faces the marginal tax rate of 35 percent: then the gain from the new roster depreciation amendments of 2004 is $G = 41.5 - 2.6E$, where E is net operating revenues after other nonroster depreciation and amortization. If net operating revenues are zero, the gain under the new rules is $41.5 million. If net operating revenues are $16.0 million, the gain goes to zero.

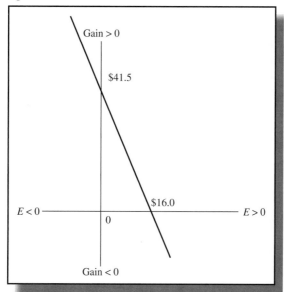

before roster depreciation is subtracted exceeds $16.0 million, then the owner is actually worse off under the new version compared to the old because $G < 0$. Apparently this is what the IRS thinks will be true.

But Figure 12.1 also shows that as E decreases, the gain under the new version of roster depreciation increases. The gain turns positive once $E < \$16.0$ million and grows larger from there. Once $E = 0$, the gain is $41.5 million. The gain grows ever larger as E continues to become increasingly negative. So, whether or not the IRS ends up being correct depends on the level of E.

Some data cast doubt on the IRS claims. *Forbes* listed 2004 operating revenues of MLB teams before taxes, depreciation, and amortization, and the average of those values is $4.4 million. Reports from the same source for the other leagues are available only up to 2003; calculating the averages yields $9.6 million for the NBA, $26.6 million for the NFL, and −$3.2 million for the NHL. Even before nonroster depreciation and amortization, only the NFL is a candidate for $G < 0$ and higher tax payments under the new version of roster depreciation. At the average, NFL teams must have nonroster depreciation and amortization of less than $10.2 million as well in order to pay more taxes under the new version.

All of this suggests that existing teams with some remaining depreciation will see some benefit, and it appears pretty likely that all future buyers are better off under the new version of roster depreciation. This last observation means that current owners who already have exhausted their depreciation will nonetheless be able to sell their teams for more because future owners will enjoy a larger tax shelter value. Estimates by financial analysts at Lehman Brothers back this up. They have publicly stated that the new version of depreciation will add about 5 percent to sports team values across all leagues (Wilson, 2004). *Forbes*'s total franchise values for all four major leagues in 2004 were $45.9 billion, so owners might expect a windfall gain of $2.3 billion, or an average of about $19 million for all 121 team owners.

A number of notables have downplayed that owners are typically better off under the new version of depreciation (the quotes in this paragraph are from Rovell, 2004). NBA Commissioner David Stern: "It's definitely not a significant motivating factor in purchasing a team. No matter what the tax treatment is, if the team isn't profitable, it can't provide a substantial benefit." Jeff Smulyan, previous owner of the MLB Mariners:

"When owners are losing millions of dollars in real money, it's crazy to think that they're fine with it because they are not paying as much tax."— Previous Mariners owner Jeff Smulyan, commenting on the new version of roster depreciation in 2004

"When owners are losing millions of dollars in real money, it's crazy to think that they're fine with it because they are not paying as much tax." David Samson, president of the Marlins: "The benefit of depreciation is far outweighed by the reality of cash losses when you are losing money operationally." Now, especially at today's high team purchase prices, the depreciation value may be relatively small, but none of these notables suggests they are zero. The analysis above, plus the assessment by Lehman Brothers, suggests millions of dollars gained, certainly for owners in all leagues except the NFL and probably for many individual owners in that league as well.

While public statements downplay the value of depreciation, it also is true that MLB actively lobbied for the revisions and that the NFL also supported the new version of depreciation (Wilson, 2004). Further, Smulyan also is a principal in one of the groups vying to buy the new Washington Nationals. Don't forget, while it should be the case that disputes over allowable write-offs would decline and so would their costs to the IRS, this is just sauce for the goose; legal fees for team owners should fall as well, increasing net operating revenues.

Bill Veeck cracked his joke about taxes and the National Anthem relative to just the original version of roster depreciation. One can only expect that he's smiling in that great grandstand in the sky over the new and improved version! IRS claims of higher tax payments appear unjustified, so owners will do better under the new rules and their legal costs should fall. Later in the chapter, we'll explore just how it is that team owners end up with this special type of tax treatment.

Roster depreciation is far from the end of the tax advantages enjoyed by owners. Another special tax decision allows owners both to postpone tax payments and

"Nevertheless the apparent irrationality of even the worst sports investment is largely explained by the effects of full utilization of the available tax benefits."
—Economist Benjamin Okner (1974)

to pay at a lower rate than the prevailing personal income tax rate. Things have changed in the past 30 years, but the first to observe this type of tax advantage was Okner (1974). Okner pointed out, "Nevertheless, the apparent irrationality of even the worst sports investment is largely explained by the effects of full utilization of the available tax benefits" (1974, p. 164). Ambrose (1995) also detailed the tax law changes of 1976 that determined tax status at the time of team sale. Let's look at these tax advantages in more detail.

Capital Gains Tax Advantages for Sports Owners

Suppose an owner has run out the player roster depreciation advantage after 15 years. That owner faces two options: continue on or sell the team. Either choice confronts the owner with tax problems.

Reorganizing After Roster Depreciation Runs Out   If the owner continues on after 15 years organized as a pass-through firm, the outcome can be very costly. At this point, the team is organized in order to pass all profit or loss directly through to the owner's personal 1040 Form. If the pass-through is positive, then the owner pays taxes at the personal income tax rate. At the end of the 15 years, the owner starts paying back what was made in the first few years from the depreciation advantage in terms of the higher personal income tax rate. However, if the team were organized as a corporation, taxes would be at the lower corporate tax rate.

It is in the owner's best interest to change the structure of the business. Under IRS rules, any firm organized to pass business income through to a personal 1040 Form can **reorganize for tax purposes** just once. Once reorganized into a regular corporation or limited partnership rather than a pass-through corporation or partnership, the tax obligation is at the lower corporate tax rate. For owners who intend to keep the team, the special tax status of pro sports allows them to take advantage of the depreciation tax shelters for the first few years. Then, the owners can reorganize the team for tax purposes once the depreciation shelter runs out. After reorganization, the owners never pay back any of the shelter and suffer no other disadvantages into the future relative to any other corporation.

IRS Rules and the Avoidance of Excess Depreciation and Capital Gains
But what happens if the owner decides to sell, rather than continue to run the team reorganized for tax purposes? In this case, it is important to note that player rosters did not really depreciate during the tenure of the previous owner despite the fact that the owner took out millions in roster depreciation. Therefore, the previous owner will sell the team for the discounted future profitability it represents. In a sense, this type of owner was in it for the tax shelter and sells the asset at market value after the tax advantages have run out. The market value of the team will include the tax shelter value to the next owner.

There is one inconsistency with this practice. If the previous owner claims the roster is worth something when selling it to the new owner, it is an admission that the depreciation never really took place even though millions were claimed. In such a case, the IRS would typically rule that there was **excess depreciation** by the previous owner, and that owner would be liable for taxes on the amount of excess depreciation.

When the IRS pursues excess depreciation, it does so at the higher personal income tax rate, and two things happen to the team owner. First, all of the income sheltered by the pass-through depreciation losses is taxable at the personal income tax rate. Second, any actual net operating revenue net of real depreciation is also taxable. Because the firm was organized at the time to pass that income through to the owner's personal 1040 Form, it would be taxed at the higher personal income tax rate as well.

However, no excess depreciation cases have ever been brought by the IRS against sports owners selling teams. For years, the IRS just agreed that the "new" team (for tax purposes) was a collection of new players ready to be depreciated all over again. By this IRS ruling, the previous owner did not have to reduce the sale value of the team because the roster was already completely depreciated. Thus, there never was any revelation of any excess depreciation. The new owner could start all over again doing precisely the same thing as the previous owner. This **roster depreciation rollover** suggests a strategy: Use the depreciation shelter for 15 years and then continue to run the team or sell it as an entirely depreciable new team.

Of course, the previous owner still must pay capital gains tax on any increase in the sale value of the team. However, even here the depreciation shelter is valuable. Capital gains taxes are paid on the difference between the sale value of the team and the owner's report of its profitability based on the book value of the firm over time. This reported profitability based on book value is called the **basis** at sale. Capital gains taxes are not meant to double tax the owner who would already have paid taxes on the profits during ownership.

Because of the depreciation shelter, the book value of the team is very low during the early years as the owner reports losses or profits of zero. This means that the sale value minus the basis is larger during the early years of ownership than it would be without the depreciation shelter. However, the owner still pays less in taxes as long as the capital gains tax is lower than the personal income tax. Rather than paying at the personal income tax rate for what profits could have been shown, the owner only pays at the lower capital gains tax rate at the time of sale. Owners enjoy the tax shelter from team losses on their 1040 Forms.

Playing off the **personal and capital gains tax gap**, the depreciation shelter raises the amount subject to capital gains, but some of the amount would have been taxed at the higher personal tax rate without the shelter. From the perspective of the current owner, this is a very attractive special tax advantage to sports teams that cannot be had anywhere else.

Typical Sports Team Organization for Tax Purposes

Here is how a team is typically organized for tax purposes. For 15 years, organized as a pass-through firm, the team shows losses due to player depreciation. The owner earns the entire net operating revenue after depreciation but pays no tax on the team. Any paper losses go straight through to the owner's personal Form 1040 as a tax shelter. After the depreciation shelter runs out, if the owners continue on, they reorganize to take advantage of a better tax situation and reduce future tax payments. If the owners sell, they have postponed payments on actual income taken out of the team and, at the time of sale, pay a possibly lower tax bill on their capital gain. Any new owner buys into exactly the same proposition starting from scratch. The sum of these tax advantages has been worth millions of dollars to sports team owners. James Quirk and I (1992) reported that these advantages could triple an owner's rate of return on team ownership. An interesting question is why the sale price faced by new owners would not have already incorporated the tax advantage value in the first place. If all owners understand the tax advantages, then the price of the team should include **imputed tax advantage values**. This just means that the value of any tax advantages represents a value of owning a team. As such, it will be counted in the price that potential owners are willing to pay for the team. In such a case, no owner should earn more than a normal return including the tax shelter. As we will see in a later section of this chapter, sale prices appear to be greater than the normal rate of return would dictate.

The personal income tax rate and the capital gains tax rate were set equal to each other in the 1986 tax reforms, and a large part of the tax advantage to team ownership disappeared. The player roster depreciation advantages remained but not the value of the difference between the capital gains and personal tax rates. However, the capital gains rate was changed to 20 percent in 1997. We are now back to the situation of the days before 1986. The capital gains rate is lower than the personal income tax rate, resulting in millions of dollars in tax value for owners.

ANTITRUST

The antitrust laws are designed to protect consumers from market power. In a nutshell, the laws dictate that firms cannot exercise their market power unhindered by government. They cannot attempt to extend their market power into other economic endeavors either on the input or output side, and they are subject to scrutiny by the Federal Trade Commission (FTC). The Department of Justice (DOJ) carries out the legal battle when the FTC finds an antitrust violation. Individuals also can bring antitrust actions if they feel a firm has violated these important market power laws.

From our studies in Chapters 5 and 8, it would seem that sports leagues are prime candidates for lawsuits under the antitrust laws. Leagues are organized to guarantee that teams enjoy market power through territorial exclusivity. Leagues also offer superior outcomes for member owners in negotiations with media providers, players, and host cities. Finally, leagues by and large put teams where they please, either through expansion or decisions over team relocation. All of these exercises of market power are possible violations of the antitrust laws.

MLB enjoys a long-standing antitrust exemption that resulted from the *Federal Baseball* decision (discussed in Chapter 8), but no similar restriction on antitrust intervention exists for other pro sports. Let's revisit some of the issues presented in Chapter 8 and raise some new ones that lay bare the antitrust status of sports leagues.

Players and Antitrust

The antitrust issue in player markets concerns how owners have turned their league market power over the production of sports into market power over players. If players have only one major league option, teams will recognize their superior position and try to take advantage of it. The history of league power over players, primarily through the reserve clause and player drafts, does not need to be repeated here, and players have gained significant ground in this regard. Long-standing league impositions such as the reserve clause were removed by court decision and the rise of unions.

Easing of Restrictions on Players' Antitrust Rights   Players' rights to take individual antitrust action against sports team owners remain quite restricted. Until 1998 the National Labor Relations Act required players to yield their individual antitrust rights when they entered into collective bargaining through certified unions. Recent changes allow players in all pro sports leagues to sue individually if behavior prohibited under the antitrust laws leads to a breakdown in labor negotiations.

MLB players were the last group of players to gain this protection. Following the MLBPA strike in 1994–1995, Congress sought a way to reduce the chances of future work stoppages. The result was the **Curt Flood Act of 1998**. The Flood Act puts MLB players on the same antitrust footing as other professional athletes. However, this act only grants rights in the special case where antitrust violations lead to a breakdown in labor negotiations.

Limitations of the Flood Act   Congress made it clear that the Flood Act was very limited, providing an itemized list of exemptions. These crucial limitations guarantee that market power over output will continue in its current form in every important respect. Specifically exempted are:

- Minor league players (especially in draft matters)
- The entire relationship between the minor and major leagues
- Expansion and team location issues
- Team ownership and ownership transfer
- The relationship between owners and the MLB commissioner
- All marketing of the entertainment product
- The joint marketing of broadcast rights, under the Sports Broadcasting Act of 1961

Therefore, almost all MLB business remains exempt, from franchise exclusivity, team movement, and expansion to output management activities such as season length, playoff structure, and broadcasting sales.

The Role of Decertification   In other leagues, players decertified their unions in order to sue under antitrust laws. As discussed in Chapter 9, NFL players voted to decertify the NFLPA as their collective bargaining agent. Then, individual players brought suit under the antitrust laws, earning free agency victories in the courts (*McNeil v. NFL*). After their victory, the union was recertified.

However, players may face **decertification dangers** using this approach. For example, a videotape distributed by Michael Jordan to other NBA stars practically guaranteed that any reformation of the NBPA would have been contentious. Jordan urged the stars of the league not to allow decertification and argued that if decertification did occur, then the union leadership should be replaced. Had the players decertified the NBPA, the reformed union would look much different from its current makeup. It would have happened due to the actions of a few stars rather than through majority rule of the union rank and file.

Franchise Moves and Antitrust

Under the operating rules in all leagues, a three-fourths majority is required before a team can move (and unanimous consent is required in any move that puts a team in an existing franchise area). If that rule is not arbitrarily applied, leagues have nearly complete control over franchise moves and team location. This, as we have discussed in Chapters 2 and 5, is the main source of the market power enjoyed by individual team owners.

The Raiders Case and Recent NFL Team Movements
The three-quarters rule was found unreasonable in the famous NFL **Raiders case** (*L.A. Memorial Coliseum Commission v. NFL*), an antitrust lawsuit brought by Raiders owner Al Davis against the NFL. Essentially, the court said that the three-quarters rule had been arbitrarily applied when the league denied Davis the chance to move his Raiders from Oakland to Los Angeles.

At the time, this ruling was expected to reduce the power of leagues over the movement of individual teams. However, over time, it barely made a dent in that power. The NFL cited the Raiders case as justification for not blocking the move of the Cleveland Browns to Baltimore in the late 1990s. However, it ignored the Raiders case entirely when dealing with Ken Behring's proposed move of the Seahawks to the Los Angeles area. The NFL also hindered the move of the Rams from Los Angeles to St. Louis, discussed in Chapter 11, until a mutually agreeable payment was made to the league stadium fund. As you can see, the Raiders case has not effectively constrained the NFL in its ability to decide where to put teams.

It is easy to see why the league behaved this way regarding these team moves. The NFL's behavior had nothing to do with fan happiness and everything to do with owner and league wealth maximization. The move of the Browns to Baltimore saved one of the league's owner-icons, Art Modell, a considerable amount of money at no cost to the league. A team was lost from one longtime NFL city, Cleveland, but gained by another longtime NFL city that had gone without a team for a few years, Baltimore. On net, Modell was better off and the league was not hurt, especially because it expanded back into Cleveland shortly thereafter. In the Seahawks case, a move from Seattle to Los Angeles would have erased a prospective large expansion fee from the future owner of the extremely valuable and, at that time, vacant Los Angeles market. League members were better off with that decision, looking forward to expansion fees that are rapidly approaching the $1 billion mark. Finally, the NFL earned $43 million or so from the Rams when they moved to St. Louis.

Congressional Hearings on Team Location
Because it is clear that leagues will continue to exercise power over team location and movement to the detriment of fans, government has the opportunity to step in under the antitrust laws. However, as history shows, government has chosen not to protect consumer (fan)

interests in the case of franchise movement and location (a history of early Congressional activity in sports, up to 1978, can be found in Johnson [1979]).

The Celler Hearings of 1951   As early as 1951, Congress investigated the power of leagues over team location and movement. Congressman Emanuel Celler began the proceedings with some opening remarks:

> Organized baseball affords this subcommittee with almost a classroom example of what may happen to an industry which is governed by rules and regulations among its members rather than by the free play of competitive forces. Without knowing at this time whether such regulation is in the best interest of baseball because of its many unique characteristics, we may at least learn something of importance about how an industry operates itself instead of being forced to comply with the antitrust laws.

However, at the end of the 1951 hearings, Congress chose not to revisit the antitrust status of MLB on the output side. Congress did, however, make it clear to MLB that its reluctance to expand westward was puzzling and encouraged the league to consider such movement.

Shortly thereafter, the Dodgers and Giants moved to California. As discussed in Chapter 5, this instigation on the part of Congress probably doomed the potential for a reduction in MLB's market power. When MLB moved west with its ready-made Dodger–Giant rivalry, the very successful PCL was reduced to minor league status despite its demands to join in as another major league. Congress could certainly have facilitated competition between MLB and the PCL but chose not to.

The Kefauver Hearings of 1961   Similarly, after hearings in 1961 led by Senator Estes Kefauver, Congress again chose to let stand the market power of MLB. Almost instantly, in 1962 the New York Metropolitans (the Mets) and Houston Colt-45s (now the Astros) were added to the National League. The American League quickly followed with the addition of the Los Angeles Angels and the last incarnation of the Washington Senators. However, as we saw in Chapter 5, these MLB actions doomed the Continental League of Branch Rickey and William Shea.

Another franchise move with antitrust implications occurred between Congressional hearings. Noll and Zimbalist (1997) reported on Congressional inquiry into antitrust after the last version of the Washington Senators left for Texas in 1971 (the Rangers began play in 1972). That inquiry led to a recommendation that MLB's antitrust exemption be removed. However, Congress only recommended further study and no further action by the entire House.

The Sisk Hearings of 1976 and After   In 1976, Congressman B. F. Sisk led Congressional hearings on the issue of market power in sports in general. Despite the clear testimony of every leading analyst on the harm done to consumers by the market power of the leagues, Congress again made no moves against the power of pro leagues over team location.

In the early 1990s, another wave of antitrust interest followed the possible move of the San Francisco Giants to Florida, but no action was ever taken. Interestingly, the most recent Congressional inquiry into franchise movement and location, concerning the movement of the NFL's Cleveland Browns to Baltimore, actually attempted to give the NFL an exemption similar to the one enjoyed by MLB. The hope was that location stability would return to the NFL. No further action beyond the inquiry occurred.

Broadcasting and Antitrust

Now let's turn to the antitrust status of pro sports in broadcasting. In the late 1950s, the DOJ held that league negotiations on the part of all member teams for a league-wide broadcasting contract were an antitrust violation. This move could have been heralded as a solid move forward for consumers of broadcast games, but Congress is nothing if not consistent. It basically reversed the DOJ's ruling. Under the **Sports Broadcasting Act of 1961**, league-wide TV contracts in all sports are exempted from antitrust. This exemption continues to the present day, despite the fact that the Supreme Court struck down precisely the same type of behavior by the NCAA.

Congress also took one further step that harms broadcast viewers and benefits leagues. If a team does not sell out a game, it can kill a contracted broadcast in its own home viewing area. The effect of these so-called **blackout laws** is to reduce the number of people who can enjoy a given game if the game is not sold out. As you can see, acts of Congress reinforce market power in broadcasting rather than suppress it.

Mergers and Antitrust

Congress has been an active facilitator of pro sports league mergers (Quirk and Fort, 1992; 1999). In MLB, the American League was a successful rival to the National League in 1902–1903. Players were jumping between the two leagues and pushing their payment closer to their marginal revenue product. For the 1904 season, an agreement was reached between the two leagues to observe each other's reserve clauses and crown a champion. That agreement established the modern version of MLB, the league we know today. Despite the fact that the antitrust laws had been in force and used in other areas for over 10 years, Congress made no effort to even investigate this agreement. The rest is market power history.

In other cases, Congress actually took formal **merger facilitation** steps in pro sports rather than carefully applying antitrust laws to the benefit of sports consumers. The fourth incarnation of the American Football League (AFL, with Al Davis at the helm) established itself as a successful rival to the NFL in the mid-1960s. However, Congress acted to formally exempt the AFL-NFL merger from antitrust in 1966, producing the modern NFL with the American and National Football Conferences. In other sports, Congress did not act to formally exempt a merger, but it brought pressure to bear on both the NBA-ABA and the NHL-WHA mergers. As James Quirk and I (1997) argue, this merger activity has played a primary role in the elimination of effective economic competition in pro sports.

Thus, despite repeated investigation, Congressional action either has not been forthcoming or has been directed toward enhancing market power in pro sports. Congress has failed to intervene in league practices concerning team movement and location, reversed antitrust decisions by the DOJ, passed blackout

Did You Know?
Congress has failed to intervene in league practices concerning team movement and location, reversed antitrust decisions by the DOJ, passed blackout laws in broadcasting, and acted to exempt or facilitate league mergers in every sport.

laws in broadcasting, and acted to exempt or facilitate league mergers in every sport. Why has Congress behaved this way? Before we apply the rational actor explanation to this question, let's have a look at what this behavior is worth to team owners.

THE IMPACTS OF SPECIAL TAX AND ANTITRUST STATUS

The impacts of the special tax and antitrust status of pro sports leagues are felt by all participants—fans, taxpayers, media providers, advertisers, owners, and players. In this section, we will focus mainly on the impacts on owners and players, but we will briefly examine the impact on the other participants.

Impacts on Fans and Taxpayers

From the fans' perspective, market power has the general tendency to reduce output and increase price. In the case of sports, consider the control that leagues and conferences have over team location and movement. Clearly, because so many cities line up when a team announces that it wishes to move or when a league announces expansion, the number of teams is restricted below the level that fans prefer. The reason leagues maintain control over location and expansion is to accumulate all of the value of increases in fan willingness to pay for the sport output for themselves. This value comes either from increases in demand for a given number of teams or from expansion fees. Fans pay more for less in the presence of market power.

From the taxpayers' perspective, tax breaks for some taxpayers raise the tax bill for the rest of the taxpayers for a given level of spending by governments. All of the types of tax breaks that have been discussed in this text have the effect of reducing the taxes paid by team owners. This is perhaps most clear for property tax forgiveness and the use of tax-exempt bonds that goes along with occupation of a publicly owned facility. Without that publicly owned facility, another tax-paying activity would occupy that space. Because property taxes typically go into both local and state treasuries, other revenue sources must make up the rest for some chosen level of public spending. The same goes at the federal level for the depreciation-driven shelter enjoyed by owners.

Impacts on Media Providers

The antitrust status of pro sports has clear negative impacts on media providers and advertisers. The special antitrust status of pro sports means that media providers must negotiate with the league or conference rather than individual teams. This reduces competition and raises the price of programming. As we saw in Chapter 3, leagues collect the value of this market power. Subject to the relationship between the supply and demand for ad slots, media providers pass a part of this higher price of programming on to advertisers. The higher price is shared between the media providers and advertisers.

Impacts on Owners and Players

Now we turn to the main beneficiaries of special tax and antitrust status—owners and players. For owners, we will see that special tax and antitrust status increases franchise values. Interestingly, the existing group of players also benefits. As long as they are free to move between teams, players earn more when teams have market power than when they do not.

Team Values and Growth in Team Sale Prices Table 12.1 presents the most obvious starting place for an analysis of the value of these types of advantages for pro sports team owners. Although popular estimates of sports team values like those

Table 12.1   Team Values, 2004 ($Millions)

MLB Team	Value	NBA Team	Value
New York Yankees	$832	Los Angeles Lakers	$510
Boston Red Sox	$533	New York Knicks	$494
New York Mets	$442	Dallas Mavericks	$374
Los Angeles Dodgers	$399	Houston Rockets	$369
Seattle Mariners	$396	Chicago Bulls	$368
Atlanta Braves	$374	Detroit Pistons	$363
San Francisco Giants	$368	Phoenix Suns	$356
Chicago Cubs	$358	Philadelphia 76ers	$342
Houston Astros	$320	Boston Celtics	$334
St. Louis Cardinals	$314	Sacramento Kings	$330
Texas Rangers	$306	San Antonio Spurs	$324
Baltimore Orioles	$296	Indiana Pacers	$311
Cleveland Indians	$292	Cleveland Cavaliers	$298
Colorado Rockies	$285	Toronto Raptors	$297
Philadelphia Phillies	$281	New Jersey Nets	$296
Arizona Diamondbacks	$276	Minnesota Timberwolves	$291
San Diego Padres	$265	Miami Heat	$279
Chicago White Sox	$248	Washington Wizards	$273
Cincinnati Reds	$245	Denver Nuggets	$268
Anaheim Angels	$241	Utah Jazz	$257
Detroit Tigers	$235	Portland Trail Blazers	$247
Pittsburgh Pirates	$217	Memphis Grizzlies	$238
Oakland Athletics	$186	Atlanta Hawks	$232
Milwaukee Brewers	$174	Golden State Warriors	$228
Florida Marlins	$172	New Orleans Hornets	$225
Kansas City Royals	$171	Los Angeles Clippers	$224
Toronto Blue Jays	$169	Orlando Magic	$218
Minnesota Twins	$168	Seattle SuperSonics	$205
Tampa Bay Devil Rays	$152	Milwaukee Bucks	$199
Montreal Expos	$145		

(Continued)

NFL Team	Value	NHL Team	Value
Washington Redskins	$1,104	New York Rangers	$272
Dallas Cowboys	$923	Dallas Stars	$270
Houston Texans	$905	Toronto Maple Leafs	$263
New England Patriots	$861	Philadelphia Flyers	$252
Philadelphia Eagles	$833	Detroit Red Wings	$245
Denver Broncos	$815	Colorado Avalanche	$229
Cleveland Browns	$798	Boston Bruins	$223
Chicago Bears	$785	Chicago Blackhawks	$192
Tampa Bay Buccaneers	$779	Los Angeles Kings	$183
Baltimore Ravens	$776	Montreal Canadiens	$170
Miami Dolphins	$765	Minnesota Wild	$166
Carolina Panthers	$760	New York Islanders	$151
Green Bay Packers	$756	St. Louis Blues	$147
Detroit Lions	$747	New Jersey Devils	$145
Tennessee Titans	$736	Columbus Blue Jackets	$144
Pittsburgh Steelers	$717	San Jose Sharks	$137
Seattle Seahawks	$712	Tampa Bay Lightning	$136
Kansas City Chiefs	$709	Washington Capitals	$130
St. Louis Rams	$708	Vancouver Canucks	$125
New York Giants	$692	Phoenix Coyotes	$120
Jacksonville Jaguars	$688	Ottawa Senators	$117
New York Jets	$685	Pittsburgh Penguins	$114
Cincinnati Bengals	$675	Florida Panthers	$113
Buffalo Bills	$637	Mighty Ducks of Anaheim	$112
San Francisco 49ers	$636	Atlanta Thrashers	$110
New Orleans Saints	$627	Carolina Hurricanes	$109
Oakland Raiders	$624	Nashville Predators	$101
San Diego Chargers	$622	Calgary Flames	$ 97
Indianapolis Colts	$609	Buffalo Sabres	$ 95
Minnesota Vikings	$604	Edmonton Oilers	$ 91
Atlanta Falcons	$603		
Arizona Cardinals	$552		

Source: www.forbes.com.

in Table 12.1 end up a bit low relative to actual observed sale values, they do give a general feel for the value of ownership. As you can see, teams are worth a lot. The majority of teams in hockey and baseball are valued at more than $137 million and $265 million, respectively. The majority of NBA teams are valued at more than $291 million. However, the NFL is at the top of the heap, with the majority of teams valued at more than $712 million.

Leagues protect territories, and the market power position in these territories is valuable. The special tax and antitrust status plays an important role in creating that value. The special status of teams makes all of the following more valuable than they would be without that status:

- Revenues at the gate
- Venue revenues
- Media rights contracts
- Claims on future expansion fees

The result is that teams are worth hundreds of millions of dollars.

Table 12.2 shows that the rate of increase in the actual sale price of teams has been, at times, simply staggering. The rate of return on the Standard & Poors Index (a weighted average of common stock prices) in Table 12.2 is meant to give a feel for the opportunity cost faced by team owners. Owners could certainly invest the amounts paid for their teams at that rate of increase rather than continue on with ownership at any point in time. The lowest rate of increase in sale value is in MLB, at times nip and tuck with the Standard & Poors Index. Teams in the other leagues are no-brainers. If you have the money, get an NFL or NBA franchise!

As the value of teams has increased, the character of ownership has changed as well. Few owners now depend exclusively (or even to any large extent) on the earnings of their team. The team is just one element in the portfolio that helps them gain wealth. The sports team contributes hundreds of millions of dollars over the owner's planning horizon. Special treatment by government makes for part of this value, relative to other investments. If teams in sports leagues did not have special tax or antitrust status, they would not be worth as much.

Interestingly, this all relates back to our discussion of the values of team ownership in Chapter 4. One type of value does follow from annual operating revenues. But all of the other values, including imputed values from special tax advantages

Did You Know?

The increase in price from one sale to the next, for NFL and NBA teams, always beats a diversified portfolio of common stock holdings. MLB prices almost always beat that index.

Table 12.2   Value Increases for Various Decades

LEAGUE	1940s	1950s	1960s	1970s	1980s	1990s
MLB		7.2%	6.9%	7.4%	7.9%	11.3%
NBA			43.8	8.1	16.1	17.7
NFL	59.9%		19.2	21.8	17.2	12.7
NHL						10.7
S&P Industrial Common stocks Rate of return	10.8%	16.7%	7.4%	7.7%	14.0%	15.9%

Sources: For 1940s–1980s, James Quirk and Rodney D. Fort, *Pay Dirt: The Business of Professional Team Sports* (Princeton, NJ: Princeton University Press, 1992); for 1990s, estimated annual rate of return on team sale values from James Quirk and Rodney D. Fort, *Hard Ball: The Abuse of Power in Pro Team Sports* (Princeton, NJ: Princeton University Press, 1999); S&P estimate 1990s, EFMoody.com.

and antitrust status, also are part of the sale price. Remember, a well-respected financial group like Lehman Brothers has already gone on the record that the most recent change in pro sports team special tax status will raise franchise prices in all sports by around 5 percent. In a recent article (Fort, 2006), I was able to use the franchise valuations published annually in *Forbes*, compared to actual team sale prices, to try to untangle these values. The results suggest that values of ownership other than annual operating profits (if any) can be in the tens of millions of dollars.

Team Sale Value Puzzles   In a world where everything was certain, the most anyone would pay for a team would be the present value of the profits that the team would generate. This is one of the most basic notions of finance. If the price were lower than the present value of profits, a prospective owner could just borrow the lower amount, buy the team, and later sell it for a profit over and above the interest paid on the loan. If the price were higher than the value of discounted profits, then anyone who owns the team would just sell, put the money in the bank, and earn more than the team would have generated over the same period of time. Thus, in a world of certainty, the price must be equal to the present value of profits, and the team value could only grow at the rate of interest. However, the observation from Table 12.2 is that franchise prices have consistently (but not always) beaten a reasonable opportunity rate of return, the Standard & Poors Index. How can this result be explained?

Benchmark Case: No Uncertainty   Let's stick with a world of certainty. Team values can beat the normal rate of return, but the flow of profits must be negative. If the franchise price were expected to increase at greater than the interest rate, then a prospective owner would do the following: borrow the money, buy the team, and make more than enough at the end of the period to pay off the loan. Any positive profit on top of that is gravy. However, all prospective owners would know this (it being a certain world, after all), so they would bid up the price to an amount equal to the excess over borrowing plus the leftover profits. The only thing that can stop the price from rising to meet the rate of interest is **negative expected profits**. However, profits cannot be negative for all years because a team with negative profits for all years cannot have a positive price. Thus, the explanation for team prices growing in excess of the rate of interest in a world of certainty requires a very special circumstance of predictable negative profits.

Uncertainty Case 1: Team Owners as Bayesian Updaters   Let's look at an explanation in the more realistic situation of uncertainty. One kind of decision maker in an uncertain world is a **Bayesian updater** (after the famous statistician, Bayes). Bayesian updaters are people who dampen their own expectations about the future based on prior experience. All this really means is that they must be shown something (repeatedly) before they really believe it. Thus, a lag occurs before Bayesian updaters update their beliefs about a change that has already occurred.

Let's suppose that the returns to owning a team have been steadily chugging along, generating a 3 percent real rate of return for a number of years, shown in Figure 12.2 by the dotted line. Then suppose a new media source (like the advent of cable TV) makes its appearance at time T^0. This new media source raises media revenue so that a team generates a 5 percent real return, shown in Figure 12.2 as the top dashed line. Thus, at time T^0, the return stream jumps discontinuously from the dotted line to the dashed line.

Figure 12.2 Bayesian Updating

For Bayesian updaters, it can take time to adjust to new information. At time T^0, the actual real rate of return to owning a team jumps from 3 percent to 5 percent. Rather than embracing this change immediately, adjustment occurs over the adjustment path until time T^1 is reached. Then all owners come to realize that the rate of return really is 5 percent. The slope of the adjustment path, or the rate of adjustment in returns, can be much larger than the eventual 5 percent.

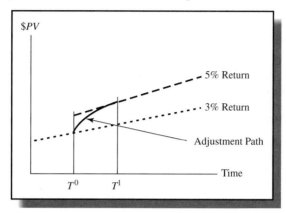

However, Bayesian updaters will not believe the discrete jump at time T^0. Instead, based on their prior belief about steady returns at 3 percent, they will only come to realize that returns have increased after some time has passed, say, at time T^1. In this case, instead of having franchise prices increase immediately to reflect the new 5 percent return, they grow over time from T^0 to T^1. The slope of the adjustment path represents the rate of growth in the actual present value as it approaches the new higher 5 percent return.

You can now see that the average rate of growth over the adjustment period can be dramatically larger than some typical opportunity rate such as the Standard & Poors Index. Indeed, during the adjustment period, growth rates double the opportunity interest rate may occur. At time T^0, the slope of the adjustment path is easily twice as steep as the eventual 5 percent return. Therefore, if owners are Bayesian updaters, then growth rates in franchise prices can beat the rate of interest for as long as it takes these decision makers to believe in the new, higher franchise price growth rate. However, barring any other increase in returns, eventually, growth rates must reflect the present value of team profits.

Uncertainty Case 2: Team Prices as Speculative Bubbles   Owners do not have to be Bayesian updaters for franchise values to grow at greater than the opportunity rate of interest. Instead, some episodes of high rates of growth in franchise prices may be examples of what is called a **speculative bubble**. It is easy to see what a speculative bubble is from an old story.

A stockbroker touts a given stock to a client. The client then buys 1,000 shares at $10 each. The broker proudly reports that the price has risen to $12 in only a week. The client is impressed by that stock performance and buys another 1,000 shares. This goes on for several weeks. The price rises and the client buys more. When the price reaches $25 per share, the client decides to do a little profit taking and tells the broker to sell

3,000 shares. The broker responds, "To whom?" Clearly, the price rise was fueled by the expectations of this single investor. When those expectations collapse, those buying just before the end of the bubble are left holding the bag and suffer losses equal to their holdings. The important requirement for a bubble in prices is that somebody continues to believe the price will rise. If somebody believes the price will rise, it will.

Data on sports team prices do not support arguments that teams are overvalued. James Quirk and I, in *Hard Ball* (1999), noted that over the past 30 years, NBA team prices have increased around 26 percent per year, MLB teams at around 14 percent per year, and NFL teams at around 22 percent per year. Thirty years seems too long a period of increases to be explained by a bubble. It is possible that it is a bubble but not very likely. If any teams are artificially overvalued, the bubbles eventually will burst. When they do, those unlucky few holding teams that are overpriced due to inflated expectations will have to eat their losses.

The Role of Government in Rising Franchise Prices   Government affects the expectations of team owners. Some choices by state and local governments, for example, can lead to extended periods of increases in the returns to those holding teams. For example, as we saw in Chapter 11, NFL teams have been the beneficiaries of 13 votes in a row to fund new NFL stadiums. These new stadiums increase team franchise values. If owners, league-wide, are Bayesian updaters, this series of increases in franchise values could take a long time to update. The result would be extended periods where franchise prices increase at greater than the standard rate of return.

These same types of impacts may occur at the federal level. As we saw in the preceding section of this chapter, periodically the federal government maintains league market power and often facilitates its growth. These actions by the federal government increase the value of franchises, league wide. If owners are Bayesian updaters and slow to adjust their beliefs after these federal tax and antitrust decisions, then franchise values might grow at greater than the rate of interest for a prolonged period.

The Value to Players   The value of special taxes and antitrust status to players can be seen in an analysis of MRP in the presence of these circumstances. Figure 12.3 facilitates our discussion. In the absence of market power, MRP in a competitive output situation determines the value of athletic services offered by players. The result in a competitive player market would be S_0 units of athletic service hired at a wage equal to W_0. However, owner profits are greater with market power. Because players contribute to a higher value in this situation, the owner demand for athletic services rises, as shown by the MRP with market power in Figure 12.3. The result would be an increase in the quantity of talent hired to S_{MP} and an increase in the wage to W_{MP}.

Players contribute to an enterprise that generates more than it would without special tax and antitrust status. This is no different from the idea that if the demand for cars increases, so does the demand for autoworker skills. Both the quantity of autoworker skills hired and autoworker pay would increase. So it is for players. Imagine if the market power of sports leagues disappeared. Profitability would fall and so would the value that players create. One would expect that salaries would fall as well. Thus, harkening back to Chapter 9 on labor relations, it is no wonder that players are staunch supporters of the market power positions of their respective leagues.

Figure 12.3 Impact of Tax and Antitrust Status on Players

If a league had no market power, player MRP would be the lower representation and S_0 athletic services would be hired at wage W_0. With market power, the contribution that athletes make is now more valuable, shifting to the higher MRP function depicted. As long as the market for athletic services is competitive, both the level of services hired, S_{MP}, and the wage, W_{MP}, increase.

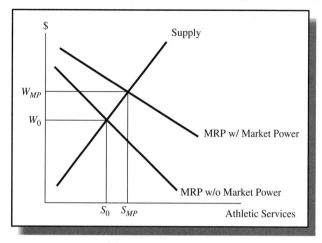

RATIONAL ACTOR POLITICS, TAXES, AND ANTITRUST

Let's examine the rational actor explanation of the relationship between government and the sports business. As with labor union governance and the stadium mess, we will use a rational actor model of politics to investigate the special tax and antitrust status of pro sports team owners.

Rational Actor Politics and Taxes

The rational actor model explanation of why there is special tax status for sports teams is the same as the explanation for any federal tax loophole. In a given tax setting, a particular group presents their elected official with a reason why they should be afforded special tax treatment. If the loophole favors a particular group, then the cost of that loophole is spread thinly across the rest of the taxpayers in terms of higher taxes to maintain the same level of government spending. As long as the specific, politically potent reelection constituency in favor of the loophole delivers in terms of votes and vote-generating resources, they get what they want.

Groups can also make their case at the agency level. The IRS hears cases from special interests about just why the interpretation of a particular part of the tax laws should go a given way. The IRS, sensitive to its Congressional overseers, makes a ruling. If Congress likes the IRS decision, the IRS receives more resources and approval, which matters to the agency leadership in their career pursuits. Through either the direct Congressional route or the indirect agency route, the important interest group gets its way.

Figure 12.4 Rational Actor Politics and Taxes

The special tax status of pro sports team owners follows rational actor politics. A powerful constituency of owners and supporters influences the electoral chances of federal elected officials. Those officials choose tax policy (carried out by the IRS) that owners and supporters evaluate in terms of their own economic welfare. If the tax policies are best for the owners and supporters, elected officials get reelected. The general constituency is relegated to the sidelines but makes up the difference in taxes avoided by owners.

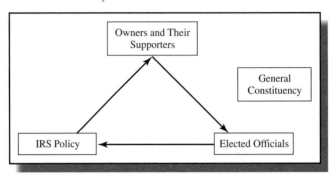

Figure 12.4 is our familiar triangle model applied to tax policy for pro sports teams. Pro sports team owners and their various supporters are an important special interest. Elected officials are interested in pleasing the strong sports reelection constituency. The costs of serving them are borne in small ways by the rest of the taxpayers. The IRS, in this case, is just the agency that carries out the desires of Congress to do this service. In this way, owners managed to "convince" the IRS that players were depreciable assets.

How is it that sports constituencies are powerful enough to gain legislative approval of their demands? To the extent that pro owners are located in the top 30 cities, nationwide, they and their supporters are important constituents to about 50 very influential members of the Senate (a few states have more than one team) and at least that many members of the House. This means that the logic we have developed is binding on many of the most important members of Congress. Because so many elected officials share a similar interest, it should come as no surprise that owners and their supporters get their way. Opposition to owner benefits may be vocal and may make the news, but apparently it is not strong enough to pose much of a challenge to the status quo powers in sports policy.

In short, if elected officials wanted to alter the tax status of pro sports teams, they certainly could. However, they have not done so, either directly through legislation or indirectly through dictates to the IRS. We are left to conclude that pro sports enjoy their special tax status because special interest groups and elected officials benefit from it.

Rational Actor Politics and Antitrust

Figure 12.5 is the triangle diagram for the antitrust outcome. Suppose you are a member of Congress with a team in your geographic jurisdiction. The team is enjoyed by some of your constituents, but it also contributes to the wealth of your

Figure 12.5 Rational Actor Politics and Antitrust

The special antitrust status of pro sports team owners follows rational actor politics. A powerful constituency of owners and supporters influences the electoral chances of federal elected officials. Those officials choose antitrust policy (carried out by the DOJ) that owners and supporters evaluate in terms of their own economic welfare. If the antitrust policies are best for the owners and supporters, elected officials get reelected. The general constituency is relegated to the sidelines.

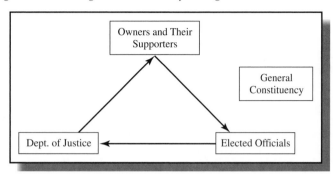

reelection constituency. A vote to limit sports league market power will change that. As long as reelection drives your decisions, you will not vote against sports or encourage the DOJ to do so.

You have just walked yourself through the predicament facing members of Congress in roughly the top 30 population areas in the United States. All have at least one sports team in their jurisdiction. This means that the pro sports league support group in Congress will include many influential politicians. Asking them to support antitrust intervention in pro sports leagues is asking them to act against their own reelection interest.

However, it cannot be denied that the political margins do not always weigh in favor of market power. The Flood Act of 1998 is one example of how political margins sometimes change, even in the world of sports. Baseball work stoppages are killers, politically speaking, because nobody is happy. The MLB strike hurt sports interests and the fans. Members of Congress had little to lose in making small changes to MLB's antitrust status in the interest of preventing future strikes.

Reality and Theory May Not Match   Before we move on, let's remember that the real world is not as cut and dried as our simple rational actor model. Sometimes, outcomes are more of a two-way street. For example, it appears that MLB is cognizant of the market power that is granted to it by Congress and responds, occasionally, to the needs of elected officials.

Shortly after the Celler hearings in 1951, MLB teams moved to the Pacific Coast. Partly in response to Congressional interest (and partly due to the threat of the Continental League), MLB added a team in New York in 1962. Although the Giants did not move to Florida, the Florida Marlins and Colorado Rockies did come into existence after that threat. Interestingly, this happened after hearings instigated by Florida Senator Connie Mack and Colorado Senator Tim Wirth. As recently as 2000, hearings led by Senator Mike DeWine of Ohio saw MLB promising to mend its competitive balance problems, as detailed in the Learning Highlight: Professor Fort Goes to Washington. It appears that Congress can get concessions out of sports leagues and owners every once in a while.

LEARNING HIGHLIGHT
Professor Fort Goes to Washington

In November of 2000, I was honorerd to have been asked to testify before the Senate Committee of the Judiciary, Subcommittee on Antitrust, Business Rights, and Competition. The title of the hearings was "Baseball's Revenue Gap: Pennant for Sale?" I saw and heard many interesting things in this up-close look at the rational actor explanation of sports outcomes.

The focus of the hearings was competitive balance, and the deck was pretty well stacked in favor of MLB's position. Commissioner Selig went first. The gist of his presentation was that baseball has real problems but that baseball could solve them without government intervention. Former Senator and peace negotiator George Mitchell followed. He had served on the Blue Ribbon Panel 2000, appointed by MLB to make recommendations about how to solve its competitive imbalance problems. Senator Mitchell argued that at this triage stage, there was no more time to waste in saving a clearly sick patient, MLB.

The final testimony came from a panel consisting of Bob Costas (noted commentator and true baseball enthusiast), George F. Will (another true enthusiast, member of the boards of MLB teams, and nationally syndicated political columnist), Frank Stadilus (CEO of USFans, a fan interest group with a strong Internet presence), and yours truly. I was the token analyst and, I must admit, I felt more like window dressing than anything else once the panel was over.

Now, except for me, think of the composition of the testimony with reference to Figure 12.5. On baseball's side, we have Selig, Mitchell, Costas, and Will. In addition, Cincinnati Reds owner Carl Lindner was in the audience and received special recognition from the chair, Senator Mike DeWine of Ohio. Indeed, Senator DeWine made it clear there was a constituency interest here: "As a lifelong fan of baseball, I am concerned about the future ability of Ohio's teams—the Cleveland Indians and the Cincinnati Reds—to compete with big-money teams, like the Yankees, the Braves, and the Diamondbacks." The fans received recognition through the presence of Mr. Stadilus. The players had no representative on the panel.

What transpired in this real-life example of the policy triangle in action? My testimony showed that (at that time) there is competitive imbalance in baseball but probably no more than had existed historically. Senate staffers refuted my testimony with a few vague charts. Costas eloquently pleaded for fiscal sanity and a return of baseball's soul. Will pointed out that there is nothing like a sports league, implying MLB knew what was best for MLB, and finished with the idea that baseball is not Bangladesh. It could be healed, but both players and owners would have to do it. Stadilus reminded everybody that the fans are the whole point, and without them the whole thing comes tumbling down.

It is my opinion that the point of the hearing was to publicize MLB's problems as extraordinary, the line from all the baseball people and clearly the belief of Senator DeWine. Then the senator, representing the antitrust investigating arm of the Senate, suggested that the commissioner and MLB could take care of its problems. Indeed, Commissioner Selig had emphasized that MLB had found solidarity and willingness by owners to do whatever it takes to create the economic blueprint for the future. Senator DeWine concluded his remarks as follows:

> While there is no consensus on the correct approach to remedy the decline in competition in the business of baseball, one thing is very clear: The status quo is simply unacceptable. Unless something is done to correct the payroll and revenue disparities among the teams—unless we untie the stranglehold around the small and medium-market teams by increasing competition—baseball cannot survive. We look this morning to Bud Selig to outline his blueprint as Commissioner of Baseball on what he plans to do to save baseball. We know the problems, we will hear about the recommendations, but what the game really needs now is leadership. The immediate challenge is clear. How will the commissioner convince the owners, particularly the larger market owners, as well as the players, that their future is tied to the health and survival of their sport? It is now up to them—owners and

players—to step up to the plate. And, as always, we, the fans will be watching. To put it simply, I look forward to hearing how the commissioner will lead the owners and players toward real solutions to the problems that plague baseball. I hope that for the sake of the game, they do the right thing.

Interestingly, nobody was there to speak for the players. Perhaps that was because collective bargaining began again at the end of the 2001 season. You can download all of the testimony at www.gpoaccess.gov/chearings/106scat2.html. It is pretty good bedtime reading.

Hearings on MLB's imbalance problems led this author to believe that the special antitrust status enjoyed by that league really is a rational actor political outcome.

Source: "Revenue Gap: Baseball's Pennant for Sale?" www.gpoaccess.gov/chearings/106scat2.html.

COMPETITION POLICY

Throughout this text, we have exploded myths, enhanced your ability to explain sports business outcomes, answered questions, and generated new ones. By way of a basic understanding of the economics of pro sports, there is only one more thing to cover, namely, **competition policy**. Competition policy concerns market power problems and what can be done about them.

The Market Power Problem

The problem addressed by sports league competition policy is market power (the discussion in this subsection follows Quirk and Fort [1999]). Most sports fans can easily identify the results of market power. High ticket prices have made it practically impossible for the average fan to enjoy many home games in person. Growing revenue imbalance has made the final league standings a forgone conclusion. Fans have lost touch with players as player salaries skyrocket. Don't even get a fan started about work stoppages!

Fans could point their fingers at any one of a number of culprits responsible for these problems—the media, owners, leagues, players, unions, and politicians. A fitting summary of what you have learned in this text is a review of the role each of these potential culprits plays in the problems confronting pro sports. We will then get back to the real problem, market power, and discuss the types of competition policy that can be used against it.

The Media   In Chapter 3, we learned that media providers do nothing more than collect revenue from advertisers and pass most of it on to pro sports leagues and teams. To media providers, sports are just another type of programming that reaches demographic groups of interest to advertisers. Because teams are allowed to act jointly through their leagues and college conferences in the sale of TV rights, it should come as no surprise that it is the leagues and teams that earn the bulk of the return from sports broadcasts.

Owners   The lesson of Chapter 4 was that owners simply act to maximize their wealth. Their team is just a very valuable asset that contributes to that pursuit. Owners will temper their pursuit of winning because it costs more to field a winning team. Thus, love them or hate them, it is not the personalities of owners that result in many of the problems facing sports; it is the discipline of the bottom line. Moreover, as future profits are imputed into the original price of the team, we should expect owners to exploit their market power. If they do not, then they will fail to recoup their initial purchase costs.

Pro Sports Leagues   Chapter 5 explained how owners act jointly through leagues to further their individual economic interests. Leagues exercise market power over both inputs and outputs. On the input side, Chapter 8 discusses how owners acting through leagues enjoyed the lion's share of player marginal revenue product under the reserve clause and player drafts. The result for fans, on the output side, has been clear since the time of Adam Smith—restricted output, prices greater than marginal cost, and profits greater than the normal rate of return.

However, we should exercise caution before we pass judgment on leagues. Remember, market power and the single dominant league outcome do not necessarily have to happen. The market power that is exercised is the culprit, not those who exercise it. After all, if the existing owners did not exercise this power through leagues, there are plenty of potential buyers who would. If the antitrust laws were enforced, market power could be regulated as it is in other industries.

Players   Many find players' seeming insatiable demands at least partly to blame for rising ticket prices. However, in Chapter 7 we covered two ideas that dispel this notion. First, why do fans think that players are any greedier than anybody else, including themselves? How many fans would be willing to take less than they could possibly make? Second, sports salaries simply reflect the value that fans place on player talent. Changes in players' salaries do not cause changes in ticket prices. Instead, it is the willingness of fans to pay ever more for sports that raises player salaries or encourages owners to seek new ways to collect revenue.

Players are no more to blame for the high price of sports than fast-food workers are responsible for the rising price of hamburgers. Fan demand drives the high-return activity that players engage in. Beside, if players did not take their share, would anybody reasonably suggest that owners would rebate the balance to fans?

Admittedly, some players may not be very likable, and some run afoul of the law, but the economics of player pay makes them no different than any other star entertainer. They are paid much the same as any person is paid, according to their contribution to the value of their employer.

Players' Unions   There can be no doubt that unions have fundamentally altered the face of professional sports. In Chapter 9 we studied how unions have displaced nearly all of the mechanisms that owners previously used to restrict the free movement of players between teams. The result is that players now receive salaries much closer to the value of their contribution to team revenues.

But are unions responsible for the ills that many claim plague sports? Some fans might begrudge players their huge salaries, but the money that fans spend on sports will not go away. As we just mentioned, if players do not get the money, then owners will keep it. Salaries are large because leagues earn more than the normal rate of return; it is the profit earned by leagues that is up for grabs in player–owner negotiations. Without these profits, unions would not have much to do except negotiate minimum salaries and benefit packages. Unions have not created the fabulous wealth available to athletes. They have just been proficient at moving that wealth from owners to players.

Politicians   Typically, when market power runs wild, we hope for government intervention to protect consumers. However, this appears to be frightfully optimistic in the case of pro sports. If anything, the behavior of politicians has facilitated market power all the way back to *Federal Baseball.* Witness the stadium mess plaguing so many current pro sports team hosts.

But are politicians, per se, to blame for these outcomes? The lesson in this chapter is that the reelection imperative confronting politicians drives their decisions. Politically potent groups control reelection by providing money and votes to politicians who serve their interests. In this sense, it is difficult to blame politicians as opposed to the system in which they operate. If politicians work against the powerful group, they risk losing in the next election. It seems unreasonable to expect politicians to commit political suicide on a regular basis.

An Indictment of the Process

It appears that the market power problem is ultimately caused by failures with the political process. Special interest politics at the state and local level are responsible for the stadium mess. Special interests also influence politics at the federal level, maintaining the special tax and antitrust status of pro sports leagues. The results of this special status are exclusive franchise rights for teams, league control over market power, and a complete stifling of competing leagues. It is a testament to the political power of owners, fans, and other sports supporters that leagues have enjoyed this special status for nearly 100 years.

There you have it. Ticket prices are high because there are no competing teams in the same geographic market to push prices to marginal cost. Competitive balance is lacking because leagues restrict the number of teams in large-revenue markets. Salaries are higher than they would be under competition because some of the profits from market power accrue to players in a labor market that is carefully managed by unions. Strikes and lockouts occur as owners and players lock horns over the division of league profits. As leagues carefully manage the number of teams, output is restricted and prices rise, and some cities are held open as relocation threats against current host cities. Host cities are confronted with all-or-nothing propositions because of the lack of substitutes for professional sports teams. All of this is the result of the pursuit of self-interest through the political process.

Rational Actor Politics and Pessimism about Reform

If market power is the problem, then its regulation or removal is the answer. There are a variety of approaches to enhancing economic competition or introducing new economic competition into pro sports. However, we would be naïve to think that just listing the good things about economic competition is enough to make it happen. After all, current political margins dictate the ongoing state of affairs in pro sports in the first place. Calls for alterations in the level of economic competition in sports must first come to grips with this simple fact of life: Unless new powerful interest groups replace the current ones, politicians will not change the economic outcomes in pro sports. This is the same observation made in Chapter 11 on changing the stadium mess, only generalized to the special tax and antitrust status of pro sports.

New powerful interest groups must arise to do battle with the status quo. In our various triangle diagrams, those on the outside looking in at the current triangle outcome must become insiders. Until this happens, our rational actor approach suggests that the chances for strident competition policy to be applied in sports are pretty low. In their 1997 book *Sports, Jobs, and Taxes*, Noll and Zimbalist put it this way:

> Unfortunately, the same forces that have impeded effective legislation also stand in the way of antitrust action that would lead to divestiture. Like Congress, the Antitrust Division of the Department of Justice is susceptible to political pressure not to upset sports, and so a large, influential monopoly remains unregulated and de facto immune from antitrust prosecution by the government. (p. 505)

However, those with an interest in reforming pro sports do have some hope. When a problem becomes important enough to enough voters, a new political mobilization can occur that alters the status quo. This is an expensive process. Those bent on such change must successfully accomplish an overwhelming educational mission and overcome the high costs and free-riding behavior associated with organizing a politically potent group. Then, once mobilized, the dog-eat-dog world of advocate politics begins. Small wonder that market power has ruled in pro sports given the obstacles to bringing it down.

There are signs that a change may be coming. Fan dissatisfaction, although perhaps not at a fever pitch, is quite high on the heels of lost seasons in both MLB and the NBA. As we learned in earlier chapters, Web pages advocating the rights of fans and alternative ownership arrangements have begun to appear. The Internet dramatically reduces the costs of forming organizations. Perhaps fan interest groups will rise to do political battle with the current pro sports supporters.

Remedies Through Competition Policy

Pessimism over the chances for reform does not stop us from examining the type of competition policy that might work if changes in rational actor politics ever occur. Two kinds of interventions come to mind: direct regulation and enforcement of antitrust laws.

Regulatory Approaches Regulatory approaches to sports problems were suggested as early as 1972. Senator Marlow Cook introduced federal legislation creating a separate federal agency to regulate sports. It never gained broad legislative support, but in 1993 columnist Charles Rhoden, writing in the *Sporting News* (April 5, 1993, p. 8), tried to resurrect the idea. Rivkin (1974) suggested that a national sports council was the best way to facilitate cooperation between leagues, Congress, and the public. Zimbalist (1992) argued that sports are a commodity supported through public expenditure and called for public-utility style regulation. Others suggest fan ownership of teams. All of these ideas have good and bad aspects. The Learning Highlight: Would Public Owners Do Any Different? provides examples of fan ownership and municipal ownership.

Did You Know?
The first call to officially regulate professional sports with its own regulatory agency was promulgated by Senator Marlow Cook in 1972.

Antitrust Approaches Noll (1976), Horowitz (1976), Ross (1989, 1991), Fort and Quirk (1997), Quirk and Fort (1999), and Fort (2000) detail the usual **antitrust approach** of breaking up the leagues. Suppose the NFC and AFC were turned into two separate competing pro football leagues. The idea is that competition between the leagues would remedy many of the ills currently attributable to NFL market power. However, two things must be kept in mind when considering this option. First, there have been competitive leagues in the past, but the tendency has always been back toward a single dominant league. Economic competition has not been self-sustaining in pro sports historically. Owners in rival leagues ultimately see the value in reforming into a single entity.

Second, owners in the current dominant leagues have established their reputations and created a strong sense of fan identification at some expense. These owners suffered low or negative profits during the early years of their leagues and have paid public relations expenditures since that time. The returns to such an investment are the profits earned by sports teams under their current market power structure.

A rival league planning to compete with existing leagues must make the same kind of investment, in addition to competing for talent, in order to demonstrate that it really is in it for the long haul at the big-league level. However, vigorous economic competition

LEARNING HIGHLIGHT
Would Public Owners Do Any Different?

Joseph Bast, president of the educational organization the Heartland Institute, argues that fan ownership will curb pro sports market power abuses. He cites the Green Bay Packers as a case in point. A private nonprofit corporation with over 400,000 shares owns the Packers. Only the CEO is paid, and a 45-member board rotates 15 positions annually. Shares cannot be sold for more than the purchase price, and no dividends are paid. If the team is ever sold, nearly all of the proceeds will go to a local Green Bay VFW post.

Because profits cannot be taken from operations or from the sale of the team, all net operating revenues go back into the team with the goal of keeping the team in Green Bay. The success of the Packers on the field is obvious from Green Bay's nickname, Titletown. We saw in Chapter 11 that Lambeau Field in Green Bay has been the least subsidized venue in pro sports until just recently being renovated. Interestingly, NFL rules enacted after the Packers joined the league now forbid corporate ownership, nonprofit or for profit, for all teams. (In other leagues, for-profit corporate ownership is allowed, but nonprofit ownership is not.)

Bast argues that municipal ownership is no substitute for fan ownership, citing "the inefficiencies of public management of enterprises of any sort." However, the city of Harrisburg, Pennsylvania, bought its minor league Senators baseball team when the previous private owner appeared to be moving the team to Springfield, Massachusetts. The club is now run by the nonprofit Harrisburg Senators Baseball Club, Inc. The team draws about 250,000 fans and earns $2 million annually. The Senators were Eastern League champs from 1996 to 1999 and currently have a new stadium under design. In this case, municipal ownership has worked out just fine.

Properly designed, it appears that public ownership of teams, like the Green Bay Packers, does help reduce the excesses against taxpayers seen in other forms of team organization.

Sources: Joseph L. Bast, "Stadium Madness: Why It Started, How To Stop It," Policy Study No. 85. Chicago, IL: Heartland Institute, February 23, 1998; Associated Press, "Minor League Teams Create Dreams for Grimy Towns," 1998.

would make it difficult to recover these costs. A new league just would not survive. With these two factors in mind, let's think about breaking up the pro sports leagues.

The Historical Precedent for Separate Leagues   History suggests that breaking up the pro sports leagues might work. Prior to 1903, the American and National Leagues in MLB were economic competitors. The same is basically true of the American and National Football Conferences in the NFL. With only a few crossover teams, the conferences are about the same as the most recent version of the AFL and the NFL prior to the merger in 1969. The two leagues were so economically competitive that then-AFL commissioner Al Davis (the current Raiders owner) urged the AFL owners not to merge with the NFL. In his opinion, the AFL would have taken over the NFL.

As we saw in Chapter 5, the current structure of the NBA and NHL is built on mergers of previously economically competitive rival leagues. Although some would argue that the merger was necessary to salvage any sort of pro basketball league, the strength of the remaining teams in the NBA belies this. The evidence does not suggest that a merger was required for economic stability in the NFL or NHL. Therefore, a breakup of existing leagues would recreate a state of economic competition that existed in the past.

One of our concerns about intervention is covered by this approach. Remember that large investments are required to generate fan loyalty and media ties. The breakup of existing leagues would allow individual owners in the resulting competing leagues to retain the fan loyalty and media ties they already have built over so many years. The leagues already are major in every sense of the word—and they wouldn't lose the fan identification that they have cultivated over the years.

However, remember that rival leagues have a tendency to fail or merge with another league. Enforcement of league breakups under existing antitrust laws would be required for competition to flourish. If leagues tried to regroup and merge, antitrust enforcement would preclude the new merged league result.

Breaking Up the Leagues: Economic Impacts   Of course, any change away from the current sports outcome will impact the welfare of leagues, players, fans, and taxpayers. Owners and players could be characterized as the losers because their welfare will fall. Overall, fans will be winners because there will be more sports to enjoy at lower prices. Taxpayers should win as subsidies would be reduced. However, some fans at locations with marginal teams could be losers; competition would drive marginal teams out of business or to other locations. But remember that our analysis of the value of owning teams in Chapter 4 shows that there are few marginal teams to worry about.

Competition pushes prices to marginal cost and increases output relative to market power situations. Believe it or not, competition would create more and cheaper sports for fans to enjoy! It would drive down the price of television contracts as more teams entered into the offer process. Media providers would have substitutes if one league got out of line in their rights fee demands. There would be more games at a lower price for fans watching games on TV.

Competitive balance problems would be resolved as well. Currently, larger-revenue-market teams buy more talent than smaller-revenue-market teams. Economic competition would drive profits to zero, economically speaking, because entry by new teams would equalize drawing potential, driving down revenue differences between teams. The result would be more equal revenues, more equal talent, and more balanced outcomes.

With true competition, bloated player salaries could become a thing of the past. Talent hiring and competitive payments to labor in a market power setting occur where the marginal revenues for teams are equal to each other. However, the evaluation of marginal revenue comes from a market power situation. Player salaries would fall in the presence of competition because monopoly profit would be driven to zero. Players simply would not be as valuable to owners as they are now. An offsetting feature would be if fan demand continues to increase over time. Salaries can still rise in a competitive economic environment. However, those same players would have earned even more during periods of increasing demand if leagues and teams had market power.

What about labor–management hegemony? Again, in a competitive environment, profits are driven to zero, and if there is nothing to fight over, there should be no fights. Unions would still have issues to negotiate, such as an inherent trade-off between decreased employment overall and higher pay for players who do get hired. But mostly, unions would be left to deal with pensions and health plans and, possibly, the inequality of salary distributions in sports.

Economic competition would also have impacts on team location and expansion. Currently, the decision rests with existing leagues that base team location on expansion fees, TV impacts, owner group stability, lost threat value, and preclusion of rival leagues. Under competition, there would be no such luxury. Every location that is economically viable would simply have a team. The only way a locality wouldn't have a team is if no team could make a go of it there. The tables would be turned on teams that threatened to move. Cities could just deny team demands and rest safe in the knowledge that they would get another team by virtue of their economic viability.

Because all viable locations would have a team, there wouldn't be any believable threats. Power would be transferred away from leagues, owners, and players toward fans and taxpayers. If one league threatened to leave a viable location, another competing league would bid for that location by lowering the demand put upon the city. Indeed, this could have the potential to turn subsidies to teams into payments by teams.

Breaking Up the Leagues: Team Quality Impacts One of the usual questions posed at this point is, "What will the quality of competition on the field be under increased economic competition?" One of these worries concerns spreading talent too thin. However, this can only be a short-term problem, like the talent spreading that occurs with any expansion. Eventually, among all teams, talent reaches the level that fans are willing to pay for in various cities. If fans in an expansion city are willing to pay for it, the level of talent they enjoy will rise. The level of talent in pro sports leagues always rebounds from short-term dips due to expansion. The clear offset to even any short-term talent diminution is that many more fans get to enjoy pro sports in more locations.

Another worry about the quality of talent in a more economically competitive structure concerns its distribution. With increased competition, profits from exclusive territories will fall. Because talent will be less valuable in the highest return cities, the value of talent will fall there as well. This worry is real. The distribution of quality will change. Some fans will not be as happy as they were, but their previous level of happiness was dictated by a market power situation that left many fans without any team at all. Under competitive leagues, many more fans would enjoy pro sports entertainment than ever did before.

Of course, it's never the case that everybody agrees on anything in sports, and antitrust is no exception. Famed sports lawyer Gary Roberts (1991, 2003) argues that the special antitrust status enjoyed by pro sports team owners and leagues is, on net, a good thing. According to Roberts, MLB's antitrust exemption has a host of characteristics that enhance fan enjoyment from the sport. First, if MLB were subject to antitrust, it would be exposed to "irrational, ad hoc regulation by judges and juries." The problem with leagues is their exercise of market power as a single entity (recall this definition from Chapter 5), not that they are illegal combinations of trade. Applying laws aimed at the second problem to try to fix the first would be irrational and costly (Shugart [1997] makes this identical argument as well).

Ross (2004) shows that antitrust intervention in sports leagues actually has served the public interest in the past, but here is an example consistent with Roberts's fears. Suppose antitrust intervention was successful and resulted in freedom of movement for all teams in MLB. If the league still controlled *the number of teams*, then some cities would gain from the moves, but the fans in cities losing teams would be clearly worse off. Johnson (1997, 2000) points out that the teams would move to larger-revenue markets, reducing the economic advantages of the previous single-occupant team owners. But it is the uncertainty of the results of antitrust applications that worries Roberts; the result could be a net loss.

Second, according to Roberts, applying antitrust laws to the major leagues could dramatically reduce the number of minor league teams to the detriment of minor league fans. This could happen because of the intricate financial relationships between major league teams and minor league teams (recall the discussion of the Professional Baseball Agreement in Chapter 2). If champions of antitrust see these relationships as anticompetitive, antitrust intervention could break the relationships, reducing payments from major league teams to minor league teams. If the payments from major to minor league owners were severe enough, some minor league teams wouldn't survive. Once again, however, we should all remember that the current situation concerning the minor leagues also is an artifact of their past contracts with major league teams that have enjoyed market power positions.

CHAPTER RECAP

In this chapter we examined the relationship between pro sports and government in detail. The history of the special tax status of pro sports dates back to when Bill Veeck convinced the IRS that the player roster was a depreciable asset. The modern version of this provides a write-off of the entire team purchase price for the first 15 years of team ownership. No real value is lost, and the owner gets to reduce both taxable team income and, if organized carefully, taxable personal income as well. In addition, when the capital gains tax rate is lower than the personal income tax rate, owners can postpone any tax payments on the team and pay at the lower capital gains rate. All this requires is a reorganization of the firm that is allowable under the tax laws. The IRS has also ruled that the next owner can start the depreciation all over again, even though the previous owner may already have depreciated the roster asset completely. These special tax advantages have been estimated to triple the owners' rates of return on team ownership relative to a case where the advantages did not exist.

In any other sphere of economic endeavor, the behavior of sports leagues would draw almost immediate antitrust scrutiny. In their relationship with players, leagues in the past sought to extend their market power on the output side over to the input side. The reserve clause was a prime example. Now, all players in all leagues can sue under the antitrust laws in the event that leagues exercise their market power in a way that leads to a negotiation stalemate. In any other case, players must decertify their union in order to sue under the antitrust laws. This is risky because the union can be quite different if and when it reforms. On the output side, leagues remain free to exercise market power over territory, franchise location and movement, broadcast rights, and merger activity with rival leagues. Indeed, Congress historically seems willing to preserve and extend this power.

Both owners and players benefit from these special tax and antitrust advantages. On the owner side, the value of franchises indicates how financially advantageous this special tax and antitrust status really has been. Franchises sell for hundreds of millions of dollars, and expansion fees have been rising at astronomical rates. These franchise value increases often exceed reasonable estimates of the opportunity cost confronting owners. This raises two interesting possibilities. First, if there is little uncertainty in the world of sports ownership, teams must generate significant negative cash flows. Second, in the much more likely case of an uncertain world, franchise price increases in excess of opportunity costs indicate that either owners are slow to update their beliefs about franchise value increases or there are speculative bubbles in ownership. Government enters into the structure of franchise price increases by being the source of many of the increases in rates of return. By protecting market power and raising the level of subsidies going to owners, government fuels increased franchise values. Players benefit because the value of their services and, hence, their pay is greater as teams reap the harvest of tax and antitrust special status.

Why does government facilitate the special tax status and market power position of pro sports leagues? The answer offered here centers on a rational actor model of the political process. In the tax case, the explanation for sports is the same as for any tax loophole. Directly, special interests seek favorable tax treatment from Congress. Indirectly, politically powerful groups can influence decisions made by the IRS. Owners and their supporters represent a strong political constituency for representatives in roughly the top 30 population centers in the United States. Their strength in Congress cannot be denied.

The explanation in the case of antitrust also is amenable to the rational actor model of politics. Powerful sports special interest groups demand antitrust protection from Congress. In the usual course of the rational actor explanation, the Department of Justice fails to enforce the antitrust laws because of pressure from special interests and members of Congress. When necessary, Congress itself has acted to make sure that market power is preserved by passing laws making joint venture TV negotiations legal, upholding blackout laws, and facilitating mergers.

It is clear that there are problems in pro sports; just ask any fan. Because these problems stem from market power, competition policy that encourages economic competition would fix these problems. However, Congressional encouragement of competition should not be expected unless fan and taxpayer interest groups become politically potent relative to the current sports support groups.

A number of arrangements could facilitate economic competition in sports leagues. These include a federal sports regulatory agency, a sports council, a public utility type commission, and a breakup of the existing leagues. The latter has an important factor to recommend it; namely, it preserves the current values of investments made in the past that need to earn a return in order for existing owners not to lose their teams. However, all of the options would require ongoing vigilance because the tendency has been to reform any form of competitive league structure into a less competitive one.

KEY TERMS AND CONCEPTS

- Reorganize for tax purposes
- Excess depreciation
- Roster depreciation rollover
- Basis
- Personal and capital gains tax gap

- Imputed tax advantage values
- Curt Flood Act of 1998
- Decertification dangers
- Raiders case
- Sports Broadcasting Act of 1961
- Blackout laws

- Merger facilitation
- Negative expected profits
- Bayesian updater
- Speculative bubble
- Competition policy
- Regulatory approaches
- Antitrust approach

REVIEW QUESTIONS

1. What is the corporate income tax? What is the personal income tax? What is the capital gains tax?
2. What is a pass-through firm? How does a pass-through firm benefit pro sports team owners?
3. What is roster depreciation? How does it benefit team owners?
4. What is excess depreciation? Logically, is there any excess depreciation when a team owner sells a team?
5. What is roster depreciation rollover? Logically, should such a thing exist?
6. What is the basis? What is meant by the personal and capital gains tax gap?
7. What are imputed tax advantage values in pro sports?
8. What is the general purpose of the antitrust laws? List the practices of pro sports leagues that seem to run afoul of the antitrust laws.
9. What is the Raiders case, and why is it important to antitrust considerations in pro sports leagues?
10. What is the Sports Broadcasting Act of 1961? Why is it important in considerations of antitrust in pro sports?
11. What are blackout laws?

12. Explain merger facilitation. What is its importance in pro sports?
13. Explain what is meant by the term *Bayesian updater*.
14. What is a speculative bubble? How can a bubble persist over time?
15. Define competition policy. What are the two competition policy approaches listed in the text? Give examples of each.

THOUGHT PROBLEMS

1. Is being organized as a pass-through firm a bad thing for sports team owners once roster depreciation has run out? Explain. What step can an owner take after roster depreciation has run out?
2. If you bought a team, how would you structure it for tax purposes? Explain your actions. If you intended to keep the team, what would you do once the roster depreciation had run out? Again, explain your actions.
3. What are the possible costs to a pro sports team owner of being hit with an IRS excess depreciation penalty? Carefully explain the way that the penalty would be assessed and the tax rates that would apply. Why isn't there any excess depreciation when a team owner sells the team to a new owner after fully depreciating the roster, even though the sale price includes roster value?
4. How do team owners use the personal and capital gains tax gap to reduce tax payments? How did the tax law changes of 1986 change this outcome?
5. What does it mean to say that once tax advantages are imputed into the value of a team the owner will only earn a normal return on the purchase of the team? Do owners earn just the normal rate of return? Explain.
6. Why would it seem on the face of it that sports leagues are prime candidates for antitrust lawsuits? Give examples. Explain why MLB has special status under the antitrust laws.
7. Explain the relationship between collective bargaining and the ability of players to take individual antitrust action against owners. How was that changed for MLB players by the passage of the Curt Flood Act of 1998?
8. List the limits of the extension of antitrust rights under the Curt Flood Act of 1998. What did players gain from the act?
9. What are the dangers of union decertification to players interested in having union representation? Explain.
10. Does the Sports Broadcasting Act of 1961 reduce market power or promote it? Explain. Who benefits from the act? Who loses?
11. Have Congressional decisions on mergers facilitated market power or reduced it? Explain.
12. If there is no uncertainty over team values, how can the growth in team sale prices exceed the normal rate of return? Explain. Can your answer persist for a long period of time? Why or why not?
13. Use the speculative bubble explanation to explain the growth rate in franchise values in excess of the normal rate of return. Can speculative bubbles last over a long period of time? Why or why not?
14. What problem is addressed by competition policy? List all of the usual suspects and discuss their role in that problem. Name the ultimate culprit.

15. What are reasons for pessimism for solving market power problems in pro sports? Be sure to include the lessons from rational actor politics in sports in your answer.

ADVANCED PROBLEMS

1. Explain the progression of organizational forms that a team owner will choose over the time of ownership. Be sure to include the tax implications of each choice.
2. Did the Raiders case have any impact on NFL control over the location of teams? Explain the outcome of the Raiders case using the logic behind Figure 12.5.
3. Characterize the behavior of Congress toward sports league market power. In particular, summarize the outcomes of the Celler, Kefauver, and Sisk hearings. In terms of the explanation in Figure 12.5, what was Congress up to during these hearings?
4. Summarize Congressional behavior toward tax issues in sports (roster depreciation, firm reorganization, excess depreciation). What explains this behavior? Use an explanation based on the discussion of Figure 12.4.
5. Summarize Congressional behavior toward antitrust issues in sports (team location, broadcasting, and league mergers). What explains this behavior? Use an explanation based on the discussion of Figure 12.5.
6. If team values are uncertain, how does Bayesian updating lead to growth rates in team prices that exceed the normal rate of return? Explain fully using Figure 12.2. Can your answer persist for a long period of time? Why or why not?
7. Of the three explanations for why the growth rate in franchise prices has been higher than the normal rate of return, which is most plausible? Justify your answer. What is the role of government at both the state and local levels in your answer?
8. Demonstrate graphically how players are better off if leagues are able to keep their market power. Figure 12.3 should prove useful in forming your answer. Given your answer, are unions necessarily against the restrictions on players' rights to sue individually under the antitrust laws? Explain.
9. Refer to the Learning Highlight: Professor Fort Goes to Washington. Draw a figure similar to Figure 12.5 based on my discussion of the competitive balance hearings in November 1999. Of the three main participants—owners and their supporters, elected officials, and antitrust authorities—who appears to have the most power in the competitive balance hearings?
10. Explain the benefits of breaking up pro sports leagues. Would you favor a breakup? Justify your answer (remember to discuss winners and losers).

INTERNET RESOURCES

For a host of additional material and questions for thought, visit this book's Web site at www.prenhall.com/fort.

REFERENCES

Ambrose, James F. "The Impact of Tax Policy on Sports," in *Government and Sport*. Arthur Johnson and James Frey, eds. Totowa, NJ: Rowmand and Allenheld, 1985.

Associated Press. "Minor League Teams Create Dreams for Grimy Towns," 1998.

Bast, Joseph L. "Sports Stadium Madness: Why It Started, How To Stop It," Policy Study No. 85. Chicago, IL: Heartland Institute, February 23, 1998.

Fort, Rodney. "Market Power in Pro Sports: Problems and Solutions," in *The Economics of Sports*. William S. Kern, ed. Kalamazoo, MI: W. E. Upjohn Institute for Employment Research, 2000.

Fort, Rodney. "The Value of Major League Baseball Ownership," *International Journal of Sport Finance* 1 (2006): forthcoming.

Fort, Rodney and James Quirk. "Introducing a Competitive Economic Environment into Professional Sports," in *Advances in the Economics of Sports*, Vol. 2. Wallace Hendricks, ed. Greenwich, CT: JAI Press, 1997.

Horowitz, Ira. U.S. House Select Committee on Professional Sports. Inquiry into Professional Sports, 94th Cong., 2d sess., part 2, September 1976, 131–136.

Johnson, Arthur T. "Congress and Professional Sports, 1951–1978," *Annals AAPSS* 445 (1979): 102–115.

Johnson, Bruce K. "An Overlooked Implication of Baseball's Antitrust Exemption," in *Diamond Mines: Baseball and Labor*. Paul D. Staudohar, ed. Syracuse, NY: Syracuse University Press, 2000.

Johnson, Bruce K. "Why Baseball's Antitrust Exemption Must Go," in *Stee-Rike Four! What's Wrong with the Business of Baseball?* Daniel R. Marburger, ed. Westport, CT: Praeger Publishers, 1997.

L. A. Memorial Coliseum Commission v. NFL, 486 F. Supp. 154 (C.D. Cal. 1979), 726 F. 2d 1381 (9th Circ. 1984), 791 F. 2d 1356 (9th Circ. 1986).

Noll, Roger. U.S. House Select Committee on Professional Sports. Inquiry into Professional Sports, 94th Cong., 2d sess., part 2, September 1976, 131–136.

Noll, Roger G. and Andrew Zimbalist. "Sports, Jobs, and Taxes: The Real Connection," in *Sports, Jobs, and Taxes: The Economic Impact of Sports Teams and Stadiums*. Roger G. Noll and Andrew Zimbalist, eds. Washington, D.C.: Brookings Institution, 1997.

Okner, Benjamin A. "Taxation and Sports Enterprises," in *Government and the Sports Business*. Roger G. Noll, ed. Washington, D.C.: Brookings Institution, 1974.

Quirk, James and Rodney D. Fort. *Pay Dirt: The Business of Professional Team Sports*. Princeton, NJ: Princeton University Press, 1992.

Quirk, James and Rodney D. Fort. *Hard Ball: The Abuse of Power in Pro Team Sports*. Princeton, NJ: Princeton University Press, 1999.

"Revenue Gap: Baseball's Pennant for Sale?" www.gpoaccess.gov/chearings/106scat2.html.

Rivkin, Steven R. "Sports Leagues and the Federal Antitrust Laws," in *Government and the Sports Business*. Roger G. Noll, ed. Washington, D.C.: Brookings Institution, 1974.

Roberts, Gary R. "Professional Sports and the Antitrust Laws," in *The Business of Professional Sports*. Paul D. Staudohar and James A. Mangan, eds. Urbana, IL: University of Illinois Press, 1991.

Roberts, Gary R. "The Case for Baseball's Special Antitrust Immunity," *Journal of Sports Economics* 4 (2003): 302–317.

Ross, Stephen F. "Monopoly Sports Leagues," *Minnesota Law Review* 73 (1989): 643–761.

Ross, Stephen F. "Break Up the Sports League Monopolies," in *The Business of Professional Sports*. Paul D. Staudohar and James A. Mangan, eds. Urbana, IL: University of Illinois Press, 1991.

Ross, Stephen S. "Antitrust, Professional Sports, and the Public Interest," *Journal of Sports Economics* 4 (2003): 318–331.

Rovell, Darren. "Tax Break Losing Value," ESPN.com, April 15, 2004.

Shugart, William F. II. "Preserve Baseball's Antitrust Exemption: Or, Why the Senators Are Out of Their League," in *Stee-Rike Four! What's Wrong with the Business of Baseball?* Daniel R. Marburger, ed. Westport, CT: Praeger Publishers, 1997.

Veeck, Bill with Ed Linn. *The Hustler's Handbook*. New York: G. P. Putnam's Sons, 1962.

Wilson, Duff. "Bill Would Raise Franchise Value of Sports Teams," NYTimes.com, August 2, 2004.

Zimbalist, Andrew. *Baseball and Billions: A Probing Look Inside the Big Business of Our National Pastime*. New York: Basic Books, 1992.

Chapter

13

College Sports

Chapter Objectives

After reading this chapter, you should be able to:

■ *Describe the workings of supply and demand in college sports, as well as revenue imbalance results, competition between conferences in the pursuit of TV revenues, and the relationship between the university and its athletic department.*

■ *Discuss the role of colleges acting through conferences and the NCAA in managing conference memberships, negotiating TV broadcasts, and battling competitive imbalance and cheating.*

■ *Understand how the amateur requirement, recruiting regulations, and rules regarding the movement of players between colleges affect college athletes.*

■ *Recognize the discrimination problems that plague college sports and the role of Title IX in fighting gender discrimination.*

■ *Discuss the special tax and market power status enjoyed by colleges in their sports activities and explain why rational actor politics helps to explain that special status.*

I still chuckle to some degree when people don't acknowledge that this is a business. Because it is and it's a big business.

—University of Oklahoma Athletic Director Joe Castiglione
Sports Business Journal, June 7, 2004, p. 24

The Association of Intercollegiate Athletics for Women (AIAW), founded in 1971, was an effective body that promoted women's sports. It served more than 800 member colleges, providing organizing principles, meetings and conferences for the membership, and a national women's championship structure. In 1980, the NCAA began a relentless move to undo the AIAW. The NCAA established its own competing women's national championship system and used its relatively greater resources to induce colleges to abandon the AIAW. The NCAA offered free trips to the championships and waived membership fees if the university already was an NCAA member. However, the straw that finally broke the AIAW's back was the NCAA's inclusion of the women's basketball championship tournament in the men's championship TV package and scheduling it at precisely the same time as the AIAW's championship. The AIAW folded in 1982.

In this chapter, we will examine the same economic issues we did with pro sports—demand and revenue, advertising, costs and profit, market outcomes, talent issues, subsidies and their economic impact, and stadium issues. We will also look at government's role in the college sports business. Our examination of supply and demand will focus on revenue imbalance results and the relationship between the university and its athletic department. We will see that sports market outcomes are the result of colleges acting through conferences and the NCAA, and that their joint ventures include the management of conference membership and TV negotiations. The understanding gained concerning the NCAA will help us understand their behavior toward the AIAW. In this chapter we will also examine the power of colleges acting through the NCAA to restrict earnings and player mobility. We will also see that discrimination problems plague college sports and that federal legislation has been enacted to overcome these problems. Finally, we will take a look at the reasons why colleges enjoy special tax and market power and show that rational actor politics provides an interesting explanation of that outcome.

COLLEGE SPORTS REALLY ARE BIG BUSINESS

As with our analysis of pro sports, in our discussion of college sports we will look past the character building and other life lessons college sports might offer and instead adopt a clear business perspective on college sports. I think you will find it most revealing if we stay the course set throughout this text and follow the money.

As with pro sports in Chapter 1, we can cite many examples that prove that college sports is big business. Most understand the linkage between spending and success in college sports. But then why don't all directors of intercollegiate athletics just spend more to increase their success? And if college sports are not a business, why charge admission? Why sell broadcast and sponsorship rights? And why not pay those players who are worth it more than the in-kind payments they already receive? If all of these questions sound familiar, they should. All come straight from Chapter 1 and are just as appropriate for college sports as they were for the pro version. We'll see some answers as we continue through this final chapter.

We can also take a lesson from a couple of long-time observers of the college sports scene. Nearly 15 years ago, Louisiana State University's basketball coach Dale Brown had this to say: "When I entered coaching 43 years ago, athletics was a component of education. Today it is about making money and winning big. There is a professional intensity creeping into intercollegiate sports" (*Sporting News*, 1992). According to Texas Tech basketball coach Bob Knight, not much has changed, "If it isn't a business, then General Motors is a charity" (*Sports Business Journal*, December 27, 2004).

"If it [college sports] isn't a business, then General Motors is a charity." —Texas Tech Coach Bob Knight

DEMAND AND COLLEGE SPORTS REVENUE

College sports fans demand the same scarce items as pro sports fans—athletic grace, commonality, relative and absolute quality, and winning. In terms of commonality, college sports games and their coverage by the media provide a common bond among many people. Most people at least know the tune to their local college fight song—and real boosters know the song to the last verse. In terms of quality, once the absolute level is determined, relative competition becomes the object of fan attention. If the best that fans can support at a particular location is Division III sports, they still will care deeply about how their team does against other Division III opponents. Let's not forget about winning. Fans love the home team, but they love it even more when it is a winner.

Demand for College Sports

From an economic perspective, commonality, quality, and winning are scarce commodities. Therefore, demand is an operational concept in college sports. Indeed, our first example in Chapter 2 was about demand for college sports—men's and women's college basketball. Those demands are reproduced in Figure 13.1. As you can see, demand is simply the relationship between prices and quantities demanded. However, let's not forget that willingness to pay, and all of the elements that determine willingness to pay, are captured in this deceptively simple concept.

Market Power Our first observation is that demand slopes downward for individual college sports. The lack of substitutes required for downward sloping demand and market power follows purposeful choices by college conferences and their enforcement arm, the **National Collegiate Athletics Association (NCAA)**. The NCAA is an association made up of member colleges that supervises the

Figure 13.1 Demand Functions for Men's and Women's Basketball Season Tickets (Typical Class Size = 100)

In this example, the instructor chooses a subset of the class and asks, "How many season tickets to men's or women's basketball would you buy at various prices?" Plotting price against student responses gives two different demand functions for the two sports. For example, 70 students are willing to buy a men's ticket at a price of $20. However, the price would have to fall to $10 before 70 students would buy a women's ticket.

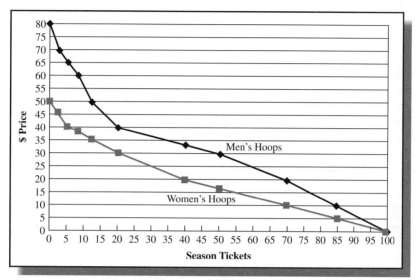

economic welfare of its members. College conferences and the NCAA perform the same functions for college teams that leagues perform for pro team owners.

For example, the Washington State University Cougars and the University of Idaho Vandals are in different athletic conferences and, until recently, played NCAA football at different levels. The Vandals, previously Division IAA, just finished a drawn out process proving that they deserve Division IA status in football. Why couldn't they just declare their intent and move up a level? The answer is that the NCAA has tight controls over who may and who may not play Division IA football. A team must prove itself "worthy" to move up to Division IA.

The conferences and the NCAA offer a number of explanations for this exclusionary practice. Essentially, they all boil down to quality control. Each conference wants to maintain the quality of its product in the eyes of fans, and the NCAA helps member conferences at different levels do so. However, regardless of the justification, the result is that the number of close substitutes is reduced and individual conferences are endowed with some market power.

The Determinants of Demand Let's look at attendance. As you can see in Figure 13.1, if ticket price changes, movement along the given demand function shows changes in quantity demanded. Demand shifters, on the other hand, such as preferences, income, price of other goods, expectation, and population, change demand itself. A couple of these demand shifters are particularly interesting in college sports.

Experience is one of the determinants of college fan preferences. Not that long ago, interest in women's basketball was so low that athletic departments did not even charge admission. However, judging by the rising importance of women's sports at the college level, especially basketball, as experience with women's sports has increased, so has the attention of fans. Thus, the demand for women's hoops probably was once to the left of its location in Figure 13.1. The demand for women's basketball has been increasing over time, shifting to the right. We will see how this translates into increased revenues for women's sports shortly.

Expectations are another determinant of the location of demand curves. Expectations play a large role in "lifetime" booster privileges for college sports fans. Boosters put up large sums and are promised their seat at the agreed upon price for many years into the future. Lifetime booster privileges are a common way to raise money for the school's endowment or for a new stadium or arena. By offering such booster privileges, development officers in athletic departments are trying to convert the avoidance of future price increases into a payment in the present for current capital needs. Because most boosters can just wait and buy seats on an annual basis, we are led to conclude that they must be getting a price break on their seat, given their expectation that prices will rise over time.

Population, another demand shifter, is part of the explanation for larger- and smaller-revenue markets in college sports. Consider two universities, one in a densely populated area, the other in a rural area. Suppose their football teams were of equal quality. On a map, think about how large a circle you would draw around the large-population university before you included enough boosters to regularly fill the stadium. Do the same exercise for the rural university. The circle for the rural school typically is many times larger. This is the heart of the issue of defining large- and small-revenue markets in college sports.

Demand, Total Revenue, and Price Elasticity

The relationship between demand and total revenue that we see in college sports is similar to the one we saw with pro sports in Chapter 2. Attempts at shifting demand are behind the myriad of promotions aimed at changing preferences for a particular college team. Willingness to pay, buyers' surpluses, and price elasticity matter for college sports for the same reasons they do in pro sports. They are the very foundation of the athletic department's pricing decisions.

Pricing and Inelastic Demand Looking only at attendance, athletic directors would never price in the inelastic portion of their gate demand function. By raising price and lowering attendance, total revenues would increase and total costs would fall. But, as with pro sports, other revenues also accompany attendance (parking, concessions, and merchandise). Consider the case of Arizona State University. In 2003, despite a losing record, football attendance increased by 27 percent. Clearly, this was facilitated by lowering the price of attendance. According to Senior Associate Athletic Director Tom Collins (USAToday.com, August 30, 2004), "Instead of looking at making more money [just on ticket sales], we are trying to fill in all our seats at a lesser cost. If we get everybody in there and our team performs, they'll buy a Coke, a T-shirt, a program, and they'll come back." Indeed, even if the team doesn't perform, lowering the price into the inelastic region of demand still sells the attendance-related parking, concessions, and merchandise, a key lesson from Chapter 2.

Sellouts A puzzle from Chapter 2 also remains for college sports. Why are prices for some games and events set clearly below the market clearing price? In these cases in pro sports, we saw in Chapter 2 that markets for scalpers are introduced whenever this happens. That the same occurs for college sports is a matter of your author's own experience and investigations you could perform for yourself. On the experience side, when Washington State played the University of Michigan in the 1998 Rose Bowl, I was fortunate enough to get six tickets at $50 face value. It ended up that I couldn't attend after all, so after giving two to family members, I sold the other four. A "broker" advertised in the local paper and set up in a local motel. The transaction took just a few minutes. I left quite a few hundred dollars richer but the tickets left before I did, neatly tucked into a FedEx envelope and on their way to Michigan.

On the investigation side, I looked into ticket prices for the Men's 2005 Final Four (all three sessions) in the Edward Jones Dome in St. Louis. The face value on the tickets, available from the NCAA, was $110 and $130 per pair. But these were only available by lottery from the NCAA on a relatively small number of seats. But have no fear, other tickets were available. A quick Internet check revealed that the NCAA prices were far below equilibrium. One could easily spend $1,200 for a pair. The highest advertised price I discovered was $14,000 for a pair of luxury box tickets. Just why it is that the NCAA prices their own tickets as they do and distributes the rest as they do is a puzzle. Perhaps some of the explanations from Chapter 2 will also end up being enlightening here.

Price Discrimination Price discrimination mechanisms such as variable seat prices and two-part pricing are common in college sports. Two-part pricing explains **donation seating**, one of the mainstays of college sports pricing. Boosters contribute money to the athletic department; in return, the department allows them access to priority seating. The boosters also receive membership in booster organizations. To the extent that these boosters would have purchased the same seat anyway, the price to the fan is higher. As long as booster organization membership benefits do not offset the entire amount of the contribution, the athletic department earns higher revenues from the same seats.

Interestingly, even some athletic departments with football teams typically ranked in the Top 25 held off on two-part contribution seat pricing until very recently. Among the Top 25 in 2004, Michigan, Iowa, and Wisconsin had no such policy. But all three implemented contribution seating for 2005. A few, like Oklahoma and Minnesota, do not require any contribution but use contributions for preferential seating. All of the remaining 20 schools had long used contribution seating, and most of the legendary programs collect a contribution from every season ticket holder (Southern Cal, Georgia, Miami, Texas, and Florida). As with PSLs in the pros, apparently there are other factors that determine just when the right time occurs to implement contribution seating in college sports. The same holds true for differential seat prices over the season for the same seat, also in use in college sports.

The Revenue Data for College Sports

The NCAA sponsors surveys of college team financial outcomes. Table 13.1 shows the results of this survey for Division IA from 1985 to 2001. The data, where possible, are shown both with and without "institutional support." **Institutional support** is money that is allocated directly from the university's operating budget to be spent on athletics. It may or may not be identified separately in an athletic department's report of revenues, but it is revenue nonetheless. This separation will prove crucial later in the chapter where we try judge the economic independence of college sports.

As you can see from Table 13.1, if we include institutional support, modern revenue averages are in the tens of millions of 2004 dollars, and the largest report was nearly $80 million. Revenues rose over the entire period, 1985 to 2001, by 124 percent in real terms, for a real growth rate of 5.2 percent per year. Remember, the typical real annual growth rate in the U.S. economy is around 3 percent. So the growth of revenues at the highest level of college football is a remarkable 1.7 times higher than the typical growth rate in the U.S. economy.

Revenue Inequality in College Sports Table 13.1 also reveals substantial **revenue imbalance in college sports**. The ratio of the top reported revenues to the average always exceeds two and has exceeded three since 1999. We must exercise caution in our conclusions about the behavior of revenue imbalance over time because the survey data may be affected by better response rates in recent years. However, Zimbalist (1999, p. 117) also showed that the ratio of top to average revenues grew from 1.81 to 3.38 over an earlier period, 1962 to 1985.

Here are some cautious conclusions about revenue inequality. From Table 13.1, we see that revenue imbalance in college sports did not change much in the 1980s but rose steadily in the 1990s, leveling off for 2001. This is dramatically different from the revenue disparity in pro sports outlined in Chapters 2 and 6. There, we saw the top-revenue teams gain dramatically against the bottom, but the average held its own against the top. In college sports, the top teams are outpacing the average and, by simple arithmetic, the bottom as well. In my own state, for example, it is common for the University of Washington's athletic department revenues to be 40 to 60 percent greater than those at Washington State University. As we will later see, revenues are just as important for winning in college sports as they are in pro sports, and this revenue inequality will help to explain competitive imbalance.

Another interesting observation from Table 13.1 is that the ratio of the top reported expenditure to the average rose steadily from 1993 to 1999, but then it fell for 2001. While we should always be careful about generalizing a single change at a point in time, it is true that the top spending report fell relative to the average, but average spending increased by nearly 9 percent from 1999 to 2001. At least for 2001, spending at the average rose to meet a falling amount at the top. Judging whether this narrowing of the gap between top and average revenues is a phenomenon or an aberration awaits the passage of time and the generation of more data.

Table 13.1 Revenues and Expenses of Division IA College Athletic Departments ($2004)

Year	Average Total Revenue ($Millions)	Average Total Expenditures ($Millions)	Average Net ($Millions)	Percent Showing Profit	Maximum Total Revenue ($Millions)	Total Revenue Ratio[a]	Maximum Total Expenditures ($Millions)	Total Expenditures Ratio[b]
With institutional support								
1985	$11.8	$12.0	–$0.2	42	$31.0	2.6	$28.7	2.4
1989	$14.8	$14.7	$0.1	55	$34.3	2.3	$33.4	2.3
1993	$17.6	$16.9	$0.7	72	$39.1	2.2	$36.3	2.2
1995	$19.0	$17.6	$1.4	75	$48.3	2.5	$39.6	2.3
1997	$20.8	$20.2	$0.6	60	$55.7	2.7	$55.7	2.8
1999	$24.6	$22.5	$2.1	71	$82.1	3.3	$71.6	3.2
2001	$26.5	$24.5	$2.0	63	$84.2	3.2	$55.1	2.2
Without institutional support								
1993	$16.6	$16.9	–$0.3	51				
1995	$17.3	$17.6	–$0.3	46				
1997	$19.3	$20.2	–$0.9	43				
1999	$22.5	$22.5	$0.0	46				
2001	$23.9	$24.5	–$0.6	35				

[a]Total Revenue Ratio = Maximum Total Revenue/Average Total Revenue.

[b]Total Expenditures Ratio = Maximum Total Expenditures/Average Total Expenditures.

Source: Author's calculations from tables in Fulks (2002).

Revenue and Spending Differences: Men's and Women's Sports   Table 13.2 compares revenues and expenses for men's and women's programs. A number of things jump out. First, revenues for men's sports are dramatically larger than for women's sports. In every year in the table, men's revenues are about ten times those generated by women's sports. Second, while men's sports revenues have grown at a healthy 4 percent real annual rate, the growth in women's sports revenues has grown in real terms at 10.9 percent annually, more than 2.7 times higher. As noted earlier, women's sports have gained in acceptance over time, and this is reflected in tremendous revenue growth. Third, the growth in spending on women's sports is more than 3 times higher than for men's sports, even though the level of spending still lags dramatically behind spending on men's sports. Finally, we shouldn't make too much of the result in Table 13.2 that shows losses on women's sports increasing dramatically over time. This is the point of Title IX programs aimed at equalizing college sports opportunities for women, a topic we'll cover later in this chapter.

Table 13.2

Revenue and Expenses of Men's and Women's Division IA College Sports ($2004)

Year	Average Total Revenue ($Millions)	Average Total Expense ($Millions)	Average Operating Profit ($Millions)
Men's			
1993	$12.2	$9.1	$3.1
1995	$24.3	$9.1	$15.2
1997	$13.5	$9.7	$3.9
1999	$15.2	$10.7	$4.5
2001	$16.7	$11.5	$5.2
%Increase	37.1%	27.1%	66.6%
Growth	4.0%	3.0%	6.6%
Multiple of 3 percent real growth rate	1.3	1.0	2.2
Women's			
1993	$0.6	$2.3	−$1.7
1995	$0.7	$2.8	−$2.1
1997	$1.1	$3.6	−$2.5
1999	$1.7	$4.4	−$2.7
2001	$1.5	$4.9	−$3.4
%Increase	128.5%	108.5%	100.8%
Growth	10.9%	9.6%	9.1%
Multiple of 3 percent real growth rate	3.6	3.2	3.0

Source: Author's calculations from data in Fulks (2002). Only years from 1993 on are used because the data are consistent with respect to values specific to men's and women's programs. The data include institutional support.

Table 13.3 2001 Revenue and Expenditure Distribution by Sport for Division IA College Athletics

| | MEN | | WOMEN | |
SPORT	PERCENT TOTAL REVENUES	PERCENT TOTAL EXPENDITURES	PERCENT TOTAL REVENUES	PERCENT TOTAL EXPENDITURES
Football	69	56	—	—
Basketball	23	18	25	24
Other sports	5	21	46	70
Unrelated to particular sport	3	5	28	6

Source: Excerpted from Fulks (2002). The data include institutional support.

Table 13.3 shows revenue source percentages for different men's and women's sports. It is no surprise that football dominates men's sports. Interestingly, basketball generates about the same percentage of total revenues for both men's and women's programs, but a much higher percent of the women's sports budget is spent on basketball. It also is interesting to note those women's sports revenues are not dominated by any one sport. Basketball is important, but the other-sports category swamps it.

Sponsorship

Sponsorships have become the norm in college sports. Every college team sells space on its uniforms for advertising, typically to athletic shoe and apparel companies such as Nike, Reebok, and Adidas. Conference championships are sponsored by corporations for millions of dollars. Lately, as with the pros, colleges are selling stadium and arena naming rights. Recent naming-rights amounts are shown in Table 13.4. As you can see, the amounts are typically a few hundred thousand dollars annually. These amounts pale compared to bowl game sponsorships, but we'll leave that discussion to our next topic, college sports on TV.

THE MARKET FOR COLLEGE SPORTS BROADCASTS

Believe it or not, at the origin of television in the late 1930s, there was a trade-off between broadcasting games and attendance at the gate. By the 1950s, the NCAA had noticed an 11.4 percent drop in football attendance from the late 1940s coincident with increased appearance of games on TV (Brown, 1999). In 1952, the NCAA instituted its first restrictive broadcast policy, overwhelmingly endorsed by a referendum of the membership. An interesting difference between college and pro sports is that this anticompetitive behavior by the NCAA was ruled illegal under the antitrust

Table 13.4 Naming Rights in College Sports

FACILITY	COLLEGE	TOTAL PAID ($MILLIONS)	DURATION OF RIGHTS (IN YEARS)	END YEAR
Save Mart Center	Fresno State	40	23	2022
Comcast Center	University of Maryland	20	25	2026
Jones Stadium	Texas Tech	20	20	2019
United Spirit Center	Texas Tech	10	20	2015
Value City Arena	Ohio State	12.5	Indefinite	
Cox Arena	San Diego State	12	Indefinite	
Bank of America	Washington	5.1	10	2008
Colonial Center Arena	University of South Carolina	5.5	12	2015
Cox Pavilion	University of Nevada, Las Vegas	5	10	2009
Wells Fargo Arena	Arizona State	5	Indefinite	
Papa John's Cardinal Stadium	Louisville	5	15	2012
Movie Gallery Veterans Stadium	Troy State University	5	20	2022
Coors Events Center	Colorado	5	Indefinite	
Carrier Dome	Syracuse	2.75	Indefinite	
Alltel Arena	Virginia Commonwealth University	2	10	2008
Cessna Stadium	Wichita State	0.3	Indefinite	

Source: Sports Business Journal, June 5, 2000, p. 30; December 29, 2003 (By the Numbers), p. 14.

Did You Know?
Early on, television was a strong substitute for attendance at college football games; by 1950, the NCAA had noticed an 11.4 percent decline in attendance.

laws. We'll see just how, and to what effect, when we examine the NCAA in detail later in the chapter.

In Chapter 3, we developed an approach for analyzing the market for broadcast rights that followed the flow of programming and money. From that perspective, there is one important difference between college and the pros. In college sports, conferences negotiate contracts with media providers under a special **three-tier broadcast rights structure**.

The first tier is a national contract between a conference and a major media provider. Any games that the major networks do not choose to show revert to the second tier, national cable, primarily ESPN. The games not chosen by the first- or second-tier providers are available to the third tier, regional cable or local broadcasters. For sanity's sake—and for the sake of some advance notice on advertising slot sales—there is a time limit for final decisions on which games are chosen for the first tier. Second- and third-tier broadcasters then make their choices.

More economic competition exists on the supply side of sports programming in college sports than in pro sports. In pro markets, if media providers want sports programming, they have no alternative but to deal with a single league. In the market for college broadcast rights, if one conference is unreasonable in its negotiations with media providers (competitively speaking), there are other college conferences that can provide sports programming. As a result, we cannot be quite as sure that the bulk of the value of market power flows primarily to college conferences as it does to pro sports leagues.

Broadcast Revenues

Table 13.5 shows the most recent TV contracts for some major college football conferences. The amounts in Table 13.5 make clear the regional appeal of college sports conferences compared to the nation-wide appeal of professional sports leagues. For

Table 13.5 Annual Values of College Football TV Contracts

FOOTBALL				
CONFERENCE	NETWORK	DURATION	ENDS	AMOUNT
ACC	ABC/ESPN	7	2010	$258
Big 12	ABC/ESPN	7	2007	n/a
	FSN	12	2011	$214
Big East	ABC/ESPN	7	2007	$105
Big Ten	ABC/ESPN	10	2007	n/a
*Notre Dame	CBS	5	2010	$45
Pac-10	ABC/ESPN	10	2006	$169
	FSN	10	2006	$153
BASKETBALL				
CONFERENCE	NETWORK	DURATION	ENDS	AMOUNT
ACC	Raycom	10	2010–11	$300
Big 12	ABC/ESPN	7	2007–08	n/a
Big East	ESPN	4	2006–07	$28
Big Ten	ESPN	10	2007	n/a
Pac-10	FSN	9	2005–06	$52.5
COMBINED				
CONFERENCE	NETWORK	DURATION	ENDS	AMOUNT
Conf USA	ESPN	8	2008–09	$80
Mid-America	ESPN	5	2007–08	$3
**Mountain West	ESPN	7	2005–06	$48
SEC	CBS	n/a	2008–09	n/a
Sun Belt	ESPN	n/a	2007–08	n/a
WAC	ESPN	6	2008–09	$8

*6 home games per year.
**Mountain West already has a 7-year contract, starting 2006, with CSTV for $82 million.
n/a is "not available."
Source: Gleaned from *Sports Business Journal*, September 6, 2004, and USAToday.com, December 22, 2003.

example, NFL TV rights are about $17.6 billion for their current contract ending in 2005, and NBA TV rights are about $4.6 billion (Chapter 3). Even if we assigned the highest comparative values for the unavailable data in Table 13.5 and added in other values earned by college conferences from postseason TV (see Tables 13.6 and 13.7, discussed shortly), college football and basketball come nowhere close to the level of TV revenue enjoyed by their professional counterparts.

Table 13.6

2004–05 Bowl Sponsors and Payouts to Teams ($Millions)

Bowl	Payout	
Wyndham New Orleans	$750,000	
Champs Sports	$850,000	
GMAC	$750,000	
Plains Capital Forth Worth	$750,000	
Pioneer Pure Vision Las Vegas	$750,000	
Sheraton Hawaii	$750,000	
MPC Computers	$750,000	
Motor City	$750,000	
Independence	$1,200,000	
Insight	$750,000	
EV1.net Houston	$1,100,000	
MasterCard Alamo	$1,550,000	
Continental Tire	$750,000	
Emerald	$750,000	
Pacific Life Holiday	$2,000,000	
Silicon Valley	$750,000	
Gaylord Hotels Music City	$780,000	
Vitalis Sun	$1,500,000	
AutoZone Liberty	$1,350,000	
Chick-fil-A Peach	$2,200,000	
Outback	$2,750,000	
SBC Cotton	$3,000,000	
Toyota Gator	$1,600,000	
Capital One	$5,187,000	
BCS Bowls		
Rose	$12,986,000	Big Ten
	$6,000,000	Big 12
Tostitos Fiesta	$12,936,000	Big East
	$11,780,000	Mt. West
Nokia Sugar	$12,936,000	ACC
	$12,936,000	SEC
FedEx Orange	$12,936,000	Pac-10
	$11,780,000	Big 12

Source: ESPN.com.

Table 13.7

2004–05 Football
Bowl Game and
2004 March
Madness Revenues
by Conference
($Millions)

	FOOTBALL BOWL GAMES	MARCH MADNESS	
CONFERENCE	TOTAL CONFERENCE PAYOUT	TOTAL CONFERENCE PAYOUT	TOTAL
SEC	$26.9	$10.7	$37.6
Big 12	$26.6	$10.9	$37.5
Big Ten	$24.7	$13.3	$38.0
ACC	$19.1	$9.9	$29.0
Pac-10	$17.9	$10.0	$27.9
Big East	$16.9	$10.4	$27.3
Mountain West	$14.6	$1.7	$16.3
CUSA	$4.3	$4.9	$9.2
MAC	$4.2	$2.3	$6.5
WAC	$2.6	$3.9	$6.5
Sun Belt	$1.5	$0.8	$2.3
All Others		$26.5	

Sources: Bowls: Author calculations from ESPN.com and *Sports Business Journal*, December 29, 2003 (By the Numbers), p. 150.

College conferences do have one thing in common with the pros—TV revenues are unevenly distributed. Comparing national football contracts and adjusting for differences in contract duration, the ACC's is twice any other conference's contract value. But note that a single school, Notre Dame, has a contract worth about half the revenue earned by some entire conferences (my own Pac-10 for example). Further, within conferences, those teams that appear on television more often make more than those that do not. Again, in my close-to-home example, TV and radio revenues for the University of Washington Huskies are typically about twice the amount collected by the Washington State University Cougars.

The Interesting Case of Notre Dame

"We covet our association with Notre Dame, the most powerful brand in college sports." —Dick Ebersol, NBC Sports Chairman

The case of the University of Notre Dame is interesting in this regard. It remains the only major independent team in the country. Because its fan base is nationwide, major networks find it valuable enough to contract separately with Notre Dame. According to Dick Ebersol, NBC Sports Chairman (USAToday.com, December 22, 2003), "We covet our association with Notre Dame, the most powerful brand in college sports." Whether you agree with him or not, the result is $9 million per year for Notre Dame.

Bowl Game Revenues

As you can see from Table 13.6, the largest sponsorships go to postseason bowl games. In the past, college football bowl games were just tourist attractions, drawing people to the southern United States during the onset of winter in the North. As such, they typically were organized and run by local business interests such as the Chamber of Commerce. Although the organization and promotion of the bowl remain primarily the job of local officials, large financial injections by sponsors have dramatically increased the value of these activities. As fans became even more interested in bowl games for their national championship implications, first through the Bowl Alliance and currently through the Bowl Championship Series (BCS), firms have become much more interested in sponsoring the major bowl games.

In Table 13.6, note that all major bowls (and a few of the lesser bowls) are sponsored events. Based on data from past bowl seasons, all of the BCS bowl payouts have grown dramatically over the last 15 years. For example, measured in 2004 dollars, the Sugar Bowl (the highest payout for 2004–2005) has grown from an $8.4 million total payout to a $25.8 million total payout. The highest payout 15 years ago was the Rose bowl at $18.2 million (adjusted to 2004), and it has increased hardly at all. So while the Rose Bowl has about the same payout it did 15 years ago in real terms, the payout for the Sugar Bowl has grown at a real rate of nearly 8 percent annually. The non-BCS games show small increases, at best, over the last 15 years (the Liberty Bowl and Cotton Bowl have actually decreased in real terms). Clearly, fan interest is in the national championship outcome, and sponsors know it.

Postseason money is a mainstay at the conference level, as shown in Table 13.7. For the 11 Division IA conferences shown in the table, the average bowl revenue per conference was about $14.5 million. For some conferences, postseason football revenues almost equal their other broadcast revenues (refer back to Table 13.4).

NCAA Basketball Tournament Revenues

All of the conferences that earned bowl revenues also earned revenues from participation in the NCAA basketball tournament, known as March Madness. So did many other conferences. All of this money flows from the $6.2 billion contract for this tournament between the NCAA and CBS. In 2004, revenues earned by the NCAA from CBS were $389 million, but the amount will grow to $764 million by 2013, the last year of the contract. This amount is larger than the last published NHL contract on an annual basis.

As with championship bowl revenues, the March Madness TV contract has increased dramatically over time. Fifteen years ago, CBS paid about $1.5 billion (adjusted to 2004) for 7 years, or about $216 million annually. That's a real growth rate of about 4 percent annually to 2004. For the conferences in Table 13.7 that received both bowl revenues and March Madness revenues, the average from March Madness is $7.2 million, much larger than nearly all of the regular season basketball TV revenues for these conferences (again, see Table 13.5). Clearly, in terms of overall earnings, the postseason is where it is at for basketball.

In our pro sports analysis, we assumed that owners were motivated by profit maximization. Given this, we developed long-run and short-run cost notions and the long-run profit-maximizing quality choice. We then found that profit pursuits constrained winning, and that profit variation could harm competitive balance. We then tried to determine what we could learn from operating revenue statements relative to the true economic value of owning a team.

We will follow a similar approach for college sports. However, we need to be careful in choosing our level of analysis. Where the owner was the unit of analysis in pro team sports, in college sports, it is the university that makes decisions about athletic quality, considering the value of that activity to its overall pursuits. Universities are unlikely to act to maximize profits. Indeed, many are explicitly directed not to behave that way. Most state colleges are charged with many different tasks that have nothing to do with profits.

The University and Its Goals

Let's consider a university's goals and organization and then turn to the relationship between the university and its athletic department. Who are the actors and what are their goals? How is the university organized to pursue those goals? What does this all suggest about the way that the university fits athletics into its scheme of operations?

Figure 13.2 shows the organization of a typical university. As with all generalizations, this simple diagram will not hold for every university, but it will be instructive for our purposes. The university provides the structure and support for research, teaching, and service to the state. It employs its inputs, organized into departments and administration, to generate the funding required for these tasks. The funding can come directly from the tasks done by its faculty and administrators or indirectly through political support.

The University and the Athletic Department

The diagram in Figure 13.2 helps make clear what the university expects of all its component parts. In this section, we will compare how the athletic department contributes to the university relative to the business school. We will stress the similarities of the two entities, the most important being that the university does not expect individual units to show profits but to contribute to its overall goals.

The Business College vs. the Athletic Department Figure 13.3 depicts the organization of a college of business. Faculty members of like interests are grouped into departments and each department has a chairperson. For example, the economics department in a business college will have a number of faculty members of different teaching and research interests organized under its chair. Departments with a common thread to their disciplines are then organized into colleges, in this case, the college of

Figure 13.2 The University and the Athletic Department

All major elements of the university (shown inside the triangle) produce outputs (research, teaching, and service) that generate money and political support for the university. The university provides the most support to those elements that generate money and political support.

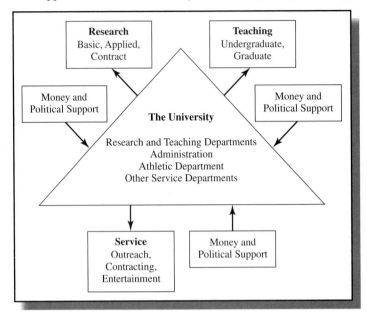

Figure 13.3 The Business College Organizational Chart

At the bottom of the chart, chairs of academic departments are responsible to their dean. The line of responsibility and oversight moves upward through the provost, the board of regents and, ultimately, to the governor.

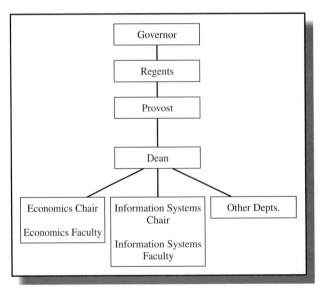

business. Thus, the accounting, marketing, information systems, finance, management, economics, and decision science departments might comprise a typical business college. At the top of the college, in terms of administration, is the dean. Typically, the dean has assistant deans who handle the day-to-day tasks of running the college so that the dean can perform fundraising and external relations duties. The dean answers to the provost and on up the ladder through the board of regents to the governor.

Only two departments are shown in Figure 13.3. The economics department usually cannot generate enough funding to pay for itself. The information systems department, on the other hand, is more likely to generate enough grant and contract activity to more than cover the cost of its faculty. The ability of the college to grow or at least to avoid cuts in its budget depends on the success of its departments. Success is measured along the lines of the university's objectives—research, teaching, and service. As you would expect, successful colleges do better during the university's budget allocation process.

Interestingly, the athletic department is not organized much differently, as shown in Figure 13.4. In this case, each sport is like a department. Each sport has its faculty equivalent, assistant coaches, and its chair equivalent, the head coach. The sports are organized around their own dean equivalent, the athletic director. The athletic director has assistant directors who oversee the day-to-day operation of the athletic department while they attend to fundraising and other activities. As with the college of business, the remaining part of the chart runs right up to the governor.

Here we will look at football and women's volleyball. The former typically more than pays its bills, whereas the latter does not. In a sense, the football program is like

Figure 13.4 The Athletic Department Organizational Chart
At the bottom of the organization, individual team coaches are responsible to their athletic director (the equivalent of the dean for academic departments). The line of responsibility and oversight moves upward through the president (not the provost as in academic departments), the board of regents and, ultimately, to the governor.

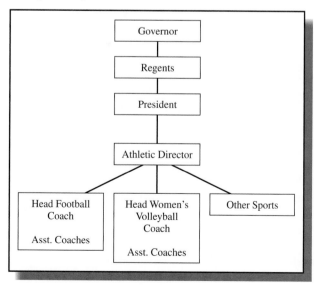

the information systems department in the college of business; both the football program and the information systems department pay for themselves and contribute dramatically to the success of their immediate organization by performing well along the dimensions that matter to the university. In the information systems department, the contributions are teaching and research. In the athletic department, it is service in terms of entertainment enjoyed by thousands, as well as in terms of producing some productive sports professionals (either professional players or future coaches). Although I know of no university that offers a degree in the subject, athletic departments certainly do teach athletes their sport, and many athletes make a living from that knowledge through playing or coaching.

Academic departments contribute to the university's goals of research, teaching, and service. The rewards are dollars directly from students, a budget from state legislative allocations, and research grants and contracts. Athletic departments also generate resources for the university's pursuits. These contributions will not be direct dollar amounts (athletic departments do not have any money left over). However, the university benefits from indirect contributions that follow from the activities of the athletic department. One of the most important types of indirect support is political support.

Political Support Political support is usually analyzed by looking at political individuals. Some of these individuals are politicians who are sports fans. Others are boosters who happen to be politically influential individuals even though they are not elected officials. These boosters may not be interested in the rest of the university's mission, but they will throw their political support to the university as long as the university supports the athletic department. In addition, athletics appeals to fans who also are taxpayers.

"For better or worse, recognition results in more alumni donations, more student applications and, most important, more support from state politicians, who control the university budget."
—Jim Norton in a letter to the editor, *Sports Illustrated*, 1994

The political support of athletic departments is common knowledge. In a letter to *Sports Illustrated*, a Mr. Jim Norton wrote, "For better or worse, recognition results in more alumni donations, more student applications and, most important, more support from state politicians, who control the university budget" (November 28, 1994, p. 4). The last part of the quote shows that political support really does matter. Thus, it shouldn't be surprising that the governor of the state typically attends the college football intrastate rivalry game every year. However, the rest of the quote hints that there are other dimensions of support, such as alumni contributions and increased visibility with potential students. But what does the evidence show on these spillover benefits?

Athletic Department Spillover Benefits Athletic departments are purported to provide **spillover benefits to the university**, including:
- Greater giving by alumni and other boosters to the general university fund
- A larger and better set of student applicants
- Better faculty and administrators
- Value added to athletes, many of whom would not be at the university without athletics

University of Washington President Mark Emmert puts it this way (*Tacoma News-Tribune* Web page, accessed September 3, 2004):

> Sport becomes this enormously powerful lens through which people see and reflect on your university. They use it as a proxy—grossly inaccurate, but nonetheless a proxy—of what the university is about. So if the football team, for example, is doing very well, and the players and the coaches represent the values of the university—they're well behaved, they're good students, they're people of good character, they're highly competitive and they're winning—then those are exactly the things that people think about the university: good values, strong place, successful, lets people compete at the highest levels.

There is some scattered evidence showing that college sports provide these spillover benefits. Goff (2004) surveys the literature in the first two of these areas, updates a few with his own empirical analysis, and offers some general conclusions. Major achievements (significant postseason appearances) appear to spark general giving. But marginal increases in winning during the season don't. Major achievements also appear to spark increased student interest even at colleges that already have high academic reputations. But the quality of the pool is better only at very select institutions. Goff also reminds us that there actually are only a few works in each area and that those works do not address the same data. Tucker (2004, 2005) adds that the success increases the percentage of alumni that give to the general university fund, increases the SAT scores of entering freshmen, and enhances graduation rates. Much more remains to be done before there is anything resembling a consensus on these first two of the listed claims, and I know of no work at all on the last two.

Institutional Support The university typically spends money on both academic and athletic departments. Academic departments receive shares of the state budget allocation to the university, determined in a competitive budgeting process at the university level. The direct payments to athletic departments out of the university budgets are referred to as institutional support. There are also other indirect subsidies from the university to the athletic department. Given our model, institutional support and other subsidies make perfectly good sense from the perspective of the university. This finding sheds light on arguments that college sports do not belong at the university because they are a losing proposition, financially.

The university is willing to pay for both the economics department and the football program because of the contribution that each makes to the university's goals. Primarily through service to fans, and politically potent boosters in particular, the athletic department generates political support for the university. It is not just the bottom line of this division that determines its worth to the university. It is its contribution to the bottom line of the organization, taken as whole, that determines its worth. Here is where the ultimate similarity between the athletic department and other university divisions lies: All make their contribution and receive their reward.

Uniqueness of the Athletic Department

Academic departments are teaching and research oriented, whereas athletic departments are service (entertainment) oriented. We should expect the university to allow each to play to their respective strengths in order to get the highest return from each. After we examine how athletic departments differ from academic departments, we will see how the university treats them differently, primarily through the budgeting process.

Differences Between Athletics and Academics

Success is much more objective in the athletic department than in academic departments. Contests on the field with objective scoring pretty much guarantee very little disagreement on this point. In contrast, analysis of the success of individual faculty careers is much more subjective and may vary by discipline. In addition, a successful academic career may take many years to come to fruition.

Further, the relation between quality and the output that actually is sold at a unit price is clear in the athletic department. This is not true of academic departments. Departments do not charge students by the lesson or by the hour. Research is performed in small pieces that may take a long time; thus, grants and contracts can run over extended periods.

These differences mean that the university will treat the athletic department differently than it treats its academic branches. From the perspective of the university, differential treatment allows the athletic department to contribute to the university's goals in the most beneficial way. Some view this differential treatment as preferential treatment. I think you will see that it is not.

The Athletic Department Budgeting Process

Differential treatment between athletics and academics is most apparent during the budgeting process. The budgeting process in research and teaching branches of universities is as follows: Individual colleges in the university determine the needs of their departments, put them together in a budget request, and turn it over to the university administration. During the budget period, colleges spend what they are given. If spending is lower or revenues are greater than anticipated, the university retains the balance for future budgets.

The situation is quite different for most athletic departments. Like the academic departments, the athletic department determines its members' needs and receives part of its budget from the university. However, if the department generates unexpected revenues, revisions can be made during the budget period to reallocate it into special projects and salaries. Thus, the athletic department is allowed to spend surplus funds however it sees fit.

This situation is easy to illustrate using my own university as a case in point. Table 13.8 shows the athletic department balance sheets for the 1997–1998 Washington State University Rose Bowl season and the year before (the data are a bit old, but the example is timeless). Revenues increased $2.9 million during the Rose Bowl year, an increase of about 21 percent (the inflation rate was only about 2 percent, so this is quite a large real increase). The bulk of

Did You Know?
Washington State University athletic department revenues increased $2.9 million in 1997–1998 when they went to the Rose Bowl, but just as the year before when they missed the postseason, the department just broke even.

Table 13.8 Budgets at Washington State University

	1996–1997	1997–1998	DIFFERENCE
Revenues			
Booster club scholarship contributions/endowment	$1,968,286	$2,451,854	$483,568
Corporate support	$314,476	$302,739	−$11,737
Football away guarantees	$1,102,150	$1,344,020	$241,870
Football tickets	$928,230	$1,502,620	$574,390
Men's basketball	$898,643	$1,312,020	$413,377
NCAA & conference	$349,224	$447,081	$97,857
Other	$361,144	$432,316	$71,172
Radio/sports video	$539,105	$472,114	−$66,991
Student fees and tickets	$1,408,431	$1,557,302	$148,871
TV-football conference	$2,589,232	$3,178,349	$589,117
University support/ tuition waivers	$3,042,047	$2,941,530	−$100,517
Royalties		$490,000	$490,000
Concessions/merchandise		$277,810	$277,810
Carry forward	$419,269	$111,197	−$308,072
Total revenue	$13,920,237	$16,820,952	$2,900,715
Expenses			
Capitalized equipment	$234,795	$733,373	$498,578
Employee benefits	$551,972	$1,054,600	$502,628
Goods and services	$2,799,511	$3,814,930	$1,015,419
Recruiting/professional development	$617,401	$586,998	−$30,403
Salaries	$4,140,899	$4,067,257	$273,642
Scholarships	$3,192,773	$2,425,524	−$767,249
Student and other wages	$629,740	$1,118,885	$489,145
Team travel	$1,310,911	$2,328,934	$1,018,023
University overhead	$437,505	$563,375	$125,870
Total expenses	$13,915,507	$16,693,876	$2,778,369
Net Operating Revenue	$4,730	$127,076	$122,346

Source: Washington State University Department of Intercollegiate Athletics.

the revenues came in identifiable large quantities—about $630,000 from TV broadcasts, another $391,000 in contributions, $219,000 in royalties, $350,000 in miscellaneous, and $141,000 in merchandising. In light of this surge in revenue, how in the world can it be that the athletic department only managed to break even? In this case, as in most, the excess revenues were simply kept by the athletic department and spent.

One way the athletic department keeps the excess revenues is through salary increases. In our Washington State example, salaries rose after the Rose Bowl. The head coach's contract, worth about $253,000 (including all payment sources as well as base salary) for the 1997–1998 season, was increased to about $450,000 after the Rose Bowl (*Spokane Spokesman-Review*, January 13, 1998, p. C1). Clearly, gains are sent straight back to the expense side of the ledger.

The university does not have to let this happen, and many athletic department observers argue that it should not. However, it makes sense from the perspective of the university's goals that the department be allowed this special budget freedom. The additional spending by the athletic department is parlayed into political support for the university.

Paying the Bills Athletic departments also differ from academic departments in how the bills are paid. Academic departments pay overhead on all grants and contracts. If faculty members receive outside funding for their work, the university requires that the granting agency pay between 20 and 45 percent of the grant to the university. This is justified because university facilities and resources are used to pursue funding and research.

Typically, athletic departments do not pay overhead to their university. At athletic events, the athletic department pays for game management (the personnel to collect tickets and control crowds, including armed police presence). They may also incur cleanup and minor repair costs. The university picks up the rest of the costs, including rent and maintenance that other facility users would have to pay. The university also typically handles student pass production and distribution. Summer activities, including camps and training sessions, receive the same benefits from the university.

An athletic department that paid the same overhead charges that academic departments pay would contribute between $25,000 and $45,000 per $100,000 earned. At my university, judging from the revenues in Table 13.8, the athletic department's overhead payment would have been as much as $6.75 million in 1997–1998.

However, this is all just a matter of incentives and rewards. The university does not take its return out of the athletic department in terms of the department's bottom line result. As long as the athletic department contributes more to the goals of the university than it costs the university, then the athletic department is worth it. The athletic department keeps its net revenue and the university helps pay its bills. If the athletic department does not contribute to the university's goals or it becomes costly to the university in embarrassing ways (covered in a later section), then it may be punished.

Did You Know?
The University of Chicago Maroons won seven Big Ten championships under legendary coach Amos Alonzo Stagg, but the university president terminated the program in 1939 citing the cheating that was required to succeed in big-time college sports.

Indeed, in one of the most famous cases in the history of college sports, intercollegiate football was banned at the University of Chicago in 1939 by then president Robert Maynard Hutchins. Under legendary coach Amos Alonzo Stagg, the Maroons were a storied team winning seven Big Ten titles and never once losing to Notre Dame. Hutchins is reputed to have based his decision on unwillingness to cheat on NCAA rules when (in his opinion) all about him were doing so. But it also is true that the Maroons lost every game in 1939 and never scored a point (Stagg had left for Pacific two years earlier). It took 30 years for the game to return—the university has played Division III football since 1969.

The Results for Athletic Departments

College athletic departments receive considerable support from their universities. In general, for Division IA, this can be seen in Table 13.1, where net operating revenue outcomes are shown for departments with and without institutional support. With institutional support, in all years but 1985, the vast majority of athletic departments show some positive net revenue. Without that support, except for 1993 where the average is break-even, the majority of departments would report losses rather than profits. This leads some to argue that, given the other problems with college sports, if they can't stand on their own financially, then they should be abandoned by universities (Sperber, 1991).

But this view misses the point entirely. First and foremost, the university helps cover the department's costs as long as it contributes enough to the final goals of the university. Arguing that the athletic department should be abandoned because it doesn't cover all of its costs holds just as true of English departments (like Professor Sperber's) or economics departments (like my own) at most universities. But the economic way of thinking suggests that universities view their English, economics, and athletics departments similarly—as long as their contribution to the university's goals exceeds the costs, they all are worth the money. Beside, if institutional support were withdrawn, the athletic department would simply reduce spending, just as any department at the university would under the same circumstances.

Again, Washington State University is a perfect case in point. Returning to Table 13.8, note that the department broke even for 1997–1998 (the net operating revenue surplus of $127,076 represents only about 0.8 percent of revenues and is hardly worth mentioning). However, without direct institutional support and a little bit of funding from the legislature (the University support/tuition waivers revenue category), this athletic department would be in the hole by about $2.8 million, or 17 percent of revenues.

But breaking even is not always the goal of either the university or its athletic department. Table 13.9 contains a comparison of Washington State and its cross-state rival, the University of Washington. We'll use most of these data for our upcoming examination of gender equity. But for now, the relevant observation is that both universities reported budget surpluses for 2003–04 (refer to the far-right totals column). Net before amortization is just under $1 million for Washington State and just over $1 million for Washington. Interestingly, neither athletic department returned any of its surplus to the university. Instead, long-term capital ambitions took up the surplus balance. Our diagram of this process and the earlier statement by the president of that university suggest that this occurs because athletic department spending flexibility helps the university reach its goals.

Postseason Money and Athletic Department Budgeting   We have neglected to discuss one important source of funds. What about bowl revenues and the revenue sharing from the championship basketball tournament shown in Table 13.7? In general, the sharing of postseason revenues already is built into a team's expected spending. All athletic departments know the amounts that will come to the conference and how much will be shared among the schools. The athletic departments know how much their conference will bring in, and make plans to spend it.

Table 13.9 Operating Revenues and Expenses, Washington State University and the University of Washington, 2003–2004

	WSU			
REVENUES	MEN'S TEAMS	WOMEN'S TEAMS	RATIO	TOTAL
Basketball	$2,148,239	$316,975	6.8	$2,465,214
Football	$12,630,209			$12,630,209
Other sports	$418,866	$1,422,675	0.3	$1,841,541
Not allocated by gender				$13,538,665
Grand total	$15,197,314	$1,739,650	8.7	$30,475,629
Expenses				
Basketball	$1,653,650	$1,253,920	1.3	$2,907,570
Football	$7,668,687			$7,668,687
Other sports	$1,710,020	$4,275,601	0.4	$5,985,621
Not allocated by gender				$12,951,738
Grand total	$11,032,357	$5,529,521	2.0	$29,513,616
Net before amortization				$962,013
	UW			
REVENUES	MEN'S TEAMS	WOMEN'S TEAMS	RATIO	TOTAL
Basketball	$4,235,886	$1,083,993	3.9	$5,319,879
Football	$28,569,263			$28,569,263
Other sports	$675,941	$1,811,108	0.4	$2,487,049
Not allocated by gender				$6,175,329
Grand total	$33,481,090	$2,895,101	11.6	$42,551,520
Expenses				
Basketball	$2,492,670	$1,661,035	1.5	$4,153,705
Football	$12,640,090			$12,640,090
Other sports	$3,970,979	$5,875,726	0.7	$9,846,705
Not allocated by gender				$14,749,393
Grand total	$19,103,739	$7,536,761	2.5	$41,389,893
Net before amortization				$1,161,627

Source: Author's calculations from data reported at the Office of Post-Secondary Education Equity in Athletics Disclosure Web site, ope.ed.gov, accessed August 8, 2005.

But what about those teams that are fortunate enough to actually go to a bowl or other postseason play? They get a larger share of the postseason revenues, but they also spend it. Partly, this spending is expected by the localities that put on bowl games, especially for lower-level bowls as shown in the Learning Highlight: Washington State University Copper Bowl Spending. The university also sees the reinvestment of these revenues as important to the contribution made by the athletic department to the university's overall goals.

The *Sports Business Journal* (March 12, 2001, p. 40) cites another example. In its first trip to the Rose Bowl since 1967, the Purdue University athletic department managed to retain just $713 after expenses and sharing with the Big 10 Conference.

LEARNING HIGHLIGHT
Washington State University Copper Bowl Spending

Bowls were invented as local economic development tools to lure winter tourists. This means that the bowl hosts expect the teams to bring spenders and to spend themselves. The result for participation in lesser bowls is that participating teams typically do not make any money on their bowl appearances. Many observers on the academic side of the university think that spending it all is just gluttony by the athletic department, but nothing could be farther from the truth. Competition simply pushes participating teams to spend all of their bowl payout and to encourage as many people as possible to attend the game; if the teams chosen do not do that, other teams will. The participating teams take their reward in terms of advertising and other types of recruiting exposure and, of course, a good time had by all in a nice place in December.

When the Washington State University (WSU) Cougars went to the Weiser Lock Copper Bowl in Tucson in 1992, many got an education on the finer points of participating in lower-level postseason bowl games. The Washington press was quick to point out that the Cougars intended to spend all of the $650,000 payout. The reasons for spending it all soon were made very clear. As Copper Bowl executive director Larry Brown said, "That's why bowl games are in existence, to stimulate the local economies . . . The economic impact is expected to be $10 million to $12 million from 5,000 to 6,000 fans that come and spend about $300 a day doing the town and having a good time."

WSU Athletic Director Jim Livengood also pulled no punches in justifying the spending: "If we were to say we will spend $325,000 [half the Copper Bowl payout to each team, at that time], we will never play another bowl game again. Why do you think the cities have bowls? They wouldn't have a Copper Bowl if it wasn't trying to bring people to Tucson. . . . It's the expectation of the Copper Bowl people that WSU bring a lot of people." The Copper Bowl people expected fans to spend in Tucson and bolster that local economy. The opponent University of Utah Athletic Department finance director, Peter Hart, echoed this: "The goal of bowl games is to sell hotel rooms in soft markets. I think they have a sense of vacancy rates around the time of the bowl." These statements make it clear that the payout was to be used to stimulate the local Tucson economy.

WSU spent all of its $650,000 allotment, bringing approximately 200 players, coaches, administrators, faculty, staff, and their families to the Copper Bowl, all expenses paid. Spending for transportation (chartered airfare), lodging, and food was budgeted at $345,000. An additional $30,000 was set aside for gifts and awards to players. Part of the WSU payment came in the form of 10,000 tickets worth $290,000 face value. WSU sold about 5,000 tickets. The rest were framed and offered as mementos for those who did not choose to go to Tucson. The WSU athletic department left itself a $75,000 buffer, apparently against the contingency that they did not sell all of the tickets. Otherwise, they would have gone in the hole going to Tucson.

Sources: The *Daily Evergreen*, December 8, 1992, pp. 1–2; December 7, 1992, p. 1; The *Daily News*, December 7, 1992, p. 8A.

Net of revenue sharing, by conference rules, the Boilermakers had $1.8 million, $1.4 million for being conference representative to a BCS bowl and another $400,000 estimated from additional ticket handling charges and private donations related to the trip—and yet they spent it all except for the meager $713 balance.

SPORTS MARKET OUTCOMES: ATHLETIC DEPARTMENTS, CONFERENCES, AND THE NCAA

We went into great detail about the relationship between pro teams and leagues in Chapters 5 and 6. Much of what we discussed there is also true for college teams and their conferences. Conferences enable teams to pursue goals and objectives that they cannot pursue as successfully acting alone. Coordinated conference activity provides teams with opportunities along many dimensions, both on and off the field. Conferences provide play and profit for colleges, just as leagues do for pro teams.

Conferences produce the competition that fans desire, including their own championships. In the process, conferences enhance the economic welfare of member athletic departments. But college sports fans also want a national champion, and that involves cooperation across conferences. To enhance that cooperation, colleges and conferences invented the NCAA. In the simple organizational role, the NCAA enforces agreements among member institutions. In this section, we'll explore the single-entity and joint-venture activities of athletic departments, conferences, and the NCAA. Enforcement of agreements across conferences by the NCAA, ostensibly to protect athletes and competitive balance, is for the next section. We will see that the NCAA enhances the economic welfare of member institutions, just as pro sports leagues do for their member team owners.

Single-Entity Cooperation in College Conferences

Conferences accomplish the single-entity aims of creating a schedule, developing rules, and organizing conference championship play. Everything said about these factors in Chapter 5 need not be repeated here, and the conclusion is the same. Colleges that join conferences determine that they are better off doing so than going it alone. Nearly all colleges have made this determination in all sports; Notre Dame actually is the exception that proves the rule (indeed, in all other sports besides football, Notre Dame is a member of the Big East Conference).

However, one thing distinguishes college sports from pro sports. In the pros, because there is only one dominant league in each sport, the national championship follows from lower-level champions under league playoff rules. College conferences must cooperate with each other to make a national championship happen. In order to cooperate with each other, college conferences invented the NCAA. Originally, the NCAA came about because individual colleges could not deal with society's discontent with college football violence in the early 1900s. But member institutions now demand that their NCAA do much more than this.

In terms of single-entity activity, the NCAA was never asked by its membership to provide a college football national championship for Division IA. But the NCAA does organize the national championship tournaments in all lower levels of football. Its membership also has absolutely demanded that the NCAA handle the determination of a national champion in all other sports, especially college basketball through March Madness.

One last note about college championships further distinguishes them from the professionals. Economically speaking, championships need not be anticompetitive. They end up that way in pro sports because of single league dominance. They also end up that way in all college sports except football because of the NCAA.

We saw that the monopoly power of the NFL has made the Super Bowl the most expensive ticket on earth. However, championships are not inherently anticompetitive as long as alternative leagues or conferences are available to teams and fans. For example, college basketball has competitive postseason venues, the National Invitational Tournament (NIT) and the NCAA Championship Tournament (believe it or not, the NIT once was the more prestigious). The NCAA tournament established its preeminence by expanding from an original field of the "Sweet 16" to its current field of 64 teams. Member institutions voluntarily chose to move to the NCAA tournament, much to the chagrin of NIT organizers. But the NIT did continue on, partly dampening the ability of the NCAA to control postseason play entirely.

At this writing, the courts are wrestling with precisely this question. The NIT organizers have sued the NCAA because a recent NCAA rule *requires* member teams to play in its tournament if invited. The complaint is that this action by the NCAA is a pretense to the monopolization of college basketball postseason play. It will be interesting to see the court ruling because the economics here is straightforward. When championships happen in a monopoly setting, prices increase and opportunities decrease to the detriment of fans.

In Division IA football, the BCS determines the national champion, but this was not always the case. Earlier on, competitive nation-wide polls crowned the champion. Indeed, if the competing polls chose different teams, the champion from each poll was referred to as a cochampion. Again, movement to the BCS doesn't have to be an economically anticompetitive determination of the champion as long as colleges and conferences are free to choose to enter that particular arrangement.

Joint-Venture Cooperation in College Sports

Athletic departments would like to take advantage of the same type of joint-venture activities as their professional league counterparts. Although there is no exclusive franchise agreement, athletic departments would prefer to maintain some market power through territory protection. In an interesting twist, there also will be a role for conferences and the NCAA in terms of handling potential rival organizations. Most members of college conferences would also admit that joint venture negotiations could be more valuable than individual negotiations over TV broadcast rights. Finally, while players are not unionized, joint-venture cooperation may strengthen the position of conference members relative to the players. As a reminder, at the pro level, leagues facilitate joint ventures. However, because there are so many college conferences, competition among themselves may hinder the pursuit of the usual goals of concerted joint ventures. In response, conferences rely upon the NCAA for much of their joint-venture activity.

Territory Protection   Individual colleges at a particular level of play do not want economic competition from rival colleges in their own backyard. If they and their rivals are playing at the same level, fans perceive more substitute possibilities, and geographic market power is reduced. Athletic departments rely on both their conference and the NCAA to protect geographical territories. Because this type of protection is not required to "make play happen," it falls outside of single-entity requirements, and basic economic intuition suggests that it occurs because the economic welfare of college athletic departments is enhanced.

It can make perfectly good sense for a conference to expand to bring in very tough rivals. When a team enters a conference, it brings its heritage, tradition, a shot at postseason play, and a television market. Stronger sports programs bring the most value along these dimensions. Therefore, it is unlikely that an athletically weak college would be allowed into a conference over a strong one. Member colleges must weigh any geographical territory issues against these benefits when they decide to accept new conference members.

In addition, member institutions have endowed the NCAA with the power to determine membership in the hierarchy of conferences from Division IA down through Division III. No team can move between divisions without NCAA approval based on minimum attendance requirements and stadium capacities. The earlier example of Idaho's bid for Division IA status is a nice case in point. Idaho and Washington State are separated by a state border but lie within 8 miles of each other. Initially, Idaho satisfied the NCAA by joining the Sun Belt Conference playing far-away schools in Arkansas, Texas, Louisiana, and Florida. Currently, Idaho plays a bit closer to home in the WAC (although there remain two long trips to Louisiana Tech and Hawaii). But neither the Sun Belt nor the WAC were ever close substitutes for Pac-10 football at Washington State. It should come as no surprise that the Pac-10 didn't invite Idaho to join it in the first place, despite the fact that recently Idaho was victorious against Washington State on the field.

Rival Associations and the NCAA   Similar to the pro leagues, the NCAA also has acted against rival associations, resulting in a single dominant association outcome. At the beginning of the chapter, we mentioned one particularly brutal episode concerning the now defunct AIAW (Zimbalist, 1999, pp. 59–60). Founded in 1971, that association served over 800 member colleges and had its own set of national women's championships. According to Zimbalist (p. 59), NCAA members saw a threat coming with the passage of gender equity laws and moved to curtail the AIAW. The NCAA took direct and concerted action to win over AIAW members, causing the AIAW to fold in 1982.

The NCAA also faces challenges from rivals in basketball. The case of the NIT has already been covered, but there is more. The NCAA has a virtual lock on pre-NBA basketball talent. However, threats from rivals, such as the Continental Basketball Association, the Collegiate Professional Basketball League, and recently the NBA's own development league have arisen. The idea driving these rivals is unbundling the student-athlete into one part student and another part athlete. Some basketball players would like to invest in becoming NBA caliber players, but they would rather not do so by going to college. These rivals pay college-aged players professional salaries and help those who desire it with their education. And they pose direct competition for college athletic departments providing training for future professional athletes.

Negotiations: Regular-Season Broadcasting and the NCAA Decision

Member teams sell their league-play TV rights through conferences under the three-tier system described in the earlier section on the broadcast rights market. But it wasn't always this way. Before 1984, the NCAA actually negotiated a single football contract for all of Division IA. The current system was created after one of the most important court cases in sports history, *NCAA v. Board of Regents of the University of Oklahoma* (otherwise known as the 1984 **NCAA Decision**).

The NCAA Decision and Football Rights   Beginning with the Television Plan of 1952, the NCAA negotiated the broadcast rights contracts for all of Division IA college football, just as the NFL does for its member team owners (Brown, 1999). Sponsors had to provide national coverage and received no more than 12 Saturday games in total. While no member college had to provide a game, no member college could appear more than one time per year. In Table 13.10, you can see the number of games, the rights fees paid, and the payment per game that resulted (all adjusted to 2004 dollars). The gap from 1953 to 1977 is due to my lack of knowledge of the number of games. But the value of the contract rose from $7.1 to $55.6 million (2004 dollars), or a real annual growth rate of 8.6 percent.

Table 13.10
College Games and Rights Fees ($Millions 2004)

Year	# Games	Total Contract	Per Game
1952	12	$7.07	$0.59
1978	23	$89.63	$3.90
1979	23	$74.82	$3.25
1980	24	$70.46	$2.94
1981	24	$68.00	$2.83
1982	28	$114.52	$4.09
1983	28	$120.35	$4.30
1984	36	$39.66	$1.10
1985	42	$47.00	$1.12
1986	42	$49.56	$1.18
1987	42	$46.17	$1.10
1988	43	$44.33	$1.03
1989	43	$42.29	$0.98
1990	43	$40.13	$0.93
1991	71	$79.76	$1.12
1992	71	$80.10	$1.13
1993	71	$79.07	$1.11
1994	71	$77.09	$1.09
1995	71	$76.20	$1.07

Source: Author's calculations from data in Brown (1999), for 1952; Fort and Quirk (1997) for the rest.

Under this approach, the NCAA limited the number of available broadcasts and the teams that could be included in this limited number of appearances. Football powerhouses like the University of Oklahoma felt that they could be on TV even more than they already were, dramatically increasing revenues. Examining Table 13.10 shows why they became particularly interested at this point in time—the value per game had risen from $2.8 to $4.3 million in the three years leading to 1983. These powerhouses joined together, forming the College Football Association, and attempted to negotiate their own, much more liberal broadcast contract. The NCAA sued the teams for failing to abide by its negotiations. Oklahoma countered that the NCAA practice restricted output and raised prices, and that they would not abide by actions that ran afoul of the antitrust laws.

Ultimately, the U.S. Supreme Court decided that the actions of the NCAA in the broadcast rights market for college football did violate the antitrust laws. Output was restricted and prices were raised above the level that would prevail under a more competitive bidding structure. Note how this stands in stark contrast to the current practices of pro sports leagues that sell broadcast rights through national contracts.

Did You Know?

Prior to 1984, the NCAA negotiated the entire Division IA television deal, and contract values typically rose in real terms at over 8 percent annually. The Supreme Court struck that down as illegal, and the per game value of Division IA contracts, with many more games shown, was constant to 1995.

It is easy to see that the courts were correct by looking again at Table 13.10. After the 1984 NCAA Decision, conferences were free to make their own TV deals with two very predictable results. There was a dramatic increase in the number of games offered (facilitated in part by the advent of cable TV) and a reduction in the price per game paid by media providers. Indeed, in real terms, the price per game changed hardly at all from 1984 to 1995. Plain and simple, the court decision invoked competition, resulting in lower prices and increased output for fans to enjoy. In addition, powerhouses were broadcast more often, and more schools were on TV than ever before.

Negotiations: Postseason Play, the BCS, and the NCAA Postseason rights in football also are handled primarily by conferences. The BCS makes this championship happen. But the BCS is nothing more than a coalition of major conferences, Notre Dame, and the ABC television network. All participants in the BCS agree to send their best teams to the four major bowls—Sugar, Rose, Fiesta, and Orange—in order to guarantee that the number one and two ranked teams meet for the national championship. There are also two at-large slots allowing the BCS some leeway in selection. The formula that determines the BCS rankings for this purpose is a complicated function of season records, opponent quality, and national polls. As we saw in Table 13.6, the eight teams in BCS games were paid $56.6 million for the 2004–2005 BCS bowl games. But there also are significant promised payments at the Division IA and IAA conference levels. According to their Web page (www.bcsfootball.org), the BCS distributed $93.15 million to participants and other designated recipients for 2005. These amounts are significantly larger than any other payments, historically, from bowl games. So it seems clear that conferences have done well for their member athletic departments through the BCS relative to what they could have done separately and individually.

Apparently, the members of the NCAA do not harbor the same feelings about basketball as they did about football. The NCAA manages and sells the broadcast rights to March Madness. This appears to satisfy NCAA members because they have never organized anything similar to the BCS in football to strike out on their own in the basketball postseason. Small wonder. As stated earlier, the $6.2 billion March Madness TV rights contract with CBS generated $389 million in 2004, but the amount will grow to $764 million by 2013. Table 13.7 shows how $105.3 million from March Madness was distributed to various conferences under the 2004 arrangement. The rest goes to fund the operations of the NCAA itself.

College Sports, the NCAA, and Athletes All dealings between athletic departments and college athletes are handled through the NCAA. This provides a unified front for athletic departments, and it isn't surprising that they need one. The relationship is very one-sided. First and foremost, amateur requirements reduce payments to players. Athletic departments and conferences also require that players remain at their original college of choice (or lose eligibility), making player movement between teams fairly difficult. Because there are incentives for individual athletic departments to cheat on these rules, member institutions give the NCAA the important role of policing compliance and punishing violators. This relationship is so important to college sports that we will examine it in great detail later in this chapter.

All Things Considered: The Changing Face of Conference Membership

College sports teams cannot relocate (universities cannot be moved to a new location for the sake of enhancing the athletic department's welfare). Thus, there is no college equivalent to a pro league's careful balancing act between expansion and believable threat locations. However, there are some similarities between pro and college sports in terms of changing conference membership. This decision roughly parallels the example in Chapter 5 about professional basketball teams choosing between the National Basketball League (the forerunner of the modern NBA) and the Basketball Association of America in the 1940s.

In a broad sense, all college conferences are rivals. In the face of this competition, conferences must provide services to their members or risk losing them to another conference. Athletic departments will simply find another organization that will provide the desired services. Table 13.11 shows athletic department movement from three previous college conferences. The Western Athletic Conference continues in name only because nearly all of the faces have changed. The Pacific Coast Athletic Association was so altered by migration that it was renamed the Big West Conference.

The most famous conference realignment ever concerns the Southwest Conference, now no longer in existence. Although the Southwest Conference was once one of the most storied conferences in college football history, Texas, Texas A&M, Texas Tech, and Baylor bolted to join the Big Eight Conference and form the Big 12 in 1994. The reasons mainly concerned dissatisfaction over revenue sharing and the chance to form a conference with two divisions and a postseason championship game. As Bill Carr, Houston's athletic director at the time puts it

Table 13.11
New Conferences,
Old Affiliations

TEAM	CURRENT CONFERENCE	PREVIOUS CONFERENCE
Air Force	Mountain West	WAC
Baylor	Big 12	SWC
BYU	Mountain West	WAC
Colorado State	Mountain West	WAC
Fresno State	WAC	PCAA
Houston	ConferenceUSA	SWC
New Mexico	Mountain West	WAC
Rice	WAC	SWC
San Diego State	Mountain West	PCAA
San Jose State	WAC	PCAA
SMU	WAC	SWC
TCU	WAC	SWC
Texas	Big 12	SWC
Texas A&M	Big 12	SWC
Texas Tech.	Big 12	SWC
UNLV	Mountain West	PCAA
Utah	Mountain West	WAC
UTEP	WAC	PCAA
Wyoming	Mountain West	WAC

(*Sports Business Journal*, December 8, 2003, p. 32), "The economics of the Southwest Conference weren't working, so we no longer had a Southwest Conference." Conferences clearly run the risk of losing members. The best example of late is covered in the Learning Highlight: Miami Joins the Big East . . . No, Make that the ACC.

SPORTS MARKET OUTCOMES: COMPETITIVE BALANCE

Exclusive territories, based on the historical happenstance of college location, can lead to conferences with competitive imbalance and low fan interest. The uncertainty of outcome hypothesis may be as important in college sports as in pro sports. Indeed, the stated goal of NCAA compliance rules is the preservation of a "level playing field," that is, enhancing competitive balance. Let's look at the data and then explore how colleges, acting through conferences and the NCAA, have come to handle this problem.

Competitive Balance Data in College Sports

As you can imagine, with so many college conferences even for just football and basketball, we would have to spend a lot of time and space for a complete analysis of

While technically no college sports team can change its physical location, the University of Miami has changed its conference location twice in the last 15 years. In 1990, Miami joined the Big East, a conference more noted for basketball than for football. This occurred just after Penn State joined the Big Ten, Arkansas the Southeastern Conference, and Florida State the Atlantic Coast Conference. With so many teams changing conferences, the Big East feared that its stronger football schools might bolt and take their basketball programs with them. To strengthen its football offerings, the conference recruited Miami as a football anchor and also added West Virginia.

Here is how valuable Miami was to the goals of the Big East. The Big East allowed Miami to keep its TV and bowl revenue for a few years, and after that period elapsed, only schools in the Big East that played Division IA football would share the revenues. To top it all off, the eventual makeup of the Big East for football featured only eight teams. With such a small number of conference games to play to determine the Big East championship, a powerhouse like Miami was free to schedule nonconference games and command large appearance fees. In essence, to save a solid basketball conference, the Big East created a solid Division IA football conference and essentially gave Miami all its football money in order to do so.

It worked until 2003. Along with Boston College and Virginia Tech, Miami left the Big East for the ACC. The ACC didn't expand to avoid catastrophe. As Commissioner John Swofford puts it, "But as the saying goes, 'It wasn't raining when Noah built the ark.' Our feeling within the majority of our schools was that we needed to be a bit larger to maintain our relative place in the future of college athletics." (*Sports Business Journal*, December 8, 2003, p. 25). As you can see looking forward to Table 13.13, after its expansion the ACC ranked second in per team revenue distributions. The ACC has only 11 teams because the Boston College move won't be final until 2005. When that happens, a postseason conference championship (and a few more million dollars) is a sure thing for the ACC.

Economically speaking, did it make sense for the ACC to expand in this way? Just prior to expansion, the ACC distributed around $88 million to its 9 members, or about $9.8 million each on average (even though equal shares do not occur). To keep that amount constant when Miami and Virginia Tech joined, the conference needed to generate another $19.6 million. But immediately, it's clear that this amount was met and then some. The ACC drew 3 million in total attendance for the first time in its history. Season ticket sales were at record levels at both Maryland and Clemson. And the TV contract with ABC doubled relative to the value of the contract signed in 1998, adding another $37 million.

None of this was lost on the old sage, Florida State coach Bobby Bowden, "[The East Coast] is where everyone lives, you know. I don't care what the SEC says, there's not that many people over in Starkville [Mississippi]." Duke's coach Ted Roof put it succinctly, "I think we're the premier football conference in America." Admittedly, a conference once dominated in football by Florida State now will be more competitive with the addition of Miami. But over $2 million more for each of the original 9 members, plus a conference championship game in 2005, and a future as a premiere conference should soften the blow.

Sources: Sports Illustrated, October 22, 1990, pp. 64–66; *Sports Business Journal*, December 8, 2003, pp. 25, 32–33; *Washington Post*, August 25, 2004, p. H01; and Citizen-Times.com, accessed August 7, 2005.

competitive balance. Instead, let's opt for a look at revenue imbalance in general for NCAA Division IA colleges and examine winning percent imbalance and championship imbalance for just a couple of major conferences.

Revenue imbalance was already presented in Table 13.1. It is worth a reminder that revenues are imbalanced and have become increasingly so through the 1990s in Division IA college sports. The top teams are gaining against teams at the average and at the bottom.

Our **winning percent imbalance** observations come from Table 13.12. The table shows our usual measure, the ratio of the actual to idealized standard deviations, for the Big Ten and the Pac-10. Winning percent imbalance is the rule in football in these two conferences. Over the last 35 years, the decade average standard deviation ratio is always greater than 1.5 (except for the Pac-10 in the 1980s but still much greater than one). Also, the level of winning percent imbalance is larger in the Big Ten than it is in the Pac-10, except for the last five years, when they are essentially equal. From the data in Table 13.12, there does not appear to be any trend in imbalance over time for either conference. But using more sophisticated techniques and all of the historical data on all Division IA teams, Depken and Wilson (2004b) find a negative trend in regular season competitive balance in college football.

The data on **championship imbalance** for football in the same two conferences also are in Table 13.12. In the Pac-10, Southern California won or tied for the championship 15 times. UCLA and Washington tied for second with 8 first-place finishes. Including ties, there were 45 first-place finishers in total in the Pac-10 in the last 35 years. These three teams were responsible for 69 percent of first-place finishes. In the Big Ten, Michigan (20 times), Ohio State (15 times), and Iowa (5 times) had the most first-place finishes. Because there were 54 first-place finishers over the period in Table 13.12, these three teams garnered 74 percent of the total. Thus, a distinct minority of teams in each of these conferences won the majority of the championships (by a landslide in the Big Ten). Therefore, it appears that winning percent imbalance and championship imbalance go hand in hand with revenue imbalance in college sports.

But an interesting occurrence between the 1980s and the 1990s partially mitigates this view of championship imbalance. Far more teams began to finish first in both the Big Ten and the Pac-10. In the 1980s, four teams finished first; UCLA and USC took 8 of the 11 occurrences. In the 1990s, eight teams finished first, and UCLA and USC took only 5 of the 15 occurrences. In the Big Ten, five teams finished first in the 1980s. Michigan and Ohio State finished first in 8 of the 12 occurrences. While those two teams finished first the same number of times in the 1990s, eight teams finished first. The share going to Michigan and Ohio State fell to 8 of 17 occurrences. Furthermore, there was only one tie for first in the Pac-10, and there were two in the Big Ten in the 1980s. But in the 1990s, ties for first occurred four times in each conference. Only halfway through the 2000s, there already have been two ties in the Pac-10 and three in the Big Ten. Thus, while it is true that just a few teams dominate, historically, more teams are finding their way into first-place finishes.

Did You Know?
Pac-10 and Big Ten championships have always been concentrated in a few teams but in the 1990s nearly twice as many teams won or shared titles, and the number of ties essentially doubled relative to the 1980s.

Table 13.12   Standard Deviation Ratio of Winning Percents and Conference Champions, Pac-10 and Big Ten, 1970–2004

| | Pac-10 | | Big Ten | |
YEAR	RATIO	CHAMPS	RATIO	CHAMPS
1970	1.37	Stanford	1.94	OSU
1971	1.13	Stanford	1.61	Michigan
1972	1.46	SC	1.64	Michigan/OSU
1973	1.81	SC	1.96	Michigan/OSU
1974	1.67	SC	1.72	Michigan/OSU
1975	1.74	Cal/UCLA	1.53	OSU
1976	1.71	SC	1.37	Michigan/OSU
1977	1.62	Washington	1.62	Michigan/OSU
1978	1.44	SC	1.86	Michigan/MSU
1979	1.35	SC	1.85	OSU
1970s Ave.	*1.53*		*1.71*	
1980	1.41	Washington	1.89	Michigan
1981	1.63	Washington	1.44	Iowa/OSU
1982	1.45	UCLA	1.81	Michigan
1983	1.28	UCLA	1.98	Illinois
1984	1.66	SC	1.44	OSU
1985	1.20	UCLA	1.63	Iowa
1986	1.37	ASU	1.46	Michigan/OSU
1987	1.58	SC/UCLA	1.55	MSU
1988	1.50	SC	1.72	Michigan
1989	1.20	SC	2.00	Michigan
1980s Ave.	*1.43*		*1.69*	
1990	1.30	Washington	1.83	Illinois/Iowa/MSU/Michigan
1991	1.80	Washington	1.66	Michigan
1992	1.31	Stanford/Washington	1.13	Michigan
1993	1.34	Arizona/SC/UCLA	1.92	OSU/Wisconsin
1994	1.49	Oregon	1.60	PSU
1995	1.70	SC/Washington	1.94	NWU
1996	1.67	ASU	2.03	NWU/OSU
1997	1.86	UCLA/WSU	2.10	Michigan
1998	2.02	UCLA	2.10	Michigan/OSU/Wisconsin
1999	1.54	Stanford	1.78	Wisconsin
1990s Ave.	*1.60*		*1.81*	
2000	1.71	Oregon/OSU/Washington	1.34	Michigan/NWU/Purdue
2001	1.90	Oregon	1.22	Illinois
2002	1.48	SC/WSU	2.00	Iowa/OSU
2003	1.31	SC	1.84	Michigan
2004	1.90	SC	1.70	Iowa/Michigan
2000s Ave.	*1.66*		*1.62*	

Sources: Pac-10 and Big Ten Web pages; www.pac-10.org and www.bigten.org.

Competitive Imbalance Remedies in College Sports

Competitive imbalance exists in college sports, and the same conclusion about pro sports appears to hold for college sports. There are different revenue potentials in different geographical territories, and successful teams collect on those higher revenues more than unsuccessful teams. Winning percent and championship imbalances follow, as we would expect. As with their pro counterparts, college conferences and their coordinating organization, the NCAA, have adopted measures to deal with revenue imbalance and competitive imbalance.

Like their pro counterparts, college conferences typically share revenues. However, their primary approach to solving competitive imbalance is through restrictions on players. Just as with pro leagues, a cursory analysis reveals that none of the restrictions on players actually have anything to do with competitive imbalance. Instead, they transfer value produced by players away from the players and toward the athletic department.

Revenue Sharing First, let's review some recent data that serve to highlight revenue sharing. Conference sharing rules cover the conference TV contract, conference tournament revenues, and post-season revenues. Table 13.13 shows the total amount of these types of revenues available for revenue sharing for major college conferences. In addition, the table shows what an equal distribution of these revenues would look like. Even if distributed evenly, as calculated in the last column of Table 13.13, there is substantial variation in shared amounts across conferences—a range of $6.4 million to $8.9 million with an average of $7.7 million. But remember, the differences among athletic departments, compared to conferences, would be magnified because revenue sharing is not equal within a conference.

Members of college conferences share local revenues generated at the gate. However, the percentages are not constant across teams, and larger-revenue market teams typically get a higher share both at home and away in the form of appearance guarantees. If anything, this type of sharing compounds competitive imbalance because it shifts larger-revenue market team marginal revenue functions down by less than it shifts small-revenue market team marginal revenue functions, as shown in Figure 13.5. In this figure, the larger-revenue market college's sharing is a smaller percentage of its revenue than the percentage shared by the smaller-revenue college. The proportion kept by the larger-revenue college is larger; that is, $\alpha < \beta$ so that the shift down for the larger-revenue market team is less than for the smaller-revenue market team. As a result, the larger-revenue market team actually wins more than it would under no sharing at all.

As stated before, college conference rules require sharing of revenues from conference TV contracts, conference championship tournaments, March Madness, and bowl games. As with local revenues, none of these actually are shared equally. Under the three-tier system, conference TV revenues are not shared in the usual sense of that word. Instead, the conference contract typically promises a minimum number of appearances for each team so that even bottom-dwellers get some TV money. Better teams appear much more often and keep a higher share of their appearance money. The TV sharing system compounds competitive imbalance because TV money is strictly allocated according to winning.

Table 13.13 Conference Distributions, 2003

Conference	Conference TV	Conference Basketball Tournament	Conference Football Tournament	March Madness	Bowls	Total Distribution	# Teams	Equal Share
ACC	49.1	5.3	—	7.6	20.5	87.6	11.0	8.0
Big East	28.0	—	—	7.3	18.7	55.4	7.0	7.9
Big Ten	62.4	3.9	—	8.9	24.7	97.8	11.0	8.9
SEC	51.0	3.5	12.0	7.9	30.7	95.7	12.0	8.0
Big 12	43.0	4.0	5.0	6.4	26.6	84.0	12.0	7.0
Pac-10	37.8	4.0	—	6.9	19.3	64.0	10.0	6.4

Source: Author's calculations from data presented in *Sports Business Journal*, December 29, 2004 (By the Numbers), p. 149. Total distributions do not match the sum of other elements due to amounts not reported in the original source.

Figure 13.5 Disproportionate Revenue Sharing

When revenues are shared disproportionately, competitive balance is harmed. If the proportion of revenues kept by larger-revenue schools is greater than that kept by smaller-revenue schools, as when $\alpha < \beta$, the result is that MR_L shifts down by less than MR_S. The result is an even higher winning percent for the larger-revenue college in the presence of disproportionate sharing than there would be without any sharing ($W_L' > W_L^*$)!

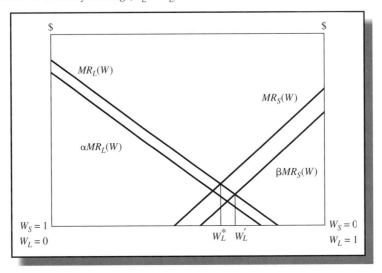

Turning to the postseason, conference championship tournament revenues are distributed equally after some traveling expenses for participants. However, nothing could be farther from the truth for March Madness and bowl game revenues. A disproportionate share of the NCAA basketball championship revenues goes to the teams that appear in the tournament, and bowl revenues are only shared after expenses. As we saw in the examples in the last section, often nothing is left after expenses, and even if some revenues are left, this is a very important reduction in sharing with the rest of the conference. Once again, shared revenue rewards are tied to winning, and the impact will be to reinforce competitive imbalance.

Player Restrictions and Competitive Balance Restrictions on players are highly touted by colleges and the NCAA as good for players and good for competitive balance. Many arguments are offered in favor of these restrictions, from paternalistic ones about caring for players to the idea that players should have a sense of obligation to the colleges that provide their scholarships. In actuality, only some of these restrictions may enhance competitive balance, but another thing is certain. They all transfer value from players to athletic departments. Because there are so many conferences and schools, it is unlikely that any joint venture aimed at restricting the choices of athletes and athletic departments would be self-enforcing. Enforcement of these restrictions is the job of the NCAA.

Recruiting Restrictions   There is no draft in college sports. However, **recruiting restrictions** preserve part of the value of talent to colleges in the same way that the draft does for pro teams. Athletic departments are restricted in how much money they can spend on recruiting and how they spend it. For example, coaches can only make a specific number of visits to any given potential recruit, and potential recruits can only make so many visits to a given university. Additionally, payment to players or anybody with influence over players is not allowed. The athletes must also comply with various restrictions on their behavior during the recruiting process.

At the end of the recruiting period, athletes must commit to a particular team on a particular date by signing a **national letter of intent**. Once signed, these letters bind a player to a particular college team. Only if that athletic department agrees (or if there is a coaching change) can a player walk away from that commitment. All of these restrictions reduce the level of compensation that goes to players and stops athletic departments from burning up the value players produce for them. As R. C. Slocum, head football coach at Texas A&M University, put it after losing a prize recruit to the Florida Marlins' lucrative contract offer, "I have a lot of rules and no money. Baseball has a lot of money and no rules" (*Sports Illustrated*, August 24, 1998, p. 20).

Interestingly, many believe that these recruiting restrictions create a level playing field that enables poorer athletic departments to compete with richer ones for talent. Nothing could be farther from the truth. Instead, these restrictions entrench power at departments at the top end of the winning percent distribution. Imagine two colleges, A and B. College A provides a better education and a better chance at a shot at the pros than college B. All else constant, competitive recruiting finds college A getting better talent than B—it is a no-brainer for athletes to choose the college that provides more of both opportunities. In such a case, the only way that college B might be able to entice recruits is with other types of compensation.

In this case, what happens when restrictions are put in place? Some of the ways that college B might compete are eliminated. Even if they wanted to try to "recruit harder" than college A, they are restricted from doing so. College B cannot win under this system, so why do they stand for it? The reason this system persists is that players' contributions to some teams' values are preserved, and richer teams share (albeit unequally) with weaker teams through conference revenue sharing. Quite simply, it pays to live under these restrictions even though there may be a chance for some teams to be better without the restrictions. Because stronger teams have an advantage under recruiting restrictions, such restrictions cannot increase competitive balance.

Restrictions on Player Movement   College players are not free to move and play elsewhere after they sign their letter of intent. They cannot move between teams without forfeiting an entire year of eligibility unless they move to a lower division. Having to sit out a year is a huge cost to college players, so most of them stay put.

Because players cannot be traded in college sports, **sit-out restrictions** definitely affect competitive balance. Unless all players choose the college where they are most valuable, without error, then some colleges get better players than they would be able to keep in a system where players either are free to move between teams or could be traded. Because they do not pay their athletes, athletic departments get to keep the benefits of mobility restrictions.

We would expect the impact of players selecting the wrong school to have an asymmetric effect. Strong programs will not

Did You Know?
Of all the restrictions on players administered by the NCAA, only the sit-out restriction actually may enhance competitive balance.

accept weak recruits, so the only errors that can happen there involve which strong team strong players choose. However, weak programs will certainly accept strong players who err in their consideration of where to play. Thus, restrictions on player movement enhance competitive balance as strong players who mistakenly select teams of lower quality enhance the quality of those lower quality teams.

The second type of restriction on college player movement concerns players trying their chances in the pro draft. In all college sports except baseball, players who declare their entry into the draft must **forfeit remaining playing eligibility**. This dampens players' incentive to enter the draft and keeps some players earning revenue streams for their athletic departments longer than they otherwise would. But because this restriction only helps maintain restricted mobility, it cannot enhance competitive balance. The players were already stuck with their team to begin with, and forfeiting eligibility just keeps them there longer across all of college sports.

Competitive Balance Impacts of the NCAA Amateur Requirement Through the NCAA, athletic departments impose an **amateur requirement** on college athletes. Athletes may not take pay for their sport. Instead, players are compensated with what is called a full tuition grant (in some sports, only partial tuition grants are allowed). Their tuition is paid, plus the calculated amount for room and board and books. In addition, they can obtain limited need-based grants and can earn no more than $2,000 working in the off-season. From an economic perspective, the amateur requirement quite simply is a salary cap (we will discuss this thoroughly in the next section). It should come as no surprise that the cap is chosen so that the actual level of compensation just equals the opportunity cost of players who can make it into college—essentially, tuition, room and board, and books. (See Byers [1995] for details on the evolution of this system.)

Clearly, the amateur requirement cannot enhance competitive balance. The full tuition grant cap is higher at colleges with higher tuition. Thus, those colleges have a talent recruiting advantage along this dimension. The source of this recruiting advantage is that higher tuition typically signals higher quality of education and degree value. Because the cap imposed by the NCAA amateur rules does not impose equal spending by all athletic departments (i.e., there is no minimum requirement), this cannot improve competitive balance. Finally, as with all caps, players make less than they would in a competitive system.

Enforcement Problems and the NCAA

The NCAA was invented to enforce the rules designed by member colleges. All of the restrictions on players are carried out through rules that must be enforced on individual athletic departments. Because there is a value to violating the rules, especially if all other schools follow them, the NCAA has an enforcement problem.

The Logic of Cheating Suppose that colleges agree not to pay athletes and codify this agreement in NCAA rules. If all the teams follow the agreement, but one college breaks the bargain and pays athletes, it will gain a talent advantage that generates additional television appearances and postseason play. Because **cheating on NCAA rules** can be worth millions of dollars, we should expect cheating to occur unless expected sanctions prevent colleges from doing so.

If all cheat, the value of the NCAA agreement is completely undone, and all teams are worse off because nobody gains any advantage from an amateur requirement. Colleges would no longer keep the money that now is spent by all teams on players. Ultimately, fans who cherish the amateur aspect of college athletics would be betrayed if players were paid. Therefore, colleges must be able to monitor each other, preempt cheating, and punish the offending athletic department if cheating is found.

James Quirk and I (1997) analyzed cheating with the following simple model. Let P denote the probability of getting caught cheating on NCAA rules. G is the gain achieved, and L is the loss under NCAA sanctions if caught. The expected value of cheating is

$$EV = (1 - P)G - PL$$

Although simple, this expression helps organize some thoughts about whom to expect to cheat.

First, cheating is more likely the lower P or L is and the higher G is. Those with high potential gains from additional winning are most likely to have higher gains, G, from cheating. These likely cheaters might have low winning percents, large unused stadium capacity, and large potential, but low actual gate and TV revenue. Possible losses if caught cheating, L, are largest for the most successful programs (lucrative TV values, wealthy donors, perennial postseason play). Cheating would be less likely for older established coaches, whereas younger coaches trying to build a team would be more likely to cheat. If P were the same for all colleges, then a program with a currently weak record and high potential for financial gain with a young coach would be a prime suspect.

Because all of the cheating opportunities concern paying athletes, the NCAA enforces the recruiting restrictions and amateur imposition among member conferences. *Sports Illustrated* (November 11, 1993, p. 96) reported that USC basketball coach George Raveling once sent 900 letters to the home of a single recruit in 2 weeks. Although this seems trivial and was well within the NCAA recruiting rules at the time, it points out some of the problems confronting the NCAA.

The Verdict on Cheating and Enforcement   Like all crime analyses, ultimately we only have observations about those cheaters who are caught. Care must be exercised in extending any findings based on actual violations and sanctions because those violations that are not caught may be quite different from those that are. However, some analysis of NCAA enforcement and sanctions has been conducted, and the results are insightful.

Fleisher, Goff, and Tollison (1992) found that "crime pays," so that violators had higher revenues and profits, but they also noted that athletic departments monitor each other's activities. So apparently some athletic departments find value in aiding the NCAA. It is also in the university's interest to watch for cheating in its own athletic department, as donations to academics appear to decline for colleges hit with NCAA sanctions (Grimes and Chressanthis, 1994). This may help explain why athletic departments often turn themselves in and suggest their own punishment.

Padilla and Baumer (1994) also found that programs with a history of violations had higher revenues and profits than those that were "clean." However, they also noted that the negative impacts of sanctions on programs did not seem to last long.

In a related vein concerning the pattern of punishment, Zimbalist (1999, p. 179) noted that the number of infractions detected has risen steadily over the decades from the 1950s to the 1990s, but the pattern of punishment has eased over time. The length of probation has risen from the decade of the 1970s to the 1990s (from 1.11 to 1.73 years), but the length of prohibitions on postseason play has fallen since the 1960s (from .85 to .49 years). Further, the length of prohibitions on TV appearances (implying reduced TV revenues) has fallen steadily from the decade of the 1950s to the 1990s (from .73 to .14 years).

Another interesting finding on NCAA enforcement concerns whether it even has had the desired effect of leveling the playing field. In essence, warts and all, does NCAA investigation and punishment improve competitive balance? According to Depken and Wilson (2004a), a sophisticated view of how athletic directors respond to the success of NCAA enforcement activity suggests enhanced competitive balance. If a higher share of departments are caught cheating, the remaining athletic directors would decrease cheating because the chances of being caught have increased. Competitive balance would increase. Depken and Wilson find just such a result on a sample of major college programs.

Did You Know?

If you just look at NCAA enforcement impacts on individual programs, these efforts appear ineffectual. But there is evidence that NCAA enforcement does enhance competitive balance.

So if one looks at the measurable impacts on athletic departments, there is cause for pessimism about NCAA enforcement. Zimbalist (1999) concludes, "In short, the NCAA enforcement apparatus is ineffectual. . . . Businesses do not usually punish themselves for doing good business" (p. 181). On this same issue, Noll (1991) offers the following, "Cheating against the NCAA rules will continue—indeed, increase—because it is the profit-maximizing strategy for nearly all universities and the income-maximizing strategy for coaches" (p. 198). But if one looks at the outcome on competitive balance, there is cause for optimism in the Depken and Wilson findings.

THE VALUE OF COLLEGE SPORTS TALENT

As in pro sports, marginal revenue product (MRP) is the primary concern when discussing the value of college sports talent. A common question at many universities is why the team cannot become more competitive. Why doesn't the athletic department just go out and hire a million-dollar coach and build state-of-the-art facilities? Better recruiting and an improved team would surely follow.

These questions echo those from Chapter 4 by those dissatisfied with the level of team quality chosen by pro owners. The answer to these questions boils down to the same comparisons at the margin that are made by pro team owners. What good is hiring a million-dollar coach or pouring millions into facilities if enough revenues cannot be generated to cover their costs?

In this section we will examine the value generated by sports talent. First, the MRP idea will be presented for college athletes along with an analysis of the value of restricting payment below MRP. Second, we will examine some estimates of what

college athletes' MRPs actually are, compared to their lev...
we will touch on the play-for-pay issue. Finally, we will ad...
college sports, primarily, gender issues in student-athlete oppor... sation. Third,
hiring for coaches.   ·ination in
                                                                     ·ay and

What Is the Value of Restricting Player Compensation?

MRP theory provides important insight into the value of college players. Players c...
tribute to winning outcomes for their team, that is, their marginal product (*MP*). The
athletic department is able to sell that contribution to generate marginal revenue (*MR*).
As was the case with pro players, the MRP of college players is equal to $MP \times MR$.

In pro sports, players are paid in cash. In college sports, athletes receive a full
tuition grant. It is possible that the value of this type of compensation to college
athletes approximates their MRP, but it is also possible that it does not, especially
for star college players who may contribute significantly to athletic department
revenues. If the latter is the case, then value is created for the athletic department
by the amateur requirement.

The Economics of Amateurism   Amateur requirements, simply put, reduce
payment to players by definition. Historian Ronald A. Smith (1988) emphasized that
the implementation of amateurism and the restriction of player movements were
driving forces behind early NCAA actions. These restrictions have evolved over time
and continue almost untouched today. The NCAA has enforced the extraction of
the value of player talent for nearly 90 years.

In practice, recruiting restrictions reduce payments to players as they enter college sports. In the absence of such restrictions, the history of pro scouting suggests
that players would be paid to sign with college teams. Once players have signed their
letters of intent, mobility restrictions also reduce payments to players. If players were
free to seek their highest-valued alternative, they might move about a bit between
teams. That they cannot means that they are not free to pursue higher-valued alternatives. These values, denied to athletes, do not just go away, and they are not given
back to the ultimate source of the funds—the fans who buy tickets and advertised
products. Athletic departments keep the money.

Graphical Analysis of the Value of Amateurism to Athletic Departments   Let's
explore the value of amateurism a little further. Suppose that a competitive market
for college players existed, just as it does for pro players. In such a setting, players
are recruited and hired to play for college teams. Once in college sports, they are free
to move from one team to another. Further, imagine a two-team college conference
with a larger-revenue college and a smaller-revenue college. This situation results in
a "free-agent" college player market shown in Figure 13.6.

Figure 13.6 shows the competitive equilibrium outcome for a two-team college
conference. The equilibrium price of talent is *P**, and the level of winning percents is
$W_L^* = 1 - W_S^*$. What is it worth to athletic directors to reduce the payment to talent? First,
we need to recognize that there is a next-best opportunity available to athletes. Suppose
the opportunity cost outside the sport is *N*. If teams acting together through the NCAA
can reduce the price paid to *N*, they get to keep the rest. Talent bills are reduced to the

the price of college talent would be determined by $P^* = MR_S = MR_L$.
$1 - W_S^*$. The value of immobilizing college talent comes from reducing
Figure 13.6 ng the going price of talent to the level of college athletes' next-best alterna-
In a competit then reduces spending on talent. The reduction for the larger-market college
Winning w whereas the reduction for the smaller-market college is $(P^* - N)^* W_S^*$.
alterna
tive
i

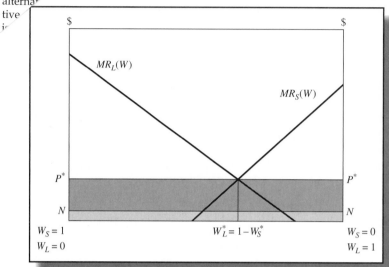

much smaller shaded areas, and the league keeps the amount shown by the top shaded
rectangle, namely, $(P^* - N) \times (W_L^* + W_S^*)$. (Note that this savings is actually $P^* - N$
because the summed winning percents are equal to 1 for a two-team league.)

The College Version of the Invariance Principle   We gain an extremely important
insight from our analysis of Figure 13.6. The largest possible amount that athletic directors can keep is generated when the distribution of talent between the two teams is such
that $MR_L = MR_S$. At any other outcome than $W_L^* = 1 - W_S^*$, the price of talent would
have to be lower so that the total area would be less than under the price P^*. Therefore,
if the athletic directors want to make as much as possible from players, both directors
want to play at their revenue-maximizing level and hire the revenue-maximizing level
of talent. Thus, the level of college athletic talent hired and its distribution between the
two teams in this conference is the same regardless of whether amateurism is imposed.

This is our old friend from Chapter 8, Rottenberg's invariance principle. Let's state
the **college version of the invariance principle** clearly:

> The distribution of talent in a college sport is invariant to who gets the
> revenues generated by players; talent moves to its highest valued use in
> the sport whether players or athletic directors receive players' MRPs.

Athletic directors and NCAA executives alike argue that competitive balance would
be harmed if competition were to dictate college player compensation. However, the
invariance principle suggests that competitive balance is invariant as to who gets to
keep the MRP of players. Under the amateur requirement, players simply earn less
but go to the same schools they would otherwise choose.

What Is the MRP of College Players?

The MRP of college stars can be quite high. You already have some insight into this idea if you recall our earlier example of the WSU Cougars and their 1998 Rose Bowl appearance. In that year, revenues rose $2.9 million for the WSU athletic department. Even though football is a team sport, it is reasonable to say that most of this value was created by star quarterback Ryan Leaf. Leaf already had an MRP even if the Cougars did not go to the Rose Bowl. However, because revenues rose $2.9 million with the WSU Rose Bowl appearance, Leaf's MRP was at least $2 to $3 million.

Economist's Estimates of MRP   Following Scully's procedure laid out in Chapter 7, Brown and Jewell (2004) estimated that a star football player could have generated about $406,914 for his athletic department for the 1995–1996 season. On average, net of the tuition paid to the university (remember, universities bill the athletic department for the full scholarship cost), they estimate that the athletic department extracted close to $400,000 of this amount (that's $492,000, adjusted to 2004 dollars). Turning to basketball, these economists estimate that many star college players are easily worth $871,310 and could be worth up to $1,283,000 to their athletic departments. Again, after tuition and other support, athletic departments could easily extract $1 million from these athletes (or about $1.2 million in 2004 dollars).

Did You Know?
Economic estimates put the marginal revenue product of star players in football at over $400,000 and in basketball at over $1 million.

Roger Noll (1991) reached a similar conclusion. He noted that quarterback John Paye was the only major roster difference on the Stanford football team in 1987. Revenues increased by $200,000 for the 1987 season. Net of the scholarship payment to the university of around $17,000 per year, the athletic department kept about 92 percent of Paye's value. In 2004 dollars, that's $330,000 and surely in the ballpark compared to the estimates by Brown and Jewell.

The clear conclusion is that star athletes are not paid anything near their marginal revenue product. This does not mean that all college athletes receive less in compensation than they contribute to athletic department revenues. For example, nonscholarship football players probably earn close to their value, namely, close to zero. For some players, the in-kind value of their full tuition grant comes close to their contribution. But star players do receive far less than the dollar value of their full tuition grant.

What If Competition Ruled the College Player Market?

If competition ruled the market for college players rather than colleges working through the NCAA, there would be no amateur requirement, no recruiting restrictions, and players would be free to move between teams subject to any contractual obligations with their current college team. The absence of an amateur requirement would mean that players would be free to negotiate whatever compensation arrangement was mutually agreeable to them and their university. For some players, the current scholarship arrangement might suffice. For others, it would not.

Few topics evoke the same level of gut-reaction disapproval than **play for pay**, that is, paying salaries to college players in addition to, or instead of, full tuition grants. Economists have commented on this issue for nearly 20 years (Gary Becker in *Business Week*, September 30, 1985, p. 18; Robert E. McCormick in *Wall Street Journal*, August 20, 1985, p. 27), and it is a hot topic even today. Here we will use our model of a competitive player market to make two important observations about implementing an economically competitive college player market. We will then address a few of the arguments against doing so.

Implications from the Theory on Amateurism
Our theoretical development of the amateur requirement yields two important observations about play for pay. First, money that is currently kept by the athletic department would flow back to players, although the amount would be no more than player MRP dictates. Returning to Figure 13.6, the shaded area defined by a competitive price, P^*, would go back to players but no more than that. Thus, denizens of the athletic department would have less and players would have more, but no more product would be created or lost.

The second observation from Figure 13.6 is that the level of talent hired by different colleges would not change if players earned the competitive rate, P^*, rather than something less. Again, in Figure 13.6, talent choices so that $W_L^* = 1 - W_S^*$ were the ones that generated the most money for redistribution away from players in the first place. Further, that level of talent choice by each college is the level of quality that makes athletic departments as successful as possible. This is just a restatement of the invariance principle. The distribution of college talent is invariant to who gets to keep player MRP. With these two observations, let's have a look at some of the arguments against play for pay.

Topical Arguments Against Play for Pay
If you think that college players should not be paid more than their current level of compensation, you are in the majority. Surveys have revealed that nearly 64 percent of those polled were against play for pay (*Sporting News*, April 18, 1994, p. 54). Let's look at the four main arguments against play for pay and make of them what we can from an economic perspective.

Where Will the Money Come From?   One argument against play for pay is that athletic departments barely break even in the first place, as shown in Table 13.1. A few make money, mostly on football and men's basketball, but not the vast majority. So where will the money to pay players come from?

This argument is confused for two reasons. First, it really is not the case that athletic departments break even in any meaningful sense of that term. Universities allow athletic departments to spend all excess revenues on an updated basis during any given budget period. Thus, a department whose costs do not rise over budgeted amounts but whose revenues are higher than expected will appear to break even because it is allowed to spend the excess. So there can be plenty of revenue to be rearranged.

The second confusion is that one does not need to worry where the money will come from because it is already there. Under the current amateur requirements, players generate their MRP. And athletic departments collect it from boosters, sponsors, and media providers. Athletes see some of it but the amateur requirement reduces compensation below this MRP, especially for star players.

But competition is relentless; the next most valuable use for these funds is where the money will be spent. Likely candidates are athletic department salaries, coaches' salaries, recruiting expenses, and facility investment. So player MRP does not go away, it is just spent elsewhere in the athletic department rather than on players. If players were paid their MRP, funds currently spent elsewhere in the athletic department budget would just be reallocated to players. The money is already there.

Athletic director compensation is an interesting case in point. Athletic director salaries (not including other compensation) in the Big 12 Conference range from $163,000 at Oklahoma State to $420,000 at Kansas University (rockymountainnews.com, accessed March 28, 2005). In 1984, the athletic director at Kansas earned $60,000 in salary, or about $108,000 adjusted to 2004 dollars. That implies a real annual growth rate of 4.2 percent, about 1.4 times the typical growth rate in the U.S. economy. No doubt this type of growth partly covers the fact that the job is very demanding. But it also includes portions of the increase that fans are willing to spend to watch college athletes who do not receive their MRP.

At the main College Park campus of the University of Maryland, the head basketball coach is guaranteed $1.3 million and the head football coach $1.1 million (www.baltimoresun.com, accessed April 28, 2004). Maryland's governor is paid $140,000, the chancellor of the University of Maryland system is paid $375,000, and the president at the main College Park campus is paid $357,999. Once again, college coaching is a demanding job. But fierce competition also leads athletic directors to spend portions of the growth in MRP produced by players procuring top coaches.

Won't Non-Revenue-Generating Sports Be Harmed, Especially Women's Sports? The argument that play for pay would harm non-revenue-generating sports recognizes that the money that would go to players under play for pay would come from other parts of the athletic department. But the argument conveniently avoids a complete list of sources within the athletic department. Setting the argument in this way pits play for pay against allocations to *other sports* in the athletic department but not against administrative salaries, coaches' salaries, recruiting, and facilities. Opponents of play for pay forecast dire consequences for low-revenue sports. A common fear is that the ability of the high-revenue sports, typically football and men's basketball, to support the rest would be reduced. This fear is especially worrisome to those supporting gender equity if the high-revenue sports are supporting women's sports (actually, they aren't, but more on that below).

So the clue to the confusion here is in the way the argument sets revenue sports against so-called non-revenue-generating sports but omits all of the other lines in the athletic department budget from consideration. If the world changed to play for pay, where would play for pay funds come from? The answer, of course, is from those areas that currently are overpaid relative to their actual MRP. Suppose it is other men's sports that are currently overpaid. This would mean that prior to play for pay, the athletic director was investing in those sports at a higher rate than their MRP would support. The same goes for women's sports, with one additional feature. Federal and state laws require spending to ensure gender equity; therefore the athletic director would spend on women's sports until that margin was met. The athletic director would have no reason to wastefully overspend on either men's or women's sports.

If athletic directors cut a sport or reduce spending on a sport, they are cutting their department's net revenue position. If sports are cut or reduced, the success of the department falls below the best level the athletic department can obtain. Athletic directors might wish they could rearrange money in this fashion, and they may use such threats to try to sway others against play for pay, but that option simply is not believable. At least it is not believable as long as athletic directors care about the bottom line of their department.

This suggests that the portion of player MRP that goes to athletic departments under NCAA amateur requirements goes mostly to salaries, recruiting, and facilities. Some would say that salaries are just a market outcome and that there is nothing that colleges can do about it. On this issue, Duke University law professor John Weistart cuts to the heart of the matter:

> It is sometimes suggested that the coaches' high incomes are simply the product of natural market forces. But the market in which coaches function is neither free nor natural. It is more likely that college coaches are able to receive their extraordinary rewards because potential competitors are tightly constrained. Most important, star players are absolutely prohibited from claiming any of the commercial value of their athletic achievement. (*Wall Street Journal*, September 11, 1992, p. A12)

The clear corollary is that if athletic department administrators and coaches had to compete for salary in a play-for-pay world, there simply would be less money around to bid up their salaries.

Figure 13.7 depicts the department's willingness to pay for salaries. Under NCAA amateur requirements and when all sports are operated close to their MRP, the athletic department's willingness to pay for coaches and administrators includes an amount that would otherwise be payments to athletes. This is portrayed as the MRP + Extraction function in Figure 13.7. In a play-for-pay world, players would be paid what is currently extracted from them under NCAA rules. This means that the willingness to pay for coaches and administrators would fall back to the MRP function in Figure 13.7. As a result, pay to these other inputs would fall, and less of those services would be purchased. Market forces that now send payments that otherwise would go to players to coaches and administrators would reduce payments to those same coaches and administrators. Nobel Prize winning economist Gary Becker sums it up well:

> Why should the viability of athletic programs depend on what amounts to subsidies from athletes, rather than on such resources as larger gifts from alumni, higher tuition from students, bigger subsidies from tax-payers, or higher ticket prices for spectators? . . . The NCAA's efforts to justify its restrictions on competition for athletes should be viewed with suspicion because they increase the financial benefits colleges receive from football, basketball, and other sports. (*Business Week*, September 30, 1985, p. 18)

Figure 13.7 Play for Pay and Coaching/Administrative Services

When athletes are not paid, what would have been their payment accrues to coaches and administrators. The higher MRP represents this case because it includes extraction of value from athletes. If players were paid, that extra value would no longer go to coaches and administrators. The MRP of coaches and administrators would fall to the lower function. The level of their services hired and their wages would follow the arrows.

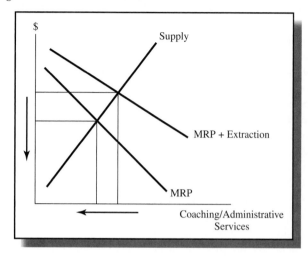

Won't Wealthy Athletic Departments Just Buy All the Best Players? In a play-for-pay world, some argue that wealthy schools would buy the best players. The idea behind this argument is that rich, successful athletic departments would be able to outbid their competitors for athletic talent and would buy up all the top-quality players. The result, according to this argument, would be competitive imbalance that would ruin college sports for fans. Fans of all but the top teams would lose interest, and their teams would suffer even further revenue declines. Ultimately, those colleges might simply drop out of Division IA. Fans at all but a few colleges would be as bad off as they possibly could be.

There is a single response to this misunderstanding—Rottenberg's invariance principle. As our theory shows, there is one and only one winning percent combination that makes all teams in the conference as well off as they can possibly be. If the teams in a conference are not at that combination, players already go to the athletic departments where they are most highly valued. This means that the richer, stronger schools already get the bulk of the most talented players. Play for pay will not change the distribution of talent because talent already is distributed in a way that generates the best bottom line for athletic departments. Coupled with our answer to the last question, play for pay would just make coaches and administrators in athletic departments poorer, but talent would still be distributed in approximately the same way.

Won't Different Players in Different Sports Be Paid Differently (Especially Women)? Another argument against play for pay rests on an inescapable observation about markets and pay: People are paid different amounts. The issue raised by this question is the usual one of the fairness of such an outcome. How can differential payment to athletes be fair? Also, in an era where departments are striving for gender equity, how can it be fair to pay those in revenue-producing sports, primarily men, more than those playing non-revenue-generating sports, primarily women?

In a play-for-pay world, there would be differential pay. Players would be paid just enough more than their second highest college sport MRP to keep them at their current school. Because $MRP = MP \times MR$, players will be paid differently if either their contribution to team success (MP) is different from that of other team members or if fans are willing to pay different amounts for the contribution to winning by different players (MR). Therefore, we would expect that quarterbacks would be paid more than second-string offensive linemen. Figure 13.1 speaks directly to the difference in pay between men's and women's sports. The figure shows that a sample of undergraduate students was willing to pay more for men's basketball than for women's basketball. This difference in willingness to pay would certainly result in higher payment for men's team members.

The argument against differential pay is one of fairness. However, in debates on differential pay, nobody argues that people should not be paid at all. Besides, even if you want a fairer way of paying players, then you still want them to be paid. In short, different people are paid different amounts in all employment markets. College sports would be no different. Again, coaches and administrators would see their pay reduced under play for pay, but it is hard to imagine that any athlete can be worse off if all are getting paid (albeit different amounts).

Enough Already! They're Already Given a Free Education The final argument against play for pay centers on the fact that scholarship athletes are given a subsidized chance to earn the future income returns and quality of life that go along with a college education. Some judge that to be more than enough. In addition, a select few are given the chance to pursue the mammoth incomes earned by professional athletes. However, this argument has two shortcomings.

The first shortcoming is that some (I repeat, *some*) athletes do not value the educational component of their time spent in college very highly. This irritates many people who hold a college education in high regard. However, the preferences of athletes cannot be invalidated just because some observers wish they had a greater appreciation for their educational opportunity. In fact, as with all things, the value of this type of payment is an entirely subjective exercise. Because it is value received that matters when discussing compensation, the athletes are the only persons who can know the value of their individual scholarships. This means that for some athletes compensation in the form of educational opportunity is worth little.

This actually is what drives some of the fortunate few players to leave early, declaring themselves eligible for professional drafts before they run out of college eligibility. They simply assess the additional value of staying in school, including their personal assessment of the value of education, versus the value of moving on to the pro level. Roger G. Noll of Stanford University showed, in the Learning Highlight: Investing in an Athletic Career (Chapter 7), it can certainly pay to invest in a shot at the pros by playing college sports. The simple corollary is that it can also pay to take that reward before finishing an education. It also is clear that this logic confronts players who do value their education highly as well.

"You're asking a player who has a chance to make money he never had before—a young, desperate, black male —to stay at a school that can't really help me out as much as I can help myself? That's ludicrous. I may be young, but I'm not stupid." —Stanford University All-American offensive lineman Bob Whitfield as he left early for the NFL in 1992

Here is a quote from another person from Stanford, All-American offensive lineman Bob Whitfield (*Sports Illustrated*, May 4, 1992, p. 78). "You're asking a player who has a chance to make money he never had before—a young, desperate, black male—to stay at a school that can't really help me out as much as I can help myself? That's ludicrous. I may be young, but I'm not stupid." Whitfield left Stanford early and was chosen eighth overall in the 1992 NFL draft by Atlanta. His career lasted 14 years, including 12 straight years with Atlanta, where he missed only one game from 1993 to 2001. The Pro-Bowler earned (2004 dollars) over $2 million in 8 of those years and also earned a high of $3.8 million in 2000. Data on his NFL compensation only run from 1995 to 2004, but in that time he earned a total of $28.7 million (again, adjusted to 2004 dollars).

Now, only Whitfield knows how much his education was worth, and not all players necessarily assess their pro potential correctly. But apparently for Whitfield, finishing even a prestigious and economically valuable Stanford degree couldn't compare to these types of earnings plus his enjoyment from competing at the professional level. The value of an education is a subjective thing even for those not as fortunate as Whitfield.

A second shortcoming to the argument that an education is sufficient compensation is that some athletes contribute more revenue to the athletic department than the value of their scholarships. As we saw earlier in this chapter, the MRP of star athletes can be between $400,000 and $1 million (and possibly more at times). Players do receive compensation, but it can be much lower than their MRP. In this context, arguing that athletes are paid enough is now a value judgment, and any person is free to pass such judgments. But consider this: Do you think that you should be paid your MRP at your job, even though you might be willing to work for less if you had to?

Postscript: Why Don't College Athletes Just Organize?

In the face of monolithic owners determined to extract the MRP of players, professional athletes organized under the labor laws of the U.S. and Canada (Chapter 9). College athletes face the same monolithic approach by athletic departments through their enforcement arm, the NCAA. So why don't college athletes organize or at least challenge the amateur requirement in court? The answer actually is quite simple. To date, courts have typically decided that college athletes are not employees of their institutions and labor law only guarantees the rights of employees to organize. This also affects their standing to sue in the court system. Until athletes are employees, they will have to be satisfied with the access to the process that they currently have—an advisory role granted by NCAA and efforts to organize outside the protection of the labor laws (see the Learning Highlight: The College Athletic Revolution?).

LEARNING HIGHLIGHT
The College Athletic Revolution?

One way to think about college athletes is as full-time students who have full-time jobs in order to cover the costs of attending their university. The NCAA has an official limit of 20 practice hours per week. Including Saturdays for a 6-day week, that's 3 hours and 20 minutes per day. But Division IA athletes typically also have many hours per week in other "suggested" sport-related activities and also travel extensively during their season. It's easy to see how this is a full-time job. Further, these days it is a year-round activity; outside of their season all athletes attend "voluntary" workout sessions and other activities.

Now, the full cost of attendance may be higher, but suppose tuition, room and board, and books for an in-state student-athlete are about $8,000. Further, suppose the same coverage for a nonresident is about $12,000. At the NCAA limit of 20 hours, for a full year resident athletes would earn about $7.69 per hour and nonresidents about $11.54 per hour. But if athletes spend fully 40 hours per week on their sports, the numbers drop to $3.85 and $5.77 per hour for resident and nonresident athletes, respectively. This latter case clearly violates the minimum wage laws in effect in every state in the country. For this, a very few athletes will have pro chances in addition to their education, but the vast majority are just like their nonathlete counterparts. The education is what they get for their toil (plus the satisfaction of competing).

Now picture this: The fans in the arena and watching on TV wait breathlessly for the college basketball national championship game to begin, but the CBPA (College Basketball Players Association) has not reached an agreement with the NCAA on seasonal wage structures or the share of postseason revenues that will go to players (perhaps they've seen Table 13.7). In protest, the CPBA brings a work stoppage and there is no NCAA championship that year.

Of course, there is no CPBA. Unlike their professional counterparts, college athletes have not organized themselves in any meaningful way to offset the power their athletic departments have over them. Why haven't college athletes organized? Technically, the answer is that athletes are not employees, so labor laws do not apply and their right to organize is not guaranteed. If athletes want to organize, they must do it without the protections afforded by labor law.

The obstacles are many. The usual obstacles to organization apply, such as educating the athletes, overcoming organization costs and free riding, and ultimately winning something for the membership. There is good reason to suspect these obstacles to be difficult to overcome. Remember we are talking about people who do not reach the age of majority until well into their college careers. In addition, they have stars in their eyes; they finally have their college shot and might be reluctant to "rock the boat" (remember the Learning Highlight: Pro Athletes as "Company Men" back in Chapter 9).

Further, without the protection of labor law, the history of those who organize labor suggests that retribution would be expected. Indeed, athletic scholarships at most major colleges have become an annually renewable affair. In some cases, coaches have pressured athletes to give up their scholarships. In a survey that deserves to be run again (*Sporting News*, April 25, 1994, p. 50), 25 percent of juniors and seniors stated that their coaches had threatened to terminate their scholarships.

However, despite these obstacles, athletes are organizing. Formed in January 2001 by a group of former UCLA football players, the

Collegiate Athletes Coalition (CAC) is backed by the United Steelworkers of America. Rather than wages and shares of postseason contracts, the CAC seeks much more modest benefits. They seek year-round medical coverage (not just during the season), insurance coverage above student policy minimums, scholarships at the full cost of attendance (typically adding around $2,000 annually), and more flexibility to earn money during the off-season (currently, the NCAA limits such earnings to $2,000).

As Stanford All-American guard Casey Jacobsen put it, "We feel that because of the success of our sport and all the money that's being generated, we want to see more of it coming back to us." But to pull it off may take something like a strategic hold-out at a crucial time, like the NCAA Final Four. It is understandable that college athletes might not find the costs worth the benefits.

The chances that college players will ever bring a work stoppage are slim to none.

Sources: Sports Illustrated, November 23, 1992, p. 124; *Seattle Times*, April 25, 1995, p. L1; Jack Scott, *The Athletic Revolution* (New York: Free Press, 1971); *Sports Business Journal*, January 29, 2001, p. 23; ESPN.com, May 21, 2001.

A SYNOPSIS OF REMAINING ISSUES

A litany of issues remain, including race and sex discrimination, subsidies and economic impact assessment for college sports, stadium issues, and the relationship between government and the college sports business concerning taxes and market power. Because the economic insights are a bit broader for two of these, we'll pay particular attention to gender discrimination under Title IX and government relations. But let's note the following in passing.

Pay differences for college coaches appear to be mostly explained by differences in revenue potential across men's and women's sports (Humphreys, 2000). Where women's sports are extremely successful, coaches of the women's teams have been paid more than their male counterparts. *The Racial and Gender Report Card*, cited heavily in Chapter 7, reports on college sports as well as pro. In the 2003 edition, it is clear that women and minorities are underrepresented in upper administration, especially at the level of athletic director.

Not much work has been done on the size of the subsidies paid to college sports, but there is work on economic impact assessment for major college sports events. As we would expect given our coverage in Chapter 10, economic activity value estimates for college sports and events appear grossly overstated (Baade and Matheson, 2004). But there are consumers' surpluses and externality values from the construction of college facilities worth a few million dollars (Johnson and Whitehead, 2000). Further work on surpluses and externalities will prove enlightening.

Finally, it isn't clear whether there is a college equivalent of a stadium mess (Chapter 11). Athletic departments appear not to be constrained by the university as long as they build within the means of their booster supporters through fund raising activities. But it is clear that athletic departments are seeking more lavish surroundings for their fans in attendance in order to capture higher revenue streams. I find *Street & Smith's Sports Business Journal* a wonderful resource on college stadium issues.

Economic Insights into Discrimination Policy in College Sports: Title IX

"No person in the United States shall, on the basis of sex, be excluded from participation in, or denied the benefits of, or be subjected to discrimination under any educational program or activity receiving Federal financial assistance. . . ." —Title IX of the Educational Amendments of 1972

Title IX of the Educational Amendments of 1972 (**Title IX** for short) recognizes that discrimination is much more than just a pay or hiring problem. It is also about access. Title IX states, "No person in the United States shall, on the basis of sex, be excluded from participation in, or denied the benefits of, or be subjected to discrimination under any educational program or activity receiving Federal financial assistance. . . ." Because almost all schools receive federal funds, Title IX applies to nearly all education institutions.

The change mandated by Title IX has been slow in coming, and participation gaps still remain. Spending parity isn't required under Title IX, but relative spending on men's and women's sports is one index of equality. The example of the major universities in my own state in Table 13.9 is representative of Title IX outcomes across college sports. In Table 13.9, three things are quite clear concerning relative spending. First, the amount of money spent on football swamps all other considerations. But so do football revenues. This gives rise to an interesting debate (covered next) about whether football subsidizes other sports, including women's sports. Second, in terms of revenues generated, women's sports pale in comparison; men's sports generate 8.7 times and 11.9 times the revenue of women's sports at Washington State and Washington, respectively. Third, the athletic department at Washington State spends twice as much on men's sports, and the multiple at Washington is 2.5. Interestingly, the two departments spend almost identical shares of total revenue on women's sports, about 18 percent.

Even 30 years after the passage of Title IX, equity remains elusive. Inequality has evolved over a long time, and very well established interest groups like the way that money has traditionally been spent. Boosters, athletic directors, and coaches all are doing quite nicely under the traditional arrangement. It should come as no surprise that the shriek is clearly audible when university presidents, who fear reductions in their federal funds, require athletic directors to meet the requirements of Title IX. Addressing some of the arguments against Title IX helps to clarify why this remains the case.

Won't Gender Equity Gains Harm Football and Kill Minor Men's Sports?

The main justification for how slow institutions have been to respond to the requirements of Title IX follows a line of logic that is practically a perfect echo of arguments against play for pay. Athletic administrators argue that they barely break even as it is. Therefore, to pay for gender equity, either non-revenue-generating men's programs will have to suffer or revenues will have to come out of men's revenue sports, primarily football. Some argue diverting money from football could so weaken the ability of the football program to continue to prosper and subsidize other sports that all of the sports at any college could be worse off.

It is true that on occasion non-revenue-generating men's sports have been cut. In one notable case, the University of Kansas athletic department cut men's swimming and tennis to stay in the black, saving about $600,000 per year and reducing participation by 50 male athletes (*Sports Business Journal*, March 12, 2001, p. 20). Among the reasons cited for the cuts were increasing scholarship costs, a 115 percent increase in team travel costs for the other sports, and increases in coaches' and administrators' salaries. The Kansas athletic department also noted that the cuts were made in order to meet gender equity requirements; cutting men's sports may free some funds to spend on women's sports, and the arithmetic of increasing the ratio of women is obvious if participation by men is reduced.

But do these cuts happen because athletic directors have no other way to meet gender equity requirements? Or do they happen because cutting minor men's sports preserves other spending that athletic directors value more. It is extremely interesting that, as in the case of play for pay, athletic department and coaches salaries never seem to make it into the discussion of where to find money for Title IX compliance.

Let's look first at the premise that the ability of football to subsidize other sports will be harmed. This can only be true if football indeed even generates enough net revenue to carry out this subsidization. There is some startling evidence that this simply is not true. Leeds, Suris, and Durkin (2004) find that colleges have continued to underfund women's athletics, but more importantly only a few of the most profitable football programs provide any actual subsidy to women's sports. Almost all other athletic departments, including some with highly profitable football programs, actually drain money from women's sports. So not only have Title IX gains to date proven no danger to big-time college football, but just the opposite appears to be true. The authors conclude, "One is forced to conclude that many collegiate athletic departments view violating Title IX as an optimal strategy" (p. 150).

The case at my home-state universities yields another look at the relationship between football and spending on gender equity. In Table 13.9, take Washington State first. Football generated $4.9 million over its own expenses, and the net sum across all men's sports was $4.0 million. Some $3.8 million in excess of women's sports revenues were spent on those sports. So men's sports, including football, just cover the excess spending on women's sports. But would any increment to gender equity have to come from football? The answer is clearly no. In addition to all of the other amounts, $13.5 million, or 44 percent of the budget, was spent on the rest of the athletic department. If the athletic director spent optimally on men's sports, additional spending on women's sports would have to come from this other spending. Similar calculations for Washington show that football generated $16.0 million after its costs. The sum across all men's sports is $14.4 million. After covering women's sports, men's sports including football yield $9.8 million on net for other spending in the athletic department. Clearly, in this case, additional spending on women's sports could be had just out of the current men's surplus.

Our observations on this argument when it was encountered against play for pay serve us just as well in the case of Title IX. Athletic departments do not really break even because they adjust their budgets to spend any excesses within budget periods. The money is already there. It is just being spent on other parts of the athletic department budget. At a place like Washington, a highly successful athletic program, enough surplus from men's sports exists to increase spending on gender equity by nearly $9.8 million, in fact, 1.3 times more than is currently spent on women's sports there. At a more typical athletic department, Washington State, additional spending on gender equity would need to come out of money not spent on men's sports, but there are quite a few million dollars there to draw from.

If discrimination has reduced investment in women's sports below the amount preferred by those taxpayers supporting Title IX, then there may have been overinvestment in other areas in these departments. Equalizing the resources devoted to men and women will just reduce these overpayments. Part of the overinvestment is in terms of salaries and administration, but some of the overinvestment will also be in terms of spending on men's sports. Therefore, Title IX will prompt athletic departments to correct for past overinvestment in men's sports. As in the case of play for pay, we should expect that those who currently benefit from past distortions in spending will not be happy about reallocations that will come out of their paychecks. However, their arguments only thinly veil the obvious reason they have dragged their feet on Title IX compliance.

Some Unintended Consequences of Title IX When Title IX dramatically increased the value of offering more opportunities for women to participate in sports, inputs to that process became more valuable to athletic departments. This is easy to see by looking at the gender balance of coaches for women's sports. In 1972, women coached more than 90 percent of women's college teams. By 1996 that had fallen to 47.7 percent (Zimbalist 1999, p. 60). Through the end of the 1990s, women coached about 51 to 52 percent of women's college teams (*Racial and Gender Report Card*, 2001).

Apparently, as the value of women's basketball rose because of Title IX compliance, the price of coaches was bid up. This led many male coaches to enter the market to coach women's teams. The final result of that market outcome was a larger number of male than female coaches. Sticking to the MRP theory of pay, this would tend to indicate that women coaches at the time were outdone by an influx of men who had higher demonstrated abilities to produce winning for college programs. In terms of our discussion of discrimination in Chapter 7, women's coaching resumes at the time were less impressive than their male counterparts because they did not have the same access to training and experience. Of course, that raises the more important issue of why that access was limited in the first place, a topic economics cannot address.

Government and the College Sports Business

We can take a look at the relationship between government and college sports through the same lens we used in pro sports. College sports enjoy some special tax advantages and have had run-ins with the antitrust laws. The NCAA provides market power for its member colleges in their sports endeavors, and our model of the government process may lead us to wonder just why that occurs.

Taxes   The tax laws are an important contributor to athletic department welfare. Public universities and private not-for-profit universities must be careful with revenue-generating activities. If revenues exceed the percentage specified under the law, tax liability looms. From this perspective, an important behavior from earlier in this chapter safeguards universities from tax scrutiny. The accounting practices of athletic departments allow them to plow all of their net revenues back into the department during the year that they are earned. Under this practice, no profits ever are shown to draw the scrutiny of tax authorities.

Another form of tax advantage to universities concerns **tax-deductible contributions to the athletic department**. The idea of such a contribution is that the contributor expects nothing in return. The estimated value of such contributions is tax deductible. To date, the IRS has treated contributions to athletics departments just like any other charitable contribution—they are tax deductible to the contributor. However, this is a questionable practice by the IRS for nearly all contributions to athletics departments. Most contributions come from boosters and sponsors, and these "contributors" definitely expect and receive something in return.

Boosters are rewarded with prime seating and other types of services (guest tent privileges and close proximity to players and coaches) by the athletic department. Indeed, prime seating is available only if a booster makes a contribution and, typically, the higher the contribution, the better the seating. This clearly is payment for benefits received and, in all cases except college sports, eliminates tax-deductible status.

Business sponsors clearly get something in return for their contribution. During breaks in the action, sponsors are announced and broadcast on scoreboard TV screens. Sponsor signage is all around the stadium. So, their "contribution" generates recognition. Even though this bears a striking resemblance to a fee paid for services rendered, sponsorship contributions are, by and large, tax deductible.

Market Power and Antitrust   Member colleges acting through conferences and the NCAA create market power. At the basic level, joint venture activity is not required, so economic intuition leads us to believe that college athletic departments are better off pursuing conference membership restrictions, TV negotiations, and player restrictions through conferences and the NCAA than going it alone.

Just like the *Federal Baseball* decision did in pro sports, the NCAA Decision set the stage for most of these issues in college sports. Interestingly, Congress has chosen the same approach to both decisions, namely, to do nothing. Congress has not overturned the ability of pro leagues to completely control team location; it has encouraged mergers and the single dominant league outcome; and it has codified joint venture TV negotiations for pro sports leagues. Likewise, Congress has done nothing to interfere with the operations of college conferences or the NCAA on a similar array of issues. Conference membership is tightly controlled; the NCAA takes actions to guarantee its sole authority against potential rivals; joint venture TV negotiations are the rule; and players' earnings are restricted. The one behavior that was ruled illegal by the courts in the NCAA Decision, joint venture sports management by the NCAA in college football, continues in basketball as the NCAA manages March Madness in both men's and women's basketball.

Government intervention clearly has benefits for college sports consumers. This can be seen in the analysis of the competitive impacts of the NCAA Decision. Bennett and Fizel (1995) reported three main findings on the impact of this decision. First, in the long run, the NCAA Decision had no overall impact on the standard deviation of winning percent (compared to the idealized standard deviation in the usual way). Second, winning percents of strong teams declined, whereas those of weak teams increased (enough to reduce the difference by two games per year). Finally, there was a decline in the difference in playing strength between traditional powers and nonpowers. In summary, the NCAA Decision, by imposing more economic competition among NCAA athletic departments, enhanced competitive balance.

James Quirk and I (1997) also looked at a few of these measures and some others for college football. On average, top-10 finishers before the NCAA Decision finished higher after the decision. However, they did so much less often. Quirk and I also examined the Pac-10 and Big Ten in some detail. We found that the conference winning percents became more balanced after the NCAA Decision. Inequality in winning percents declined nearly 24 percent in the Pac-10 and almost 6 percent in the Big Ten. Finally, literally the same teams won all of the conference championships just prior to the NCAA Decision (USC, UCLA, and Washington in the Pac-10, and Michigan, Ohio State, and Iowa in the Big Ten). However, these same teams won 20 percent fewer championships in the Pac-10 and almost 10 percent fewer in the Big Ten after the decision (harken back to Table 13.12).

The lesson from these analyses is that a little economic competition appears to be good for competition on the field. We also saw in Table 13.10 that a little economic competition reduced the price of games to media providers, which increased the viewing alternatives for sports fans at home. These lessons cannot be lost on Congress, so we are left to try to explain why it remains noncommittal in its treatment of college conferences and the NCAA.

The Rational Actor Politics Behind the Status of College Sports

In college sports, so-called booster and sponsorship "contributions" are tax deductible as charitable donations. It is a funny kind of donation that earns boosters prime seat locations or firms a service in return for the contribution. However, this practice is permitted by the government. Further, Congress has allowed colleges acting through conferences and the NCAA completely free reign over college sports output and players.

I think you can probably see how a **rational actor politics model of college sports** would explain the special tax and market power status afforded colleges regarding their sports activities. Here, the concentrated interest occurs in every single state. Any revision of the tax or market power status enjoyed by colleges would hurt all college athletic departments. However, larger, richer college athletic departments would probably be harmed more than smaller ones. Therefore, politicians pursue the welfare of colleges under the IRS interpretation of charitable gifts and allow colleges to do as they will in running sports. Universities favor this outcome because their boosters and sponsors enjoy greater net benefit from their contributions than if those contributions were taxed. In addition, they are also able to price according to their market power position and keep nearly all of the value produced by college athletes.

CHAPTER RECAP

For the most part, there is very little new in terms of economics when we turn from pro sports to college sports until we get to college sports market outcomes. Demand concepts provide similar insights into college sports, especially the impact of preferences for women's and men's sports and the importance of population as a revenue determinant. Market power exists for individual colleges, but they need the NCAA to help maintain that power because so many conferences compete with each other for talent and TV dollars.

Revenues are much smaller for college athletic departments than for pro sports teams. However, revenue inequality is just as apparent for college sports, and it appears to be growing over time. The top revenue schools are gaining against the middle as well as the bottom. In terms of TV revenues, conferences are much more competitive in providing programming to media providers than are pro leagues. Total college broadcast revenues are much lower than even the NHL but are unequally distributed among teams in a conference even though some revenue sharing does occur. Bowl payouts to colleges are simply spent, with colleges taking their value out in terms of exposure and advertising for recruiting purposes.

On the supply side, comparisons to other parts of the university reveal that the value of athletic departments is in terms of money and political support. From that perspective, it is clear that even though most athletic departments lose money (absent institutional support), they are worth having. Nonstandard treatment of the athletic department, such as budgeting process differences and cost forgiveness, are understandable given the values they provide to the university.

Turning to college sports market outcomes, colleges join conferences for the same reasons that pro owners join leagues—they are better off financially in conferences than going it alone as independents. In college sports, the NCAA performs the joint entity cooperation function for colleges. The NCAA maintains exclusivity for Division IA sports and negotiates the TV deal for college basketball's national championship. The famous NCAA Decision (1984) precludes the NCAA from doing the same for anything but the postseason.

Competitive imbalance follows from revenue imbalance and exclusive conference membership. Broadcast and bowl revenues are shared, but better teams get a larger slice. Competitive balance is maintained through restrictions on players (the amateur requirement, recruiting restrictions, and mobility restrictions). The main result of those restrictions is to redistribute money from college players to their athletic departments. Of course, all of these requirements generate an incentive to cheat by individual coaches and departments, and it does not appear that the NCAA's heart is in its enforcement job.

Theoretical analysis of the amateur restriction suggests the college version of the invariance principle. Colleges can make the most off their athletes at the same distribution of talent between colleges whether athletes earn their MRP or athletic departments keep it. The range of estimated values of individual star players to their athletic departments is from $400,000 to $1 million. Following the theory, paying college players their MRP, rather than just paying their tuition, room and board, and books, should not change anything except to reduce the level of spending on administrative salaries, coaches' salaries, and facilities. However, different athletes would be paid different amounts.

For two remaining items, economics offers substantial insights. Title IX (1972) was passed to bring about gender equity in terms of participation for male and female athletes in college. From an economic perspective, all of the fears voiced about paying for gender equity are as groundless as those concerning play for pay. However, gender equity has proven elusive, even after more than 30 years since passage of Title IX. Turning to government and the college sports business, athletics enjoys tax advantages, primarily the tax-deductible status of donations despite the fact that these "donations" typically provide goods and services to the contributor. Congress has made no moves to investigate the market power enjoyed and promulgated by the NCAA for member schools. The same rational actor politics model used to explain pro sports advantages also explains this college sports outcome.

KEY TERMS AND CONCEPTS

- National Collegiate Athletics Association (NCAA)
- Donation seating
- Institutional support
- Revenue imbalance in college sports
- Three-tier broadcast rights structure
- Spillover benefits to the university

- Institutional support
- NCAA Decision
- Winning percent imbalance
- Championship imbalance
- Recruiting restrictions
- National letter of intent
- Sit-out restrictions
- Forfeit remaining playing eligibility
- Amateur requirement

- Cheating on NCAA rules
- College version of the invariance principle
- Play for pay
- Title IX
- Tax-deductible contributions to the athletic department
- Rational actor politics model of college sports

REVIEW QUESTIONS

1. Which has higher absolute quality of play, Division IA or Division IAA? Explain. Give an example of relative competition in college sports.
2. Explain why it must be preferences that explain the difference between the demand functions in Chapter 2.
3. Explain the effect that each of the following would have on the demand for UCLA college football games:
   a. All else constant, some UCLA fans do not like the cheating that occurs in college football.
   b. All else constant, incomes of Los Angeles residents increase.

c. All else constant, the price of a season ticket to the MLB Los Angeles Dodgers falls to equal the price of a UCLA season ticket.

d. All else constant, UCLA fans expect season ticket prices to rise next year.

4. Describe donation seating. Is it price discrimination? Explain.

5. What does "institutional support" mean when describing college sports revenues? Describe the behavior of revenues in college sports over time using Table 13.1. Does it grow over time nearly as much without institutional support?

6. Describe the three-tier broadcast rights structure used in college sports. Explain each tier fully.

7. Why is there more competition on the supply side of sports programming in college sports than in pro sports?

8. Describe the four types of sponsorship currently occurring in college sports.

9. What was the original purpose of college bowl games? Has this changed for all bowl games or just for some? If just for some, which ones? Explain.

10. Why isn't a focus on the athletic department the most insightful level of analysis when discussing college sports? What is the object of analysis that is most insightful? What are the goals of that decision maker? Explain, with special attention to Figure 13.2.

11. List the spillover benefits that are purported to flow from the athletic department to the university. What actually is known about these spillover benefits?

12. Why do colleges join conferences? How does the example of Notre Dame's remaining independent help explain this motivation?

13. What is the NCAA? What purpose does it serve for college sports programs?

14. What is Title IX? What does it require?

15. What special tax advantages are enjoyed by college sports? Provide examples.

THOUGHT PROBLEMS

1. Has institutional support grown over time in college sports (use Table 13.1)? Why or why not? Provide an explanation for your answer using Figure 13.2.

2. Examine the revenue disparity data in Table 13.1. What has happened to the ratio of highest to average revenue over time? What does this suggest about the level of competitive balance in Division IA college sports?

3. How does just looking at Notre Dame's broadcast rights value indicate that broadcast rights revenues are unequally distributed throughout Division IA? (*Hint:* Remember that there are 106 Division IA football schools.)

4. A clever sports economics student asked the athletic director at that university to dig back into the records for data on attendance and prices at the college's tennis matches. The student's research revealed the following attendance demand function for alumni and other boosters:

$$P_B = \$24 - \frac{1}{20} A_B$$

P_B = booster price and A_B = booster attendance. Draw this attendance demand function. Does this tennis team have market power over boosters? Why or why not? What is the highest possible total revenue that the team can hope to collect? At what level of attendance? At what price?

5. In what ways is the football program just like any academic department at the university? In what ways is it different? How does this help determine the different ways that the university administration treats each? Explain fully using Figures 13.3 and 13.4.

6. College athletic departments are rarely economically self-sufficient. Why is this the case? If athletic departments cannot break even, why do coaches' salaries increase year after year? Explain fully.

7. Pac-10 members are required to have a minimum number of varsity sports. What role does this restriction play in the welfare of conference members?

8. What essential service did the Big East provide for Miami to get it to join that conference? Why was the Big East so easy on Miami in terms of it sharing revenues with the rest of the conference? (Refer to the Learning Highlight: Miami Joins the Big East . . . No, Make That the ACC.)

9. Why do colleges need the NCAA? What does the NCAA accomplish for colleges that their conference cannot accomplish? Give examples.

10. Give an overview of revenue, winning percent, and championship imbalances in college sports using the data in Table 13.1 and 13.12. What is the ultimate source of these imbalances?

11. List the ways that colleges acting through conferences and the NCAA try to reduce competitive imbalance. Are these methods effective? Why or why not?

12. Using the Fort and Quirk (1997) expression for the expected value of cheating, if the probability of getting caught is the same across all colleges, explain why cheating would be more likely in a program with a currently weak record and high potential for financial gain with a young coach.

13. What is the main lesson from the graphical analysis of the NCAA's amateur requirement? How does this generate the college version of the invariance principle? Be sure to use Figure 13.6. in your explanation.

14. About 49 percent of the head coaches of women's sports were women according to the *Race and Gender Report Card*, 2001. Does this mean that there is hiring discrimination against women at that position? State the arguments against that position. State the arguments supporting that position. Can you draw any conclusions about this problem from economic analysis? Explain.

15. How is it that special tax advantages and market power for the NCAA persist in college sports? Detail a rational actor politics response.

ADVANCED PROBLEMS

1. Performance-enhancing drugs are an issue in college sports. Are players looking to gain absolute or relative advantage through these drugs? What is the outcome on the field if all players use performance-enhancing drugs? What are the benefits and costs of outlawing these drugs?

2. A common story is that cost escalation plagues college athletic departments. However, over the last few years, more athletic departments are showing a positive

balance (Table 13.1). Reconcile these conflicting stories. (*Hint:* Which elements on athletic department balance sheets are increasing in cost? Rent? Players?)

3. In addition to the booster demand function in Thought Problem 4, our clever student also discovers that the demand by students for attendance at the same tennis matches and the same seat types is as follows:

$$P_S = \$12 - \frac{1}{23} A_S$$

P_S = student price and A_S = student attendance. Show why students will be charged a lower price for the same event and seat type than boosters. What is the ratio of booster to student price if the athletic director cares about the bottom line? Is this price discrimination?

4. Pro owners, due to the imputed profit charge when they obtain a team either through purchase or expansion, can be expected to behave like rapacious monopolists (Chapter 5). Does the same force operate in college sports? What drives college athletic departments to behave the same way?

5. Suppose that the NCAA was not allowed to run March Madness. What do you expect would happen to broadcast rights fees for the championship series? Who would host it and set it up?

6. Patrick Ewing played college basketball at Georgetown University. According to the *Chronicle of Higher Education* (January 8, 1986), Ewing's presence was worth about $12 million over his 4-year college career—the value of attendance at home games tripled; sales of memorabilia skyrocketed; and additional TV appearances went with the success of the team. The athletic department paid for the cost of Ewing's scholarship over the period, about $48,600. What percent of Ewing's MRP did Georgetown keep? Compare this to the other estimates in the text and explain any discrepancy between the Ewing case and those estimates.

7. Suppose through a legal finding that college athletes were deemed employees of the athletic department. How would this change the structure of the relationship between college athletes and their universities? Is it possible that the amateur requirement could be in danger? How? (*Hint:* As employees, athletes would enjoy the same labor rights under federal law as any other group of employees.)

8. Why is it important to athletic departments that the competitive equilibrium level of talent on all teams be maintained when the amateur requirement is in force? (Use Figure 13.6 in your explanation.) What is the implication of this important observation for arguments against play for pay? Examine each argument one at a time in your explanation.

9. Give the MRP explanation for why most male college basketball coaches make more than most female coaches. Again, using the MRP explanation, when will female coaches make more than male coaches? What is the most obvious evidence that there is discrimination against women college basketball coaches? (*Hint:* How many female coaches of men's programs are there, using the *Race and Gender Report Card*, 2001, data given in the text?)

10. Why is participation in college sports still 60–40 in favor of men over women, even though federal law has dictated equality for more than 30 years under Title IX?

INTERNET RESOURCES

For a host of additional material and questions for thought, visit this book's Web site at www.prenhall.com/fort.

REFERENCES

Baade, Robert A. and Victor A. Matheson. "An Economic Slam Dunk or March Madness? Assessing the Economic Impact of the NCAA Basketball Tournament," in *The Economics of College Sports*. John Fizel and Rodney Fort, eds. Westport, CT: Praeger Publishers, 2004.

Bennett, Randall W. and John L. Fizel. "Telecast Deregulation and Competitive Balance: Regarding NCAA Division I Football," *American Journal of Economics and Sociology* 54 (1995): 183–198.

Brown, Gary T. "The Electronic Free Ticket: Early NCAA Feared Televised Football Would Harm Attendance," *NCAA News*, November 22, 1999.

Brown, Robert W. and R. Todd Jewell. "Measuring Marginal Revenue Product in College Athletics: Updated Estimates," in *The Economics of College Sports*. John Fizel and Rodney Fort, eds. Westport, CT: Praeger Publishers, 2004.

Byers, Walter with Charles Hammer. *Unsportsmanlike Conduct: Exploiting College Athletes*. Ann Arbor, MI: University of Michigan Press, 1995.

Depken, Craig A. II and Dennis P. Wilson. "The Impact of Cartel Enforcement in NCAA Division I-A Football," in *The Economics of College Sports*. John Fizel and Rodney Fort, eds. Westport, CT: Praeger Publishers, 2004a.

Depken, Craig A. II and Dennis P. Wilson. "Institutional Change in the NCAA and Competitive Balance in Intercollegiate Football," in *The Economics of College Sports*. John Fizel and Rodney Fort, eds. Westport, CT: Praeger Publishers, 2004b.

Fleischer, Arthur A., Brian L. Goff, and Robert D. Tollison. *The National Collegiate Athletic Association*. Chicago, IL: University of Chicago Press, 1992.

Fort, Rodney and James Quirk. "Introducing a Competitive Economic Environment into Professional Sports," in *Advances in the Economics of Sport*, Vol. 2. Wallace Hendricks, ed. Greenwich, CT: JAI Press, 1997.

Fort, Rodney and James Quirk. "The College Football Industry," in *Sports Economics: Current Research*. John Fizel, Elizabeth Gustafson, and Lawrence Hadley, eds. Westport, CT: Praeger, 1999.

Fulks, Daniel L. *Revenues and Expenses of Divisions I and II Intercollegiate Athletic Programs: Financial Trends and Relationships, 2001*. Overland Park, KS: National Collegiate Athletic Association, 2002.

Goff, Brian. "Effects of University Athletics on the University: A Review and Extension of Empirical Assessment," in *The Economics of College Sports*. John Fizel and Rodney Fort, eds. Westport, CT: Praeger Publishers, 2004.

Grimes, Paul W. and George A. Chressanthis. "Alumni Contributions to Academics: The Role of Intercollegiate Sports and NCAA Sanctions," *American Journal of Economics and Sociology* 53 (1994): 27–40.

Humphreys, Brad R. "Equal Pay on the Hardwood: The Earnings Gap Between Male and Female NCAA Division I Basketball Coaches," *Journal of Sports Economics* 1 (2000): 299–307.

Johnson, Bruce and John Whitehead. "Value of Public Goods from Sports Stadiums: The CVM Approach," *Contemporary Economic Policy* 18 (2000): 48–58.

Leeds, Michael A., Yelena Suris, and Jennifer Durkin. "College Football and Title IX," in *The Economics of College Sports*. John Fizel and Rodney Fort, eds. Westport, CT: Praeger Publishers, 2004.

Noll, Roger G. "The Economics of Intercollegiate Sport," in *Rethinking College Athletics*. Judith Andre and David N. James, eds. Philadelphia, PA: Temple University Press, 1991.

Padilla, Arthur and David Baumer. "Big-Time College Sports: Management and Economic Issues," *Journal of Sport and Social Issues* 18 (1994): 123–143.

Race and Gender Report Card. Center for the Study of Sports, Northeastern University, Boston, MA, 2001.

Scott, Jack. *The Athletic Revolution*. New York: Free Press, 1971.

Smith, Ronald A. *Sports and Freedom: The Rise of Big-Time College Athletics*. New York: Oxford University Press, 1988.

Sperber, Murray. *College Sports, Inc.: The Athletic Department vs. the University*. New York: Henry Holt and Company, 1991.

Tucker, Irvin B. "A Reexamination of the Effect of Big-Time Football and Basketball Success on Graduation Rates and Alumni Giving Rates," *Economics of Education Review* 23 (2004): 655–661.

Tucker, Irvin B. "Big-Time Pigskin Success: Is There an Advertising Effect?" *Journal of Sports Economics* 6 (2005): 222–229.

Zimbalist, Andrew. *Unpaid Professionals: Commercialism and Conflict in Big-Time College Sports*. Princeton, NJ: Princeton University Press, 1999.

GLOSSARY

absolute quality Clearly different levels of quality, as in the difference between minor and major league sports.

advertising bans A government-imposed ban on advertisements for a particular product (e.g., cigarette ads on TV).

advertising dilemma Situation where product competitors spend more on advertisements than the value of the extra product sold because each would lose sales in the absence of increased advertising.

advertising reach The number of people of a specific demographic that will see a particular advertisement.

advertising slots Short time periods set aside for advertisements during a broadcast.

amateur requirement The requirement by NCAA member schools that college athletes only receive compensation in the form of tuition, room and board, and books.

annual hiring risk The risk team owners would confront in terms of rising player salaries if players only had annual contracts.

antitrust approaches Methods of reducing the impacts of market power on consumers; methods rely on the antitrust laws.

arbitration A process where a mutually agreed upon independent third party determines a disputed outcome.

asymmetric information Information known to one party but not the other in an economic confrontation.

bargaining in good faith Sincerely seeking a mutually agreeable end to a bargaining situation.

basis, the The difference between the sale value of an asset and its accumulated book profits; used to determine capital gain obligations at time of sale.

Bayesian updater A decision maker who only updates their beliefs about the value of an asset as information is revealed over time.

believable threat locations A city that current host cities believe could be an economically viable location for their current team.

between-league revenue variation The observed outcome that some leagues generate greater cumulative owner revenues than others.

biased information In the political process, the observed outcome that information tends to be polarized rather than centralized toward the truth.

biased turnout The observed outcome in elections that only those with the most to gain or lose turn out to vote.

bidding war The observation that bids will exceed the expected value of the asset under bid when coming in second is costly.

blackout laws Laws that prohibit broadcasting a game in the home area unless that game is sold out at the gate.

brand choice Selection of a specific brand from among competing brands once a consumer has determined a particular type of consumption.

buyer's surpluses For a given buyer, the sum of that consumer's willingness to pay for all units of consumption in excess of the actual price that was paid.

buyers' surpluses The sum of each individual buyer's surpluses across all buyers.

championship imbalance The observed outcome that particular teams consistently win more championships than the rest of the teams in a given league or conference over time.

collective bargaining Negotiation between a labor union and an employer of a labor contract that sets the terms of employment for members of the labor union.

collective bargaining agreements The contract reached between owners and the players' union through the process of collective bargaining.

Collusion I, II, and III Arbitration cases in the 1980s that found that Major League Baseball owners had colluded to repress player salaries.

competition policy Government policy consisting of antitrust approaches or regulations that aim to reduce the impacts of market power on consumers.

competitive imbalance The observed outcome that particular teams win consistently more games during the regular season than the rest of the teams in a league or conference over time.

competitive talent market A process that determines the price and allocation of talent in a competitive market.

concentrated benefits Benefits allocated to special interest groups due to their level of political potency.

control of ballot alternatives In some initiatives or referendums, particular groups interested in the outcome control the alternatives that appear before the voters on ballots.

cost of fan discrimination The amount that must be paid to players of a particular race or ethnicity, in excess of their actual market value, because of fan preferences for that particular race or ethnicity.

cost of owner discrimination The reduction in profits at a given level of winning that must be paid by owners hiring players of a particular race or ethnicity based strictly on owner preferences for players of that particular race or ethnicity.

cost-benefit analysis Assessment of the net value of an investment that compares the values generated by the investment with the complete opportunity costs of obtaining them.

Curt Flood Act of 1998 Act of Congress that allows baseball players to sue under the antitrust laws if behavior by owners that is counter to those laws also hinders labor negotiations.

defined gross revenues Under collective bargaining, revenues that are defined for the purposes of calculating a team-level salary cap.

demand The functional relationship between the price of a good and the quantity of units purchased by consumers.

demand shifters Factors other than price (income, preferences, closeness and availability of substitutes, and expectations) that determine the shape and location of the demand function.

development value Economic growth at a particular location that can be attributed solely to the existence and/or number of pro sports teams at that location.

differential alternatives The value of the next highest-valued activity that a party in a labor negotiation may turn to if negotiations fail.

diminishing returns The economic characteristic of production where, eventually, the marginal product of the next unit hired is smaller than the one hired just before it.

direct democracy Initiatives and referendums that allow each voter to vote on a single issue.

direct economic activity The value of the economic activity associated with construction of a stadium and stadium occupancy once it is completed.

discrimination in pay and hiring Pay and hiring outcomes based on worker characteristics other than their contribution to the value of output, such as race, sex, or ethnicity.

dispersed costs The observation that the costs of providing political benefits to particular special interests are spread out in small amounts over all taxpayers.

donation seating In college sports, the required flat payment in addition to ticket prices that must be paid to guarantee a particular seat to a fan.

economic impact analysis (EIA) An approach that determines the value of economic activity associated with an investment in a pro sports facility.

education costs The costs to a union of educating employees about the economic gains to be had by collective bargaining.

excess depreciation Any depreciation for the purpose of reducing tax payments in excess of those allowed by the law and tax court findings.

exclusive territory By the rules of league franchising, the territory of any given team that is kept intact and exclusive to that franchise owner.

expansion draft During a league expansion, a draft that is designed to move players from existing teams to the expansion teams.

expansion fee An amount paid by expansion owners to existing owners in the league.

expected local revenue impacts The impacts of expansion teams on the local revenues of the existing owners in the league, such as local TV contracts and gate ticket prices.

expected marginal revenue product Estimate, due to the fact that performance is a random variable, of a player's contribution to the value of team winning.

expected national TV impacts The impacts of expansion teams on a league's national TV contract value.

experience-earnings profile The data showing the relationship between a player's experience and their earnings over the length of their career.

experience-earnings relationship The graph showing the relationship between experience on the x-axis, and earnings on the y-axis; earnings start low, increase quickly, and then level off with experience.

external benefit A benefit created by a producer that the producer cannot collect by charging a price.

external benefit inefficiency The prediction that a producer will produce less than the true value of their output to buyers due to the presence of external benefits.

fan consumer movements Growth of organizations that seek to protect fans from the actions of pro sports leagues that lead to high prices, restricted expansion, and team relocation.

fan discrimination Socially unacceptable fan preferences in favor of players and/or coaches of a particular race, ethnicity, or sex.

federal subsidy component Funding mechanisms that reduce federal taxes paid during stadium construction that represent a subsidy that must be made up by federal taxpayers.

50-50 split The prediction from the simplest bargaining situation where both parties independently reach the same conclusion to split the value under negotiation equally and without any work stoppage.

final offer salary arbitration (FOSA) A sports arbitration process where both parties agree that an independent third-party arbitrator must choose the proposal of one party or the other.

financial value of expansion That portion of the league's consideration of the value of expansion that has to do only with financial gain or loss.

forfeit remaining playing eligibility One element of the NCAA amateur requirement where players lose their remaining college-playing eligibility if they enter a pro draft.

franchise agreements The contract between a league and an owner that specifies the rights of each party relative to granting the owner a league franchise.

franchise sale values The market value of a franchise to a particular owner.

free agents Players who have reached the end of their contract and have met the experience requirements required by the collective bargaining agreement who are free to sell their services to the highest bidder.

free-riding behavior A common behavior where people enjoy gains obtained by the actions of others without paying their share of the costs of obtaining the gains.

game theory The branch of economics that studies strategic behavior in economic situations in the presence of full or limited information.

gate revenue sharing Sharing of ticket revenue by the home team and the visiting team under rates specified in league rules.

imputed expansion fee The inclusion of the price paid for an expansion team into the costs that must be recouped by the new owner over time.

imputed tax advantage values The inclusion of the value of special tax advantages enjoyed by team owners into the sale price of a team.

incentive-compatible mechanisms Economic mechanisms designed to take into account actions that might be taken in response to the mechanism.

indirect economic activity The value of the economic activity around, but not directly at, a stadium during and after its construction.

individual bargaining rights   In sports, individual players retain the right to negotiate only over salary. Player unions negotiate all other aspects of employment.

inelastic attendance pricing   Outcome where owners price their tickets in the inelastic portion of gate demand.

infrastructure subsidies   Payments by cities and states for roads and public services that facilitate stadium construction and operation.

institutional support   The portion of college athletic department budgets that come directly from the university budget.

invariance principle   Attributable to Simon Rottenberg, the principle that states the distribution of talent is invariant with respect to whether owners or players get to keep the value generated by players.

joint venture negotiations   Cooperation among teams in league or conference negotiations with players, media providers, and host cities.

joint ventures   Cooperative behavior by owners that is not required to make play happen, includes territory protection and negotiations with players, media providers, and host cities.

labor relations   The relationship between organized labor and ownership.

league expansion   The process of adding teams to an existing league.

limit to management ability in the long run   The inability to manage talent and stadium inputs yielding the result that costs must eventually rise with higher quality (winning percent) in the long run.

local broadcasting contract   A contract between an individual team and a local media provider to broadcast games not covered by the league's national contract.

local revenue sharing   Sharing of local revenue (gate, concessions, parking, and local TV) by higher-revenue owners with lower-revenue owners under a process specified by league rules.

lockout   Work stoppage instituted by owners after collective bargaining fails.

long run   A production planning period where owners consider all production factors, including contracts and stadiums, to be variable.

long-run profits   All of the possible different profit outcomes associated with all the possible quality teams that an owner might put on the field.

long-run quality choice   The choice of winning percent when all production factors are variable.

long-run total cost   The cost of all the possible quality teams that an owner might put on the field.

long-run winning percent production function   The relationship between player quality and winning percent when all factors are variable.

long-term contract   A player contract that lasts more than a single season.

managerial efficiency   How close a team manager comes to the idealized best possible winning percent that the players on a team are capable of producing.

marginal revenue   How revenues change when output is changed by one unit (attendance in the short run or winning percent in the long run).

marginal revenue product (MRP)   The product of player marginal product (*MP*) (contribution to the team's winning percent) and the marginal revenue (*MR*) earned by that contribution.

marginal revenue product of broadcast rights   The contribution of the last bundle of sports programming to a media provider's revenue.

market failures   Situations where markets fail to include all costs and benefits, e.g., externalities and market power.

market power   When a producer faces limited substitute products and is able to set the price of their product based on how much they produce.

McNeil vs. NFL   The court case where NFL players won free agency.

media providers   Network, cable, and satellite broadcasters.

media revenue disparity   The observed outcome that some teams consistently earn higher local media revenues than the rest of the teams in a league.

merger facilitation Government facilitation of sports league mergers.

minimum subsidy The minimum subsidy required to keep a money-losing owner in town.

monitoring effort Actions required to determine if players are exerting maximal effort to perform at the highest levels.

movement along demand All else constant (for a given demand function), the change in consumption caused by a change in the price of the good.

national broadcasting contract Contract between sports leagues or college conferences and media providers to broadcast games to regional and national audiences.

National Collegiate Athletic Association (NCAA) Governing organization of college sports composed of individual member colleges.

National Labor Relations Act (NLRA) The law that governs labor relations, including the formation of unions and the collective bargaining process.

National Labor Relations Board (NLRB) The administrative agency created under the NLRA to oversee the collective bargaining process.

national letter of intent Letter signed by college recruits committing them to a particular college athletic program.

***NCAA* Decision** The court case where the negotiation of college football TV rights contracts by the NCAA, for all teams, was ruled illegal.

new economic activity Direct and indirect economic activity that would not exist in the absence of a pro sports team and its stadium.

new value added New economic activity, net of the costs required to produce it.

operating subsidies Subsidies to ongoing team operations, typically through clauses in the lease contract between team owners and government stadium authorities.

opportunity cost of time The value of the next best use of an individual's time.

outcome uncertainty Uncertainty of the outcome on the field, even between two unequally matched teams; a primary reason that fans are willing to pay for sports.

owner discrimination Owner preferences in favor of players and/or coaches of a particular race, ethnicity, or sex.

owner retaliation Owner behavior injurious to the careers of players active in the formation and operation of a union.

owner viability The long-term ability of owners to be financially successful.

pass-through firm A firm structure that allows owners to pass the net financial outcome of their team through to their personal income tax report.

payroll imbalance When larger-revenue owners have higher player payrolls than smaller-revenue owners.

payroll luxury tax In some leagues, a tax on purchases of talent beyond a specified total payroll level.

performance and injury risks Revenue risks faced by owners and compensation risks faced by players due to variability in player performance and chances of player injury.

personal and capital gains tax gap The difference between an owner's marginal personal income tax rate and the corporate tax rate.

personal seat licenses (PSL) In pro sports, the required flat payment in addition to ticket prices that must be paid to guarantee a particular seat to a fan.

play for pay The popular description of paying college athletes a market-determined salary in addition to any compensation for tuition, room and board, and books.

player agent A person who represents a player in salary negotiation/arbitration activities.

player exploitation A measure of the power of owners to extract the marginal revenue product of players, typically the ratio of the difference between MRP and the player's actual wage divided by MRP.

player loyalty The idea of a player staying with one team throughout their entire career.

player moves versus performance moves. Distinguishing between the total number of player moves versus movements by players of higher quality since the introduction of free agency in a league.

player representative A team's representative to the players' union.

price discrimination Charging different customers different amounts for the same type of consumption or the same customer less for increased units of consumption at a point in time based on willingness to pay rather than on cost of service.

price elasticity The responsiveness of consumption to changes in price; technically, the percentage change in consumption divided by the percentage change in price that caused the change.

profit maximization hypothesis The hypothesis that sports team owners act to maximize profits.

profitable work stoppage A work stoppage that may have been undertaken simply because the expected value of the work stoppage to the party that brought it is large enough to justify the expected costs.

quantity restrictions In the case of market power, reduction in output to consumers in order to charge a price in excess of the underlying costs of production.

***Raiders* Case** The court case where the ability of the NFL to overrule the movement of the Oakland Raiders to Los Angeles was ruled illegal.

ratings A measurement of the total number of viewing households for a given broadcast.

rational actor explanation An explanation of political outcomes that recognizes voters, owners of firms, and politicians can act in their best economic interests in political situations.

rational actor model A model of politically determined outcomes that assumes elected officials (e.g., union leaders, politicians) seek reelection and must provide benefits to powerful reelection groups in order to obtain it.

rational ignorance The idea that it is rational for a person to know nearly nothing about almost everything; a primary element in the reduction of political participation.

rational level of voting Because of the costs of voting and rational ignorance, all eligible voters will not vote. Only those who find voting important enough, relative to the costs, will actually vote.

rationing Choosing a mechanism (price, waiting in line) to distribute scarce commodities among competing uses.

recruiting restrictions NCAA rules that restrict the amount and type of resources that can be devoted to recruiting college athletes.

regulatory approaches Appoaches to handling market power that involve the implementation of regulations governing league behavior and creation of administrative agencies to oversee that behavior.

relative quality The closeness of competition that occurs at a particular level of quality.

reorganize for tax purposes Selection of a different form for a firm (corporation, subchapter S, partnership, etc.) in order to minimize tax liability.

reserve clause A clause in player contracts that, for many years, allowed owners to continue the previous contract if they simply informed the player that they were going to do so by a particular date.

revenue imbalance The observed outcome that some teams have larger revenues than the other teams in the league.

revenue shifting and cross-ownership The practice of distributing the revenues from various holdings across the financial statements of those holdings to the financial advantage of the owner of the holdings.

reverse-order-of-finish draft A draft of incoming league players where the teams with the worst records in the previous season make the first selections.

rights fee A fee paid by media providers to a league or conference for the right to broadcast their games.

rival leagues Leagues that are economic competitors bidding for the same talent, venues, and legitimacy in the eyes of fans.

roster depreciation The right (determined by past tax court rulings) of an owner to depreciate up to half of the purchase price of their team under the heading of roster value despite the fact that they also are able to expense player salaries as a cost of doing business.

roster depreciation rollover   The ability of a new owner to practice roster depreciation on a roster even though it already was completely depreciated by the previous owner of the team.

Rozelle Rule   Compensation paid by teams gaining free agents to teams losing them, popularized by former NFL Commissioner Pete Rozelle.

salary caps   A mechanism where a portion of defined gross revenues, equally allocated across all teams, determines the most that any team in the league can spend on all of its players combined.

scarcity   The simple economic fact of life that there are not enough goods and services freely available to satisfy our wants.

shirking   When an agent acts counter to the best interests of their principal, as when players under long-term contracts do not exert maximal effort at their sport.

short run   A production time period where some inputs are fixed; for example, labor contracts or fixed stadium capacity.

short-run fixed costs   Costs determined by fixed inputs in the short run.

short-run fixed inputs   Inputs that are fixed in the short run due to contractual obligations.

short-run profits   With team quality fixed, the amount of profits that can be made selling that particular level of quality.

short-run total costs   The sum of short-run fixed costs and short-run variable costs.

short-run variable costs   Costs that are variable in the short run due to use of inputs that remain variable, for example, marketing effort.

short-run variable inputs   Inputs that are variable in the short run, such as marketing effort.

single dominant league   The observation that rival pro leagues tend not to survive due to their failure or merger with another league so that one league dominates.

single-entity cooperation   Cooperation from team owners that allows competition to occur; for example, the creation of rules and set up of a schedule.

sit-out restrictions   NCAA requirements that any Division IA player changing teams must sit out a full year of eligibility unless released by their previous coach.

slot fees   The fee charged by media providers for particular times slots.

speculative bubble   Continual increase in the price of an asset beyond its apparent expected value.

spending multiplier   A factor that, if multiplied by an initial injection of spending, would reconcile the injection and the final amount of economic activity it creates.

sponsorship   Spending by a business to have a corporate name attached to a particular sports event, game, or stadium.

Sports Broadcast Act of 1961   Act of Congress that explicitly granted professional sports leagues the ability to negotiate TV contracts for their member teams.

stacking   The observed practice of putting people of a particular race, ethnicity, or sex in secondary (less publicly conspicuous) positions on the field or in the front office.

stadium subsidies   Payments by taxpayers for the construction and/or operation of a stadium where a team plays.

standard deviation of winning percents   A statistically defined measure of dispersion, or imbalance, in winning percents; the larger the standard deviation, the less competitive balance in a league.

start-up consumption   A consumer's decision to engage in a particular type of consumption for the first time.

statistical discrimination   "Rule-of-thumb" discrimination based on previous perceptions of the productivity of individuals based on race, ethnicity, or sex.

strategic advertising   Advertising choices made to adversely affect the economic position of a rival firm.

strategic expansion/relocation   The placement of teams by sports leagues to cover the main population centers in order to preclude entry by rival leagues.

strategic misrepresentation   Misrepresentation of facts or a situation in order to gain economically.

strategic player effort The idea that players may only exert maximal effort at economically opportunistic times, such as just before an upcoming contract renegotiation.

strike A work stoppage brought by players.

tacit cooperation Concerted action by rival firms that raise the profits of both without direct communication or collusion.

talent dumping Trading of star players in order to reduce payroll and enhance profits.

talent market equilibrium A price and distribution of talent at which owners no longer wish to trade or sell talent among themselves.

target demographic group The group that a given advertiser most wishes to see their ads (typically described by age, sex, and income).

tax-deductible contributions Payments to college athletic departments that are tax deductible as a charitable deduction, despite the fact that services are provided to the contributor.

team relocation The movement of a team from one geographic location to another.

teammate discrimination Preferences by team members in favor of players and/or coaches of a particular race, ethnicity, or sex.

three-tier broadcast rights structure The structured broadcast rights contracts that allows national/regional broadcasters first rights at games to broadcast, followed by regional cable, and then by local broadcasters.

Title IX The federal statute requiring equal access to college athletics for women at all universities accepting federal funds.

total revenue Price multiplied by the quantity sold.

trading down draft picks Trading of higher-ranked draft picks for lower-ranked draft picks by an owner in order to increase the probability that those players drafted will actually sign with the drafting team.

unbiased expectations Estimates of the value of an asset, such as player performance, that are correct on average, even though any particular estimate may be off the mark after the fact.

union decertification A vote by players to revoke the ability of an organization to represent them in labor negotiations with owners.

wealth redistribution The use of league rules, collective bargaining, and the legal and political process to move wealth created by a league from players to owners or vice versa.

winner's curse In a competitive bidding situation with naïve and/or inexperienced bidders where there is a broad range of estimates of the value of the asset up for bid, the highest bidder is certain to have bid well in excess of the actual expected value of the asset.

winner-take-all explanation The hypothesis that when fans only want to see the best performers and the technology exists to provide them what they want, very few performers will obtain nearly all of the total spending by all fans.

winning percent equilibrium A talent market equilibrium where talent is measured so that one more unit of talent increases winning percent by one more unit (the choice of talent is synonymous with the choice of team quality or winning percent).

within-league revenue variation The observed outcome that some team locations in a given league generate greater owner revenues than do other locations.

worker job preferences Worker preferences for safety, location and other nonpay factors associated with a particular job at a particular location.

INDEX